REMAINS

OF A

VERY ANTIENT RECENSION

OF THE

FOUR GOSPELS IN SYRIAC,

HITHERTO UNKNOWN IN EUROPE;

DISCOVERED, EDITED, AND TRANSLATED

BY

WILLIAM CURETON, D.D., F.R.S.

HON. D.D. OF THE UNIVERSITY OF HALLE; HON. MEM. OF THE HISTORICO-THEOLOGICAL SOCIETY OF LEIPSIC; COR. MEM. OF THE INSTITUTE OF FRANCE (ACAD. DES INSCRIP. ET BELL. LETT.); COR. MEM. OF THE ORIENTAL SOCIETY OF GERMANY; MEMBER OF THE ASIATIC SOCIETY OF PARIS, &c. &c. &c.

CHAPLAIN IN ORDINARY TO THE QUEEN;
RECTOR OF ST. MARGARET'S; AND CANON OF WESTMINSTER.

WIPF & STOCK • Eugene, Oregon

Wipf and Stock Publishers
199 W 8th Ave, Suite 3
Eugene, OR 97401

Remains of a Very Ancient Recension of the Four Gosples
in Syriac, Hitherto Unknown in Europe
By Cureton, William
ISBN 13: 978-1-60608-917-0
Publication date 3/29/2010
Previously published by John Murray, 1858

TO HIS ROYAL HIGHNESS

THE PRINCE CONSORT, K.G.,

&c. &c. &c.

SIR,

IT affords me the highest gratification to be allowed to dedicate this Volume to your Royal Highness. The position which your Royal Highness occupies so near to the Throne makes this a peculiar distinction, while your Royal Highness' own personal qualities enhance the honour in a very eminent degree.

It is a source of great satisfaction for me to know, that whatever may be the imperfections of this work, your Royal Highness can estimate the amount of labour and research which was requisite to undertake it; and I therefore feel assured, that by your Royal Highness at least it will be leniently and kindly judged.

No defects on the part of the Editor can preclude these venerable Remains of Christian Antiquity, now for the first time brought to light, from taking their place in the ranks of Christian Literature; and on this account I have solicited the favour of being permitted to inscribe on this page a record both of my gratitude to your Royal Highness, and of my respect.

I have the honour to be,

SIR,

with the greatest respect,

your Royal Highness'

very obedient and grateful Servant,

WILLIAM CURETON.

WESTMINSTER,

May 24, 1858.

PREFACE.

THE manuscript from which the text of these Fragments of the Gospels contained in this volume has been printed was one of those obtained in the year 1842, by Archdeacon Tattam, from the Syrian monastery dedicated to St. Mary Deipara, or Mother of God, in the valley of the Natron Lakes. It consisted of portions of three antient copies, bound together to form a volume of the Four Gospels, with a few leaves in a more recent hand added to make up the deficiencies.

The following note at the end of the book shews the time at which it was bound together in that condition: ܫܘܒܚܐ ܠܐܒܐ ܘܠܒܪܐ ܘܠܪܘܚܐ ܩܕܝܫܐ ܠܥܠܡ ܥܠܡܝܢ ܐܡܝܢ. ܒܫܢܬ ܐܬܠܓ ܕܝܘܢܝܐ ܐܬܚܕܬܘ ܟܬܒ̈ܐ ܕܕܝܪܐ ܕܥܕܬܐ ܕܝܠܕܬ ܐܠܗܐ ܕܣܘܪ̈ܝܝܐ ܒܝܘܡ̈ܝ ܪܝܫܘܬܗ ܕܩܘܡܣ ܡܪܝ ܝܘܚܢܢ ܘܒܣܝܠܝܘܣ ܪܝܫ ܕܝܪܐ ܘܡܪܝ ܝܘܣܦ ܦܪܢܣܐ ܐܠܗܐ ܒܪܚܡܘܗܝ ܢܬܠ ܠܗܘܢ ܘܠܟܠܗܘܢ ܐܚ̈ܐ ܐܓܪܐ ܛܒܐ ܗ̇ܢܘܢ ܕܐܫܬܘܬܦ ܒܗܘܢ ܐܘ ܒܡܠܬܐ ܐܘ ܒܥܒ̈ܕܐ ܐܠܗܐ ܢܚܣܐ ܠܗܘܢ ܘܠܥܢܝ̈ܕܝܗܘܢ ܒܨܠܘܬܗ̇ ܕܝܠܕܬ ܐܠܗܐ ܘܕܟܠܗܘܢ ܩܕܝ̈ܫܐ ܐܡܝܢܐܝܬ ܐܡܝܢ ܟܠ ܕܩܪܐ ܒܟܬܒܐ ܗܢܐ ܢܨܠܐ ܥܠ ܚܛܝܐ ܕܟܬܒ ܀

"Glory to the Father, and to the Son, and to the Holy Ghost, for ever and ever, Amen. In the year 1533 of the Greeks (A.D. 1221), the books belonging to the Convent of the Church of Deipara of the Syrians were repaired, in the days of the presidency of the Count our lord John, and Basil the Head of the convent, and our lord Joseph the Steward. May God in his mercy grant to them and to all the Brethren a good reward! Those with whom he has communicated in word or in deed may God spare them, and the dead belonging to them, through the prayers of the Mother of God, and of all the Saints continually! Amen. Whoso readeth in this book, let him pray for the sinner who wrote this."

This is found at the bottom of the last leaf of the volume, which also comprises the ten last verses of the Gospel of St. Luke, in the same hand as this note, on palimpsest vellum, which was formerly part of a manuscript of the sixth or seventh century, and originally contained a portion of the first chapter of St. Luke in Syriac.

On the first page of the first leaf of this volume the following inscription occurs in a more antient hand: ܐܝܬܘܗܝ ܟܬܒܐ ܗܢܐ ܕܫܡܥܘܢ ܕܕܝܪܐ

ܕܝܗܒܗ ܠܕܝܪܐ ܩܕܝܫܬܐ ܕܥܕܬ ܝܠܕܬ ܐܠܗܐ ܕܣܘܪܝܝܐ ܕܒܡܕܒܪܐ ܕܐܣܩܛܐ.
ܕܐܠܗܐ ܦܝܫ ܪ̈ܚܡܐ ܘܪܘܚܡܐ ܗܘ ܕܡܛܠ ܫܡܗ ܡܫܒܚܐ ܦܪܫ ܘܝܗܒ.
ܣܝܡܬܐ ܗܕܐ ܪܘܚܢܝܬܐ ܗܘ ܢܫܒܘܩ ܚ̈ܛܗܘܗܝ، ܘܢܚܣܘܡ ܒܨܝܪ̈ܘܬܗ، ܘܢܡܢܝܘܗܝ،
ܥܡ ܓܒ̈ܝܐ ܕܝܠܗ ܒܝܘܡܐ ܕܢܘܚܡ ܪ̈ܚܡܘܗܝ، ܒܨ̈ܠܘܬܐ ܕܟܠܗ ܣܕܪܐ ܕܩܕ̈ܝܫܐ
ܐܡܝܢ ܐܡܝܢ ⁘

ܒܪܗ ܕܐܠܗܐ ܚܝܐ ܗܘ ܒܫܥܬܐ ܕܕܝܢܟ ܚܘܣ ܥܠ ܚܛܝܐ ܕܟܬܒ ܐܡܝܢ ⁘

"This book belonged to the monk Habibai, who presented it to the holy convent of the Church of Deipara belonging to the Syrians in the desert of Scete. May God, abounding in mercies and compassion, for the sake of whose glorious name he set apart and gave this spiritual treasure, forgive his sins, and pardon his deficiencies, and number him among his own elect in the day of the resurrection of his friends, through the prayers of all the circle of the Saints! Amen. Amen.

"Son of the Living God, at the hour of thy judgement, spare the sinner who wrote this!"

The volume containing these Fragments of the Gospels was made up, as I have stated above, of parts of several different manuscripts. These were taken, as it would appear, almost by hazard, without any other consideration than that of their being of the same size, and then arranged so as to form a complete copy of the Four Gospels. There were several other volumes in the Nitrian Library made up in this manner. The person who arranged them seems to have had no idea of selecting the scattered parts of the same original volume which had fallen to pieces, but merely to have taken the first leaves that came to his hand which would serve to complete a copy of the Gospels, and then to have bound them together. In this way it came to pass that parts of three or four manuscripts were found mixed up with portions of three or four others, written at different times, and by different scribes; and sometimes, indeed, not even of the same exact size, apparently without regard to any other circumstance than merely to render the context perfect. In re-binding these volumes since they have been deposited in the British Museum, this injury has been in most cases repaired; and the parts of the same copy have been collected, and again bound together in one. Those portions, therefore, of other manuscripts which had been mixed up with these Fragments now printed, have been restored to the original copies to which they formerly belonged.

They consisted, First, of eight leaves of thick vellum, transcribed apparently in the sixth or seventh century, in a very large, bold hand, with the divisions of the sections and canons of Ammonius and Eusebius marked by numeral letters in the margin in red ink; and the canons themselves in the same colour at the bottom of the page. In these eight leaves is comprised Matt. xxiii. 28—xxviii. 42.

Secondly. Ten leaves of very thin and white vellum, in a large hand, in two columns, similar to the former, but apparently rather older. In these leaves is contained Mat. xxviii. 42—Mark vi. 49.

Thirdly. Nineteen leaves, containing Mark. vi. 49—Luke ii. 37, belonging to the same original manuscript as the eight above mentioned.

Fourthly. One leaf without any division of columns, in a more recent hand, comprising Luke ii. 10—iii. 13. This had been added to supply the deficiency caused by the loss of one leaf; and the first page of it, containing Luke ii. 10—37, has been marked as superfluous by several lines drawn through it with a pen.

Fifthly. Twenty-three leaves belonging to the same book as the above-mentioned eight and nineteen, in which is comprised Luke iii. 13—xvii. 28.

On all of these numerous points have been added, to designate the vowels, by a subsequent hand.

Of the original copy of the Syriac Gospels, to which these Fragments now printed belonged, eighty-two leaves and a-half only have reached the British Museum. They have been collected together, and form the volume numbered 14,451. Eighty of these leaves were found in the volume of the Four Gospels above mentioned, and were brought to England in the year 1842. One more leaf I discovered in the binding of another volume, which also arrived at the same time. This contained Luke ii. 48—iii. 16. Another, on which is written Luke xiv. 35—xv. 21, was obtained from M. Pacho in the year 1847; and amongst the small fragments which he brought in the same year I found the part of a leaf containing John xiv. 10—12, 16—18, 21—23, 26—29. This was not discovered in time to insert it in its proper place. It has therefore been printed at the end of the book.

The volume, as at present arranged, consists of the eighty-two leaves and a-half belonging to the original manuscript and five others, which appear to have been added to them in the year of the Greeks 1533 (A.D. 1221), when the volume was bound up in the manner in which it was found at the time that it was obtained from the Syrian monastery. These eighty-two leaves are of large quarto, written in a bold hand in two columns. There are no indications of any division of the Gospels into ecclesiastical Lections, or portions appointed to be read on stated days in the churches, of the same period as the transcription of the volume; but such indications of Lections as have been added subsequently in several places are by different hands, and were written apparently at various periods, sometimes in red ink, and at others in black. The heading at the beginning of the Gospels, and the running title occurring at the top of some of the pages, as well as the colophons, are written in red letters. At the beginning of the Gospel of St. John the following inscription has been added in red letters by a hand several centuries later than the original manuscript ܐܘܢܓܠܝܘܢ ܩܕܝܫܐ ܟܪܘܙܘܬܐ ܕܝܘܚܢܢ ܫܠܝܚܐ ܕܡܠܠ ܝܘܢܐܝܬ ܒܐܦܣܘܣ ܀ ܩܪܝܢܐ ܕܒܝܬ ܕܢܚܐ. "The Holy Gospel—the preaching of the Apostle St. John, which he spake in Greek at Ephesus. Lection of the Epiphany."

The first words of the Benedictions in the Sermon on the Mount in St. Matthew's Gospel are also written in red letters. In the punctuation the single points are almost always red. When there are more than one point at the end of a section—thus, ∘∘ ∘∘ ∘∘ or ∘∘∘ or thus ∘⁘∘—the outer points are usually red, and the inner black. The vellum formerly was extremely white, and in such leaves as have not been much exposed to the atmosphere it still remains so.

I have no doubt that this copy of the Gospels is of the fifth century—probably transcribed about the middle of it. When it first came into my hands, I laid it aside among the other earliest manuscripts of the Gospels without further examination at that time, concluding, from its external marks of antiquity, that it must have been written at a period even more remote than the time of Philoxenus, and that it could not therefore be other than an early copy of the Peshito. The next time I took it up I was struck by observing that several erasures had been made in the fifth and seventh chapters of the Gospel of St. Matthew and other words supplied. This led me to examine the matter more closely, when I ascertained that this had been done with regard to words and passages which had differed from the text of the Peshito; they had been erased, and the others from the Peshito had been supplied. A little further examination shewed that the text before me was very different from that of the Peshito; and, indeed, belonged to a recension of the Gospels in Syriac hitherto altogether unknown in Europe.

The first cursory reading of these remnants of the Gospels, which, beyond all question, are of very high antiquity, convinced me of the great importance of this recension for the critical arrangement of the text of the Gospels, as being one of the earliest testimonies extant; and all my subsequent study of them has tended to confirm this opinion. I resolved, therefore, to edit the Syriac text with a literal English translation, and to illustrate it with notes in which I purposed to point out all the variations which it exhibits from the ordinary

Textus Receptus of the Greek; and to shew by what antient authorities they were supported from the earliest period down to the date of the manuscript. In the course of this examination several curious and important questions relative to the text arose, these I purposed to discuss according to my ability, and to insert them in the notes at the places where they would occur. This latter part of my undertaking, although considerably advanced, I have thought it better to defer for the present, to wait till I shall have had opportunity of considering these subjects more fully myself, and also have had the benefit of the critical opinion of other scholars, especially those of Germany, who doubtless will examine these Fragments of the Gospel fully and accurately; and, as I have reason to know, have been long looking forward for their publication. On a subject of such deep weight as that of the Gospels, I feel that no one can be too cautious how he propounds any theory or speculation at all varying from that which has been most generally received, even if he have almost demonstrative evidence to support the views which he takes. For myself I should much prefer that another have the credit of being the first to make known any facts or illustrations founded upon this recension, which may seem to go very far towards determining some doubtful or disputed matters, than that, from a desire to appropriate this credit to myself, I should run the risk of advancing any arguments which, although apparently conclusive, still may be defective, and lead to error; or should keep back any longer the text itself of these Fragments from the perusal of other scholars who have been anxiously looking for their publication, and who may be able to use them with much advantage in their critical examination of the Gospels. I shall confine myself, therefore, at present, to the task of pointing out a few of the leading characteristics of this recension, and more especially in the Gospel of St. Matthew, with the hope of taking up and completing my undertaking in a subsequent volume.

The Gospels are arranged in this manuscript in the following order, Matthew, Mark, John, Luke. All that exists at present of this copy, and printed in this volume, is, Matthew i. 1—viii. 22; x. 32—xxiii. 25; Mark xvi. 17—20; John i. 1—42; iii. 6—vii. 37; xiv. 10—12, 16—18, 19—23, 26—29; Luke ii. 48—iii. 16; vii. 33—xv. 21; xvii. 24—xxiv. 44.

GOSPEL OF SAINT MATTHEW.

This has a title different from the rest; for while that of Mark is simply ܐܘܢܓܠܝܘܢ ܕܡܪܩܘܣ "Gospel of Mark," and that of John, ܐܘܢܓܠܝܘܢ ܕܝܘܚܢܢ "Gospel of John," St. Matthew is ܐܘܢܓܠܝܘܢ ܕܡܦܪܫܐ ܡܬܝ, which I have rendered, "The distinct Gospel of Matthew." There is a small defect in the vellum immediately before the word ܡܬܝ. It seems probable that the particle ܕ occupied this space, and that it ought, therefore, to be supplied. I cannot venture to assert that this translation is certainly the correct one. In my doubts upon this matter I applied to my very learned friend, Professor Bernstein, at Breslau, the father of Syriac scholars of the present day, for his opinion as to the proper mode of rendering this title. He conceives the correct translation to be "Evangelium per anni circulum dispositum," and refers to Assemani's Bibliotheca Orient. Clemen. Vat., vol. ii. p. 230, where ܐܘܢܓܠܝܘܢ ܕܡܦܪܫܐ is so translated by Assemani, by which he intends it to mean a copy of the Gospels divided into *αναγνωσματα*, or lections, that is, portions appointed to be read on certain days throughout the course of the year. There are several such copies found among the volumes of the Nitrian collection to which this belongs. But the great objection to this interpretation is in the fact, that this copy is not so arranged, nor are there any indications whatever of such lections, written at the same period at which this title with the rest of the volume was copied. In a few places indications of lections have been subsequently added, but by a much later hand—indeed, several centuries after this copy of the Gospels was transcribed. Nor have I seen any volume of the Gospels in this collection so arranged into lections for the year that is not of much more recent date than this. It seems to me that whatever meaning is to be given to the word ܡܦܪܫܐ, it is intended to denote that, in some way or other, the Gospel of St. Matthew is to be regarded as distinct from the other three Gospels in this copy; and certainly it is in every way to be considered as a text far superior to the others: they exhibit several marks of blunders and mistakes in the translation from the Greek into Syriac, while this Gospel of St. Matthew appears at least to be built upon the original Aramaic text, which was the work of the Apostle himself.

CHAPTER I.

v. 1. *Generations*—In the plural, like the Hebrew ספר תולדות, Gen. v. 1, which the Peshito also has in the plural, as here, while the Septuagint reads γενεσεως, as in the Greek in this place.

2. *Isaac*—This name, according to the Syriac, should be pronounced *Ishac.* I have, however, given the proper names as they are read in our English version, except where there is some peculiarity to shew that the Syriac varies from the Greek. In this copy, as well as in the printed editions of the Peshito, these proper names approach much nearer to the Hebrew form than in the Greek. The version commonly called the Philoxenian, which was made directly from the Greek at a later period, follows the Greek orthography exactly in the proper names, and also adds the particle ܕܝܢ for δε of the Greek, which is not found either in this copy or in the Peshito. It would carry me too far to speak here at any greater length respecting the variation or peculiarity in the proper names of this genealogy, this will be more appropriately considered in the notes.

8. The three kings in the line of the descent omitted in the Greek, Ahazia, Joash, and Amuzia, 1 Chron. iii. 11, are added here. It appears that these names formerly existed in some antient copies of the Syriac or Aramaic Gospel in use in the East; and the reason for their subsequent omission stated by Dionysius Bar Salibi seems to be not improbable. Indeed, long before I read the passage of Bar Salibi, which I am about to quote, this had suggested itself to my own consideration. In a treatise by Mar Yakub the Persian, entitled ܬܚܘܝܬܐ ܕܦܪܕܬܐ, and composed in the year of the Greeks 656, or A.D. 342, of which there are two copies in the British Museum—the one, 17,182, transcribed as early as the fifth century, and the other,* 14,619, written about a hundred years later—these three names are found in the genealogy of Jesus, which he gives and makes to consist of sixty-three races from Adam to Christ.† They are also

* This volume is in two parts: the first was written in the year of the Greeks 785 (A.D. 473): the second, although apparently not in the same hand, is certainly of the same period.

† I transcribe the whole of this genealogy from 14,619, fol. 163.b, which appears to be the more correct: ܡܢܝܢ ܡܢܝܢ ܫܘܒܥܒܢܐ ܕܫܠܡܝܢ ܫܬܝܢ ܘܬܠܬ ܫܪܒܢ ܡܢ ܐܕܡ ܠܡܫܝܚܐ
ܕܐܬܡܠܝ: ܡܫܝܚܐ ◦◦◦ ܐܕܡ. ܫܝܬ. ܐܢܘܫ. ܩܝܢܢ. ܡܗܠܠܐܝܠ. ܝܪܕ. ܚܢܘܟ.
ܡܬܘܫܠܚ. ܠܡܟ. ܢܘܚ. ܫܡ. ܐܪܦܟܫܕ. ܫܠܚ. ܥܒܪ. ܦܠܓ. ܐܪܥܘ. ܣܪܘܓ. ܢܚܘܪ.
ܬܪܚ. ܐܒܪܗܡ. ܐܝܣܚܩ. ܝܥܩܘܒ. ܝܗܘܕܐ. ܦܪܨ. ܚܨܪܘܢ. ܐܪܡ. ܥܡܝܢܕܒ.
ܢܚܫܘܢ. ܣܠܡܐ. ܒܥܙ. ܥܘܒܝܕ. ܐܝܫܝ. ܕܘܝܕ. ܫܠܝܡܘܢ. ܪܚܒܥܡ. ܐܒܝܐ. ܐܣܐ.
ܝܗܘܫܦܛ. ܝܘܪܡ. ܐܚܙܝܐ. ܝܘܐܫ. ܐܡܘܨܝܐ. ܥܘܙܝܐ. ܝܘܬܡ. ܐܚܙ.
ܚܙܩܝܐ. ܡܢܫܐ. ܐܡܘܢ ܝܘܫܝܐ. ܝܘܝܩܝܡ. ܝܘܟܢܝܐ. ܫܠܬܐܝܠ. ܙܘܪܒܒܠ.

found in the book called the "Cave of Treasures," ܡܥܪܬ ܓܙܐ,* fol. 37. We have here, in the Greek, *Οζιας*, like this Syriac text, and not *Αζαριας*, as it is in the Septuagint and עזריה in the Hebrew, 1 Chron. iii. 12. The Peshito, however, in that place reads ܥܘܙܝܐ Uzia. The variation has doubtless arisen from the similarity of the words עזיה and עזריה. In 2 Kings xv. 1, 30, we find the name written both ways; and in 2 Chron. xxv. the name of the king is given as Uzziah, and that of the priest Azariah. Various reasons have been assigned by different authors from very antient times to account for the omission of these three names. I will give here only such as I have found mentioned by Dionysius Bar Salibi, who compiled a commentary upon the Scriptures from earlier writers in the twelfth century.† Assemani has cited a part of his commentary upon this place, with a Latin translation, in the second volume of his Bibliotheca Orientalis, p. 160. Dudley Loftus, the friend, and afterwards successor, of the very learned Ussher in the Archiepiscopal see of Armagh, has also translated this passage into English; ‡ but his translation has so many

ܐܒܝܘܕ. ܐܠܝܩܝܡ. ܥܙܘܪ. ܨܕܘܩ. ܐܟܝܢ. ܐܠܝܘܕ. ܐܠܥܙܪ. ܡܬܢ. ܝܥܩܘܒ. ܝܘܣܦ.
ܘܝܫܘܥ. ܒܪܗ ܕܐܠܗܐ ܕܐܬܝܠܕ ܡܢ ܡܪܝܡ ܒܬܘܠܬܐ ܘܐܬܩܪܝ، ܝܘܣܦ ܐܒܘܗܝ،

"Now receive the reckoning of these sixty-three races from Adam up to the birth of the Messiah. Adam, Seth, Enos, Cainan, Mahallael, Jared, Henoch, Methushelah, Lamek, Noah, Shem, Arphacshar, Shelah, Eber, Peleg, Areu, Serug, Nahor, Therah, Abraham, Isaac, Jacob, Juda, Pharez, Hezron, Aram, Aminadab, Nashon, Shela, Boaz, Ober, Jesse, David, Solomon, Rehoboam, Abia, Asa, Jehoshaphat, Jehoram, Ahazia, Joash, Amuzia, Uzia, Jotham, Ahaz, Hezekia, Manasse, Amon, Joshia, Joiakim, Joiacin, Shealthiel, Zurbabel, Abiud, Eliakim, Azor, Zadok, Acin, Eliud, Eleazar, Mathan, Jacob, Joseph, and Jesus the Son of God, who was born of Mary the Virgin, and Joseph was called his father"—In this list given by Mar Yakub the Persian the names correspond very closely with those in this copy of St. Matthew. We have here Shela, as in verse 4, instead of Salmon of the Greek and Peshito; but at Ruth iv. 20 the Peshito reads ܫܠܐ. and the Hebrew שלמה, and in the next verse שלמון. At 1 Chron. ii. 10 the Hebrew reads שלמא, and the Peshito ܣܠܡܐ: Septuagint, Σαλμων. In the copy of the *Cave of Treasures* ܡܥܪܬ ܓܙܐ fol. 27.a, this name is written ܫܠܐ. and 27.b, ܫܝܠܐ, with a note in the margin, ܫܝܠܐ ܗܘܝܘ ܣܠܡܘܢ. "Shela, that is, Salmon;" so that at fol. 36 we find Salmon in the genealogy. In the genealogy by St. Luke, iii. 35, the name is *Σαλα*, which the Peshito represents by ܫܠܚ. The word ܫܝܠܐ is the same as Silas, Acts xv. 22, with which the Hebrew שֵׁלָה corresponds, see Numbers xxvi. 20, where the Peshito has ܫܠܐ, as here, and the Septuagint Σηλωμ: see Genesis xlvi. 12. The reading of Arphacshar and Ober arises from the confusion and interchange of ר for ד, which is of very common occurrence. See what Kirsch has written on this head in the preface to his edition of the Syriac Pentateuch, p. x.

* See Assemani Bibl. Orient. Clem. Vat. ii. p. 498, iii. p. 281.

† See Assemani Bibl. Orient. Clem. Vat. ii. p. 156.

‡ In his book entitled "A Clear and Learned Exposition of the History of our Blessed

errors, that I have thought it better to supply another English version of my own.

"But why did he omit Ahazia, and Joash, and Amuzia? Some say that Africanus, bishop of Emmaus,* declares the reason that he omitted them to be because they were sinners and of the seed of Jezebel. To him we reply that they were not of the seed of Jezebel; for Jezebel was the wife of Ahab, but Joram took to wife Athalia, the daughter of Omri, the sister of Ahab, and of her he begat Ahazia. Nevertheless, in one place, according to the sense of the Septuagint, she is called the daughter of Ahab, on account of her wickedness being of the same kind, as St. Severus explains it. But the mother of Joash was named Zauba† of Beersheba, and the mother of Amuzia was Jehoaddan of Jerusalem. They were not, therefore, of the seed of Jezebel; neither were they greater sinners than Solomon, Ahaz, and Menasse, whose names are written in the genealogy. St. Severus saith that Joram, the son of Jehosaphat, married Athalia, the daughter of Ahab, and of her he begat Ahazia, Joash, and Amuzia; and Matthew omitted them because the Hebrews hated the idolatry of the house of Ahab, and therefore he made no mention of these, who were born of an idolatrous marriage, calling to mind the words, *I punish the sins of the fathers upon the children unto the third and fourth generations of them that hate me.* To him some reply, that Athalia, the wife of Joram and mother of Ahazia, was not the daughter of Ahab, but Omri's daughter, and Ahab's sister; and if it were out of regard to the Hebrews that he abstained from making mention of those who were descended from Athalia, how comes it to pass that he has mentioned Uzia who was a leper, and more abominated by the Jews than these? Origen ‡ says that he omitted them in order that the generations from

Saviour Jesus Christ, taken out of above thirty Greek, Syriack, and other Oriental Authors, by way of *Catena*: by DIONYSIUS SYRUS, who flourished most illustriously in the *tenth* and *eleventh centuries*, and faithfully translated by DUDLEY LOFTUS. 4to., Dublin, 1695.

* Julius Africanus, being himself a Syrian, is cited also by other Syriac authors, as Barcephas, Barhebræus, George, metropolitan of Arbela, &c. See Assemani, Bibl. Orient. ii. 158, 283, 310, iii. 520. The passage alluded to here is probably taken from his Epistle to Aristides on the supposed disagreement of Matthew and Luke in the genealogy of Christ. See Eusebius Hist. Eccl. vi. 31: or his Commentary on the Gospel. See Assemani, ibid. iii. 14.

† ܨܘܒܐ as in the Peshito, Heb. סִבְיָה, Sept. Σαβια, 2 Kings xii. 1.

‡ The passage to which he refers is in the twenty-seventh homily of Origen on the Book of Numbers—De *Mansionibus Filiorum Israel.* "Sed primo omnium, intuere mysterii rationen: quam qui diligenter observaverit, in scripturis inveniet in egressione filiorum Israel de Ægypto, quadraginta et duas habitas esse mansiones; et rursum adventus Domini et Salvatoris nostri in hunc mundum per quadraginta et duas generationes adducitur. Sic enim Matthæus

David to the captivity might be so arranged as to make the number fourteen, because three times fourteen amount to forty-two generations; and this was a type shewing, that as, at the end of forty-two encampments, the people of Israel entered upon the inheritance of the land of promise, so at the end of forty-two generations Christ arose and conferred the inheritance of this temporal earth upon the saints. George of the Gentiles * says that Matthew did not omit these three persons, nor did he change the number of the generations, and say fourteen instead of seventeen; but inasmuch as he wrote his Gospel for the Jews, and many of them were learned in the Greek language, when they desired to translate into the Greek from the Hebrew, inasmuch as the Greek language was not able to express the letters ח, ע, and צ like the Hebrew and Syriac tongues, nor indeed has it at all in its alphabet deep guttural letters, when the translators came to Joram, and it is said that he begat Ahazia, and he Joash, and he Amuzia, and Amuzia Uzia, and wanted to express these in Greek, they wrote their names thus, *Ιωραμ* begat *Οχοζιαν*, and *Οχοζιας Ιωαν*, and *Ιωας Ομοσιαν*, and *Ομοσιας Οσιαν*. But others afterwards, desiring to copy the Gospel in the Greek language, when they began from hence that Joram begat *Οχοζιαν*, wrote "Joram begat *Οζιαν*," on account of the similitude of the names, and their variation in the single letter Caph. This, perhaps, they did unintentionally; or they might have done it on purpose to accommodate the series of generations to fourteen, because the septenary number was much cherished by those who had embraced Christianity from among the Jews; and by such means corrupted copies were transmitted to the Gentiles.—To him we reply that this is not correct; for had it been an error or a blunder of the transcriber, and Matthew himself had not omitted them, then Matthew ought to have said, that from David to the Captivity there were seventeen generations; but inasmuch

Evangelista commemorat, dicens: "Ab Abraham usque ad David regem generationes quatuordecim, et a David usque ad transmigrationem Babylonis generationes quatuordecim, et a transmigratione Babylonis usque ad Christum generationes quatuordecim." Istas ergo quadraginta et duas generationes, quas velut mansiones Christus fecit descendens in Ægyptum mundi hujus, ipso numero quadraginta et duas mansiones faciunt, qui ascendunt de Ægypto.—Igitur in quadraginta duabus mansionibus perveniunt filii Israel usque ad principium capiendæ hæreditatis." &c. Origenis Opera. Omm. edit. Delarue, vol. ii. p. 375.

* Assemani has given the text of this part with a Latin translation in the second volume of his Bibl. Orient. p. 160; but it varies a little from that of the two manuscripts in the British Museum which I have compared (7184 and 12,143). George of the Gentiles, or George of Arabs, as he is otherwise called, was consecrated bishop in the year of the Greeks 998, A.D. 686 (see Assemani, ibid, p. 335). He is also cited by Barhebræus (see ibid 283, &c.)

as Matthew wrote fourteen generations, we therefore perceive that Matthew himself did not omit them."

"Others say that the Christians of the Hebrews removed these three, in order to accommodate the generations from David to the Captivity to the number fourteen, because this number was cherished by them ; for there is found occasionally a Syriac copy made out of the Hebrew, which inserts these three kings in the genealogy ; but that it afterwards speaks of fourteen and not seventeen generations is because fourteen generations has been substituted for seventeen by the Hebrews, on account of their holding to the septenary number, which is much cherished by them, because on the fourteenth they were delivered from the bondage of the Egyptians."

"Others again say that Matthew omitted these names because they were abominable in the eyes of the people : for Ahazia connected himself with the house of Ahab when he sent ships to fetch gold ; and he went up with Ahab to Ramoth Gilead, and the prophet rebuked him, and he was afterwards slain by Jehu : and Joash, because he put to death the sons of Jehoiada the priest : Amuzia also was slain in rebellion, having stirred up the king of Israel to war with him ; and on his account, and by his hands, the wall was broken down and the Sanctuary violated ; and for this reason Matthew omitted them. Let the reader, however, choose that which pleases him."

11. *Josia begat Jeconia*—as in the Greek. Some Syriac copies, however, inserted Jehoiakim.* The same George of the Gentiles who is quoted above by Dionysius Bar Salibi declares that it did originally stand so.† ܘܡܛܠ ܠܐ ܟܬܒ ܡܬܝ، ܘܝܘܫܝܐ ܐܘܠܕ ܠܝܘܝܩܝܡ. ܘܝܘܝܩܝܡ ܠܝܘܟܢܝܐ. ܘܓܐܘܪܓܝܣ ܐܡܪ ܕܗܟܢ ܟܬܝܒ ܗܘܐ ܐܠܐ ܟܬܘܒܐ ܛܥܐ ܘܟܬܒ ܚܠܦ ܝܘܝܩܝܡ ܝܘܟܢܝܐ, "And why did not Matthew write, *and Josia begat Jehoiakim, and Jehoiakim Jeconia.* But George says that it was so written, but the transcriber made a mistake, and wrote Jehoiakim instead of Jeconia."

16. *To whom was espoused Mary the Virgin, which bare Jesus the Messiah*—With this the Old Latin version, before it was corrected by Jerome, agrees : ***a b c d***,‡ "Cui desponsata virgo Maria : Maria autem peperit Jesus qui dicitur

* See Versio Syriaca Philoxeniana, edit. J. White, Oxon, 1778, pp. 2, 563.

† Add. MSS., Mus. Brit., 7184, f. 4.

‡ I use here the signs generally employed by the critical editors of the Greek Testament to distinguish certain well-known manuscripts—(*a*) Codex Vercellensis, (*b*) Veronensis, (*c*) Colbertinus, (*d*) Cantabrigiensis, Bezæ ; and for the Greek—(A) Codex Alexandrinus, (B) Vaticanus, (C) Regius Ephraemi palimpsestus, (D) Catabrigiensis, Bezæ.

Christus." The Greek reads, *τον ανδρα Μαριας, εξ ης εγεννηθη Ιησους ο λεγομενος Χριστος*, which the printed editions of the Peshito follow.

17. According to the text of this copy, which introduces the three kings omitted in the Greek, the number from David to the Captivity ought to be seventeen races or generations, instead of fourteen. George of the Gentiles, cited above, says that Matthew did write here originally seventeen ; and, indeed, the two words in the Hebrew character שבעסרא and ארבעסרא are sufficiently similar to have easily caused such an error, especially when one of them in either case must have occurred twice.

18. *The Messiah*—And so the Peshito, the Old Latin *a b c d*, and the edition corrected by Jerome : Irenæus also read it so, but the Greek adds *Ιησου*.

19. *But Joseph, because he was a righteous man*—The Old Latin *a b c* has *cum esset homo justus*, but the Greek *Ιωσηφ δε ο ανηρ αυτης, δικαιος ων*. In the next verse, 20, we find *thine espoused* instead of *την γυναικα σου*. The Peshito follows the Greek. In Luke ii. 5 she is called *Μαριαμ τῇ μεμνηστευμενῃ αυτῳ* ; and Joseph, in the Protevangelium of James, is made to call her his *espoused*, but to deny that she was his *wife*. *η δε ειπεν, Και τις εστιν η γεννωσα εν τῃ σπηλαιᾳ; και ειπον εγω, Η μεμνηστευμενη μοι. Και ειπε μοι, Ουκ εστιν σου γυνη ; και ειπον αυτῃ, Μαριαμ εστιν η ανατραφεισα εν τῳ ναῳ κυριου, και εκληρωσαμην αυτην γυναικα. Και ουκ εστιν μοι γυνη, αλλα συλληψιν εχει εκ πνευματος αγιου.** In this verse we have "in a *vision* of the night" for *κατ' οναρ* (see ii. 12).

21. *He shall save the world*—Greek *τον λαον αυτου* ; Peshito, ܠܥܡܗ. The variation must have arisen from the similarity of לעלמא and לעמא.

22. *By the mouth of Esaia the prophet*, Greek *δια του προφητου* ; and Peshito ܒܝܕ ܢܒܝܐ, "*by the hand* of the Prophet," which is merely an Aramaism, signifying the instrument, like *δια* of the Greek.

23. *Shall be called—our God with us.* Mar Yakub the Persian, mentioned above, cites this passage as follows, ܗܐ ܒܬܘܠܬܐ ܬܒܛܢ ܘܬܐܠܕ. ܘܢܬܩܪܐ ܫܡܗ ܥܡܢܘܐܝܠ ܕܐܬܦܫܩܗ، ܐܠܗܢ ܥܡܢ, "Lo a virgin shall conceive and bring forth, and his name shall be called Emmanuel, which is, *Our God with us*."

25. *Took Mary, and dwelt purely with her till she bare the son, and she called his name Jesus.* Here again we have *Mary* instead of *την γυναικα αυτου*.

CH. II. v. 1. *of Juda*—with which the Peshito concurs ; Greek *της Ιουδαιας* ; but *Juda* was the reading of the Hebrew Gospel which Jerome had in his

* See Evangelia Apochrypha, edit. Const. Tischendorf, 8vo. Lips. 1853. p. 34.

hands: "Putamus enim ab Evangelista primum editum, sicut in ipso Hebraico legimus, *Judæ* non Judææ.*

7. *To them*—omitted in the Greek, but the Old Latin *a b c* reads "paruit *eis* stella."

11. *The boy*—in the masculine; but the Greek *το παιδιον*; the Codex Bezæ D has here, and in the places where it occurs below, *τον παιδα*; and at v. 16 the Greek text also has *παντας τους παιδας*.

18. *In Ramtha*—and so the Peshito. . The Greek has *Ραμα*. This word signifies *the height*, and some of the translators of the orginal Aramaic Gospel into Greek rendered it so. Origen tells us, that in his days there were some copies which had this reading: *Τοπον υψηλον σημαινει το ραμα· διο και εν τισι των αντιγραφων βιβλιων ουτω γεγραπται, Εν τη υφηλη ηκουσθη*.† Jerome also writes "Quod autem dicitur in *Rama*, non putemus loci nomen esse juxta Gabaa, sed *Rama* 'excelsum,' interpretatur, ut sit sensus; Vox in excelso audita est, id est, longe lateque dispersa." ‡ It seems, however, to be certainly a proper name, and the same as that which, xxvii. 57, is called in the Greek *Αριμαθαια*; in the Peshito the same word ܪܡܬܐ is always used where *Αριμαθαια* occurs in the Greek, Mark xv. 43, Luke xxiii. 51, John xix. 38. The Greek seems to have originated in the form ܐܪܡܬܐ with the Olaph prefixed, to facilitate the pronunciation of the Rish. This was very common in words of which the first radical was Rish, as is well known to all who are familiar with the Syriac language. I may state that I have found this form the most common in the earliest manuscripts.§ *The voice of Rachel*—the Greek omits *voice*.

20. *To take it away*—is not found in the Greek. It is like the passage, 1 Kings xix. 10, "and they seek my life to take it away." But it would swell this preface to too wide an extent were I to proceed to notice the variations in this text, even at no greater length than I have done in these two first chapters, although I have omitted many which suggest several important considerations as to which were the very words of the Evangelist. I shall therefore only notice a few of the principal variations that occur in the remaining chapters, chiefly those which relate to additions or omissions, or such

* See Jerome's Commentary on St. Matthew at this verse.

† See Origen. Cat. Gr. in Matt. ii. 18, cited by Simon. Hist. Crit. du Text du N. T. p. 399.

‡ See Jerome, ibid, at this verse.

§ See the passage cited from Mar Yakub, p. 7 above, when we have ܐܪܥܘ Areu for רעו Reu.

as may seem especially to bear upon the subject of the original Aramaic text.

CH. III. v. 3. *written*—Greek ο ρηθεις, and Peshito ܐܬܐܡܪ *spoken of*; but Luke in the parallel passage, iii. 4, has ως γεγραπται. In the quotation from Isaiah xl. 3, we have *the paths of our God*, as in the Hebrew לאלהינו, which Mar Yakub the Persian also confirms, and one copy of the Old Latin *b*; but Mark and Luke both have τας τριβους αυτου as in the Greek text here.

4. *Was clad in raiment of the hair*—Greek ειχεν το ενδυμα αυτου απο τριχων. Mark i. 6, ην ενδεδυμενος τριχας.

5. *The children of Jerusalem*—an Aramaism, signifying simply the people or inhabitants of Jerusalem: οι Ιεροσολυμιται, as Mark gives it. The Greek has only Ιεροσολυμα, with which the Peshito concurs. Of the copies of the Old Latin, *a* reads *omnis Hierosolyma, b ex Herosolymis, c ab Ierosolymis*; the two latter as if it had been read מן אורשלם for בני אורשלם; all seeming to shew that there existed in the original from which they were taken some additional word, which afterwards was omitted. The Old Latin *a b c* agrees with this in having the plural *were coming*; and also *loins* in the preceding verse; while the Greek has both in the singular εξεπορευετο and την οσφυν. The word *river*, omitted in the Greek, is here added to *Jordan*, and so frequently throughout this text.

9. *and say not*—Greek και μη δοξητε λεγειν. Luke iii. 8, και μη αρξησθε λεγειν.

10. *Lo the axe is arrived*—Greek ηδη δε—κειται, and so Luke iii. 9. The variation must have arisen either from confounding ιδε with ηδη in the Greek, or הא ιδε with השא, ηδη in the Aramaic, while the difference between *arrived* and *laid* probably arose from the transposition of the letters in סים and מטי.

11. *to bear*—Greek βαστασαι. In the parallel passage both Luke iii. 16 and Mark i. 7 have λυσαι; and in the latter some copies add κυψας, although this word is omited in the Codex Bezæ D and in the Old Latin *a b c*. Did this variation arise from their having read in the Aramaic document למשריו, *to lose*, instead of למשקל, *to bear?*

14. *and John forbad*—with the Old Latin *a b c d*: Greek ο δε διεκωλυεν only. In the account of the baptism of our Lord there are several variations from the Greek text, which are suggestive of some interesting critical inquiries. I can, however, only mention one or two here.

16. The Spirit of God *rested* upon him; while the Greek has ερχομενον επ' αυτον, which the Peshito follows. The Gospel according to the Hebrews, which doubtless had the original Aramaic of Matthew for its basis, reads here, *et requievit super eum* (see Jerome's Com. on Isaiah ii. 1). John i. 32 has also και εμεινεν επ'

αυτον; and in Mark i. 10 several Greek manuscripts add *και μενον*: the Old Latin *b* has also *et manentem*, which the Coptic and Æthiopic versions confirm. *The Spirit of God* is here in the feminine according to the usage of the Aramaic, and so in the Peshito. In the Philoxenian version the masculine is employed to agree with the Greek, and probably with a doctrinal view.

17. *Thou art my son and my beloved*—Greek *ουτος εστιν ο υιος μου ο αγαπητος*; but the Codex Bezæ D has *συ ει ο υιος μου*, and also the Old Latin *a*. This is likewise the reading both of Mark, i. 11 and Luke, iii. 22. Justin Martyr cites it, *συ μου ει ο υιος* (Dialog. Tr. 88). The Gospel according to the Hebrews also reads *tu es filius meus* (see Jerome, Com. on Isaiah xi. 1); and in like manner the Gospel of the Ebionites, *συ μου ει ο υιος ο αγαπητος* (Ephiphanius, Contra Hæres. 30. 13). The variation seems to have arisen from the Greek translator reading איח הו instead of אנת הו, and then having rendered it *ουτος εστιν* instead of *συ ει*. In this same verse for the reading *and a voice was heard from heaven* וקלא אשתמע מן שמיא the Greek has *και ιδου φωνη εκ των ουρανων*. Probably the Greek translator was led to omit a word from the alliteration of אשתמע and שמיא. for Mark i. 11 has *και φωνη εγενετο εκ των ουρανων*, and Luke iii. 22 *και φωνην εξ ουρανου γενεσθαι*, both differently from the Greek of Matthew. I may observe here, that in parallel passages of the Gospels, where the Greek of Matthew varies in some word from this Aramaic text, Mark and Luke generally vary likewise.

CH. IV. v. 1. *Spirit of Holiness*—that is, the Holy Spirit. The Greek has only *του πνευματος*: Luke iv. 1, has *πληρης πνευματος αγιου υπεστρεψεν απο Ιορδανου, και ηγετο εν τῳ πνευματι*. We have here *Satan*: Greek *του διαβολου*; but Mark i. 12 has *του Σαταvᾶ*.

2. *Forty days*—Greek adds *και νυκτας τεσσαρακοντα*, which the Peshito follows; but both Mark i. 13 and Luke iv. 2 omit the *forty nights*.

4. *Jesus*—although omitted in other Greek copies, is found in Cod. Bezæ D, and in the Old Latin *b c*, as well as in the corresponding passage of Luke. *thing*—I have given this rendering of the original ܦܬܓܡܐ to distinguish it from ܡܠܬܐ *word*, of the Peshito, which has followed the Greek *ρηματι*, and because of the original meaning of the Hebrew (Deut. viii. 3), כל מוצא פי יהוה, "whatsoever cometh out of the mouth of Jehovah (or the LORD)." The Peshito of Deuteronomy has rendered the Hebrew exactly, ܟܠ ܡܕܡ ܕܡܦܩ ܒܦܘܡܗ ܕܡܪܝܐ, "every thing that cometh out of the mouth of the LORD." The *Lord* is the reading of our copy; but the Greek of Matthew has *Θεου*; and, indeed, this quotation, as we find it in the Greek of Matthew, is word for word from the Septuagint.

9. *worship before me*—Greek μοι only, which the Peshito follows, reading ܠܝ. Luke iv. 7 has προσκυνησῃς ενωπιον μου, and the Peshito has rendered it there exactly as it is here ܬܣܓܘܕ ܩܕܡܝ. This, which is more peculiarly an Aramaic idiom, is also more in accordance with the expression ***Get thee behind me*** in v. 10, which, although omitted in several Greek manuscripts and in the Peshito, is confirmed by the palimpsest Codex Ephraemi C, the Codex Bezæ D, and the Dublin Codex Z, as well as by the Old Latin *a b c*.

11. *for a season*—omitted in the Greek and in the Peshito. If it did not belong to the original Aramaic Gospel it has probably been added from Luke iv. 13, αχρι καιρου, which the Peshito renders in that place as this copy has it here ܥܕ ܠܙܒܢܐ.

16. *have seen*—Greek in the singular ειδε, except the Codex Bezæ C, which has ειδον, and is supported by the Old Latin *a b c*. χωρᾳ και of the Greek is omitted here and also by *a c*.

17. μετανοειτε and γαρ, are omitted, thus marking a difference between the commencement of the preaching of Jesus and that of John the Baptist, iii. 2.*

18. *Andrieus*—as if it had been ανδρειος instead of ανδρεας. I find the same form also in an ancient martyrology dated A.D. 411.

19. *fishers*—The word ܨܝܕܐ, which I have translated thus, as in the English version, means *hunters* or *catchers* of any kind, and not simply *fishermen*, αλιεις, as we find it in the Greek. Luke, v. 10, has more accurately expressed the meaning of the Aramaic term by ανθρωπους εσῃ ζωγρων.

21. *while they were sitting*—this is not in the Greek.

22. *their nets*—The received reading here, chiefly upon the authority of B D *a*, is το πλοιον και τον πατερα αυτων, but the Old Latin *b c* and the edition of Jerome have *relictis retibus et patre*. Mark i. 20 reads, τον πατερα αυτων Ζεβεδαιον εν τῳ πλοιῳ μετα των μισθωτων.

24. This verse varies otherwise from the Greek, but principally by the addition of the words *and upon each one of them he was laying his hand*: this might have been added from Luke iv. 40, ο δε ενι εκαστῳ αυτων τας χειρας επιτιθεις; or it might have been omitted by the Greek translator of the original Gospel from error on account of the similarity of the ending of the two consecutive sentences סאם הוא and מאסא הוא. *all*—generally omitted in the Greek, is found also in Cod. Bezæ D and in the Old Latin *a b c*.

* Some Greek copies omit these words according to the authority of a Scholiast on this verse cited by Griesbach.

CH. V. verses 4 and 5 are not in the order in which they are at present found in most Greek manuscripts; but in that in which they were read by Origen. This is also the order of the Eusebian canons and the Sections of Ammonius, and of the Old Latin, as well as of the copies revised by Jerome.*

6. *Justice*—is the rendering of ܙܕܝܩܘܬܐ; and so at verse 10. The Greek is δικαιοσυνη, which the Peshito has represented by ܟܐܢܘܬܐ.

11. *persecute you and revile you*—The Codex Bezæ D *d* confirms this order.

12. *in that day*—omitted in the Greek, but found in the parallel passage of Luke vi. 23. *your fathers* אבהיכון—This also is omitted. Two copies of the Old Latin *b c* read *patres eorum,* אבהידהון which Irenæus and Cyprian confirm. Luke also has οι πατερες αυτων,

15. *and no man lighteth a candle*—Greek ουδε καιουσιν λυχνον; but Luke has twice, viii. 16 and xi, 33, ουδεις δε λυχνον αψας.

18. *Letter Yod—letter* is omitted in the Greek.

23. *enmity,* אכתא—omitted in the Greek, but retained in the Peshito, with the addition of ܡܕܡ to correspond with τι.

25. *Exactor,* ܬܒܥܐ or collector of tribute, which the Peshito retains; Greek τῳ υπηρετῃ. At Luke xii. 58 the Greek πρακτωρ is rendered, both in this copy and the Peshito, by the same word ܬܒܥܐ.

26. *Schamún*—which the Peshito also retains: Greek κοδραντην. In the parallel passage of Luke xii. 59, we read λεπτον, for which the Peshito, as well as this copy, has ܫܡܘܢܐ. In Mark xii. 42, λεπτα δυο, ο εστιν κοδραντης is rendered in the Peshito ܬܪܬܝܢ ܡܢܝܢ ܕܐܝܬܝܗܘܢ ܫܡܘܢܐ, "two Mnas which are a Shamún." This word seems to be derived from the Hebrew שמנה, and to signify the eighth part—probably the eighth part of a shekel, and the half of a quarter shekel רבע שקל, see 1 Sam. ix. 8.

29. *should go*—The Textus Receptus here reads βληθῃ, which is also, the reading of the Codex Vaticanus B; but Codex Bezæ D agrees with this text απελθῃ, which the Old Latin *a b c* confirms. The variation must have arisen from mistaking words containing the same letters either in the Aramaic נאזל and נפל, or in the Greek απελθῃ and βληθῃ. Justin Martyr has πεμφθηναι.

39. *thy cheek*—omitting δεξιαν, which is found in several Greek copies, the Old Latin *a b c*, and the Peshito, but is omitted in the Codex Bezæ D, and by Luke, vi. 29, and by Mar Yakub the Persian ܡܢ ܕܡܚܐ ܠܟ ܥܠ ܦܟܟ ܩܪܒ ܠܗ ܐܚܪܢܐ, fol. 63.

47. *what is your grace,* מנאהיטיבותכון—Greek τι περισσον ποιειτε, as if it

* See Tregelles, Account of the Printed Text of the New Testament, p. 187.

had been read מנאהייתירותכון. The Peshito has מנאיתירעבדיןאנתון, following the Greek. Luke vi. 32 has ποια υμιν χαρις εστι, which the Peshito renders ܐܝܢܐ ܗܝ ܛܝܒܘܬܟܘܢ, "what is your grace," as here. Justin Martyr, Apol. i. 15, has τι καινον ποιειτε.

CH. VI. In the Lord's Prayer we have, v. 11, *constant of the day*, ܐܡܝܢܐ ܕܝܘܡܐ, which agrees exactly with *quotidianum* of the Old Latin *a b c*, and with the reading of Cyprian. The Gothic version also uses a term meaning *continual.** This would seem to imply that there was originally some other word in the place of επιουσιον, if the rendering of the Greek by Jerome, *super-substantialem*, be correct. Origen informs us that this term, which had not been previously used by any Greek author, was invented by the Evangelists themselves; and it seems to be not an improbable conjecture that it was suggested in some way by the original Aramaic. The Greek word in Hebrew letters would be אפיוסיא. Will the comparison of this with אמינאדיומא suggest any probable solution? The words of Origen are η λεξις η επιουσιον παρ' ουδενι των Ελληνων, ουτε των σοφων ωνομασται, ουτε εν τῃ των ιδιώτων συνηθειᾳ τετριπται. αλλ' εοικε πεπλασθαι υπο των Ευαγγελιστων. De Orat. 16.† Jerome informs us that in the Gospel according to the Hebrews he found the word מחר, and this also implies that there was formerly a different reading here. It would almost seem that our Lord referred to the precept of Numbers iv. 7, ולחם התמיד עליו יהיה, "and the continual bread shall be thereon," which the Peshito renders ܘܠܚܡܐ ܐܡܝܢܐܝܬ ܥܠܘܗܝ ܢܗܘܐ, using the same expression as here. The Peshito has here ܕܣܘܢܩܢܢ ܝܘܡܢܐ, "of our need to day."

12. *and forgive us our debts so that also we forgive our debtors.* Compare Luke xi. 2 of this copy. The Greek of Luke also has και γαρ αυτοι αφιομεν instead of ως και ημεις αφηκαμεν of the Greek of Matthew. The meaning of this petition, according to the text before us, would seem to be, "Forgive us, so that the sense of thy forgiveness may induce us to do the same to our brethren:" not as it is in the Greek, "Let thy forgiveness extend to us according as we extend our forgiveness to our brethren.

13. *Thine is the Kingdom and the Glory*—omitting και η δυναμις of the Textus Receptus. The whole of this doxology is omitted by the Old Latin *abc*, by Greek copies B D Z,‡ and Luke. Recent editors have therefore removed it from the Text, as having been probably inserted from the antient Liturgies.

* See Th. Marseschalli Observatt. in Versionem Gothicam Evangeliorum, p. 393.

† See J. Jac. Wetstenii, Edit. Nov. Test., Vol. i. p. 325.

‡ See Simon, Histoire Crit. du Texte du N. T. cxxxii. p. 404.

24. *sustain the one,* ܢܣܝܒܪ—with the Latin *sustinebit.* This may perhaps be translated as correctly in this place by *bear* or *endure,* to agree with the reading *patietur* of the Old Latin *a c.* The Greek is ανθεξεται, which Luke also has, xvi. 13, and is rendered in both places in the Peshito by ܢܝܩܪ *honor,* but in the Philoxenian version by ܢܬܒܛܠ, *take care of.* The Greek should have been ανεξεται here to correspond with this and the Latin text. Thus, in Matthew xvii. 17 for ανεξομαι υμας we have in this copy, and also in the Peshito, ܐܣܝܒܪܟܘܢ.

25. We have nothing here for η τι πιητε, which is also omitted in the Old Latin of *a b,* and in the edition of Jerome. *for the soul*—Luke also has, as here, η γαρ ψυχη, but the Greek reads ουχι η ψυχη, which the Peshito follows.

27. μεριμνων of the Greek is omitted, and also by the Old Latin *a b.*

30. *is gathered and*—This is not in the Greek.

32. *Your Father*—omitting ο ουρανιος with the Old Latin *a b c* and Cyprian.

CH. VII. v. 21. *he shall enter into heaven's kingdom*—These words, which seem to have fallen out on account of the repetition, are not found in most of the Greek copies, although there be some that retain them. They are, however, read in the Old Latin *a b c,* "ipse intrabit in regnum cœlorum," and are cited by Cyprian and Hilary.

22. *have we not in thy name eaten and drunk*—These words, although not found now in the Greek copies, existed in those which were used by Origen, and are several times cited by him.* They are also quoted by Justin Martyr in his first Apology, 18, Κυριε, κυριε, ου τῳ σῳ ονοματι εφαγομεν και επιομεν και δυναμεις εποιησαμεν ; and also in the Dialogue with Trypho the Jew, 76, Κυριε, ου τῳ σῳ ονοματι εφαγομεν και επιομεν και προεφητευσαμεν και δαιμονια εξεβαλομεν. The fact that they existed originally in the Aramaic Gospel of St. Matthew seems also to be confirmed by the passage of Luke xiii. 26, *We have eaten and drunk in thy presence,* εφαγομεν ενωπιον σου και επιομεν.

CH. VIII. v. 2. *One man a leper,* גברא חד גרבא—the Greek has only λεπρος ; but Luke v. 12, nearer to this, ανηρ πληρης λεπρας. The word גברא ανηρ might easily have been omitted by the Greek translator on account of its similarity, consisting of exactly the same letters, with גרבא πληρης λεπρας immediately following.

3. *was cleansed from him the leprosy*—Greek εκαθαρισθη αυτου η λεπρα : Mark i. 42, απηλθεν απ' αυτου η λεπρα και εκαθαρισθη : Luke v. 13, η λεπρα απηλθεν απ' αυτου.

* See De Principiis, edit. Redepenning, p. 46. Griesbach, Nov. Test. at this verse; and Symbol. Crit. ii. p. 262.

4. *(beware) lest thou tell*—דלמא. The Greek supplies the ellipse of the original and reads ορα μηδενι ειπης, which the Peshito follows and adds חזי *see*, and so Mark; but Luke has it differently, και αυτος παρηγγειλεν αυτῳ μηδενι ειπειν. *as commanded*—Greek ο προσεταξεν; Mark α προσεταξεν; but Luke, as here, καθως.

5. *after these things*—omitted in the Greek; but the Old Latin *a b c* has *post hæc.*

9. *And there is to me authority also*—These words omitted in the Greek, although they may not seem to be necessary, render the sense more complete; and might have been omitted on account of the repetition of the same words, תחית שולטנא and ואית לי שולטנא. In the first place the centurion states that he was subject to a superior power, and then that he also had power over others set under him. The expression *under authority*, υπο εξουσιαν, is an Aramaism ܬܚܝܬ ܫܘܠܛܢܐ; and thus we find εκ της εξουσιας Ηρωδου εστιν, Luke xxiii. 7, rendered, both in this copy and the Peshito, by ܡܢ ܬܚܝܬ ܫܘܠܛܢܐ ܗܘ ܕܗܪܘܕܣ.

14. *Simon Cepha*—Greek πετρου only. *Simon* is generally added throughout this copy. *a fever held her*—Greek πυρεσσουσαν; but Luke iv. 38 συνεχομενη πυρετῳ μεγαλῳ.

16. *But at the sun's setting came near before him all those that had devils.* The Greek is οψιας δε γενομενης προσηνεγκαν αυτῳ δαιμονιζομενους πολλους. Luke, in the parallel passage, iv. 40, has δυνοντος δε του ηλιου, which exactly corresponds with this reading and Mark i. 32, οψιας δε γενομενης; οτι εδυσεν ο ηλιος. The variation probably arose from confounding the original רמשא οψια with שמשא ηλιος. Both Mark and Luke, although varying here in some respects, confirm the reading *all*, παντες, instead of the Greek πολλους of Matthew here. The word קרבו, *came near*, which I have translated in the neuter sense, may also have a transitive signification if it be taken in the Pael form: and as the cases here are not distinguished by terminations, as in the Greek, the following words כלהוןאילין, *all these*, may either be the subject or the object. The Greek προσηνεγκαν, therefore, in this latter case would be also correct. Mark has εφερον: Luke ηγαγον, and comes still nearer to this text, reading παντες οσοι ειχον, *all those that had.*

21. *and I will come*—These words are not in the Greek. They are also added twice in the parallel passage of St. Luke in this copy, although the Greek does not contain them, Luke ix. 59, 61.

22. *and thou come after me*—does not exist in the Greek, but in the corresponding passage Luke has in their stead συ δε απελθων διαγγελλε την βασιλειαν του Θεου.

CH. X. v. 33. *and before his angels*—Not in the Greek. In Luke xii. 9, there is found *ενωπιον των αγγελων του Θεου,* from whence it seems this addition was made, if it did not exist in the original Aramaic Gospel.

CH. XI. v. 2. *Jesus*—Greek *του χριστου*; but the Codex Bezæ B has *του ιησου*. *dispatched his disciples and sent to him*—Greek, *πεμψας δια των μαθητων αυτου ειπεν αυτῳ*. The Textus Receptus here has *δυο*, evidently by an error for *δια*, which is also the reading of the Peshito, ܫܕܪ ܒܝܕ ܬܠܡܝܕܘܗܝ, ܘܐܡܪ ܠܗ. Luke, in the parallel passage, vii. 19, has *δυο*. The Old Latin *a b c* reads *discipulos* only. If the original Aramaic stood as in this text, the variation may have arisen from the Greek translator not fully perceiving the difference between the two words שדר *to send away* or *dispatch*, and שלח *to send with a message*. In this text the word ܫܠܚ, which I have rendered *sent to*, conveys in itself the force of sending a message, and from it is derived ܫܠܝܚܐ *messenger*, which the Greek expresses by *αποστολος*: thus in this copy, v. 16, the children are represented as sitting in the market, and *sending messages* to their companions, ܫܠܚܝܢ ܠܚܒܪܝܗܘܢ, where the Greek is *προσφωνουντα* or *προσφωνουσι*, which the Peshito has rendered by ܩܥܝܢ *calling*. Luke vii. 32 has also *προσφωνουσιν*, where the Peshito translates by the same word ܩܥܝܢ. That part of Luke is lost from this copy.

5. *The poor are sustained*—Greek, *ευαγγελιζονται*. The difference here is between the מסטברין and מסטיברין, or if the י be omitted, which is often the case, simply in the pronunciation. In the Apochryphal Gospel of Matthew, edited by Tischendorf, p. 96, this seems to have been the reading followed: "et videant cæci et claudi ambulent recte et pauperes *fruantur bonis*, et reviviscant mortui.

8. *and if not,* ואלא—Greek *αλλα*, probably suggested by אלא in the original Aramaic. *among kings*—בית מלכא. The word בית means a *house*, and also, when used as a particle, *among*. We find, therefore, in the Greek Matthew, *εν τοις οικοις των βασιλεων*; and in Luke vii. 25, *εν τοις βασιλειοις*, either of which the reading of this text may express.

18. *to you*—This, although omitted in most of the Greek manuscripts, is found in some of considerable antiquity, as the L of Griesbach or *η* of Stevens, and others indicated by Griesbach and Birch. *And ye say*—the Greek here is *λεγουσι*. Luke, in the parallel passage, vii. 33, reads as here, *λεγετε*, and also in the next verse. The variation might have arisen from mistaking ואמרין אנתון for ואמרין אית.

20, *he shewed*—Greek *εγενοντο*. The variation must have arisen from the similarity of חוי חילא *εδειξε δυναμεις* and הוו חילא *εγενοντο δυναμεις*, which occurs in the next verse.

23. *art thou not exalted?*—Lachmann, on the authority of the Codex Vat. B. Cod. Ephr. C, and Cod. Bezæ D, and the Old Latin *a b c*, has adopted this reading in his text.

27. *No man knoweth the Son but the Father*—The Greek here reads επιγινωσκει, and Luke, in the parallel passage, x. 22, γινωσκει; but Origen, Irenæus, Justin Martyr, and the Clementine Homilies, read εγνω, in the past tense. The Aramaic ידע, as here, is either past or present, according to the enunciation by the vowels; and this may account for the variation of the tenses.

CH. XII. 1. *And rubbing in their hands*—This is not in the Greek, but it is found in the Old Latin *c*, *et confricantes eas manibus suis manducebant.* Luke has, vi. 1, και ησθιον ψωχοντες ταις χερσιν; and Mark, ii. 23, οδον ποιειν τιλλοντες τους σταχυας; almost as if he had read the original Aramaic כרכין or מתכרכין instead of פרכין. Codex Bezæ D and the Old Latin *b c* omit οδον ποιειν.

2. *Why*—The Greek here is ιδου, apparently from confounding מנא and הא. The Old Latin *a* reads with this text *quid faciunt.* Luke vi. 2 reads τι ποιειτε, and Mark ii. 24 has ιδε τι, combining the two. εν τῳ σαββατῳ of the Greek is omitted here.

4. *Face-bread*—literally rendered from ܠܚܡ ܐܦܐ which exactly corresponds with the Hebrew לחם הפנים, 1 Sam. xxi. 6. This is translated in the Peshito there ܠܚܡܐ ܕܐܦܐ, "bread of faces;" and by the Septuagint, τους αρτους της προθεσεως, which is followed in the Greek text of Matthew. The Peshito of Matthew has rendered ܠܚܡܐ ܕܦܬܘܪܗ ܕܡܪܝܐ "bread of the table of the Lord." The Philoxenian version servilely ܠܚܡܐ ܕܣܝܡܘܬ ܩܘܕܡܐ, "bread of setting before."

6. *For I say to you that lo*—Greek λεγω δε υμιν οτι. Cod. Bezæ D*d* reads γαρ, as here: and at verse 42 the Greek also has ιδου.

10. *whose right hand was withered*—Greek χειρα εχων ξηραν only; but Luke vi. 6 has και η χειρ αυτου η δεξια ην ξηρα; and so in the next words Luke reads exactly as here, ινα ευρωσιν κατηγορειν αυτου. The word ευρωσιν is an Aramaism, literally rendered from ܢܫܟܚܘܢ *find*, and signifying *be able.* The Greek text here has ινα κατηγορησωσιν αυτου only.

13. *was restored*—and so the Peshito. Greek απεκατεσταθη υγιης. Both Mark iii. 5 and Luke vi. 10 omit υγιης, as well as the Old Latin *a b c* and Hilary.

15. *many men*—The Codex Vat. B has only πολλοι, with which the Old Latin *a b c* agrees. The Codex Bezæ D and the Textus Receptus, with which the Peshito agrees here, have οχλοι πολλοι. The variation may be accounted for

by the reading of כנשא סגיאא for אנשא סגיאא, the former being οχλοι πολλοι, and the latter being sufficiently expressed by πολλοι only, without adding ανθρωποι. In the next verse לאנשא *to any*, literally ανθρωπῳ, is also omitted in the Greek.

19. *He shall not cry and not strive*—Greek ουκ ερισει ουδε κραυγασει: but Hilary follows the order of this text, *non clamabit non contendet.*

22. *Then they brought before him one Man upon whom was a devil*—This reading will explain the variations in the Greek copies. The Aramaic use of the plural transitive is a very common method of expressing a passive sense. the Syriac, as it stands here, may be rendered equally well by προσηνεχθη δαιμονιζομενος, as it is read in Cod. Bezæ D, which was also the reading of the Old Latin *a b c*; or still more literally by προσηνεγκαν—δαιμονιζομενον, as it is found in the Cod. Vat. B. The omission or retention of the word *man* in the Greek was not important, being implied: the Old Latin *ab c*, however, retained it.

And heard—omitted in the Greek, but found in the Old Latin *b*, *et audiret.* The term חרשא, which I have translated *dumb*, means one who is deaf as well as dumb: the addition, therefore, here makes the sense more complete.

25. *But when he saw*—The Cod. Vat. B and the Textus Receptus read ειδως δε, which the Old Latin *abc* follows, *Jesus autem sciens*; but the Cod. Bezæ D and some others have ιδων δε.

27. *From your children*—This is not in the Greek. It is also added in this copy at Luke xi. 19, but it is not found there in the Greek. It may have fallen out from the repetition of the consecutive words בניכון בניכון.

31. *All sins and blasphemies shall be forgiven to men's sons: but every one that against the Spirit of Holiness shall blaspheme, it shall not be forgiven to him*—Greek πασα αμαρτια και βλασφημια αφεθησεται τοις ανθρωποις, η δε του Πνευματος βλασφημια ουκ αφεθησεται. The reading of Mark iii. 28 comes nearer to this text, παντα αφεθησεται τοις υιοις των ανθρωπων τα αμαρτηματα και αι βλασφημια—ος δ'αν βλασφημησῃ εις το Πνευμα το αγιον ουκ εχει αφεσιν. Origen, in quoting this passage, has retained the Aramaic form υιοις των ανθρωπων, *men's sons*, as well as Mark. It is, however, identical in meaning with the simple ανθρωποις of the Greek of Matthew. The latter part of the verse is also confirmed by the Old Latin *b*, *qui autem in Spiritum Sanctum blasphemaberit non remittetur illi.*

32. *Every one that against the Spirit of Holiness shall blaspheme*—Greek ος, δ' αν ειπῃ κατα του πνευματος του αγιου. Origen reads βλασφημησῃ εις το αγιον πνευμα.

34. *the mouth bringeth forth*—This reading is confirmed by Cyprian, *emittit.* The Greek is λαλει.

38. *Then came near to him*—Greek *τοτε απεκριθησαν αυτῳ*—The Old Latin *b* agrees with this text in reading *adierunt* ; and also in adding *aliquid* in this verse, *some sign.*

47. This verse is omitted in this text. The Cod. Vat. B also omits it, and the antient Paris manuscript, L of Griesbach or *η* of Stevens.*

CH. XIII. 2. *and he went up*, וסלק—Greek *ωστε—εμβαντα.* Assuming this to be as it stood in the original, the use of *ωστε* by the translator instead of *και* would seem to have been suggested by the two first letters וס *ως*.

4. *The fowl of the heaven*—Greek, *τα πετεινα* only, although three important manuscripts, E K M of Griesbach, add *του ουρανου.* This is also added in the Old Latin *b*, and was the reading used by Origen. In Mark iv. 4 and Luke viii. 5 some manuscripts add, and others omit, *του ουρανου.*

6. *and in the shining of the sun which was upon it, it sank down*—The word שבת, which I have rendered *it sank down*, from the root שבב, may perhaps be even more correctly rendered *was burnt*, from שוב. It would then come nearer to the Greek, *ηλιου δε ανατειλαντος εκαυματισθη.* *And because it had not cast root in the earth it withered*—Greek has *δια το μη εχειν ριζαν εξηρανθη.* Luke viii. 6 has *και φυεν εξηρανθη δια το μη εχειν ικμαδα,* leaving out *δια το μη εχειν βαθος γης, ηλιου δε ανατειλαντος* (Mark, *και οτε ανετειλεν ο ηλιος*) *εκαυματισθη* of both the Greek Matthew and Mark iv. 6. If he had an original Aramaic text like this before him, it is easy to perceive how he might have omitted this passage, on account of the similarity both of its beginning and ending with the next מטל דלית—שבת and מטל דלא—יבשבת. The similarity of the first syllable of עקרא, *root*, with *ικμαδα*, *moisture*, and perhaps some defect in the copy by which ד might have been read for ר, thus making עקדא *ικδα* instead of עקרא, might have caused the substitution of one for the other when the material signification would scarcely be altered.

7. *among*—Greek *επι*, Mark *εις*, but Luke *εν μεσῳ.* *and the thorns rose up with it*—Greek omits *with it*; but Luke reads *συμφυεισαι αι ακανθαι* ; Mark also seems to point to this having originally existed by reading *συνεπνιξαν αυτο.*

8. *and they increased and gave*—This is not in the Greek, but *αναβαινοντα και αυξανοντα* occupy the place of these words in the parallel place of Mark, and seem to imply their existence in the original Aramaic.

13. *That that which they see they may not see; and that which they hear they may not hear, and may not understand*—The Greek here is *οτι βλεποντες ου*

* See Griesbach Prolegomena, edit. D. Schultz, p. xcix; and Schultz's note, ibid.

βλεπουσιν, και ακουοντες ουκ ακουουσιν ουδε συνιουσιν. But the Codex Bezæ D agrees with this text in reading *ινα βλεποντες μη βλεπωσιν κ. τ. λ.*, which the Old Latin *a b c* and Irenæus also confirm, as well as Luke viii. 10 and Mark iv. 12. The Aramaic particle ד, representing both *ινα* and *οτι*, might have given rise to this difference. *That they may never be converted*—This, although omitted in most of the Greek copies, is found in Cod. Bezæ D, and in other manuscripts indicated by Griesbach, as well as in the Old Latin *b c*, and in the parallel place of Mark.

14. *may be fulfilled*—*impleatur* as Irenæus has it: or it may be rendered *shall be fulfilled*, *πληρωθησεται*, as the Codex Bezæ D, and *complebitur* as the Old Latin *c*, have it. The Aramaic ותשלם bears either meaning. The Codex Vaticanus B, and others which read *αναπληρουται*, would seem to have followed a reading ושלמת or ושלמא, as in the Peshito.

16. *Happy your eyes that see, and happy your ears that hear*—The Greek has *οτι βλεπουσιν*—*οτι ακουουσιν*. The Aramaic דחזין and דשמעין, on account of the twofold signification of the particle ד, may be rendered either way, *that see* and *that hear*, or *because they see* and *because they hear*: consequently we find in the Old Latin *a b c qui vident* and *quæ audiunt*, with which Irenæus and Hilary concur, almost seeming to indicate that they followed another Greek version or recension which had understood the original Aramaic in this manner. This view seems to be confirmed by the fact of Hegesippus citing this passage thus, *μακαριοι οι οφθαλμοι υμων οι βλεποντες, και τα ωτα υμων τα ακουοντα*;* and Eusebius † informs us that Hegesippus used the Gospel according to the Hebrews and the Syriac.

19. *The seed*—Greek Cod. Vat. B. *εσπαρμενον*, with which the Old Latin *a b c* agrees; Cod. Bezæ D *σπειρομενον*; Mark has *τον λογον τον εσπαρμενον*, like the Peshito here ܡܠܬܐ ܕܙܪܝܥܐ and Luke *τον λογον* only.

22. *And that which fell among thorns*—Greek, *ο δε εις ακανθας σπαρεις*; and Mark, *οι εις τας ακανθας σπειρομενοι*; but Luke viii. 14, nearer to this, *το δε εις ακανθας πεσον*. Above, verse 7, Luke also agrees with *among thorns* of this by reading *εν μεσω των ακανθων*, where the Greek of Matthew has *επι τας ακανθας*, and Mark *εις*. These also have the former, *τα πετρωδη*, and the latter, *το πετρωδες*; while Luke exactly as this text, *την πετραν*. In the next verse, 23, *fell in the good ground*—the Greek and Mark have *σπαρεις* and *σπαρεντες*, but Luke *το δε εν τη καλη γη* only, where Codex Bezæ D reads *εις την καλην γην*, carrying on

* See Grabe: Spicilegium SS. Patrum; Edit. alt., vol. ii. p. 213.

† *Εκ τε του καθ' Εβραιους ευαγγελιου και του Συριακου, και ιδιως εκ της Εβραιδος διαλεκτου τινα τιθησιν, εμφανων εξ Εβραιων εαυτον πεπιστευκεναι*: Hist. Eccl. lib. iv. 22.

πεσον from the verse preceding. In this copy of the Syriac the word נפל is supplied, viii. 15. The Old Latin *c* also has *quod vero cecidit.*

33. *Another parable*—without any thing more, which reading Codex Bezæ D supports. It seems probable that it originally stood so; for while the palimpsest of Ephraim C has here *παρεθηκεν αυτοις λεγων*, the Codex Vat. B reads *ελαλησεν αυτοις*, with which the Old Latin *a b c* agrees. At verse 31 also above, the Codex Bezæ D, supported by the Old Latin *a b c*, comes nearer to this text, by reading *ελαλησεν*, than the Codex Vaticanus B *παρεθηκεν*, which the Vulgate of Jerome follows. In this verse the woman is called חכימתא, *wise* or *prudent*; and this is omitted from the Greek, while *τρια σατα* not found in this text, occupies its space. It seems obvious that there was another word in the original. This perhaps might have been partially effaced or illegible, and the words *τρια σατα* have been suggested by Gen. xviii. 6. I ought to state that the observance of many such passages where similar variations occur in this text and the Greek of Matthew, and, indeed, in the parallel places of the other Evangelists, has led me to the conclusion that in some instances this must have arisen from a defect in the copy of the original rendering some words obscure and almost illegible.

35. *of old*: מן קדים, and in the original Hebrew, Ps. lxxviii. 2, מני קדם, which the Septuagint renders there *απ' αρχης*, and the Peshito ܡܢ ܩܕܝܡ as here. The Greek of Matthew is *απο καταβολης*, according to the Codex Vat. B, and Origen; but this seeming to represent an imperfect sense, *κοσμου* has been added in the Codex Bezæ D, which reading is supported by the Old Latin *a b c* and by Jerome's recension, as well as by the Peshito, ܡܢ ܩܕܡ ܬܪܡܝܬܗ ܕܥܠܡܐ. The original seems to have stood as it is read in this text, and the word *καταβολης* to have been suggested by the similarity of the first syllable קד and *κατ*. It would not be difficult to point out several other instances where the choice of the Greek word appears to have suggested itself to the translator from this circumstance, a thing of usual occurrence in all translations. Compare especially xi. 22, where the word *ανεκτοτερον* seems to have suggested itself on account of the similarity of sound, ניח יתיר. This, taken in connection with verse 29 following, explains and shews the peculiar force of ניח as here applied to Christ and the last Judgment, and the rest, ניח, which he promises.

48. *The fishes that were good, good*—ܢܘܢܐ ܕܛܒܝܢ ܛܒܝܢ: The Greek has *τα καλα εις αγγεια* or *τα καλιστα*, as we read in Codex Bezæ D, or *optimos pisces* of the Old Latin *a b*. The repetition of the word טבין טבין, has either an intensive or successive force. Assuming that it stood thus in the original

Aramaic, the translator into Greek must have confounded טבין, *good*, with במנין, *into baskets*. In the Peshito, which follows the Greek, we have במאנא, and, according to Buxtorf Lex. Chal., this word is written either with or without the aleph. Scribitur promiscue cum א et absque eo. It appears from chapter xxi. 41, where he has rendered *κακους κακως απολεσει αυτους*, which is doubtless a misunderstanding of the original idiom ביש ביש, of not unfrequent occurrence, that the translator was not quite familiar with this reduplication, and the change, therefore, from טבין to במנין might very easily have arisen. In the Peshito, *κακως κακους απολεσει* has been restored to the idiomatic form ביש ביש נובד, as it is in this text.

55. *Is not this Joseph's son the carpenter*—The Greek omits *Joseph*, but the Old Latin *a b* have *filius Joseph fabri*.

CH. XIV. v. 5. *The people*: Greek, *τον οχλον*; but the Old Latin version *a b c* has *populum*; and so the Peshito. Again, in the next verse, *in the midst of the banquet*, *b c* have *in medio triclinio*, Peshito, ܩܕܡ ܣܡܝܟܐ, *before the guests*, and so the Armenian, while the Greek has *εν τῳ μεσῳ* only.

6. *came in and danced*—the Greek *ωρχησατο* only; but in Mark vi. 22, although there is otherwise a considerable variation in the narrative, we find *εισελθουσης—και ορχησαμενης*.

13. There is nothing here to correspond with *εν πλοιῳ* of the Greek and ܒܐܠܦܐ of the Peshito, which might have been inserted as a counterpart to *πεζῃ*, which represents ברגל of this text, although perhaps not correctly. *and the villages*—this is omitted in the Greek.

19. *And the disciples gave to the multitude*—The Greek has nothing to correspond with *gave*, but the Old Latin of the Codex Veronensis *b* has *posuerunt*; and the Peshito agrees with it in reading ܣܡܘ *set*. Compare xv. 36, where the Old Latin *a b c* agrees with this text in reading *dederunt*, omitted in the Greek.

20. *The remnants*—in the plural with the Old Latin *a b c d*. The Greek has *το περισσευον*. In the next verse also *a b c* agree with this text in omitting *ωσει* of the Greek. *from before them*—this is not in the Greek.

22. *And he commanded*: Greek *ηναγκασεν*, which the Peshito has rendered by ܐܠܨ, *he constrained*; but the Old Latin *a b c* has *jussit*. The Palimpsest of Ephraem C also omits *ευθεως*, as here.

24. *was separated from the land many stadia*—this is the same as the Codex Vat. B, *σταδιους πολλους απο της γης απειχε βασανιζομενον*; and so the Jerusalem Syriac. The Peshito also, in this place, substitutes רחיקא *distant* for פריקא *separated*. The Textus Receptus, and most Greek copies, have *ηδη μεσον της θαλασσης ην βασανιζομενον*, which is the reading supported by Origen:

the Old Latin *a b c*, has *in medio mari jactabatur*: this text *and they were tormented.*

25. *The waters*—The Textus Receptus and Codex Bezæ D here read επι της θαλασσης, and *a b c* of the Old Latin *super mare.* Origen states that the true reading was *upon the waters*, and not *upon the waves*, ου γεγραπται ηλθε προς αυτους περιπατων επι τα κυματα αλλ' επι τα υδατα. But in the next verse we have here *upon the waves of the sea.* The Greek omits *waves*, and has only επι της θαλασσης, and the Peshito *on the waters* ܥܠ ܡܝܐ only. In the original Aramaic the words מיא *waters* and ימא *sea* consist of the same three letters, and hence doubtless arose the variation. At verse 29 all agree in the reading *waters.*

32. *when he went up*—Greek, αναβαινοντων αυτων; but the Old Latin *b c*, as here, *cum ascendisset.* Mark vi. 51 has και ανεβη.

34. *And when he went up to the dry land they came to Genesar*—Greek, και διαπερασαντες ηλθον εις την γην Γεννησαρεθ. The Codex Bezæ D by the first hand before it was corrected has γεννησαρ, and the Old Latin *a b c d Genesar* and *Gennasar.* The Peshito also retains *Genesar*, adding from the Greek *to the land.*

CH. XV. v. 2. *Commandments*—פוקדנא: and so in verses 3 and 6, where the Greek has παραδοσιν, which the Peshito follows.

3. *because that* (or *in order that*) *ye may establish*—the Greek has only the particle δια, and so again in verse 6.

5. *each*—ܐܢܫ, literally *man.* Greek ος εαν ειπῃ; but Mark εαν ειπῃ ανθρωπος. If the Aramaic stood as here, εαν might have orginated in the first syllable ܐܢ of ܐܢܫ: Mark, although using εαν ειπῃ as in Matthew, has also retained ܐܢܫ in εαν ειπῃ ανθρωπος.

9. *The doctrines of the commandments*—Greek, διδασκαλιας ενταλματα. The Old Latin *a b c* has *doctrinas et mandata.* The instances of ו and ד being confounded are very frequent, and this would bring the Latin to agree with this text.

12. *this word*—with which the Old Latin *a b c* agree, reading *audito hoc verbo.* Greek has τον λογον only.

14. *They are blind leaders*—Greek, τυφλοι εισιν οδηγοι τυφλων; but the Codd. Vat. B and Bezæ D omit the latter τυφλων.

15, *Explain*—פשק: Greek, φρασον.

17. *In the purging* or *purifying*, ܒܬܕܟܝܬܐ: Greek, εις αφεδρωνα. Mark seems to have had this word before him, and has therefore added καθαριζων

παντα τα βρωματα, vii. 19. This same word ܬܕܟܝܬܐ is used in the Peshito, Luke ii. 22, for the Greek term καθαρισμος.

19. *Evil thoughts of murder and of adultery, &c.*—Greek only διαλογισμοι πονηροι, φονοι, μοιχειαι.

20. *for when a man shall eat bread while his hands are not washen, he is not defiled*—Greek το δε ανιπτοις χερσιν φαγειν ου κοινοι τον ανθρωπον.

23. *because lo! she crieth and cometh after us*—Greek has only οτι κραζει οπισθεν ημων; but the Old Latin of the Codex Veronensis *b* agrees with this, and reads *quia sequitur et clamat post nos*.

27. *and live*—not found in the Greek, but in the Peshito and the Jerusalem Syriac.

31. κυλλους υγιεις of the Greek is omitted here. These words are also omitted in the Old Latin of *b c*, and by Jerome.

32. *lo, three days*—Greek ηδη ημεραι τρεις, substituting ηδη for ιδε or ιδου, which the Peshito and Coptic retain. Cod. Vat. B omits ηδη. This Aramaic construction is easy and clear, however obscure the Greek may be*. *This multitude*—Cod. Bezæ D adds τουτον: the Old Latin *b c* and Hilary, *huic*.

33. *a desert place*—Greek, ερημια; but C and Origen have ερημῳ τοπῳ.

34. *a few fishes*—Greek, ολιγα ιχθυδια, which seems to have arisen from ܢ̈ܘܢܐ ܙܥܘܪ̈ܐ meaning either *little fishes* or *few fishes*. In the next verse the Greek has ιχθυας.

36. *His disciples gave*—Greek οι δε μαθηται only; but the Old Latin *a b c* has *et discipuli dederunt*.

37. *From before them*—This is not in the Greek. Compare xiv. 20 and xvi. 9.

39. *Magadun*—The Textus Receptus has Μαγδαλα; Codd. Vat. B and Bezæ D, Μαγαδαν; Palimp. Ephr. C, Μαγδαλαν; and the Old Latin *abc* and Jerome, *Magedan*; Peshito, ܡܓܕܘ.†

CH. XVI. verses 2 and 3: οψιας—δυνασθε of the Greek are omitted here. They are also omitted in the Cod. Vat. B and some other copies, and do not seem to have been read by Origen. They are, however, found in the Peshito.

6. *Beware* אזדהרו—The Greek has ορατε και προσεχετε; but the Old Latin *a b c* has only *attendite vobis*, which exactly agrees with this text. Mark reads (viii. 15); ορατε, βλεπετε, which would be written in Aramaic חוזרו. This comes very near to our word אזדהרו, and hence might have originated ορατε και προσεχετε of the Greek of Matthew, and ορατε, βλεπετε of Mark.

* See Griesbach Com. Crit., par. i. p. 131.

† See ibid, p. 133.

7. *And they were reasoning among themselves that they had not taken for them bread*—This is much nearer to Mark viii. 16, *και διελογιζοντο προς αλληλους οτι αρτους ουκ εχουσιν*, than to the Greek of Matthew, *εν εαυτοις λεγοντες οτι αρτους ουκ ελαβομεν.* The variation seems to have arisen from the similarity in the original Aramaic between נסבו *ελαβον* and נסבן *ελαβομεν*. The word *λεγοντες* is omitted in Cod. Ephr. C.

9. *also the five thousand*—The Old Latin *a b* agrees with this in reading *et quinque milium.* Cod. Vat. B and Textus Receptus have *των πεντακισχιλιων*, but Cod. Bezæ D *τοις πεντακισχιλειοις*, as if the translator had taken the Aramaic prefix of ܠܚܡܫܐ in the second instance to represent the dative, which it may do, instead of being a repetition of the accusative as in the first. *which ate of them*—is not found in the Greek, and so also in the next verse.

12. *The leaven of the Pharisees and Sadducees*—Greek *της ζυμης των αρτων* only. *That, Beware*—in the imperative with the particle ד prefixed according to the Aramaic idiom. The Old Latin *d* has retained this in *attendite*; but the Greek translator has *προσεχειν* in the infinitive, apparently as if not quite familiar with this idiom he had taken the ד to indicate the subjunctive, and read, as the Peshito has translated *προσεχειν*, ܕܬܙܕܗܪܘܢ.

19. *The keys of the gates*—Greek has *τας κλειδας* only.

21. *Should endure much, and suffer from the elders*—Greek only *πολλα παθειν απο των πρεσβυτερων*: but in the parallel passages both Mark viii. 31 and Luke have *πολλα παθειν και αποδοκιμασθηναι*, which the Peshito renders ܕܢܚܫ. ܣܓܝ ܘܢܣܬܠܐ. This is also the translation of Luke ix. 22 in this copy.

22. *and Simon Cepha came near and said, Spare thyself my Lord*—Greek *και προσλαβομενος αυτον ο Πετρος ηρξατο αυτῳ επιτιμâν λεγων Ιλεως σοι, κυριε.* The Cod. Vat. C has the latter part thus, *λεγει αυτῳ επιτιμων.* The phrase of the Greek *ιλεως σοι* is perhaps borrowed from the Septuagint *ιλεως μοι* to represent חלילה לי, 2 Sam. xx. 20, xxii. 17; or it might have originated in the similarity of sound to some original Aramaic expressions. חס, as it is found in this text, which is equivalent to *μη γενοιτο*,* and is often used by the Peshito to translate it, might have suggested *εως*. Perhaps it might have stood חלילה חס.

27. *works*—Greek, *την πραξιν*; but the Old Latin *a b c, opera.*

28. *And his glory*—This is not in the Greek text, although some copies cited by Griesbach have *εν τῃ δοξῃ* for *εν τῃ βασιλειᾳ.* Origen has both.†

* See Rom. iii. 4, 6, &c.. In Luke xxvi. 16 *μη γενοιτο* is rendered in this copy חס ולא נהוא, but the Peshito ܠܐ ܢܗܘܐ ܗܕܐ.

† See Griesbach Com. Crit. in textum Græcum N. T. part 1, p. 143.

CH. XVII. v. 2. *changed was the vision of his face to their eyes*—Greek *μετεμορφωθη εμπροσθεν αυτων* only; but Codex Bezæ D and the Old Latin *a b c* add *ο Ιησους* between *μετεμορφωθη* and *εμπροσθεν*, as if there had been some other word in the original Aramaic. Luke, in the parallel passage, ix. 28, seems to shew that this manuscript has retained the original words *εγενετο—το ειδος του προσωπου αυτου ετερον*. In this verse we have *snow*, which reading is also confirmed by D and the Old Latin *a b c*; and in the parallel passage of Mark ix. 3 *ως χιων*.

5. *a cloud of light*—Although there are but few authorities for *νεφελη φωτος* rather than *φωτεινη*, Griesbach had inferred that this was the true reading.* *A voice was heard*—The Greek has only *ιδου φωνη*. The Old Latin *a* adds *audita est*, and Hilary. Mark ix. 7 has *ηλθε*, Luke ix. 35 *εγενετο*, but in the Clementine Homilies, iii. 53, it is read *ηκουσθη*, as here.

11. *that he may prepare*—which is equivalent to the infinitive *αποκαταστησαι* of Cod. Bezæ D, with which the Old Latin *a b c* concur. The Cod. Vat. B and Cod. Dubl. Z, with others, have *και αποκαταστησει*, which variation the common error of interchanging ו and ד sufficiently accounts for. Compare note on xv. 9 above

14. *and when Jesus came*—Greek *ελθοντων*; but Cod. Bezæ D reads *ελθων*, which the Old Latin *a b c d* and Jerome confirm. *And was entreating of him*—These words are not found in the Greek copies, but they exist in the Latin of the Cod. Veron. *b*, *rogans eum*; and Luke ix. 38 adds *δεομαι σου*.

15. *Be compassionate towards me: my son has a lunatic spirit,* literally a *son of the roof,* which the Greek renders *σεληνιαζεται*. The Greek here is *ελεησον μου τον υιον*, and the variation seems to have arisen from the repetition of בר in עלי ברי בר אגרא אית לה.

20. *The smallness of your faith*—with *ολιγοπιστιαν* of the Cod. Vat. B; but Cod. Bezæ D, and the Old Latin version *a b c*, and the edition of Jerome, read *απιστιαν*.

21. *τουτο δε το γενος ουκ εκπορευεται ει μη εν προσευχῃ και νηστειᾳ* is omitted here, as also in Cod. Vat. B and the Jerusalem Syriac, Coptic, and Æthiopic versions. It bears the appearance of an explanatory note added from the margin. It is rejected by Mill but defended by Griesbach.†

27. *there*—with the Cod. Bezæ D and the Old Latin *a b c*, but omitted by others.

CH. XVIII. v. 3. *One of these children*—Greek *τα παιδια* only. In the

* See *ibid*, p. 143.

† See *ibid*, 1, p. 146.

preceding verse the Cod. Bezæ D*d* agrees with this in reading *εν παιδιον*, *one child*, and so Origen.

6. *In the depths of the sea*—Greek *εν τῳ πελαγει της θαλασσης*: *a b c* of the Old Latin *in profundum maris*, and so Hilary.

7. *Woe to the world from the offences that are coming*—The last words, *that are coming*, are not in the Greek copies.

8. *Gihanna of fire*—as in the next verse. The Greek *το πυρ το αιωνιον* The Old Latin *a* has *Gehennam æternam.*

10. *that believe in me*—These words, although omitted in the editions, are also found in the Cod. Bezæ D and in the Old Latin *b c*, and in the Coptic, Sahidic, and Anglo-Saxon versions, and Hilary.

11. *and that the Son of Man came that he might save that which was lost*—The only antient Greek manuscript which has these words is the Codex Bezæ D. They are, however, found in the Old Latin *a b c*, and in Jerome's version, as well as in the Peshito and Philoxenian Syriac.

17. *Let him be accounted by thee*—Greek *εστω σοι* only.

25. *and all that he had should be taken*—Greek *και παντα οσα εχει και αποδοθηναι.*

30. *but he did not receive his entreaty*—Greek *ο δε ουκ ηθελεν* only.

35. The Textus Receptus adds here *τα παραπτωματα αυτων*, but this is omitted in the later critical editions.*

CH. XIX. v. 4. *he who made the male from the beginning, also the female he made*—With this the Old Latin of the Cod. Vercel. *a* agrees. The Greek varies by the addition of *αυτους.*

7. *whoso wisheth that he should put away his wife, let him give her a letter of divorcement*—The Greek has *δουναι βιβλιον αποστασιον και απολυσαι*, omitting the preceding words.

9. *towards her*—omitted in the Greek, which has only *μοιχαται*, and this is also the reading of the Old Latin *a b c*, and of Jerome's edition. The Cod, Vat. B, the Ephr. Palimp. C and Origen read *ποιει αυτην μοιχηθηναι.* This difference I suspect to have arisen from the original standing as it does here in the form מגר גאר לה, where the word מגר, which is the infinitive intensive, might have been mistaken for the participle transitive. Compare Matt. v. 32 in this text, where we have מגיר לה for *ποιει αυτην μοιχευθηναι*, and מגר גאר for *μοιχαται*, while the Peshito closely following the Greek has ܥܒܕ ܠܗ̇ ܕܬܓܘܪ, and ܓܐܪ only. Mark x. 11 has it *μοιχαται επ' αυτην* גאר לה, as here. The following of the Greek *και ο απολελυμενην γαμησας μοιχαται* is

* See Simon, Hist. Crit. du texte du N. T., p. 409. Griesbach Com. Crit., part 1, p. 151.

omitted here, in which omission Cod. Bezæ D and the Old Latin *a b* concur.

11. *from God*—is not found in the Greek copies.

12. *For there are eunuchs*—The Aramaic term מהימנא, for eunuchs, means literally *faithful* or *believers;* and in our Lord's discourse there might have been an intention of double meaning in the word which he used in the original. *that he should endure, let him endure.*—דנסיבר נסיבר. The Greek is *χωρειν χωρειτο*, which the Peshito renders דנספק נספק. In the verse immediately preceding, we find in this text ספק for *χωρουσι*. The meaning in both cases is nearly the same, and the variation probably has arisen for the similarity of דנסבר and דנספק.

14. *coming to me*, i.e. *to come to me.* These words are not found in the Greek copies; but both Mark and Luke, in the parallel passages, x. 14 and xvii. 16, have *αφετε τα παιδια ερχεσθαι προς με*, omitting *ερχεσθαι* in the latter part of the sentence.

16. *and one Man came near*—Greek *και ιδου εις προσελθων*. The alliteration of קרב גברא חד might have caused the omission of גב, and the reading רא have suggested הא *ιδου*. Some manuscripts read here *νεανισκος τις*: Hilary, *juvenis*: Luke xviii. 18, *τις αρχων*; all perhaps implied in the word גברא "vir." *Good teacher, what shall I do?* I have translated the original, ܡܠܦܢܐ ܛܒܐ ܡܢܐ ܐܥܒܕ. thus, referring ܛܒܐ *good* to ܡܠܦܢܐ *teacher*, which the more usual order of the syntax would seem to require. From the next verse, however, which reads here, *Why askest thou me concerning good*, it would appear that the proper rendering in this place should be *Master, what good shall I do*, as in the Greek of Matthew, *διδασκαλε, τι αγαθον ποιησω*, and, in some copies, *διδασκαλε αγαθε, τι αγαθον.* Mark, however, has it *διδασκαλε αγαθε, τι ποιησω*; and Luke, omitting the word *good* altogether, has only *διδασκαλε, τι ποιησας.* The Old Latin *b c* and Jerome's version follow the copies in which it is made to serve both ways, *Magister bone, quid boni?* There seems to be little doubt but that all these variations must have arisen from the original Aramaic having stood as here, and having admitted of both renderings. The word מלפנא *Teacher*, standing alone, is the usual style of addressing our Lord; and the following word, טבא *good*, is capable of being referred either to that or to the next word מנא. The alliteration also might have contributed to this, *Malfono tobo mono.* The reading of the next verse, *why askest thou me concerning good?* *τι με ερωτας περι του αγαθου*; has been already introduced into the text in the editions of Griesbach, Lachmann, Tischendorf, and Tregelles, instead of that

usually received, τι με λεγεις αγαθον, which is also the reading of Mark.* *That I may inherit*—Most Greek manuscripts have σχω or εχω, and the Old Latin *a b c habeam.* Cod. L of Griesbach or η of Stevens, and some others, as well as Mark x. 17 and Luke xviii. 18 and x. 25 have, as here, κληρονομησω.

17. *God*—Omitted in the Greek, but it is added in the Old Latin *b c* and in Jerome's edition. Mark and Luke have in the parallel passages ουδεις αγαθος ει μη εις ο θεος.

20. *Lo, since I was a boy*—This is supported by Cod. Bezæ D, εκ νηοτητος μου, the Old Latin *a b c* and Origen, as well as Mark and Luke in the parallel passages. The Greek has been literally translated in the Peshito ܡܢ ܛܠܝܘܬܝ *from my youth.*

21. *go sell thy property*—Greek, υπαγε, πωλησον σου τα υπαρχοντα; Mark, υπαγε, οσα εχεις πωλησον: Luke παντα οσα εχεις πωλησον, omitting υπαγε, as if he had read in an Aramaic text like this כל παντα for זל υπαγε. *and take up thy cross and come after me*—The Greek is και δευρο ακολουθει μοι only. Mark adds, x. 21, αρας τον σταυρον. Compare Matt. x. 38, xvi. 24.

25. *and feared*—This is supported by the Codex Bezæ D, και εφοβηθησαν, by the Old Latin *a b c, et timebant,* and Hilary, *et metuunt.*

29. *in the world that cometh*—These words are not in the Greek; but the parallel passages, both of Mark x. 30 and Luke xviii. 30, have εν τῳ αιωνι τῳ ερχομενῳ. Irenæus also has *in hoc seculo et in futuro,* perhaps by error for *in seculo futuro* only. This might have been omitted in the Aramaic on account of the ομοιοτελευτον, but not so in the Greek.

CH. XX. v. 7. *That which is just I will give you*—The Textus Receptus has here και ο εαν η δικαιον ληψεσθε; but these words are omitted in the Cod. Bezæ D and Cod. Vat. B and others, and therefore have been removed from the text by Lachmann, Tischendorf, and Tregelles. The Coptic and Jerusalem Syriac agree with this in reading *I will give you* instead of ληψεσθε. Compare the next verse, *to them he would give more*: Greek, οτι πλειον λημψονται.

11. *and when they saw*—כד חזו: Greek λαβοντες, as if the translator had taken חזו from אחזו of the Hebrew for חדו of אחדו, dropping the א, which letter not unfrequently falls out in this text.†

* See Tregelles, Account of the Printed Text of the Greek New Testament, p. 135. Simon, Hist. Crit. du Texte du N. T., p. 409, and Griesbach, Com. Crit., par. 1, p. 154.

† See xxi. 36, 37, where two instances occur of א falling out before ח: חרנא for אחרנא, and בחריתא for באחריתא.

13. *do not trouble me*—Greek *ουκ αδικω σε.* The Aramaic לא תהרני is used in the Peshito, Luke xi. 7, for *μη μοι κοπους παρεχε.*

17. *his twelve*—The Textus Receptus reads *τους δωδεκα μαθητας* with the Cod. Vat. B and others; but Codd. Bezæ D, Dubl. Z, and Origen omit *μαθητας*; and the Old Latin *a c* adds *his.*

19. *and they shall mock at him*—Greek *εις το εμπαιξαι.* The difference between these is only in the reading of ד for ו, which change frequently occurs. Had it been written דנבזחון, the Greek rendering would have been correct; but Mark has it exactly as here, *και εμπαιξουσιν,* ונבזחון. At ch. xi. v. 10, xvii. 12, compare דנתקן, which I have translated *that he may prepare,* but it may also be *who shall prepare, ος κατασκευασει,* as we find it in Luke, with which the Codd. Vat. B, Bezæ D, Dubl. Z, and Origen agree in reading *ος*: while the Cod. Guelf. P and the Old Latin *a b c* have *και,* all of which the interchange of ו and ד in the original will at once account for.

21. *My Lord, that these my two sons may sit*—Instead of *My Lord* the Greek reads *ειπε.* This has doubtless arisen from the similarity of מרי *My Lord* and אמר *bid,* which the Peshito following the Greek has,. *and in thy glory*—This is not in the Greek. Mark, in the parallel passage, x. 37, has *εν τη δοξη σου,* instead of *εν τη βασιλειᾳ σου,* and hence, perhaps, this addition here. Compare ch. xvi. v. 28 above.

22, 23. Many copies of the Greek add here *και το βαπτισμα ο εγω βαπτιζομαι βαπτισθηναι*; and these words are found in the Textus Receptus. Griesbach, Lachmann, Tischendorf, and Tregelles have removed them from the text. Origen, in his commentary on Matthew, says that they belong to Mark, *η ως ο Μαρκος ανεγραψε, Δυνασθε το ποτηριον πιειν ο εγω πινω, η το βαπτισμα ο εγω βαπιζομαι βαπτισθηναι*: Mark x. 38, 39.*

28. *But you, seek ye that from little things, &c.*—This addition is found also in the Old Latin version *a b c*: and in the Codex Bezæ, Greek and Latin, in the terms following.

Υμεις δε ζητειτε εκ μεικρου αυξησαι και εκ μειζονος ελαττον ειναι. Εισερχομενοι δε και παρακληθεντες δειπνησαι, μη ανακλεινεσθαι εις τους εξεχοντας τοπους, μη ποτε ενδοξοτερος σου επελθη, και προσελθων ο δειπνοκλητωρ ειπη σοι, ετι κατω χωρει· και κα-

Vos autem quæritis de minimo crescere, et de magno minui. Introeuntes autem et rogati cœnare, ne discubueritis in eminentibus locis, ne forte dignior te superveniat, et accedens cœnæ invitator dicat tibi: Adhuc deorsum

* See Origen, Com. in Matt. Opp. edit, Delarue iii. p. 717; Tregelles, ibid, p. 140; and Simon, ibid, p. 411.

ταισχυνθηση. Εαν δε αναπεσης εις τον ηττονα τοπον, και επελθη σου ηττων, ερει σοι ο δειπνοκλητωρ, συναγε ετι ανω· και εσται σοι τουτο χρησιμον.

accede, et confundaris. Si autem discubueris in minimum locum, et superveniat minor te, dicet tibi invitator cœnæ: Collige adhuc superius, et erit tibi utile.*

This same passage is also read in the margin of the Philoxenian version in the Vatican, and is cited by Adler in full:† and I have found it in the margin of a copy of the Peshito of the Nitrian manuscripts, No 14,456 in the British Museum. As it stands in these copies, it is plain that it has been translated immediately from the Greek and not been taken from another copy of this Syriac text, from which, indeed, it varies in language considerably, as it will be seen by comparing them. This passage is found likewise in the Anglo-Saxon version in not less than four copies indicated by Mareshall‡ in his notes on this place. He renders the Saxon into Latin in the following words :—"In rebus exiguis crescere vos cupitis, et in maximis rebus minui. Cum autem vos ad refectionem *vel* convivium, vocati fueritis, ne discumbite in primis (*i.e.* summis) sedibus: ne forte vir te honorabilior accedat post te, et paterfamilias te surgere jubeat, et alteri locum dare; et tu confundaris. Si in convivio discubueris in sede ultima

* For the variations in this text see the editions of Griesbach and Tregelles.

† Novi Testamenti Versiones Syr. 4to Hafniæ, 1789, p. 90. ܐܢܬܘܢ ܕܝܢ ܒܥܝܢ ܐܢܬܘܢ.
ܡܢ ܙܥܘܪܬܐ ܠܡܪܒܐ ܘܡܢ ܪܒܬܐ. ܠܡܙܥܘܪܬܐ. ܟܕ ܕܥܐܠܝܢ ܐܢܬܘܢ
ܕܝܢ ܘܟܕ ܡܬܩܪܝܢ ܐܢܬܘܢ ܠܡܣܬܡܟܘ. ܠܐ ܬܣܬܡܟܘܢ ܒܕܘ̈ܟܝܬܐ ܡܥܠܝܬܐ.
ܕܠܡܐ ܕܝܬܝܪ ܡܢܟ ܒܬܪܟ ܢܐܬܐ. ܘܟܕ ܢܩܪܘܒ ܗܘ ܩܪܐ ܠܚܫܡܝܬܐ.
ܢܐܡܪ ܠܟ ܬܘܒ ܐܬܚܬ ܠܬܚܬ ܘܬܬܒܗܬ. ܐܢ ܕܝܢ ܬܣܬܡܟ ܒܕܘܟܬܐ ܒܨܝܪܬܐ.
ܘܢܐܬܐ ܒܬܪܟ ܕܒܨܝܪ ܡܢܟ. ܢܐܡܪ ܠܟ ܗܘ ܩܪܐ ܠܚܫܡܝܬܐ ܐܬܟܢܫ ܬܘܒ
ܠܥܠ. ܘܬܗܘܐ ܠܟ ܗܕܐ ܕܝܬܝܪ ܚܫܝܚܐ (ܡܫܒܚܐ .Ass. ii).

ܗܠܝܢ ܡܢ ܒܨܚܚܐ ܥ̈ܬܝܩܐ ܒܠܘܩܐ ܠܚܘܕ. ܡܬܩܪܝܢ ܒܦܘܩ. ܕܢܓ̄ ܐܫܬܟܚܘ ܕܝܢ
ܒܨܚܚܐ ܝܘܢܝܐ ܗܪܟܐ ܘܡܛܠܗܢܐ ܐܦ ܡܢܢ ܐܬܬܘܣܦܘ ܗܠܝܢ

"Vos autem quæritis, de pusillo crescere, et de majore minoris esse. Introeuntes autem et rogati cœnare, ne discubueritis in eminentibus locis, ne forte dignior te superveniat, et accedens cœnæ invitator dicat tibi, Adhuc deorsum accede, et confundaris. Si autem discubueris in minimum locum, et superveniat minor te, dicet tibi invitator cœnæ, Collige adhuc superius, et erit tibi hoc utile (Ass. ii. honorificum).—Hæc quidem in exemplis antiquis in Luca tantum leguntur, capite (κεφαλαιω) LIII. Inveniuntur autem in exemplis Græcis hoc loco, quapropter hic etiam a nobis adjecta sunt."

‡ Observationes in Versionem Anglo-Saxonicam, p. 496. See Quatuor Euang. Verss. Goth. et Anglo-Sax., 4to, Amstel. 1684.

(*i.e.* infima) et post te accedat alius conviva, dicatque tibi invitator, Amice interius (*i.e.* eminentius) discumbe: tunc tibi honorificentius erit, quam *si* te exterius (*i. e.* inferius) detrudant." This passage was also known to Hilary, and seems to have had a place in the copy of St. Matthew used by Juvencus in the first half of the fourth century, when he wrote his poetical paraphrase of the Gospels, which, according to Jerome, represented the text almost literally in hexameter verses.* He has rendered it thus:—

> At vos ex minimis opibus transcendere vultis,
> Et sic a summis lapsi comprenditis imos.
> Si vos quisque vocat cœnæ convivia ponens,
> Cornibus in summis devitet ponere membra
> Quisque sapit, veniet forsitan si nobilis alter,
> Turpiter eximio cogetur cedere cornu,
> Quem tumor inflati cordis per summa locaret.
> Sin contentus erit mediocria prendere cœnæ
> Inferiorque dehinc, si mox conviva subibit,
> Ad potiora pudens transibit strata tororum.†

We have therefore in favour of this passage, in the East, the testimony of this very early Syriac copy; among the Greeks,‡ that of the antient Codex Bezæ, and of the Greek copies made use of by the author of the note in the margin of the Philoxenian version, and the Peshito above mentioned; and in the West, that of the Old Latin and not less than four venerable MSS. in Anglo-Saxon, which, as Mareshall, and, after him, Simon, observes, must have been made from the Latin previously to its having been corrected by Jerome; as well as the evidence of Hilary, and of Juvencus in Spain in the time of Constantine. Whether it formed a part of the original Gospel of St. Matthew, and, from some cause or other, came to be omitted in the greater part of the Greek copies,§ and those versions which followed their authority, or whether it be an addition from some of the

* De Script. Ecc. "Quatuor Evangelia hexametris versibus pene ad verbum transferens."

† See Juvencus, Hist. Evang. Lib. iii. Simon, Hist. Crit. par. iii. ch. 23.

‡ Griesbach rejects the opinion of Bengel and others who supposed that this addition was made to the Greek of the Cod. Bezæ from the Latin. Com. Crit., par. 1, p. 167. Symbl. p. cx.

§ Ne pourroit-on pas même conjecturer, qui celuy qui a traduit d'Ebreu en Grec l'Original de Saint Matthieu, la abrege en quelques endroits, et qu'il a quelquefois pris la liberté d'en traduire plûtôt le sens que les mots? Au moins il semble qu'il ait usé de cette liberté dans les passages du Vieux Testament qui y sont citez, et qui ont plus de conformité avec la Version Grecque des Septante, qu' avec le Texte Ebreu. See Simon, Hist. Crit. du Texte N. T. ch. ix. p. 98.

uncanonical Gospels, similar to that which the history of the woman taken in adultery, in St. John viii. 2—11, is by many supposed to be, every reader must judge for himself.* It certainly belongs to the most antient times of Christianity; and the fact of the same advice of our Lord in very similar words being found in the Gospel of St. Luke would at least make it appear that it is to be referred ultimately to him, whatever might have been the channel through which it has been derived.

34. *and we may see thee*—These words are not found in the Greek. In the same manner, we find in this copy, at Luke xviii. 41, *I may see thee.*

CH. XXI. 1. *and when he came near*—Greek, ηγγισαν in the plural; but the Old Latin *b*, and the Cod. Palat. edited by Tischendorf, the Jerusalem Syriac, Origen, and others have the singular as here. *Two of his disciples*—Greek, δυω μαθητας only; but the Old Latin *a b c* adds *his*; and Mark and Luke exactly as here, δυο των μαθητων αυτου. *The mount of Beth Zaithe*—This is the Mount of Olives—Ορος των ελαιων, as the Greek has it. The proper name of the place seems, however, to be as I have given it here—Mount of *the Place* of Olives, like the preceding word Beth Phage, the Place of unripe Figs. In the one instance the Aramaic name has been retained in the Greek, Βηθφαγη: in the other it has been translated Ορος των ελαιων. Any reader of the New Testament must have observed that the word Beth, literally meaning a house or abode, very frequently enters into the composition of proper names, as Bethabara, the Place of the Fords or Passes; Bethsaida, the Place of Fishing, &c.

2. *lo*—Greek, και ευθεως; omitted in the Old Latin *a b c* and by Luke. *and her colt at her side*—Greek και πωλον μετ' αυτης; but both Mark xi. 2 and Luke xix. 30 have instead εφ' ον ουδεις ανθρωπων κεκαθικε. Whence this variation? Might it not have arisen from their having read the original Aramaic differently from the translator into Greek, with the change of ד for ו so frequently oc-

* Il se peut faire que cette histoire ait été prise de quelque ancien Livre apoccryphe, où elle étoit commune dans les premiers siecles du Christianisme; et peut-être croyoit-on qu'elle venait des Apôtres, ou de leurs Disciples. C'est pourquoi ceux qui ont osé retoucher en tant d' endroits les premiers Exemplaires du Nouveau Testament dans la seule vûë de les rendre intelligibles à tout le monde, n'auront aussi fait aucune difficulté d'y ajoûter ces sortes d'histoires qu'ils croyoient être veritables. Nous avons vû cy-dessus de semblables examples dans l'Evangile des Nazaréens. Si nous avions aujourd'hui un assez grand nombre de cette sorte d'Exemplaires qui étoient avant Saint Jerôme, principalment dans les Eglises d'Occident, on pourroit y découvrir quelques autres additions qui nous sont presentiment inconnües, parce qu'il ne nous reste presque rien des Livres de ces premiers temps.—Ibid, ch. xxx. p. 376. See also Griesbach, Com. Crit. par. i. p. 167.

curring? The slight transposition of one letter and the omission of a slight stroke turns ועילה על גבה of this text into דעליה על גבר, *εφ' ον ανθρωπος κεκαθικε*; or perhaps דעליה לא גבר *εφ' ον ουδεις ανθρωπων*.

5. *Cometh to thee just and meek*—The word *just* is not found in the Greek copies, but it is in the passage of Zechariah ix. 9. צדיק ונושע הוא עני ורכב על חמור ועל עיר בן אתנות, which the Peshito has rendered זדיקא ופרוקא ומכיכא ורכיב על חמרא ועל עילא בר אתנא, as in this text, only with the omission of פרוקא, which might easily have fallen out on account of the *ομοιοτελευτον* after זדיקא, or have been intentionally omitted from among epithets indicative of meekness. Compare what Origen says on the variation of this citation in Matthew and John.*

9. *and many went out to meet him, and were rejoicing and praising God concerning all that which they saw*—This passage is not found in the Greek. If it be not a part of the original Aramaic of St. Matthew, it would appear to have been supplied from the parallel passages of Luke and John conjointly; for in Luke we read *ηρξαντο απαν το πληθος των μαθητων χαιροντες αινειν τον Θεον φωνῃ μεγαλῃ περι πασων ων ειδον δυναμεων*, xix. 38; and in John *και εξηλθον εις υπαντησιν αυτῳ*, xii. 13.

12. *temple of God*—the addition *of God* is supported by the Codex Bezæ D and the Old Latin *a c*. At verse 6 above, *c* also adds *Jesus* with this text.

13. *for all nations*—These words are not found in the Greek copies, but they exist in the original of Isaiah lvi. 7, and in the parallel place of Mark xi. 17, *πασιν τοις εθνεσιν*, and also in Luke xix. 46 in this copy.

14. *the blind and deaf*—The Greek has *τυφλοι και χωλοι*.

16. *They say, Hearest thou not*—אמרין לא שמע אנת: Greek, *ειπον αυτῳ, Ακουεις*; as if the translator had read לה *αυτῳ* for לא *ουκ*, thus אמרין לה שמע אנת. Two Greek manuscripts, F, H, cited by Tregelles, have *ουκ*; and so reads the Memphitic version.

21. *shall be to you so*, i.e. *ye shall have it so*—Greek, *γενησεται* only.

23. There is nothing here that corresponds with *διδασκοντι* of the Greek, nor is there in the Old Latin *a b c*.

24. *this word*—Greek, *λογον ενα*. The variation must have arisen from the similarity of הדא *this*, and חדא *one*, seeming to prove that this text was originally written in the square Hebrew character, as there is not the same similarity between ܚܕܐ and ܗܕܐ

28. *και προσελθων* of the Greek is omitted here.

* Com. in Matt. Edit. Delarue, vol. iii. p. 738. Cited also by Lachmann at this verse.

29. *to the vineyard*—This, omitted in most of the Greek copies, is found in the Codex Bezæ D, and in the Old Latin *a b c*.

30. *Yea, my Lord*—Greek εγω, Κυριε, which the Peshito renders אנא. The difference lies between אין ναι and אנא εγω. The Old Latin has *eo, Domine*, probably a corruption for *ego*, and Cod. Bezæ D εγω Κυριε, υπαγω: Chrysostom απερχομαι.*

31. *seemeth to you that he*—This is not in the Greek: probably omitted because occurring two verses above. *The first*—with the Textus Receptus, the Old Latin *c*, and Jerome. Lachmann and Tregelles have in their editions ο υστερος.†

34. *that they might send to him the fruits*—Greek λαβειν τους καρπους αυτου. Luke xx. 10, has ινα απο του καρπου του αμπελωνος δωσουσιν αυτῳ.

37. *perhaps*—This is not in the Greek; but the Old Latin *b c* have *forsitan*, which is supported by the Peshito as well as by other versions and Irenæus. Luke also reads ισως τουτον εντραπησονται.

39. *and the inheritance shall become ours*—Greek και σχωμεν την κληρονομιαν αυτου; but the Old Latin *a b c* have *et habebimus hereditatem*, which exactly agrees with this: and so Mark xii. 7, και ημων εσται η κληρονομια; and Luke xx. 14 the same, only changing ד for ו, ινα ημων γενηται η κληρονομια; though in Luke the Old Latin *c* read as here *et fiet*; and in this copy in Luke we have ותהוא ירתותא דילן.

41. *Evilly, evilly will he destroy them*—The intensive form of ביש ביש repeated: the translator does not seem to have been familiar with this, and therefore has rendered κακους κακως απολεσει αυτους, and the Latin *malos male perdet*. The Peshito retains the idiomatic expression as here.‡ Both Mark and Luke have substituted for ביש ביש *evilly, evilly*, ελευσεται, probably from some defect in the original MS. almost as if there had been read in Hebrew בוא יבוא.

CH. XXII. 2. *banquet*—משתותא, literally, a *Symposium* or *drinking party*. The Greek has γαμους. Luke in the parallel passage, xiv. 16, has δειπνον μεγα. Γαμου was probably supplied for the sake of euphemy by the translator, having also perhaps regard to the marriage feast mentioned in John ii.

7. *and the king was wroth*—The Greek copies add ακουσας, but the Cod. Vat. B omits it. *his army*—Most Greek copies have στατευματα; but Cod. Bezæ D has the singular form as here, and so the Old Latin *a b c*. *with fire*—Greek omits this.

* See Griesbach Com. Crit., par. ii. p. 7.

† See ibid, p. 2.

‡ Compare iv. 24 and xiv. 35 above, where the Greek for ביש ביש עבידין of this text is κακως εχοντας.

9. *amongst the highways*—לבית אורחתא, or literally *to the house* or *place of highways*. Greek, επι τας διεξοδους των οδων, which the Peshito follows ܠܡܦܩܢܐ ܕܐܘܪܚܬܐ. In the next verse we have the same Aramaic expression, but the Greek is εις τας οδους only. Luke xiv. 21 has εις τας πλατειας και ρυμας της πολεως, which this copy translates ܠܫܘܩܐ ܘܠܫܘܝܩܐ ܕܡܕܝܢܬܐ, "the streets and lanes (little streets) of the city." *the banquet house*—בית משתותא : Greek τους γαμους; and in the next verse *banquet house* is represented by ο γαμος; but Cod. Vat. B has ο νυμφων. Luke, in the parallel passage, has ινα γεμισθη ο οικος μου, introducing the word *house*, which is not found in the Greek of Matthew.

13. *Seize him by his hands and by his feet, and take him out*—This reading is supported by the Cod. Bezæ D, αρατε αυτον ποδων και χειρων και βαλετε αυτον, and the Old Latin *a b c*, and Irenæus. The Textus Receptus has δησαντες αυτου ποδας και χειρας αρατε αυτον και εκβαλετε.

15. *catch him*—that is, like a hunter, or fowler, or fisherman. The Greek has παγιδευσωσιν, but Mark xii. 13 exactly as here, αγρευσωσιν.

16. *The servants of Herod*—Greek των Ηρωδιανων, which the Peshito expresses by ܕܒܝܬ ܗܪܘܕܣ, *those of the house of Herod*. It would appear that they were servants of Herod, from whose province Jesus came (see Luke xxiii. 7), who went with the disciples of the Pharisees prepared to seize upon Jesus, and deliver him up to the secular power of Herod, should he have given any answer to their question that would have denied the right of the Roman emperor to collect tribute from the Jews (compare Luke xxiii. 2). *For thou acceptest not the person* (literally, "takest not by the face") *of man*, that is, *of any* דאנש—Greek ου γαρ βλεπεις εις προσωπον ανθρωπων; and so Mark xii. 14; but Luke xx. 21 retains the idiom ου λαμβανεις προσωπον, omitting των ανθρωπων, but still accurately rendering the Aramaic דאנש, which, although it be literally *of man*, really means *of any*, and was therefore not necessary for the sense in Luke. Had the meaning been των ανθρωπων it would have been דאנשא, as the Peshito has rendered the Greek; or, perhaps still more properly, דבנינשא, *of men's sons*, as I have always translated it in these Gospels, to mark the distinction. Hegesippus, himself a Jew and well acquainted with the language, has retained the Aramaism and translated literally the words of the Jews addressed to James the Just οτι δικαιος ει, και οτι προσωπον ου λαμβανεις.* There is sufficient resemblance between βλειπεις εις and λαμβανεις to warrant the conjecture that the change might have been made by a transcriber ignorant of the Aramaic idiom λαμβανειν προσωπον.

* See Eusebius, Hist. Ecl. ii. 23.

17. *Head-money*—The Greek Matthew and Mark have *κηνσον*, the Latin *Census*; and Luke *φορον*.

18. *their thoughts*—Greek *την πονηριαν αυτων*. One antient Latin manuscript, Cod. Rehdigeranus, cited by Schulz*, reads *cogitationes*. Hilary has *interna cogitationum secreta*. Mark xii. 15 has has *υποκρισιν*; Luke xx. 23 *την πανουργιαν*, which reading Origen also confirms; and this is rendered in this manuscript בישותהון, the same word as the Peshito employs here in Matthew. There is sufficient resemblance between מחשבתהון "thoughts," and בישותהון "wickedness," to lead to the conjecture that this variation might have arisen from some defect in the Aramaic copy.

22. *and left him*—Greek *και αφεντες αυτον*: Luke xx. 26 has *εσιγησαν*; and Mark omits this. The similarity between שבקו *they left* and שתקו, *they were silent* seems to have caused the variation.

24, *Moses said to us*—Greek *ειπεν* only, omitting *to us*; but the Aramaic אמר means *commanded* as well as *said*. Mark xii. 19 and Luke xx. 28 have both *εγραψεν ημιν*, substituting *wrote*, instead of *said*, and retaining *to us*; although therefore the Aramaic אמר might be employed in both cases, the Greek translation *ειπεν* would seem to be properly applied only in the case of those to to whom Moses actually spake. This might have been the reason why Luke and Mark substituted *εγραψεν* for *ειπεν*, and the Greek translator dropped, *to us*.

25. *died and left not children*—Greek *ετελευτησε, και μη εχων σπερμα*; Mark xii. 20, *αποθνησκων ουκ αφηκε σπερμα*; but Luke xx. 29, *απεθανεν ατεκνος*.

28. *unto the seven of them she was*, i.e. *the seven of them had her*—Greek *παντες γαρ εσχον αυτην*. The Old Latin of Codd. Veron. *b* and Palat. *e* has *septem enim eam habuerunt*; and both Mark and Luke *οι γαρ επτα εσχον αυτην γυναικα*.

31. *That God said*—Greek *το ρηθεν υμιν υπο του Θεου λεγοντος*: Mark xii. 26 also varies here, *εν τη βιβλῳ Μωυσεως επι του βατου, ως ειπεν αυτῳ ο Θεος λεγων*. Justin Martyr, Apol. i. 63, has *το ειρημενον εκ βατου τῳ Μωσει*.

34. *when they saw*—Greek *ακουσαντες*; Peshito ܟܕ ܫܡܥܘ. *assembled near him*—Greek *επι το αυτο*, which the Peshito renders ܐܟܚܕܐ *together*; but Cod. Bezæ D and the Old Latin *b c* read as here, *επ' αυτον*, *ad eum*: Hilary *adversus eum*.

35. *one of them a scribe*—Greek *νομικος*, which the Peshito here has rendered ܝܕܥ ܢܡܘܣܐ, *knowing of the law*. Mark xii. 28 has *εις των γραμματεων*, and, v. 32, *ο γραμματευς*. In the next verse, 36, we have *great and first*; Greek *μεγαλη* only, but Mark *πρωτη*: at verse 38 the Greek has both. We have the

* See his edition of Griesbach's New Testament at this place.

Aramaic באוריתא rendered in the Greek *εν τῳ νομῳ*, and the Peshito following retains the Greek word ܢܡܘܣܐ. *and said to him*—This is omitted in most of the Greek copies, but it is found in Cod. Bezæ D, the Textus Receptus, and the Old Latin of *b c*.

37. *from all thy heart, and from all thy soul, and from all thy strength*—which the Greek has *εν ολῃ τῃ καρδιᾳ σου και εν ολῃ τῃ ψυχῃ σου και εν ολῃ τῃ διανοιᾳ σου*, while Mark has the passage exactly as here, *εξ ολης της καρδιας σου και εξ ολης της ψυχης σου και εξ ολης της ισχυος σου*, and so the Peshito. Instead of *strength* or *της ισχυος*, as Mark has it, which seems undoubtedly to be the true reading, referring to Deut. vi. 5, whence the words are quoted, we have in the Greek *διανοιᾳ*. Whether *διανοιᾳ* be a corruption from the word *δυναμει*, which we find used to translate the Hebrew מאד in the Septuagint, or whether the Greek translator of Matthew read הונך *thy mind*, for חולך *thy strength*, or from what other cause this variation arose, the reader must judge for himself.

42. *What say ye?*—Greek *τι υμιν δοκει*. Both Mark and Luke have *πως λεγουσιν οι γραμματεις*.

43. *by the Spirit of Holiness*—Most of the Greek copies have *εν πνευματι* only. Griesbach cites one or two which add *αγιῳ*. The Jerusalem Syriac reads as here. Mark xii. 36 also has *εν τῳ πνευματι τῳ αγιῳ*; but Luke xx. 42 *εν βιβλῳ ψαλμων*. *My Lord*—Greek *κυριον*.

46. *from that hour*—Greek *της ημερας*; but Cod. Bezæ D reads as here, and so the Old Latin *a*.

CH. XXIII. 3. *Be ye hearing and doing*—Greek *ποιησατε και τηρειτε*. Origen once has, as here, *audite et facite*.* The Clementine Homilies, iii. 18, *παντα οσα λεγωσιν υμιν ακουσατε*.

4. *heavy*—Greek *βαρεα και δυσβαστακτα*. The Old Latin *a b* and Irenæus omit *δυσβαστακτα*. Luke xi. 46 has *δυσβατακτα* only, whence it seems probable that it became inserted in the text here, both Greek words being different translations of the one Aramaic יקירתא. *and they with one of their fingers touch them not*—Greek *αυτοι δε τῳ δακτυλῳ αυτων ου θελουσιν κινησαι αυτα*. Luke xi. 46 is much nearer to this, *και αυτοι ενι των δακτυλων υμων ου προσψαυετε*.

5. *straps of their Tephillas*—Greek *φυλακτηρια*, which word occurs for the first time in this place, and was probably adopted not less on account of the sound suggested by the Aramaic than because it represents to a certain degree the sense. The letters of these two Aramaic words, ערק תפלא, when transposed, may be used to write the Greek *φυλακτηρια*, פלקתערא; and

* Op. Edit. Delarue, iii. 382.

it seems to me that this is the origin of the Greek word used by the translator of Matthew's Gospel, in the same way as the name of Jerusalem, *Ιεροσολυμα,* for the Hebrew ירושלם, has been modified from the name *Σολυμα.* common to several other cities, and the prefix *Ιερο* to represent the Hebrew ירו, and also at the same time to indicate its sacred character. If I be not mistaken, I have discovered traces of several Greek words used by the translator, suggested by the similarity of sound, although others more logically correct might have been employed. The Hebrew or Aramaic תפלין, תפלא, is the word used to express the very meaning that the Greek *φυλακτηρια* is intended to convey; and consequently, in the Peshito, accommodated to the Greek, we find ܬܦܠܐ only, the word ܐܣܘܪܐ straps being omitted.

10. *Teachers*—מלפנא: Greek *καθηγηται.*

13 and 14. These verses are found transposed in different Greek manuscripts. 14 has been omitted by Lachmann, Tischendorf, and Tregelles in their editions.

16. *hurteth not*—Greek *ουδεν εστιν.* The variation seems to have arisen from confounding לא מכא and לא מדם, as it is in the Peshito; and so in *sinneth,* where the Greek is *οφειλει,* from the similarity of חטא and חאב.

18. There is omitted here, probably by an error of the transcriber, *και ος αν ομοση εν τῳ θυσιαστηριῳ.*

19. *Blinded*—with D Z and the Old Latin *a*: others add *μωροι και.*

GOSPEL OF MARK.

CHAPTER XVI.

This very small remaining Fragment of St Mark is an early testimony to the authenticity of the last twelve verses of this Gospel, which have been deemed spurious by some critics.*

18. *In their hands*—Codd. Ephr. Palimp. C, Reg. 62, L. Monac. X, and Sangal. Δ have also *εν ταις χερσιν.* This is omitted in other Greek copies, and in the Peshito. *any poison of death*—and so Peshito: Greek *θανασιμον τι.*

19. *after he had commanded his disciples*—Greek *μετα το λαλησαι αυτοις,* with which the Peshito agrees.

20. *the Lord was with them in all*—Greek *του κυριου συνεργουντος,* which Peshito renders ܘܡܪܢ ܡܥܕܪ ܗܘܐ ܠܗܘܢ, "and the Lord was helping them. *By the signs which they were doing*—and so also the Peshito: Greek *δια των επακολουθουντων σημειων.*

* See Griesbach's Com. Crit. ii. p. 298, and Tregelles' Edition of the Greek New Testament, p. 213.

GOSPEL OF JOHN.

CH. I. v. 1. *The word,* ܗܘ ܡܠܬܐ—here in the masculine to accommodate itself to the Greek ο λογος.

4. *But that which was in him is life*—This punctuation, instead of that of the Textus Receptus, has been already adopted both by Lachmann and Tischendorf in their editions, upon the weight of other authorities.

13. *by blood,* ܒܕܡܐ—Greek εξ αιματος. *of the body,* ܕܦܓܪܐ—and so in the next verse for the Greek σαρξ. The Peshito has corrected both of these, to bring them nearer to the Greek, and reads ܡܢ ܕܡܐ *of blood* and ܒܣܪܐ *flesh.*

14. *and the word became body and dwelt among us*—The translator here seems to have forgotten himself, and has used ܡܠܬܐ *word,* in the feminine, in its natural grammatical construction, and not in accordance with the Greek, as in the first verse. *The only* son, יחידא—the same as the Hebrew יחיד (See Genesis xxii. 2. The Greek is μονογενους, and so in v. 18 below.

18. *to us*—which the Old Latin *c* supports, is omitted in the Greek.

19. *when they sent to him from Jerusalem, the Jews, and the chief priests, and the Levites*—The Greek οτε απεστειλαν προς αυτον οι Ιουδαιοι εξ Ιεροσολυμων ιερεις και Λευιτας. The translator seems to have read ιερεις and λευιται in the nominative.

21. Τι ουν; Ηλιας ει συ; και λεγει Ουκ ειμι of the Greek is omitted here.

22. *Tell us*—left out in the Greek, but the Old Latin *b c* has *dic ergo nobis.*

24. *and they were sending and saying to him*—For this the Greek has και οι απεσταλμενοι ησαν εκ των Φαρισαιων, και ηρωτησαν αυτον και ειπαν αυτῳ.

26. *said to him*—omitting απεκριθη. See also below, iii. 27; iv. 10, 13, 17, &c.

27. ος εμπροσθε μου γεγονεν—These words are omitted in this text, and also in Codd. Vat. B, Palimps. Ephr. C, and the Old Latin *b* and Origen.

28. *spake*—Greek εγενετο. *Beth Abara*—Most copies of the Greek and Latin have here *Bethany,* but Origen was persuaded that *Beth Abara* was the true reading: Βηθανιᾳ σχεδον εν πασι τοις αντιγραφοις και παρα Ηρακλεωνι· επεισθην δε δειν αναγινωσκειν Βηθαβαρᾳ.* *the river*—omitted in the Greek.

29. *Lo*—This is not repeated in the Greek, but it is in *a b c* of the Old Latin,

* See Origen, Opp. v. iv., p. 140; Griesbach's Edition of N. T.; and Birch's note on this verse. "Quatuor Evangelia Græce," 4to., Havniæ, 1788, p. 536.

ecce qui tollit, and by Cyprian; and so by Eusebius in his "Theophania," book iii. c. 59.*

34. *the chosen of God*—Greek ο υιος του Θεου. The Old Latin *a b* has *electus filius dei*, and one Greek copy cited by Griesbach, εκλεκτος, and the Jerusalem Syriac ܓܒܝܗ, *his chosen*.†

35. *Jesus*—evidently an error for Ιωαννης of the Greek.

36. *Lo, the Messiah*—omitted in the Greek. One manuscript cited by Birch has here ο Χριστος. The Greek ο αιρων την αμαρτιαν του κοσμου, found in some copies and left out in others, is also omitted here.

37. *and when those disciples of John heard*—for the Greek και ηκουσαν αυτου οι δυω μαθηται λαλουντος.

39. *Our Master*—ܪܒܢ: Greek ραββι. The explanation in the Greek, ο λεγεται μεθερμηνευομενον διδασκαλε, was unnecessary to the Syriac reader who knew the meaning of the term, and is therefore omitted, if, indeed, this and similar explanations be not marginal notes which have found their way into the text subsequently to the time when this version was made.

41. *of those disciples of John*—in which sense the Syriac translator seems to have understood the words των ακουσαντων παρα Ιωαννου. *Andrius* or *Andreius*—for Ανδρεας, as in Matthew. *was his name*—omitted. The order of the words also is changed here: and ܚܙܐ *saw* or *seeth* for ευρισκει.

42. *The Messiah*—omitting ο εστιν μεθερμηνευομενον χριστος, as in verse 39.

CH. III. v. 6. *because of the flesh it is born*—omitted in the Greek, but found in the Old Latin *a b*, *quia de carne natum est*. *because God is a spirit*—This is also omitted in the Greek, but exists in the Old Latin *a*, *quia deus spiritus est*. These words are likewise found in the margin of one of the Greek manuscripts collated by Birch. St Ambrose also read them in his copies, and accuses the Arians of having erased them for dogmatical purposes.‡

8. *of water and*—omitted in the Greek, but found in the Old Latin *a b*, *de aqua et*.

15. μη αποληται αλλ'—is omitted here, and also by Cod. Vat. B, the Old Latin *a*, by Cyprian, and the Jerusalem Syriac.§

16. μη αποληται αλλα of the Greek is also omitted here.

* Edited by Dr. Lee, 8vo., London, 1842, p. 58.

† See Adler, N. T. Vers, Syrr., p. 186.

‡ De Sprit. Sanc., lib. iii. c. 11. See respecting this Simon, Hist. Crit. du N. T., c. xxix. p. 355.

§ Adler, p. 186.

19. *the world*—repeated in the second place: Greek *οι ανθρωποι*.

23. *Æn Yon*—ܥܝܢ ܝܘܢ "Doves' fountain." Greek *Αινων*.

CH. IV. 1. *Jesus*—with Cod. Bezæ D, the Old Latin *b c*, and the Peshito. But Codd. Alex. A and Vat. B, and the Textus Receptus have *ο κυριος*.

7, 8. The order of these two verses is inverted in the Greek.

9. *Lo, thou art a Jew: how askest thou me water to drink, because, lo, I am a Samaritan*—Beside the addition of *water*, in this as well as in the preceding verse, the rendering here is much more free than in the Peshito.

14. *αλλομενου* of the Greek is omitted here.

20. *the house of worship*—בית סגדתא. An Aramaism, meaning "the place of worship." Greek *ο τοπος οπου προσκυνειν δει*, which the Peshito follows literally, ܗܘ ܐܬܪܐ ܕܘܠܐ ܠܡܣܓܕ.

22. *from Juda*—Greek *εκ των Ιουδαιων*. The Old Latin *b* has *Judea*.

24. This verse is obscured, evidently by some error of the Syriac translator or transcriber.

25. *ο λεγομενος Χριστος* of the Greek omitted, being unnecessary for a Syriac reader, as above.

27. *But speaking they spake not to him*—Greek, *ουδεις μεντοι ειπεν*. *What asked she*, as if the translator had read *τι ζητει* for *τι ζητεις*; but more probably an error of the transcriber in confounding ܒܥܬ and ܒܥܝܬ.

31. *But His disciples were entreating of him that he should eat with them bread*—This is a free and not very correct rendering of the Greek text, *εν δε τῳ μεταξυ ηρωτων αυτον οι μαθηται λεγοντες Ραββι, φαγε*.

33. *they*—Greek, *οι μαθηται*.

45. *εις την Γαλιλαιαν* of the Greek omitted.

46. *Catna* or Catne, ܩܛܢܐ; and so Peshito: Greek, *Κανα*.

47. *one king's servant*—and so at verse 49; as also the Peshito: Greek, *τις βασιλικος*. *from Galilee to Judæa*—Evidently a blunder, because at verse 54 below is read, "from Judæa to Galilee," as it is in the Greek in both places. *and see his son*—Greek, *ιασηται*. This seems to have been an error of the scribe in confounding, from the similarity of the sound, ܢܚܙܐ *see* with ܢܐܣܐ *heal*, as it is correctly found in the Peshito.

48. *Marks*, or signals ܪ̈ܡܙܐ—for *σημεια*. The Peshito has ܐܬܘܬܐ.

50. *to thy house*—omitted in the Greek, while *ον ειπεν αυτῳ, και επορευετο* of the Greek is omitted here.

52. *The ninth hour*—Greek *ωραν εβδομην*: evidently an error of the scribe, confounding ܬܫܥ with ܫܒܥ.

CH. V. 2. εν τη προβατικη of the Greek is omitted here.

3. *in the porches*—Greek εν ταυταις. The rest of the verse, εκδεχομενων την του υδατος κινησιν, is omitted with B, and also A C in the first hand before corrected.

4. This verse, αγγελος γαρ—νοσηματι of the Greek is also omitted, with B C D.

8. *go to thy house*—omitted in the Greek, and probably added from Matt. ix. 6.

9. και ηρεν τον κραβαττον αυτου of the Greek omitted here.

10. *to him*—Greek, τῳ τεθεραπευμενῳ.

13. *had turned himself from the place to another on account of the multitude of men*—This is a very free rendering of the Greek ο γαρ Ιησους εξενευσεν οχλου οντος εν τῳ τοπῳ.

14. *him that was healed*—Greek αυτον only: see verse 10. *what is worse than the first*—Greek χειρον τι only.

15. *that hath made me whole*—with D and the Old Latin *a d.* The Textus Receptus and A B have ο ποιησας αυτον υγιη.

16. και εζητουν αυτον αποκτειναι of the Textus Receptus omitted, with B C D and the Old Latin *a b c.*

17. *on this account*—omitted in the Greek.

18. *on account of this word*—Greek δια τουτο. *He called God, My Father*—Greek, πατερα ιδιον ελεγε τον Θεον.

19. *neither that which he seeth not his Father do*—Greek εαν μη τι βλεπῃ τον πατερα ποιουντα.

20. *that he may do*—omitted in the Greek. *and marvel not that I said to you*—Greek, ινα υμεις θαυμαζητε.

21. *Those that believe in him*—Greek ους θελει.

25. *that also*—Greek οτε. In this verse οι ακουσαντες is omitted.

28. *because, lo*—for this, Greek has οτι ερχεται ωρα εν η. *and live*—omitted in the Greek, but read by Origen.

32. *ye know*—with Cod. Bezæ D and the Old Latin *a*. Most copies have οιδα. The Syriac translator might have read οιδατε for οιδα οτι. At verse 25 he seems to have read οτι for οτε.

39. *those which ye suppose that in them ye have life, they testify respecting me*—This is omitted in the Greek; but the Old Latin *a b* also adds *in quibus putatis vos vitam habere, hæ sunt quæ de me testificantur.*

45. προς τον πατερα omitted here.

CH. VI. 1. *of Tiberius*—Gr. Τιβεριαδος.

3. *the passover*—The Syriac translator has here taken the word by the

sound from the Greek πασχα, and written ܦܣܟܐ instead of the correct Aramaic term ܦܨܚܐ; from which the Greek itself was borrowed.

10. *Go* and *the men in sitting and sittings*—omitted in the Greek, and probably borrowed from Mark vi. 39.

11. The Textus Receptus, supported by Cod. Bezæ D and the Old Latin *b*, adds here τοις μαθηταις, οι δε μαθηται; but this has been omitted by Lachmann and Tischendorf in their editions.

15. *They were seeking*—Greek, οτι μελλουσιν ερχεσθαι. *left them and fled*—Greek, ανεχωρησεν; but the Old Latin *a c* has *fugit.*

16. *He went down and his disciples*—Greek κατεβησαν οι μαθηται. The variation here, from what follows, is evidently a blunder, and probably is to be referred to the scribe writing by mistake ܢܚܬܗܘܘ for ܢܚܬܘ.

18. *and the wind was risen vehemently, and the lake was troubled over them*—This is a very free rendering of the Greek, η τε θαλασσα ανεμου μεγαλου πνεοντος διεγειρετο.

19. *on the waters*—Greek, επι θαλασσης: see on Matthew xiv. 25 above.

20. μη φοβεισθε of the Greek is omitted here.

22. αλλα μονοι οι μαθηται αυτου απηλθον omitted here.

23. ευχαριστησαντος του Κυριου is omitted; and so by Cod. Bezæ D and the Old Latin *a*.

33. *and is living and given to the world*—This is a mistaken translation of και ζωην διδους τῳ κοσμῳ.

37. *My Father*—Greek ο Πατηρ.

38. *of the Father which sent*—Greek, του πεμψαντος only.

40. *of my Father*—with C D and the Old Latin *a b*; but the Textus Receptus, with A B, has του πεμψαντος. The Old Latin of *c* combines both, *Patris mei qui misit me.*

42. *and we know his father*—Greek, ου ημεις οιδαμεν τον πατερα και την μητερα. The Old Latin *b* omits, as here, "and mother."

46. *which is with God*—as if the translator had read παρα τῳ Θεῳ instead of του Θεου, or had confounded the meaning of the particle.

47. *believeth God*—Greek, ο πιστευων εις εμε. Codd. Vat. B and Borg. T omit the last word altogether.

48. *which came down from heaven*—omitted in the Greek.

50. *that a man may eat of it and die*—Greek, ινα τις εξ αυτου φαγῃ και μη αποθανῃ. The Syriac translator, referring to verse 31, evidently understood the words "this is the bread which came down from heaven" to relate

to the Manna, the "bread from heaven," of which the Israelites ate in the wilderness and died, in contradistinction to that "living bread" Christ, which came down from heaven that a man may eat of it and live for ever, or *not* die, spoken of in the following verse 51. Compare also verse 58.

64. τινες εισιν οι μη πιστευοντες και of the Greek omitted here.

69. *The Son of God*—Greek Textus Receptus, ο Χριστος ο υιος του Θεου ζωντος; but Codd. Vat. B, Ephr. Palimp. C, and Bezæ D, have ο αγιος του Θεου, which Griesbach, Lachmann, Tischendorf, &c., have adopted in their editions.

70. *all of you*—Greek, υμας τους δωδεκα. *and lo, even of you one is Satan*—and so Hilary, "ecce ex vobis unus est satanas." Greek, και εξ υμων εις διαβολος εστιν.

CH. VII. 1. *for he had not power*—and so *a b* of the Old Latin, *non enim habebat potestatem.* Greek, ου γαρ ηθελεν.

12. *he is not good*—Greek ου only.

14. *and when the days of the feast of Tabernacles were divided*—Greek ηδη δε της εορτης μεσουσης.

19. *keepeth its commandments*—Greek, ποιει τον νομον.

21. *before your eyes*—omitted in the Greek.

23. *do ye murmur against me*—Greek, εμοι χολατε.

26. *he standeth and speaketh*—Greek, λαλει only. *the elders*—Greek, οι αρχοντες.

29. *with him*—Greek παρ' αυτου: compare above, vi. 45.

32. ταυτα and υπηρετας of the Greek omitted here.

35. *to the seed of the Aramæans then goeth he teaching, that we find him not?*—Greek, μη εις την διασποραν των Ελληνων μελλει πορευεσθαι και διδασκειν τους Ελληνας. The translator has confounded the meaning of διασποραν with σποραν.

37. τη εσχατη of the Greek omitted here.

CH. XIV. 10. *is in me*—Greek, εν εμοι μενων. *these works*—Greek, τα εργα αυτου.

11. *and if me ye believe not*—Greek, ει δε μη only.

22. *Juda Thoma*—Greek, Ιουδας, ουχ ο Ισκαριωτης; and the Old Latin *b c* adds "sed alius." There seems to be no doubt that the real name of Thomas was Juda, or Judas in the Greek form; the appellation Thoma or Thomas, answering to the Greek διδυμος, having been added to distinguish him from other Apostles bearing the same name. Afterwards, in the West, he came to be known by this appellation only. In the East, however, he still retained his original name, and was called Juda Thoma, or Judas the

Twin, as here. Even in the Greek Acts of St. Thomas he is called *Ιουδας Θωμας*,* as well as in the Syriac copy in the British Museum; Cod. Add. 14,645, and in a very antient copy of the Doctrine of the Apostles, ܡܠܦܢܘܬܐ ܕܫܠܝ̈ܚܐ, Cod. Add. 14,531; and by Ephraem Syrus.†

26. *it shall teach*—The Spirit is put here in the feminine, according to the genius of the language. και υπομνησει of the Greek is omitted.

GOSPEL OF LUKE.

CH. II. 48. ο πατηρ σου καγω of the Greek omitted, as also in the Old Latin *a b*; and in the apocryphal Gospel of St. Thomas, ιδου οδυνωμενοι εζητουμεν σε, ch. xix.‡ *with anxiety and much grief*—Greek, οδυνωμενοι only; but Cod. Bezæ D, supported by *a*, adds και λυπουμενοι.

CH. III. 2. *and he was preaching in the wilderness, and in all the country of the borders of Jordan*—εν τῳ ερημῳ και ηλθεν εις πασαν περιχωρον του Ιορδανου κηρυσσων.

3. *in the prophecy*—Greek, εν βιβλῳ λογων.

4. The passage cited here from Isaiah xl. 3 is taken word for word from the Peshito version of that Prophet, and not rendered from the Greek text of Luke. The Peshito of Luke has also retained this in a great measure, but it has been brought nearer to the Greek by substituting ܣܘܪܒܐ for ܡܟܪܙܐ, and ܛܝܒܘ ܐܘܪܚܗ ܕܡܪܝܐ for ܦܢܘ ܐܘܪܚܐ ܠܡܪܝܐ, and ܢܚܙܐ ܟܠ ܒܣܪ ܚܝܐ ܕܐܠܗܐ for ܢܚܙܘܢܗ ܐܟܚܕܐ ܟܠ ܒܣܪ; as well as by omitting ܘܢܬܓܠܐ ܐܝܩܪܗ ܕܡܪܝܐ, "and the glory of the Lord shall be revealed," and ܡܛܠ ܕܦܘܡܗ ܕܡܪܝܐ ܡܠܠ, "because the mouth of the Lord hath spoken." See Matthew iii. 3.

7. *were coming to him*—Greek, εκπορευομενοις βαπτισθηναι υπ᾽ αυτου.

8. εν εαυτοις of the Greek omitted here; and so likewise by the Old Latin *abc*.

10. *and live*—with ινα σωθωμεν of Cod. Bezæ D, and *vivamus* of *b*, and *salvi simus* of *d* in the Old Latin: omitted in other copies.

12. διδασκαλε omitted here.

15. *and the men which were hearing him were meditating in themselves and saying, Is this then the Messiah? He said to them*—This varies widely from

* See Acta S. Thomæ Apostoli, edit. I. C. Thilo., p. 5.

† See Assemani, Bibl. Or. Clem. Vat. vol. i. pp. 100, 318.

‡ See Evangelia Apocrypha, edit. Const. Tischendorf, p. 148.

the Greek, *προσδοκωντος δε του λαου, και διαλογιζομενων παντων εν ταις καρδιαις αυτων περι του Ιωαννου, μη ποτε αυτος ειη ο Χριστος, απεκρινετο ο Ιωαννης απασιν λεγων.*

CH. VII. 33. *The Son of Man*—The translator shews here that he was not accurately acquainted with the Greek language, and therefore translates *ο υιος του ανθρωπου* by ܒܪܗ ܕܓܒܪܐ, "Son of Man," "filius *viri*," not *hominis.*

35. *παντων* of the Greek omitted here, and so in D, as in Matt. xi. 19.

38. *ηρξατο* of the Greek omitted here, and by D and the Old Latin *a b c.*

39. *what is the fame of that woman, the sinner, which touched him*—and the Peshito in the same words, but slightly transposed. Greek, *ποταπη η γυνη ητις απτεται αυτου, οτι αμαρτωλος εστιν.*

46. *Thou anointedst me not*—Greek, *ελαιῳ την κεφαλην μου ουκ ηλειψας.*

CH. VIII. 1. *And after these*—Greek, *και εγενετο εν τῳ καθεξης*: also *κηρυσσων και* of the Greek is omitted.

2. *he had cast out*—like Mark xvi. 10. Greek, *εξεληλυθει.*

3. *to them*—and so D, Old Latin *c*, and Peshito. Greek, *αυτῳ.*

7. *αι ακανθαι* omitted here.

5. *τον σπορον αυτου* of the Greek omitted with Old Latin *c* : *του ουρανου* also omitted, with D and the Old Latin *a b.*

8. *good and fruit-giving*—Greek, *την αγαθην* only ; but D adds *και καλην*, supported by the Old Latin *a c d* and the Peshito.

10. *those without*—as in Mark iv. 11, *εκεινοις δε τοις εξω.* The Greek here is *τοις δε λοιποις. It is not given to them to know: on this account it is spoken to them*—omitted in the Greek: probably added from Matt. xii. 12, 13.

12. *the word of God*—with *b* of the Old Latin. *c* has *verbum* only. This is omitted in the Greek.

13. *immediately*—omitted in the Greek : added from the parallel passages of Matthew and Mark ; as also *offended* instead of *αφιστανται* of the Greek here.

14. *are occupied*—probably from mistaking the sense of the Greek *πορευομενοι*, and confounding it with that of *πορος* or some other word. *and produce not fruits*—with the Old Latin *a b c d*: Greek *ου τελεσφορουσιν.*

16. *another parable he spake*—omitted in the Greek. *or in a hidden place*—omitted in the Greek, and taken apparently from xi. 33. Mar Yakub the Persian,* has the passage in this form, ܠܐ ܐܢܫ ܒܣܬܪ ܫܪܓܐ

* It may, perhaps, be as well to state that this Mar Yakub, to whom I have already referred above, p. vii., is the same writer as the one spoken of by Gennadius in the first chapter of his work, "De Viris Illustribus," as "Jacobus cognomine sapiens, Nisibenæ nobilis Persarum

ܘܣܐܡ ܠܗ ܬܚܝܬ ܣܐܬܐ ܐܘ ܬܚܝܬ ܥܪܣܐ. ܐܘ ܣܐܡ ܠܗ ܒܐܬܪܐ ܛܫܝܐ
ܐܠܐ ܣܐܡ ܠܗ ܥܠ ܡܢܪܬܐ ܕܟܠ ܐܢܫ ܢܚܙܐ ܢܘܗܪܗ ܕܫܪܓܐ, "No man lighteth a candle and placeth it under a measure, or under a bed, or placeth it in a hidden place; but placeth it on a candlestick, that every man may see the light of the candle."

18. *and be added to him*—omitted in the Greek, and inserted here from Matt. xiii. 12.

19. *were standing without*—omitted in the Greek: added from Matt. xii. 46.

23. *and their boat was filled from the waves, and was near to sink*—Greek, και συνεπληρουντο και εκινδυνευον. The Old Latin *b c* has *implebatur a fluctibus navicula.*

24. και επαυσαντο of the Greek omitted.

25. *and the sea*—with *et mari* of the Old Latin *c*: Greek, τῳ υδατι. See on Matt. xiv. 25 above.

27. *and he was crying every cry and smiting himself with stones*—This is not in the Greek, and has been added from Mark v. 5, ην κραζων και κατακοπτων εαυτον λιθοις.

29. *was cleaving to him*—for the Greek συνηρπακει, probably from a blunder of the translator, as if he had understood it συνυπαρχει.

30. *because we are many in him*—from Mark, v. 9, οτι πολλοι εσμεν, with which the Old Latin *b* agrees, *quia multi sumus.* The Greek of Luke here is οτι εισηλθεν δαιμονια πολλα εις αυτον.

31. *that he would not send them to Gihanna, and not cast them out*—Greek, ινα μη επιταξη αυτοις εις αβυσσον απελθειν.

33. *and all*—omitted in the Greek, but added here from Matt. viii. 32, πασα η αγελη.

37. *they that saw again*—not in the Greek; and της περιχωρου omitted.

39. *and to thy men's house*—that is, "those that belong to thee." Omitted in the Greek, but added from Mark v. 19, εις τον οικον σου προς τους σους.

43. *and she meditated in herself and says, if going I touch even the garments of Jesus I am healed*—omitted in the Greek, and added here from Matt. ix. 21, ελεγεν γαρ εν εαυτῃ· Εαν μονον αψωμαι του ιματιου αυτου, σωθησομαι, and Mark v. 28.

modo civitatis episcopus." An Armenian translation of this work was published by N. Antonelli at Rome, 1756. I trust to be able to give to the public very shortly the original Syriac of this writer, so highly interesting and important in every point of view, as contemporary with the Nicene Fathers, from the two very antient copies in the Nitrian Collection.

So likewise, v. 45, *turned and*, omitted in the Greek, but added from Matthew and Mark.

44. *παραχρημα* of the Greek omitted here.

45. *και οι συν αυτῳ* omitted here, and likewise in B.

47. *she confessed before every man*—omitted in the Greek.

50. *that they said so*—omitted in the Greek; but D has *τον λογον*, and so *b c* of the Old Latin *audito hoc sermone*, and Mark v. 36, *τον λογον λαλουμενον*.

52. *the girl*—as in Mark, and the Old Latin *c* has *puella*. Greek omits this.

54. *εκβαλων εξω παντας*, of the Textus Receptus and A C, omitted here with B D and the Old Latin *a b c*.

CH. IX. 2. *τους ασθενεις* omitted here, and likewise in B.

6. *in the countries and in the cities*—with *castella et civitates* of the Old Latin *b c*. Of the Greek, A B have *κατα κωμας*, and D *κατα πολεις*.

10. *πολεως καλουμενης Βηθσαιδα* omitted here.

12. *his disciples*—Greek, *οι δωδεκα*. *we are here in the desert*—the Greek has this at the end of the verse; but in the parallel passages of Matt. xiv. 15 and Mark vi. 35 *ερημος εστιν ο τοπος* is at the beginning of the verse. They both have also *οι μαθηται* instead of *οι δωδεκα*.

17. *and those men which ate of the bread were about five thousand, besides women and children*—This, which is omitted in the Greek, has been added from Matt. xiv. 21. The translator here again betrays his ignorance of the difference between *ανδρες* and *ανθρωποι*.

18. *προσευχομενον*—omitted here, is also omitted in D.

19. *αλλοι δε, οτι προφητης τις των αρχαιων ανεστη*—omitted here.

20. *του Θεου*—omitted.

25. *lose his soul*—and so the Greek, *εαυτον δε απολεσας*, adding also *η ζημιωθεις*, which probably found its way into the Greek text from the parallel expression of Matthew and Mark, *την δε ψυχην αυτου ζημιωθῃ*.

26. *before men's sons and those that are mine*—for this the Greek has *και τους εμους λογους*; but D, the Old Latin *a*, and Origen omit *λογους*.

27. *that it cometh in glory*—omitted in the Greek; but Cod. Bezæ D and Origen read the passage thus, *τον υιον του ανθρωπου ερχομενον εν τῃ δοξῃ αυτου*, and Mark ix. 1 adds here *εληλυθυιαν εν δυναμει*.

29. *like snow*—omitted in the Greek, added from Mark ix. 3, *ως χιων*. Matt. xvii. 2 has *ως φως*, but in this copy *like snow*, as here. See above, p. xxxi.

34. *when they saw*—omitted in the Greek.

35. *was heard*—Greek, *εγενετο*: compare Matt. xvii. 5.

38. *be compassionate*—Greek, επιβλεψον; but Matt. xvii.15 ελεησον, as here.

40. *and they were not able to heal him and to cast it out*—Greek, ινα εκβαλωσιν αυτο, και ουκ ηδυνηθησαν. "to heal him" is added from Matt. xvii. 16, αυτον θεραπευσαι.

54. ως και Ηλιας εποιησε omitted, and also by B.

59. *and I will come*—and so in verse 61: omitted in the Greek.

CH. X. 16. *and whoso heareth me, heareth him that sent me*—omitted in the Greek.

22. και στραφεις προς τους μαθητας ειπεν—omitted with D and the Old Latin *ab*.

25. *while he said these*—Greek, και ιδου only; but the Old Latin *b c* has *hæc eo dicente, ecce.*

30. υπολαβων δε omitted here.

33. *in the same way*—omitted in the Greek.

41. *my care and the anxiety of me is with thee about many*—Greek, μεριμνας και θορυβαζη περι πολλα. The word ܠܘܪܒܐ, which I do not find in the lexicons, and which must have the same meaning as ܠܘܪܦܐ was doubtless suggested by the word τυρβαζη or θορυβαζη, which the translator did not perhaps understand. It is near to the Latin *turbaris.* The Peshito has ܨܦܬܟܝ, ܘܪܗܒܘܬܟܝ, ܥܠ ܣܓܝܐܬܐ, which agrees exactly with the Greek.

CH. XI. 1. *after he ceased a little from the prayer*—Greek, ως επαυσατο only.

2. γενηθητω το θελημα σου ως εν ουρανῳ και επι γης—omitted here, and also in the Cod. Vat. B, and by Jerome in his recension. Origen says that these words were omitted by Luke, ο Λουκας μετα το, Ελθετω η βασιλεια σου, ταυτα παρασιωπησας εταξε, Τον αρτον ημων τον επιουσιον διδου ημιν καθ' ημεραν. Διοπερ ας προεταξαμεν λεξεις, ως παρα μονῳ τῳ Ματθαιῳ κειμενας, εξετασωμεν ακολουθως τοις προ τουτων. See Περι ευχης, Opp. i. p. 240.

9. ζητειτε, και ευρησετε omitted.

15. *of the Pharisees*—and so *b* of the Old Latin, *ex Pharisæis*: Greek, εξ αυτων.

17. *divided* is not repeated in the Greek, but it is in Matthew xii. 25 and Mark iii. 25.

19. *from your children*—omitted in the Greek. See on Matt. xii, 27 above.

29. ει μη σημειον Ιωνα του προφητου—omitted here.

31. των ανδρων—omitted here, with C.

36. *and if the light which is within thee be dark, thy darkness how great will it be*—This is like Matt. vi. 23, ει ουν το φως το εν σοι σκοτος εστιν, το σκοτος ποσον. The Greek of Luke here is ει ουν το σωμα σου ολον φοτεινον, μη εχον μερος τι σκοτεινον, εσται φωτεινον ολον ως οταν ο λυχνος τη αστραπη φωτιζη σε.

38. *had begun saying in his mind*—and so D, ηρξατο διακρινομενος εν εαυτῳ λεγειν; and the Old Latin *a b c d*, with slight variations, *cœpit intra se reputans dicere*, as at v. 21. The other Greek copies have here, ιδων εθαυμασεν.

42. *scribes and*—omitted in the Greek. The Old Latin *c* has *scribæ et pharisæi.*

44. γραμματεις και φαρισαιοι, υποκριται omitted with B C and the Old Latin *a c*. *ye are sepulchres*—and so D and *a c* of the Old Latin, *monumenta estis*. Greek, εστε ως τα μνημεια τα αδηλα.

46. *and set them on the shoulders of men's sons*—like Matt. xxiii. 4. Greek, φορτιζετε τους ανθρωπους.

47. *and ye are the sons of these murderers*—also from Matt. xxiii. 31, υιοι εστε των φονευσαντων τους προφητας. The Greek here is οτι αυτοι μεν απεκτειναν αυτους, υμεις δε οικοδομειτε αυτων τα μνημεια.

51. *Barachia's son*—also in D: omitted in the Greek, and added apparently from Matthew xxiii. 35.

52. *have hidden*—and so D, εκρυψατε, and the Old Latin *a b c*: Greek, ηρατε.

53. *in the sight of all the people*—and so D, ενωπιον παντος του λαου, and the Old Latin *b c*: omitted in other copies of the Greek. *he began to be abominated by the Scribes and Pharisees*—Greek, ηρξαντο οι γραμματεις και οι Φαρισαιοι δεινως ενεχειν.

54. *seeking to lay hold of a cause against him*—Greek, ζητουντες θηρευσαι τι εκ του στοματος αυτου.

CH. XII. 3. *ye have whispered*—and so Peshito: Greek, ελαλησατε.

13. *the land and*—omitted in the Greek.

14. η μεριστην of the Greek omitted; and so by D and the Old Latin *a c*.

18. και ειπε τουτο ποιησω of the Greek omitted. και τα αγαθα μου—omitted; and also by D and the Old Latin *a b c*.

27. *lilies of the plain*—Greek, τα κρινα only, but *ab c* of the Old Latin, *lilia agri*.

28. *of the hills* and *drieth up and*—omitted in the Greek.

29. *and what ye shall be clad with*—omitted in the Greek: added from Matt. vi. 31.

36. *banquet-house*—Greek, των γαμων.

38. *and if in the first watch he shall come and find them watching, happy they, because he will make them sit down and will minister*—This is omitted in the Greek.

39. εγρηγορησεν αν και—omitted with D.

42. *and good*—omitted in the Greek copies, but found in D and the Old Latin *c*.

53. *and the woman*, or *wife*—Greek, *μητηρ.*

56. *and its signs*—omitted in the Greek.

58. *convict thee*, or *condemn thee*—so D, *κατακρεινη*, and *b d* of the Old Latin, *condemnet*: other Greek copies, *κατασυρῃ.*

CH. XIII. 9. *to the quick*—Syriac, ܠܡܚܝܝܢ. The Peshito has ܠܡܢܐ ܚܝ, "why does it live?" I am by no means confident that this translation which I have given, supposing that the Syriac translator might have read *μυελον*, is correct: perhaps it may be rendered ܠܡܢ ܚܝ, "for whom does it live?" much in the same sense as the Peshito. The Greek is *εις το μελλον*, which the Philoxenian version gives, ܒܗܝ ܕܥܬܝܕܐ.

11. *had a spirit*—omitting *ασθενειας* of the Greek. D varies here, and reads *εν ασθενειᾳ ην πνευματος.*

15. *Jesus*—Greek, *ο Κυριος*, but D, *Ιησους.*

26. *Thou hast walked*—Greek, *εδιδαξας.* It is probably an error of the scribe in mistaking אלפת, "taught" for הלכת, "walked;" either giving a good sense, and *walking* being more common than *teaching* in the streets.

35. *until the day shall come*—with *donec veniat dies* of the Old Latin *a b.* Greek, *εως αν ηξει* only.

CH. XIV. 1. *that they might see what he did*—omitted in the Greek.

5. *His son shall fall, or his ox, or his ass*—The Textus Receptus has *ονος η βους.* See the remarks of Dr. Tregelles* upon this passage, who, however, in citing this text, has omitted to state, that after the reading *his son, or his ox*, is also added *or his ass.*

12. *the lord of the supper*—Greek, *τῳ κεκλημοτι αυτον*, which the Peshito has rendered literally, ܠܗܘ ܕܩܪܝܗܝ; and *a b c* of the Old Latin, *invitatori.*

30. *a tower*—omitted in the Greek.

31. *καθισας* of the Greek omitted here.

32. *from the battle-place*—omitted in the Greek.

CH. XV. *In those meats which were not meet, because he was living prodigally with harlots*—Greek, *ζων ασωτως* only.

14. *και αυτος ηρξατο υστερεισθαι*—omitted here.

16. *to eat*—Greek, *γεμισαι την κοιλιαν αυτου*, which the Peshito renders literally, ܠܡܡܠܐ ܟܪܣܗ. Codd. B D have here, *χορτασθηναι. husks of the sea*—Greek, *των κερατιων.*

CH. XVII. 23. *Let them not deceive you*—omitted in the Greek: added from Matt. xxiv. 4.

* Account of the Printed Text of the Greek Testament, p. 197.

29. *και θειον* of the Greek omitted, as also in the Old Latin *a b*.

31. *in that hour*—with the Old Latin *a b c*. Greek, *εν εκεινῃ τῃ ημερᾳ*. *Let him not come down that he may take his goods from the house*—Greek, *και τα σκευα αυτου εν τῃ οικιᾳ, μη καταβατω αραι αυτα·*

CH. XVIII. 3. *a long while*—with *multum tempus* of *b c*. Greek, *επι χρονον*; but omitted here, and added in the next verse.

15. *bless*—Greek, *απτηται*.

18. *one of the chiefs of the Pharisees*—Greek, *τις αρχων*.

19. *and why askest thou me respecting the good?*—omitted in the Greek. See on Matt. xix. 17 above.

20. *if thou wishest to enter into life*—omitted in the Greek: added from Matthew, *ει δε θελεις εισελθειν εις την ζωην*.

28. *every thing that we have*—like the Old Latin *a b c*, *relictis omnibus nostris*: Greek, *τα ιδια*. Matthew has *παντα* only

29. *whoso*—Greek. *ουδεις εστιν ος*.

30. *a hundred-fold*—Greek, *πολλαπλασιονα*: Cod. Bezæ D, *επταπλασιονα*, and *a b c* of the Old Latin, *septies tantum*. *inherit*—omitted in the Greek: *a b c* have *possidebit*.

33. *and spit in his face*—Greek, *και εμπτυσθησεται*.

34. *with them*—the Old Latin *a* has *ad eos*: omitted in the Greek.

36. *voice*—and so Peshito: omitted in the Greek.

41. *and I may see thee*—omitted in the Greek: see Matt. xx. 33.

CH. XIX. 1. *and while they went up*—Greek, *και εισελθων*.

3. *τις εστιν* and *απο του οχλου* of the Greek omitted here. *Zacai*—not in the Greek.

5. *and while Jesus passed, he saw him*—Greek, *και ως ηλθεν επι τον τοπον, αναβλεψας ο Ιησους ειδεν αυτον*.

20. *in linen*—ܣܕܘܢܐ, *σινδων*: Greek here, *σουδαριῳ*, which the Peshito follows, ܣܘܕܪܐ, the variation arising from the similarity of the words.

25. *και ειπον αυτῳ Κυριε, εχει δεκα μνας* omitted; and also by D and the Old Latin *b*.

26. *and be added to him*—omitted in the Greek; but D has *προστιθεται*: added from Matthew and Mark. *that which he supposeth*—omitted in the Greek: added from ch. viii. 18.

32. *οι απεσταλμενοι* of the Greek omitted.

33, 34. *and when they asked them, they returned to them answer: that, For his Lord he is required*—Greek, *λυοντων δε αυτων τον πωλον, ειπον οι κυριοι αυτου* προς αυτους, Τι λυετε τον πωλον; οι δε ειπον οτι ο Κυριος αυτου χρειαν εχει. The Old Latin *a* has here *Domino suo necessarius est.*

37. *and when they came near*—Greek, εγγιζοντος δε αυτου ηδη; but D reads, as here, εγγιζοντων δε αυτων.

42. *thy peace, but peace has hidden itself*—Greek, τα προς ειρηνην σου· νυν δε εκρυβη.

44. *Thy greatness*—Greek, της επισκοπης σου. The translator here, at the same time that he betrays a want of knowledge of the Greek language, seems also to indicate that he performed his task at a period when the episcopal office was held in the highest dignity. The Peshito has ܣܘܥܪܢܟܝ.

46. *for all nations*—omitted in the Greek. See Matt. xxi. 13.

CH. XX. 1. *of the people*—omitted in the Greek.

3. λογον ενα—omitted, and also by the Old Latin *a.*

10. γεωργοι of the Greek omitted, with D and the Old Latin *a c d.*

12. και προσεθετο τριτον πεμψαι, οι δε κακεινον τραυματισαντες εξεβαλον omitted.

17. *of the building*—Greek, γωνιας.

19. *they feared the people*—In the Greek this precedes.

20. *to the Governor*—and so D, τῳ ηγεμονι; but the rest of the copies, τῃ αρχῃ και τῃ εξουσιᾳ του ηγεμονος.

34. *beget and are begotten*—and so γεννωνται και γεννωσιν of D, and the Old Latin *a c d*: confirmed also by Origen and Cyprian: omitted in other Greek copies.

37. *when God spake with him*—not found in the Greek.

41. *the scribes*—not in the Greek.

46. *in the porches*—ܒܐܣܛܘܐ: Greek, εν στολαις, from confounding στοαις with στολαις, each affording a good sense. The Peshito has ܒܐܣܛܠܐ.

CH. XXI. 4. *into the treasury an offering*—Greek, εις τα δωρα του Θεου.

10. τοτε ελεγεν αυτοις—omitted; and so by D and the Old Latin *a.*

11. *and terrors shall be from heaven, and great signs shall be seen and great tempests*—Greek, φοβηθρα τε και απ' ουρανου σημεια μεγαλα εσται. The Old Latin *a c* also has *erunt et hiemes*, and the Peshito, ܘܥܠܥܠܐ ܪܘܪܒܐ ܢܗܘܘܢ, "and great tempests shall be."

15. ουδε αντειπειν omitted.

18. και θριξ εκ της κεφαλης υμων ου μη αποληται omitted.

25, 26. *and affliction in the earth, and clapping of hands of the nations, and a voice that is like the sea's, and the quaking of the exit of the souls of men's sons, from terror of that which is about to come on the earth*—The Greek here is *και επι της γης συνοχη εθνων εν απορια ηχους θαλασσης και σαλου, αποψυχοντων των ανθρωπων απο φοβου και προσδοκιας των επερχομενων τη οικουμενη.* The Peshito in this place is so very like to this text, that it is impossible that it could be altogether by a different hand: yet, even here, an attempt has been made to bring the Syriac translation nearer to the Greek.

30. *when they begin branching forth and giving their fruits*—οταν προβαλωσιν ηδη only.

34. *by the eating of the flesh, and by the drunkenness of wine, and by the care of the world*—Greek, εν κραιπαλη και μεθη και μεριμναις βιωτικαις.

CH. XXII. 4. και τοις στρατηγοις omitted here, and so by D and the Old Latin *a b c*.

7. *The day of the Pescha*—and so D, η ημερα του πασχα, with which the Old Latin *a b* agrees. The other copies have των αζυμων.

14. οι δωδεκα—omitted with B D and *a b c*.

17—19. The order of these verses varies from the Greek. Verse 19, "and he took bread, &c." precedes 17, "and he took the cup, &c."

Verse 20 is omitted. As there is no mention made, either by Matthew, or Mark, or St. Paul, of our Lord having given the cup twice to his disciples at the institution of the Holy Eucharist, it seems probable that verse 20 has found its way into the text here from 1 Cor. xi. 25, being in precisely the same words.

25. *and that do well*—omitted in the Greek.

26, 27. *as a minister, and not as one sitting down. For who is great, he that sitteth down or that ministereth? Lo, am not I as minister among you?*—Greek, ως ο διακονων: τις γαρ μειζων, ο ανακειμενος η ο διακονων; ουχι ο ανακειμενος; εγω δε ειμι εν μεσω υμων ως ο διακονων.

31. *and our Lord said to Simon, Simon*—Greek, ειπεν δε ο Κυριος Σιμων Σιμων. The Old Latin *a* has *Petro,* and Cyprian *ad Petrum.*

34. Πετρε omitted here. *two times* not found in the Greek: probably added from Mark xiv. 30.

38. *rise, let us go*—omitted in the Greek: probably added from John xiv. 31.

42. *if possible*—as in Matthew and Mark. The Greek here is ει βουλει.

43. απο του ουρανου omitted here.

48. *the son of Man*—ܒܪܗ ܕܓܒܪܐ, υιος του ανδρος, as above, instead of του ανθρωπου.

52. παραγενομενους επ' αυτον omitted here.

58. *and said likewise*—Greek, εφη Και συ εξ αυτων ει. There is omitted here ανθρωπε, and *of them* added.

61. *two times*—omitted in the Greek.

64. *and they covered his face and say to him*—Greek, και περικαλυψαντες αυτον, ετυπτον αυτου το προσωπον και επηρωτων αυτον λεγοντες: but B has only και περικαλυψαντες αυτον επηρωτων.

CH. XXIII. 7. *of unleavened*—omitted in the Greek.

8. πολλα of the Greek omitted, and so in B and D.

9. *cunning words*—Greek, λογοις ικανοις. The Translator, perhaps, was not quite aware of the meaning of ικανοις. At any rate ܢܟܝܠܘܬܐ seems to have been suggested to him from the similarity of the first syllable. See above, on Matthew xiii. 6, 35. *as though he had not been there*—This is not in the Greek. The Old Latin *c* has *quasi non audiens.*

10. *rulers*—ܐܪܟܘܢܐ: Greek, οι γραμματεις. At verse 13, we have τους αρχιερεις και τους αρχοντας.

12. *and on that same day there was a reconciliation between Herod and Pilate, because they were enemies*—Greek, εγενοντο δε φιλοι ο τε Πιλατος και ο Ηρωδης εν αυτῃ τῃ ημερᾳ μετ᾽ αλληλων· προυπηρχον γαρ εν εχθρᾳ οντες προς εαυτους.

15. *and any thing that is worthy of death he has not found behind him: nor is any thing worthy of death done by him*—the Greek is και ιδου ουδεν αξιον θανατου εστιν πεπραγμενον αυτῳ only.

17. This verse is transposed here, and placed after verse 19, as in Cod. Bezæ D. It is omitted altogether in A and B and the Old Latin *a.*

19. *seditions*—The Syriac for this word is ܦܠܓܘܬܐ, which I have translated as the Greek στασιν; the corresponding Syriac term for στασιν in verse 25 is ܗܪ̈ܣܣ, *heresies.*

36. και οξος προσφεροντες omitted.

37. *Peace to thee*—identical with Χαιρε of Cod. Bezæ D, omitted in other copies; and with *Ave* of the Old Latin *c. and they had set upon his head a crown of thorns*—which D and *c* also have, although omitted by the rest. These probably have been added here from Matt. xxvii. 29.

38. γραμμασιν Ελληνικοις και Ρωμαϊκοις και Εβραικοις—omitted here, with Codd. B D and the Old Latin *c.*

39. *Art thou not the Messia?*—with ουχι συ of B and the Old Latin *a b.* The other copies have Ει συ ει ο Χριστος.

40. *we also are in the same judgment*—and so exactly D and C have the plural εσμεν: the other copies οτι εν τῳ αυτῳ κριματι ει.

43. *Eden's garden*—Greek, εν τῳ παραδεισῳ, and the Peshito, ܦܪܕܝܣܐ.

46. *and he finished*—Greek, και τουτο ειπων εξεπνευσεν. Compare John xix. 30, ειπε· Τετελεσται· και κλινας την κεφαλην παρεδωκεν το πνευμα.

48. *and saying, Woe to us! What is this?* (or *what is become of us?*) for ܗܘܝ seems here to be an error of the scribe for ܗܘܐ, as at verse 41 above. *Woe to us from our sins*—Instead of this, the Greek has υπεστρεφον only.

50. *a Man just and good from Ramtha, a fortress of Judæa; and he was looking for the kingdom of heaven. This Man, who did not equal his mind with the accusers*—The Greek here is ανηρ αγαθος και δικαιος, ουτος ουκ ην συγκατατεθειμενος τη βουλη και τη πραξει αυτων, απο Αριμαθαιας πολεως των Ιουδαιων, ος προσεδεχετο την βασιλειαν του Θεου.

55. *and those women which came with him from Galilee, came to the sepulchre in their footsteps, and saw the corpse while they laid it up there*—Greek, κατακολουθησασαι δε αι γυναικες, αιτινες ησαν συνεληλυθυιαι αυτῳ εκ της Γαλιλαιας, εθεασαντο το μνημειον και ως ετεθη το σωμα αυτου.

CH. XXIV. 1. αρωματα of the Greek omitted here. It is also omitted in Cod. Bezæ D and the Old Latin *a b c*.

5. *those men*—omitted in the Greek.

10. *Mary the daughter of Jacob*—Greek, Μαρια η Ιακωβου: The Peshito, ܡܪܝܡ ܐܡܗ ܕܝܥܩܘܒ, "Mary the Mother of Jacob."

11. *as though it was from their wonder they had spoken these words*—Greek, ωσει ληρος τα ρηματα ταυτα.

12. *and went to it*—Greek, και απηλθεν προς εαυτον. If this be not a mistake of the translator, it is, perhaps, an error of the scribe in reading ܐܙܠ ܠܒܝܬܗ instead of ܐܙܠ ܠܗ.

13. *and he appeared to two*—Greek, και ιδου δυο.

17. περιπατουντες omitted here, and so in the Old Latin *a b c*.

20. *the elders*—Greek, οι αρχοντες.

22. *also women from us went to the sepulchre where he was laid, and when they found not his body, they came and told us that they had seen angels there; and they were astonished, and told respecting him that he is alive*—Greek, αλλα και γυναικες τινες εξ ημων εξεστησαν ημας, γενομεναι ορθριναι επι το μνημειον, και μη ευρουσαι το σωμα αυτου ηλθον λεγουσαι και οπτασιαν αγγελων εωρακεναι, οι λεγουσιν αυτον ζην.

28, 29. *and he appeared to them as though he were going to a distant place: and they began and were entreating of him that he would be with them: because it was near to become dark*—Greek, *και αυτος προσεποιησατο πορρωτερον πορευεσθαι, και παρεβιασαντο αυτον λεγοντες Μεινον μεθ' ημων, οτι προς εσπεραν εστιν και κεκλικεν ηδη η ημερα.*

32. *heavy*—ܝܩܝܪ: Greek, *καιομενη*, probably a mistake of the scribe, confounding ܪ with ܕ, and so writing ܝܩܝܪ "heavy," for ܝܩܝܕ "burning," as the Peshito has it to agree with the Greek. The former, *heavy*, is, however, more in conformity with ܝܩܝܪܝ ܠܒܐ, "heavy of heart:" Greek, *βραδεις τῃ καρδιᾳ* at verse 25 above. There seems also to have been very antiently some doubt in the Greek respecting the word *καιομενη*, for the Cod. Bezæ D has, instead of it, *κεκαλυμμενη*, and *c* of the Old Latin *excæcatum*.

35. *αυτοις* omitted.

40. *και τουτο ειπων εδειξεν αυτοις τας χειρας και τους ποδους* omitted, and so in D and the Old Latin *a b*.

41. *from their fear and from their joy, and were wondering*—Greek, *και θαυμαζοντων απο της χαρας.*

43. *and he took up that which remained* and *gave to them*—omitted in the Greek. The Old Latin *c* also has *sumens reliquias dedit eis.*

GENERAL OBSERVATIONS ON THE TEXT OF THESE SYRIAC REMAINS.

It would very far exceed the limits of a Preface were I to attempt to enter at length into the discussion of several topics of the highest interest, which naturally have suggested themselves in the course of the preceding pages. I must, therefore, at present confine myself to a few observations which the comparison of the text of these Syriac Remains of Gospels with that of the Greek have given rise to, relating especially to that text itself. The facts which this comparison has established all tend to shew that these Fragments belong to an edition or recension of the Gospels which must be assigned to those very early times of the Christian religion, when the spirit was felt to be of far greater importance than the letter, and when the substance of what the Evangelists had written was more heeded than the very words themselves in which it was expressed.* At a period so near to the days when the wonders recorded in the Gospels were performed, and the lessons and doctrines which they contain were preached—while the immediate successors of those to whom Christ himself, or his Apostles, had given commission to teach and to baptize were personally engaged in spreading the glad tidings of salvation—the necessity for verbal critical accuracy was not so keenly felt,† nor its importance held to be so great as it afterwards became in times more remote, when those who had drawn the waters of life near to their source were passed away, and their personal authority and oral instruction could no longer be referred to. It is probably to this cause that the great difference existing in various antient copies of the Gospels before his own time, spoken of by Origen,‡ is to be attributed, rather than to any wilful and intentional alteration

* As a special instance of this, I would refer to Justin Martyr in the second century, whose quotations often vary, in words, considerably from the text of the Gospels, although they accurately represent its substance: see Credner's *Beiträge*, vol. i. p. 151, and Bishop's Marsh's Illustration of his *Hypothesis*, Appendix, p. 52, where the comparison is instituted. The verbal variations from the text of the Gospels in the citations by Clement of Rome in the first century, are perhaps to be referred to the fact of his having received them orally from the Apostles, rather than from any written document: see Less, Authenticity of the New Testament, translated by R. Kingdom, p. 54; Lardner's *Credibity*, vol. ii. p. 31.

† See De Wette, Lehrbuch der historisch-kritischen Einteitung, N. T., § 35, 36.

‡ *Και ει μεν μη και περι αλλων πολλων διαφωνια ην προς αλληλα των αντιγραφων, ωστε τα κατα Ματθαιον μη συνᾳδειν αλληλοις, ομοιως δε και τα λοιπα ευαγγελια, κᾳν*

of the Evangelists' words by persons desirous of accommodating them to their own views, or, indeed, to any culpable negligence on the part of the transcribers beyond that which belonged to an uncritical age.†

Jerome, in his preface to the Gospels addressed to Pope Damasus, points out more fully what was the nature of the differences in the several copies of the Gospels which had continued to be transmitted down to his own time, and in a great measure also accounts for the way in which they originated. " Novum opus me facere cogis ex veteri, ut post exemplaria scripturarum toto orbe dispersa, quasi quidam arbiter sedeam, et quia inter se variant, quæ sint illa quæ cum Græca consentiant veritate, decernam,—Si enim Latinis exemplaribus fides est adhibenda, respondeant quibus, tot enim sunt exemplaria, pene

ασεβης τις εδοξεν ειναι ο υπονοων ενταυθα προσερριφθαι, ουκ ειρημενην υπο του σωτηρος προς τον πλουσιον την Αγαπησεις τον πλησιον σου ως σεαυτον, εντολην· νυνι δε δηλονοτι πολλη γεγονεν η των αντιγραφων διαφορα, ειτε απο ραθυμιας τινων γραφεων, ειτε απο τολμης τινων μοχθηρας της διορθωσεως των γραφομενων, ειτε και απο των τα εαυτοις δοκουντα εν τῃ διορθωσει προστιθεντων η αφαιρουντων. την μεν ουν εν τοις αντιγραφοις της παλαιας διαθηκης διαφωνιαν, θεου διδοντος, ευρομεν ιασασθαι, κριτηριῳ χρησαμενοι ταις λοιπαις εκδοσεσιν. κ.τ.λ. Com. in Matt., tom. xv. Opp. Edit. C. Delarue, vol. 3, p. 671. *Ου καταφρονητεον ουν της περι τα ονοματα ακριβειας τῳ απαραλειπτως βουλομενῳ συνιεναι τα αγια γραμματα. το μεντοιγε ημαρτησθαι εν τοις Ελληνικοις αντιγραφοις τα περι των ονοματων πολλαχου, και απο τουτων αν τις πεισθειη εν τοις ευαγγελιοις.* Com. in Ioan. tom. vi. ibid. vol. 4, p. 140.

† Even before Origen, Dionysius of Corinth had intimated that some had ventured to tamper with the text of the New Testament: *ου θαυμαστον αρα, ει και των κυριακων ρᾳδιουργησαι τινες επιβεβληνται γραφων,* cited by Eusebius, Hist. Eccl. iv. 23. Clement of Alexandria also had remarked upon a variation in the copies of the Gospels: *Μακαριοι, φησιν, οι δεδιωγμενοι ενεκεν δικαιοσυνης· οτι αυτοι υιοι Θεου κληθησονται. η ως τινες των μετατιθεντων τα ευαγγελια, Μακαριοι, φησιν, οι δεδιωγμενοι υπο της δικαιοσυνης· οτι αυτοι εσονται τελειοι.* Strom. lib. iv.; Clem. Alex. Opp. edit. Colon., 1688, p. 490. Respecting this, Dr. Mill—without, however, furnishing any other authorities for what he states—writes in his *Prolegomema*, 287 : Cæterum inter Codices Ecclesiarum et privatorum hominum, hoc fere interfuit; quod isti, prout e librariorum manibus exierant, emaculati, notulisque marginalibus liberi fere, integri in Ecclesiarum tabulariis remanserint; hi vero, ab ipsis, in quorum gratiam fuerunt conscripti, statim fere inter lineas, aut ad marginem, glossis scholiisque fuerint conspersi; maximopere in id incumbentibus S. literarum studiosis, ut Textum Sacrum, quem apud se habebant, explicatiorem suisque usibus magis indies ac magis idoneum redderent. Hinc apud Clementem Alexandrinum, qui sub finem seculi secundi floruit, mentio sit *των τα ευαγγελια μετατιθεντων*, seu *Scholiastarum*, qui jam ab initio libris istis ad oram aut spatio interlineari explicatiunculas suas illiverant. Harum unam ille et alteram adducit.

quot codices. Sin autem veritas est quærenda de pluribus, cur non ad Græcam originem revertentes, ea quæ vel a vitiosis interpretibus male reddita, vel a presumptoribus imperitis emendata perversius, vel a librariis dormitantibus aut addita sunt, aut mutata corrigimus?—De Novo nunc loquor Testamento, quod Græcum esse non dubium est, excepto Apostolo Matthæo, qui primus in Judæa Evangelium Christi Hebraicis literis edidit. Hoc certe cum in nostro sermone discordat et in diversos rivulorum tramites ducit, uno de fonte quærendum est. ——. Magnus siquidem hic in nostris codicibus error inolevit, dum quod in eadem re alius Evangelista plus dixit, in alio quia minus putaverint, addiderunt. Vel dum eundem sensum alius aliter expressit, ille qui unum a quatuor primum legerat, ad ejus exemplum cæteros quoque existimaverit emendandos. Unde accidit ut apud nos mixta sunt omnia, et in Marco plura Lucæ atque Matthæi, rursus in Matthæo plura Johannis et Marci, et in cæteris reliquorum, quæ aliis propria sunt, inveniantur."

What is stated here by Jerome respecting the condition in which he found the text of the Old Latin version in his time exactly applies to that of these Syriac Gospels now before us, between which and the Old Latin there is otherwise a very close affinity. For if we turn to St. Luke, we find several examples of additions made to the text from the other Evangelists, who had related some fact or discourse in greater detail, or with some additional circumstances;* of the change of words or phrases to accommodate them and bring them nearer, or even to make them identical with the terms employed in other Gospels,† and of errors which can only be attributed to ignorance or mistakes on the part of the translator; but of this latter I shall have occasion to speak again as we proceed.

The Gospel of St. John, from its peculiarity in having less in common than the other three, will necessarily admit of fewer changes of this sort; but still, even in that small portion of it which remains, indications of this kind are observable.‡ Of Mark, only four verses of the last chapter remain. The Gospel of St. Matthew§ also seems to exhibit some signs of a similar nature, especially with regard to additions made to the text; but its approximation

* See Luke viii. 10, 13, 18, 19, 27, 33, 39, 43, 45, 52; ix. 17, 29, 40; xi. 17, 47, 51; xii. 29; xvii. 23; xviii. 19, 20; xxii. 34, 38; xxiii. 37.

† See vii. 35; viii. 2, 01, 13, 30, 50; ix. 12, 27, 35, 38; xi. 17, 36, 46, 47; xxii. 42; xxiii. 46.

‡ See iv. 50; v. 8; vi. 10.

§ iv. 11, 24; x. 33; xix. 29; xxi. 9, 13.

in numerous places to the reading found in St. Mark and St. Luke is probably to be attributed rather to another cause, to which I shall refer more fully in the sequel.

Moreover, besides these varieties in the text of one of the Canonical Gospels occasioned by reference to what is found in the others, there are also some passages added which do not appear to have been written at all by any of the Four Evangelists, but rather to have been taken from some of those uncanonical or apocryphal histories which were common in the early ages of the Church.*

Further, words and sentences which are found in the Textus Receptus of the Greek are not unfrequently omitted in these Remains; and several of such omissions are confirmed by the authority of some of the earliest Greek manuscripts extant. I leave it for others to decide whether these shew a defect in this Syriac text, or an excess in that of the Greek, originating in causes similar to those which have produced the additions of which I have just spoken.

All these circumstances taken together seem sufficient to shew that these Syriac Remains of the Gospels must be considered as belonging to those very antient times to which the Old Latin version that Jerome undertook to correct is to be assigned, as well as those Greek copies of which Origen spake. Indeed, the transcription of the manuscript in which they are contained, so far as I am competent to form an opinion, cannot have been many years subsequent to the time when Jerome wrote the words that I have cited above.

A reference to the preceding pages, in which I have noted several of the variations of this text that are supported by the Old Latin version, will shew a very close affinity in many respects between the two. The striking agreement between the Old Latin and the Peshito as first edited by Widmanstad, A.D. 1562, has been already pointed out by several critics;† and although there is a marked difference in some places between the text of the Peshito and that of these Syriac Fragments, the general similarity and agreement between the two is so great as to preclude the possibility of their having been two altogether distinct and independent versions.

Of the oldest Greek manuscripts now known to exist, it will be seen that this copy coincides most nearly, and, in some particulars, in a very striking

* See Dr. Mill, Prolegomena, 251—256.

† See Ridley, De Syriacarum Novi Fœderis Versionum indole atque usu, p. 32. J. D. Michaelis, Curæ in Versionem Syriacam, p. 163, seq. I. Wichelhaus, De N. T. Versione Syriaca antiqua, p. 240.

manner, with the Codex Bezæ D, which itself is very closely allied in many respects with the Old Latin. The remarkable agreement of this very venerable manuscript with the Peshito has already been pointed out by others ;* and it has been inferred that its language has been influenced by Oriental idiomatic expressions,† and that it must have assumed its present form from being in use among Judaizing Christians.‡ But although the text of these Syriac Fragments so often and so closely agrees with that of the Codex Bezæ, it also at other times diverges from it, and follows the reading of some one or more of the other most antient Greek manuscripts. Not unfrequently, also, when it varies from the usually received text, like the Codex Bezæ,§ it is supported by very early authorities, such as Justin Martyr, the Clementines, Irenæus, Origen, and Cyprian, all pointing to that antient period to which this recension is to be referred.||

The Gospels of St. Luke, St. John, and St. Mark evidently have been translated directly from the Greek. The fact of these having been originally composed in that language, and the great improbability of their being rendered into Syriac through any intermediate channel,¶ would have led to this inference. This is, however, proved by the comparison of the two texts together, which shews that the Syriac has been made to conform to the Greek, and that errors into which the translator has fallen, could only have arisen from mistaking and

* See J. D. Michaelis, ibid, p. 82.

† "Etiam Græcum Codicis D. sermonem ab interpretatione aliqua, eaque Orientali (forsan Syra) primitus pependisse, aut ejusmodi versionem in exarando hocce libro iis saltem locis, quos adeo multos ab omnium codicum Græcorum textu abhorrentes habet, una cum Græco quodam antigrapho adhibitam fuisse, existimo:" See D. D. Schulz: Disputatio de Codice D Cantabrigiensi, Vratis., 1827, p. 16: cited by Credner, Beiträge zur Einleitung in die biblischen Schriften. vol. i. p. 492.

‡ See Credner, ibid., p. 495.

§ Ibid., p. 452.

|| Credner has the following observation respecting the Codex Bezæ, which will also apply in this instance: "Veränderungen wie diese konnten in der katholischen Kirche nur bis um die Mitte des zweiten Jahrhunderts mit dem Texte der Evangelien vorgenommen werden; den nach dieser Zeit hat die Behauptung eines göttlicken Ursprunges der neu-testamentlichen Schriften in derselben allgemeine Anerkennung gefunden. Dieses Dogma lässt keine solche Behandlungsweise des Textes mehr zu, wie dieselbe mit dem Texte unserer Handscrift vorgenommen ist. Dann würde unserer Handshcrift ein Text aus dem zweiten Jahrhunderte zum Grunde liegen." ibid., p. 491.

¶ See Ridley, De Syriac. N. T. Verss., p. 31, 35.

confounding one Greek word with another.* Some Greek terms also are retained in this text, which have been removed, and the proper Syriac expressions substituted in the subsequent revision of the Peshito.† It is also manifest that the translator was not in all respects accurately acquainted with the precise meaning and logical force of several Greek words. For instance, he does not seem to have been fully cognizant of the difference between the terms *ανθρωπος* and *ανηρ*, and consequently has fallen occasionally into the grave error of rendering *ο υιος του ανθρωπου*,‡ as applied to our Lord Jesus Christ, by ܒܪܗ ܕܓܒܪܐ, equivalent to *ο υιος του ανδρος*. Probably, also, from having been accustomed at that period, when he performed his task, to regard the Episcopal office with great veneration, and to esteem it in the highest honour, he has translated *τον καιρον της επισκοπης σου*§ by ܝܘܡܐ ܕܪܒܘܬܟ, "the day of thy greatness." To the same cause—the want of a full and accurate knowledge of the Greek language—must be attributed the loose and paraphrastical translation of several passages,‖ which, although they represent tolerably well the general sense, are very free and wide of the literal signification. Many instances of this occur, both in St. John and St. Luke. There are also some manifest errors in the text of these two Gospels,¶ which can hardly be attributed to any other cause than ignorance or carelessness on the part of the transcriber. All these circumstances taken together seem to shew that this copy of the Gospels must belong to those very early days of Christianity when verbal critical accuracy was not esteemed to be of that essential importance which afterwards it necessarily assumed. At the same time, also, it appears to be evident that this version is the production of one or more translators who have left clear indications that they were not fully acquainted with all

* See John i. 19; iv. 48; vi. 1, 3, 16, 46,; vii. 23, 35; xiv. 10, 26: Luke vii. 33; xxi. 20; xx. 46.

† Thus Luke iii. 1, ܒܟܘܪ *χωρας*; Pesh. ܒܐܬܪܐ: viii. 3, ܐܦܛܪܘܦܘܗ, *επιτροπου*; Pesh. ܪܒܒܝܬܗ: x. 25, ܡܠܦ ܢܡܘܣܐ, *νομικος*; Peshito, ܣܦܪܐ: xii. 11, ܐܪܟܘܣ, *αρχας*; Peshito, ܪ̈ܫܐ: xii. 55, ܟܘܪܢܐ *καυσων*; Peshito, ܫܘܒܐ: xiv. 2, ܗܕܪܘܦܝܩܘܣ, *υδρωπικος*; Peshito, ܕܢܦܝܚ ܗܘܐ ܡܝܐ: xxii. 52, ܐܣܛܪܛܓܘܬܐ, *στρατηγους*; Peshito, ܪ̈ܒܝ ܚܝܠܐ

‡ Luke vii. 33; xxii. 48.

§ Luke xix. 44.

‖ John i. 19, 41; iv. 9, 31; v. 13; vi. 18, 33; vii. 35: Luke iii. 2, 15; viii. 14, 23, 31; ix. 40; x. 41; xv. 1; xvii. 31; xxi. 11, 25, 26, 34; xxii. 26, 27, 64; xxiii. 12, 15, 50, 55; xxiv. 11, 22, 28, 29, 41.

¶ See John i. 35; iv. 24, 52; vi. 16: Luke xxiii. 48; xxiv. 12, 32.

the precise shades of meaning, and the logical peculiarities of various terms in the original Greek.

It has been already observed that it seems to be scarcely possible that the Syriac text published by Widmanstad, which, throughout these pages, I have called the Peshito, could be altogether a different version from this. It would take up too much space to institute here a comparison of passages to establish this fact, which, indeed, any one may easily do for himself. The ruder and more uncultivated form will naturally be esteemed to be the more antient of the two; and the more cultivated and improved edition to be the result of revision and correction from a fresh collation with the original Greek. This seems to be sufficiently established by the fact, that while this text and that generally called the Peshito concur in a great number of instances, as to readings which do not literally agree with the Greek, in almost all cases—if, indeed, not in all—where they differ from each other the Peshito has been brought into closer conformity with the text of the Greek. This latter observation applies to the Gospel of St. Matthew equally with those of St. Luke and St. John, and even to the only four remaining verses of St. Mark.

The language, also, of the four Gospels in the Peshito, has undergone some modification from this text. Other terms and different modes of expression which appear to be purely dialectical have been substituted in the place of those which are found here.* The grammar also has been carefully revised

* I will note here a few instances which may serve to illustrate these facts. In the first place, I shall set this text, then the Greek, and afterwards, the Peshito, so that the variations may be seen at once. Math. i. 17: ܘܥܕܡܐ, εως, ܥܕܡܐ. 18: ܥܕ ܠܐ ܢܬܩܪܒܘܢ ܚܕ ܠܘܬ ܚܕ, πριν η συνελθειν αυτους, ܥܕ ܠܐ ܢܫܬܘܬܦܘܢ. 19: ܕܒܛܠܝܐܝܬ ܢܫܠܝܗ̇, λαθρα απολυσαι αυτην, ܕܒܛܫܝܐܝܬ ܢܫܪܝܗ̇. 20: ܒܚܙܘܐ ܕܠܠܝܐ, κατ' οναρ, ܒܚܠܡܐ. 25: ܘܒܕܟܝܘܬܐ ܝܬܒ ܗܘܐ ܥܡܗ̇, και ουκ εγινωσκεν αυτην, ܘܠܐ ܚܟܡܗ̇. ii. 9: ܘܐܬܚܙܝ ܠܗܘܢ, και ιδου, ܘܗܐ — ܠܥܠ ܡܢ ܒܪ ܕܗܘܐ — ܗܘܐ, επανω ου, ܠܥܠ ܡܢ ܐܝܟܐ. 13: ܘܡܢ ܒܬܪܗܘܢ, και αναχωρησαντων αυτων, ܟܕ ܕܝܢ ܐܙܠܘ. 16: ܠܡܬܚܘܬܐ ܕܙܒܢܐ ܕܐܬܚܦܛܘ ܠܗ ܡܢܗܘܢ ܡܓܘܫܐ, κατα τον χρονον ον ηκριβωσε παρα των μαγων, ܐܝܟ ܙܒܢܐ ܕܐܬܚܦܛ ܡܢ ܡܓܘܫܐ. 22: ܒܕܘܟܬܗ, αντι, ܚܠܦ. 23: ܘܐܬܡܠܝܬ ܡܠܬܐ ܕܐܡܝܪܐ οπως πληρωθη το ρηθεν, ܕܢܬܡܠܐ ܡܕܡ ܕܐܬܐܡܪ. iii. 4: ܠܒܫ ܗܘܐ ܠܒܘܫܐ ܕܣܥܪܐ, ειχε το ενδυμα αυτου απο τριχων, ܐܝܬܘܗܝ ܗܘܐ ܠܒܘܫܗ ܕܣܥܪܐ. 6: ܟܕ ܡܘܕܝܢ ܗܘܘ ܐܢܫ ܐܢܫ, εξομολογουμενοι, ܟܕ ܡܘܕܝܢ. 10: ܗܐ ܡܟܝܠ ܠܗ ܢܪܓܐ ܥܠ ܥܩܪܝܗܘܢ ܕܐܝܠܢܐ, ηδη δε και η αξινη προς την ριζαν των δενδρων κειται, ܗܐ ܕܝܢ ܢܪܓܐ ܣܝܡ ܥܠ ܥܩܪܐ ܕܐܝܠܢܐ. 12: ܢܣܟܠ, συναξει, ܢܟܢܫ. iv. 4; ܥܠ ܦܬܓܡ

and many of the more loose and less accurate points of Syntax have been corrected. This is probably due to the labours of the school of Edessa. In several points the language of this text bears a close resemblance to that of the Syriac version of the Theophania of Eusebius, published by the late Dr. Lee, Regius Professor of Hebrew in the University of Cambridge, from the

επι παντι ρηματι, ܒܟܠ ܡܠܐ. 6: ܪܘܡܐ, πτερυγιον, ܟܢܦܐ — ܐܪܡܐ, βαλλε, ܫܕܝ. 9: ܕܬܣܓܘܕ ܩܕܡܝ, προσκυνησης μοι, ܕܬܣܓܘܕ ܠܝ. 20—23: ܒܗ ܒܫܥܬܐ, ευθεως, ܡܚܕܐ. v. 18: ܝܘܕ ܐܬܘܬܐ ܚܕܐ ܐܘ ܪܘܡܐ ܚܕܐ, ιωτα εν η μια κεραια, ܝܘܕ ܚܕܐ ܐܘ ܚܕ ܣܪܛܐ. 22: ܨܦܝܐ, μωρε, ܠܠܐ. 31: ܐܓܪܬܐ ܕܕܘܠܠܐ, αποστασιον, ܟܬܒܐ ܕܕܘܠܠܐ. 34: ܕܬܡܘܡܘܢ ܠܐ ܬܐܡܘܢ, μη ομοσαι ολως, ܣܟ ܠܐ ܬܐܡܘܢ. vi. 1: ܠܩܕܡ, εμπροσθεν, ܩܕܡ. 6: ܘܐܚܘܕ ܬܪܥܐ ܒܐܦܝܟ, κλεισας την θυραν σου, ܘܐܚܘܕ ܬܪܥܟ. 30: ܕܒܪܝܐ, του αγρου, ܕܚܩܠܐ — ܗܝܡܢܘܬܐ ܚܣܝܪܝ, ολιγοπιστοι, ܙܥܘܪܝ ܗܝܡܢܘܬܐ. viii. 4: ܕܠܡܐ, ορα μηδενι ειπης, ܚܙܝ ܠܐܢܫ. 17: ܒܦܘܡ, δια, ܒܝܕ — ܫܩܠ, εβαστασεν, ܢܛܠ. xi. 16: ܥܢܝܢ, προσφῶνουντα, ܩܪܝܢ. xiii. 1: ܠܓܢܒ, παρα, ܥܠ ܝܕ. 2: ܒܣܦܝܢܬܐ, εις το πλοιον, ܒܐܠܦܐ. 6: ܘܒܡܕܢܚܐ ܕܫܡܫܐ, ηλιου δε ανατειλαντος, ܘܟܕ ܕܢܚ ܫܡܫܐ. 32: ܦܪܚܬ ܫܡܝܐ, τα πετεινα, ܦܪܚܬܐ. 35: ܐܡܠܠ, ερευξομαι, ܐܒܥ. xv. 20: ܠܡܐܟܘܠ ܠܚܡܐ, φαγειν, ܠܡܠܥܣ. 32: ܟܕ ܛܘܦܬ ܐܢܘܢ, νηστεις, ܨܝܡܝܢ. 34: ܐܝܬ ܒܝܕܝܟܘܢ, εχετε, ܐܝܬ ܠܟܘܢ. xvii. 19: ܒܠܚܘܕܝܗܘܢ ܘܠܗ, κατ' ιδιαν, ܒܠܚܘܕܝܗܘܢ. 27: ܚܟܬܐ, αγκιστρον, ܒܠܩܐ. xviii. 28: ܦܪܘܥܢܝ, αποδος μοι, ܗܒ ܠܝ. xix. 7: ܐܓܪܬܐ ܕܕܘܠܠܐ, βιβλιον αποστασιου, ܟܬܒܐ ܕܫܘܒܩܢܐ. xxi. 29: ܬܘܗ ܢܦܫܗ, μεταμεληθεις, ܐܬܬܘܝ. 32: ܬܘܗ ܢܦܫܟܘܢ, μετεμεληθητε, ܐܬܬܘܝܬܘܢ. xxii. 18: ܦܬܟܡܐ, νομισμα, ܕܝܢܪܐ. 35: ܣܦܪܐ, νομικος, ܝܕܥ ܢܡܘܣܐ. 36: ܒܐܘܪܝܬܐ, εν τῳ νομῳ, ܒܢܡܘܣܐ. 39: ܘܕܬܪܬܝܗ, δευτερα δε, ܘܕܬܪ̈ܬܝܢ. xxiii. 9: ܡܠܦܢܐ, καθηγηται, ܡܕܒܪ̈ܢܐ. Mark xvi. 18: ܡܕܡ ܣܡܐ ܕܡܘܬܐ, θανασιμον τι, ܣܡܐ ܕܡܘܬܐ — ܢܟܐ, βλαψη, ܢܗܪ. 19: ܐܬܥܠܝ, ανεληφθη, ܣܠܩ. 20: ܟܕ ܡܪܝܐ ܡܥܕܪܢܘܗܝ ܒܟܠ, του κυριου συνεργουντος, ܘܡܪܢ ܡܥܕܪ ܗܘܐ ܠܗܘܢ. John i. 3: ܒܗ, δι' αυτου, ܒܐܝܕܗ. 8: ܣܗܕܐ ܗܘ ܕܢܘܗܪܐ, ινα μαρτυρηση περι του φωτος, ܕܢܣܗܕ ܥܠ ܢܘܗܪܐ. 13: ܕܕܡܐ, εξ αιματων, ܡܢ ܕܡܐ — ܕܦܓܪܐ, σαρκος, ܕܒܣܪܐ — ܕܒܪ ܐܢܫܐ, ανδρος, ܕܓܒܪܐ. 16: ܐܢܚܢܢ ܟܠܢ ܢܣܒܢ, ημεις παντες ελαβομεν, ܟܠܢ ܚܢܢ ܢܣܒܢ. 29: ܘܠܝܘܡܐ ܐܚܪܢܐ, τη επαυριον, ܘܠܝܘܡܐ ܕܒܬܪܗ. iii. 7: ܠܡܬܝܠܕܘ ܡܢ ܠܥܠ, γεννηθηναι ανωθεν, ܠܡܬܝܠܕܘ ܡܢ ܕܪܝܫ. 18: ܡܚܝܒ ܗܘ, ηδη κεκριται, ܡܢ ܟܕܘ ܕܝܢ ܗܘ. 21: ܩܘܫܬܐ, την αληθειαν, ܫܪܪܐ. 29: ܡܫܠܡܐ, πεπληρωται, ܡܫܡܠܝܐ. iv. 31: ܕܢܐܟܘܠ ܥܡܗܘܢ ܠܚܡܐ, ραββι φαγε, ܪܒܢ ܠܥܣ. 48: ܢܝܫ̈ܐ ܘܐܬܘܬܐ, σημεια και τερατα, ܐܬܘܬܐ ܘܬܕܡܪ̈ܬܐ. v. 6: ܕܬܗܘܐ ܚܠܝܡ, υγιης γενεσθαι, ܕܬܬܚܠܡ. 13: ܥܒܪ ܗܘܐ ܠܗ ܡܢ ܕܒܟܢܫܐ ܠܡܥܪܬܗ, εξενευσεν, ܐܬܟܢܝ ܗܘܐ ܠܗ.

most antient manuscript bearing a date in the Nitrian Collection, written A.D. 412.* The peculiarities of grammar, &c., occurring in that version Dr. Lee was inclined to believe were an indication of its having been produced in the schools of Palestine, rather than of Edessa.† This seems to me also to be highly probable, but at present the means of arriving at any positive conclusion respecting these different Syriac dialects are so scanty, that it would be presumption to pronounce any decided opinion on this matter. All that I can venture to say is, that several of these peculiarities are not found in Syriac works which we know to have been written at Edessa, at a rather later

vii. 10: ܚܝܡ ܒܓܠܐ, *φανερως*, ܒܓܠܝܐ. 13–26: ܒܡܓܠܝܐ, *εν παρρησιᾳ*, ܓܠܝܐܝܬ. 24: ܐܦܝܡ ܐܦܝܡ, *κατ᾽ οψιν*, ܒܡܣܒ ܒܐܦ̈ܐ. 35: ܠܡܐ ܗܘ ܠܙܪܥܐ ܕܐܪ̈ܡܝܐ ܐܙܠ ܡܠܦ, *μη εις την διασποραν των Ελληνων μελλει πορευεσθαι και διδασκειν τους Ελληνας*, ܠܡܐ ܗܘ ܠܐܬܪ̈ܘܬܐ ܕܡܒܕ̈ܪܐ ܥܬܝܕ ܕܢܐܙܠ ܘܢܠܦ ܠܚܢܦ̈ܐ. Luke iii. 1: ܒܡܕܒܪܢܘܬܐ, *της ηγεμονιας*, ܕܡܠܟܘܬܗ. —: ܒܥܒܘܪ, *χωρας*, ܒܐܬܪܐ. 4: ܒܟܬܒܘܬܗ, *εν βιβλῳ των λογων*, ܒܟܬܒܐ ܕܡܠܐ. vii. 34: ܪܘܝܐ, *οινοποτης*, ܫܬܐ ܚܡܪܐ. viii. 3: ܡܢ ܡܕܡ ܕܐܝܬ ܗܘܐ ܠܗܝܢ, *απο των υπαρχοντων αυταις*, ܡܢ ܩܢܝܢܗܝܢ. ix. 31: ܚܘܠܦܢܗ, *την εξοδον αυτου*, ܡܦܩܢܗ. 37: ܘܡܚܪ ܝܘܡܐ ܒܬܗ, *εν τη εξης ημερᾳ*, ܘܗܘܐ ܒܝܘܡܐ ܕܒܬܪܗ. 51: ܕܡܣܩܢܗ, *της αναληψεως αυτου*, ܕܥܠܘܬܗ. x. 7: ܡܢ ܒܝܬܐ ܠܒܝܬܗ *εξ οικιας εις οικιαν*, ܡܢ ܒܝܬܐ ܠܒܝܬܐ. 16: ܛܠܡ, *αθετει*, ܛܠܡ. 30: ܟܕ ܡܝܬ ܡܝܬ ܠܗ, *ημιθανη*, ܟܕ ܩܠܝܠ ܡܥܟܐ ܗܘ ܢܦܫܐ. 35: ܬܪܥܝܘܗܝ, *επιμεληθητι αυτου*, ܝܨܦ ܕܝܠܗ. xii. 58: ܥܡܠܗ, *εργασιαν*, ܐܬܦܪܩܬ. xiii. 32: ܡܫܬܠܡ ܐܢܐ, *τελειουμαι*, ܡܫܬܠܡܐ ܐܢܐ. xiv. 15: ܫܪܘܬܐ, *αρτον*, ܠܚܡܐ. 18, 19: ܐܫܐܠܢܝ, *εχε με παρητημενον*, ܫܒܘܩܝܢܝ ܕܡܫܬܐܠ ܐܢܐ. xvii. 24: ܡܢ ܪܝܫ ܕܫܡܝܐ ܘܥܕܡܐ ܠܣܘ̈ܦܝܗ, *εκ της υπ᾽ ουρανον εις την υπ᾽ ουρανον*, ܡܢ ܫܡܝܐ ܘܟܠܗ ܬܚܝܬ ܫܡܝܐ. 27: ܫܝܨ, *απολεσεν*, ܐܘܒܕ. xx. 16: ܚܣ ܘܠܐ ܢܗܘܐ *μη γενοιτο*, ܠܐ ܬܗܘܐ ܗܕܐ. 17: ܕܙܘܝܬܐ, *γωνιας*. ܪܝܫܐ. xxi. 1: ܘܐܪܝܡ ܥܝܢܘܗܝ, *αναβλεψας δε*, ܚܪ ܕܝܢ. 28: ܐܬܕܝܩܘ, *ανακυψατε*, ܐܬܠܒܒܘ. xxii. 22: ܕܣܝܡ ܗܘܐ ܥܠܘܗܝ, *το ωρισμενον*, ܕܐܬܦܪܫ. 43: ܒܪܘܢܐ ܪܒܐ, *εν αγωνιᾳ*, ܒܐܠܨܬܐ. xxiii. 9: ܣܓܝܐܬܐ, *ικανοις*, ܣܥܝܐܬܐ. 14: ܘܡܕܡ ܠܐ ܐܫܟܚܬ ܥܠܬܗ, *ουδεν ευρον εν τῳ ανθρωπῳ τουτῳ αιτιον*, ܘܥܠܬܐ ܡܕܡ ܠܐ ܐܫܟܚܬ ܒܓܒܪܐ ܗܢܐ. 19: ܗܦܘ̈ܟܬܐ, *στασιν*, ܐܣܛܣܝܣ. 25: ܗܪ̈ܣܣ, *στασιν*, ܐܣܛܣܝܣ. 38: ܦܛܩܐ, *επιγαφη*, ܟܬܒܐ. 43: ܒܓܢܬ ܥܕܢ, *εν τῳ παραδεισῳ*, ܒܦܪܕܝܣܐ. xxiv. 18: ܠܐ ܫܡܥ ܐܢܬ, *ουκ εγνως*, ܠܐ ܝܕܥ ܐܢܬ. 19: ܘܐܫܬܟܚ ܒܚܝܠܐ, *δυνατος*, ܘܚܝܠܬܢ ܗܘܐ.

* See respecting this manuscript; my Preface to Festal Letters of Athanasius; and Edinburgh Review, No. 214, April 1857, p. 449.

† Eusebius, Bishop of Cæsarea, on the Theophania, 8vo. *Cambridge,* 1843: Preface, p. xv.

date, nor even in the work of Bardesan,* which is the most antient production by any one belonging to that district to which we can with certainty refer. Those varieties, however, which are purely grammatical, are to be attributed, perhaps, rather to antiquity than to any dialectical peculiarity; for I have observed, upon the comparison of several of the oldest copies now in the British Museum of that very text of the Gospels which has been generally received as the Peshito, that the more antient the manuscripts be, the more nearly do they correspond in this respect with the text of these Syriac Fragments.

ON THE GOSPEL OF ST. MATTHEW.

In the preceding observations upon the text of St. Matthew, it will be seen that I have assumed that his Gospel was originally written in the Hebrew dialect, generally spoken by the Jews in Palestine at the time when the events took place of which it furnishes the narrative. I have done this upon the conviction that no fact relating to the history of the Gospels is more fully and satisfactorily established.‡ From the days of the Apostles themselves, down to the end of the fourth century, every writer who has had occasion to refer to this matter has testified the same thing: Papias,[a] Irenæus,[b] Pantænus,[c]

* Printed in my "Spicilegium Syriacum."

‡ Those who wish for fuller information on this, may be referred to Simon's *Hist. Crit. du Texte du N. T.*, ch. v.; B. Lamy, *Præfatio Apparatus Chron.* cap. vi.; Dr. Mill, *Pro legomena*, § 65; B. Walton, *Proleg.* vol. ii. p. 483, edit Wrangham; J. D. Michaelis, *Einleitung.* § 132; Elsner, *Dissertatio, Matthæum Hebraico Sermone conscripsisse*, 4to.; Francof. ad Viadrum, 1791; Olshausen, *Die Echtheit der Evv.*, p. 18; Dr. Campbell, *Preface to Matthew's Gospel*; Horne, *Introduction*, p. ii. ch. ii. sect. ii. § iv., &c. &c. &c.

[a] Ματθαιος μεν ουν Εβραϊδι διαλεκτῳ τα λογια συνεγραψατο, ηρμηνευσεν δ' αυτα ως ηδυνατο εκαστος: Eusebius, *Hist. Ec.*, lib. iii. 39.

[b] Ο μεν δη Ματθαιος εν τοις Εβραιοις τῃ ιδιᾳ αυτων διαλεκτῳ και γραφην εξηνεγκεν ευαγγελιου, του Πετρου και του Παυλου εν Ρωμῃ ευαγγελιζομενων και θεμελιουντων την εκκλησιαν: Eusebius, *Hist. Ec.*, lib. v. 8. Το κατα Ματθαιον ευαγγελιον προς Ιουδαιους εγραφη: Possini, *Catena Patt. in Matt. apud Massuet*, p. 347.

[c] Ων εις γενομενος ο Πανταινος και εις Ινδους ελθειν λεγεται, ενθα λογος ευρειν αυτον προφθασαν την αυτου παρουσιαν το κατα Ματθαιον ευαγγελιον παρα τισιν αυτοθι τον Χριστον επεγνωκοσιν, οις Βαρθολομαιον των αποστολων ενα κηρυξαι, αυτοις τε Εβραιων γραμμασιν την του Ματθαιου καταλειψαι γραφην, ην και σωζεσθαι εις τον δηλουμενον χρονον: Eusebius, *Hist. Ec.* lib. v. 10.

Origen,[d] Eusebius,[e] Cyril of Jerusalem,[f] Athanasius,[g] Epiphanius,[h] and Jerome,[i] all with one consent affirm this. Such a chain of historical evidence appears to be amply sufficient to establish the fact, that St. Matthew wrote his Gospel originally in the Hebrew dialect of that time, for the benefit of the Jews, who understood and spake that language.* A careful and critical examination of the Greek text of this Gospel will afford very strong confirmation of this.

[d] *οτι πρωτον μεν γεγραπται το κατα τον ποτε τελωνην, υστερον δε αποστολον Ιησου Χριστου Ματθαιον, εκδεδωκοτα αυτο τοις απο Ιουδαϊσμου πεπιστευκασι, γραμμασιν Εβραϊκοις συντεταγμενον.* Eusebius, *Hist. Ec.*, vi. 25. *αρξαμενοι απο του Ματθαιου, ος και παραδεδοται πρωτος λοιπων τοις Εβραιοις εκδεδοκεναι το ευαγγελιον τοις εκ περιτομης πιστευουσι*: *Com. in Ioh.* Opp. Ed. Delarue, T. iv. p. 132.

[e] *Ματθαιος μεν γαρ προτερον Εβραιοις κηρυξας, ως ημελλεν και εφ' ετερους ιεναι, πατριῳ γλωττῃ γραφῃ παραδους το κατ' αυτον ευαγγελιον, το λειπον τῃ αυτου παρουσιᾳ τουτοις, υφ' ων εστελλετο, δια της γραφης απεπληρου.* *Hist. Ec.* iii. 24.

[f] *Ματθαιος ο γραψας το ευαγγελιον, Εβραϊδι γλωσσῃ τουτο εγραψεν*: *Catechesis* 14, p. 148, edit. Paris. 1640.

[g] Evangelium secundum Matthæum ab ipso Matthæo Hebraica dialecto conscriptum est: *Synopsis S. Scripturæ*, in Athanasii Opp., T. ii. p. 55. The genuineness of this document has been called in question.

[h] *Ουτος μεν ουν ο Ματθαιος Εβραϊκοις γραμμασιν γραφει το ευαγγελιον*: *Hæres*, 51, v. i. p. 426. *ως αληθη εστιν ειπειν, οτι Ματθαιος μονος Εβραιστι και Εβραϊκοις γραμμασιν εν τῃ καινῃ διαθηκῃ εποιησατο την του ευαγγελιου εκθεσιν τε και κηρυγμα*: *Hæres*, 30, v. i. p. 127.

[i] Matthæus, qui et Levi, ex publicano apostolus, primus in Judæa propter eos, qui ex circumcisione crediderant, evangelium Christi Hebraicis literis verbisque composuit; quod quis postea in Græcum transtulerit non satis certum est: *Cat. de Viris Ill.* c. 3. Matthæus primus evangelium in Judæa Hebraico sermone edidit, ob eorum vel maxime causam, qui in Jesum crediderant ex Judæis: *Proleg. in Matt.* Matthæus, qui evangelium Hebraico sermone conscripsit, ita posuit: *Epist. ad Damas.* Mihi videtur evangelistam Matthæum, qui evangelium Hebraico sermone conscripsit, non tam "vespere" dixisse quam "sero," et eum qui interpretatus est, verbi ambiguitate deceptum, non "sero" interpretatum esse sed "vespere:" *Ad Hedibiam.* Matthæus autem et Joannes quorum alter Hebraico, alter Græco sermone evangelia texerunt, testimonia de Hebraico proferunt: *Com. in Isaiam.* Cui nos breviter respondebimus: primum Matthæum evangelium Hebraeis literis edidisse, quod non poterant legere, nisi qui ex Hebraeis erant: *Com. in Oseam.* To these several other indirect testimonies may be added.

* Grotius writes respecting this, "Evangelium suum S. Matthæum Hebraice, *i.e.* Syriace scripsisse ita constanter apud veteres, quibus de hac re veritas melius quam nobis innotescere poterat, traditum est, ut nullus plane sit dubitandi locus," *Com. in Matt.* i.; and Bishop Marsh, "I am persuaded that the evidence of Papias, and the *concurrent* evidence of other Greek Fathers, establish the fact that St. Matthew wrote in Hebrew full as well as any evidence of that kind can establish a fact," *Illustration of Hypothesis*, p. 47.

It will further be observed, that in speaking of this original work of St. Matthew, I have called it Aramaic rather than Hebrew, in order to mark the distinction between it and the antient Hebrew in which the scriptures of the Old Testament were written, the vernacular use of which the Jews had ceased to be familiar with during their captivity in Babylon, and had adopted the dialect of the Chaldees, in whose country they had so long been resident.* I have also used the word Aramaic as a general term embracing all the slight varieties of dialect existing in the Syriac or Chaldaic, without attempting to define in what those varieties consist; for, as I have already observed, I do not think that we have at present sufficient data, or, at least, that they have as yet been sufficiently examined and analysed to enable us to come to any accurate decision as to what are the precise peculiarities of each.† Generally it may be observed that the language used by our Saviour and his apostles being that ordinarily employed by the Hebrews in Palestine at that time, and called by St. Luke (Acts xxi. 40, xxii. 1), Papias, and Irenæus, the Hebrew Dialect, is so very similar and closely allied with the Syriac of the New Testament, called the Peshito, that the two may be considered identical, with the exception, perhaps, of some very slight dialectical peculiarities. These facts are so well known to all who have given attention to this subject, that it is not necessary for me to enter into any proof of them in this place.‡

* See Walton, *Prolegomena*, edit. Wrangham, vol. ii. p. 400.

† Hinc quam sæpissime legas Rabbinos linguam Chaldaicam vocare Aramæam. Morinus, *Exercit. Bibl.* p. 381. The reader may see what Wichelhaus has written "De linguæ Aramææ dialectis," lib. i. c. iv. in *De Novi Testamenti Versione Syriaca Antiqua*, 8vo. Halis, 1850.

‡ To guard myself, however, against the imputation of having assumed too much, I will quote the following passages from Walton's *Prolegomena*, and add a few other references out of many. "Postea appellata est 'Syriaca' a regione Syriæ, 'Aramæa' ab Aram, et ab Assyria 'Assyriaca:' aliquando etiam dicta est 'Hebræa,' scilicet in N. T.; non quod proprie eadem sit cum Hebraïca, sed quod populus Hebræus post Captivitatem Babylonicam, hac usus sit pro vernacula cujus oblitus erat. vol. ii. p. 390. Per 'sermonem igitur Hebraicum' in Novo Testamento clarum est, Syriacum sive Chaldæo-Hierosolymitanum intelligendum esse. Vide plura apud Widmanstadium. *Præf. in N. T.* Doct. Grotium locis citatis, et Mayeri *Philol Sacr.* ii. 3. *Ibid*, p. 468. Immo, ipsi Domino et Salvatori vernacula erat, quam una cum lacte materno suxit, in qua voluntatem Dei et expressa vitæ æternæ promissa Unigenitus Dei Filius orbi revelavit. Hunc sacro ore consecravit, in hac doctrinam Evangelicam tradidit, in hac preces ad Patrem obtulit, mysteria mundo abscondita aperuit, Patrisque de cœlo vocem audivit; ita ut dicere possimus,

Lingua hominum est lingua nobilitata Dei

et ut quidam cecinit de Syro Lexicographo,

Nos docet hic unus Numinis ore loqui,

When, therefore, it was well known that the author of the first of the four canonical Gospels was no other than one of the Twelve chosen Apostles of our Lord, and that he had composed his Gospel in a dialect so very closely allied with that of the New Testament in general use in the antient Syrian churches as to be virtually identical with it, it seems to be scarcely credible that those who undertook to make a collection of the books of the New Testament in Syriac, and for that purpose to translate into that language such other of the apostolic writings as had been composed in Greek, should not have availed themselves of the original document of St. Matthew, rather than have attempted to re-translate it into Syriac from any Greek version which might have happened to be at hand. Indeed, it is only on the supposition that the original had been lost, or was not then procurable, that we can imagine that any would have undertaken a task at once not only needless in itself, but also necessarily tending to make the Gospel in a certain degree of less authority; for no translation can be considered to be altogether so authentic as the original words of the author. Moreover, if the opinion which many have held as to the very early collection of the books of the New Testament in Syriac be correct,* there is no positive proof that any Greek translation of St. Matthew's Gospel was in use at that time. And even had the original Hebrew document of the apostle been generally lost sight of in rather later times, of which, however, there is no evidence, this might easily have arisen in the Syrian churches from the fact of its having been adopted by them with some slight dialectical modifications and change of the written character, and thus having become absorbed into the Syriac Canon of the New Testament; while in the Greek and Latin Churches, which were unacquainted with the Aramaic, the canonical Greek translation and Latin version would, as a matter of course,

ibid. p. 506. "In Novo Testamento sæpe nomina Chaldaica dicuntur Hebræa, et Hebraice loqui Apostoli quoque dicuntur cum Chaldaice id faciunt." Morinus *Exercit. Bibl.* p. 379. "Syriaca lingua eadem est cum Chaldaica, et Vernacula Judæorum, *ibid.* p. 381. See also Amira, *Prœludia in Grammaticam Syriacam sive Chaldaicam;* Ridley, *De Syr. Novi Fœderis Ver. Indole*, p. 9; Car. Schaaf, *Præfat. in Opus Aramæum;* Simon, *Hist. Crit. du Texte du N. T.* c. v. p. 47, &c.; Olshausen, *Die Echtheit der Evangelien*, p. 69, &c. &c. &c.

* The reader may see what Jeremiah Jones has written on this subject in his *New and Full Method of settling the Canonical Authority of the New Testament*, part i. ch. xv.—xviii. Although I believe his conclusions in the main to be right, I cannot concur with his arguments when they are founded upon an assumed fitness and propriety of things, rather than upon the evidence of facts.

be used in its stead. Neither does this afford any ground to conclude that it had disappeared altogether at that earlier period at which the Syriac version of the other Gospels was made. Indeed, there seems to be evidence to prove that it was in existence down to the time of Epiphanius and Jerome, in its genuine, as well as in an extended and interpolated form.* If we are to place any faith in the tradition constantly maintained in the Syrian churches, the books of the New Testament originally written in Greek, which have been received into their canon, were translated into Syriac before the end of the first century, in the days of Abgar, the first Christian king of Edessa, under the superintendence of Adai or Thaddai (Thaddæus), said to have been one of the Seventy Disciples chosen by our Lord.† There is also a record preserved of the date of a copy of the Gospels in Syriac transcribed at Edessa by Achæus, the friend of one of Adai's own disciples, as early as A.D. 77 or 78.‡ And if this

* Epiphanius informs us that there was found, in the time of Constantine, in a cell at Tiberias, το κατα Ματθαιον Εβραϊκον φυτον (*Hæres.* 30, *Ebion.* § 6.), respecting which Fabricius has this note: "το Εβραϊκον φυτον" non est genealogia Hebraica, ut vult Petavius, sed integrum evangelium, integer fœtus, sive liber Hebraice scriptus sub nomine Matthæi." *Cod. Apoc. N. T.* vol. i. p. 369. Εχουσι δε το κατα Ματθαιον Ευαγγελιον πληρεστατον Εβραϊστι. Παρ' αυτοις γαρ σαφως τουτο καθως εξ αρχης εγραφη Εβραϊκοις γραμμασιν ετι σωζεται: *Hæres*, xxix. 9, respecting which Fabricius writes: "Cæterum puto vocabulum πληρεστατον eo solum spectare, quod non versionem sed ipsum originarium Hebraicum Matthæi habuerint Nazaræi:" *ibid.* p. 369. And Jerome, after having spoken of St. Matthew in the words cited above, p. lxxiv., states that his Hebrew Gospel still existed in the library of Cæsarea: "Porro ipsum Hebraicum habetur usque hodie in Cæsariensi Bibliotheca, quam Pamphilus martyr studiosissime confecit: Mihi quoque a Nazaræis qui in Berœa, urbe Syriæ, hoc volumine utuntur, describendi facultas fuit," *De Vir. Ill.* He does not, however, as Fabricius observes, say that he himself inspected the Hebrew Gospel of St. Matthew in the library at Cæsarea. It is, therefore, uncertain whether it was the same as the Gospel according to the Hebrews, used by the Nazarenes and Ebionites, which he translated, or not. As the passage stands alone, it seems plainly to imply St. Matthew's original Gospel.

† See Gregory Bar Hebræus, cited by Assemani, *Bibl. Orient.* tom. ii. p. 279: see also *ibid.* p. 392: Gabr. Sionita, *Præf. in Lib. Psal.* p. 3: see also Wichelhaus, *De N. T. Versione Syriaca*, p. 60.

‡ Annotatio ad calcem Codicis Evangeliorum ab Achæo descripti, quam amanuensis in hæc verba describit—*De quodam pervetusto Evangelio, quod extabat in sacra ecclesia Ædium Romæorum in urbe Bagdado. Erat quoddam Evangelium Edessenum (hoc est Syriacum Edessæ exaratum) pervetustum quidem, sed clarum et dilucidum, ex quo ne jota quidem unum deletum fuerat, legebatur autem clarius quam libri recens exarati, et unus dumtaxat prior quinternio præ antiquitate ex eo exciderat. Ad ejus vero calcem ita scriptum erat "Absolutus est sanctus iste liber, Feria quinta, die* 18, *Canun prioris (hoc est, Decembris) Anno Græcorum* 389 (*Christi* 78) *propria manu Achæi Apostoli, socii Mar Mæris Discipuli Mar Adæi Apostoli, cujus oratio nobiscum sit, Amen.* See Assemani, *ibid.* tom. ii. p. 486.

is to be relied upon—and the probability of its being genuine derives very great confirmation since the discovery of the Nitrian manuscripts—it is no unreasonable inference to draw, that the Gospels of St. Mark and St. Luke were translated into Syriac even before the present canonical Greek version of St. Matthew existed; for Papias, writing several years later, seems to intimate plainly that no one particular Greek version had been generally adopted by the Church at that period, but that every one interpreted the original for himself as well as he could* Jerome also tells us that it was not known who made the Greek translation.† At any rate, it seems to be the opinion, of all who have studied and written upon this subject, that the Syriac canon of the New Testament cannot be referred to a later age than the second century of the Christian era.‡ The books, therefore, of which it consists must have been collected together at a time when the original Hebrew or Aramaic Gospel of St. Matthew was still to be found: for we have positive testimony to its being in existence in the days of Pantænus, about the last quarter of the second century; and we have also inferential evidence of its having been used about the same time by Hegesippus, who, as Eusebius informs us, proved himself to have been a Jew by birth and country, by the fact of his having cited both from the Gospel according to Hebrews and from the Syriac.§ By this in all probability is meant the interpolated recension of the Hebrew Gospel of St. Matthew, which the Nazarenes and Ebionites made use of, and the Syriac canon of the New Testament as it existed at that time, containing the Syriac version of such books as had been originally composed in Greek; comprising also, perhaps, the Syriac Gospel of St. Matthew, with some slight modification of dialect from the Hebrew or Syro-Chaldaic of Palestine.‖

* See note ([a]) p. lxxiii. above.

† His words are, "Quod quis postea in Græcum transtulerit not satis certum est."

‡ See Walton, *Prolegomena*, vol. ii. p. 489; Dr. Mill, *Proleg.* 1237; Ridley, *De Syr. N. T. Vers.* sec. vi.; Simon, *Hist. Crit. des Verss. du N. T.* chap. xiii.; J. D. Michaelis, *Einleitung*, § 57; De Wette, *Einleit. in das N. T.* § 11a.

§ See passage cited p. lxxiii. above.

‖ Fabricius, *Cod. Apoc. N. T.* p. 360; and after him Olshausen (*Die Ectheit.* p. 41) thinks that by the Syriac is meant the same thing as the Gospel according to the Hebrews, which was written in the Syriac language, and he cites Jerome's words, "Evangelium juxta Hebræos, quod Chaldaico Syroque sermone scriptum est." But the terms which Eusebius uses, *του καθ' εβραϊους ευαγγελιου και του συριακου*, "the Gospel according to the Hebrews *and the* Syriac" certainly make a distinction, and mean two different things. If *του συριακου* does not bear the signification here which I have proposed, probably it is to be referred to the Syriac version of the Old Testament, the same as O Συρος, whose readings are frequently

Moreover, there is preserved a quotation by Hegesippus, taken from the Gospel of St. Matthew; and it is very remarkable, that while it varies from the Greek text of his Gospel, which must have been translated from the Original Hebrew or Aramaic, it agrees with this Syriac which I now publish; and further, that notwithstanding their difference, they both may be taken as correct renderings of this same Syriac text, the variation having arisen simply from the two-fold signification of the Aramaic particle ד.* A more complete proof could hardly have been imagined, that this Syriac text, which shews the source of the variation, is the original, which both have followed; and that in this place at least it is identical with the original Aramaic of the Apostle.

That there was some very close affinity between the Gospel according to the Hebrews and Matthew's Hebrew Gospel is evident, from the fact that in the time of Epiphanius and Jerome they were thought by many to be one and the same. Grabe† and Dr. Mill‡ believed the Gospel according to the Hebrews to have been written before any of the canonical Gospels; and Lessing, Niemeyer, Weber, and others considered it to have been the original document upon which St. Matthew himself based his Gospel.§ The opinion, however, which seems to be the best grounded, and has been most generally received, is, that the Gospel according to the Hebrews had for its basis the genuine Hebrew Gospel of St. Matthew, and was afterwards expanded in some places by various interpolations, and perhaps mutilated in others;|| but that the changes made in it were not such as to preclude it from being esteemed to be the genuine work of St. Matthew, by many even in the days of Epiphanius and Jerome. Nor does it seem to be less certain that there were two recensions of this, varying in some respects from each other—the one in use

cited by the ancient scholiasts. See Montfaucon, *Præliminaria in Hexap. Orig.* p. 20. Ο Συρος, as referred to the Old Testament, was used as early as about A.D. 170 by Melito. See Routh, *Reliq. Sacr.* Melito, iv.; Mill, *Proleg.* 1239.

* See on Matt. xiii. 16, p. xxv. above.

† "Evangelium *secundum Ebræos* appellatum esse, eo quod a primis Christianis Ebræis, qui Hierosolymis degebant, literis esset consignatum, et quidem *ante* quatuor Canonica Evangelia. *Spicil. Patrr.* vol. i. p. 17.

‡ *Prolegomena,* § 38.

§. See Bp. Marsh, *Dissertation,* p. 21—24.

|| See Simon, *Hist. Crit. du Texte du N. T.* chap. vii. viii; Lardner, *Credibility,* vol. ii. p. 84; Olshausen, *Gesh. des Ev. des Matt.* in his book above cited; Bp. Marsh, *Illustration of Hypothesis,* p. 63; De Wette, *Einleitung in das N. T.* § 64; Jones, *New and Full Method,* part ii. ch. xxv.—xxix.; J. D. Michælis, *Einleitung,* § 138.

among the sect of the Nazarenes, and the other among the Ebionites.* It would carry me too far from my present object were I to enter here into any discussion on this matter. The reader may find all the information that he can require on this matter in the authors to whom I have referred. I have only mentioned this to shew that we may very reasonably infer that in such places as have not been altered by the intrusion of interpolated matter or by mutilation, the Gospel according to the Hebrews represents the original text of St. Matthew's Gospel. In those cases, therefore, in which the Peshito and this Syriac text vary in some respects from the Greek of St. Matthew, but agree with the Gospel according to the Hebrews, they may be presumed, upon the weight of this additional evidence, to represent more accurately the precise words of the Evangelist himself than the Greek translation.

Further, in my previous observations I have taken it for granted, upon the authority of Jerome, and other antient writers whom I have quoted, that the original Gospel of St. Matthew, although composed in Syro-Chaldaic, the vernacular tongue of the Hebrew people in Palestine at that time, was, nevertheless, written in Hebrew characters,† similar to those still used by the Jews; and not in those commonly employed by others who wrote in the Syriac language, resembling in a great measure the type in which the text of this volume is printed. That, in fact, in this respect it was like the interpolated copies of the Ebionites and Nazarenes, which were held by many at that time to be the authentic work of the Apostle: as Jerome describes it, "In Evangelio juxta Hebræos, quod Chaldaico quidem Syroque sermone, sed Hebraicis literis scriptum est, quo utuntur usque hodie Nazareni, secundum Apostolos, sive ut plerique autumnant, juxta Matthæum." He gives precisely the same description of the Books of Daniel and Ezra, in which the Chaldaic as well as the Hebrew seems always to have been written in Hebrew letters.‡ These letters, Jerome tells us, were introduced by Ezra after the Return from Babylon, and continued unchanged down to the time when he himself was writing.§ The distinc-

* See Fabricius, *Cod. Apoc. N. T.* p. 367.

† See Montfaucon, *Prælim. in Hex. Orig.* p. 22.

‡ "Sciendum quippe est, Danielem maxime et Esdram Hebraicis quidem literis sed Chaldæo sermone conscriptos." *Præfat. in Danielem.*

§ "Certum est, Esdram Scribam Legisque Doctorem, post captam Hierosolymam et instaurationem templi sub Zorobabel, alias literas reperisse, quibus nunc utimur cum ad illud usque tempus iidem Samaritanorum et Hebræorum characteres fuerint." *Præfat. in Lib. Regum.*

tion made by Jerome, as to the letters and the language, could not perhaps formerly be so clearly understood as it is at present. The recent recovery of the very antient collection of Syriac manuscripts from the Nitrian Desert has shewn us with certainty what was the form of the letters commonly used in writing Syriac about Jerome's own time, and how they differed from those which had been employed by the Jews since the days of Ezra.

Taking, therefore, for granted from the arguments which have preceded that this Syriac copy now before us is a more antient recension of the Gospel of St. Matthew, in use among the Syriac churches, than the Peshito published by Widmanstad; and that the variations between the two have arisen chiefly from the fact of the latter being a revised text, which, from collation with the Greek, has not only undergone some change in its terms and modes of expression, but also has been brought into closer conformity with the Greek text; assuming, likewise, that the original work of the evangelist, being in the Syro-Chaldaic language or the vernacular Hebrew of the Jews in Palestine at that time, and written in Hebrew characters, was adopted with, perhaps, some slight dialectical modifications, into the Syriac canon from the first, and not retranslated from any Greek version previously made; admitting, moreover, that the Gospel according to the Hebrews, in the form in which it was used both by the Nazarenes and the Ebionites, was no other than the original Aramaic document of St. Matthew modified by additions and interpolations, with, perhaps, some omissions*—let us now compare this Syriac text before us with such fragments of the Gospel according to the Hebrews as have been preserved to us, in order to see how far the resemblance between them will tend to confirm these admissions, and, consequently, to bear out the pretensions of this Syriac copy to be considered as more nearly representing the exact words of St. Matthew himself than any other yet discovered.

It will, perhaps, be the most convenient method to consider the passages taken from the Gospel used by the Nazarenes and Ebionites in the chronological order of the authors by whom they have been cited. The first, perhaps, is in the

* Epiphanius, while he describes the Gospel used by the Nazarenes thus—εχουσι δε το κατα Ματθαιον Ευαγγελιον πληρεστατον Εβραϊστι. παρ' αυτοις γαρ σαφως τουτο, καθως εξ αρχης εγραφη, Εβραϊκοις γραμμασιν ετι σωζεται· Ουκ οιδα δε ει και τας γενεαλογιας, τας απο του Αβρααμ αχρι Χριστου, περιειλον, *Hær.* xxix. 9—speaks of it as among the Ebionites in these terms—Εν τῳ γουν παρ' αυτοις Ευαγγελιῳ κατα Ματθαιον ονομαζομενῳ, ουχ ολῳ δε πληρεστατῳ, αλλα νενοθευμενῳ, και ηκρωτηριασμενῳ, Εβραϊκον δε τουτο καλουσι. *ibid.* xxx. 13.

Ignatian Epistle to the Smyrnæans, c. 3, *Λαβετε, ψηλαφησατε με και ιδετε, οτι ουκ ειμι δαιμονιον ασωματον.* These words, Jerome tells us, were taken from a Gospel that he had recently translated ;* which, he informs us in another place, was the Gospel used by the Nazarenes and the Ebionites.† They are evidently an interpolation into the original Gospel of St. Matthew from Luke xxiv. 39: *ψηλαφησατε με και ιδετε, οτι πνευμα σαρκα και οστεα ουχ εχει, καθως εμε θεωρειτε εχοντα*; differing, however, in substituting *δαιμονιον ασωματον* for *πνευμα.* To this Jerome again adverts in another place. "Cum enim Apostoli eum putarent *spiritum*, vel juxta Evangelium, quod Hebræorum lectitant Nazaræi, *incorporale dæmonium*, dixit eis, quid turbati estis, et cogitationes ascendunt in corda vestra? Videte manus meas et pedes, quia ego ipse sum.‡ The difference seems to have arisen from the original word in the Aramaic having been ܫܐܕܐ, rendered *δαιμονιον*; or, perhaps, to express it more fully, *διαμονιον ασωματον.* In this text (Matt. viii. 16) we find ܫܐܕܐ where the corresponding term in the Greek is *πνευματα*: ܟܠ ܐܝܠܝܢ ܕܐܝܬ ܗܘܐ ܠܗܘܢ ܫܐܕܐ ܘܐܦܩ ܐܢܘܢ ܒܡܠܬܐ, "all those that had devils (*δαιμονια*), and he cast them out with his word," *προσηνεγκαν αυτῳ δαιμονιζομενους πολλους, και εξεβαλε τα πνευματα λογῳ.* In Luke also, viii. 27 and 29, *δαιμονιον* and *πνευμα ακαθαρτον*, or ܫܐܕܐ and ܪܘܚܐ ܛܢܦܬܐ, are used as synonymous terms. At Matt. xiv. 26 in this text, "when the disciples saw Jesus walking on the sea they were troubled, and were saying, 'it is a *devil*,'" ܫܐܕܐ, the Greek is *φαντασμα*: and it is remarkable that our English version has here, *It is a spirit.* It is not improbable that the Greek translator, for the sake of euphemy, to avoid referring the term ܫܐܕܐ, *δαιμονιον*, to our Lord, used the word *φαντασμα* instead; and the Peshito, although retaining this text here in other respects, has accommodated itself to the Greek in this word, and substituted ܚܙܘܐ ܕܓܠܐ, "a vain vision."

Of the coincidence of the passage cited by Hegesippus with this text I have

* "Scripsit et ad Smyrnæos, proprie ad Polycarpum commendans illi Antiochensem ecclesiam, in qua et de evangelio, quod nuper a me translatum est, super persona Christi ponit testimonium dicens, 'Ego vero post resurrectionem in carne eum vidi, et credo quia sit. Et quando venit ad Petrum, et ad eos qui cum Petro erant, dixit eis, Ecce palpate me et videte, quia non sum dæmonium incorporale.'" *De Viris Illust. Ignat.*

† "In evangelio, quo utuntur Nazareni, et Ebionitæ, quod nuper in Græcum de Hebræo sermone transtulimus, et quod vocatur a plerisque Matthæo authenticum." *Com. in Matt.* xii. 13. Evangelium quoque quod appellatur secundum Hebræos et a me nuper in Græcum Latinumque sermonem translatum est." *De Viris Illust. Jacob.*

‡ *Com. in Esaiam,* Proœmium, lib. xviii.

already spoken. Those quoted by Clement of Alexandria* from the Gospel according to the Hebrews do not afford any means of direct comparison. They are but two sentences: one, *ο θαυμασας βασιλευσει, και ο βασιλευσας αναπαυσεται,* is distinctly stated to be from the Gospel according to the Hebrews ;† and the other, *Μυστηριον εμον εμοι και τοις υιοις του οικου μου,*‡ although the name of Gospel is not mentioned, is probably from the same source. Both seem to be from the interpolated parts. The latter, however, in the expression *τοις υιοις του οικου μου* resembles this text (Matt. x. 36), "the enemies of a man are *the sons of his house*," ܒܢܝ̈ ܒܝܬܗ, equivalent to *οι υιοι του οικου αυτου.* The Greek is *οι οικιακοι αυτου.*

The passage from the Gospel according to the Hebrews, quoted by Origen, in his commentary on Matthew at xix. 16, seems to be an interpolation in order to add another instance of the same thing; for in Matthew we find at this verse "Lo, *one* came and said to him, 'What good thing shall I do,'" &c.? and here "*another* of the rich said, 'What good thing shall I do.'" "Dixit ad eum alter divitum, Magister quid bonum faciens." It does not, however, afford any thing for the purpose of comparison. Another quotation, in his commentary on St. John, is *αρτι ελαβε με η μητηρ μου, το αγιον πνευμα, εν μιᾳ των τριχων μου, και απενεγκε με εις το ορος το μεγα Θαβωρ.* The Holy Spirit here is called our Lord's *Mother*, doubtless from the circumstance of the voice which was heard at the time of the descent of the Spirit upon him at his baptism, declaring, "Thou art my beloved son;" and the word רוחא, *spirit*, in the Aramaic, being of the feminine gender,§ as it is found in this text, iii. 17. The passage has reference to our Lord's being led up of the Spirit into the wilderness to undergo the temptation, which immediately followed his baptism: and it is to be observed, that while the Greek of Matthew iv. i. has only *του*

* The reader will find all the passages which have been cited by various writers down to the 5th century collected in J. A. Fabricius, *Codex Apoc. N. T.* vol. i. p. 355; Jones, *New and Full Method*, par. ii. ch. 25; *J. Kirchhofer Quellensammlung*, p. 448.

† *Strom.* lib. 2. Edit. Colon. p. 380.

‡ *Ibid.* lib. 5. p. 578.

§ See Fabricius, note on this, *Codex. Apoc.* vol. i. p. 361; and Origen's own explanation, *Com. in Johan*, tom. 2. Jerome writes, *Com. in Esai*, lib. xi. xl. ii., Hebræi asserunt, nec de hac re apud eos ulla dubitatio est, Spiritum Sanctum lingua sua appellari genere fœminino. Sed et in Evangelio quod juxta Hebræos Nazaræi lectitant, Dominus loquitur, "Modo tulit me mater mea, Spiritus Sanctus." Nemo autem in hac parte scandalizari debet, quod dicatur apud Hebræos Spiritus genere masculino, et Græco sermone, neutro. In divinitate enim nullus est sexus: see also *Com. in Mich.* lib. ii. 7, 6.

πνευματος, this Syriac text has ܪܘܚܐ ܕܩܘܕܫܐ, *Spirit of Holiness*, or Holy Spirit, *το αγιον πνευμα*, as it is found in this place of the Gospel according to the Hebrews. At verse 8 we read *εις ορος υψηλον λιαν*, for which this text has לטורא אינא דטב רם. Perhaps the word *θαβωρ* might have got into the text of the Gospel according to the Hebrews from דטבר of the last two words. In the Peshito of Ezekiel xl. 2, we read טורא דטב רם.

Jerome gives the following quotation from the Gospel according to the Hebrews respecting our Lord's baptism: "Factum est autem, quum ascendisset Dominus de aqua, descendit fons omnis Spiritus Sancti et requievit super eum ac dixit ei: Fili mi, in omnibus prophetis expectabam te, ut venires et requiescerem in te, tu es enim requies mea, tu es filius meus primogenitus, qui regnas in sempiternum." On this it is to be observed that the Holy Spirit is said to have *rested* or *remained* upon Jesus, as we find it in this Syriac Text; and also the voice from heaven to have addressed him directly, "My son," while the Greek of Matthew is *ουτος εστιν ο υιος μου*: see note on Matt. iii. 16, 17, p. xiv. above.

He also alleges this same Gospel again in his tract against the Pelagians, l. iii. c. i.: "Et in eodem volumine, 'Si peccaverit, inquit, frater tuus in verbo, et satis tibi fecerit, septies in die suscipe eum. Dixit illi *Simon* discipulus ejus: septies in die? Respondit Dominus et dixit ei, etiam ego dico tibi, usque septuagies septies." This has reference to Matt. xviii. 21, where we have *τοτε προσελθων αυτῳ ο Πετρος ειπε*, but in this text we have *Simon Cepha*. Moreover, the passage to which we have already referred, relating to *another* of the rich, who inquired what good he must do, ends thus: "Et conversus dixit *Simoni*, discipulo suo, sedenti apud se. *Simon*, fili Jonæ, facilius est camelum intrare per foramen acus, quam divitem in regnum cælorum." This refers to Matt. xix. 23, 24; but there our Lord is said to have spoken to *his disciples*. It is evident, however, that he addressed his discourse to them when Peter was present, and probably directed it especially to him; for we find that it was Peter who made the reply, v. 27, *τοτε αποκριθεις ο Πετρος ειπε*. In this Syriac text of St. Matthew we always find the name *Simon*, as it is in the Gospel according to the Hebrews; sometimes, indeed, with the addition of *Cepha*, equivalent to *Peter*, but never *Cepha* alone: while in the Gospel of St. Luke, whenever the word *Πετρος* occurs (being not less than thirteen times), the text of this recension has translated it by *Cepha* alone, with one single exception, where *Simon* has been substituted; thus causing a marked distinction in this respect between the two Gospels of this Syriac copy. In the Ignatian Epistle to the Smyrneans the name *Peter* is mentioned, but not in the part cited; and as to this we should not omit to state that Origen, the most antient writer who alludes to the passage, says that it was taken from the *Διδαχη Πετρου*.*

In the Greek the common name *Simon* is generally dropped, probably out of respect to St. Peter and perhaps, in order that he might not be called by the same appellation as his great antagonist Simon Magus,† in the same way as Thomas became the usual designation of another of the Apostles, probably to avoid calling him by the same name as Judas the traitor. See note above, p. l. on John xiv. 22.

In his commentary on Matt. vi. 11, Jerome writes: "In Evangelio quod appellatur secundum Hebræos, pro supersubstantiali pane reperi מחר, quod dicitur crastinum, ut sit sensus, Panem nostrum crastinum, id est, futurum da nobis hodie." This varies from the Syriac text: see note p. xviii. above. It is not, however, improbable that this passage might have undergone some change after the Greek translation had been made, and the word מחר have been substituted or added, as seeming to represent the same signification as *επιουσιον* of the Greek. At any rate we find in Acts vii. 26, *τῃ επιουσῃ ημερᾳ*, having the same meaning as מחר, rendered in the Peshito יומאאחרנא, from which, indeed, מחר seems to be an abbreviated derivative, as in the Hebrew. At Exodus ii. 13, whence the place in Acts is taken, the Septuagint has *τῃ ημερᾳ τῃ δευτερᾳ*, a literal rendering of the Hebrew ביום השני ; but the Peshito has there also יומא אחרנא.

I have already observed upon Matt. ii. 6, p. xii. above, that Jerome quotes the ***Hebrew***, "Et tu Bethlehem terra Judæ," exactly as it is in this Syriac text. Whether by the Hebrew he meant the orignal work of St. Matthew or the Gospel according to the Hebrews is much the same for our present consideration. It is quite evident, from what he writes in another place, that he did not mean the original Hebrew text of Micah, v. 2.‡

* Si vero quis velit nobis proferre ex illo libro, qui Petri Doctrina appellatur, ubi Salvator videtur ad discipulos dicere: "Non sum dæmonium incorporeum:" primo respondendum est ei, quoniam ille liber inter libros ecclesiasticos non habetur: *De Principiis* sive Περι *αρχων*, edit. Redepenning, p. 94.

† See the Clementine Homilies, where the distinction between the names of these two, Peter and Simon, is distinctly maintained.

‡ "Quanta sit inter Matthæum et Septuaginta verborum ordinisque discordia, sic magis admiraberis, si Hebraicum videas, in quo scriptum est: *Et tu Bethlehem Ephrata, parvulus es in millibus Iuda, ex te mihi egredietur, qui sit dominator in Israel.* Considera gradatim quæ ab Evangelista sint posita. *Et tu Bethlehem terra Iuda.* Pro *terra Iuda,* in Hebraico habet *Ephrata,* in Septuaginta, *domus Ephrata.* Et pro *nequaquam minima es in ducibus Juda,* in Septuaginta legitur, *modicus es, ut sis in millibus Juda.* In Hebræo, *parvulus es in millibus Juda.* Sensusque contrarius est; Septuaginta sibi in hoc duntaxat loco et Hebraico concordante: see *De optimo genere interpretandi, ad Pammachium.*

Further, in speaking of the Hebrew Gospel, Jerome says that it is to be observed, that whenever the Evangelist cites any testimonies from the antient scriptures, either in his own person or that of Christ, he does not follow the authority of the Septuagint, but that of the Hebrew; and he then quotes the two sentences, "Out of Egypt have I called my son," and "He shall be called a Nazarene;"* both of which exactly coincide with the Greek of St. Matthew, *εξ Αιγυπτου εκαλεσα τον υιον μου* and *οτι Ναζωραιος κληθησεται.*† This proves, that in these places at least the Greek translator of St. Matthew's Gospel has rendered the words for himself, without having reference to the Septuagint. As to the rest of the citations from the Old Testament, it may be observed, that in this Syriac they do not in all cases agree with the Hebrew, as we now read it; but whenever there is any variation between them, as they occur in this text and in the Greek of St. Matthew, they always come nearer in the Syriac to the Hebrew original than they do in the Greek. It is plain that the Greek translator sometimes rendered the Aramaic in his own words, and at others adopted the very words of the Septuagint instead of translating the passage afresh. The latter, however, might have been the work of subsequent revisors or transcribers of the Greek version, in order to bring it into closer conformity with the Septuagint as generally cited by other evangelists. I may also observe that there is a great similarity in many cases between the Peshito of the Old Testament and this text in the places quoted by St. Matthew.

* Porro ipsum Hebraicum habetur usque hodie in Cæsariensi bibliotheca, quam Pamphilus martyr studiosissime confecit. Mihi quoque a Nazarenis, qui in Berœa, urbe Syriæ, hoc volumine utuntur, describendi facultas fuit. In quo animadvertendum, quod ubicumque Evangelista, sive ex persona sua, sive ex persona Domini Salvatoris, Veteris Scripturæ testimoniis utitur, non sequatur Septuaginta translatorum auctoritatem, sed Hebraicam, e quibus illa duo sunt: "Ex Ægypto vocavi filium meum," et "Quoniam Nazaræus vocatur." *De viris illust.* Ex quo apparet, Matthæum Evangelistam non veteris interpretationis auctoritate constrictum, dimisisse Hebraicam veritatem, sed quasi Hebræum ex Hebræis et in lege Domini doctissimum ea gentibus protulisse, quæ in Hebræo legerat.—Quod beatum Matthæum non solum in hoc testimonio, sed etiam in alio loco fecisse legimus: *Ex Ægypto vocavi filium meum*; pro quo Septuaginta transtulerunt, "*Ex Ægypto vocavit filios suos*; quod utique nisi sequamur Hebraicam veritatem, ad Dominum Salvatorem non pertinere, manifestum est.—Et non solum in præsenti loco, sed ubicunque de Veteri Instrumento Evangelistæ et Apostoli testimonia protulerunt, diligentius observandum est, non eos verba secutos sed sensum: et ubi Septuaginta ab Hebraico discrepant, Hebræum sensum suis expressisse sermonibus," *Ad Algasiam*, quæst. ii.

† The reader may see what Jerome has written further on these two passages in his *Com. in Es.* xi. 2, and *De optimo gener. interp.*: also Morinus, *Exercitationes Biblicæ*, pp. 149, 153.

Besides these passages from the Gospel according to the Hebrews, upon which I have made observations, there are also several others that Jerome alleges from the same source; but as some of them evidently belong to the interpolations, and others relate to parts of the Gospel which no longer exist in this Syriac copy, we cannot institute any comparison. We may, however, infer, that had the leaves of the manuscript which have been lost still existed, they would have enabled us to throw much additional light upon this subject; for it is evident, that when the volume was bound up in the state in which it was found in the convent of Nitria, those leaves which contained passages that varied too far from the Peshito recension of the Syriac Gospels then generally read in the Churches were removed, and others in accordance with the usual text inserted to supply their place.

Epiphanius* likewise gives some indications of the Gospel according to the Hebrews used by the Ebionites. Among the names of the Apostles in one passage which he cites, we read *Σιμωνα τον Ζηλωτην*, as it is correctly given in St. Luke; and not *Σιμων ο Κανανιτης*, as it is erroneously found in the Greek version of Matthew, from the translator confounding two words similar in sound, ܩܢܢܝܐ and ܟܢܥܢܝܐ. The part containing ch. x. v. 4 is lost in this text; but here the Peshito has not been made to conform with the Greek, and has retained the true reading, ܩܢܢܝܐ "zealot." A little further on in the same passage from the same Gospel it is said that John came baptizing in the *River* Jordan, and so again in the next chapter. In the Greek of Matthew iii. 6, we have *τῳ Ιορδανῃ* only; but in the Syriac text we have in this place ܒܝܘܪܕܢܢ ܢܗܪܐ, "the *River* Jordan; and so generally: see note p. xiv. In the account of our Lord's baptism, also, the reading is the same as in this Syriac text, "*Thou art* my beloved son;" but in this Ebionite copy an addition has been made, and the voice is said to come a second time, "*This is* my beloved,"† as it is in the Greek of St. Matthew. It would almost appear as if this latter sentence had been interpolated after the Greek version was made.

Although, then, the passages from the Gospel according to the Hebrews which have been preserved to us be but few, still they are sufficient upon the comparison to establish the fact that there was a closer relationship between

* *Hæres* 30, c. 13 and 14.

† Και φωνη εγενετο εκ του ουρανου λεγουσα· Συ μου ει ο υιος ο αγαπητος, εν σοι ηυδοκησα. Και παλιν, Εγω σημερον γεγεννηκα σε, και ευθυς περιελαψε τον τοπον φως μεγα, ον ιδων, φησι, ο Ιοαννης λεγει αυτῳ, Συ τις ει, Κυριε; και παλιν φωνη εξ ουρανου προς αυτον; Ουτος εστιν ο υιος μου ο αγαπητος, εφ' ον ευδοκησα.

that Gospel, which, even in its interpolated form, was esteemed by many to be the authentic work of St. Matthew himself, and this Syriac text which I now publish, than between it and the canonical Greek translation of St. Matthew's Gospel; and so far, at least, to justify the inference, that in such places this Syriac text exhibits the precise words which the Apostle himself originally employed. For had this Syriac text of St. Matthew been a re-translation, it would have followed the Greek in such places as varied from the original Aramaic, which was the groundwork of the Gospel according to the Hebrews, and not have agreed with that Gospel when it differed from the Greek. The reason, also, for the variation of the Greek from the original is apparent in the Aramaic. The Greek translator or transcriber might readily have mistaken one letter for another in such a case as אנת הו, "thou art," and אית הו "this is," especially if the characters had been a little effaced, and the manuscript was not perfectly clear and legible; while a Syriac translator could not so readily have confounded *ουτος εστιν* with *συ ει* in the Greek. Moreover, this comparison, by proving the agreement between the two, tends also to confirm the historical testimony as to the fact that St. Matthew originally wrote his Gospel in Hebrew or Syro-Chaldaic, and that the Gospel according to the Hebrews was often taken for the authentic work of the Apostle.

The Gospel of St. Matthew, the same historical testimony informs us, although composed in the Aramaic or Syro-Chaldaic language, was written in Hebrew letters—that is, in the same character as was always used by the Jews from the time of Ezra in their sacred books, not only for the ancient Hebrew, but even for such parts of their more recent scriptures as were in the Chaldaic language, as I have already observed. In my preceding notes upon the Gospel of St. Matthew, I have assumed this to be true. Any one who will be at the trouble to compare the numerous passages where I have brought this to bear will hardly fail to find ample grounds to convince him that this must be correct as to the original Aramaic Gospel of St. Matthew; that it also equally applies to this text, and that the manuscript before us, although transcribed in the character commonly employed by others who used the Syriac language, has followed, in the Gospel of St. Matthew, a copy, the original of which either immediately or more remotely must have been written in Hebrew letters. See note on Matt. xxi. 24, p. xxix.

Another means of enabling us to form some opinion as to the claims of this Syriac to be considered as having retained the original words which St. Matthew himself employed will be found in the comparison of the parallel passages of the first three Evangelists. Unless we admit the verbal inspiration of the Gospels, a theory long since abandoned by all scholars and critics, which, indeed, could only be maintained by those who are entirely ignorant of the way in which the New Testament has been transmitted to our own times, and which, if persisted in, must involve very serious objections against these inspired writings, and tend to infidelity, it is impossible to account for the close and even verbal coincidence of many parallel passages in the first three Gospels upon any other ground, than that one Evangelist copied from the other, or that they all borrowed from a common source. But even this, although it may account for the material and verbal agreement between them, gives no satisfactory explanation of the discrepancies which exist in the midst of this agreement. Among the various hypotheses which have been advanced, the only one which appears to be sufficient to explain this, and which, therefore, has been most generally adopted, is, First, that in such passages as these three Greek Gospels have matter in common, they contain translations of some original Hebrew or Aramaic document made use of in them all, and that these three translations at the first were made independently of each other. This will account for different but synonymous Greek terms being so often employed in relating the same thing. And, Secondly, that the translation which followed next in order of time had been compared with that which had been already incorporated in the preceding Gospel; and, in certain cases where it was deemed proper, had been made to conform with it, even to the employment of the same terms. This will account also for the verbal identity wherever it occurs. If we, therefore, take this view of the matter, we may easily perceive how it came to pass that the same thing has been related by the separate Evangelists, sometimes in the very same words, and at others in different but synonymous terms.

It does not at all belong to my present purpose to enter upon the question as to the extent of the original Aramaic document which the other two Evangelists used: whether it was the entire Hebrew Gospel of St. Matthew himself, or some shorter history of the acts and sayings of the Lord Jesus Christ already existing in that language when he wrote, which he also used as well as the other Evangelists, and incorporated into his own narrative.*

* The reader will find what he may wish to know on this head in the works already cited of the able and really learned English bishop, Dr. Herbert Marsh, "*Dissertation on the Origin and Composition of the Three First Canonical Gospels*, and *Illustration of the Hypothesis proposed in the Dissertation.*

The object which I have now in hand is simply to apply this Syriac text as a test to the alleged fact, that certain parallel passages in the three Greek Gospels are translations from an Aramaic original. For if, while the hypothesis of their being translations from the same original accounts for their agreement, the application of this text will also explain the reason of certain discrepancies of the Greek Gospels in the midst of this agreement, it will afford a very strong confirmation of the presumption that they do contain passages translated from the same original Aramaic document; and also will give much additional weight to the pretensions of this text to be considered in such places, at least, as exhibiting the very words which St. Matthew himself employed, even were we to go so far as to admit that he also made use of a previously existing Aramaic narrative in common with St. Mark and St. Luke, and not, as I believe to be the case, that they used his Hebrew Gospel in the composition of their own.

It seems to me that no candid person who is sufficiently acquainted with the language and the subject, after having fully entered into the examination, can fail to acquiesce in the conclusion arrived at by Bishop Marsh, that "*The table of parallel and coincident passages*," as shewn in his Dissertation, "*is one continued proof, either that the Hebrew text of St. Matthew was the basis of the Gospels of St. Mark and St. Luke, or that some common document*," that is, Hebrew or Aramaic, "*was the basis of all three Gospels.*" It has been no part of my present purpose to enter into this matter generally, but only so far as it relates to this Syriac Text and the canonical Greek version of the Gospel of St. Matthew; but in my preceding observations I have assumed this statement of Bishop Marsh to be correct, and have therefore applied it in the examination of passages in which these two differed from each other, in order to ascertain what light the comparison of parallel places of the other Evangelists would throw upon the discrepancies between them. It is not necessary for me to repeat here what I have already stated in the foregoing notes on St. Matthew's Gospel. I must, therefore, request the reader to peruse them with this object in view, and then to draw his own conclusions. He will find that, in many instances where this text and the Greek version of St. Matthew differ from each other, the variation may easily be accounted for, upon the highly probable supposition that the translator, or the scribe who copied the manuscript made use of by him, read the original Aramaic in a slightly different manner; sometimes substituting one Hebrew letter for another that closely resembled it, or confounding one similar word with another; and sometimes making omissions in consequence of the close repetition of the same word or syllable—things which every one who has had any experience in the collation of manuscripts knows to be of very frequent occurrence; and that, upon reference to several parallel passages in which the other Evangelists are presumed to have made use of the same original Aramaic, this text is found to agree with them, while it differs from the Greek of Matthew; and, further, that, if we place this Syriac text by the side of them, some slight variations in the Greek of those parallel passages themselves can not only be explained and accounted for in the same manner, but sometimes, also, upon the ground of a different Greek meaning having been given to an Aramaic particle of a twofold signification. Moreover, I have observed in several instances, where there is a difference between the Greek of St. Matthew and this Syriac text, that the other Evangelists also, in the parallel passages, vary, not only from the Greek text of St. Matthew, but likewise from each other. For this I can assign no other probable reason, than that it must have arisen from some defect in the original copy, which they all more immediately or remotely followed, rendering it in such places obscure and partly illegible. Had we, then, direct and positive evidence that such parallel passages in the Greek Gospels were translations made by three different persons from several copies of an Aramaic original in Hebrew characters, we should certainly expect to find, simply as a matter of course, these very phenomena. The phenomena themselves, therefore, may very reasonably be taken conversely as so much internal evidence of such being really the case, even with respect to the other two Gospels; but when we have so great an amount of historical testimony to the fact itself, with regard to the Gospel of St. Matthew, the evidence, both external and internal, concurring, seems to be complete, and fully to bear out the conclusion that this Syriac text, so far as it explains these phenomena, may be deemed, to that extent at least, to exhibit the very words which that Evangelist himself employed.

To recapitulate the arguments which have been already advanced in order to shew the pretensions which this Syriac text of the Gospel of St. Matthew has to be considered as representing more nearly the exact words which the Evangelist himself made use of than any other that has hitherto been discovered, they are briefly these:—

First, the great improbability that those who undertook to collect the books of the New Testament received into the Syriac canon for the use of the churches should have neglected to avail themselves of the original Hebrew or

Syro-Chaldaic Gospel of St. Matthew, which must have been still in existence, and rather have undertaken to re-translate it back again into the same language from some Greek version ; especially when there is no evidence that any such version had been generally adopted into the Greek canon at the very early period when the Syriac translation of the rest of the books of the New Testament is said to have been produced. That this text is evidently a more antient recension of the same Syriac Gospel of St. Matthew, which, so far as we have the means of tracing it, appears to have been always in use in the Syriac canon, and that the variations in the subsequent recension, called the Peshito, have arisen from comparison with the Greek, by which it has been modified and brought in many places into closer conformity with the Greek ; that there is a marked difference between this Syriac text of St. Matthew and that of the other Gospels in the same copy, proving them to be by different hands ; that while the others evidently shew that they have been translated from the Greek, and exhibit plain signs of the Syriac translator mistaking and misunderstanding some Greek words, I have discovered nothing of this kind in the text of St. Matthew, although there be, perhaps, some traces of subsequent modification according to the Greek text, and several Greek terms employed. The use, however, of Greek words, which had already been generally adopted into the Syro-Chaldaic language at the time when St. Matthew wrote, affords no evidence of translation from the Greek, as some writers have supposed, even with respect to the Peshito recension of this Gospel.

Secondly : Direct testimony as to certain peculiarities in the original Hebrew Gospel of St. Matthew, which are found in this text and not in the Greek. Such is the statement of a Syriac writer of the seventh century, George of the Gentiles, that St. Matthew, in his original Gospel, did not omit the three kings in the genealogy, ch. i. v. 8, but that these fell out in the Greek, for the reasons which he has stated; and that they were thenceforth omitted by those who had embraced Christianity from among the Gentiles, and generally used the Greek tongue: see above, p. x. That also of Dionysius Bar Salibi, who states, that in his days there was sometimes found a Syriac copy made out of the Hebrew which retained the three generations ; thereby implying that this copy was made out of the Hebrew, that is, adopted from the Hebrew Gospel of St. Matthew with some slight change of dialect, and transcribed in ordinary Syriac letters: see above, p. xi. And that, too, of Jerome, who writes that he had found in the original Hebrew of St. Matthew, at ch. ii. v. i., *Juda*, as it is in this text, and not Judæa, as it is in the Greek: see p. xii. To these should be added the testimony of Origen who informs us, that in his time, there were still existing some Greek copies, that instead of ***Rama*** read εν τῃ υψηλῃ, which is a literal translation of ***Ramtha***, as it is found in this text, p. xii., and that of the citation of Hegisippus, who, being of Jewish origin, used the Hebrew and Syriac, to which I have already referred, pp. xxv. lxxviii. Nor should I omit the fact that the very antient Syrian writer, Mar Yakub the Persian, alleges the three kings in his genealogy, p. vii.

Thirdly, the agreement of this Syriac text, on certain points in which it varies from the Greek, with the Gospel according to the Hebrews, which was in the same language as the Hebrew Gospel of St. Matthew, and had so much in common with it as to be supposed by many, even so late as the fourth century, to be the authentic work of the Evangelist himself.

And, Fourthly, the internal evidence afforded by the fact that upon comparing this text with the Greek of St. Matthew and the parallel passages of St. Mark and St. Luke, they are found to exhibit the very phenomena which we should, *a priori*, expect certainly to discover had we the plainest and most incontrovertible testimony that they are all in reality translations from such an Aramaic original as this.

Whatever conviction these arguments may bring to the mind of others, I have no hesitation in stating that they have fully satisfied my own, that this Syriac text of the Gospel of St. Matthew which I now publish has, to a great extent, retained the identical terms and expressions which the Apostle himself employed; and that we have here, in our Lord's discourses, to a great extent the very same words as the Divine Author of our holy religion himself uttered in proclaiming the glad tidings of salvation in the Hebrew dialect to those who were listening to him, and through them, to all the world.

I have said to *a great extent*, because I believe that even this text is not entirely free from changes and alterations arising from subsequent collation with the Greek, such as were afterwards carried to a much greater degree, when that revised recension, usually called the Peshito, came to be generally adopted in the churches. I think it would not be a very difficult task for an acute and judicious critic to mark precisely those passages which have undergone the greatest change. At some future time I may, perhaps, myself venture to undertake the work, having been already led to make many observations on this head; but the text itself being now before the public, it will be open to all scholars to give it that full consideration which it so well merits ; and the united criticism of many may arrive at more certain results than the single labours and efforts of any one individual.

It may perhaps be necessary to add a word respecting the English translation from the Syriac. My great object has been to make it as literal as I could, in order to enable those who may not be acquainted with the Syriac to use the English for comparison with the Greek. For this purpose, I have even retained the order of the Syriac words, so far as it seemed possible to do so without obscurity. It has been my intention also to render always the same Syriac term by the same English word; and I have kept up such distinctions as ܐܢܫ, *man*; ܓܒܪܐ, *Man*, ανηρ; and ܒܪ ܐܢܫܐ, ܒܢܝ ܐܢܫܐ, *man's son, men's sons*, ανθρωπος, ανθρωποι; and ܒܪܗ ܕܐܢܫܐ, *The Son of man*, the peculiar appellation of our Lord Jesus Christ, together with other similar distinctions with which the reader will become familiar upon the perusal.

I give on another page a list of the few errata which I have discovered in the Syriac text, it being very important that this should be as accurate as possible. I regret to find also that some typographical errors have escaped my eye in the Preface and the English Translation. I believe, however, that they are such as will cause no difficulty to the reader, and may easily be corrected by him wherever they occur. This he is entreated to do for himself. For the Facsimile of the Manuscript I am indebted to the willing and skilful hand of my wife.

And now I commit this work into the hands of the public with a deep sense of the importance and responsibility of the task that I have undertaken, a task which I felt that I dare not shrink from, for it seemed to be thrown in my way by Providence. I was led, in the first place, to make every effort that I could, to neglect no available means, in my endeavours to obtain the rescue of the invaluable Nitrian collection of Syriac manuscripts from the chance of being destroyed and lost for ever, a danger to which they were exposed so long as they lay mouldering in the cellars of the convent in the Desert ; and when, happily, they were secured for the British nation, it fell to my lot to discover amongst them these venerable remains of the Gospels. No one, indeed, can be so fully alive to the defects in my task as myself. I have, however, honestly and fearlessly sought for the truth in my labours ; and during their progress I have had the vast satisfaction of continually obtaining additional conviction of the genuineness and authenticity of these documents of our faith, of the impossibility of their being other than what they are represented to be, and of the wonderful fidelity of the transmission of the text in all essential matters whatever, in the midst of some variations which nothing but a constant miracle could prevent, by several processes of philological argument and reasoning, which rest solely upon the free critical examination of numerous questions into which this task has led me.

CORRIGENDA.

MATTHEW.

vi. 1.	for	ܒܢܝܐ	read	ܒܢܝ
xiii. 30.	..	ܕܠܘܩܕܢܐ	..	ܕܠܘܩܕܢܐ
32.	..	ܘܙܪܥܗ̇	..	ܘܙܪܥܗ
xvi. 14.	..	ܐܚܪܢܐ	..	ܐܚܪܢܐ

MARK.

xvi. 19.	for	ܡܬܪ	read	ܒܬܪ

LUKE.

iii. 15.	for	ܒܢܦܫܘܢ	read	ܒܢܦܫܗܘܢ
ix. 21.	..	ܟܐܦܐ	..	ܟܐܦܐ
xii. 38.	..	ܒܪ	..	ܒܕ

THE DISTINCT GOSPEL OF MATTHEW.

---

1 THE book of the generations of Jesus
the Messiah, the son of David, the son
2 of Abraham. Abraham begat Isaac;
Isaac begat Jacob; Jacob begat Ju-
3 da and his brethren; Juda begat Pha-
rez and Zarah of Thamar; Pharez
begat Hezron; Hezron begat Aram;
4 Aram begat Aminadab; Aminadab
begat Nahshon; Nahshon begat She-
5 la; Shela begat Boaz of Rahab;
Boaz begat Ober of Ruth; Ober be-
6 gat Jesse; Jesse begat David the
king; David begat Solomon of the
7 wife of Uria; Solomon begat Reho-
boam; Rehoboam begat Abia; Abia
8 begat Asa; Asa begat Jehoshaphat;
Jehoshaphat begat Jehoram; Jehoram
begat Ahazia; Ahazia begat Joash;
Joash begat Amuzia; Amuzia begat
9 Uzia; Uzia begat Jotham; Jotham
begat Ahaz; Ahaz begat Hezekia;
10 Hezekia begat Manasse; Manasse
begat Amon; Amon begat Josia; Jo-
11 sia begat Jeconia and his brethren,
in the captivity of Babylon: but after
12 the captivity of Babylon, Jeconia be-
gat Shealthiel; Shealthiel begat Ze-
13 rubbabel; Zerubbabel begat Abiur;
Abiur begat Eliakim; Eliakim begat
14 Azor; Azor begat Zadoc; Zadoc be-
15 gat Acin; Acin begat Eliur; Eliur
begat Eleazar; Eleazar begat Mat-
16 than; Matthan begat Jacob; Jacob
begat Joseph, to whom was espoused
Mary the Virgin, which bare Jesus
the Messiah.

All the races, therefore, from Abra- 17
ham even to David, are fourteen
races; and from David even to the
captivity of Babylon fourteen races;
and from the captivity of Babylon to
the Messiah fourteen races.

But the birth of the Messiah was 18
thus: While was espoused Mary his
mother to Joseph, while they come not
near one to the other, she was found
pregnant from the Spirit of Holiness.
But Joseph, because he was a righ- 19
teous Man, was not willing that he
should expose Mary, and had medi-
tated that quietly he should divorce
her. But while he meditated these 20
things, appeared to Joseph the angel
of the Lord in a vision of the night,
and said to him, Joseph, son of David,
fear not to take Mary thine espoused:
for that which is to be born of her is
conceived of the Spirit of Holiness.
But she shall bare for thee a son, and 21
his name shall be called Jesus: for
he shall save the world from its sins.
But this which was, *was* that might be 22
fulfilled that which was spoken from
the Lord by the mouth of Esaia the
prophet, which had said, Lo, the virgin 23
shall conceive, and shall bear a son,

and his name shall be called Emma-
nuel, which is interpreted, Our God
with us.
24 But when Joseph rose from his sleep
he did as the angel of the Lord com-
manded him, and took Mary and
25 purely dwelt with her until she bare
the son: and she called his name
Jesus.

Ch. II. 1 And when Jesus was born *in*
Beth Lehem of Juda in the days of
Herod the king, and lo, Magi came
from the east to Jerusalem, and
2 say, Where is the King of the Jews
that is born? for we have seen his star
in the east, and come to worship him.
3 But when Herod the king heard,
he was moved, and all Jerusalem
4 with him. And he assembled all
the chief priests and scribes of the
people, and said to them, Where is to
5 be born the Messiah? They say to
him, *In* Beth Lehem of Juda: for thus
6 it is written by the prophet, Even
thou Beth Lehem of Juda hast not
been the least of the kingdom of Juda:
for from thee shall come forth the
king, that shall tend my people Israel.
7 Then Herod privily called those Magi,
and was examining them, that he
might know at what time appeared
8 to them the star; and he sent them to
Beth Lehem, and said to them, Go,
examine concerning this same boy di-
ligently; and when that ye have found
him, come, shew me, that I also may
go, worship him. But they, when 9
they received the command from the
king, went; and to them appeared
that star, which they had seen in the
east, it was going before them, until
it came and stood over where the
boy was. But they, when they saw 10
the star, rejoiced a great rejoicing.
And entered into the house, and 11
saw the boy with Mary his mo-
ther, and fell down, worshipped him:
and opened their treasures, and of-
fered to him an offering; gold, and
myrrh, and frankincense. And it 12
appeared to them in a vision that
they should not return to Herod, and
they by another way went to their
country. And after them appeared 13
to Joseph the angel of the Lord in
a dream, and said to him, Arise,
take the boy and his mother, and
flee into Egypt, and there be until
I tell thee: because Herod is about
to seek the boy so that he may de-
stroy him.

But Joseph arose, and took the 14
boy and his mother by night, and went
into Egypt: And was there until 15
Herod the king was dead: that
might be fulfilled that which was
spoken from the Lord by the hand of
the prophet, which had said, that,
From Egypt I have called my son.

Then Herod, when he saw that 16
those Magi mocked at him, was very
wroth, and sent, slew all the boys

that were *in* Beth Lehem, and in all
its coasts, from the son of two years
and under, to the likeness of the
time that these Magi said to him.
17 Then was fulfilled the word which
18 spake Jeremia the prophet, A voice
was heard in Ramtha, lamentation,
and weeping, and many groans, the
voice of Rachel, who is weeping over
her children, and not willing to be
19 comforted, because they are not. But
when Herod the king was dead, ap-
peared to Joseph in Egypt the angel
20 of the Lord in a dream, and said
to him, Arise, take the boy and
his mother, and go to the land of
Israel: because they are dead which
were seeking the life of the boy to
21 take *it* away. But he arose, took the
boy and his mother, and came to the
land of Israel.

22 But when Joseph heard that Arche-
laus was king in Judea in Herod
his father's room, he was afraid that
he should go thither; and it appeared
to him in a vision, that he should go
23 to the country of Galilee: And he
came thither, and was dwelling in one
city which is called Nazareth: and
the word was fulfilled which was
spoken by the prophet, that, Naza-
rene shall he be called.

Ch. III. 1 And in those days came John the Bap-
tist, and was preaching in the wilder-
2 ness of Judea, and was saying, that, Re-
pent ye: because the kingdom of hea-
ven is come near. For this is he con- 3
cerning whom it is written by Esaia the
prophet, which had said, The voice that
crieth in the wilderness, Prepare the
way for the Lord, and make straight
the paths of our God. But he, John, 4
was clad *in* raiment of the hair of
camels, and was bound *with* a strap on
his loins; and his food was locusts and
honey of the field. Then were coming 5
to him the children of Jerusalem,
and all Judea, and all the other side
of the coasts of the river Jordan, and 6
he was baptizing them in the river
Jordan, while each confessed his sins.
But when he saw the Publicans and 7
the Pharisees and the Sadducees that
come to his baptism, he said to
them, Offspring of vipers, who hath
shewed you to flee from the wrath
that is coming? Produce therefore 8
fruits that are worthy for repentance:
And say not in yourselves, that the 9
father to us is Abraham: for I say to
you, that God is able from these stones
to raise up children to Abraham.
And lo, the ax is arrived upon the root 10
of the trees: every tree, therefore,
that good fruits produceth not is
cut down, and goeth into the fire.
But I, lo, I baptize you with water to 11
repentance: but he that cometh
after me is mightier than I, and not
worthy am I his shoes to bear: he shall
baptize you with the Spirit of Holiness,
and with fire: he who holdeth the fan 12

in his hand, and purgeth his floor, and
the wheat he gathereth into his gar-
ners; and the chaff he burneth with
fire that is not quenched.
13 Then cometh Jesus from Galilee to
Jordan unto John, that he might bap-
14 tize him. And John forbad him, and
said to him, I need that thou shouldest
baptize me, and art thou come to *me?*
15 Jesus said to him, Leave what is
now: because thus it is becoming
to us that we should fulfil all righte-
ousness. Then he left him to be bap-
16 tized. And Jesus was being baptized;
and while he was baptized, at the same
moment that Jesus came up from the
water, and lo, were opened the heavens,
and he saw the Spirit of God, which
descended as a dove, and rested upon
17 him: And a voice was heard from hea-
ven, which said to him, Thou art my
Son, and my beloved, that in thee I am
CH. IV. 1 well pleased. Then Jesus was led of
the Spirit of Holiness to the wilderness,
that he might be tempted of Satan.
2 And after forty days that he was fast-
3 ing, he was hungry. And he that
tempteth came near to him, and said
to him, If thou be the Son of God,
command that these stones may be
bread. Jesus answered and said to him,
4 It is written, that, It is not by bread
alone liveth man's son, but by every
thing that proceedeth from the mouth
5 of the Lord. Then the Devil took
him and brought him to Holiness's
City, and set him upon a corner of
the temple, and said to him, If thou 6
be the Son of God, cast thyself down:
for it is written, that, His angels he
shall charge concerning thee: that
upon their arms they should bear thee,
that thou shouldest never stumble with
thy foot against a stone. Again Jesus 7
said to him, It is written, that, Thou
shalt not tempt thy Lord and thy
God. Again, the Devil took him to 8
that mountain which is very high,
and shewed him all the kingdoms of
the world, and their glory; and said 9
to him, These all I will give thee, if it be
that thou fall down and worship before
me. Then Jesus said to him, Get thee 10
behind me, Satan: for it is written, that,
Thy Lord thy God shalt thou worship,
and him by himself shalt thou serve.
Then the Devil left him for a season, 11
and, lo, angels came near and were
ministering to Jesus.

But when Jesus heard that John 12
was delivered up, he went to Galilee;
and left Nazareth, and came, dwelt in 13
Capernaum, which is upon the side of
sea, in the border of Zebulun and of
Naphthali: That might be fulfilled that 14
which was spoken by the hand of Esaia
the prophet, which had said, The land 15
of Zebulun, and the land of Naphthali,
the way of the sea, the other side of the
river Jordan, Galilee of the nations;
The people which was sitting in dark- 16
ness have seen great light; and those

which were sitting in the shadows of
death great light is risen upon them.
17 From then began Jesus to preach,
and to say, The kingdom of heaven is
18 come near. And while our Lord was
walking on the side of the lake of Gali-
lee, he saw two brethren, Simon who
is called Cepha, and Andreius his bro-
ther, while they were casting their
nets into the sea, because they were
19 fishers. Jesus said to them, Come after
me, and I will make you fishers of men's
20 sons. And they in the same moment
left their nets, and went after him.
21 And when he turned from thence,
he saw other two brethren, Jacob
and John his brother, Zebedee's
sons, while they were sitting in the
boat with Zebedee their father, and
mending their nets; and Jesus called
22 them. And they in the same moment
left their nets, and went after him.
23 And he was going about in all Galilee,
and was teaching in the synagogues,
and was preaching the gospel of the
kingdom, and was healing all torments
24 and all diseases in the people. And his
fame was heard in all Syria: and they
brought to him all those which were
badly, badly affected, and those which
were diseased with difficult diseases
and with hateful torments, and many
on whom paralysis was fallen, and
lunatics; and upon each one of them
he was laying his hand, and was
25 healing them all. And after him went
great multitudes from Galilee, and
from the Ten Cities, and from Jerusa-
lem, and from Judea, and from the
other side of Jordan. But when he saw 1 CH. V.
the multitudes, he went up, sat him on
the mountain, and his disciples came
near to him: And he opened his mouth, 2
and was teaching them, and said,

Happy they, to the poor in their 3
spirit: because their's is the king-
dom of heaven.

Happy they, to the meek: because 5
they shall inherit the earth.

Happy they, to the sorrowful: be- 4
cause they shall be comforted.

Happy they, to those which hun- 6
ger and thirst for justice: because
they shall be satisfied.

Happy they, to the merciful: be- 7
cause upon them shall be mercies.

Happy they, to those which are 8
pure in their heart: because they
shall see God.

Happy they, to the peacemakers: 9
because the sons of God they shall
be called.

Happy they, to those which are per- 10
secuted on account of justice: be-
cause their's is the kingdom of heaven.

Happy ye, when men's sons perse- 11
cute you, and revile you, and say against
you every thing that is bad with
falsehood, on my name's account. But 12
you, rejoice and be glad in that day, be-
cause your reward is much in heaven:
for thus your fathers were persecuting

the prophets, which were before you.
13 Ye are the salt of the earth : but if the
salt become insipid and foolish, with
what shall it be salted? It goeth not for
anything, but that they should cast it
out, and men's sons should be treading
14 on it. Ye are the light of the world;
and a city that is built on an hill is not
15 able that it should be hid. And no
man lighteth a candle, and setteth it
under a bushel, but setteth it on a can-
dlestick; and it lighteth all those which
16 are in the house. Thus let shine
your light before men's sons, that they
may see your fair works, and glorify
your Father which is in heaven.

17 Suppose not that I came that I
should destroy the law, and the pro-
phets; I came not that I should de-
18 stroy them, but to fulfil them. For
verily I say to you, That until heaven
and earth shall pass, one letter Yod or
one corner shall not pass from the law,
19 until every thing shall be. Every
one that shall break therefore one of
these commandments the least, and
shall teach so to men's sons, shall be
called little in the kingdom of heaven:
but every *one* that shall do and teach,
this *man* shall be called great in the
20 kingdom of heaven. For I say to
you, That unless your justice shall
abound more than the Scribes and
Pharisees, ye shall not enter into the
21 kingdom of heaven. Ye have heard
that it was said to the ancients, That
thou shalt not kill; and whosoever
shall kill shall be condemned in the
judgment: But I say unto you, That 22
whosoever shall be angry against
his brother unreasonably shall be ob-
noxious to the judgment: and whoso
shall say to his brother, Raca, shall
be obnoxious to the synagogue: and
whosoever shall say to his bro-
ther, Shatya, shall be obnoxious to
the Gihanna of fire. When therefore 23
thou offerest thine offering before the
altar, and there shalt remember that
thy brother holdeth any thing against
thee *in* enmity; Leave thine offering 24
there before the altar, and go, first
be reconciled with thy brother, and
then come and offer thine offering.

Be agreeing with thine adversary 25
quickly, whilst thou art with him in
the way; lest thine adversary deliver
thee to the judge, and the judge de-
liver thee to the exactor, and thou
fall into prison. And verily I say 26
unto thee, that thou shalt not come
out from thence, until thou shalt give
the last Schamún.

Ye have heard that it was said 27
to the ancients, That thou shalt not
commit adultery: But I say unto 28
you, that whosoever seeth a woman
and lusteth for her hath committed
adultery with her in his heart. But 29
if thy right eye make thee offend,
pluck out and cast it from thee: for
it is profitable for thee that one

member of thee should perish, and not
thy whole body should go to Gi-
30 hanna. And if thy right hand make
thee offend, cut off, cast it from thee:
for it is profitable for thee that
one of thy members should perish,
and not thy whole body should go to
31 Gihanna. It hath been said that
Whoso putteth away his wife, let him
32 give her a letter of divorcement: but
I say to you, That whoso putteth
away his wife, against whom adul-
tery hath not been spoken, he it is
maketh her commit adultery: and
whoso taketh the *woman* left com-
mitteth adultery.

33 Again, ye have heard that it hath
been said to the ancients, Thou shalt
not swear an oath of lying, but shalt
34 give to the Lord thine oath: but
I say to you, That yourselves swear
not: not by the heavens; because they
35 are the throne of God: and also not
by the earth; because it is the foot-
stool which is under his feet: and also
not by Jerusalem; because it is the
36 city of the great King. And also
by thy head swear not, because thou
art not able to make in it one thread
37 of the hair black or white. But be
your word, Yea, yea; and Nay, nay:
but that which is more than these is
of the evil.

38 Ye have heard that it hath been
said that An eye for an eye, and a
39 tooth for a tooth: but I say to you,
that ye stand not up against the
evil: but whoso smiteth thee on thy
cheek, [turn] to him the other. And 40
whoso wisheth that he should liti-
gate with thee, and take thy coat,
let him take also thy cloke. Who- 41
so biddeth thee that thou should-
est go with him a mile, go [with him]
two others. And whoso asketh thee 42
give to him; and whoso wisheth that
he should borrow from thee hinder
him not. Ye have heard that it hath 43
been said to the ancients that Love
thy neighbour, and hate thine enemy.
But I say unto you that Love your 44
enemies, and pray for them which
persecute you: so that ye may be 45
the children of your Father which is
in heaven: he who maketh his sun
rise on the good and on the bad, and
sendeth down his rain on the righteous
and on the wicked. For if ye love 46
them which love you, what is your
reward? for so also the publicans do.
And if ye salute your brethren only, 47
what is your grace? Lo, do not
even the heathen so?

Be therefore perfect, as your Fa- 48
ther which is in heaven is perfect.
Beware that ye make not your gift for 1 CH. VI.
the eye of men's sons, so that ye may
be seen to them: because *if* not, there
is no reward for you with your Father
which is in heaven. When there- 2
fore thou doest justice, thou shall not
sound the horn before thee, as do the

accepters of persons in the synagogues
and in the streets, so that they may
be glorified of mens' sons. Verily I
say to you, that they have received
3 their reward. But thou, when thou
doest justice, let not thy left *hand*
know what thy right doeth: That
4 thy justice may be in secret: and thy
Father which seeth in secret shall
5 reward thee. And when thou prayest,
be not as those accepters of persons,
which love that they should stand in
the synagogues and in the corners of
the streets to pray, that they may be
seen to men's sons. I say to you,
that they have received their reward.
6 But thou, when thou prayest, enter
thou into the closet, and shut the
door in thy face, and pray to thy
Father in secret; and thy Father
which seeth in secret shall reward
thee.

7 And when ye pray, be not babbling,
as the accepters of persons: for they
think that in much speaking they
8 are heard. Be not therefore like
to them: for your Father, he knoweth
what is requisite for you before ye
9 shall ask him. But thus be praying:
Our Father which art in heaven, Hal-
10 lowed be thy name. Thy kingdom
come. And be thy wills in earth, as in
11 heaven. And our bread constant of
12 the day give us. And forgive us
our debts, so that also we forgive our
13 debtors. And bring us not into temp-
tation, but deliver us from the evil:
Because thine is the kingdom, and
the glory, for ever and ever. Amen.

For if ye forgive men's sons their 14
faults, also your Father which is in
heaven will forgive you: But if ye 15
forgive not men's sons their faults,
neither also will the Father forgive
you your faults.

And when ye are fasting, be not as the 16
accepters of persons, which make sad
their faces: that they may be seen to
men's sons that they are fasting. And
verily I say to you, that they have re-
ceived their reward. But thou, when 17
thou art fasting, wash thy face, and
anoint thy head; That thou mayest not 18
be seen to men's sons that thou art
fasting, but to thy Father which know-
eth in secret: and the Father, which
seeth in secret, shall reward thee.
Lay not up for yourselves treasure on 19
earth, where falleth the moth and cor-
rupteth, and where break through
thieves and steal: But lay up for your- 20
selves treasure in heaven, where the
moth corrupteth not, and also thieves
break not through and steal: For where 21
your treasure shall be, also your heart
will be there. For the candle of the 22
body is the eye: if thine eye be single,
also thy whole body will be luminous.
But if thine eye be evil, also thy 23
whole body is dark. If therefore the
light that is in thee be dark, thy
darkness how great will it be!

24 No man is able serving two mas-
ters, that he should not hate one,
and love the other, or should sus-
tain one, and despise the other. Ye
are not able to serve God and mam-
25 mon. On this account I say to
you, that ye should not be anxious
for your soul, what ye shall eat; nei-
ther also for your bodies, what ye
shall put on; for the soul is better
than sustenance, and the body than
26 raiment. Look at the fowl of the hea-
ven, that they sow not, and reap not,
and carry not; and your Father which
is in heaven nourisheth them. Are not
27 therefore ye better than they? But
which of you is able to add upon his
stature one cubit; that ye are anxious
28 about raiment? See the lilies of the
plain, how they grow; that they spin
29 not, and toil not. And verily I say
to you, That not even Solomon in
all his glory was arrayed like them.
30 But and if the grass of the plain,
which to day is, and to-morrow is
gathered and falleth into the oven,
God clotheth, how much therefore
will he be careful over you, defi-
31 cient of faith? Be not therefore anx-
ious, and say, What shall we eat? and,
What shall we drink? and, What shall
32 we be covered with? For all these
things, the nations it is of the earth
seek them: for your Father know-
eth that also for you these things are
33 requisite. But you, seek first the
kingdom of God, and his justice; and
these all of them shall be added to
you. Be not therefore anxious about 34
the morrow's, because the morrow is
anxious about its own. Sufficient
for the day is its evil. Judge not, that 1 CHAP. VII.
ye be not judged. For with that 2
judgment which ye judge, are ye
judged: and with the measure which
ye mete, is it measured to you. But 3
what is the mote that in the eye of thy
brother thou seest, and the beam
that is in thine eye thou perceivest
not? Or how art thou able to say to 4
thy brother, Leave, I will pull out the
mote from thine eye; because, lo, in
thine own eye a beam is set? Accep- 5
ter of persons, pull out first the beam
from thine eye; and then it shall be
perceived for thee to pull out the
mote from the eye of thy brother.

Give not the holy thing to dogs, 6
and cast not the pearls before
swine, that they may not trample
them with their feet, and turn, rend
you. Ask, and ye shall receive; 7
seek, and ye shall find; knock,
and it shall be opened to you: For 8
whosoever asketh receiveth; and
whoso seeketh findeth; and whoso
knocketh it is opened to him. For 9
who is he of you, that his son shall
ask him bread, does he offer him 10
a stone? Or if he shall ask him
a fish, does he offer him a serpent? 11
If, therefore, ye which are evil

know good gifts to give to your chil-
dren, how much more your Father
which is in heaven, that he should give
good things to them that ask him?
12 Every thing therefore that ye wish
that men's sons should do to you, be
ye doing to them: for this is the law
and the prophets. Enter at the
13 strait gate: because wide is the gate,
and broad is the way, that leadeth
to destruction, and many are they
14 which go by it. How strait is the
gate, and narrow is the way, which
leadeth unto life, and few are they
that find it!

15 Keep yourself from the prophets
of lying, which come to you in the
clothing of lambs, and from within
16 they are plundering wolves. From
their fruits therefore ye shall know
them. For they gather not from
thorns grapes, neither figs from this-
17 tles. Every good tree produceth good
fruits; and the bad tree produceth
18 bad fruits. The good tree is not able
that it should produce bad fruits, nei-
ther also the bad tree that it should
19 produce good fruits. Every tree there-
fore that produceth not good fruits
is hewn down, and falleth into the fire.
20 From their fruits therefore ye shall
recognize them.

21 It is not therefore every *one* that
shall say to me, My Lord, my Lord,
entereth into the kingdom of heaven;
but he that doeth the will of my
Father which is in heaven, he shall
enter into heaven's kingdom. For 22
many will say to me in that day,
Our Lord, our Lord, have we not
in thy name eaten and drunk, and
in thy name prophesied? and in thy
name have cast out devils? and in thy
name have done many mighty works?
Then will I say to them, that I never 23
knew you: get you from me, doers
of wickedness.

Every man that heareth these my 24
words, and doeth them, I will liken
him to the wise Man, which built
his house upon the rock: And the 25
rain descended, and the rivers came,
and the winds blew, and dashed against
the same house; and it fell not: be-
cause its foundations upon the rock
were set. And every man that heareth 26
these my words, and doeth not them,
shall be likened to the foolish Man,
which built his house upon the sand:
And the rain descended, and the 27
rivers came, and the winds blew, and
dashed against that same house; and
it fell: and its fall was great.

And when Jesus finished these his 28
words, astonished were the multitudes
at his doctrine, because as *one* au- 29
thorized he was teaching them, and
not as their scribes and the Pharisees.
And when he descended from the 1 CHAP. VIII.
mountain, great multitudes were
coming after him. And, lo, one Man, 2
a leper, came, fell, worshipped him,

and said to him, My Lord, if thou
wilt, thou art able to cleanse me.
3 And Jesus extended his hand, and
touched him, and said to him, I will;
4 be cleansed. And in the same moment
was cleansed from him the leprosy.
And Jesus said to him, *Beware*
lest thou tell to any; but go, shew
thyself to the priests, and offer the of-
fering as commanded Moses, that thou
mayest be to them for a testimony.

5 After these things, when he entered
into Capernaum, came near to him
one centurion, and was entreating of
6 him and beseeching him, and saying,
My servant is paralyzed, and lieth in
7 the house in great torment. Jesus
saith unto him, I will come and heal
8 him. That centurion answered and
said to him, My Lord, I am not
worthy that thou shouldest enter
under my shelter: but only speak with
the word, and my boy shall be healed.
9 For I also am a Man that is under
authority, and there is to me authority,
also to me, and soldiers are under my
hand: and I say to this, that, Go, and
he goeth; and to another, that, Come,
and he cometh; and to my servant
I say, that, Do so and so, and he doeth.
10 But when Jesus heard, he mar-
velled, and said to the men that come
after him, Verily I say to you, that
not even in a man of the house of Israel
11 have I found like this faith. But I
say to you, That many shall come
from the east and from the west, and
shall sit down with Abraham, and
Isaac, and Jacob, in the kingdom of
heaven; and the children of the 12
kingdom shall go out to outer dark-
ness: there shall be weeping and
gnashing of teeth. Then said Jesus 13
to that centurion, Go: as thou hast
believed, it shall be to thee. And
in the same moment was healed his
boy.

And Jesus came to the house of 14
Simon Cepha, and saw his mother
in law who was lying, and a fever
held her. And he touched her hand, 15
and in the same moment the fever
left her: and she arose, and was
ministering to them.

But *at* the the sun's setting came 16
near before him all those that had
devils: and he cast them out with his
word, and those that were badly, badly
affected he healed them: That might 17
be fulfilled that which was spoken
by the mouth of Esaia the prophet,
which had said, that, He shall take our
pains, and shall bear our diseases.

But when Jesus saw the great mul- 18
titude that surrounded him, he com-
manded his disciples that they should
go across to the other side. And one 19
scribe came near, and said to him,
Teacher, I will come after thee whither
thou goest. Jesus said to him, For 20
the foxes, there are holes for them, and
for the fowl of the heaven shelter;

but for the Son of man, there is not for
21 him where he may lay his head. But
another from his disciples said to
him, My Lord, permit me first that I
may go, bury my father, and I will
22 come. Jesus said unto him, Leave
the dead burying their dead; and
thou, come after me.

* * * * * *
* * * * * *
* * * * * *
* * * * * *
* * * * * *
* * * * * *
* * * * * *
* * * * * *
* * * * * *
* * * * * *

CHAP. X. 32 Every man therefore that shall con-
fess in me before men's sons, even I also
will confess in him before the Father
33 which is in heaven. And whoso shall
deny me before men's sons, also I will
deny him before my Father which is in
34 heaven, and before his angels. I came
not that I might cast peace on earth,
but division of wills, and the sword.
35 For I came that I might divide the
son against his father, and the daugh-
ter against her mother, and the
daughter in law against her mother
36 in law; and the enemies of a Man
are his house's children.

37 But whoso loveth his father or
his mother more than me, he is not
worthy for me: and whoso loveth his
son or his daughter more than me,
he is not worthy for me. And every 38
one that taketh not his cross, and
cometh after me, is not worthy for
me. For whoso findeth his soul 39
shall lose it: and whoso shall lose his
soul on account of me shall find it.
Whoso receiveth you, me he re- 40
ceiveth, and whoso receiveth me re-
ceiveth him that sent me. Whoso 41
receiveth a prophet in a prophet's
name shall receive the reward of a
prophet; and whoso receiveth a just
man in a just man's name shall
receive the reward of a just man.
And whosoever shall give to drink 42
to one of these little ones a cup of
cold water in the name of the disci-
pleship, verily I say to you, that he
shall not lose his reward.

And it was, when Jesus finished 1 CHAP. XI.
to charge his twelve disciples, he
turned him from thence to teach and
to preach in their cities.

But John, when he heard in the 2
prison the works of Jesus, dispatched
his disciples, and sent to him, Art 3
thou he that cometh, or another is it
we expect? And Jesus answered and 4
said to them, Go, shew to John that
which ye see, and that which ye hear: 5
For lo, the blind see, and the lame walk,
and the lepers are cleansed, and the
deaf hear, and the poor are sustained,
and the dead rise: And happy he 6
unless he shall be offended in me.

7 But after that these were gone,
began Jesus to say to the multitudes
concerning John, What went ye out
to the wilderness to see? A reed that
8 is moved by the wind? And if not,
what went ye out to see? A Man
that was clad in soft garments? lo,
they that are clad in soft *garments*
9 are among kings. And if not, what
went ye out to see? A prophet? yea,
I say to you, that he is more than
10 the prophets. This is he, concerning
whom it is written, that, Lo, I send
my angel before thy face, that he
may prepare the way before thee.
11 Verily I say to you, That there
is not risen among those born of
women that is greater than John
the Baptist: but the least in the
kingdom of heaven is greater than
12 he. But from John the Baptist's
days and until now the kingdom
of heaven is oppressed, and its op-
13 pressors seize upon it. For all the
prophets and the Law until John
14 prophesied. And if ye wish to re-
ceive, he is Elia, which was about
15 to come. Whoso hath ears to hear,
let him hear.

16 But to what shall I liken this
race? It is like to boys that are
sitting in the market, and sending
17 to their fellows, and saying, We
have tuned to you, and ye have not
danced; and have mourned to you,
18 and ye have not lamented. For John
came to you while not eating, and
also not drinking, and ye say, A devil
in him. And the Son of man came 19
eating and drinking, and ye say, Lo, a
Man a glutton, a drinker, and a friend
of publicans and of sinners. And
wisdom is justified from her children.

Then began Jesus to upbraid the 20
cities, those in which he shewed many
mighty works, and they repented not;
and said, Woe to thee, Chorazin! woe 21
to thee, Beth Saida! because if in Tyre
and in Sidon had been the mighty
works which have been in you: per-
haps then in sackcloths and ashes they
had repented. On this account I say 22
to you, That for Tyre and for Sidon it
shall be mild in the day of the judgment
rather than for you. And thou, Ca- 23
pernaum, art not thou exalted unto
heaven? but to hell shalt thou de-
scend: because if in Sodom had
been those mighty works which have
been in thee, standing had it been
until to-day. On this account I say 24
to you, That for the land of Sodom
it shall be mild in the day of the
judgment rather than for thee.

But at that time answered Jesus and
said, I thank thee, the Father, Lord 25
of heaven and of earth, that thou hast
hid these *things* from the wise, and
hast revealed them to boys. Yea,
my Father; because so was the will
before thee. Every thing is delivered 26
to me from my Father: and no man 27

knoweth the Son, but the Father;
nor also the Father, but the Son,
and whoso the Son shall wish that
he reveal to him.
28 Come to me, all ye weary and
bearing heavy burdens, and I will
29 refresh you. And take my yoke up-
on you, and learn from me, that mild
am I and meek am I in my heart:
and ye shall find rest for your souls.
30 For my yoke is gentle, and my bur-
den is light.

CHAP. XII. 1 And at that time Jesus was walk-
ing on the sabbath among the corn;
and his disciples were hungry, and
began plucking the ears, and rub-
bing in their hands, and eating.
2 When the Pharisees saw them, they
say to him, Why are thy disciples
doing that which is not lawful to
3 do? He said unto them, Have ye
not read what did David, when he
was hungry, and they that were with
4 him; How he entered into the house
of God, and ate of the face-bread,
which for him was not lawful to eat,
neither for them that were with
5 him, but for the priests only? Or
have ye not read in the Law, that the
priests in the temple they profane the
sabbath itself, and that they are with
6 out sin? For I say to you, That lo,
one that is greater than the temple *is*
7 here. And if ye were knowing what
it is, pity I ask, and not sacrifice,
ye would not condemn the inno-
cent. For the Lord of the sabbath 8
is the Son of man.

And when he turned from thence, 9
and came to their synagogue: And, 10
lo, one Man whose right hand was
withered. And they were asking him,
and saying, that, Is it that it is lawful
on the day of the sabbath to heal? that
they might be able *that* they should
calumniate him. He said to them, 11
Who is the Man of you, that has a
sheep, and it fall into a ditch on the day
of the sabbath, and does not draw, lift-
ing it up? How much therefore rather 12
a man's son than a sheep? Wherefore
it is lawful on the sabbath to do
what is becoming. Then he said to 13
that Man, Stretch out thine hand.
And he stretched out his hand, and
it was restored like its fellow.

And when the Pharisees went out, 14
they took against him council, so
that they might destroy him. But 15
Jesus knew, and turned him from
thence: and many men went after
him, and he healed them all; And 16
enjoined them that they should not
disclose him to any; That might be 17
fulfilled that which was spoken by
the mouth of Esaia the prophet, which
had said, that, Lo, my servant, in whom 18
I have been pleased; and my beloved,
in whom my soul delighted: my spirit
will I set upon him, that he may
preach judgment to the nations. He 19
shall not cry, and shall not strive;

and no man shall hear his voice in
20 the street. The bruised reed shall
not be broken, and the candle that
flickereth shall not be quenched, till
he send forth judgment to victory.
21 And to his name the nations shall
hope.

22 Then they brought near before him
one Man upon whom was a devil, and
blind, and dumb: and he healed
him, and that dumb spake, and saw,
23 and heard. And marvelling were all
the multitudes, and were saying, that,
24 Is not then this the son of David? But
the Pharisees, when they heard, said,
This *man* doth not cast out devils, but
by Beelzebub the head of the dæmons.
25 But when he saw their mind, he said
to them, Every kingdom that shall
be divided against itself shall be de-
solated; and every house and city
that shall be divided against it-
26 self shall not stand: And if Satan
cast out Satan, against himself he is
divided; how therefore shall stand his
27 kingdom? And if I by Beelzebub cast
out devils from your children, your
children by what cast they them out?
on this account they shall be for you
28 judges. But if I by the Spirit of God
cast out devils, then is come near upon
29 you the kingdom of God. For how
is a man able that he should enter
into the house of the strong *man*,
and spoil his goods, unless first he
bind the strong *man?* and then he
will spoil his house. Whoso is not 30
with me is against me; and whoso
gathereth not with me scattering scat-
tereth. On this account I say to 31
you, That all sins and blasphemies
shall be forgiven to men's sons: but
every *one* that against the Spirit of
Holiness shall blaspheme it shall not
be forgiven to him. And every *one* 32
that shall speak a word against the
Son of man, it shall be forgiven to
him: but every *one* that against the
Spirit of Holiness shall blaspheme, it
shall not be forgiven to him, not in
this world, and not in the world that
is about to be. Either make the tree 33
good, and its fruits good; or make
the tree bad, and its fruits bad:
but from its fruits is the tree known.
Offspring of vipers, how are ye 34
able good things to speak who are
bad? for from the superfluities of the
heart the mouth bringeth forth. And 35
the good Man from the good treasures
which are in his heart bringeth forth
good things: and the bad Man from
the bad treasures which are in his
heart bad things speaketh. But I 36
say to you, That every idle word that
men's sons shall speak, they shall give
respecting it answer in the day of
judgment. For from thy words thou 37
shalt be justified, and from thy words
thou shalt be condemned.

Then came near to him men from 38
the scribes and Pharisees, and say

to him, Teacher, we wish that we
39 may see from thee some sign. But
he answered and said to them, This
race bad and adulterous seeketh
a sign; and a sign shall not be
given to it, but the sign of Jonan
40 the prophet: For as Jonan was in
the belly of the fish three days and
three nights; so also the Son of man
shall be in the heart of the earth
41 three days and three nights. The
Men Nineveh's sons shall stand
in the judgment with this race,
and shall condemn it: because they
repented at the preaching of Jonan;
and, lo, *one* that is greater than Jonan
42 *is* here. The queen of the south
shall stand in the judgment with
this race, and shall condemn it:
because she came from the boun-
ries of the earth that she might hear
the wisdom of Solomon; and, lo, *one*
that is greater than Solomon *is* here.
43 But the unclean spirit when it is
gone out of a man's son, goeth wander-
ing about in places in which there is
no water, that it may find for itself rest.
44 And when it hath not found it, then
it saith, I will return, go to my
house from whence I came out; and
if it came, found it that it is empty,
45 swept, and garnished; then it goeth,
taketh with it seven other spirits that
are worse than itself, and they enter
and dwell in him: and the end of that
Man is worse than his beginning.
So shall it be to this bad race.

And while he was speaking to the 46
multitude, and lo, his mother and his
brethren were standing without, and
were seeking to speak with him.
But he answered and said to him 48
that told him, Who is my mother? 49
and who are my brethren? And he
stretched out his hand toward his dis-
ciples, and said, Lo my mother, and
lo my brethren! For whosoever 50
doeth the will of my Father which is
in heaven, this is my brothers and
my sisters and my mother.

CHAP. XIII.

And on that day went out Jesus from 1
the house, and sat him on the side of
the lake. And they were gathered 2
together to him a great multitude,
and he went up and sat him in the
boat; and all the multitude was
standing on the sea's shore. And 3
he spake with them much in allegories,
and said, Lo, the sower went out to
sow; and while he sowed, some 4
fell on the side of the way, and came
the fowl of the heaven and devoured
it. But other fell upon the rock, 5
and there was not much soil, and in
the same hour it germinated, because
there was not the depth of much soil:
and in the shining of the sun which 6
was upon it it sank down; and be-
cause it had not cast root in the
earth, it withered. Other fell among 7
thorns; and the thorns rose up with
it, and choked it: But other also fell 8

on good ground, and gave fruits; and
they increased and gave, some a hun-
dred, and some sixty, and some
9 thirty. Every *one* that hath ears to
hear, let him hear.
10 And his disciples came near, and
say to him, Why in allegories speakest
11 thou with them? And he answered
and said to them, Because that to
you it is given to know the mystery
of the kingdom of heaven, but to
those, it is not given to them to know.
12 For whoso hath, it shall be given to
him, and it shall be added to him:
and whoso hath not, even that which
he hath shall be taken from him.
13 On this account in allegories speak I
with them: that that which they see
they may not see; and that which they
hear they may not hear, and may not
14 understand, that they may never be
converted, and may be fulfilled the
prophecy of Esaia the prophet, which
had said that, Hearing ye shall hear,
and shall not understand; and the
15 vision ye shall see, and shall not see:
For become gross is the heart of this
people, and their ears they have made
heavy that they may not hear, and
their eyes they have closed; that
they may not see with their eyes, and
hear with their ears, and understand
with their heart, and be converted,
16 and I should heal them. But yours,
happy your eyes, that see: and
17 happy your ears, that hear. For
verily I say to you, That many
prophets and just *men* have de-
sired that they might see that which
ye see, and have not seen; and
to hear that which ye hear, and
have not heard. But you, hear ye 18
the parable of the sower. Every 19
man that heareth the word of the
kingdom, and understandeth not,
cometh the evil *one*, and snatcheth
the seed from his heart: This is that
which was sown by the side of the
way. And that which was sown upon 20
the rock, this is he that heareth the
word, and with joy hastily receiveth
it; and because that it hath not root, 21
a little time it abideth in him: but
when there is affliction or persecu-
tion on account of the word, quickly
he is offended. And that which fell 22
among the thorns, this is he that
heareth the word; and is in the
care of this world, and in the deceit-
fulness of riches, and they choke
it, and fruitless he is. And that 23
which fell in the good ground is he
that heareth the word, and under-
standeth it; and giveth fruit, some
a hundred, and some sixty, and some
thirty.

But another parable he added 24
and said to them, Like is the king-
dom of heaven to a Man which sowed
good seed in his field: and while 25
men slept, came the enemy and
sowed zizany among the wheat, and

26 went. And when the blade grew
up, and produced fruit, then ap-
27 peared the zizany. And the servants
of the lord of the house came near
and say to him, Our Lord, was
it not good seed thou sowedst in
thy field? whence is there in it
28 zizany? But he said to them, A
Man an enemy hath done this. His
servants say to him, If thou wishest,
we will go pick them up. He
29 saith to them, No; lest while ye pick
up the zizany, ye root up also the
30 wheat with them. But leave *them*
growing together until the harvest:
and in that time of harvest I will say to
the reapers, Pick up first the ziza y,
and bind them *in* bundles as for the
fire: and the wheat gather it into
barns of mine.

31 And he spake to them another
parable, Like is the kingdom of
heaven to a grain of mustard-seed,
which a Man took, and sowed it in his
32 field: And it is less than all seeds:
and when it is grown, it is greater
than all herbs, and becometh a tree,
and cometh the winged animal of
heaven and lodgeth in its branches.

33 Another parable; Like is the king-
dom of heaven to leaven, which a wise
woman took, and hid in meal, until
it was all leavened.

34 These all spake Jesus in allegories
to the multitudes; and without alle-
gories he was not speaking with them:
And the word was fulfilled which was 35
spoken by the prophet, which had said,
I will open my mouth in parables; and
I will speak secrets which are of old.

Then he left the multitudes, and 36
came to the house: and his disciples
came near before him, and say to
him, Explain to us that parable
of the zizany of the field. But he 37
answered and said to them, The
sower of the good seed is the Son of
man; And the field is the world; 38
but the good seed they are the chil-
dren of the kingdom; and the zizany
are the children of the evil *one*, and 39
the sower he is the evil *one*; and
the harvest is the end of the world;
and the reapers are the angels. As 40
therefore that the zizany are picked
up and burned in the fire; so shall it
be in the end of the world. The 41
Son of man shall send his angels, that
they may gather from among his
kingdom all offences, and all those
which do wickedness; And cast them 42
into the furnace of fire: there shall
be weeping and gnashing of teeth.
Then the just shall shine as the sun in 43
the kingdom of their Father. Whoso
hath ears to hear, let him hear.

Like is the kingdom of heaven to a 44
treasure which is laid up in a field;
and when a Man found it, he hid it,
and from his joy went sold every thing
that he had, and bought for himself
that field.

45 Again, like is the kingdom of hea-
ven to a Man, a merchant, who was
46 seeking good pearls: And when he
found a good pearl, and valuable of
price, he went and sold every thing
that he had, and came and bought it
for himself.

47 Again, like is the kingdom of hea-
ven to a great net, that fell into the
sea, and of every kind gathered:
48 But and when it was full, they
lifted it upon the sea's shore, and
sat down, chose the fishes that
were good, good; and those which
49 were bad they cast them out. So
shall it be at the end of the world:
the angels shall go forth, and separate
50 the bad from among the just, And
shall cast them into the furnace of
fire: there shall be weeping and
gnashing of teeth.

51 Jesus said to them, to his dis-
ciples, Have ye understood all these?
They say unto him, Yea. He saith to
52 them, On this account every scribe
that is instructed for the kingdom
of heaven is like to a Man, the
lord of a house, that bringeth out
of his treasures the new and the old.

53 And when Jesus finished these
parables, he turned him from thence,
54 And came to his *own* city: and
Jesus was teaching them in their
synagogues, so that they wondered,
and they say, Whence to this *man*
55 this wisdom, and this power? Is
not this Joseph's son the carpenter?
and the name to his mother Mary?
and his brethren, Jacob, and Joseph,
and Simon, and Juda? And his sisters, 56
all of them are with us? Whence to
him all these *things*, to this *man*? And 57
they were offended at him. But
Jesus said to them, There is not a pro-
phet which is despised, except in his
city, and in his house. And he did 58
not there many mighty works, on
account of the lack of their faith.

CHAP. XIV.

But at that time heard Herod the 1
tetrarch the fame of Jesus, And
said to his servants, This is John 2
the Baptist; he is risen from among
the dead; on this account much is
his power. For he Herod had seized 3
John, and bound him, and cast him
into prison on account of Herodia,
his brother Philip's wife. For John 4
had said to him, That it is not
lawful for thee that she should be
to thee a wife. And he was wish- 5
ing to kill him, and he was afraid
of the people, because as a prophet
they were holding John.

And when it was the birthday of 6
Herod, the daughter of Herodia
came in, danced in the midst of the
banquet, and pleased Herod. On 7
this account he promised to her with
an oath that whatsoever she should
ask him he would give to her. But 8
she, because she was instructed of her
mother, said, Give to me here in a

dish the head of John the Baptist.
9 And it grieved the king: and on ac-
count of the oath, and on account of
the guests, he commanded that it
10 should be given to her. And he sent,
cut off the head of John in the pri-
11 son. And they brought the head of
John in a dish, and it was given to
the girl: and that girl took it to
12 her mother. And the disciples of
John came near, and took up his
corpse, and buried it, and they came
13 and informed Jesus. But Jesus when
he heard turned himself from thence
to a desert place by themselves: and
when the multitudes heard which
were from the cities and the villages,
14 they went after him on foot. And
when he saw the great multitudes, he
was compassionate towards them, and
their diseased he healed.

15 And when it was the evening, his
disciples came near to him, and say to
him, The place is desert, and the time
is past; send away the multitudes,
they may go to the villages, and buy
16 for themselves sustenance. And he
said to them, It is not requisite for them
17 to go; give ye to them to eat. They
say to him, We have not here but five
18 loaves, and two fishes. He said to
19 them, Bring them to me. And he
commanded the multitudes to sit
down on the grass, and took those
five loaves, and two fishes, and looked
to heaven, and blessed, and brake
the bread, and gave to his disciples,
and they, his disciples, gave to the
multitudes. And they ate all of them, 20
and were satisfied: and they took up
the remnants of the fragments from
before them twelve baskets being
full. And those men which ate were 21
five thousand Men, besides the women
and the children. And he commanded 22
his disciples that they should sit in a
ship, and should go before him to the
other side, while he sent away those
multitudes. And when he sent them 23
away, he went up to a mountain by
himself to pray: and when it was
evening, he was there by himself. 24
And the boat was separated from the
land many stadia, and they were tor-
mented by the waves: because the wind
was against them. But in the fourth 25
watch of the night came to them
Jesus, walking upon the waters. And 26
when his disciples saw him that *he was*
walking on the waves of the sea, they
were moved, and were saying that, It is
a devil; and from their fear they gave
a cry. And in the same moment he 27
talked with them, Be strengthened; it
is I; fear not. Simon Cepha said to 28
him, My Lord, if it be thou, permit me
that I may come to thee upon the
waters. He said to him, Come. And 29
Simon Cepha descended from the boat,
and was walking upon the waters, and
coming towards Jesus. And when he 30
saw the wind that it was strong, he

feared; and began to sink, and he
cried with a loud voice, and said,
31 My Lord, save me. And in the same
moment stretched out Jesus his hand,
and seized him, and said to him, De-
ficient of faith, why didst thou doubt?
32 And when he went up into the boat,
33 the wind ceased. And they that were
in the boat came near, worshipped
him, and say, Truly thou art the
34 Son of God. And when he went up
to the dry land, they came to Genesar.
35 And the sons of that place recognized
him, and they sent to all their country,
and brought near before him all those
36 that were badly, badly affected; And
were entreating of him that they might
touch only the fringe of his robe: and
those that touched were healed.

CHAP. XV. 1 Then came near to Jesus the
scribes and Pharisees, which were
2 from Jerusalem, and say to him, Why
transgress thy disciples against the
commandments of the aged? for
they wash not their hands when they
3 eat bread. But he answered and
said to them, Why also do even
ye transgress against the command-
ment of God, because that ye may
4 establish your commandments? For
God said, Honour thy father and
thy mother: and, Whoso revileth
his father or his mother shall be
5 slain. But ye say, each to his fa-
ther and his mother, My offering, thou
shalt be benefited from me. This
honoureth not his father. And ye 6
have made vain the word of God, be-
cause that ye may establish your com-
mandments. Accepters of persons, 7
well prophesied concerning you Esaia
the prophet, which said, This people 8
with its lips it honoureth me; and in
its heart is far from me. But in vain 9
they fear me, and teach the doctrines
of the commandments of men's sons.

And he called the multitude, and 10
said to them, Hear, and understand:
That it is not that which entereth 11
into the mouth defileth a man's son;
but that which cometh out of the
mouth, it defileth a man's son. Then 12
came near his disciples, and say
to him, Knowest thou that the Pha-
risees, when they heard this word,
were offended? But he answered 13
and said to them, Every plant that
my Father which is heaven hath not
planted, shall be rooted up. Let 14
them alone: they are blind leaders.
But the blind that leadeth the
blind, with him into the ditch shall
fall. Simon Cepha answered and 15
said to him, Explain to us this
parable. He said to him, Do not 16
ye even until now understand?
Know ye not, that whatsoever 17
entereth into the mouth to the
belly it goeth, and from thence is
ejected in the purging? But that
which cometh out from the mouth
from the heart it cometh out; and

19 this it is defileth a man's son. For
from the heart it is come out the bad
thoughts of murder, and of adultery,
and of fornication, and of theft, and
of the witness of lying, and blas-
20 phemy: These are they which defile
a man's son: for when a man shall
eat bread while his hands are not
washen he is not defiled.
21 And Jesus went out from thence,
and went to the coast of Tyre and of
22 Sidon. And lo, one woman, a Ca-
naanite, came out of those same coasts,
and was crying and saying, Be com-
passionated to me, my Lord, son of Da-
vid; my daughter is badly conducted
23 by a devil's hands. And he gave not to
her an answer. And his disciples came
near, and were entreating of him, and
were saying to him, Send her away;
because lo, she crieth and cometh
24 after us. But he answered and said
to them, I am not sent but after those
flocks which have strayed from the
25 house of Israel. Then she came
near, worshipped him, and saith to
26 him, My Lord, help me. But he
answered and said to her, It is not fit
to take the bread of the children, and
27 to cast to the dogs. She saith to him,
Yea, my Lord: for even the dogs eat of
the crumbs which fall from the tables
28 of their masters, and live. And he
answered and said to her, O woman,
great is thy faith: it shall be to
thee as thou wilt. And her daugh-
ter was healed from that moment.
And Jesus turned from thence, and 29
came upon the side of the lake of
Galilee; and went up, sat him on
the mountain. And great multi- 30
tudes came near to him, while were
with them the lame, and the blind,
and the dumb, and the maimed, and
many of other afflictions, and they cast
them at his feet; and he healed them:
And those multitudes were marvel- 31
ling, while they were seeing the dumb
that speak, and the lame that walk,
and the blind that see: and they
were praising the God of Israel. But 32
Jesus called his disciples, and said to
them, I am compassionate towards this
multitude, because lo, three days they
have continued with me, and there is
not for them what they may eat:
and that I should send them away
while they are fasting I am not
willing, lest they faint them in the
way. His disciples say to him, 33
From whence for us in a desert
place bread to satisfy all this mul-
titude? Jesus said to them, How 34
many loaves are with you? They
say to him, Seven loaves, and a few
fishes. And he commanded the 35
multitudes that they should sit down
on the ground. And he took up the 36
seven loaves and the fishes, and glo-
rified, and brake, and gave to his
disciples, and his disciples gave to the
multitudes. And they ate, all of them, 37

and were satisfied: and they took
up from before them the remainder
of the fragments filling seven pan-
38 niers being full. And they were,
those men that ate, four thousand
Men, besides children and women.
39 And when he sent away the multi-
tude, he went up, sat him in a boat,
and came to the coast of Magadún.
CHAP. XVI. 1 And the Pharisees and the Sadducees
came near, and were tempting him,
asking him a sign from heaven, that
2 he should shew them. But he said to
4 them, A race bad and adulterous
seeketh a sign; and a sign shall
not be given to it, but the sign of
Jonan the prophet. And he left
5 them, and departed. And when they
came to the other side, his disciples
forgot that they should take for
6 them bread. Jesus said to them,
Beware of the leaven of the Phari-
7 sees and of the Sadducees. And they
were reasoning among themselves,
that they had not taken for them
bread. But Jesus knew, and said to
them, What are ye reasoning among
yourselves, deficient of faith, that ye
have not taken for you bread? Even
8 until now do ye not understand, and
do ye not remember the five loaves,
also the five thousand which ate of
them, and how many baskets ye took
9 up from before you? And also not
those seven loaves that the four thou-
sand ate of them, and how many
panniers ye took up? How is it ye 11
do not understand that it is not con-
cerning bread I said to you, that Be-
ware of the leaven of the Pharisees
and of the Sadducees? Then they 12
understood that it was not concerning
the leaven of the Pharisees and of
the Sadducees he said to them, that
Beware; but of the doctrine of the
Pharisees and of the Sadducees.

But and when Jesus came to the 13
country of Cæsarea of Philippus,
he was asking his disciples, and saying,
What say men concerning me that I
am? Who forsooth is this Son of
man? His disciples say to him, 14
There are who say that he is John the
Baptist; others say that he is Elia;
others say he is Jeremia; others
say he is one of the prophets. He 15
said to them, And you, what say
ye that I am? Simon Cepha an- 16
swered and said, Thou art the Mes-
siah, the Son of the living God. Jesus 17
said to him, Happy thou, Simon, son
of Jona: because flesh and blood hath
not revealed to thee, but my Father
which is in heaven. Also I say to 18
thee, That thou art Cepha (stone),
and upon this stone I will build my
church; and the gates of hell shall
not overcome it. To thee I will 19
give the keys of the gates of the
kingdom of heaven: and whatso-
ever thou shalt bind in earth shall
be bound in heaven: and what

thou shalt loose in earth shall be
20 loosed in heaven. Then he rebuked
his disciples, that to any they should
not tell concerning him that he is
the Messiah.

21 From then began Jesus to shew to
his disciples, that he was about that he
should go to Jerusalem, and should
endure much, and suffer from the
elders and chief priests and scribes,
and they should kill him, and at
22 the third day he should rise. And Si-
mon Cepha came near, and said, Spare
thyself, My Lord: this shall not be.
23 But he, Jesus, turned, and rebuked
him, Simon, and said to him, Get thee
behind me, Satan: thou art an of-
fence to me: because thou mindest
not what is God's, but what is men's
24 sons'. Then said Jesus to his disci-
ples, Whoso willeth that he should
come after me, should deny him-
self, and take up his cross, and
25 come after me. For whoso willeth
that he should save his soul shall
lose it: and whoso shall lose his
26 soul for my sake shall find it. For
what is man's son profited, if the whole
world he shall gain, and his soul shall
lose? or what shall man's son give *in*
27 exchange of his soul? For the Son of
man is about that he should come in
the glory of his Father with his angels;
and then he shall recompense each
28 man according to his works. Ve-
rily I say to you, That there be
men of those that are standing here,
which shall not taste death, till they
shall see the Son of man while coming
in his kingdom and in his glory.

CHAP. XVII.

After six days Jesus took Simon 1
Cepha, and Jacob, and John his
brother, and brought them up to a
high mountain by themselves. And 2
changed was the vision of his face to
their eyes: and his countenance shone
as the sun, and his garments were
white as the snow. And to them ap- 3
peared Moses and Elia while talking
with him. Simon Cepha said to Jesus, 4
It is well for us that here we should
be: if thou wilt, we will make here
three tabernacles; for thee one, and
for Moses one, and for Elia one. And
while he was speaking, lo, a cloud 5
of light shadowed over them: and a
voice was heard from that cloud,
which said, This is my Son, and my
beloved, in whom I am pleased;
him hear. And when his disci- 6
ples heard, they feared much, and
fell on their faces. And Jesus came 7
near and raised them, and said
to them, Fear not. And they lifted 8
up their eyes, and they saw not, but
Jesus by himself. And while they 9
come down from the mountain,
Jesus was charging them, and said
to them, Tell not to any the vision,
until the Son of man shall rise from
the dead.

And his disciples were asking him, 10

and saying, Why say the scribes that
11 Elia cometh first? He said to them,
Elia cometh, that he may prepare every
12 thing. But I say to you, That Elia is
come, and they knew him not, but have
done by him whatsoever they willed.
So also the Son of man is about that he
13 should endure from them. Then un-
derstood his disciples that concerning
John the Baptist he spake to them thus.
14 And when Jesus came to the multi-
tude, came one Man and fell upon his
knees, and was entreating of him and
15 saying to him, My Lord, be compas-
sionate towards me, my son has a lunatic
spirit, and endureth evil: for how
many times into the fire falleth he,
and how many times into the water.
16 And I brought him near to thy disci-
ples, and they were not able to heal him.
17 Jesus answered and said to them, O
race perverse, and without faith, until
when shall I be with you, and en-
dure you? bring him to me, thy son,
18 hither. And Jesus rebuked him, and
out from him came the devil; and from
that moment was healed that boy.
19 Then came near to Jesus his dis-
ciples, and say to him, between them-
selves and him, Why were not we able
20 to cast him out? He said to them,
Because of the smallness of your faith;
for verily I say to you, That if it be
that there shall be in you faith as a
grain of mustard-seed, ye shall say
to this mountain that it should re-
move from hence, and it shall re-
move; and nothing shall surpass you.

And while they were going about in 22
Galilee, Jesus said to them, But the
Son of man is about that he should
be delivered into men's sons' hands:
And they shall kill him, and at the 23
third day he shall rise. And it grieved
them much.

And when they came to Caper- 24
naum, came those that collect two,
two drachms to Simon, and say to
him, Thy master, doth he not give his
two drachms? And Simon saith, Yea. 25
And when they entered into the house,
Jesus prevented him, and said to him,
What seemeth to thee, Simon? the
kings of the earth, from whom
collect they tribute and head money?
from their children, or from strangers?
Simon saith to him, From strangers. 26
Jesus saith to him, Then children of
the free are the children. But that 26
we may not offend them, go to the
sea, and cast a hook, and the first fish
that cometh up, take and open his
mouth, and thou shalt find there a
Stater; take it, and give it for me
and for thee.

Chap. XVIII.

And on that day came near the disci- 1
ples of Jesus, and say to him, Who then
shall be great in the kingdom of hea-
ven? And Jesus called one boy, and set 2
him up amongst them, And said, Verily 3
I say to you, That unless ye be con-
verted, and be as one of these children,

ye shall not enter into the kingdom
4 of heaven. For whoso humbleth
himself as this boy, he *is* great in the
5 kingdom of heaven. And every *one*
that shall receive such as one of these
children in my name, me he receiveth.
6 And every *one* that shall offend one of
these little ones which believe in me, it
were expedient for him that should
be hanged a millstone of an ass on his
neck, and he be drowned in the depths
7 of the sea. Woe to the world from
the offences that are coming! for it is
necessity that offences should come;
but woe to the Man by whose hand
8 come the offences! But if thy hand or
thy foot make thee offend, cut off, cast it
from thee: for it is expedient for thee
that thou shouldest come into life when
thou art halt or when thou art maimed,
and not when thou hast two hands
and two feet shouldest fall into the
9 Gihanna of fire. And if it be that
thine eye make thee offend, pluck out,
cast it from thee: it is expedient for
thee that thou shouldest enter into life
when thou hast one eye, and not
when thou hast two eyes shouldest
10 go into the Gihanna of fire. See
that ye despise not one of these little
ones which believe in me; for I say
to you, That their angels in hea-
ven at all times see the countenance
11 of my Father which is in heaven, And
that the Son of man came that he
might save that which was lost.

But how seemeth it to you? if a 12
man have an hundred sheep, and
one of them stray, doth he not
leave the ninety and nine in the
mountain, and go seek that which
strayed? And when he hath found 13
it, verily I say to you, that he re-
joiceth in it more than those ninety
and nine which strayed not. So 14
willeth not your Father which is
in heaven, that should perish one
of these little ones.

But if thy brother have sinned 15
against thee, reprove him between
thee and him alone: if he hear thee,
thou hast gained thy brother. And 16
if he shall not hear thee, take with
thee again one or two, that at
two and three witnesses' mouth
may stand every word. But if he 17
shall not hear them, tell to the
church: and if the church he shall
not hear, let him be accounted by
thee as a heathen and as a pub-
lican. And verily I say to you, That 18
whatsoever ye shall bind on earth
shall be bound in heaven: and that
which ye shall loose on earth shall
be loosed in heaven. Again, verily 19
I say to you, That if two of you
shall agree on earth concerning what
they shall ask, it shall be to them
from my Father which is in heaven.
For where are assembled two or three 20
in my name, there am I amongst them.

Then drew near to him Simon Cepha, 21

and said to him, my Lord, how many
times if it be that my brother sin against
me shall I forgive him? until seven
22 times? He saith to him, Not seven:
but above seventy seven seven.

23 On this account like is the king-
dom of heaven to a Man, a king, who
wished to take the reckoning from his
24 servants. And when he began to take
the reckoning, came near before him
one of them that was owing to him
25 ten thousand talents. And when he
had not to pay, he commanded that
he should be sold, he and his wife,
and his children, and all that he had
26 should be taken. And that servant
fell, and worshipped his lord, and
said, Have patience toward me, and
27 every thing I will pay thee. And his
lord was compassionate toward him,
and loosed him, also the debt he
28 forgave him. And that servant went
out, and found one of his fellow-
servants, that was owing to him a
hundred denars: and he caught him,
and was throttling him, and was say-
ing to him, Pay me that which thou
29 owest to me. And that his fellowser-
vant fell down, and was entreating of
him, and was saying to him, Have pa-
tience toward me, and I also will pay.
30 But he did not receive his entreaty,
but went, cast him into prison, until
he should pay him that which he
31 owed. But when his fellowservants saw
those *things* which were *done*, it grieved
them much, and they came and shewed
to their lord every thing that was *done*.
Then his lord called him, and said to 32
him, Bad servant, that whole debt I
forgave thee, because thou entreatedst
of me: Wast not thou also indebted 33
that thou shouldest pity thy fellowser-
vant, as I pitied thee? And his lord 34
was angry against him, and delivered
him that he should be tormented, un-
til he should pay all the debt. So 35
shall do to you my Father which is in
heaven, unless ye forgive each his
brother from your hearts.

CHAP. XIX.

And it was when Jesus finished 1
these words, he turned him from
Galilee, and came to the coasts of
Judæa to the other side of Jordan;
And a great multitude came after 2
him; and he healed them there.

And the Pharisees came near to 3
him, and were tempting him, and
were saying, that, Is it lawful for
a Man that he should put away his
wife upon every cause? But he 4
answered and said to them, Have
ye not read, that he who made the
male from the beginning also the
female he made, and said, That 5
on this account the Man shall leave
his father and his mother, and shall
cleave to his wife; and they shall be
both of them one flesh? Wherefore 6
they are not two, but are one flesh.
That which God therefore hath joined,
let not man's son separate. They 7

say to him, Why therefore commanded
Moses that whoso wisheth that he
should put away his wife, let him give
8 her a letter of divorcement? He said
to them, Moses on account of your
heart's hardness he permitted you
that ye should put away your wives:
but from the beginning it was not so.
9 But I say to you, That whoso leaveth
his wife, without the word of adultery,
and taketh another, committeth adul-
10 tery towards her. His disciples say to
him, If so be the case between the
Man and the wife, it is not expedient
11 to take a wife. Jesus said to them, It
is not every man sufficeth for this
same word, but those to whom it
12 is given from God. For there
are eunuchs, that from the womb of
their mother were eunuchs: and there
are eunuchs, that men's sons have
made them: and there are that have
made themselves eunuchs on account
of the kingdom of heaven. But whoso
is able in strength that he should en-
dure let him endure.

13 Then they brought near to him chil-
dren, that he should lay his hand on
them, and pray: and his disciples re-
14 buked them. Jesus said to them, Suffer
the children coming to me, and forbid
them not that they should come to me:
for they which are as these, theirs is the
15 kingdom of heaven. And he laid his
hand on them, and went from thence.

16 And one Man came near and said
to him, Good Teacher, what shall I do,
that I may inherit the life which is for
ever? Jesus said to him, Why askest 17
thou me concerning good? for one
is good, God; but if thou wishest
that thou shouldest enter into life,
keep the commandments. He said 18
to him, Which? Jesus said to
him, Do not kill, and, Do not com-
mit adultery, and, Do not steal,
and, Do not witness the witness of
lying. Honour thy father and thy 19
mother: and, Love thy neighbour
as thyself. That young man said 20
to him, These all of them I have kept
them lo, since I was a boy: what
again am I lacking? Jesus said to him, 21
If thou wishest that thou shouldest
be perfect, go, sell thy property, and
give to the poor, and thou shalt
have treasure in heaven: and take
thy cross and come after me. And 22
when that young man heard this
word, he went while it grieved him,
because he had much property. But 23
Jesus said to his disciples, Verily
I say to you, That it is difficult for
a rich man that he should enter
into heaven's kingdom. But again I 24
say to you, It is easier for a camel
that it should pass through the eye
of a needle, than for a rich man to
the kingdom of heaven. But again 25
when his disciples heard, they were
astonished, and feared much, and
were saying, Who then is able to be

26 saved? Jesus looked on them, and said
to them, This among men's sons is not
possible that it should be; but God is
27 able to do every thing. Then an-
swered Simon Cepha and said to him,
Lo, we have left every thing, and come
after thee; what then shall be to us?
28 Jesus said to them, Verily I say to
you, That ye which are come after
me, in the new birth, when sitteth
the Son of man on the throne of his
glory, also ye shall sit upon twelve
thrones, and shall judge the twelve
29 tribes of the house of Israel. And
every man that hath left houses, and
brethren, or sisters, or mother, or
wife, or children, or lands, on account
of my name, mine, shall receive an
hundredfold, and in the world that
cometh shall inherit the life which is
30 for ever. But many *are* first that shall
be last; and last that shall be first.

CHAP. XX. 1 But like is the kingdom of heaven
to a Man, the lord of a house, which
went out in the morning to hire
2 labourers for his vineyard. And he
agreed with them, with the labourers,
from one denar for one labourer on
one day, and sent them to his vineyard.
3 And he went out at the third hour, and
saw others while standing in the
4 street, and idle. And said to them;
Go also ye to the vineyard, and that
which is right I will give to you. And
5 they went. And he went out again at
the sixth hour, and at the ninth hour,
and did likewise. And he went out 6
at the eleventh hour, and found others
while standing, and said to them, Why
are ye standing and idle all the day?
They say to him, No man hath hired 7
us. He saith to them, Go also ye to
the vineyard; and that which is just
I will give to you. And when it was 8
evening, the lord of the vineyard said
to the master of his house, Call those
labourers, and give to them their hire,
and he began from the last until the
first. But when came those which *were* 9
hired in the eleventh hour, they re-
ceived a denar, a denar. And when the 10
first came, they were supposing that
to them he would give more; and
they also received a denar, a denar.
And when they saw, they murmured 11
against the lord of the house, And say 12
to him, These last have cultivated one
hour, and thou hast made them equal
with us, which have borne the burden
of all the day, and the heat. But he 13
answered and said to one of them,
My friend, do not trouble me: was
it not for a denar thou agreedst with
me? Take thine own, and go; and if 14
I wish that I should give to this last
as to thee, am I not authorized that I 15
should do with mine own that which I
wish? Or is thine eye evil, because I
am good? So shall be the last first, 16
and the first shall be last: for many
are the called, and few the chosen.

And when Jesus was going up to 17

Jerusalem, he was taking with him
his twelve in the way, and said to
18 them between him and them, Lo,
we go up to Jerusalem; and the
Son of man is delivered to the chief
priests and to the scribes, and they
19 shall condemn him to death, And
shall deliver him to the nations, and
they shall mock at him, and scourge
him, and crucify him: and the third
day he shall rise.

20 Then came near to him the mother
of Zebedee's sons, she and her sons,
and she fell, worshipped him, and
21 was asking him something. But he
said to her, What wishest thou? She
saith to him, My Lord, that these
two my sons may sit, one on thy
right, and one on thy left, in thy
22 kingdom and in thy glory. Jesus
answered and said to her, Ye know
not what ye ask. Are ye able
to drink this cup that I am about
to drink? They say, We are able.
23 Jesus saith to them, That ye should
drink this cup ye are able; but
that ye should sit one on my right,
and one on my left, this is not mine
that I should give to you, but to those
for whom it has been prepared by my
24 Father. And when the ten heard, they
were angry against these two brothers.
25 And Jesus called them, and said to
them, Ye know that the chiefs of the
nations are their lords, and their
great ones are authorized over them.
But among you it shall not be so: 26
but whoso wisheth among you that
he should be great, shall be to you a
minister; And whoso wisheth among 27
you that he should be first, shall be
to you a servant: As the Son of man 28
came not that he should be mini-
stered to, but that he should mini-
ster, and that he should give his soul
a ransom for many. But you, seek
ye that from little things ye may be-
come great, and not from great things
may become little.

Whenever ye are invited to the
house of a supper, be not sitting down
in the honoured place, lest should
come he that is more honoured than
thou, and to thee the Lord of the
supper should say, Come near below,
and thou be ashamed in the eyes
of the guests. But if thou sit down
in the little place, and he that is less
than thee should come, and to thee the
Lord of the supper shall say, Come
near, and come up and sit down,
thou also shalt have more glory in
the eyes of the guests.

And while they were going out from 29
Jericho, a great multitude was coming
after him. And, two blind *men* were 30
sitting on the way's side, and when
they heard that Jesus passed, they
were crying and saying, Be compassio-
nate towards us, son of David. And 31
those multitudes were rebuking them,
that they should be silent: but they

lifted up their voice, and say, Be com-
passionate toward us, our Lord, son of
32 David. And Jesus stood, and called
them, and said, What wish ye that I
33 should do for you? They say unto
him, Our Lord, that our eyes may be
34 opened and we may see thee: and he
was compassionate toward them, and
touched their eyes; and in the same
moment they saw, and went after him.

CHAP. XXI. 1 And when he came near to Jeru-
salem, and came to Beth Phage, on the
side of the mount of Beth Zaithe,
then sent Jesus two of his disciples,
2 And said to them, Go to this vil-
lage which is opposite you, lo, ye find
one ass while tied, and her colt at
her side: loose, bring them to me.
3 And if any shall say to you some-
thing, say to him, For their Lord
they are required; and immediately
4 he sends them. But this which
was, *was* that might be fulfilled
that which was spoken of the prophet,
5 which had said, Tell ye to Zion's
daughter, Lo, thy King cometh to
thee, just and meek, and riding upon an
ass, and upon a colt a she-ass's foal.
6 And those disciples went, and did as
7 Jesus commanded them, And brought
the ass, and the colt, and spread their
cloaks, and Jesus rode on the top them.
8 And the great number of that multi-
tude spread their cloaks in the way;
but others were cutting branches
from the trees, and casting them in
the way. And those multitudes that 9
were going before him, and with him,
were crying, and saying, Hosanna to
the son of David: Blessed is he that
cometh in the name of the Lord;
Hosanna in the height; and many
went out to meet him, and were re-
joicing and praising God concerning
all that which they saw.

And when he entered Jerusalem, 10
the whole city was moved, and they
say, Who is this? Those multitudes 11
say to them, This is Jesus the prophet,
which is from Nazareth of Galilee. And 12
Jesus entered into the temple of God,
and expelled from the temple of God
all the buyers and sellers, and Jesus
overthrew the tables of the money-
changers, and the seats of those that
sold doves, And said to them, It is 13
written, that, My house shall be called
the house of prayer for all the nations;
but ye have made it a den of thieves.
And the blind and the deaf came 14
near to him in the temple; and he
healed them. And when the scribes 15
and chief priests saw the wonders
that he did, and the children which
were crying in the midst of the temple,
and were saying, Hosanna to the son
of David, it displeased them, And
they say, Hearest thou not what these 16
say? Jesus said to them, Yea; have
ye never read, that, Out of the mouth
of children and babes I will make
praise? And he left them, and went 17

out to the outside of the city to Beth
18 Any; that he might be there. But
in the morning while he was passing
19 by to the city, he hungered. And he
saw one fig tree in the way, and he
came to it, and found not on it any
thing but leaves only, and said to it,
Again fruits shall not be on thee for
ever. And in the same moment that
20 fig tree withered. And when his
disciples saw, they marvelled and
were saying, How immediately
withered this fig tree! Jesus an-
swered and said to them, Verily I
say to you, That if faith shall be in
you, and ye doubt not, not only like
this of the fig tree shall ye do, but if
ye shall say to this mountain, that,
Be removed, and fall into the sea;
22 it shall be to you so. And what-
soever ye shall ask in prayer, and
believe, ye shall receive.

23 And when he came to the temple,
came near to him the chief priests and
the elders of the people, and say to
him, By what authority doest thou these
things? and who gave to thee this
24 authority? Jesus answered and said
to them, Also I will ask you this word
that ye may tell me, and I will tell you
by what authority I do these *things.*
25 The baptism of John, from whence was
it? from heaven, or from men's sons?
But they were meditating among them-
selves, and were saying, That if we
shall say to him, That from heaven
it is; he will say unto us, And why did
ye not believe in him? And if we 26
shall say, That from men's sons it is;
we are afraid of the multitude; for all
men were holding John as a prophet.
And they say to him, We know not. 27
Jesus said to them, And I also tell
not to you by what authority I do
these *things.*

But how seemeth it to you? There 28
were to one Man two sons; he said to
the first, Go, my son, to-day do work in
the vineyard. He said to him, I do not 29
wish; but afterward his soul repented
him, and he went to the vineyard.
And he said to the other likewise. 30
And he answered and said, Yea, my
lord: and went not. Which of these 31
two seemeth to you that he did the
will of his father? They say to him,
That first. Jesus saith to them, Ve-
rily I say to you, That the publicans
and the harlots go before you to the
kingdom of God. For to you came 32
John in the way of righteousness, and
ye believed him not: but the publicans
and the harlots believed in him:
but ye, not even when ye had seen,
did your soul repent you afterward,
that ye should believe him.

Hear another parable: There was 33
one Man, the Lord of a house, he
planted a vineyard, and surrounded it
with a hedge, and digged in it a wine-
press, and built in it a tower, and de-
livered it to the cultivators, and went.

34 And when drew near the time of
fruits, he sent his servants to the
cultivators, that they might send to
35 him the fruits. And they took them,
those cultivators *took* his servants,
one they beat, and one they stoned,
36 and one they killed. Again, he sent
his servants others which *were* more
than the first: and they did to them
37 likewise. But at the last he sent to
them his son, and said, Perhaps they
38 will have reverence for my son. But
those cultivators, when they saw his
son, said among themselves, This is his
heir; come, we will kill him, and the
39 inheritance shall become ours. And
they took him, and brought him out to
the outside of the vineyard, and killed
40 him. When therefore shall come the
lord of the vineyard, what he will do to
41 those cultivators? They say to him,
that, Evilly, evilly, will he destroy
them, and the vineyard he will deliver
to other cultivators which give the
42 fruits in their season. Jesus saith to
them, Have ye not ever read in the
scripture, that, That stone which the
builders rejected, it is become the
head of the corner: from the Lord
was this, and it is a marvel in our
43 eyes? On this account say I to you,
That from you shall be taken the king-
dom of God, and shall be given to a
44 nation that produceth fruits. For every
one that shall fall on that stone shall
be broken: and every *one* on whom
it shall fall, it will crush him. But 45
the chief priests and Pharisees, when
they heard the allegory, knew that
against them he spake. And they 46
sought that they might take him, and
they were afraid of the people, because
as a prophet they were holding him.

CHAP. XXII.

Again answered Jesus and said to 1
them in allegories, Likened is the king- 2
dom of heaven to a Man, a king, which
made a banquet for his son, And sent 3
his servants that they should call those
that *were* invited to the banquet: and
they did not wish to come.

Again, he sent other servants, and 4
said, Say to those that were invited,
Lo, my supper is prepared, and
my oxen of fatness are killed, and
every thing is prepared: come to
the banquet. But they despised, 5
and one went to the farm, and one
went to the merchandise: But the rest 6
which remained took his servants,
and insulted them, and killed. And 7
that king was wroth: and sent his
army, and destroyed them, those mur-
derers, and their city he burned
with fire.

Then he said to his servants, The 8
banquet is prepared, and those that
were invited were not worthy for it.
Now go out amongst the highways, 9
and whomsoever ye find, call to the
banquet house. And those servants 10
went out amongst the highways, and
collected all that they found, bad

and good: and the banquet house
11 was filled *with* guests. And the
king went in that he might see
the guests, and he saw there a Man
that was not clad in the clothes
12 of the banquet. He saith to him,
My companion, how camest thou
hither, because thou hast not the gar-
ments of the banquet. And he was
13 silent. Then said the king to the
ministers, Seize him by his hands and
by his feet, and take him out to outer
darkness; there shall be weeping and
14 gnashing of teeth. For many are
called, and few chosen.

15 Then went the Pharisees, and took
counsel how they might catch him
16 in talk. And they sent to him their
disciples with the servants of Herod,
and say to him, Teacher, we know
that thou art true, and the way of
God in truth thou teachest, and thou
carest not for man: for thou ac-
17 ceptest not the person of man. Tell us,
What seemeth to thee? *Is it* lawful
to give head-money to Cæsar, or
18 not? But Jesus knew their thoughts,
and said to them, Accepters of per-
19 sons, why tempt ye me? Shew me
the impress of the head-money. And
20 they brought to him a denar. And
Jesus said to them, This image and su-
21 perscription of whom *are they?* They
say to him, Of Cæsar. Then saith he
to them, Give Cæsar's to Cæsar; and
22 God's to God. And when they heard,
they marvelled, and left him, and
went.

On that day came near before him 23
the Sadducees, and say to him, that
there is no resurrection: and they
asked him, and say to him, Teacher, 24
Moses said to us, That if it be that a
man die, while he has no children, his
wife shall be unto his brother, and he
shall raise up seed for his brother.
But there were with us seven bre- 25
thren: the first of them took a wife,
and died, and left not children, and
his wife was unto his brother: Also 26
another likewise, and also the third,
until the seven of them. And last 27
after all of them died that woman her-
self. In the resurrection therefore, 28
unto which of them shall the wife be?
for lo! unto the seven of them she was.
Jesus answered and said to them, 29
Much ye err, and ye know not the
scriptures, nor the power of God. For 30
in the vivification of the dead the Men
take not women, neither are women
unto Men, but as the angels are they of
heaven. But also concerning the re- 31
surrection of the dead, have ye not
read, that God said, that, I am the God 32
of Abraham, and the God of Isaac,
and the God of Jacob? and lo, God
is not of the dead, but of the living.

And when those multitudes heard, 33
they were marvelling at his doctrine.
But the Pharisees, when they saw that 34
he had silenced them, the Sadducees,

35 were assembled near him. And one of
them, a scribe, asked him, while tempt-
36 ing him, and said to him, Teacher,
which commandment is great and
37 first in the law? Jesus said to him,
that, Thou shalt love the Lord thy
God from all thy heart, and from all
thy soul, and from all thy strength.
38 This is the great commandment and
39 the first. And that after it which
is like to it, that, Thou shalt love
40 thy neighbour as thyself. On these
two commandments hangs the law,
41 and the prophets. And while the
Pharisees were assembled, He was
42 asking them, And said, What say
ye respecting the Messiah? the son
of whom is he? They say to him,
43 David's son. He saith to them,
How therefore doth David by the
Spirit of Holiness call him My Lord,
44 for he says that The Lord said to
my Lord, Sit thou on my right, until
I place thine enemies under thy feet.
45 If therefore David call him My Lord,
46 how is he his son? And no man was
able that he should give him an an-
swer, neither also dared any from
that hour to ask him again.

CHAP. XXIII.

1 Then said Jesus to the multi-
2 tudes, and to his disciples, On the
seat of Moses sit the Scribes and
3 the Pharisees. Whatsoever they
say to you, be hearing and doing;
but like their works do ye not: for
4 they say, and do not. And they bind
heavy burdens, and lay them on the
shoulders of men's sons; and they
with one of their fingers touch them
not. For whatsoever they do *is* that 5
they may be seen to men's sons: and
they widen the straps of their Te-
philla, and extend the fringe of their
cloaks. And love the chief sittings and 6
suppers, and the first seats in the syna-
gogues, And greeting in the streets, 7
and wish that men's sons should be
calling them, My Master, My Master.
But you, call ye not, My Master; for 8
one is your Master, the Messiah; and
ye are brethren. And call not Father 9
for you on the earth: for one is your
Father, which is in heaven. And 10
be ye not called Teachers: because
your Teacher is the Messiah. And 11
whoso desireth among you that he
should be great, shall be to you a mi-
nister. For every man who shall exalt 12
himself shall be abased; and whoso
shall abase himself shall be exalted.

Woe to you, Scribes and Pharisees, 13
accepters of persons! because ye shut
the kingdom of God before men's
sons: for ye enter not, neither those
that come to enter suffer ye.

Woe to you, Scribes and Pharisees, 14
accepters of persons! because ye de-
vour the houses of widows, with the
pretence that ye lengthen your
prayers: on this account ye shall
receive more condemnation.

Woe to you, Scribes and Phari- 15

sees, accepters of persons! because ye
compass sea and dry *land* that ye may
make one proselyte, and when that
he is, ye make him the son of Gi-
hanna double over yourselves.
16 Woe to you, blind guides, because
ye say, Whoso sweareth by the temple,
hurteth not; and whoso sweareth by
the gold that *is* in the temple, sinneth!
17 Fools, blinded: which is greater, the
gold, or the temple which itself sanc-
18 tifieth the same gold? And, Whoso
sweareth by the oblation that *is* upon
19 the altar, sinneth. Blinded: which
is greater, the oblation, or the altar
which itself sanctifieth the same obla-
20 tion? Whoso sweareth, therefore, by
the altar, sweareth by it, and by what-
21 soever is upon it. And whoso sweareth
by the temple, sweareth by it, and by
him who dwelleth in it. And whoso 22
sweareth by heaven, sweareth by the
throne of God, and by him that sitteth
upon it.

Woe to you, scribes and Phari- 23
sees, accepters of persons! because
ye tithe mint and anise and cummin,
and have omitted the weighty *things* of
the law, judgment, and pity, and faith:
but these ye should have done, but
those also not have left. Blind guides, 24
because ye strain out from gnats, and
ye swallow camels.

Woe to you, scribes and Phari- 25
sees, accepters of persons! because
ye cleanse the outside of the cup and
of the dish, and from within * *

* * * * * * *
* * * * * * *
* * * * * * *

---

* * * * * * *
* * * * * * *
* * * * * * *

17 that believe in me; these in my
name shall cast out dæmons; with
new tongues they shall speak; ser-
18 pents they shall take up in their
hands; and if any poison of death
they drink, it shall not hurt them; on
the diseased they shall lay their hands,
and they shall become sound.

But our Lord Jesus after that he 19
had commanded his disciples, was
exalted to heaven, and sat on the
right *hand* of God. But they went 20
forth, and preached in every place,
while the Lord *was* with them in all,
and their word he was confirming by
the signs which they were doing.

ENDETH GOSPEL OF MARK.

GOSPEL OF JOHN.

Chap. I. IN the beginning was the Word, and
the Word was with God, and God
2 was the Word. This was in the be-
3 ginning with God. Every thing by
him was; and without him even not
4 one *thing* was. But that which was
in him is life; and the life is the light
5 of the men's sons. And the light in
the darkness was shining; and the
darkness apprehended it not.

6 There was a man's son that was
sent from God, his name was John.
7 This came for testimony that he
might witness respecting the Light,
and that every man might believe at
his hand. He was not that Light, but 8
was a witness of the Light. But it was 9
the Light of the truth, which lighteth
every man's son that cometh into
the world. In the world he was, and 10
the world by him was, and the world
knew him not. To his own he came, 11
and his own received him not. But 12
those which received him, he gave
to them power that they may be the
sons of God, those that on his name

13 believe: Those that not by blood,
and not of the will of the body, and not
of the will of man's son, but of God
14 were born. And the Word became
body, and dwelt among us, and we
saw his glory, as the glory of the
only *son* which *is* of the Father,
while full of grace and truth.

15 And John witnessed respecting
him, and cried, and said, This is he
of whom I said, that he cometh after
me and is before me: because he is
16 anterior to me. And of his fulness
we all of us receive, and grace for
17 grace. Because the law by Moses'
hand was given, and grace and truth
was by the hand of Jesus the Mes-
18 siah. God never has man seen him;
the only Son, which *is* from the bo-
som of his Father, he hath declared
19 to us. And this is the testimony of John
when they sent to him from Jerusa-
lem, the Jews and the chief priests
and the Levites, and ask him, Who
20 art thou? And he confessed, and
21 said, that I am not the Messiah. And
they say to him, And art thou a pro-
22 phet? He said to them, No. They say
to him, And who art thou? tell to us,
that we may give an answer to those
that sent us. What sayest thou respect-
23 ing thyself? He said, I *am* a voice
that crieth in the wilderness, Pre-
pare the way for the Lord, as said
24 Esaia the prophet. And they were
25 sending and saying to him, Why
therefore baptizest thou, if thou
be not the Messiah, nor Elia, nor
a prophet? John said to them, I 26
baptize with water: but among you
standeth he, whom ye know not;
He that cometh after me, he that I 27
am not worthy that I should loose the
straps of his shoes. These *things* he 28
spake *in* Beth Abara beyond the river
Jordan, where John was baptizing.

And on the next day he saw Jesus 29
while coming to him, and said, Lo,
the Lamb of God! Lo, he that bear-
eth the sin of the world! This is 30
he respecting whom I said, that, A
Man cometh after me: and he was
before me, because he is anterior to me.
And I had not known him: but on ac- 31
count that he should be known to
Israel: on this account I came that
with water I should baptize. And 32
John testified, and said, I saw the Spi-
rit that descended like a dove from
heaven and rested upon him. And I 33
had not known him: but he that sent
me to baptize with water, he said to
me, That he whom thou seest that the
Spirit descendeth, and resteth upon
him, he it is baptizeth with the Spirit
of Holiness. And I saw, and testified 34
that this is the chosen *one* of God.

And on the next day was standing 35
Jesus, and two of his disciples
with him; And he looked at Jesus 36
while walking, and said, Lo, the Mes-
siah! Lo, the Lamb of God! And 37

when those disciples of John heard,
38 they went after Jesus. And Jesus
himself turned, and saw them that
they come after him, and said to
them, What seek ye? They say
to him, Our Master, where art
39 thou? He said to them, Come
and ye shall see. And they came
after him and saw where he was,
and with him they were that day: and
40 it was about the tenth hour. And one
of them, of those disciples of John, An-
drius was his name, *was* the brother
41 of Simon Cepha. And he Andrius
saw Simon Cepha, and said to him,
42 We have found the Messiah. And he
took him and came to Jesus. And
Jesus looked at him, and said, * *

* * * * * *

Chap. III. * * to the kingdom of
6 God. That which is born of the
flesh is flesh, because of flesh it is
born; and that which is born of the
spirit is spirit, because God is a
spirit, and of God it is born. And
7 marvel not that I said to thee, That it
is meet for you to be born from above.
8 The wind where it wisheth bloweth,
and its voice only thou hearest,
but not from whence it is come
knowest thou, neither whither it
goeth: so is every man that is born
9 of water and of the Spirit. Nicode-
mus answered and said to him, How
10 is this able to be? Jesus answered
and said to him, Art thou a teacher
of Israel, and these *things* knowest
not? Verily, verily, I say to thee, 11
That that which we know we speak,
and that which we have seen we
testify; and our testimony ye re-
ceive not: if respecting those things 12
that are on earth I have told to you,
and ye believe not, how if respecting
those things which are in heaven I
tell to you, shall ye believe me? No 13
man hath ascended to heaven, but he
that descended from heaven, the Son
of man, which was in heaven. And 14
as Moses lifted up the serpent in
the wilderness, so is it meet for
the Son of man to be lifted up: that 15
every man that believeth in him
should have the life which is for ever.
For thus loved God the world, so that 16
his only Son he gave, that every man
that believeth in him should have the
life which is for ever. For God 17
sent not his Son to the world that
he should judge the world; but
that the world by him might be
saved. Whoso believeth on him is 18
not judged: but also whoso be-
lieveth not is obnoxious, because he
believed not on the name of the
only Son of God. But this is the 19
judgment, that light came to the
world, and the world rather loved
darkness more than the light, because
evil were its deeds. For whoso 20
doeth hateful *things* hateth the

light, and cometh not to the light, that
there may not be reproof to his deeds.
21 But he that doeth the truth cometh to
the light, that his deeds may be seen,
that in God they *are* done.
22 After these things went out Jesus
and his disciples to the land of Judæa;
and there he was going about with
23 them, and was baptizing. Also John
was baptizing in Æn Yon which is
on the side of Salem, because much
water was there: and men were
24 coming, and being baptized. For not
until now was John fallen into prison.
25 But there had been a question be-
tween the disciples of John with the
26 Jews concerning purification. And they
came to John, and say to him, Our
Master, he that was with thee beyond
Jordan and thou testifiedst concerning
him, lo! also he baptizeth, and all men
27 come to him. John said to them, A
man's son is not able to receive even any
thing, unless it be given to him from
28 heaven. But witness ye to me, that I
said, that I was not the Messiah, but I
29 am sent before him. For whoso hath
the bride he is the bridegroom: and
the friend of the bridegroom, he
which standeth and listeneth to him,
and rejoiceth a great joy on account of
the voice of the bridegroom: this there-
30 fore my joy, lo! it is absolute. For to
him it is meet to increase, * * * to
31 decrease. For he * * * above
cometh is above * *: and he
which is of the * * * is of the earth,
* * * the earth speaketh: and he
that from heaven cometh, what 32
* * * * * and heard, testifieth;
and * * * * not every man
* * * * * *. He that hath re- 33
ceived his testimony * * * * *
* * * that God * * true.
For he * * * * * * hath sent 34
him the words * * * * * * *
speaketh: not * * * * * * *
by measure * * * * * * * *
* *. The Father the Son * * 35
loveth * * * * * * * given *
* * * thing * * * * * * *.
He that believeth * * * * * * 36
* hath * * * * * *: and he
that * * * * * * Son shall not
see life; but the wrath of God
abideth upon him.
But * * Jesus knew * * * Chap. IV. 1
Pharisees * * * * that his disci-
ples * * * was more * * * *
John, And Jesus was not baptizing, 2
* * his disciples, * * * Judæa,
and went * * * * to Galilee. * 3
* * * was for him * * * * that 4
he should pass by * * *. And he 5
came * * * * of the Samaritans,
* * * * was * * * * * * * a
village * * * * * * * * seph his
son * * * * but there * * of 6
Jacob * * * sat * * of the fountain
* * * from the labour of the way, 7
And his disciples were entered unto the
fortress that they might buy for them

sustenance. And when Jesus sat, it
7 was about the sixth hour. And one wo-
man had come from Samaria that she
may fill water: Jesus said to her,
Give to me water *that* I may drink.
9 That Samaritan woman saith to him,
Lo, thou art a Jew, how askest thou
me water to drink, because lo, I am
a Samaritan? for the Jews deal not
10 with the Samaritans. Jesus said to
her, If thou wert knowing the gift of
God, and who is this that saith to thee,
Give to me *that* I may drink; thou
wouldest be asking him, and he would
11 give to thee living waters. That wo-
man saith to him, My Lord, thou also
hast not a bucket, and the well is deep:
whence hast thou the living waters?
12 Art thou greater than our father
Jacob, who himself gave to us this
well, and also he drank of it, and his
13 children, and his flock? Jesus said
to her, Every *one* that shall drink
of these waters shall thirst again:
14 And every *one* that shall drink of
those waters which I shall give to him
shall not thirst again for ever; but
those waters that I shall give to him
shall be in him a fountain of waters
15 for the life which is for ever. That
woman saith to him, My Lord, give
to me of those waters that I be not
thirsting, and come drawing from
16 hence. Jesus saith to her, Go, call to
me thy husband, and come hither.
17 She saith to him, I have not a husband.

Jesus saith to her, Well hast thou
said, that I have not a husband: For 18
thou hast had five husbands; and
this whom thou hast now is not thy
husband: this thou hast said true.
That woman saith to him, My Lord, 19
I see thou art a prophet. Our fathers 20
in this mountain worshipped; but ye
also say, that in Jerusalem is the house
of worship. Jesus saith to her, Wo- 21
man, believe me, that the hour com-
eth, that not in this mountain, nor
at Jerusalem, shall ye worship the
Father. Ye worship that which 22
ye know not: and we worship that
which we know, because salva-
tion is from Juda. But the hour 23
cometh, and now is, that the true
worshippers shall worship the Father
in spirit and in truth: for also the Fa-
ther too such worshippers seeketh. For 24
God is a Spirit: and they that worship
him in spirit also it is meet for them to
worship, for those that worship him
in spirit and in truth. That woman 25
saith to him, I know that the Messiah
cometh: and when he cometh, he
declareth to us every thing. Jesus 26
saith to her, I am he that talk with
thee. And while they talk came his 27
disciples, and were marvelling that
with a woman he was talking: But
speaking they spake not to him, that
either, What asked she? or, What
wast thou saying to her? And that 28
woman left her waterpot, and went to

29 the city and saith to the men, Come, see
a Man, which told to me every thing
that I have done: is he the Messiah?
30 And they went out from the city, and
31 were coming to him. But his disci-
ples were entreating of him that he
32 should eat with them bread. He
said to them, I have meat that I may
33 eat which ye know not. They say
one to another, Hath then any brought
34 to him something to eat? Jesus saith
to them, My meat, my own, *is* that I
should do the will of him that sent
35 me, and should finish the work. Say
not ye, That there are four months,
and the harvest cometh? Lo! I say
unto you, that, Lift up your eyes, and
see that the lands are white and ar-
36 rived at the harvest. And already
the reaper receiveth wages, and ga-
thereth fruit to the life which is for
ever: and the sower and the reaper
37 together shall rejoice. For in this
is the word of truth, That another
38 soweth, and another reapeth. And I
sent you to reap that which it is not
you have laboured on it, but those which
have laboured, and ye are entered upon
39 the labour of those. And from that
city many believed on him of the Sa-
maritans on account of the testimony of
that woman, which was saying, Every
thing that I have done he told to me.
40 And when those Samaritans came to
him, they were entreating of him
that he would be with them: and he
was with them two days. And many 41
believed on him on account of his
word; And were saying to that wo- 42
man, that, Now it is not on account of
thy word we believe in him: for we
have heard from him, and know that
truly he is the Saviour of the world.

After those two days Jesus went out 43
from thence to Galilee. For Jesus 44
himself was testifying, that a prophet
in his own city is not honoured.
And when he came the Galilæans re- 45
ceived him, since they saw that which
he did in Jerusalem at the feast: for
also they too had come to the feast.
And He came again to Catna of Gali- 46
lee, where he had made the water wine.

And there was at Capernaum one 47
king's servant, whose son was sick.
When he heard that Jesus came from
Galilee to Judæa, he came to him,
and was entreating of him that he
would come down, and see his son:
because he was near to die. Je- 48
sus said to him, If marks and
signs ye see not, ye will not be-
lieve. The king's servant saith to 49
him, My Lord, come down ere the
boy die. Jesus saith to him, Go to 50
thy house; Lo! thy son liveth. And
that Man believed on the word of
Jesus. And while he was going, his 51
servants met him, and told him, and
said to him that, Thy son liveth. And 52
he asked them that, At what hour be-
came he well? They say to him, Yes-

terday at the ninth hour the fever
53 left him. And his father knew that
it was at that hour, that Jesus said to
him that, Thy son liveth: and he be-
54 lieved, and all his house. This
is the second sign that Jesus did,
when he came from Judæa to Galilee.
CHAP. V. 1 After these *things* was a feast of the
Jews; and Jesus went up to Jerusa-
2 lem. And there was at Jerusalem
one place of bathing, which is called
in Hebrew, Beth Hesda, and there is
3 in it five porches. And in the porches
were lying a multitude of diseased,
and blind, and withered, and lamed.
5 And one Man was there, which
was diseased thirty and eight years.
6 And when Jesus saw him lie, he
knew that he had a long time: he
said to him, Wishest thou that
7 thou shouldest be sound? He said to
him, My Lord, I have not a man which,
when the waters are moved, should
take me down the bathing: and while
I am coming, another before me
8 goeth down. Jesus saith to him, Rise,
take up thy bed, and walk, go to thy
9 house. And at the same moment that
Man was made whole, and walked:
and that same day was the sabbath.
10 The Jews say to him, It is the sab-
bath: it is not lawful for thee that
11 thou shouldest take up thy bed. He
said to them, the same that made me
whole, he said to me that, Take up
12 thy bed, and walk. They say to him,
Who is this Man which said to thee
that, Take up thy bed, and walk?
And he that was healed did not know 13
who he was: for Jesus had turned
himself from the place to another,
on account of the multitude of men
After these *things* Jesus found him 14
that was healed in the temple,
and said to him, Lo! thou art
whole: again sin not, lest should
happen to thee what is worse than
the first. And that Man went, and 15
told to the Jews that, Jesus it is that
hath made me whole. And on his 16
account the Jews were persecuting
Jesus, respecting why he did these
things on the sabbath. But Jesus 17
said to them, My Father until now
doeth works, on this account also
I too work. But the Jews on account 18
of this word were seeking to kill him,
not only because he had broken the
sabbath, but because he had called
God My Father, and was comparing
himself with God. Jesus said to them, 19
Verily, verily, I say to you, That the
Son is not able to do any thing of
his own self: neither that which
he seeth not his Father do: but
what his Father doeth, also the Son
resembles him. For the Father 20
loveth his Son, and whatsoever he
doeth sheweth to him, that he may
do: and what are more than these
works he sheweth him: and marvel
not that I said to you: for as the 21

Father quickeneth the dead and
raiseth them up, so also the Son
quickeneth those that believe in him.
22 For the Father will not judge man,
but all the judgment to his Son he
23 will give it: That every man should
honour the Son, as he honoureth the
Father. And whoso honoureth not
the Son, also honoureth not the Fa-
24 ther which sent him. Verily, verily,
I say to you, That whoso heareth
my word, and believeth him that sent
me, hath the life which is for ever,
and to the judgment cometh not;
because he hath turned himself from
25 death to life. Verily, verily, I say to
you that, Coming is the hour, and even
now is, that also the dead shall hear
the voice of the Son of God, and
26 shall live. For as the Father hath life
in his essence; so hath he given also
to the Son that he should have life in
27 his essence; And hath empowered him
over the judgment, because he is the
28 son of man. And marvel not at this:
because lo! all those that are in the
graves shall hear the voice of God, and
29 live; and shall come forth; and those
that *are* doers of good *things*, shall
be for the resurrection of life; and
those that are doers of evil *things*, shall
30 be for the resurrection of judgment. I
am not able to do any thing of mine
own mind: but as I hear, I judge:
and my judgment is righteous; for I
seek not my will, but I seek the
will of him that sent me. If I tes- 31
tify respecting myself, my testimony
is not true. Another is testifying 32
respecting me; and ye know that
true is his testimony which he testi-
fied concerning me. Ye sent to 33
John, and he testified in the truth.
But I it is not from man's son I re- 34
ceive testimony: but these *things*
I say, that ye might live. He was a 35
candle that burneth and lighteth:
but ye were willing that ye should
exult for a moment in his light. But 36
I have testimony that is greater than
John's: for the works which my Fa-
ther hath given to me that I should
accomplish them, those works which
I do, testify concerning me, that the
Father hath sent me. And the Father 37
which hath sent me, he hath testified
concerning me. His voice ye have
never heard, and his vision ye have not
seen, and his word abideth not in you: 38
because in him whom he hath sent, ye
believe not. Search the scriptures; 39
because in them ye suppose that ye
shall live for ever: and those Scrip-
tures testify respecting me, those
which ye suppose that in them ye have
life, they testify respecting me. And 40
to me ye wish not that ye should
come, that ye might have life.
Glory from men's sons I receive not. 41
But I know you, that the love of God 42
is not in you. I am come in the 43
name of my Father, and ye receive

not me: and if another shall come
in the name of himself, him ye will
44 receive. How are ye able to be-
lieve, which receive glory one of
another, and the glory which *is* from
45 one God ye seek not? Suppose ye
that I am your accuser? Moses is
your accuser, he in whom ye hope.
46 For if in Moses ye had believed, also
in me too ye would believe: for he
47 wrote respecting me. But and if in
the writings of him ye believe not,
how believe ye my words?

CHAP. VI. 1 After these *things* went Jesus to the
other side of the lake of Galilee, of Ti-
2 berius. And after him went a great
multitude, because they were seeing
the signs which he was doing on the
3 diseased. And Jesus had gone up to
a mountain, and there he was sitting
4 with his disciples. And nigh was
the passover, a feast of the Jews.
5 And Jesus lifted up his eyes, and
saw great multitudes that come to
him, and said to Philip, Whence
shall we buy bread, that these men
6 may eat? But he, as trying him,
asked him: for himself was knowing
7 what he *was* about to do. Philip said
to him, Bread of two hundred denars
is not sufficient for them, when
they should eat a little, a little.
8 One of his disciples said to him, An-
drius was his name, the brother of
9 Simon Cepha: There is here a boy,
and there are with him five loaves of
barley and two fishes; but what do
they for these all? Jesus said, Go, 10
make them sit down, the men *in* sit-
tings *and* sittings, but much grass was
in that same place. And the men sat
down, the number five thousand. And 11
Jesus took up those loaves and blessed,
and gave to those that *were* set down;
and so likewise also respecting the
fishes as much as they wished. And 12
when they were satisfied, he said to his
disciples, Collect the fragments which
remain, that not any thing at all be
lost. And they collected, and filled 13
twelve baskets of the fragments of the
five loaves of barley, which remained
from those that had eaten. But 14
those men, when they saw this sign
which he did, were saying, Truly
this is the prophet that cometh
into the world. And Jesus was 15
knowing that they were seeking that
they might seize him, and make him a
king: he left them, and fled again
to a mountain by himself. But when 16
it was evening he went down and his
disciples to the sea, And they sat in a 17
boat, and were coming to the other
side of the lake of Capernaum. And
it had become dark, and Jesus came
not to them. And the wind was risen 18
vehemently, and the lake was troubled
over them. And they had rowed the 19
boat twenty and five stadia, or thirty,
and they saw Jesus while walking on
the waters, and when he came near to

20 the ship, they were afraid. But Jesus
21 said to them, I am. And they were
wishing that they should receive him
into the boat; and at the same moment the boat had drawn near to
the land to which they were going.
22 And on the next day, that multitude which was on the other side of
the lake, which saw that no other
boat was there, but the one in
which the disciples of Jesus went
over, and Jesus was not with his dis-
23 ciples in the boat; And when other
boats came from Tiberius to where
24 they ate the bread, And they saw that
Jesus was not there, neither his disciples, they went down into a boat,
and came to Capernaum, and were
25 seeking Jesus. But and when they
found him on the other side of the
lake, they say to him, Our Master,
26 when camest thou hither? Jesus
said to them, Verily, verily, I say to
you, That it is not because ye saw
the signs ye have sought me, but
because ye ate the bread, and were
27 satisfied. Cultivate not the meat
that perisheth, but cultivate the
meat which abideth to the life that
is for ever, which the Son of man
giveth to you: for this hath God the
28 Father sealed. They say to him,
What shall we do, that we may cul-
29 tivate the works of God? Jesus said
to them, This is the work of God,
that ye should believe on him whom
he hath sent. They say to him, 30
What sign therefore doest thou, that
we may see, and believe in thee?
what cultivatest thou? Our fathers 31
ate manna in the wilderness; as it is
written, that, Bread from heaven he
gave them to eat. Jesus said to them, 32
Verily, verily, I say to you, It was
not Moses gave to you bread from
heaven; but the Father giveth to you
the bread of truth from heaven.
For the bread of God came down 33
from heaven, and is living, and given
to the world. They say to him, Our 34
Lord, at every time give to us this
bread. Jesus said to them, I am 35
the bread of life: whoso cometh to
me shall not hunger; and whoso believeth on me shall not ever thirst.
But I said to you, That ye see, and 36
ye believe not. Whomsoever my 37
Father giveth to me he will come to
me: and whoso shall come to me I
will not cast him out. Because I came 38
down from heaven, it is not that I
should do my will, but that I should
do the will of the Father which sent
me. But this is the will of him that 39
sent me, that every thing which he hath
given to me I should not lose of it any
thing, but should raise it up at the
last day. For this is the will of my 40
Father, that every man that seeth the
Son, and believeth in him, hath the life
which is for ever: and I will raise
him up at the last day. But the 41

Jews were murmuring at him, because
he said, that, I am the bread which
42 came down from heaven; And were
saying, Is not this Jesus, the son of
Joseph, and we know his father?
how saith he, that I came down from
43 heaven? Jesus said to them, Mur-
44 mur not one with another. For no
man is able that he should come to
me, but he whom the Father which
sent me shall draw: and I will raise
45 him up at the last day. For it is writ-
ten in the prophet, that, They shall
be all taught of God. Whosoever
hath heard therefore from the Father,
46 and learned, cometh to me. It is
not because man hath seen the Fa-
ther, but he which is with God, he
47 hath seen the Father. Verily, verily,
I say to you, That whosoever be-
lieveth God, hath the life which
48 is for ever. I am the bread of life
49 which came down from heaven. Your
fathers ate bread in the wilderness,
50 and died. But this is the bread
which came down from heaven, that
51 a man may eat of it, and die. I
am the living bread which came
down from heaven, that whoso shall
eat of this bread, may live for ever:
and that bread which I will give is
my body, which *is* for the life of the
52 world. And the Jews were striving
one with another, and were saying,
How is this *man* able that he should
53 give to us his body to eat? Jesus said
to them, Verily, verily, I say to you,
That unless ye shall eat the body of
the Son of man, and drink his blood,
ye have not life in you. And whoso 54
eateth my body, and drinketh my
blood, hath the life which is for ever;
and I will raise him up at the last
day. My body truly is meat, and 55
my blood truly is drink. Whoso 56
eateth my body, and drinketh my
blood, in me abideth, and I in him.
As the living Father hath sent me, 57
and I live on account of the Father:
whoso shall eat me, shall be living
on account of me. This is the 58
bread which came down from hea-
ven: it is not as that which your
fathers ate, and died: whoso shall
eat of this bread shall live for ever.
These *things* he spake in the synagogue, 59
while teaching in Capernaum. And 60
many from his disciples, when they
heard, were saying, Hard is this
word; who is able to hear it? But 61
Jesus when he knew that his disciples
murmur at this, said to them, Doth
this offend you? But if ye shall see 62
the Son of man while ascending to
where he was of old? It is the spirit 63
that quickeneth; or the body profit-
eth nothing: the words which I have
spoken with you, are spirit, and are life.
But there are of you those that believe 64
not. For Jesus was knowing of old who
it was that betrayeth him. He said 65
to them, On this account I said to you,

that no man is able that he should
come to me, unless it be given to
66 him from the Father. On account
of this many from his disciples went
from with him, and were not walk-
67 ing with him. Jesus said to his
twelve, Do ye also wish to go?
68 Simon Cepha said to him, My Lord,
to whom shall we go? thou hast the
word of the life which is for ever.
69 And we have believed and known
70 that thou art the Son of God. Jesus
said to them, Have not I chosen
you all of you, and lo! even of you
71 one is satan? But he was speaking
concerning Juda the son of Simon
Iscariot: for it was he was about to
betray him, one of the twelve.

CHAP. VII. 1 After these *things* Jesus was walk-
ing in Galilee: for he had not power
to walk in Judæa, because the Jews
were seeking to kill him.

2 And the feast of the Jews was draw-
3 ing near, of tabernacles. And his
brethren had said to him, Turn thee
hence, and go to Judæa, that thy
disciples may see the works which
4 thou doest. For there is not a man
that doeth any thing in secret, and
wisheth that he may be manifest.
If thou do these *things*, shew thyself
5 to the world. For until then not
even his brethren had believed on
6 him. Jesus said to them, My time
until now is not arrived: but yours,
7 your time, always is ready. And the
world is not able to hate you; but
me, the world hateth me, because I
testify concerning it, that evil are
its works. Go ye up to this feast: 8
I go not up to this feast; because
not until now is my time com-
plete. When he said these things, he 9
remained in Galilee. And when his 10
brethren went up, then also he went
up to the feast, not openly, but in se-
cret. But the Jews were seeking him 11
at the feast, and were saying, Where
is he? And much murmuring there 12
was concerning him among the
people: and there were *some* that
say, He is good; and there were *some*
that say, He is not good, but he de-
ceiveth the people. But no man 13
openly was speaking concerning him
on account of the fear of the Jews.

And when the days of the feast of 14
tabernacles were divided, Jesus went
up to the temple, and was teaching.
And the Jews were marvelling, and 15
saying, How knoweth this *man* letters,
who hath not learned? Jesus said to 16
them, My doctrine is not my own, but
of him that sent me. And whoso 17
wisheth that he should do his will,
knoweth this doctrine, if from God it
be, or I from mine own self am speak-
ing. For whoso from his own mind 18
speaketh, seeketh the glory of himself:
and whoso seeketh the glory of him
that sent him, is true, and wickedness
is not in him. Was it not Moses gave 19

you the Law, and no man of you
keepeth its commandments? Me,
20 why seek ye to kill me? Men say to
him, A dæmon is in thee: who seek-
21 eth to kill thee? Jesus said to them,
One work I have done before your
22 eyes, and ye all marvel. On this ac-
count Moses gave to you circumcision;
it is not because it is from him, from
Moses, but because it is from your fa-
thers; and on the day of the sabbath
23 ye circumcise a man's son. And if a
man's son be circumcised on the sab-
bath, that the law of Moses should not
be broken; against me murmur ye,
because a whole man's son I have
made sound on the day of the sabbath?
24 Be not judging *by* faces, *and* faces, but
25 righteous judgment judge. And men
of Jerusalem's children were say-
ing, Is not this he, whom they were
26 seeking to kill? And, lo, openly he
standeth and speaketh, and no man
sayeth any thing to him. Perhaps
truly the elders know that this is the
27 Messiah. But this *man*, lo, we know
him from whence he is: and the
Messiah when he cometh, no man
knoweth from whence he is.

28 And Jesus lifted up his voice in
the temple while teaching, and said,
Me ye know, and from whence I am ye
know: Of myself I am not come, but
he is true that sent me, he whom ye
29 know not. But I know him: because
30 I am with him, and he sent me. And
they sought to take him: and no
man laid on him hands, because his
hour was not come. And many from 31
the multitude had believed on him,
and were saying, When the Messiah
cometh, doeth he more than these
signs, which this *man* hath done?
And the Pharisees heard that men 32
murmured concerning him; and the
chief priests and the Pharisees sent
that they might take him. And Je- 33
sus said, A little other time am I
with you, and I depart to him that sent
me. And ye shall seek me, and shall 34
not find me: and where I go, ye are
not able to come. The Jews say one 35
to another, Whither then goeth this
man, that we find him not? to the seed
of the Aramæans then goeth he teach-
ing, that we find him not? Or what is 36
this word that he spake, that, Ye shall
seek me, and shall not find me: and
where I *am*, ye are not able to come?

And on the great day of the feast, 37
Jesus was standing and cried, and said,
Whoso thirsteth, let him come to
me, * * * * * * * * * *
* * * * * * * * * * * *
* * * * * * * * * * * *
It is not of my own mind I speak with 10 CHAP. XIV.
you, but my Father that is in me,
doeth these works. Believe me that 11
I am in my Father, and my Father
is in me: and if me ye believe not,
even on account of the works believe.
Verily, verily, I say to you, That whoso 12

believeth in me, these works which I
do also he shall do; and what *are* more
than these works * * * ; * *
* * * * * * * * * * * *
15 * * * * * * * * * * keep
16 And I will entreat of my Father, that
he may give to you another Paraclete,
that he may be with you for ever;
17 The Spirit of truth; which the
world is not able to receive, for it
hath not seen it, and not known it:
but ye know it; and with you it
18 dwelleth, and is in you. And I will
19 not leave you orphans: Lo, a little *
* * * * * * * * * * * *
* * * * * * * * * * * *
21 them, he it is loveth me: and whoso
loveth me the Father shall love him,
also I will love him, and also will
22 shew him myself. Juda Thoma
saith to him, Our Lord, what is it that
to us thou art about to shew thyself,
and not to the world? Jesus said to 23
him, Whoso loveth me, keepeth my
word: and my Father will love him,
and I will come unto him, and abode *
* * make * * * * * * * *
* * * * * * * * * * * *
my Father in my name, it shall 26
teach you every thing that I say to you.
Peace I leave to you, my own peace 27
I give to you: it is not as the world
giveth, give I to you. Let not your
heart be troubled, and let it not fear.
Ye have heard that I said to you, 28
that I go, and I come to you. If ye
were loving me, ye would rejoice,
because I go to my Father: because
great * * * * now lo * * * 29

* * * * * * * *

* * * * * * * *

* * * * * * * *

* * * * * * * *

GOSPEL OF LUKE.

* * * * * * * *

* * * * * * * *

* * * * * hast thou done to us so?
because, lo, we with anxiety and
49 much grief were seeking thee. He
said to them, Why seek ye me? know
ye not that it is meet for me that I
should be of the Father's house?
50 But they understood not the word
51 which he spake to them. And he
went down with them, and came to
Nazareth, and was subject to them:
but his mother was keeping all these
52 words in her mind. But Jesus be-
came great in his stature and abun-
dant in his wisdom, and in his favour
with God and with men's sons.

CHAP. III. 1 But in the fifteenth year, in the ad-
minstration of Tiberius Cæsar, and in
the government of Pontius Pilate in
Judæa, while Herod *was* tetrarch in
Galilee, and Philip his brother te-
trarch in the country of Ituræa and
in the region of Trachona, and
Lysania tetrarch in the country of the
2 Habilenes, in the Chief-Priesthood of
Hanan and of Caiapha, the word of
God was upon John, Zacharia's son,
and he was preaching in the wilder-
3 ness, And in all the country of the
borders of Jordan the baptism of re-
pentance for the remission of sins;
4 As it is written in the prophecy of
Esaia the prophet, The voice which
crieth in the wilderness, Prepare ye
the way for the Lord, and make straight
in the plain a path for our God. All 5
the valleys shall be filled, and all the
mountains and heights shall be
made low: and the crooked shall
become straight, and the rough place
a plain; And the glory of the Lord 6
shall be revealed, and they shall see
him all flesh together, because the
mouth of the Lord hath spoken.

And he was saying to those multi- 7
tudes that were coming to him, Off-
spring of vipers, who hath shewed
you to flee from the wrath that
cometh? Produce therefore fruits 8
that are worthy for repentance, and
begin not to say, That the father to
us is Abraham: for I say to you,
That God is able from these stones
to raise up children to Abraham.
And lo, the axe is arrived at the 9
root of the trees: but every tree that
produceth not good fruits is cut
down, and falleth into the fire.

And the multitudes were asking 10
him, What shall we do and live?
He saith to them, Whoso hath two 11
coats, let him give one of them to
him that hath not; and whoso

hath sustenance, let him do like-
12 wise. And also publicans came to
be baptized, saying to him, What
13 shall we do? He said to them,
Collect not any thing more beyond
that which is appointed for you.
14 And the soldiers also asked him,
and say to him, What shall we also
do? He said to them, Oppress
no man, and insult no man; and
let your wages suffice for you.
15 And the men which were hear-
ing him were meditating in them-
selves, and saying, Is then this the
16 Messiah? He said to them, I, lo, I
baptize you with water; * * * *
* * * * * * * * * * * *
* * * * * eating nor drinking,
CHAP. VII. 34 ye say, A devil in him. And the
Son of Man is come eating and drink-
ing; ye say, Lo, a Man a glutton, and
a drunkard, and a friend of publicans
35 and of sinners! And wisdom is jus-
tified of her children.

36 And one Pharisee came, entreated
of him that he would eat with him.
And he entered into the house of that
Pharisee, and when he sat down,
37 There was one woman, a sinner, in
that city, when she knew that he *was*
sitting in the house of that Pharisee,
she took a box of ointment which *was*
38 sweet. And stood behind him at his
feet and was weeping, and with her
tears she wet his feet, and with the hair
of her head was wiping them, and
was kissing his feet, and was anointing
them with that ointment. But when 39
that Pharisee which bade him saw,
he considered in himself, and said,
This *man*, if he were a prophet,
would know who she is, or what *is* the
fame of that woman, the sinner, which
touched him. Jesus said to him, 40
Simon, I have something that I should
say to thee. He said to him, Say,
my Master. Jesus said to him, 41
There were two debtors to one cre-
ditor: one was owing to him five
hundred denars, and one fifty denars.
And when they had not to pay, 42
he forgave them both. Which of
them will love him most? Simon 43
said to him, I suppose that he, to
whom most was forgiven. Jesus
said to him, Thou hast well
judged. And he turned to the wo- 44
man, and said to Simon, Seest thou
this woman? Into thine house I en-
tered, water for my feet thou gavest
not to me: but she with her tears
wet my feet, and with the hair of her
head wiped them. Thou kissedst me 45
not: but she since I entered hath not
ceased to kiss my feet. Thou anoint- 46
edst me not: but she with ointment
which *is* sweet hath anointed my feet.
On this account I say to thee, That her 47
many sins *are* forgiven to her; because
much she loved: for to whom little is
forgiven, he loveth little. He said to 48
her, to that woman, that, Thy sins *are*
forgiven to thee. And they that *were* 49
sitting began saying in themselves,

Who is this that also forgiveth sins ?
50 And he said to that woman, Thy
faith hath saved thee; go in peace.

CHAP. VIII. 1 And after these *things*, he was going
about in the villages and cities, and
preaching the kingdom of God : also
2 his twelve *were* with him, And those
women, which had been healed of evil
spirits and of diseases, Mary which *is*
called Magdalene, out of whom he had
3 cast seven devils, And Johan the wife of
Chuza the steward of Herod, and Susan,
and many others, which were minister-
ing to them from that which they had.
4 And when a great multitude was
collected, and those that were com-
ing to him from the cities, he spake
5 to them in parables: Lo, a sower
went out to sow : and while he sowed,
some fell upon the way side; and
was trodden upon, and the fowl
6 devoured it. And other fell upon a
rock; and because it had no moisture,
7 it failed and withered. Other fell
among thorns; and they sprang up
8 with it, and choked it. And other
fell on good and fruit-giving ground,
and sprang up and produced fruit a
hundredfold. And when he said
these *things*, with a loud voice he
was saying, that, Whoso hath ears
that he may hear, let him hear.
9 And his disciples asked him, What
10 is this parable? He said to them,
To you it is given to know the mys-
tery of the kingdom of God: but to
those without it is not given to them
to know: on this account in allego-
ries it is spoken to them; that while
seeing they may not see, and while
hearing they may not understand.
But this is the parable: The seed is 11
the word of God. And those which 12
are upon the way side are they that
hear the word of God; and the
enemy cometh, taketh the word from
their heart, that they should not be-
lieve and be saved. And that which *is* 13
on the rock are those, which, when
they have heard the word, hastily
with joy receive it; and they have
no root in it, and for a time be-
lieve, and in time of trial are of-
fended. And that which fell among 14
thorns these are they, which hear
the word, and are in care, and
in the riches of the world and in the
pleasures of living are occupied and
choked, and produce not fruits. And 15
that which fell in good ground are
they, which in a pure and good heart
have heard the word, and hold *it*, and
produce fruits with patience.

Another parable he spake, No man 16
lighteth a candle, and covereth it with
a vessel, or setteth it under a bed or
in a hidden place; but setteth it upon
a candlestick, that every man which
entereth may see its light. For there 17
is not any thing that is concealed which
shall not be made manifest; nor that
is hidden, which shall not be known
and come to manifestation. See what 18
ye have heard: for whoso hath it

shall be given to him, and be added to
him; and he that hath not, even
that which he was supposing that he
hath shall be taken from him.
19 And his mother and his brethren were
come to Jesus, and were standing without,
and were not able that they should
see him on account of the multitude of
20 men. And they told to him, Thy mother
and thy brethren stand without,
21 and desire to see thee. But he answered
and said to them, These are
my mother and my brethren, they
which hear the word of God, and do it.
22 And it was on one of these days
Jesus went up *and* sat in a boat, he
and his disciples with him: and he
said to them, Let us go over to that
23 other side of the lake. And while
they were advancing on the sea he
fell asleep: and there was a storm of
wind on the lake; and their boat
was filled from the waves, and was
24 near to sink. And they came near,
awoke him, and say to him, Our
Lord, we are perishing. And he
arose, and rebuked the wind and the
tempest of the waters: and there
25 was a calm. And he said to them,
Where is your faith? But they
while fearing were marvelling, and
saying one to another, Who then is
this, that even commandeth the winds
and the sea, and they obey him!
26 And they arrived at the country of
the Gadarenes, which is over against
7 Galilee. But when he went out to the
land, one Man met him, upon whom
was a devil from a long time, and
he was not clad with clothes, and
he was not dwelling in a house, but
among the tombs, and he was crying
every cry, and smiting himself with
stones. And when he saw Jesus, 28
he cried, and fell down, worshipped
him, and with a loud voice said, What
to me and to thee, Jesus, Son of the
high God? I entreat of thee, torment
me not. For he had commanded 29
that unclean spirit to come out from
the man's son. For a long time
it was cleaving to him: and he was
bound with chains and with fetters
that he might be kept; and he was
breaking his bands, and was cutting,
and was driven of the same devil into
the desert. But Jesus asked him, 30
and said, What *is* thy name? And
he said to him, Legion: because we
are many in him. And those devils 31
were entreating of him that he would
not send them to Gihanna, and not
cast them out. But there was there 32
on the mountain one herd of many
swine which were feeding there: and
those devils were entreating of him
that he would permit them to enter
into that herd of swine. And he
permitted them. And the devils 33
went out from that Man, and entered
into the swine: and all that herd went
straight to a precipice, and they fell
into the sea, and were choked. But 34
when those herdsmen saw that which

was done, they fled, and related *it* in
35 the cities and in the countries. And
the men went out that they might see
that which was done; and they came to
Jesus, and found that Man, from whom
those devils went out, while clothed,
and right-minded, and sitting at the
feet of Jesus: and they were afraid.
36 And they related to them how that Man
37 was saved: And they that saw, again
were entreating of him, that whole
multitude of the Gadarenes, that he
would depart from them; because
great fear had seized them: but he
went up into the boat, and returned
38 from them. But that Man out of
whom those devils went was entreat-
ing of him that he might be with him:
and Jesus dismissed him, and said to
39 him, Return to thine house, and to
thy men's house, and relate to them
those *things* which the Lord hath
done for thee. And he went, and was
publishing in all the city that which
40 Jesus had done to him. And when Jesus
returned, a great multitude received
him: for they were looking for him.
41 And one Man came, Jairus was his
name, and he was a chief of the syna-
gogue: and he fell down before the
feet of Jesus, and was entreating of him
that he would enter into his house:
42 For he had an only daughter, and she
was about twelve years old, and she
was near to die. And while Jesus
went the multitude was pressing him.
43 And one woman whose blood was
running twelve years, and she had
spent all her possessions upon phy-
sicians, and was not able that she
should be healed of any, And she me- 44
ditated in herself and says, If going I
touch even the garments of Jesus I am
healed, and she came near from behind
him, and laid hold of the border of his
garment: and the running of her blood
stopped. And Jesus turned and said, 45
Who is it touched me? And when all
were denying, Cepha said to him, Our
Master, the multitudes press thee and
come, and sayest thou, Who is it
touched me? Jesus said to him, A man 46
touched me: for I know that power is
gone out of me. But when that woman 47
saw that not even this escaped him,
she came while fearing and trembling,
fell down, worshipped him, and told
to the eye of all that people, for what
purpose she had touched him: and
how immediately she was healed she
confessed before every man: but he 48
said to her, My daughter, thy faith
hath saved thee; go in peace. And 49
while he spake, came some from the
house of the master of the synagogue,
and say to him, Thy daughter is
dead; trouble not the Teacher. But
when Jesus heard that they said so, he 50
said to him, Fear not: only believing
believe, and thy daughter shall live.
And when he came to the house of 51
that Man, he suffered no man that
he should enter, except Cepha, and
Jacob, and John, and the father and

52 the mother of the girl. All the men
were weeping over her, and were
lamenting: Jesus said to them, Weep
not; for the girl is not dead, sleeping
53 she sleepeth. But they were laughing
at him, because they knew that she was
54 dead. And he took her by her hand, and
called her, and said to her, Girl, arise.
55 And her spirit returned, and imme-
diately she arose: and he commanded
that they should give to her to eat.
56 And her parents were astonished: and
he commanded them that they should
tell to no man that which was done.

CHAP. IX. 1 And Jesus called them, his twelve,
and gave to them power and authority
over all spirits and devils, and to
2 heal the sick. And he sent them
that they might preach the kingdom
3 of God, and to heal. And he said
to them, Take not any thing for
you for the way, not staff, nor
scrip, nor bread, nor money; and
4 have not two coats. And into that
house which ye enter, there be, and
5 from thence go out. And those which
receive you not, when ye go out from
that city, even the dust also of your
feet shake off, that it may be a testi-
mony for them.

6 And when his apostles went out,
they were both going about in the coun-
tries and in the cities, and were preach-
7 ing, and healing in every place; He-
rod the tetrarch also heard of all these
things that were done: and he was
marvelling, because that men of
them were saying, that John is
risen from the dead; and others say, 8
that Elia has appeared; others say,
that one of the ancient prophets is
risen from the dead. And Herod said, 9
The head of John I cut off: who is
this, of whom I hear these things
concerning him? And he was wish-
ing that he might see him.

And those apostles returned, and re- 10
lated to him every thing that they had
done. And he took them by themselves,
and went to a desert place. And when
the multitudes knew, they departed
after him on foot: and he received
them, and was speaking with them
respecting the kingdom of God: and
those that were in need of healing
he was healing them.

And when the day was near to 12
stand, his disciples came near, and say
to him, We are in the desert, dismiss
these multitudes, that they may go to
the countries that *are* round about,
and to the villages, that they may
lodge in them: or that they may
find for themselves sustenance. Je- 13
sus said to them, Give ye to them to
eat. They say to him, We have not
more than five loaves and two fishes;
except we should go, buy sustenance
for all this multitude. For they 14
were five thousand Men. He said to
his disciples, Make them sit down, fifty
and fifty Men in a sitting. And they 15
did so, and made them all sit down.
And he took those five loaves and 16

two fishes, and looked to heaven,
and blessed over them, and brake,
and gave to his disciples that they
17 should set before the multitudes. And
they all ate, and were satisfied: and
they took up the fragments, that which
they left, full twelve baskets. And
those men which ate of that bread
were about five thousand, besides wo-
men and children.

18 And when he was by himself, and his
disciples with him, he asked them, and
said, What say the multitudes respect-
19 ing me that I am? They say to him,
There are that say, that he is John the
Baptist; others say, that he is Elia;
20 He said to them, And you, what say ye
that I am? Simon Cepha answered
and said to him, Thou art the Messiah.
21 And he rebuked them, and charged
them that they should tell to no man
22 this; And he said, that it is about to
be to the Son of man that he should
suffer much, and be rejected of the
elders and scribes and priests, and be
slain, and on the third day should arise.

23 And he said, Whosoever wisheth
that he should come after me, let
him deny himself, and take up his
cross on every day, and come after me.
24 For whoso wisheth that he should save
his soul shall lose it: and whoso
shall lose his soul on account of
25 me, shall save it. For what shall a
man's son gain, if he possess the
whole world, and lose his soul?
For whoso shall be ashamed of me 26
before men's sons and of those that
are mine, the Son of Man shall be
ashamed of him, when he cometh
in the glory of his Father, and of his
holy angels. But I say to you truly, 27
that there be men that stand here,
which shall not taste death, until
they shall see the kingdom of God
that it cometh in glory.

And it was after these words about 28
eight days, and he took Cepha and
Jacob and John, and they went up to
a mountain to pray. And while 29
praying, the aspect of his face was
altered, and his garments were white
and shining like snow. And, lo, two 30
Men talking with him, Moses and Elia:
Which appeared in glory, and were 31
speaking concerning his decease which
was about that it should be accom-
plished at Jerusalem. And Simon Ce- 32
pha and they that *were* with him became
heavy with much sleep: and when
they awoke, they saw his glory, and
those two men that were standing with
him. And when they began to sepa- 33
rate from him, Cepha said to Jesus,
My Master, it is good that we be
here: and we will make here three
tabernacles; for thee one, and for
Moses one, and for Elia one: and he
was not knowing what he was saying. 34
And while he said these *things*, there
was a cloud, and shadowed over them:
and when they saw these, that they

enter into the cloud, they feared.
35 And a voice was heard from that
cloud, which said, This is my Son,
and my beloved: him hear ye.
36 And when the voice was, Jesus was
found by himself. And they were
silent, and to man's eye told not that
which they had seen in those days.
37 And on that day again, while they
come down from the mountain, a
38 great multitude met him. And one
Man from that multitude cried and
said, Teacher, I entreat of thee, be
compassionate upon my son: he is to
39 me the only *child*. And he hath a
spirit, and suddenly it casteth him;
and he foameth, and hardly it de-
parteth from him when it hath crush-
40 ed him. And I entreated of thy dis-
ciples; and they were not able to
41 heal him and to cast it out. And
Jesus answered and said, O race
perverse and without faith, until when
shall I be with you, and endure you?
42 Bring him to me, thy son hither. And
while he was bringing him, that devil
cast him down, and was agitating him.
And Jesus rebuked that same un-
clean spirit, and healed the boy, and
43 delivered him to his father. And
they all marvelled at the greatness
of God. And while every man was
marvelling at all which he had done,
44 he said to his disciples, Lay ye these
words in your ears: for the Son of
man is about that he should be de-
livered into men's sons' hands. And 45
they were not understanding this same
word, because it was hid from them,
that they should not understand it:
and they were afraid that they should
ask him respecting this same word.
And there had arisen among them this 46
reasoning, that, Which should be great
among them. But Jesus, when he 47
knew their reasonings, took one boy,
and set him up by him, and said,
Whoso receiveth this boy in my 48
name, me he receiveth: and who-
so receiveth me, him that sent me
he receiveth: for he that *is* little
among you like this boy he is great.
And John answered and said to him, 49
We saw one Man that *was* casting
out devils in thy name; and we for-
bad him, because he cometh not with
us after thee. Jesus said to him, 50
Forbid not: for whoso is not against
you is with you.

And it was when the days of his going 51
up were fulfilled, he prepared his coun-
tenance that he should depart to Jeru-
salem, And he sent messengers before 52
his face: and they went, entered into
one village of the Samaritans, that they
may prepare for him. And they re- 53
ceived them not, because his counte-
nance was set to go to Jerusalem. But 54
and when his disciples Jacob and John
saw, they said to him, Our Lord, wish-
est thou that we command that fire
should descend from heaven, and

55 consume them, And he turned, and
rebuked them, and said to them, Ye
56 know not of what spirit ye are. For
the Son of man came not to destroy
souls, but to save. And they departed
to another village.

57 And while *they were* going in the
way, came one Man, *and* said to him,
Lord, I will come after thee whither
58 thou goest. Jesus said to him, The
foxes they have holes, and the birds
of the heavens nests; but the Son of
man, he hath not where that he may
59 lay his head. And he said to another,
Come after me. He said to him, My
Lord, permit me first I may go bury
60 my father and I will come. Jesus said
to him, Leave the dead burying their
dead: and thou, go preach the king-
61 dom of God. Another said to him,
I will come after thee: but, my Lord,
first permit me *that* I may go *and* show
to the children of my house and I will
62 come. Jesus said to him, No man
casteth his hand upon the plough,
and looketh behind him, and is again
fit for the kingdom of God.

CHAP. X.

1 And after these *things* he separated
also other seventy and two, and sent
them two *and* two before his face to
every place and city, to which he
2 was about to go. He said to them,
The harvest is much, and the la-
bourers few: entreat therefore of the
Lord of the harvest so that he would
send forth labourers to his harvest.
Go now: lo! I send you as lambs 3
among wolves. Carry not for you 4
purses, nor scrips, nor shoes: and
salute not any by the way. And in- 5
to that first house which ye enter, be
saying, Peace in this house. And if 6
the son of peace be there, your peace
shall rest upon him: but and if not, it
shall turn upon yourselves. And in 7
the same house be, eating and drink-
ing of theirs: the labourer is wor-
thy of his sustenance. And turn not
from one house to another. And 8
into what city ye enter, and they
receive you, eat every thing which
is set before you: And heal the in- 9
firm that are therein, and be saying,
that, The kingdom of God is come
nigh upon you. But into what city 10
ye enter, and they shall not receive
you in it, go out and say in its streets,
And lo, even the dust, which cleaveth 11
to our feet, we wipe it off: but ne-
vertheless know this that the king-
dom of God is come nigh. I say to 12
you, that for Sodom it shall be tole-
rable in the day of judgment, rather
than for that city.

Woe to thee, Chorazin! woe to thee, 13
Beth Saida! because if in Tyre and
in Sidon had been the mighty works,
which have been in you, perhaps they
had repented, in sackcloth and ashes.
Nevertheless for Tyre and Sidon it 14
shall be tolerable in the day of judg-
ment, more than for you. And also 15

thou, Capernaum, art not thou exalted
to heaven? but to hell shalt thou
16 descend. Whoso heareth you me
he heareth; and whoso injureth you
me he injureth; and whoso injureth
me injureth him that sent me. And
whoso heareth me heareth him that
sent me.
17 And those seventy which he sent
returned with joy, and say, Our
Lord, and even the devils are sub-
18 ject to us through thy name. Jesus
said to them, I saw Satan that he fell
like lightning which falleth from hea-
19 ven. Lo, I give to you power that
ye may be treading on serpents and
scorpions, and all the might of the
enemy: and nothing shall hurt you.
20 Nevertheless in this rejoice not, that
the devils are subject to you; but
rejoice in your names which *are*
21 written in heaven. And in the same
hour he rejoiced in the Spirit of holi-
ness, and said, I thank thee, the Fa-
ther, Lord of heaven and of earth,
that thou hast hid these *things* from the
wise and from the prudent, and hast
revealed them to children: yea, my
Father; because so was the will before
22 thee. Every thing is delivered to me
from my Father: and no man knoweth
who is the Son, but the Father; nor
who is the Father, but the Son, and he
to whom the Son shall wish that he
23 should reveal to him. And he turned
to his disciples, and said to them,
Happy the eyes which see that
which ye have seen: I say to you, 24
that many prophets and kings have
wished that they might see that which
ye see, and have not seen; and to
hear that which ye hear, and have not
heard. And while he said these *things*, 25
one taught of the law came near,
who was standing, that he should
tempt him. He said to him, Teacher,
what shall I do that I may inherit the
life which is for ever? Jesus said to 26
him, In the law how *is it* written?
and how hast thou read? He said 27
to him, that, Thou shalt love the Lord
thy God from all thy heart, and from
all thy might, and from all thy soul,
and from all thy mind; and thy
neighbour as thyself. Jesus said to 28
him, Correctly thou hast said: these
do, and thou livest. But he was 29
wishing to justify himself: he said to
Jesus, And who is my neighbour?
Jesus said to him, One Man was go- 30
ing down from Jerusalem to Jeri-
cho, and fell into thieves' hands, and
they stripped him, and smote him,
and left him between dead and alive
and departed. And it happened one 31
priest was going down by that way:
and he saw him, and passed him.
And also a Levite, when he arrived at 32
that place, saw him, and passed him.
But one Samaritan, while he was jour- 33
neying in the same way and arrived
near him, saw him, and was compas-

34 sionate towards him. And went near,
and bound up his wounds, and poured
upon them wine and oil, and made
him ride upon his ass, and brought
35 him to an inn, and fed him. And
on the morning of the day, he took
out two denars, gave them to the
host, and said, Feed him; and when
I am returned, what is expended
by thee, again I repay to thee.
36 Which of these three seemeth to
thee that he was the neighbour of
him that fell into thieves' hands?
37 He said to him, He that was compassionate
upon him. Jesus said
to him, Go, and be thou also doing
likewise.

38 And while they were going in the
way, he entered into one village: and
one woman whose name *was* Martha
39 received him in her house. And she
had a sister whose name *was* Mary, and
she came, sat at the feet of our Lord,
40 and was hearing his words. But Martha
was occupied with much serving,
and came saying to him, My Lord, dost
thou not care respecting me that my
sister hath left me by myself that I
should serve? bid her *be* helping me.
41 He said to her, Martha, Martha, my
care and the anxiety of me is with
42 thee about many *things*: But one
thing is requisite: Mary hath chosen
for her the good part, and it shall
not be taken from her.

CHAP. XI. 1 But and while he was praying in one
place, after that he ceased a little
from his prayer, one of his disciples
said to him, Our Lord, teach us to
pray, as John taught his disciples.
He said to them, When ye pray, be 2
saying, Our Father which *art* in heaven,
Hallowed be thy name. And
come thy kingdom. And give to us 3
bread continual of every day. And 4
forgive us our sins; and may we also
forgive every *one* that is indebted to
us. And bring us not into temptation;
but deliver us from evil. And Jesus 5
said to them, Who is he of you that
shall have a friend, and he shall come
to him in the middle of the night,
and shall say to him, My friend,
lend me three loaves; Because my 6
friend is come to me from the way,
and I have not any thing that I
may set before him? And he shall 7
answer from within and say to him,
Trouble me not: because the door
is shut, and the children *are* with
me in bed; I am not able that I
should rise, *and* give to thee. I say 8
to you, That if on account of his
friendship he will not rise *and* give to
him, on account of his importunity he
will rise and give to him as much as
is requisite for him. And also I say 9
to you, Ask, and it shall be given to
you; knock, and it shall be opened
to you. For every man that asketh 10
receiveth; and every *one* that seeketh
findeth; and every *one* that knocketh

11 it is opened to him. But which
of you that his son shall ask him
bread offers to him a stone? or if he
ask him a fish, for a fish gives he to
12 him a serpent? And if he shall ask
him an egg, offers he to him a scor-
13 pion? And if ye that are evil, know
good gifts to give to your children:
how much rather will the Father from
heaven give the Holy Spirit to them
that ask him?

14 And it was while he was casting
out a devil from the dumb, and
when that devil was gone out, that
dumb spake; and those multitudes
15 marvelled. And men from the Phari-
sees said, By Beelzebub the head of the
dæmons this *man* casteth out devils.
16 But others while they were tempting
him, were asking him a sign from
17 heaven. But he, while he knew their
intention, said to them, Every king-
dom that shall be divided against it-
self shall be desolate; and every
house that is divided against a house
18 falleth. And if Satan be divided against
himself, how shall his kingdom stand?
because ye say that by Beelzebub I
19 cast out devils. But and if I by Beel-
zebub cast out devils from your
sons, by what do your sons cast
them out? On this account they
20 shall be for you judges. But if by
the finger of God I cast out devils,
then the kingdom of God is come near
21 upon you. But when a strong man
while been armed keepeth his palace,
in peace is his property: But if one 22
that is stronger than he shall come,
and overcome him, he shall both take
away his armour on which he was
trusting, and also divideth his spoil
for him. Whoso is not with me is 23
against me: and whoso gathereth
not with me scattering scattereth.

The unclean spirit when it is gone 24
out of a man's son goeth wandering
about in places in which there is no
water, that it may find rest for itself;
and when it has not found, it saith, I
will return, go to my house from
whence I came out. And when it is 25
come, and hath found that it *is* swept
and garnished, It goeth, taketh seven 26
other spirits that are worse than itself:
and they enter and dwell in him: and
the end of that man's son is worse
than his beginning.

And while he said these *things*, 27
one woman from the midst of the
multitude with a loud voice said to
him, Happy the womb that bare
thee, and the paps which suckled
thee. Jesus said to her, Happy they 28
which hear the word of God, and
keep it.

And when the multitudes were 29
assembled, he began to say, This race
is an evil race: it seeketh a sign;
and a sign shall not be given to it.
But as Jonan was a sign to the 30
Ninevites, so likewise also the Son of

31 man *is* to this race. The queen of the
south shall stand in the judgment with
this race, and shall condemn them:
because she came from the boundaries
of the earth that she may hear the
wisdom of Solomon; and, lo, *one* that
32 *is* greater than Solomon *is* here! The
Men, Nineveh's sons shall stand
in the judgment with this race, and
shall condemn it: because they re-
pented at the preaching of Jonan;
and, lo, *one* that *is* greater than Jonan
is here.

33 No man lighteth a candle, and
setteth it under a bushel or in a
hidden place, but setteth it upon a can-
dlestick, that they which come in may
34 see its light. For the candle of the
body is the eye: when thine eye there-
fore shall be single, also thy whole
body is luminous: but if thine eye be
35 evil, also thy whole body is dark. Be
therefore cautious lest the light which
36 *is* in thee become dark. And if the
light which *is* in thee be dark, thy
darkness how great will it be!

37 And one Pharisee was entreating of
him that he would dine with him: and
38 he went in *and* sat down. And that
Pharisee had begun saying in his mind,
that, Why washed he not before his
39 dinner? Our Lord said to him, Ye
Pharisees, the outside it is of the cup
and of the dish ye make clean; and
your inside is full of rapine and
40 evil. Little of mind, was it not he
who made that which *is* without also
made that which is within? But that 41
which is within you give it *in* justice;
and lo, every thing is clean to you.
But woe to you, Scribes and Phari- 42
sees! because ye tithe mint and rue
and all herbs, and ye pass over judg-
ment and over the love of God: but
these ye should have done, but those
also not have left.

Woe to you, Scribes and Pharisees! 43
because ye love the honoured seats in
the synagogues, and salutation in the
streets. Woe to you, because ye are 44
sepulchres, and men's sons walk over
you and know not. And one of the 45
Scribes answered and said to him,
Teacher, while thou sayest these
things even us also thou reproach-
est. He said to him, Also to you, woe, 46
Scribes! because ye take up heavy
burdens and set them on the shoulders
of men's sons, and you, not even with one
of your fingers touch ye them. Woe to 47
you! because ye build the sepulchres
of the prophets, whom your fathers
killed. Therefore ye testify and ye con- 48
fess to the deed of your fathers: and
ye are the sons of those murderers.
On this account the wisdom of God has 49
said, I will send amongst them pro-
phets and apostles, *some* of them they
shall kill and persecute: That may 50
be required the blood of all the pro-
phets, which has been shed, lo, from
when the world was created until this

51 race; From the blood of Abel
even to the blood of Zacharia, Ba-
rachia's son, who was killed between
the altar and the temple: verily
I say to you, That it shall be re-
quired from this same race.

52 Woe to you, Scribes! because ye
have hidden the keys of knowledge:
ye entered not, and those that enter
53 ye hindered. And when he had said
these *things* against them in the sight
of all the people, he began to be abo-
minated by the Scribes and Pharisees,
and they were disputing with him con-
54 cerning many *things:* And they were
seeking to lay hold of a cause against
him, that they might be able that they
CHAP. XII. 1 should accuse him. And when a
great multitude was gathered to-
wards him, so that they should tread
upon one another, he began to say
to his disciples, First beware of the
leaven of the Pharisees, which is ac-
2 cepting of persons. For there is
not any thing which is concealed,
that shall not be revealed; nor that
is hid, which shall not be known.
3 For those *things* which ye have said
in darkness shall be heard in the
light; and that which in the closets
ye have whispered in the ears shall
be proclaimed upon the roofs.

4 But I say to you my friends, Be
not afraid of those that kill the body,
and afterwards are not able to do
5 any thing. But I will shew you of
whom ye should be afraid: Be afraid
of him, who after that he hath killed
hath power to cast into Gihanna; yea,
I say to you, that, Of this *one*, it is
meet to be afraid. Five sparrows 6
are sold for an assar, and one of them
is not forgotten before God. For even 7
the hairs of the hair of your head are
numbered by him. Be not afraid
therefore: because that ye are much
better than an abundance of sparrows.
But I say to you, That every *one* that 8
shall confess me before men's sons,
also the Son of man shall confess
him before his holy angels: And he 9
that shall deny me before men's sons
shall be denied before the angels
of God. And every *one* that shall 10
speak a word against the Son of man,
it shall be forgiven him: but whoso
shall blaspheme against the Spirit of
Holiness, it shall not be forgiven him.
But when they bring you to the syn- 11
agogues, before principalities, and
governors, be not anxious how ye
shall apologize, or what ye shall say:
For the Spirit of Holiness shall teach 12
you in that hour what it is meet that
ye should say.

And one Man of that multitude said 13
to him, Teacher, speak to my brother,
that he be dividing with me the land
and the inheritance. But he said to 14
him, Man, who set me over you a
judge? And he said to the multi-
tudes, Beware of all covetousness:

because it is not in the superfluities of
many possessions men's sons have life.
16 And he spake this parable to them,
One rich Man, his land had produced
17 him much produce: And he was con-
sidering in himself, and saying, What
shall I do, because I have not where
18 I may carry my produce? I will
pull down my barns, and build and
enlarge them, and collect in them
19 my produce. And he said to his
soul that, Lo, many good *things* are
laid up for thee for many years;
be at ease, and eat, and drink, and
20 be merry. God said to him, Defi-
cient of understanding, lo, in this night
they require thy soul of thee: those
things which thou hast prepared, for
21 whom shall they be? So is he whoso
layeth up for himself treasures, and
is not rich in God.
22 And he said to his disciples, On
this account I say to you, Be not
anxious for *the things* of your soul,
what ye shall eat; neither also
the things of the body, what ye
23 shall put on: for the soul is better
than sustenance, and the body than
24 raiment. Consider the ravens: that
they sow not and reap not; and they
have no storehouses nor barns; and
God nourisheth them: how much
25 therefore are ye better than they? For
which of you while being anxious is
able to add upon his stature one cubit?
26 But if not even a little *thing* ye are
able to do, why are ye anxious about
the rest? Consider the lilies of the 27
plain how they spin not and weave
not; and I say to you, that not even
Solomon in all his glory was clad
like them. But if the grass of the 28
hills which is to-day on the hills, and
to-morrow drieth up and falleth into
the oven, God clothe; how much
rather you therefore, deficient of faith?
Seek not therefore what ye shall eat, 29
and what ye shall drink, and what ye
shall be clad with, and be occupied
in these. For all these, the nations 30
it is of the earth seek them: but your
Father knoweth that also for you they
are requisite. You henceforth, seek 31
ye the kingdom of God; and these of
more shall be added to you.

Fear not, little flock; because your 32
Father wisheth that he should give
you the kingdom. Sell whatsoever ye 33
have, and give justice; and make
for you purses which wear not out,
and also a treasure that faileth not in
heaven, where the thief arriveth
not, neither also the moth corrupteth.
And where your treasure shall be, also 34
your heart too will be there. Be 35
your loins girded, and your candles
burning. And ye shall be like to men 36
that expect their lord, when he shall
cease from the banquet-house; that
when he cometh and knocketh, imme-
diately they may open to him. Hap- 37
py those servants, whom their lord

shall come *and* find them watching:
verily I say to you, that he shall gird
his loins, and make them sit down, and
38 will minister. And if in the first watch
he shall come and find them watch-
ing, happy they, because he shall make
them sit down and will minister;
or if in the second watch or the third
he shall come and find them watch-
39 ing, happy they. But this know,
that if the lord of the house had known
at what hour cometh the thief, he
would not have suffered that his house
40 should be broken through. Also you,
be prepared: because at an hour that
ye know not, the Son of man shall
41 come. Cepha said to him, My lord,
to us is it thou speakest this parable,
42 or even to every man? Our Lord said
to him, Who is the authorized *person*
faithful and wise and good, whom his
lord shall set over his servants, that he
may give them the portion in its sea-
43 son? Happy that servant, when his
lord shall come *and* find him that he
44 doeth so. Truly I say to you, that
he will set him over all his posses-
45 sions. But if that servant shall say
in his heart, that, My lord delayeth
to come; and shall begin to beat those
servants and handmaidens, and to eat
46 and to drink, and to be drunken; The
lord of that servant shall come also
in a day that he supposeth not, and
at an hour that he knoweth not, and
shall divide him, and shall set his
share with those that believe not. The 47
servant, which knew the will of his
lord, and prepared not for him accord-
ing to his will, shall be beaten many
stripes. And he that knew not, and 48
did any thing which is worthy of stripes,
shall be beaten few stripes. For every
one to whom shall be given much,
much he shall require at his hand: and
to whom they have committed much,
the more shall they require of him.
For it is a fire I am come that I should 49
cast on the earth; and what wish I, if
already it be kindled? And I have a 50
baptism that I should be baptized; and
how much am I straitened until it be
dismissed! Suppose ye that I am come 51
that I should make peace on earth? I
say to you, that, No; but divisions:
For from now shall be five in one 52
house, they shall be divided, three
against two, and two against three.
The father shall be divided against 53
his son, and the son against his father;
the woman against her daughter, and
the daughter against her mother; and
the mother-in-law against her daugh-
ter-in-law, and the daughter-in-law
against her mother-in-law.

And he was saying to the multitudes, 54
When ye have seen a cloud that riseth
from the west, ye say that, There is
rain; and it is so. And when the 55
south *wind* bloweth, ye say, There is
heat; and it is. Accepters of persons, 56
the face of the heaven and of the earth

ye know to prove; this time and
57 its signs search ye not? And in
yourselves judge ye not the truth?
58 When thou goest with thine adversary to the ruler, whilst thou art with him in the way, give him his convenience that thou mayest be delivered from him; lest he convict thee before the judge, and the judge deliver thee to the exactor, and the exactor
59 cast thee into prison. I say to thee, that thou shalt not come out from thence, till thou shalt pay the last Shamun.

CHAP. XIII.
1 And at that same time came men and told to him respecting those Galilæans, whose blood Pilate min-
2 gled with their sacrifices. Jesus answered and said to them, Suppose ye that these Galilæans were sinners more than all the Galilæans, that so
3 it happened to them? I say to you, that, No: but also you, unless ye shall repent, so shall all of you perish.
4 And those eighteen, upon whom the tower in Shiloh fell, and slew them, suppose ye that they were sinners more than all the men's sons that
5 dwell in Jerusalem? I say to you, that, No: but also you, unless ye repent, shall so perish.
6 And he was speaking this parable; One Man had a fig tree in his vineyard; and he came, sought on it fruit,
7 and found not. He said to the cultivator, Lo, three years since I come *and* seek fruit on this same fig tree, and I find not: cut it down; why
cumbereth it the ground? That 8
cultivator said to him, My lord,
leave it also this year, till I shall cul-
tivate it and dung it: And if it pro- 9
duce fruit, *well*, and if not, thou shalt cut it down to the quick.

And while he was teaching on the 10
sabbaths in one of the synagogues:
And one woman there was which 11
had a spirit eighteen years, and was bent, and was not able that she should
erect herself at all. And Jesus saw 12
her, and called her, and said to her, Woman, thou art loosed from thine
disease. And he laid his hands on 13
her: and immediately her stature was erect, and she was glorifying God.
And the master of the synagogue an- 14
swered while he was angry because that Jesus was healing on the sabbath, and said to the multitudes, Six are the days in which it is right to work: on them be coming and be healed, and not on the day of the sabbath.
Jesus answered and said to him, 15
Accepter of persons, each one of you doth he not loose his ox or his ass from the stall on the day of the sab-
bath, and go watering him? But this 16
woman who is a daughter of Abraham, whom the Devil hath bound, lo, eighteen years, was it not meet that she should be loosed from this bond on the day of the sabbath?

17 And when he had said these *things,*
all those that were standing against
him were ashamed: and all the people
was rejoicing in all the wonderful
things that were done by his hand.
18 And he was saying, To what is the
kingdom of God like? and to what
19 shall I liken it? It is like to a grain
of mustard seed, which a Man took,
cast it into his garden; and it grew
large, and became a tree; and the fowl
of the heaven lodged in its branches.
20 Again he said, To what shall I liken
21 the kingdom of God? It is like
to leaven, which a woman took and
mixed in three measures of meal, till
22 it all should be leavened. And he was
going about in the villages and cities,
and was teaching.
23 And while he went to Jerusa-
lem, came one and was asking him,
and saying, My lord, are they few
that be saved? Jesus said to him,
24 Strive to enter by the strait gate:
for I say to you, that many shall
seek to enter, and shall not be able.
25 From the hour that the Lord of the
house shall rise, and shall shut the
door, and ye be standing without, and
knocking at the door, and saying, Our
Lord, Our Lord, open to us; and he
shall answer and say to you, I know
26 you not whence ye are: Then shall
ye begin to say, Before thee we have
eaten and drunk, and in our streets
27 thou hast walked. Then he shall say
to you, Verily I say to you, that I
know you not whence ye are; sepa-
rate you from me, for all ye are
workers of falsehood. There shall 28
be weeping and gnashing of teeth,
when ye shall see Abraham, and
Isaac, and Jacob, and all the prophets,
in the kingdom of God, and ye shall
be expelled to the outside. And they 29
shall come from the east, and from the
west, and from the south, and from
the north, and shall sit down in the
kingdom of God. And there are last 30
which shall be first, and first last.

And in those same days came near 31
men from the Pharisees, and say to
him, Get thee out, depart hence: be-
cause Herod seeketh to kill thee.
He said to them, Go, tell to this same 32
fox, Lo, I cast out devils, and my cures
I perform to-day and to-morrow, and
on the third day I am perfected. Ne- 33
vertheless it is right for me that to-day,
and to-morrow, and after to-morrow,
I should go about: because it is not
possible that a prophet should perish
outside of Jerusalem. Jerusalem, 34
Jerusalem, which hast killed the pro-
phets, and stoned them that were sent
unto thee; how many times have I
wished to gather together thy children,
as a hen that gathereth her chickens
under her wings, and ye would not!
Lo, your house left to you desolate: I 35
say to you, that ye shall not see me,
until shall come the day that ye shall

Chap. say, Blessed is he that cometh in the
XIV. 1 name of the Lord. And when he
entered into the house of one of the
chiefs of the Pharisees that he might
eat bread on the day of the sab-
bath, they were watching that they
2 might see what he did. And one
3 Man dropsical was before him. Jesus
answered and said to the scribes and
to the Pharisees, that, Is it authorized
4 to heal on the sabbath or not? And
they were silent. And he took him,
and healed him, and let him go;
5 and said to them, Who is he of you
that his son shall fall or his ox or his
ass into a pit on the day of the sabbath,
and doth not immediately draw him
6 up? And they were not able to give to
him an answer respecting these *things*.
7 And he was speaking this parable, to
those which were invited, and were
choosing the chief seats; saying to
8 them, When thou art invited to a ban-
quet, go not *and* sit down in the ho-
noured place; lest there be there
he who is more honoured than thou;
9 And he shall come that invited thee
and him and shall say to thee, that,
Give place to this *man;* and then while
ashamed thou shalt sit down in the last
10 place; But when thou art invited, go
sit down in the last place; that when
he cometh that invited thee, he may
say to thee, My friend, go up above:
and thou shalt have glory in all the
11 guests' eyes. For every *one* that shall
exalt himself shall be abased; and
every *one* that shall abase himself shall
be exalted. And he was saying also 12
to the lord of the supper, When thou
makest a dinner or a supper, call not
thy friends, nor also thy brethren,
nor thy kinsmen, nor thy neighbours
which be rich; lest they also call
thee, and a recompence be to thee.
But when thou makest a supper, 13
call the poor, and the blind, and the
lame, and the afflicted: And happy 14
thou; because they have not that
they may recompense thee: and thy
recompense shall be at the resurrec-
tion of the just. And when one of 15
them that were sitting heard these
things, he said to him, Happy he that
shall eat dinner in the kingdom of
God. Our Lord said to him, One Man 16
had made a great supper, and called
many: And sent his servant at the time 17
of sitting down that he should tell to
them that were invited, that they
should come; For lo, every thing is
ready. And they began immediately 18
to make excuse. The first said to him,
I have bought a field, and I am pressed
that I should go out *and* see it: I en-
treat of thee, Excuse me. And another 19
said, Five yoke of oxen I have bought,
and I go that I may prove them: I
entreat of thee, Excuse me. And the 20
third said, I have taken a wife, I am
not able that I should come. And 21
that servant came, told these *things*

to his lord. Then the lord of the
house was angry and said to his ser-
vant, Go out quickly to the streets
and lanes of the city, and bring in
hither the poor, and the maimed, and
22 the afflicted, and the blind. And the
servant said, My lord, lo, that which
thou commandedst is done, and yet
23 there is room in the sitting. The lord
said to his servant, Go out to the ways
and among the hedges, and make
that they come in, that my house
24 may be filled. For I say to you,
That they shall not one of those men
which were called taste of my supper.

25 And while the multitudes were
going with him, he turned *and* said to
26 them, Whoso cometh to me, and hateth
not his father, and his mother, and
his brothers, and his sisters, and his
wife, and his children, even him-
self, is not able that he shall be a
27 disciple to me. And whoso taketh
not up his cross, and cometh after
me, is not able that he should be a
28 disciple to me. For who is he of you,
that wisheth that he should build a
tower, and does not first sit reckoning
its costs, if it be *that* he have to finish
29 it? Lest if he should lay the founda-
tion, and was not able that he should
finish, all that see may be mock-
30 ing at him and saying, This Man
began that he shall build a tower,
and was not able that he should
31 finish. Or, who is the king, that goeth
to contend with another king, and con-
sidereth not first whether he be able
with ten thousand to meet him that
cometh against him with twenty
thousand? And if not, while far 32
off from the battle-place, he sendeth
ambassadors, and entreateth of him
respecting peace. So every man of 33
you that leaveth not all his posses-
sions, is not able that he should be
my disciple. Good salt is: but if 34
even the salt be insipid, with what
shall it be salted? It goeth not to 35
the land, nor to the dung; but is
cast out. Whoso hath ears that may
hear, let him hear.

CHAP. XV.

And the publicans and sinners were 1
coming near to him that they might
hear him. And the scribes and Pha- 2
risees were murmuring and saying,
This Man receiveth sinners, and eat-
eth with them. He spake to them this 3
parable, Who is he of you, that hath
an hundred sheep, and one of them 4
shall be lost, leaveth he not the ninety
and nine in the plain, and goeth, seek-
eth that which was lost, until he shall
find it? And when he hath found it, 5
he layeth it upon his shoulders, and
rejoiceth; And cometh to his house, 6
and calleth his friends and his neigh-
bours, and saith to them, Rejoice with 7
me; because I have found my sheep
which was lost. But I say to you, 8
that so shall be joy in heaven over
one sinner that repenteth, rather

than ninety and nine just *persons*, for
whom repentance is not requisite.
8 Or who is the woman that hath
ten drachms, and shall lose one of
them, lighteth she not a candle, and
sweepeth the house, and seeketh it
9 diligently till she shall find it? And
when she hath found it, she calleth
her friends and her neighbours and
saith to them, Rejoice with me; be-
cause I have found my drachm which
10 was lost. I say to you, that so
joy shall be before all the angels
of God over one sinner that repenteth.
11 He was saying to them again, One
12 Man had two sons: The younger said
to him, My father, give me the in-
heritance that cometh to me from thy
house. And he divided to them all
13 his possessions. And after a few days
that his younger son collected what-
soever came to him, and went to a
distant country, and there dissipated
his possessions in those meats which
were not meet, because he was living
14 prodigally with harlots. And when
he finished every thing that he had,
and there was a severe famine in
15 that country; He went, joined himself
to one of the sons of that country;
and he sent him to the field to feed
swine. And he was lusting to eat of
16 those husks of the sea which the swine
were eating: and no man gave to
him. And when he came to him-
17 self, he said, How many hirelings are
there now in my father's house to
whom bread abounds, and I am
perishing here from my hunger! But 18
I will arise, go to my father, and say
to him, My father, I have sinned
against heaven, and before thee, And 19
am not worthy henceforth that I should
be called thy son: make me as one of
thy hirelings. And he arose, *and* came 20
to his father. And while he was dis-
tant, his father saw him, and was com-
passionate towards him, and ran, fell
upon his neck, and kissed him. And 21
his son said to him, My father, I have
sinned against heaven, and before
thee, and henceforth I am not wor-
thy that I should be called thy son.

* * * * * *
* * * * * *
* * * * * *
* * * * * *
* * * * * *
* * * * * *
* * * * * *
* * * * * *
* * * * * *
* * * * * *

CHAP. XVII.

Let them not deceive you, and 23
go not. For as the lightning light- 24
eneth from the top of heaven, and
even unto its extremities: so shall
be the the day of the Son of man.
But first he is about that he should 25
suffer in many *things*, and that
he should be rejected of this race.

26 And as it was in Noah's days, so
shall it be in the days of the Son of
27 man, that they were eating, and drink-
ing, and were taking wives, and were
giving to husbands, until the day that
Noah entered into the ark, and the
28 flood came, and took them all. Thus,
as it was in Lot's days; that they
were eating, and drinking, and
were buying and selling, and were
29 planting and building; And on the
day that Lot went out from Sodom
it rained fire from heaven, and de-
30 stroyed them all, So shall it be in
the day that the Son of man is re-
31 vealed. But in that hour whoso is
upon the housetop, let him not
come down that he may take his
goods from the house: and whoso is
in the field, let him not turn behind
32 him. And remember the wife of Lot.
33 Whoso wisheth that he should save
his soul shall lose it; and whoso shall
34 lose his soul shall find it. But I say
to you, that in that night shall be two
in one bed; one shall be taken, and
35 one shall be left. And two *women*
shall be grinding with one mill toge-
ther; one shall be taken, and one
36 shall be left. And two shall be in
the field; one shall be taken, and
37 one shall be left. They say to him,
Whither, our Lord? He said to them,
Where the body *is*, there will be
gathered together the eagles.

CHAP. XVIII.

1 He spake to them again also this
parable, that they should be praying
at all times, and it should not weary
them. There was one judge in one city, 2
which was not afraid of God, and of
men's sons was not regardful: And one 3
widow was in the same city; and she
was coming to him a long while, and
saying to him, Avenge me of mine ad-
versary. And he was not willing: and 4
afterwards that judge said within him-
self, Although of God I am not afraid,
and of men's sons am not regard-
ful; And this widow always troubles 5
me, I will avenge her, lest she be
always coming *and* harrassing me.
And our Lord said, Hear what saith 6
the evil judge. Shall not God there- 7
fore rather make avenging for his
elect, which cry to him by day and
by night, and have patience with
them? I say to you that he will 8
make their avenging speedily. Ne-
vertheless shall the Son of man come
then, and find faith upon the earth?

And he was speaking this parable 9
against men which *were* trusting upon
themselves that they are just, and were
despising the many: Two men went 10
up to the temple to pray; one a Pha-
risee, and the other a publican. And
that Pharisee was standing by himself, 11
and was praying these *things*, I thank
thee, God, that I am not as the rest of
men, extortioners, and evil, and adul-
terers, and not as this publican. But 12
I fast twice in the week, and I tithe

13 every thing that I possess. But that
publican was standing from afar, and
was not daring *that* even his eyes
he should raise to heaven, but was
smiting upon his breast, and saying,
God be compassionate upon a sinner.
14 I say to you, that this went down to his
house justified rather than that: for
every man that shall exalt himself
shall be abased; and every *one* that
shall abase himself shall be exalted.

15 And they had brought near to him
also infants, that he should bless them:
and when his disciples saw, they were
16 rebuking them. And he, Jesus, said
to them, Leave the children that
they may come to me, and forbid
them not: for those that are like
these, theirs is the kingdom of heaven.
17 Verily I say to you, That whoso shall
not receive the kingdom of God as
this child shall not enter into it.

18 And one of the chiefs of the Pharisees
had asked him, and said to
him, Good Teacher, what shall I do
that I may inherit the life which is
19 for ever? Jesus said to him, Why
callest thou me good? And why
askest thou me respecting the good?
There is not good, except one, God.
20 But the commandments thou knowest
them, If thou wishest to enter into
life, Kill not, and Commit not adultery,
and Steal not, and Witness not
the witness of falsehood, Honour
21 thy father and thy mother. He said
to him, These all I have kept them
lo, since I was a boy. When Jesus 22
heard, he said to him, One *thing*
still *is* lacking to thee: sell every thing
that thou hast, and give to the poor,
and there shall be for thee treasure in
heaven: and come after me. But 23
when he heard these *things* it grieved
him: for he was very rich. When 24
Jesus saw that it grieved him, he
said, How difficult is it for those
that have riches that they should
enter into the kingdom of God! For 25
it is easier for a camel that it should
pass through the eye of a needle,
than a rich man that he should enter
into the kingdom of God. And they 26
that heard were saying, Who is
able to be saved? He said to them,
Those *things* which with men's sons are 27
not able to be, with God nevertheless
are able. Cepha said to him, lo, We 28
have left every thing that we have and
come after thee. Jesus said to him, 29
Verily I say to you, That whoso hath
left house, or parents, or brethren, or
wife, or children, on account of the
kingdom of God, Shall receive a 30
hundred fold in this time, and in the
world that cometh shall inherit the
life which is for ever.

And he took his twelve, and said to 31
them, Lo, we go up to Jerusalem, and
all those *things will be* fulfilled which
are written in the prophets respecting
the Son of man. For he *will be* de- 32

livered to the Nations, and they shall
mock at him, and revile him, and
33 spit in his face: And shall scourge
him, and kill him: and on the third
34 day he shall rise. And they under-
stood not one of these *things:* but
the word was hid from them, and
they perceived not those things which
were spoken with them.

35 And when he was near to enter unto
Jericho, one blind Man was sitting by
36 the side of the way and begging: And
when he heard the multitude's voice
that passed by, he was asking, that,
37 Who is this? They say to him, Jesus
38 the Nazarene passeth by. And he
cried, and said, Jesus, son of David,
39 be compassionate towards me. And
those that were going before Jesus
were rebuking him, that he should be
silent: and he was crying the more,
Son of David, be compassionate to-
40 wards me. And Jesus stood, and was
commanding that they should bring
him: and when he came near to
him, he asked him, and said to him,
41 What wishest thou I should do to
42 thee? He said to him, My Lord, that
my eyes may be opened, and I may see
thee. He said to him, See: thy faith
43 hath saved thee. And immediately
he saw, and was coming after him,
and was glorifying God: and all the
people which saw, they glorified God.

CHAP. XIX.

1 And while they went up and he
2 passed by Jericho, One Man, whose
name *was* Zacai, and he was a master
of the publicans, and was rich: And 3
he was wishing to see Jesus; and
he was not able, because that in his
stature Zacai was little; And he ran, 4
went before him, and climbed up
into a tasteless fig-tree that he might
see him: because so Jesus was pass-
ing. And while Jesus passed, he 5
saw him, *and* said, Hasten, come
down, Zacai; for to-day in thy house
it is meet for me that I should
be. And he hasted, came down, and 6
received him joyfully. And when 7
all those saw, they were murmuring,
that with a Man, a sinner, he was
gone that he may lodge. And Zacai 8
stood, and said to our Lord; Lo, my
Lord, half my goods I give to the
poor; and every *one* that I have
injured, I recompense fourfold. Jesus 9
said to him, To day is salvation in
this house, and also this is a son of
Abraham: And that, The Son of man 10
is come that he may seek and save
that which was lost.

And while they were hearing these 11
things, he added to speak a parable, be-
cause he was nigh to go up to Jerusa-
lem, and they were supposing that at
that hour the kingdom of God was
about to be revealed. He said to them, 12
One Man, the son of a great house,
went to a distant country to receive
a kingdom, and to return. And he 13
called his ten servants, and gave to

them ten pounds, and said to them,
Be occupied with them till I come.
14 And his city's sons were hating him,
and sent messengers after him, and
say to him, We do not wish that
15 this *man* should reign over us. And
when he received the kingdom, and
returned, he commanded that they
should call to him those his servants
to whom he had given the money, that
he might know what they had traded.
16 And the first came and said, My
Lord, thy pound hath gained ten
17 pounds. He said to him, Well,
good servant: because thou hast been
found faithful in a little, thou shalt be
18 authorized over ten fortresses. And
the second came, *and* said to him, My
Lord, thy pound hath made five
19 pounds. He said to him also, And
thou too shalt be authorized over
20 five fortresses. And another came,
and said, Lo, that thy pound, which
has been by me laid up in linen:
21 For I was afraid of thee, because
thou art a severe Man: because thou
takest up that which thou placedst
not, and reapest that which thou sow-
22 edst not. His Lord said to him, Out
of thy mouth will I judge thee, evil
servant that *art* not faithful. Thou
knewest me that I am a severe Man,
and I take up that which I placed
not, and I reap that which I sowed
23 not. How is it thou castest not my mo-
ney upon the table, and I then should
have come *and* required mine own
with its interest? And he said to those 24
that stand by him, Take from him the
pound, and give it to him that hath
by him ten pounds. For I say to 26
you, That to every man that hath
shall be given to him and be added to
him; and whoso hath not, even that
which he supposeth that he hath shall
be taken from him. But nevertheless 27
bring hither those mine enemies,
which wished not that I should be
king over them, and slay them before
me. And when he said these *things* 28
they went out from thence.

And while he was going up to
Jerusalem, and arrived at Beth Phage 29
and Beth Any, and arrived at the
mount which is called of Beth Zaithe,
he sent two of his disciples and
said to them, Go to the village that 30
is opposite you; and while ye enter,
lo, ye find a colt tied, on which man
has not ridden: loose, bring him.
And if a man ask you, Why loose 31
ye him? say to him, For his lord he
is required. And they went, and 32
found so. And when they asked 33
them they returned to them answer,
that, For his lord he is required. 34
And they brought the colt to Jesus: 35
and they cast upon him their cloaks,
and they made Jesus ride. And while 36
he was going they were spreading
their cloaks in the way. And when 37
they came near to the descent of

the mount of Beth Zaithe, they began,
the whole multitude, *and* were re-
joicing and praising God with a loud
voice for every thing which they saw;
38 And were saying, Blessed is the King
which cometh in the name of the Lord:
peace in heaven, and glory in the
39 height. Men of the Pharisees from
among that multitude say to him,
Our Master, rebuke them that they
40 shout not. He said to them, Verily
I say to you that, if these should be
41 silent, these stones would shout. And
when he came near, and saw the city,
42 he wept over it, And said, that, But
even if in this day thou hadst known
thy peace! but peace has hidden itself
43 from thine eyes. But the days shall
come that thine enemies shall sur-
round thee, and press thee from every
44 place, And shall cast thee down
upon the ground, and thy children
in the midst of thee; and shall not
leave in thee stone upon stone; be-
cause that thou knewest not the day
of thy greatness.

45 And when he entered into the tem-
ple, he began to cast out those that sell
46 in it purchases; And said, It is written
that, My house is the house of prayer
for all nations: but ye have made it a
47 den of thieves. And he was teaching
every day in the temple. But the
chief priests and the scribes and the
heads of the people were seeking to
48 destroy him, And were not finding
what they might do to him: for all
the people was hanging upon him to
hear him.

And it was on one of the days, while 1 CHAP. XX.
he was teaching the people in the
temple, and was preaching, the chief
priests and the scribes of the people
with the elders rose against him, And 2
say to him, Tell us by what autho-
rity thou doest these *things?* or who
is he gave thee this authority? He 3
said to them, Also I will ask you;
tell me: The baptism of John, from 4
heaven was it, or from men's sons?
But they were considering among 5
themselves, and saying, If we say that
it is from heaven; he will say to us,
And how is it ye believed him not?
And if we say, that it is from men's 6
sons; all the people stone us: for
they be persuaded respecting John
that he is a prophet. They say to 7
him, We know not from whence it
is. Jesus said to them, Neither also 8
tell I to you by what authority I do
these *things.*

And he began to speak to them 9
this parable; One Man planted a
vineyard, and let it to cultivators,
and departed a long time. And at 10
one of the times he sent his ser-
vant to the cultivators, that they
should give to him of the fruits of the
vineyard: and they beat him, and
sent him away empty. And he 11
added and sent another his servant:

and this also they struck, and cast
13 him out. The lord of the vineyard
said, What shall I do? I will send
my beloved son: perhaps they will
14 reverence him. But when the culti-
vators saw him, they were considering
and saying, This is the heir: come,
let us kill him, and the inheritance
15 shall be our's. And they cast him out-
side of the vineyard, and killed him.
What shall the lord of the vineyard
16 do to them? He shall come and
destroy those cultivators, and shall
give the vineyard to others. But
when they heard these *things*, they
17 say, Spare and let it not be. But he
looked at them, and said, And what is
this which is written, that The stone
which the builders rejected, it is be-
18 come the head of the building. For
every man that shall fall upon that
stone shall be broken; and upon
whomsoever it shall fall, it will crush
19 him. And the chief priests and
the scribes sought that they might
lay hands on him in the same hour;
for they knew that against them he
spake; and they were afraid of the
20 people. And afterwards they sent
spies, which should feign them-
selves just, that they might take hold
of him by word, and deliver him
21 to the governor. And they asked
him, and say to him, Teacher, we
know that rightly thou speakest and
teachest, and thou acceptest not the
person of man, but in truth the word
of God thou teachest: Is it lawful 22
for us to give head money to Cæsar,
or no? And he understood their 23
wickedness, and said to them, Why
tempt ye me? Shew me a denar. The 24
image and superscription of whom is
upon it? And they shewed him and
say to him, Cæsar's. He said to them, 25
Give Cæsar's to Cæsar, and God's to
God. And they were not able to 26
take hold of his word before the peo-
ple: and they marvelled at his an-
swer, and were silent.

And men of the Sadducees came 27
near, those which say that there is
no resurrection; and they asked him,
And say to him, Teacher, Moses 28
wrote to us, That if the brother of
a man should die while he has no
children, and should leave a wife, his
brother should take his wife, that he
may raise up seed to his brother.
There were seven brethren: the 29
first took a wife, and died without
children. And his brother took that 30
wife, and he died without children.
Also the third took her; and even 31
the seven of them took her, and died
while they left no children. And that 32
woman also died. In the resurrection 33
whose of them shall she be? for lo,
she was to the seven of them. Je- 34
sus said to them, The children of
this world beget and are begotten,
and take women, and women are to

35 Men. But those that are worthy to
obtain that world, and that resurrec-
tion which *is* from among the dead, the
Men take not women, nor are women
36 to Men: Neither are they able to die:
for they are become equal with the
angels, as children of God *being* chil-
37 dren of the resurrection. But respect-
ing the dead that they shall rise, even
Moses also foretold when God spake
with him from the bush, and said, The
Lord the God of Abraham, and the
God of Isaac, and the God of Jacob.
38 And lo, God is not of the dead, but
of the living: for they all live to him.
39 Men of the scribes say to him,
40 Teacher, well hast thou said. And
again they durst not ask him any
thing.
41 And he said to them, How say the
scribes respecting the Messia that
42 he is the son of David? And David
himself saith in the book of Psalms,
that, The Lord said to my Lord, that
43 Sit thou on my right, until I shall
place thine enemies under thy feet.
44 If therefore David calleth him My
Lord, how is he his son?
45 And while all the people were hear-
46 ing he said to his disciples, Beware of
the scribes, which wish to walk in the
porches, and love salutation in the
streets, and the honoured seats in the
synagogues, and the chief sittings
47 at suppers; and devour the houses
of widows, on pretence that they
lengthen their prayers; and they shall
receive greater condemnation.

And he lifted up his eyes, and saw 1 CHAP. XXI.
the rich which were casting their offer-
ings into the treasury. And he saw 2
also a poor widow, too, which cast in
two Shamun. He said, The truth I say 3
to you, that this poor widow hath cast
in more than all of them: For they 4
from that which was abundant to them
cast into the treasury an offering: but
this *woman* from that which *was* lack-
ing to her hath cast in all that she
possessed.

And while men spake concerning 5
the temple, that it was adorned with
beautiful stones and with offerings,
he said, Ye see these *things*, the days 6
will come, that there shall not be left
here stone upon stone, which shall
not be thrown down.

And they asked him, and say to 7
him, Teacher, when shall these *things*
be? and what *is* the sign when these
things begin to be? But he said to 8
them, See that ye be not deceived:
for many shall come in my name,
and shall say that I am *he*; and the
time is near: go not after them.
And when ye hear war and commo- 9
tions, fear not: for these things are
about to be first; but not yet is the
end arrived. For nation shall rise 10
against nation, and kingdom against
kingdom: And great earthquakes in 11
places *and* places, and pestilences,

and famines, and terrors shall be
from heaven; and great signs shall
12 be seen and great tempests. But
before all these, they shall lay hands
on you, and persecute you, and de-
liver you up to the synagogues, and
to prisons, and they shall bring you
before kings and governors on account
13 of my name. But for you shall be this
14 testimony. And set in your hearts,
that ye be not learning to make apo-
15 logy: For I will give to you a mouth
and wisdom, which all your ene-
mies are not able that they should
16 stand against. Your wives, and your
brethren, and your kinsfolks, and
your friends, shall deliver you up,
and they shall put to death *some* of
17 you. And ye shall be hated of every
19 man on account of my name. But by
endurance ye shall possess your soul.
20 But when ye have seen Jerusalem
that an army surrounds it, know
21 that its desolation is near. And those
which are in Judæa let them flee to
the mountain; and *those* which *are*
in the midst of it let them come out
of it; and those that *are* in the coun-
tries let them not enter into it.
22 Because they are the days of venge-
ance, that every thing which is
23 written may be fulfilled. But woe
to those that are pregnant, and to
those that give suck, in those days!
for there shall be great affliction in
the earth, and mighty wrath upon this
nation. And they shall fall by the 24
mouth of the sword, and shall be taken
captive to all nations: and Jerusalem
shall be trodden down of all nations,
until the times of the nations shall be
fulfilled. But signs shall be in the 25
sun, and in the moon, and in the stars;
and affliction in the earth, and clap-
ping of hands of the nations; and
a voice that is like the sea's, And the 26
quaking of the exit of the souls of men's
sons from terror of that which is about
to come on the earth: and the powers
of heaven shall be shaken. And then 27
shall they see the Son of man while
he cometh in the clouds with much
power and glory. But when these 28
things begin to be, look up, and lift
up your heads; because your deli-
verance draweth near.

And he spake to them this parable; 29
See the fig tree, and all the trees;
That when they begin branching 30
forth, and giving their fruits, ye un-
derstand that summer is near. So 31
also ye, when ye have seen these
things that they be, know that the
kingdom of heaven is near.

Verily I say to you, that, This race 32
shall not pass until all these *things* be.
Heaven and earth shall pass: and my 33
words shall not pass. But beware in 34
yourselves, that ye overcharge not
your hearts by the eating of flesh,
and by the drunkenness of wine, and
by the care of the world, and that day

35 rise upon you suddenly. For as a
snare it shall come on all those that sit
36 on the face of the earth. Watch there-
fore always, and be entreating that
ye may be worthy to escape from these
things that are about to be, and that
ye may stand before the Son of man.
37 And in the days he was teaching
in the temple; and at the nights he
was going out, *and* lodging in the
mount that is called of Beth Zaithe.
38 And all the people they came early
to him in the temple, that they might
hear him.

CHAP. XXII. 1 And the feast of the unleavened,
which is called Pescha, was drawing
2 near. And the chief priests and scribes
were seeking how they might kill him;
for they were afraid of the people.
3 But Satan entered into Juda who
was called Iscariot, who was of the
4 number of the twelve. And he went
and spake with the chief priests and
scribes, how he might deliver him to
them. And they rejoiced, and pro-
mised that they would give him mo-
6 ney. And he promised to them, and
sought for himself opportunity how
he might deliver him to them apart
from the multitude.
7 And when the day of the Pescha
arrived in which it is the cus-
tom that the Pescha should be
8 slain, He sent Cepha and John,
and said to them, Go prepare for
us the Pescha, that we may eat.
They say to him, Where wishest thou 9
that we should prepare? He said to 10
them, Lo, when ye enter into the city,
a Man meeteth you, who is bearing
a pitcher of water; go after him to
that house which he entereth, Say 11
to the lord of the house, Our Master
saith, Where is the guestchamber,
where I may eat the Pescha with
my disciples? Lo, he sheweth to you 12
one large upper room which is fur-
nished: there prepare. And they 13
went, found as he had said to them:
and prepared the Pescha.

But and when it was the time he 14
sat down, and his apostles with him.
He said to them, Desire hath impelled 15
me that I should eat with you the Pescha
before I suffer. For I say to you, that 16
henceforth I will not eat it, until it be
accomplished in the kingdom of God.

And he took the bread, and gave
thanks over it, and brake, and gave 19
to them, and said, This is my body
which *is* for you: so be ye doing
for remembrance of me. And he 17
took the cup, and gave thanks
over it, and said, Take this, divide
among you: I say to you, That 18
from now I will not drink of this
fruit of the vine, until the kingdom
of God shall come. But, neverthe- 21
less, lo, the hand of my betrayer
is with me on the table. And the Son 22
of man goeth, as it is determined
respecting him: but nevertheless woe

to him by whose hand he is betrayed!
23 And they began to enquire among
them, that, Who then is he that *is*
about to do this *thing*.
24 And there was a strife between them,
that, Who is *he* among them that *is*
25 greatest. Our Lord said to them, The
kings of the nations are their lords;
and those that are authorized and that
26 do well are called benefactors. But you
not so: but he that *is* great among you,
let him be as the least; and he that
is chief, as a minister and not as *one*
27 sitting down. For who is great, *he* that
sitteth down, or that ministereth? Lo,
am not I as a minister among you?
28 But you that have continued with
29 me in my temptations, I also pro-
mise to you, as my Father hath pro-
30 mised to me, a kingdom; That ye may
eat and drink with me at my table in
the kingdom, and may sit on twelve
thrones and judge the twelve tribes
31 of the house of Israel. And our
Lord said to Simon, Simon, lo, Satan
seeketh that he may sift you as wheat:
32 But I have entreated for thee, that
thy faith may not lack: and thou
also in time turn and confirm thy
33 brethren. He said to him, My Lord,
with thee I am ready to go, both
34 to prison and also to death. Jesus
said to him, I say to thee, that before
the cock shall crow to day two times,
three times thou shalt deny me that
thou knowest me not.

He said to them, When I sent you 35
without purses, and without scrips, and
without shoes, did any thing lack to
you? They say to him, Not even any
thing. He said to them, From now, 36
whoso hath a purse or a scrip, let him
take *it*, and whoso hath not a sword,
let him sell his garment, and buy for
himself a sword. For I say to you, that 37
also this which *is* written *is* about that
it should be fulfilled in me, that, With
the evil he was numbered: and that
which is concerning me to be ful-
filled. And they say to him, Our 38
Lord, Lo, we have here two swords.
He saith to them, They are enough;
rise, let us go.

And he went out, and went, as he 39
was accustomed, to the mount which is
called of Beth Zaithe; and his disci-
ples also went with him. And when 40
he arrived at the place, he said to
them, Pray that ye enter not among
temptations. And he separated from 41
them about the cast with a stone, and
set his knees, and was praying, and
said, My Father, if possible, let this 42
cup pass me: but not my will be,
but thine. And an angel appeared 43
to him, strengthening him. And he 44
was in great anxiety, and was pray-
ing earnestly: and his sweat was as
drops of blood, and was falling upon
the ground. And he rose from his 45
prayer, and came to his disciples, and
found them sleeping from their sor-

46 row. He said to them, Why sleep ye?
rise and pray, that ye enter not into
temptation.
47 And while he was speaking, a
great multitude appeared, and he that
was called Juda, one of the twelve,
came before them, and drew near
48 *and* kissed Jesus. Jesus said to him,
Juda, with a kiss betrayest thou the Son
49 of Man? But when they which *were*
with him saw that which was about
to be, they say to him, Our Lord,
shall we smite them with swords?
50 And one of them smote the servant
of the chief priest, and took his right
51 ear. Jesus answered and said, Enough
until this. And he touched his ear, and
52 healed it. And he said also to those
chief priests, and the soldiers of the
temple, and the elders, As against a
thief be ye come out against me with
53 swords and with staves? Every day that
I was with you in the temple, ye were
not stretching out hands against me:
but this is your hour, and your power
54 of darkness. And they took him, and
brought him to the house of the chief
priest. But Simon Cepha was coming
55 after him from afar. And a fire was
set in the midst of the hall, and
they were sitting round it, and Cepha
56 was sitting amongst them. And one
maid saw him that he sat by the fire,
and she looked upon him, and says, And
57 this *man* also was with him. And he
denied, and said, Woman, I know him
not. And after a little another also saw 58
him, and said likewise. And Cepha
said, I am not of them. And after one 59
hour another was affirming, and said,
Truly also this *man* was with him: for
he also is a Galilæan. And Cepha said, 60
Man, I know not what thou sayest. And
at the same moment the cock crew.
And our Lord turned, *and* looked at 61
him, at Cepha. And Cepha remem-
bered the word of our Lord, who said to
him, that, Before the cock shall crow
two times, three times thou shalt deny
me. And he went out, *and* wept bitterly. 62
And the Men that were holding 63
Jesus were mocking him, and were
smiting him. And they covered his 64
face and say to him, Prophesy, who
is it smote thee? And again many 65
other *things* they were both blas-
pheming and speaking against him.
And when it dawned, assembled 66
the elders and the chief priests and
the scribes, and led him up to the
house of their assemblies, and say,
If thou art the Messia, tell us. He 67
said to them, If I tell you, ye will
not believe: And if I ask you, ye give 68
me not an answer, nor even loose
me. For from now shall be the Son 69
of man sitting on the right *hand* of
the might of God. They say all of 70
them, Art thou the Son of God? He
said to them, Ye say that I am.
They say, Why further is witness re- 71
quisite for us? for lo we have heard

CHAP. XXIII.

1 from his mouth. And they arose, the
whole multitude, and brought him to
2 Pilate. And they began accusing
him, and were saying, We found this
man that he perverteth our nation, and
forbiddeth us, that we should give head
money to Cæsar, and saith respect-
ing himself, that he is a king, the
3 Messia. Pilate said to him, Art thou
the King of the Jews? He said to him,
4 Thou hast said. Pilate said to the chief
priests and to that multitude, I find not
5 any cause against this Man. But they
shout and say, He hath stirred up the
people, while teaching in all Judæa,
and he began from Galilee even to here.
6 But Pilate when he heard that they
say that, From Galilee, asked that if he
7 is from Galilee. And when he heard
that he was from under the autho-
rity of Herod, he sent him to him,
because also Herod himself was at
Jerusalem in those days of the unleav-
8 ened. But Herod, when he saw Je-
sus, rejoiced much: for he was very
desirous to see him from a long time,
because he had heard respecting him;
and he was hoping that he should see
9 some sign from him be done. And
he was asking him with cunning
words; but Jesus returned him not
any answer, as though he had not been
10 there. But the chief priests and
rulers were standing and accusing
11 him fully. And Herod mocked him,
and his attendants, and put on him
splendid garments in mockery, and
sent him to Pilate. And on that 12
same day there was reconciliation be-
tween Herod and Pilate: because they
were enemies. But Pilate called the 13
chief priests and the rulers and all the
people, And said to them, Ye have 14
brought to me this Man, *of* whom ye
have told me that he hath stirred up
your nation: and lo, I have examined
him before your eyes: and have not
found any thing behind him of those
things of which ye accuse him: Nor 15
also Herod: for I sent him to him; and
any thing that is worthy of death he
has not found behind him, nor *is* any
thing *worthy* of death done by him. I ·16
will chastise him therefore, and dis-
miss him. And they gave voice, all 18
the people, and say, Take away this
man, and release to us Bar Aba:
Who on account of seditions, and 19
murders, was cast into prison. And 17
Pilate was accustomed that he should
release to them one man at the
feast. And again Pilate called them 20
and spake to them, because he was
wishing that he should release Jesus.
But they were crying and saying, Cru- 21
cify him, crucify him. But he the third 22
time said to them, For what that *is* evil
hath this *man* done? For any thing
that is worthy of death I find not in 23
him: I will chastise him, therefore, and
dismiss him. And they were insisting
with a loud voice, and saying to him

that he should be crucified. And their
voice was prevailing and that of the
24 chief priests with them. And Pilate
commanded that their request should
25 be. And he released to them him
that on account of murders and here-
sies was in prison, as they asked; and
Jesus he delivered to their will.
26 And while they were conducting him
they laid hold upon Simon, a Cyre-
nian, who was coming from the coun-
try, that he might carry the cross,
27 and come after Jesus. And a
crowd of the people was coming
after him, and women, which were
bewailing over him and lament-
28 ing. And Jesus turned to them and
said to them, Jerusalem's daughters,
weep not over me, but weep over
yourselves, and over your children.
29 For the days shall come, in which
ye shall say, Happy the bar-
ren, and the wombs that have not
borne, and the teats which have not
30 suckled. And then ye shall begin to
say to the mountains, that, Fall
31 on us; and to the hills, that, Cover
us. Because in a green tree they
32 do these *things*, in the dry what shall
be? And with him were coming
two others, malefactors, that they
33 may be slain. And when they came
to the place, which is called Kar-
kaptha they crucified him there, and
those malefactors, one on his right,
34 and one on his left. And Jesus an-
swered and said, My Father, forgive
them; for they know not what they do.
And they divided his garments, and
cast lots over them. And the people 35
was standing and looking. And
also with them the rulers were de-
riding him, and saying, Others he
saved; let him save himself, if he be
the Messia, the chosen of God, and
they were mocking him. And also the 36
soldiers were coming near to him,
And saying, Peace to thee: if thou be 37
the king of the Jews, save thyself. And 38
they had set upon his head a crown of
thorns, and also was written a title
and placed over him, This is the King
of the Jews.

But one of those malefactors which 39
were crucified with him, was blas-
pheming against him, and saying, Art
not thou the Messia? save thyself and
save us, also us. And his companion 40
that other rebuked him, and said to him,
Art not thou even afraid of God, be-
cause lo, we also are in the same judg-
ment? And lo, we as those who have 41
deserved; and as we have done we
are requited: but this *man* even no-
thing that *is* hateful *is* done by him.
And he said to Jesus, My Lord, remem- 42
ber me when thou comest in thy king-
dom. Jesus said to him, Verily I say to 43
thee to-day that with me thou shalt be
in the Eden's garden. But and it 44
was about the sixth hour, and dark-
ness was over all the land, until

45 the ninth hour. And the sun was
darkened, and the front of the door of
the temple was rent from the midst
46 of it. And Jesus called with a loud
voice, and said, Father, into thy hands
I place my spirit: and he finished.
47 But when the centurion saw that
which was done, he glorified God, and
48 said, Truly this Man was just. And all
those which were assembled there, and
saw that which was done, were smiting
upon their breast, and saying, Woe to
us, What is this! Woe to us from our
49 sins! And they all were standing from
afar, the acquaintance of Jesus, and
the women which came with him from
Galilee, and beholding these *things*.
50 And one Man whose name was
51 Joseph, he was a counsellor; a
Man just, and good, from Ramtha,
a fortress of Judæa, and he was look-
52 ing for the kingdom of heaven: This
Man who did not equal his mind with
the accusers, this same went near,
53 and asked for the body of Jesus. And
took it down, and wrapped it in ban-
dages, and laid it in a hewn sepul-
chre in which as yet no man was
54 buried. And that same day was Fri-
day. And the sabbath was dawning.
55 And those women which came with him
from Galilee, came to the sepulchre
in their footsteps, and saw the corpse
56 while they laid it up there, And
returned, *and* prepared spices and
ointment that *was* sweet; and on the
sabbath they rested as it is com-
manded. But on the first of the week, 1 CHAP. XXIV.
in the early morning, they came to
the sepulchre, and brought that which
they had prepared, and there were
with them other women. And they 2
found that stone that it *was* rolled
from the sepulchre. And they entered, 3
and found not the body of Jesus.
And while it grieved them concern- 4
ing this, they saw two men which
stand above them and their raiment
was shining: And they feared and 5
bowed their heads and were look-
ing upon the earth from their fear.
Those Men say to them, Why seek
ye the living among the dead? He 6
is not here, but is risen: remember
that which he spake with you while
he *was* in Galilee, And said to you, 7
that, The Son of Man is about that he
should be delivered into the hands of
wicked men, and be crucified, and on
the third day he shall rise. And they 8
remembered those words, And re- 9
turned from the sepulchre, *and* told
those words to the eleven, and to the
rest of those disciples. Mary Magda- 10
lene, and Joan, and Mary the daughter
of Jacob, and the rest that *were* with
them, these told to the apostles; And 11
they seemed in their eyes as though
it was from their wonder they had
spoken these words, and they were
not believing them.

But Simon arose, and ran to the 12

grave; and stooped, and saw the linen
only, and went to it, and was marvel-
13 ling at that which was done. And
he appeared to two of them on the
same day while they were going to a
village whose name *was* Emmaus,
which *was* distant from Jerusalem
14 sixty stadia. And they were talk-
ing one with the other concern-
ing all these *things* which hap-
15 pened. And while they talk, Jesus
came *and* approached them, and was
16 walking with them. And their eyes
were holden that they should not re-
17 cognize him. He said to them, What
are these words which ye are talking
while ye are sad?

18 One of them, whose name was
Cleopa, said to him, Art thou then
by thyself a stranger from Jerusa-
lem, that thou knowest not what has
19 been done in it? He said to them,
What? They say to him, Concerning
Jesus the Nazarene, which was a
Man, a prophet, and he was able in
might and in deeds and in word be-
fore God and before all the people:
20 And the chief priests and the elders
delivered him to the judgment of
21 death, and crucified him. And we
were supposing that it was he was
about that he should deliver Israel:
and lo, three days lo, since all these
22 things were. Also women from us
went to the sepulchre where he was
23 laid; And when they found not his
body, they came, *and* told us that they
had seen angels there, and they were
astonished and told respecting him that
he is alive. And also men of us went 24
to the sepulchre, and found so as the
women said: but him they saw not.

Then said Jesus to them, O lack- 25
ing of faith, and heavy of heart to
believe! from all those *things* which
the prophets have spoken, Was it not 26
these *things* Messia was about that he
should endure, and that he should en-
ter into glory? And he began to speak 27
to them from Moses and from all the
prophets, and he was expounding to
them concerning himself from all the
scriptures. And they drew near to 28
that village, to which they were going,
and he appeared to them as though
he were going to a distant place.
And they began, *and* were entreating 29
of him that he would be with them:
because it was near to become dark.
And he entered with them so that
he might be with them. And when he 30
sat down, he took bread, and blessed,
and brake, and gave to them. And 31
at once their eyes were opened, and
they recognized him; and he took
himself away from them. And they 32
were saying one to the other, Was it
not our heart was heavy by the way
while he *was* explaining to us the scrip-
tures? And they arose in the same 33
hour, and returned to Jerusalem,
and found the eleven assembled,

34 and those that *were* with them, Say-
ing, Truly our Lord is risen, and hath
35 appeared to Simon. And they also
related to them those *things* which
were done in the way, and how he
was recognized while he brake bread.
36 And while they were speaking, he
was found standing among them, and
saith unto them, Peace *be* with you.
37 And they were moved and affrighted,
and were supposing that they were
38 seeing a spirit. Then Jesus said to
them, Why are ye moved? and con-
cerning what arise thoughts upon
39 your hearts? Lo! see my hands and
my feet, and feel and see that I
am; for a spirit hath not flesh and
bones, as ye see that I have. And 40
when even until now they believe not
from their fear and from their joy, and
were wondering, he said to them,
Have ye here any thing to eat? 41
And they gave to him a piece of fish 42
that *was* broiled, and of an honey-
comb. And when he took he ate 43
before their eyes. And he took up 44
that which remained *and* gave to
them, *and* said to them, These words

* * * * * * * * * * *
* * * * * * * * * * *

* * * * * * *

* * * * * * *

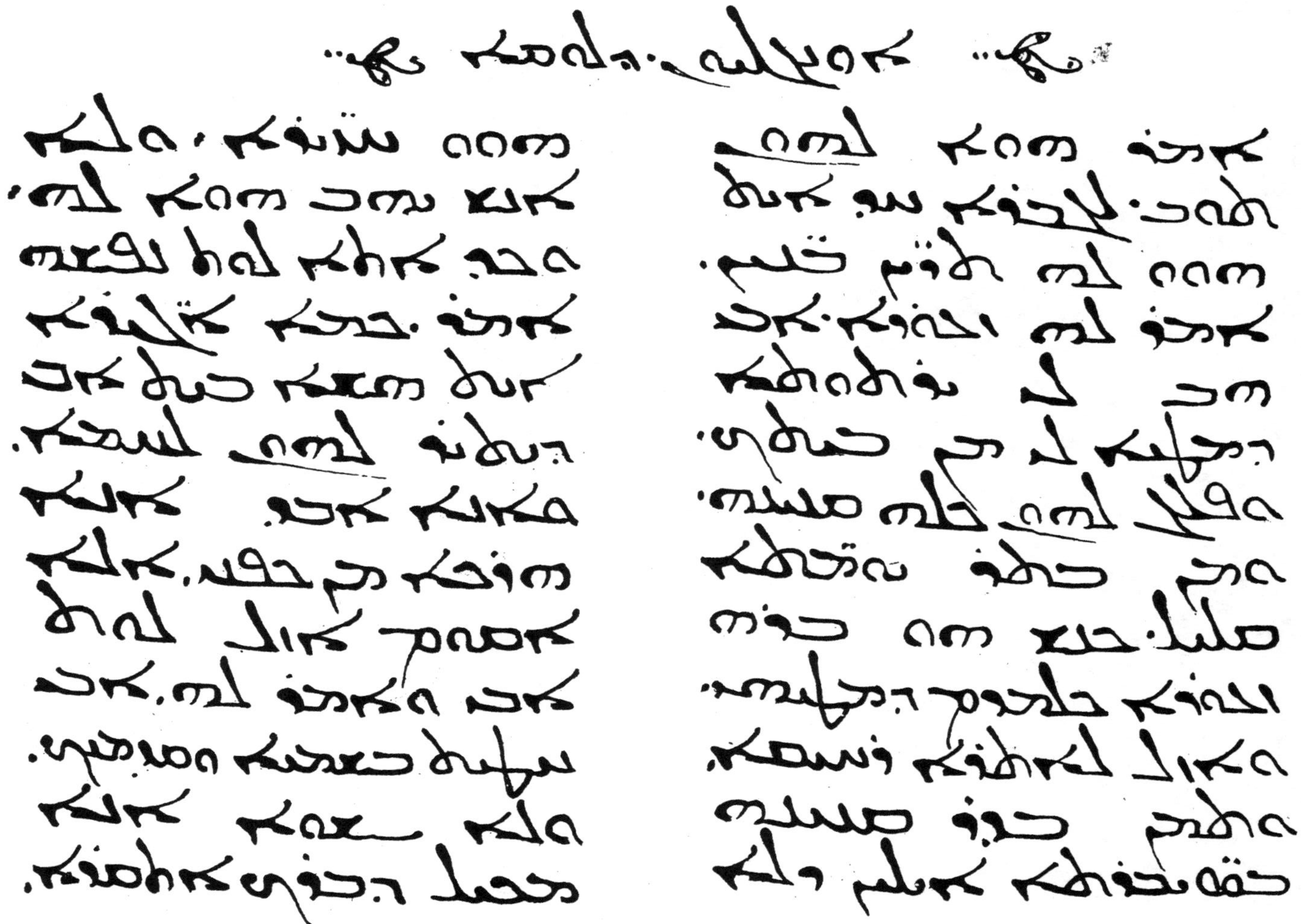

Harrietta Cureton fecit.

Cod. Add. 14451. fol. 72.b

25 ܗܝܕܝܢ ܐܡܪ ܠܗܘܢ ܝܫܘܥ. ܐܘ ܚ̈ܣܝܪܝ ܗܝܡܢܘܬܐ
ܘܝܩܝܪܝ ܠܒܐ ܠܡܗܝܡܢܘ. ܡܢ ܟܠܗܝܢ ܐܝܠܝܢ ܕܡܠܠܘ
26 ܢܒ̈ܝܐ. ܠܐ ܗܘܐ ܗܠܝܢ ܚܫ̈ܐ ܗܘܐ ܕܢܣܒܪ ܡܫܝܚܐ.
27 ܘܕܢܥܘܠ ܠܬܫܒܘܚܬܐ. ܘܫܪܝ ܗܘܐ ܠܡܐܡܪ ܠܗܘܢ
ܡܢ ܡܘܫܐ ܘܡܢ ܟܠܗܘܢ ܢܒ̈ܝܐ. ܘܡܦܫܩ ܗܘܐ
28 ܠܗܘܢ ܥܠ ܢܦܫܗ ܡܢ ܟܠܗܘܢ ܟܬ̈ܒܐ. ܘܩܪܒܘ
ܠܩܪܝܬܐ ܗܝ ܕܐܙܠܝܢ ܗܘܘ ܠܗ̇. ܘܗܘ ܐܬܚܙܝ ܠܗܘܢ
29 ܐܝܟ ܕܠܕܘܟܐ ܪܚܝܩܐ ܐܙܠ ܗܘܐ. ܘܥܨܪܘ ܗܢܘܢ ܒܥܝܢ
ܗܘܘ ܡܢܗ ܕܢܗܘܐ ܠܘܬܗܘܢ. ܡܛܠ ܕܪܡܫܐ ܗܘܐ ܗܘܬ
30 ܠܡܥܪܒ. ܘܥܠ ܥܡܗܘܢ ܐܝܟ ܕܠܘܬܗܘܢ ܢܗܘܐ. ܘܟܕ
ܐܣܬܡܟ ܢܣܒ ܠܚܡܐ ܘܒܪܟ. ܘܩܨܐ ܘܝܗܒ ܠܗܘܢ.
31 ܘܒܫܥܬܐ ܐܬܦܬܚ ܗܘܝ ܥܝ̈ܢܝܗܘܢ ܘܐܫܬܘܕܥܘܗܝ.
32 ܘܗܘ ܐܫܬܩܠ ܠܗ ܡܢܗܘܢ. ܘܐܡܪܝܢ ܗܘܘ ܚܕ
ܠܚܕ. ܠܐ ܗܘܐ ܠܒܢ ܝܩܝܪ ܗܘܐ ܒܐܘܪܚܐ. ܟܕ ܡܦܫܩ
33 ܠܢ ܟܬ̈ܒܐ. ܘܩܡܘ ܒܗ̇ ܫܥܬܐ ܘܗܦܟܘ ܠܐܘܪܫܠܡ.
ܘܐܫܟܚܘ ܠܚܕܥܣܪ ܟܕ ܟܢܝܫܝܢ. ܘܠܐܝܠܝܢ ܕܥܡܗܘܢ
34 ܟܕ ܐܡܪܝܢ. ܫܪܝܪܐܝܬ ܩܡ ܡܪܢ ܘܐܬܚܙܝ ܠܫܡܥܘܢ.
35 ܘܐܦ ܗܢܘܢ ܐܫܬܥܝܘ ܠܗܘܢ ܐܝܠܝܢ ܕܗܘܝ ܒܐܘܪܚܐ.
ܘܐܝܟܢܐ ܐܬܝܕܥ ܠܗܘܢ ܟܕ ܩܨܐ ܠܚܡܐ ܀
36 ܘܟܕ ܗܢܘܢ ܡܡܠܠܝܢ ܗܘܘ. ܐܫܬܟܚ ܩܐܡ ܒܝܢܬܗܘܢ.
37 ܘܐܡܪ ܠܗܘܢ. ܫܠܡܐ ܥܡܟܘܢ. ܘܗܢܘܢ ܐܬܙܝܥܘ
ܘܐܬܪܗܒܘ. ܘܣܒܪܝܢ ܗܘܘ ܕܪܘܚܐ ܚܙܝܢ ܗܘܘ. ܗܝܕܝܢ
38 ܐܡܪ ܠܗܘܢ ܝܫܘܥ. ܡܢܐ ܡܬܪܗܒܝܢ ܐܢܬܘܢ. ܘܥܠ

16 ܛܪܘ ܘܐܢܐ ܐܒܥܐ ܡܢ ܐܒܝ ܕܢܬܠ ܠܟܘܢ ܐܚܪܢܐ
17 ܦܪܩܠܛܐ ܕܢܗܘܐ ܥܡܟܘܢ ܠܥܠܡ ܪܘܚܐ ܕܫܪܪܐ ܗܝ
ܕܥܠܡܐ ܠܐ ܡܫܟܚ ܠܡܩܒܠܘܬܗ̇ ܠܐ ܓܝܪ ܚܙܗ̇
ܘܠܐ ܝܕܥܗ̇ ܐܢܬܘܢ ܕܝܢ ܝܕܥܝܢ ܐܢܬܘܢ ܠܗ̇
18 ܘܠܘܬܟܘܢ ܥܡܪܐ ܘܒܟܘܢ ܗܝ ܘܠܐ ܐܫܒܘܩܟܘܢ
ܝܬ̈ܡܐ ܗܐ ܡܠܠ ܐܢ*** ***ܐ ܠܐ ܝ* * *

* * * * * * * * * * * *

ܠܗܘܢ ܗܘ ܗܘ ܪܚܡ ܠܝ. ܘܡܢ ܕܪܚܡ ܠܝ ܢܪܚܡܘܗܝ
ܐܒܝ. ܐܦ ܐܢܐ ܐܪܚܡܝܘܗܝ. ܘܐܦ ܐܚܘܝܘܗܝ
22 ܢܦܫܝ. ܐܡܪ ܠܗ ܝܗܘܕܐ ܬܐܘܡܐ ܡܪܢ. ܡܢܘ ܕܠܢ
23 ܥܬܝܕ ܐܢܬ ܠܡܚܘܝܘ ܢܦܫܟ ܘܠܐ ܠܥܠܡܐ. ܐܡܪ
ܠܗ ܝܫܘܥ ܡܢ ܕܪܚܡ ܠܝ ܡܠܬܝ ܢܛܪ. ܘܐܒܝ ܢܪܚܡܝܘܗܝ.
ܘܠܘܬܗ * ܬܐ ܐܢܐ. ܘܐܒܐ *** ܐܥܒܕ ****

* * * * * * * * * * * *

ܐܒܝ ܒܫܡܝ. ܗܝ ܬܠܦܟܘܢ ܟܘܠ ܡܕܡ ܕܐܡܪܢܐ
27 ܠܟܘܢ. ܫܠܡܐ ܫܒܩ ܐܢܐ ܠܟܘܢ. ܫܠܡܐ ܕܝܠܝ ܝܗܒ
ܐܢܐ ܠܟܘܢ. ܠܐ ܗܘܐ ܐܝܟܢܐ ܕܝܗܒ ܥܠܡܐ ܝܗܒ
ܐܢܐ ܠܟܘܢ. ܠܐ ܢܬܕܪܗܒ ܠܒܟܘܢ ܘܠܐ ܢܙܝܥ.
28 ܫܡܥܬܘܢ ܕܐܡܪܬ ܠܟܘܢ ܕܐܙܠ ܐܢܐ ܘܐܬܐ ܐܢܐ
ܠܘܬܟܘܢ. ܐܠܘ ܪ̈ܚܡܝܢ ܗܘܝܬܘܢ ܠܝ ܚܕܝܢ ܗܘܝܬܘܢ
29 ܕܐܙܠ ܐܢܐ ܠܘܬ ܐܒܝ ܕܪܒ ***** * ܗܫܐ ܗܐ

* * * * * * * * * * * *

ܕܠܘܩܐ

39 ܡܢܐ ܦ̈ܠܓܢ ܡܚ̈ܫܒܬܐ ܥܠ ܠܒ̈ܘܬܟܘܢ. ܗܐ ܚܙܘ
ܐܝ̈ܕܝ ܘܪ̈ܓܠܝ. ܘܓܫܘ ܚܙܘ ܕܐܢܐ ܐܢܐ. ܠܪܘܚܐ ܓܝܪ
ܒܣܪܐ ܘܓܪ̈ܡܐ ܠܝܬ ܠܗ̇. ܐܝܟܢܐ ܕܚܙܝܢ ܐܢܬܘܢ
41 ܕܐܝܬ ܠܝ. ܘܟܕ ܒܕܘܟܐ ܠܗܝܡܢܐ ܠܐ ܡܗܝܡܢܝܢ
ܡܢ ܕܚܠܬܗܘܢ ܘܡܢ ܚܕܘܬܗܘܢ. ܘܡܬܡܗܝܢ ܗܘܘ.
42 ܐܡܪ ܠܗܘܢ ܐܝܬ ܠܟܘܢ ܬܢܢ ܡܕܡ ܠܡܐܟܠ. ܘܗܢܘܢ
ܝܗܒܘ ܠܗ ܡܢܬܐ ܡܢ ܢܘܢܐ ܕܛܘܝܐ. ܘܡܢ ܟܘܪܬܐ
43 ܕܕܒܫܐ. ܘܟܕ ܢܣܒ ܐܟܠ ܗܘܐ ܠܥܝ̈ܢܝܗܘܢ. ܘܫܩܠ
44 ܡܕܡ ܕܝܬܪ ܝܗܒ ܠܗܘܢ. ܐܡܪ ܠܗܘܢ. ܗܠܝܢ ܡ̈ܠܐ

* * * * * * * * * * * *

* * * * * * * * * * * *

ܕܝܘܚܢܢ

* * * * * * * * * * * * XIV.

ܠܐ ܗܘܐ ܡܢ ܨܒܘܬ ܪܥܝܢܝ ܡܡܠܠܐ ܒܟܘܢ. ܐܠܐ
11 ܐܡܢ ܕܟܢ ܗܘ ܒܟܕ ܒܥ̈ܒܕܐ ܗܠܝܢ ܗܝܡܢܘܢ ܕܐܢܐ
ܒܐܒܝ ܐܢܐ ܘܐܒܝ ܒܝ ܗܘ ܘܐܢ ܠܝ ܠܐ ܡܗܝܡܢܝܢ
ܐܢܬܘܢ ܐܦ ܡܛܠܬܗܘܢ ܕܥ̈ܒܕܐ ܗܝܡܢܘ. ܐܡܝܢ
12 ܐܡܝܢ ܐܡܪܢܐ ܠܟܘܢ ܕܡܢ ܕܡܗܝܡܢ ܒܝ ܥ̈ܒܕܐ
ܐܠܝܢ ܕܐܢܐ ܥܒܕܢܐ ܐܦ ܗܘ ܢܥܒܕ ܘܕܝܬܝܪܢ ܡܢ
* * * * * * * * * ܗܠܝܢ ܥ̈ܒܕܐ

ܕܠܘܩܐ

ܟܬܢܐ ܒܠܚܘܕ. ܘܐܙܠ ܠܒܝܬܗ. ܘܡܬܕܡܪ ܗܘܐ
13 ܒܡܕܡ ܕܗܘܐ. ܘܐܬܚܙܝ ܠܬܪ̈ܝܢ ܡܢܗܘܢ ܒܗ
ܒܝܘܡܐ. ܟܕ ܐܙܠܝܢ ܗܘܘ ܠܩܪܝܬܐ ܕܫܡܗ ܐܡܡܐܘܣ.
14 ܕܪܚܝܩܐ ܡܢ ܐܘܪܫܠܡ ܐܣ̈ܛܕܘܬܐ ܫܬܝܢ. ܘܡܡܠܠܝܢ
15 ܗܘܘ ܚܕ ܥܡ ܚܕ. ܥܠ ܗܠܝܢ ܟܠܗܝܢ ܐܝܠܝܢ ܕܓ̈ܕܫ. ܘܟܕ
ܗܢܘܢ ܡܡܠܠܝܢ. ܐܬܐ ܝܫܘܥ ܡܛܠ ܐܢܘܢ. ܘܡܗܠܟ
16 ܗܘܐ ܥܡܗܘܢ. ܘܥ̈ܝܢܝܗܘܢ ܐܚ̈ܝܕܢ ܗܘܝ ܕܠܐ
17 ܢܫܬܘܕܥܘܢܗ. ܐܡܪ ܠܗܘܢ ܡܢܐ ܐܢܝܢ ܡ̈ܠܐ ܗܠܝܢ
ܕܡܡܠܠܝܢ ܐܢܬܘܢ ܟܕ ܡܗܠܟܝܢ ܐܢܬܘܢ ܀
18 ܐܡܪ ܠܗ ܚܕ ܡܢܗܘܢ ܕܫܡܗ ܗܘܐ ܩܠܝܘܦܐ. ܐܢܬ
ܗܘ ܒܢܘܟܪܝܐ ܒܠܚܘܕܝܟ ܡܢ ܐܘܪܫܠܡ. ܕܡܕܡ ܕܗܘܐ
19 ܒܗ ܠܐ ܝܕܥ ܐܢܬ. ܐܡܪ ܠܗܘܢ ܡܢܐ. ܐܡܪܝܢ ܠܗ
ܥܠ ܝܫܘܥ ܢܨܪܝܐ ܗܘ ܕܗܘܐ ܓܒܪܐ ܢܒܝܐ. ܘܐܫܬܟܚ
ܚܝܠܐ ܘܡܫ̈ܒܚܐ ܘܒܡܠܠܬܐ. ܩܕܡ ܐܠܗܐ ܘܩܕܡ
20 ܟܠܗ ܥܡܐ. ܘܐܫܠܡܘܗܝ ܪ̈ܒܝ ܟܗ̈ܢܐ ܘܩܫܝܫܝ
21 ܠܕܝܢܐ ܕܡܘܬܐ ܘܙܩܦܘܗܝ. ܘܐܢܚܢ ܣܒܪܝܢ ܗܘܝܢ
ܕܗܘܝܘ ܥܬܝܕ ܗܘܐ ܕܢܦܪܘܩܝܗ ܠܐܝܣܪܝܠ. ܘܗܐ
22 ܬܠܬܐ ܝ̈ܘܡܝܢ ܗܐ ܡܢ ܕܗܠܝܢ ܟܠܗܝܢ ܗܘܝ. ܐܦ ܢ̈ܫܐ
23 ܡܢܢ ܐܙܠ ܗܘܝ ܠܒܝܬ ܩܒܘܪܐ ܐܬܪ ܕܩܒܝܪ ܗܘܐ. ܘܟܕ
ܠܐ ܐܫܟܚ ܦܓܪܗ. ܐܬܝ̈ ܐܡ̈ܪܢ ܠܢ ܕܡ̈ܠܐܟܐ ܚܙܝ
24 ܬܡܢ. ܘܬܡܗܝܢ. ܘܐܡ̈ܪܢ ܟܠܗܘܢ ܕܚܝ ܗܘ. ܘܐܦ
ܐܢܫܐ ܡܢܢ ܐܙܠܘ ܗܘܘ ܠܒܝܬ ܩܒܘܪܐ. ܘܐܫܟܚܘ
ܗܟܢܐ ܐܝܟ ܕܐܡ̈ܪܝ ܢ̈ܫܐ. ܐܠܐ ܠܗ ܠܐ ܚܙܘ ◦◦◦

ܡܢ ܓܠܝܠܐ. ܐܬܝ̈ ܠܒܝܬ ܩܒܘܪܐ ܒܬܒܥܬܗܘܢ. ܘܚܙܝ̈
56 ܠܦܓܪܐ ܟܕ ܐܬܩܒܪ ܠܬܡܢ. ܘܗܦܟܝ̈ ܛܝܒ̈ ܗܪ̈ܘܡܐ
ܘܡܫܚܐ ܕܒܣܡܐ. ܘܒܫܒܬܐ ܫܠܝ̈ ܐܝܟ ܕܦܩܝܕ.
XXIV. ܒܚܕܒܫܒܐ ܕܝܢ ܒܨܦܪܐ ܪܒܐ. ܐܬܝ̈ ܗܘܝ̈ ܠܒܝܬ
ܩܒܘܪܐ. ܘܐܝܬܝ̈ ܗܘܝ̈ ܡܕܡ ܕܛܝ̈ܒ. ܘܐܝܬ ܗܘܝ̈
2 ܥܡܗܝܢ ܢܫ̈ܐ ܐܚܪ̈ܢܝܬܐ. ܘܐܫܟܚܘ ܠܟܐܦܐ ܗܝ
3 ܕܡܓܠܠܐ ܡܢ ܒܝܬ ܩܒܘܪܐ. ܘܟܕ ܥܠܝ̈ ܠܐ ܐܫܟܚܝܗܝ
4 ܠܦܓܪܐ ܕܝܫܘܥ. ܘܟܕ ܬܘܗܐ ܗܘܬ ܠܗܝܢ ܥܠ ܗܕܐ.
ܚܙܝ̈ ܬܪ̈ܝܢ ܓܒܪ̈ܝܢ ܕܩܝܡܝܢ ܠܥܠ ܡܢܗܝܢ. ܘܡܠܒܫܝܢ
5 ܗܘܘ ܠܒܘܫܗܘܢ ܘܕܚܠ. ܘܟܦܝ̈ ܪ̈ܫܝܗܝܢ ܘܚܝܪ̈
ܗܘܝ̈ ܒܐܪܥܐ ܡܢ ܕܚܠܬܗܘܢ. ܐܡܪܝܢ ܠܗܝܢ ܗܢܘܢ
6 ܓܒܪ̈ܐ. ܡܢܐ ܒܥܝܢ ܐܢܬܝܢ ܚܝܐ ܒܝܬ ܡ̈ܝܬܐ. ܠܝܬ ܗܘ
ܗܪܟܐ. ܐܠܐ ܩܡ ܠܗ. ܒܗܕܝܢ ܡܕܡ ܕܡܠܠ ܥܡܟܝܢ
7 ܟܕ ܗܘ ܒܓܠܝܠܐ. ܘܐܡܪ ܗܘܐ ܠܟܝܢ. ܕܒܥܐ ܗܘ ܒܪܗ
ܕܐܢܫܐ ܕܢܫܬܠܡ ܒܐܝ̈ܕܝ ܐܢܫܐ ܚܛ̈ܝܐ ܘܢܨܛܠܒ.
8 ܘܠܬܠܬܐ ܝܘ̈ܡܝܢ ܢܩܘܡ. ܘܐܬܕܟܪ ܐܢܝܢ ܠܡ̈ܠܐ ܗܠܝܢ.
9 ܘܗܦܟܝ̈ ܡܢ ܒܝܬ ܩܒܘܪܐ ܐܡܪ ܐܢܝܢ ܡ̈ܠܐ ܗܠܝܢ
10 ܠܚ̈ܕܥܣܪ. ܘܠܫܪܟܐ ܕܬܠܡ̈ܝܕܐ ܗܠܝܢ. ܡܪܝܡ
ܡܓܕܠܝܬܐ ܘܝܘܚܢ. ܘܡܪܝܡ ܒܪܬ ܝܥܩܘܒ. ܘܫܪܟܐ
11 ܕܥܡܗܝܢ. ܗܠܝܢ ܐܡܪ̈ܢ ܗܘܝ̈ ܠܫܠܝܚܐ. ܘܡܬܚܙܝܢ
ܗܘܝ̈ ܒܥܝܢܝܗܘܢ ܐܝܟ ܕܡܢ ܬܘܗܪܬܗܘܢ ܗܘܘ ܐܡܪ̈ܢ
ܗܘܝ̈ ܡ̈ܠܐ ܗܠܝܢ. ܘܠܐ ܡܗܝܡܢܝܢ ܗܘܘ ܠܗܝܢ ⁘
12 ܫܡܥܘܢ ܕܝܢ ܩܡ ܘܪܗܛ ܠܩܒܪܐ. ܘܐܕܝܩ ܘܚܙܐ

43 ܡܪܝ ܐܬܕܟܪܢܝ ܡܐ ܕܐܬܐ ܐܢܬ ܒܡܠܟܘܬܟ. ܐܡܪ
ܠܗ ܝܫܘܥ. ܐܡܝܢ ܐܡܪ ܐܢܐ ܠܟ ܝܘܡܢܐ ܕܥܡܝ
44 ܬܗܘܐ ܒܓܢܬ ܥܕܢ. ܘܐܝܬ ܗܘܐ ܕܝܢ ܐܝܟ ܫ̈ܥܐ ܫܬ.
ܘܗܘܐ ܚܫܘܟܐ ܥܠ ܟܠܗ̇ ܐܪܥܐ ܥܕܡܐ ܠܬܫܥ
45 ܫ̈ܥܝܢ. ܘܚܫܟܐ ܫܡܫܐ. ܘܐܬܦܠܓܝ ܐ̈ܦܝ ܬܪܥܐ
46 ܕܗܝܟܠܐ ܡܢ ܡܨܥܬܗ. ܘܩܪܐ ܝܫܘܥ ܒܩܠܐ ܪܡܐ
ܘܐܡܪ. ܐܒܐ ܒܐ̈ܝܕܝܟ ܣܐܡ ܐܢܐ ܠܗ̇ ܠܪܘܚܝ
ܘܐܫܠܡ ܀
47 ܟܕ ܚܙܐ ܕܝܢ ܩܢܛܪܘܢܐ ܡܕܡ ܕܗܘܐ. ܫܒܚ ܠܐܠܗܐ.
48 ܘܐܡܪ ܫܪܝܪܐܝܬ ܗܢܐ ܓܒܪܐ ܙܕܝܩܐ ܗܘ. ܘܟܠܗܘܢ
ܐܝܠܝܢ ܕܐܬܟܢܫܘ ܬܡܢ ܘܚܙܘ ܡܕܡ ܕܗܘܐ. ܛܪܦܝܢ
ܗܘܘ ܥܠ ܚܕܝܗܘܢ ܘܐܡܪܝܢ. ܘܝ ܠܢ ܡܢܐ ܗܘܢ. ܘܝ
49 ܠܢ ܡܢ ܚܛܗܝܢ. ܘܩܝܡܝܢ ܗܘܘ ܡܢ ܪܘܚܩܐ ܟܠܗܘܢ
ܡܫܡܫܢܘܬܗ ܕܝܫܘܥ. ܘܢܫ̈ܐ ܐܝܠܝܢ ܕܐܬܝ ܥܡܗ
ܡܢ ܓܠܝܠܐ. ܘܚܙܝ ܗܠܝܢ. ܀
50 ܘܓܒܪܐ ܚܕ ܕܫܡܗ ܗܘܐ ܝܘܣܦ. ܒܘܠܘܛܐ ܗܘܐ.
ܓܒܪܐ ܙܕܝܩܐ ܘܛܒܐ. ܡܢ ܪܡܬܐ ܟܪܟܐ ܕܝܗܘܕ.
51 ܘܣܒܪ ܗܘܐ ܠܡܠܟܘܬܐ ܕܫܡܝܐ. ܗܢܐ ܓܒܪܐ ܕܠܐ
52 ܐܫܬܘܝ ܪܥܝܢܗ ܥܡ ܐ̈ܟܠܝ ܩܪܨܐ. ܗܘ ܗܢܐ ܩܪܒ
53 ܘܫܐܠ ܦܓܪܗ ܕܝܫܘܥ. ܘܐܚܬܗ ܘܟܪܟܗ ܒܣܕܝܢܐ.
ܘܣܡܗ ܒܝܬ ܩܒܘܪܐ ܢܩܝܪܐ. ܐܝܟܐ ܕܥܕܟܠ ܐܢܫ
54 ܠܐ ܐܬܬܣܝܡ ܒܗ. ܘܗܘ ܗܘ ܝܘܡܐ ܥܪܘܒܬܐ ܗܘܬ.
55 ܘܫܒܬܐ ܢܓܗܐ ܗܘܬ. ܘܗܠܝܢ ܢܫ̈ܐ ܕܐܬܝ ܥܡܗ

ܬܫܪܘܢ ܠܡܐܡܪ ܠܛܘܪܐ ܕܦܠܘ ܥܠܝܢ. ܘܠܪ̈ܡܬܐ
31 ܕܟܣܝܢ. ܕܒܩܝܣܐ ܪܛܝܒܐ ܗܠܝܢ ܥܒܕܝܢ. ܒܝܒܝܫܐ
32 ܡܢܐ ܢܗܘܐ. ܘܐܝܬܝܘ ܗܘܘ ܥܡܗ ܬܪ̈ܝܢ ܐ̈ܚܪܢܝܢ
33 ܥܒ̈ܕܝ ܒܝ̈ܫܬܐ ܕܢܬܩܛܠܘܢ. ܘܟܕ ܐܬܘ ܠܕܘܟܬܐ
ܕܡܬܩܪܝܐ ܩܪܩܦܬܐ. ܙܩܦܘܗܝ ܬܡܢ. ܘܠܗܢܘܢ ܥܒ̈ܕܝ
34 ܒܝ̈ܫܬܐ ܚܕ ܡܢ ܝܡܝܢܗ ܘܚܕ ܡܢ ܣܡܠܗ. ܘܒܥܐ
ܝܫܘܥ ܘܐܡܪ ܐܒܝ ܫܒܘܩ ܠܗܘܢ. ܠܐ ܓܝܪ ܝܕܥܝܢ
ܡܢܐ ܥܒܕܝܢ. ܘܦܠܓܘ ܢܚ̈ܬܘܗܝ ܘܪܡܘ ܥܠܝܗܘܢ.
35 ܘܩܐܡ ܗܘܐ ܥܡܐ ܘܚܙܐ. ܘܡܒܙܚܝܢ ܗܘܘ ܒܗ
ܒܦܘܡܗܘܢ ܘܐܦ ܐܪ̈ܟܘܢܐ ܘܐܡܪܝܢ. ܠܐ̈ܚܪܢܐ ܐܚܝ.
ܢܚܐ ܢܦܫܗ ܐܢ ܗܘܝܘ ܡܫܝܚܐ ܓܒܝܗ ܕܐܠܗܐ.
36 ܘܡܒܙܚܝܢ ܗܘܘ ܒܗ. ܘܐܦ ܣܛܪ̈ܛܝܘܛܐ ܡܬܩܪܒܝܢ
37 ܗܘܘ ܠܗ ܘܐܡܪܝܢ. ܫܠܡ ܠܟ. ܐܢ ܐܢܬ ܗܘ ܡܠܟܐ
ܕܝܗܘ̈ܕܝܐ ܐܚܐ ܢܦܫܟ. ܘܣܡܘ ܗܘܘ ܒܪܫܗ ܟܠܝܠܐ
38 ܕܟܘ̈ܒܝܐ. ܘܟܬܝܒ ܗܘܐ ܐܦ ܦܛܩܐ ܘܣܝܡ ܠܥܠ
ܡܢܗ. ܗܢܘ ܡܠܟܐ ܕܝܗܘ̈ܕܝܐ ⁘
39 ܚܕ ܡܢ ܗܢܘܢ ܕܝܢ ܥܒ̈ܕܝ ܒܝ̈ܫܬܐ ܕܐܨܛܠܒܘ ܗܘܘ ܥܡܗ.
ܡܓܕܦ ܗܘܐ ܥܠܘܗܝ ܘܐܡܪ. ܠܐ ܗܘܝܬ ܡܫܝܚܐ.
40 ܐܚܐ ܢܦܫܟ ܘܐܚܝܢ ܐܦ ܠܢ. ܘܟܐܐ ܒܗ ܚܒܪܗ ܗܘ
ܐܚܪܢܐ ܘܐܡܪ ܠܗ. ܐܦܠܐ ܡܢ ܐܠܗܐ ܕܚܠ ܐܢܬ.
41 ܕܗܘܐ ܐܦ ܚܢ ܒܗ ܚܢ ܒܕܝܢܐ. ܘܗܘܐ ܐܚܢܢ ܐܝܟ
ܕܙܕܩ ܗܘܐ ܗܘܘ. ܘܐܝܟ ܕܥܒܕܢ ܐܬܦܪܥܢ. ܗܢܐ
42 ܕܝܢ ܐܦ ܠܐ ܡܕܡ ܕܣܪܝܩ ܥܒܕ ܠܗ. ܘܐܡܪ ܠܝܫܘܥ

ܟܠܗ ܟܢܫܐ ܘܐܡܪܝܢ ܫܩܘܠܝܗܝ ܠܗܢܐ ܘܫܪܝ ܠܢ
19 ܠܒܪ ܐܒܐ. ܗܘ ܕܡܛܠ ܗܦ̈ܘܟܝܬܐ ܘܩ̈ܛܠܐ ܕܗܘܐ
17 ܗܘܐ ܒܝܬ ܐܣܘܪܐ. ܘܥܝܕ ܗܘܐ ܦܝܠܛܘܤ ܕܢܗܘܐ
20 ܫܪܐ ܠܗܘܢ ܚܕ ܐܝܟ ܕܒܥܕܥܕܐ. ܘܬܘܒ ܩܪܐ ܐܢܘܢ
ܦܝܠܛܘܤ ܘܐܡܪ ܠܗܘܢ. ܡܛܠ ܕܨܒܐ ܗܘܐ
21 ܕܢܫܪܝܘܗܝ ܠܝܫܘܥ. ܗܢܘܢ ܕܝܢ ܩܥܝܢ ܗܘܘ ܘܐܡܪܝܢ
22 ܙܩܘܦܝܗܝ ܙܩܘܦܝܗܝ. ܗܘ ܕܝܢ ܕܬܠܬ ܙܒܢܝܢ ܐܡܪ ܠܗܘܢ.
ܡܢܐ ܓܝܪ ܕܒܝܫ ܥܒܕ ܗܢܐ. ܡܕܡ ܓܝܪ ܕܫܘܐ ܠܡܘܬܐ
ܠܐ ܡܫܟܚܢܐ ܒܗ. ܐܪܕܘܗܝ ܗܟܝܠ ܘܐܫܒܘܩܝܘܗܝ.
23 ܘܗܢܘܢ ܬܒܥܝܢ ܗܘܘ ܒܩܠܐ ܪܒܐ. ܘܐܡܪܝܢ ܠܗ
ܕܢܙܩܘܦ. ܘܥܫܢ ܗܘܐ ܩܠܗܘܢ. ܘܕܪ̈ܒܝ ܟܗ̈ܢܐ
24 ܕܥܡܗܘܢ. ܘܦܣܩ ܦܝܠܛܘܤ ܕܬܗܘܐ ܫܐܠܬܗܘܢ.
25 ܘܫܪܐ ܠܗܘܢ ܠܗܘ ܕܡܛܠ ܩ̈ܛܠܐ ܘܗܦ̈ܘܟܝܐ ܗܘܐ
ܒܝܬ ܐܣܘܪܐ ܐܝܟ ܕܫܐܠܘ. ܘܠܝܫܘܥ ܐܫܠܡ
ܠܨܒܝܢܗܘܢ ◦◦◦
26 ܘܟܕ ܡܘܒܠܝܢ ܠܗ. ܐܚܕܘ ܠܫܡܥܘܢ ܩܘܪܝܢܝܐ. ܕܐܬܐ
ܗܘܐ ܡܢ ܩܪܝܬܐ. ܕܢܫܩܘܠ ܙܩܝܦܐ ܘܢܐܬܐ ܒܬܪ
27 ܝܫܘܥ. ܘܐܬܐ ܗܘܐ ܒܬܪܗ ܣܘܓܐܐ ܕܥܡܐ.
28 ܘܢܫ̈ܐ ܕܡܪܩܕܢ ܗܘܝ ܥܠܘܗܝ ܘܐܠܝܢ. ܘܐܬܦܢܝ ܝܫܘܥ
ܠܘܬܗܝܢ ܘܐܡܪ ܠܗܝܢ. ܒ̈ܢܬ ܐܘܪܫܠܡ ܠܐ ܬܒܟܝܢ
29 ܥܠܝ. ܐܠܐ ܒܟܝܢ ܥܠ ܢܦܫܟܝܢ ܘܥܠ ܒ̈ܢܝܟܝܢ. ܕܗܐ ܐܬܝܢ
ܝܘܡ̈ܬܐ ܕܒܗܘܢ ܬܐܡܪܢ. ܛܘܒܝܗܝܢ ܠܥܩܪ̈ܬܐ.
30 ܘܠܟܪ̈ܣܬܐ ܕܠܐ ܝܠܕ. ܘܠܬ̈ܕܝܐ ܕܠܐ ܐܝܢܩܘ. ܗܝܕܝܢ

ܕܠܘܩܐ

6 ܠܡܪܝܐ. ܦܝܠܛܘܣ ܕܝܢ ܟܕ ܫܡܥ ܕܐܡܪܝܢ ܕܡܢ
7 ܓܠܝܠܐ. ܫܐܠ ܕܐܢ ܡܢ ܓܠܝܠܐ ܗܘ. ܘܟܕ ܫܡܥ
ܕܡܢ ܬܚܝܬ ܫܘܠܛܢܐ ܗܘ ܕܗܪܘܕܣ ܫܕܪܗ ܠܘܬܗ.
ܡܛܠ ܕܐܦ ܗܘ ܕܝܢ ܗܪܘܕܣ ܒܐܘܪܫܠܡ ܗܘܐ
8 ܒܗܢܘܢ ܝܘܡܬܐ ܕܦܛܝܪܐ. ܗܪܘܕܣ ܕܝܢ ܟܕ ܚܙܐ
ܠܝܫܘܥ ܛܒ ܚܕܝ. ܛܒ ܓܝܪ ܨܒܐ ܗܘܐ ܠܚܙܝܘܗܝ ܡܢ
ܙܒܢܐ ܣܓܝ. ܡܛܠ ܕܫܡܝܥ ܗܘܐ ܥܠܘܗܝ ܘܣܒܪ
9 ܗܘܐ ܕܢܚܙܐ ܐܬܐ ܚܕܐ ܡܢܗ ܕܗܘܝܐ. ܘܫ̈ܐܠܐ
ܣܓ̈ܝܐܬܐ ܡܫܐܠ ܗܘܐ ܠܗ. ܗܘ ܕܝܢ ܡܕܡ
ܦܬܓܡܐ ܠܐ ܐܦܢܝܗ. ܐܝܟ ܗܘ ܕܠܐ ܗܘܐ ܬܡܢ
10 ܗܘܐ. ܪ̈ܒܝ ܟܗ̈ܢܐ ܕܝܢ ܘܣܦܪ̈ܐ ܩܝܡܝܢ ܗܘܘ
11 ܘܐܟܠܝܢ ܩܪ̈ܨܘܗܝ ܡܟܠܐܝܬ. ܘܒܣܝ ܒܗ ܗܪܘܕܣ
ܘܩܠܣܘܗܝ. ܘܐܠܒܫܗ ܫܘܬܐ ܙܚܘܪܐ ܕܒܘܨܐ.
12 ܘܫܕܪܗ ܠܘܬ ܦܝܠܛܘܣ. ܘܒܗ ܒܝܘܡܐ ܗܘ ܗܘܬ
ܬܪܥܘܬܐ ܒܝܢ ܗܪܘܕܣ ܠܦܝܠܛܘܣ. ܡܛܠ ܕܩܕܡ ܒܥܠܕܒܒܐ
13 ܗܘܘ. ܦܝܠܛܘܣ ܕܝܢ ܩܪܐ ܠܪ̈ܒܝ ܟܗ̈ܢܐ ܘܠܐܪ̈ܟܘܢܐ
14 ܘܠܥܡܐ ܟܠܗ ܘܐܡܪ ܠܗܘܢ. ܩܪܒܬܘܢ ܠܝ ܓܒܪܐ
ܗܢܐ. ܕܐܡܪܬܘܢ ܠܝ ܕܡܗܦܟ ܠܥܡܟܘܢ. ܘܗܐ ܐܢܐ
ܒܨܝܬܗ ܠܥܝ̈ܢܝܟܘܢ ܘܡܕܡ ܠܐ ܐܫܟܚܬ ܒܗ. ܡܢ
15 ܐܠܝܢ ܕܡܪܫܝܢ ܐܢܬܘܢ ܒܗ. ܘܐܦܠܐ ܗܪܘܕܣ.
ܫܕܪܬܗ ܓܝܪ ܠܘܬܗ ܘܡܕܡ ܕܫܘܐ ܠܡܘܬܐ ܠܐ
ܐܫܟܚ ܒܗ. ܘܐܦܠܐ ܗܘ ܐܡܪ ܠܗ ܡܕܡ ܕܥܒܕܗ.
16, 18 ܐܪܕܝܘܗܝ، ܗܟܝܠ ܘܐܫܒܩܝܘܗܝ. ܘܩܥܘ ܟܠܗ

63 ܘܓ̈ܒܪܐ ܕܐܚܝܕܝܢ ܗܘܘ ܠܗ ܠܝܫܘܥ ܡܒܙܚܝܢ ܗܘܘ
64 ܒܗ. ܘܡܚܝܢ ܗܘܘ ܠܗ. ܘܚܦܘ ܐ̈ܦܘܗܝ، ܘܐܡܪܝܢ ܠܗ.
65 ܐܬܢܒܐ ܡܢܘ ܡܚܝܟ. ܘܬܘܒ ܐܚܪ̈ܢܝܬܐ ܣܓ̈ܝܐܬܐ.
66 ܘܡܓܕ̣ܦܝܢ ܗܘܘ ܘܐܡܪܝܢ ܥܠܘܗܝ. ܘܟܕ ܢܓܗܬ.
ܐܬܟܢܫܘ ܩܫ̈ܝܫܐ ܘܪ̈ܒܝ ܟܗ̈ܢܐ ܘܣ̈ܦܪܐ. ܘܐܣܩܘܗܝ،
67 ܠܟܢܘܫܬ ܟܢܘ̈ܫܬܗܘܢ. ܘܐܡܪܝܢ ܐܢ ܐܢܬ ܗܘ
ܡܫܝܚܐ ܐܡܪ ܠܢ. ܐܡܪ ܠܗܘܢ ܐܢ ܐܡܪ ܠܟܘܢ ܠܐ
68 ܬܗܝܡܢܘܢ. ܘܐܢ ܐܫܐܠܟܘܢ ܠܐ ܡܦܢܝܢ ܐܢܬܘܢ
69 ܠܝ ܦܬܓܡܐ. ܘܐܦܠܐ ܫܪܝܢ ܐܢܬܘܢ ܠܝ. ܡܢ ܗܫܐ
ܓܝܪ ܢܗܘܐ ܒܪܗ ܕܐܢܫܐ ܝܬܒ ܡܢ ܝܡܝܢܐ ܕܚܝܠܐ
70 ܕܐܠܗܐ. ܐܡܪܝܢ ܟܠܗܘܢ ܐܢܬ ܗܘ ܒܪܗ ܕܐܠܗܐ.
ܐܡܪ ܠܗܘܢ ܐܢܬܘܢ ܐܡܪ̈ܝܢ ܐܢܬܘܢ ܕܐܢܐ ܐܢܐ.
71 ܐܡܪܝܢ ܡܢܐ ܬܘܒ ܡܬܒܥܝܐ ܠܢ ܣܗܕܘܬܐ. ܗܐ
XXIII. ܓܝܪ ܐܢܚܢ ܫܡܥܢ ܡܢ ܦܘܡܗ. ܘܩܡܘ ܟܠܗ ܟܢܫܐ.
2 ܘܐܝܬܝܘܗܝ، ܠܘܬ ܦܝܠܛܘܣ. ܘܫܪܝܘ ܐܟܠܝܢ ܩ̈ܪܨܘܗܝ،
ܘܐܡܪܝܢ ܗܘܘ. ܐܫܟܚܢ ܠܗܢܐ ܕܡܗܦܟ ܥܡܢ.
ܘܟܠܐ ܠܡ ܕܟܣܦ ܪܫܐ ܠܩܣܪ ܠܐ ܢܬܠ. ܘܐܡܪ ܥܠ
3 ܢܦܫܗ ܕܗܘܝܘ ܡܠܟܐ ܡܫܝܚܐ. ܐܡܪ ܠܗ ܦܝܠܛܘܣ
ܐܢܬ ܗܘ ܡܠܟܐ ܕܝܗ̈ܘܕܝܐ. ܐܡܪ ܠܗ ܐܢܬ ܐܡܪܬ.
4 ܐܡܪ ܦܝܠܛܘܣ ܠܪ̈ܒܝ ܟܗ̈ܢܐ ܘܠܟܢܫܐ ܗܘ. ܐܢܐ
ܡܕܡ ܥܠܬܐ ܠܐ ܡܫܟܚ ܐܢܐ ܥܠ ܓܒܪܐ ܗܢܐ.
5 ܗܢܘܢ ܕܝܢ ܡܬܚܡܨܝܢ ܘܐܡܪܝܢ ܐܙܝܥܗ ܒܥܡܐ.
ܟܕ ܡܠܦ ܒܟܠܗ ܝܗܘܕ. ܘܫܪܝ ܡܢ ܓܠܝܠܐ ܥܕܡܐ

ܕܠܘܩܐ

50 ܘܡܚܐ ܚܕ ܡܢܗܘܢ ܠܥܒܕܗ ܕܪܒ ܟܗ̈ܢܐ ܘܦܣܩܗ̇
51 ܐܕܢܗ ܕܝܡܝܢܐ. ܥܢܐ ܝܫܘܥ ܘܐܡܪ ܥܕܘ ܥܕܡܐ
52 ܠܗܕܐ. ܘܩܪܒ ܠܐܕܢܗ ܘܐܣܝܗ̇. ܘܐܡܪ ܘܐܦ ܠܗܘܢ
ܪ̈ܒܝ ܟܗ̈ܢܐ ܘܐܣܛܪܛܓ̈ܐ ܕܗܝܟܠܐ ܘܩ̈ܫܝܫܐ.
ܐܝܟ ܕܥܠ ܓܝܣܐ ܢܦܩܬܘܢ. ܥܠܝ ܒܣ̈ܝܦܐ ܘܒܚܘܛܪ̈ܐ.
53 ܟܠܝܘܡ ܕܥܡܟܘܢ ܗܘܝܬ ܒܗܝܟܠܐ. ܠܐ ܡܘܫܛܝܢ
ܗܘܝܬܘܢ ܥܠܝ ܐܝ̈ܕܝܐ. ܐܠܐ ܗܕܐ ܗܝ ܫܥܬܟܘܢ
54 ܘܫܘܠܛܢܟܘܢ ܕܚܫܘܟܐ. ܘܐܚܕܘܗܝ ܘܐܝܬܝܘܗܝ
ܠܒܝܬܗ ܕܪܒ ܟܗ̈ܢܐ. ܫܡܥܘܢ ܕܝܢ ܟܐܦܐ ܐܬܐ
55 ܗܘܐ ܒܬܪܗ ܡܢ ܪܘܚܩܐ. ܘܢܘܪܐ ܫܓܝܪܐ ܗܘܬ
ܒܡܨܥܬ ܕܪܬܐ. ܘܝܬܒܝܢ ܗܘܘ ܚܕܪܝܗ̇. ܘܝܬܒ ܗܘܐ
56 ܟܐܦܐ ܒܝܢܬܗܘܢ. ܘܚܙܬܗ ܐܡܬܐ ܚܕܐ ܕܝܬܒ
ܠܘܬ ܢܘܪܐ. ܘܚܪܬ ܒܗ ܘܐܡܪܐ ܗܢܐ ܥܡܗ
57 ܗܘܐ. ܘܗܘ ܟܦܪ ܘܐܡܪ ܐܢܬܬܐ ܠܐ ܝܕܥܢܐ ܠܗ.
58 ܘܒܬܪ ܩܠܝܠ ܚܙܝܗܝ ܘܐܦ ܐܚܪܢܐ ܘܗܟܘܬ ܐܡܪ.
59 ܘܐܡܪ ܟܐܦܐ ܠܐ ܗܘܝܬ ܡܢܗܘܢ. ܘܒܬܪ ܫܥܐ
ܚܕܐ ܡܬܚܪܐ ܗܘܐ ܐܚܪܢܐ ܘܐܡܪ. ܫܪܝܪܐܝܬ ܘܐܦ
60 ܗܢܐ ܥܡܗ ܗܘܐ. ܐܦ ܓܠܝܠܝܐ ܗܘ ܓܝܪ. ܘܐܡܪ
ܟܐܦܐ ܓܒܪܐ ܠܐ ܝܕܥ ܐܢܐ ܡܢܐ ܐܡܪ ܐܢܬ. ܘܒܗ̇
61 ܒܫܥܬܐ ܩܪܐ ܬܪܢܓܠܐ. ܘܐܬܦܢܝ ܡܪܢ ܚܪ ܒܗ
ܒܟܐܦܐ. ܘܐܬܕܟܪ ܟܐܦܐ ܡܠܬܗ ܕܡܪܢ ܕܐܡܪ
ܠܗ. ܕܥܕ ܠܐ ܢܩܪܐ ܬܪܢܓܠܐ ܬܪ̈ܬܝܢ ܙܒ̈ܢܝܢ. ܬܠܬ ܙܒ̈ܢܝܢ
62 ܬܟܦܘܪ ܒܝ. ܘܢܦܩ ܒܟܐ ܡܪܝܪܐܝܬ ○ ○

ܕܬܬܦܢܐ ܡܢ. ܕܒܗ ܙ̈ܘܥܐ ܐܬܡܠܝܘ. ܘܡܒܕܡ ܕܟܠ
38 ܗܘ ܠܡܬܠܡܕܘ ܠܗ. ܘܗܘܝ ܐܡܪ ܠܗ. ܦܢܝ ܗܘܐ
ܐܢܬ ܠܟ ܠܒܝܬܟ ܬܠܬ ܝܘ̈ܡܝܢ. ܐܡܪ ܠܗܘܢ ܡܫܡܫ
ܘܡܟܪܙ ܒܟܠ ܀ ܀ ܀
39 ܘܢܦܩ ܗܘܐ ܘܐܙܠ ܐܝܟ ܕܥܒܕ ܗܘܐ ܠܟܘܪܐ ܕܡܕܝܢܬܐ
40 ܕܥܒܕ ܝܫܘܥ. ܘܐܙܠ ܒܥܒܪܐ ܘܐܦ ܬܠܡ̈ܝܕܘܗܝ. ܘܟܕ
ܗܦܟ ܠܗ ܠܥܒܪܬܐ. ܐܡܪ ܠܗܘܢ ܢܦܠ ܕܠܐ ܬܬܠܘܢ
41 ܠܟܠܗ ܥܡܐ. ܘܗܘ ܦܪܩ ܡܣܟܝܢ ܐܝܟ ܡܥܕܪܐ
42 ܒܒܐܦܐ. ܘܗܘ ܒܪܒܘܬܗ، ܘܡܫܟܚܐ ܗܘܐ ܘܐܡܪ.
ܐܒܝ ܐܝ، ܡܫܡܫܐ ܢܫܪܝܬ ܒܗܘܐ ܗܢܐ. ܐܠܐ ܠܐ
43 ܢܫܒܘܩ ܫܡܘܐ ܐܠܐ ܕܒܥܐ. ܘܐܬܚܝܠ ܠܗ ܡܠܐܟܐ
44 ܟܕ ܡܫܬܠܛ ܠܗ. ܘܗܘܐ ܒܪܢܫܐ ܙܒܢܐ. ܘܫܦܠܐܬ
ܡܠܟܐ ܗܘܐ. ܘܗܘܬ ܕܒܟܠܗ ܐܝܟ ܬ̈ܠܬܐ ܕܕܒܪܐ.
45 ܘܫܠܐ ܗܘܬ ܟܠ ܐܪܒܥܐ. ܘܡܢ ܡܢ ܠܬܠܗ. ܘܐܬܐ
ܠܗܬ ܬܠܡ̈ܝܕܘܗܝ، ܘܐܬܒܥܝ ܐܝܟ ܟܕ ܕܡܒܥܝܢ ܡܢ
46 ܒܡܬܘܗ. ܐܡܪ ܠܗܘܢ ܡܢܐ ܕܡܒܥܝܢ ܐܢܬܘܢ.
ܘܡܟܪܙ ܘܠܐ ܕܠܐ ܬܬܠܘܢ ܠܫܘܥܢܐ ܀ ܀
47 ܘܟܕ ܗܘ ܡܟܠܠ ܗܘܐ. ܐܬܚܝܠ، ܒܢܫܐ ܫܦܝܪܐ. ܘܗܘ
ܕܡܬܕܝܢܐ ܗܘܐ ܢܗܘܪܐ ܚܕ ܡܢ ܬ̈ܠܡܝܕܘܗܝ. ܐܬܐ
48 ܗܘܐ ܡܕܡܫܝܚܘ. ܘܩܪܒ ܢܩܫ ܠܫܘܒ. ܐܡܪ ܠܗ
ܫܘܒ ܢܗܘܪܐ. ܒܫܡܫܬܐ ܡܫܠܡ ܐܢܬ ܠܗ ܠܒܪܗ
49 ܕܒܪܬܐ. ܟܕ ܚܙܘ ܕܝܢ ܐܢܫܝܢ ܕܒܥܝܢ ܡܕܡ ܕܢܬܠ.
ܠܡܘܬܐ. ܐܡܪܝܢ ܠܗ ܡܝܬܬ ܢܡܫܐ ܐܠܘܟ ܒܩܦܐ.

26 ܥܒܕ̈ܝ ܛܒ̈ܬܐ ܡܬܩܪܝܢ. ܐܢܬܘܢ ܕܝܢ ܠܐ ܗܟܢܐ.
ܐܠܐ ܐܝܢܐ ܕܪܒ ܒܟܘܢ ܢܗܘܐ ܐܝܟ ܙܥܘܪܐ.
ܘܡܢܐ ܕܪܝܫܐ ܗܘ ܐܝܟ ܡܫܡܫܢܐ ܘܠܐ ܐܝܟ
27 ܡܫܬܡܫܢܐ. ܡܢܘ ܓܝܪ ܪܒ ܕܣܡܝܟ ܐܘ ܕܡܫܡܫ. ܠܐ
28 ܗܐ ܐܢܐ ܐܝܟ ܡܫܡܫܢܐ ܐܝܬܝ ܒܝܢܬܟܘܢ. ܐܢܬܘܢ
29 ܕܝܢ ܕܟܬܪܬܘܢ ܥܡܝ ܒܢܣܝܘ̈ܢܝ. ܘܐܢܐ ܡܫܬܘܕܐ
ܐܢܐ ܠܟܘܢ ܐܝܟܢܐ ܕܐܫܬܘܕܝ ܠܝ ܐܒܝ ܡܠܟܘܬܐ.
30 ܕܬܐܟܠܘܢ ܘܬܫܬܘܢ ܥܡܝ ܥܠ ܦܬܘܪܝ ܒܡܠܟܘܬܐ.
ܘܬܬܒܘܢ ܥܠ ܬܪ̈ܥܣܪ ܟܘܪ̈ܣܘܢ. ܘܬܕܘܢܘܢ ܬܪ̈ܥܣܪ
31 ܫܒ̈ܛܐ ܕܒܝܬ ܐܝܣܪܝܠ. ܘܐܡܪ ܡܪܢ ܠܫܡܥܘܢ.
ܫܡܥܘܢ. ܗܐ ܣܛܢܐ ܒܥܐ ܕܢܪܒܠܟܘܢ ܐܝܟ
32 ܕܠܚ̈ܛܐ. ܐܢܐ ܕܝܢ ܒܥܝܬ ܥܠܝܟ ܕܠܐ ܬܚܣܪ
ܗܝܡܢܘܬܟ. ܘܐܦ ܐܢܬ ܒܙܒܢ ܐܬܦܢ ܘܫܪܪ ܠܐܚ̈ܝܟ.
33 ܐܡܪ ܠܗ ܗܘ. ܡܪܝ ܥܡܟ ܡܛܝܒ ܐܢܐ ܘܐܦ ܠܒܝܬ
34 ܐܣܝ̈ܪܐ ܘܐܦ ܠܡܘܬܐ ܠܡܐܙܠ. ܐܡܪ ܠܗ ܝܫܘܥ.
ܐܡܪܢܐ ܠܟ ܕܥܕܠܐ ܢܩܪܐ ܬܪܢܓܠܐ ܝܘܡܢܐ ܬܪ̈ܬܝܢ
ܙܒ̈ܢܝܢ. ܬܠܬ ܙܒ̈ܢܝܢ ܬܟܦܘܪ ܒܝ ܕܠܐ ܝܕܥ ܐܢܬ ܠܝ. ܀
35 ܐܡܪ ܠܗܘܢ ܟܕ ܫܕܪܬܟܘܢ ܕܠܐ ܟܝ̈ܣܐ ܘܕܠܐ
ܬܪ̈ܡܠܐ ܘܕܠܐ ܡ̈ܣܢܐ. ܕܠܡܐ ܡܕܡ ܚܣܪ ܠܟܘܢ.
36 ܐܡܪܝܢ ܠܗ ܐܦ ܠܐ ܡܕܡ. ܐܡܪ ܠܗܘܢ ܡܢ ܗܫܐ
ܡܢ ܕܐܝܬ ܠܗ ܟܝܣܐ ܐܘ ܬܪܡܠܐ ܢܫܩܘܠ. ܘܡܢ
ܕܠܝܬ ܠܗ ܣܝܦܐ ܢܙܒܢ ܢܚܬܗ ܘܢܙܒܢ ܠܗ ܣܝܦܐ.
37 ܐܡܪ ܐܢܐ ܠܟܘܢ ܓܝܪ ܕܐܦ ܗܕܐ ܕܟܬܝܒܐ ܥܬܝܕܐ

ܕܥܐܠ. ܐܡܪܘ ܠܡܪܗ ܕܒܝܬܐ. ܪܒܢ ܐܡܪ ܐܝܟܐ
ܗܘ ܒܝܬ ܡܫܪܝܐ. ܐܝܟܐ ܕܐܟܘܠ ܦܨܚܐ ܥܡ
12 ܬܠܡܝ̈ܕܝ. ܗܘ ܡܚܘܐ ܠܟܘܢ ܥܠܝܬܐ ܚܕܐ ܪܒܬܐ
13 ܕܡܫܘܝܐ. ܬܡܢ ܛܝܒܘ. ܘܐܙܠܘ ܐܫܟܚܘ ܐܝܟ ܡܐ
ܕܐܡܪ ܠܗܘܢ. ܘܛܝܒܘ ܦܨܚܐ. ◦ ○ ◦
14 ܘܟܕ ܗܘܐ ܕܝܢ ܥܕܢܐ. ܐܣܬܡܟ ܗܘ ܘܫ̈ܠܝܚܘܗܝ
15 ܥܡܗ. ܐܡܪ ܠܗܘܢ. ܡܪܓ ܪܓܝܬ ܕܐܟܘܠ ܥܡܟܘܢ
16 ܦܨܚܐ ܥܕ ܠܐ ܐܚܫ. ܐܡܪܢܐ ܠܟܘܢ ܓܝܪ ܕܡܟܝܠ
ܠܐ ܐܟܠܝܢܘܗܝ ܥܕܡܐ ܕܢܫܬܠܡ ܒܡܠܟܘܬܗ
ܕܐܠܗܐ ·⊙·
19 ܘܢܣܒ ܠܚܡܐ ܘܐܘܕܝ ܥܠܘܗܝ. ܘܩܨܐ ܘܝܗܒ ܠܗܘܢ.
ܘܐܡܪ ܗܢܘ ܦܓܪܝ ܕܥܠ ܐ̈ܦܝܟܘܢ. ܗܟܢܐ ܗܘܝܬܘܢ
17 ܥܒܕܝܢ ܠܕܘܟܪܢܝ. ܘܢܣܒ ܟܣܐ ܘܐܘܕܝ ܥܠܘܗܝ. ܘܐܡܪ
18 ܣܒܘ ܗܢܐ ܦܠܓܘ ܒܝܢܬܟܘܢ. ܐܡܪܢܐ ܠܟܘܢ ܕܡܢ
ܗܫܐ ܠܐ ܐܫܬܐ ܡܢ ܐܕܫܐ ܗܢܐ ܕܓܦܬܐ.
21 ܥܕܡܐ ܕܬܐܬܐ ܡܠܟܘܬܗ ܕܐܠܗܐ. ܒܪܡ ܕܝܢ ܗܐ
22 ܐܝܕܗ ܕܡܫܠܡܢܝ ܥܡܝ ܥܠ ܦܬܘܪܐ. ܘܒܪܗ ܕܐܢܫܐ
ܐܙܠ ܐܝܟܢܐ ܕܦܣܝܩ ܗܘܐ ܥܠܘܗܝ. ܒܪܡ ܕܝܢ ܘܝ ܠܗ
23 ܠܓܒܪܐ ܕܒܐܝܕܗ ܡܫܬܠܡ. ܘܫܪܝܘ ܗܢܘܢ ܕܢܒܥܘܢ
ܒܝܢܬܗܘܢ. ܕܡܢܘ ܟܝ ܗܘ ܕܗܕܐ ܥܬܝܕ ܠܡܥܒܕ ⊙
24 ܘܗܘܐ ܚܪܝܢܐ ܒܝܢܬܗܘܢ. ܕܡܢ ܐܝܬ ܒܗܘܢ ܪܒ.
25 ܐܡܪ ܠܗܘܢ ܡܪܢ. ܡ̈ܠܟܝܗܘܢ ܕܥܡ̈ܡܐ ܡܪ̈ܝܗܘܢ
ܐܢܘܢ. ܘܐܝܠܝܢ ܕܫ̈ܠܝܛܐ ܐܢܘܢ ܘܕܫܦܝܪ ܥܒܕܝܢ.

36 ܕܐܪܥܐ. ܥܝܪܘ ܗܟܝܠ ܒܟܠܙܒܢ. ܘܬܗܘܘܢ ܒܥܝܢ
ܕܬܫܘܘܢ ܠܡܥܪܩ ܡܢ ܗܠܝܢ ܕܥܬ̈ܝܕܢ ܠܡܗܘܐ.
ܘܕܬܩܘܡܘܢ ܩܕܡ ܒܪܗ ܕܐܢܫܐ ܀
37 ܘܒܐܝܡܡܐ ܡܠܦ ܗܘܐ ܒܗܝܟܠܐ. ܘܒܠ̈ܠܝܘܬܐ
ܢܦܩ ܗܘܐ ܒܐܬ ܒܛܘܪܐ ܕܡܬܩܪܐ ܕܒܝܬ ܙ̈ܝܬܐ.
38 ܘܟܠܗ ܥܡܐ ܡܩܕܡܝܢ ܗܘܘ ܠܘܬܗ ܠܗܝܟܠܐ
ܕܢܫܡܥܘܢܗ ◦
XXII. ܘܩܪܒ ܗܘܐ ܒܥܐܕܐ ܕܦ̈ܛܝܪܐ ܕܡܬܩܪܐ ܦܨܚܐ.
2 ܘܒܥܝܢ ܗܘܘ ܪ̈ܒܝ ܟܗ̈ܢܐ ܘܣ̈ܦܪܐ ܐܝܟܢܐ
ܢܩܛܠܘܢܝܗܝ. ܕܕܚܠܝܢ ܗܘܘ ܓܝܪ ܡܢ ܥܡܐ ◦
3 ܥܠ ܗܘܐ ܕܝܢ ܣܛܢܐ ܒܝܗܘܕܐ ܕܡܬܩܪܐ
ܐܣܟܪܝܘܛܐ. ܕܐܝܬܘܗܝ ܗܘܐ ܡܢ ܡܢܝܢܐ ܕܬܪ̈ܥܣܪ.
4 ܘܐܙܠ ܡܠܠ ܥܡ ܪ̈ܒܝ ܟܗ̈ܢܐ ܘܣ̈ܦܪܐ ܐܝܟ
5 ܕܢܫܠܡܝܘܗܝ ܠܗܘܢ. ܘܚܕܝܘ. ܘܐܫܬܘܕܝܘ ܗܘܘ
6 ܕܢܬܠܘܢ ܠܗ ܟܣܦܐ. ܘܐܫܬܘܕܝ ܠܗܘܢ. ܘܒܥܐ
ܗܘܐ ܠܗ ܦܠܛܐ ܐܝܟܢܐ ܕܢܫܠܡܝܘܗܝ ܠܗܘܢ. ܠܒܪ
ܡܢ ܟܢܫܐ ◦
7 ܘܟܕ ܡܛܝ ܝܘܡܐ ܕܦܨܚܐ ܕܒܗ ܐܝܬ ܗܘܐ ܥܝܕܐ
8 ܕܢܬܢܟܣ ܦܨܚܐ. ܫܕܪ ܠܟܐܦܐ ܘܠܝܘܚܢܢ ܘܐܡܪ
9 ܠܗܘܢ. ܙܠܘ ܛܝܒܘ ܠܢ ܦܨܚܐ ܕܢܐܟܘܠ. ܐܡܪܝܢ ܠܗ
10 ܗܢܘܢ. ܐܝܟܢܐ ܨܒܐ ܐܢܬ ܕܢܛܝܒ. ܐܡܪ ܠܗܘܢ ܗܐ
ܡܐ ܕܥܠܝܢ ܐܢܬܘܢ ܠܡܕܝܢܬܐ. ܦܓܥ ܒܟܘܢ ܓܒܪܐ
11 ܕܫܩܝܠ ܓܪܒܐ ܕܡ̈ܝܐ. ܙܠܘ ܒܬܪܗ ܠܒܝܬܐ ܐܝܟܢܐ

ܒܦܘܡܐ ܕܣܝܦܐ. ܘܢܫܬܒܘܢ ܠܟܠܗܘܢ ܥܡ̈ܡܐ.
ܘܐܘܪܫܠܡ ܬܗܘܐ ܡܬܕܫܐ ܡܢ ܟܠܗܘܢ ܥܡ̈ܡܐ.
25 ܥܕܡܐ ܕܢܫܬܠܡܘܢ ܙܒ̈ܢܐ ܕܥܡ̈ܡܐ. ܢܗܘܘܢ ܕܝܢ
ܐ̈ܬܘܬܐ ܒܫܡܫܐ ܘܒܣܗܪܐ ܘܒܟܘ̈ܟܒܐ. ܘܐܘܠܨܢܐ
ܒܐܪܥܐ ܘܦܘܫܟܢ ܐ̈ܢܫܐ ܕܥܡ̈ܡܐ. ܘܩܠܐ ܕܕܝܡܐ
26 ܠܕܡܐ. ܘܢܦܩܐ ܕܡܦܩ ܢܦܫ̈ܬܐ ܕܒ̈ܢܝ ܐܢܫܐ. ܡܢ
ܕܚܠܬܐ ܕܡܣܟܝܢ ܠܡܕܡ ܕܐܬܐ ܥܠ ܐܪܥܐ. ܘܢܬܙܝܥܘܢ
27 ܚ̈ܝܠܐ ܕܫܡܝܐ. ܘܗܝܕܝܢ ܢܚܙܘܢܝܗܝ ܠܒܪܗ ܕܐܢܫܐ
ܟܕ ܐܬܐ ܒܥܢ̈ܢܐ. ܒܚܝܠܐ ܣܓܝܐܐ ܘܒܫܘܒܚܐ.
28 ܡܐ ܕܫܪܝ ܕܝܢ ܗܠܝܢ ܕܢܗܘܘܢ. ܐܬܩܦܘ ܘܐܪܝܡܘ
ܪ̈ܫܝܟܘܢ. ܡܛܠ ܕܡܛܝ ܠܗ ܦܘܪܩܢܟܘܢ. ∘∘ ∘∘ ∘∘ ∘∘
29 ܘܐܡܪ ܗܘܐ ܠܗܘܢ ܡܬܠܐ ܗܢܐ. ܚܙܘ ܠܬܬܐ
30 ܘܠܟܠܗܘܢ ܐ̈ܝܠܢܐ. ܕܡܐ ܕܫܪܝܘ ܡܦܪ̈ܥܝܢ ܘܡܘܥܝܢ
ܦܐܪ̈ܝܗܘܢ. ܡܬܝܕܥܝܢ ܐܢܬܘܢ ܕܡܛܝ ܠܗ ܩܝܛܐ.
31 ܗܟܢܐ ܐܦ ܐܢܬܘܢ ܡܐ ܕܚܙܝܬܘܢ ܗܠܝܢ ܕܗܘܝܢ.
ܕܥܘ ܕܩܪܝܒܐ ܗܝ ܡܠܟܘܬܐ ܕܐܠܗܐ ◦ ◦ ◦
32 ܐܡܝܢ ܐܡܪܢܐ ܠܟܘܢ. ܕܠܐ ܬܥܒܪ ܫܪܒܬܐ ܗܕܐ.
33 ܥܕܡܐ ܕܗܠܝܢ ܟܠܗܝܢ ܢܗܘܝܢ. ܫܡܝܐ ܘܐܪܥܐ ܢܥܒܪܘܢ.
34 ܘܡ̈ܠܝ ܠܐ ܢܥܒ̈ܪܢ. ܐܙܕܗܪܘ ܕܝܢ ܒܢܦ̈ܫܬܟܘܢ. ܕܠܐ
ܢܝܩܪܘܢ ܠܒ̈ܘܬܟܘܢ ܒܡܐܟܘܠܬܐ ܕܒܣܪܐ. ܘܒܪܘܝܘܬܐ
ܕܚܡܪܐ. ܘܒܪ̈ܢܝܬܐ ܕܥܠܡܐ. ܘܢܩܘܡ ܥܠܝܟܘܢ
35 ܫܠܝܐ ܗܘ ܡܢ ܬܫܥܬ ܥܠܝܟܐ. ܐܝܟ ܦܚܐ ܓܝܪ
ܢܐܬܐ ܥܠ ܟܠܗܘܢ ܐܝܠܝܢ ܕܝܬܒܝܢ ܥܠ ܦܪܨܘܦܗ̇

ܕܠܘܩܐ

ܐܝܬ ܓܝܪ ܠܘܩܕܡ ܗܠܝܢ ܠܡܗܘܐ. ܐܠܐ ܠܐ ܗܝ ܒܥܓܠ
10 ܡܛܠ ܚܪܬܐ. ܢܩܘܡ ܓܝܪ ܥܡܐ ܥܠ ܥܡܐ ܘܡܠܟܘ
11 ܥܠ ܡܠܟܘ. ܘܙܘܥܐ ܪ̈ܘܪܒܐ ܒܕܘܟܐ ܕܘܟܐ.
ܘܡܘ̈ܬܢܐ ܘܟ̈ܦܢܐ ܘܚܙܘܢ ܕܕܚ̈ܠܬܐ ܡܢ ܫܡܝܐ.
12 ܘܢܬܚܙܘܢ ܐ̈ܬܘܬܐ ܪ̈ܘܪܒܬܐ. ܘܣ̈ܬܘܐ ܪ̈ܘܪܒܐ. ܩܕܡ
ܗܠܝܢ ܕܝܢ ܟܠܗܝܢ. ܢܪܡܘܢ ܥܠܝܟܘܢ ܐ̈ܝܕܝܐ
ܘܢܪܕܦܘܢܟܘܢ. ܘܢܫܠܡܘܢܟܘܢ ܠܟܢܘܫܬܐ. ܘܠܒܝܬ
ܐܣ̈ܝܪܐ. ܘܢܩܪܒܘܢܟܘܢ ܩܕܡ ܡ̈ܠܟܐ ܘܗ̈ܓܡܘܢܐ
13 ܡܛܠ ܫܡܝ. ܬܗܘܐ ܠܟܘܢ ܕܝܢ ܣܗܕܘܬܐ ܗܕܐ.
14 ܘܣܝܡܘ ܒ̈ܠܒܝܟܘܢ. ܕܠܐ ܬܗܘܘܢ ܡܬܒܠܝܢ ܠܡܦܩ
15 ܪܘܚܐ. ܐܢܐ ܓܝܪ ܐܬܠ ܠܟܘܢ ܦܘܡܐ ܘܚܟܡܬܐ.
ܐܝܕܐ ܕܠܐ ܡܫܟܚܝܢ ܕܢܩܘܡܘܢ ܠܘܩܒܠܗ̇ ܟܠܗܘܢ
16 ܒܥܠܕܒ̈ܒܝܟܘܢ. ܢܫܠܡܘܢܟܘܢ ܐ̈ܒܗܝܟܘܢ ܘܐ̈ܚܝܟܘܢ
ܘܐ̈ܚܝܢܝܟܘܢ ܘܪ̈ܚܡܝܟܘܢ. ܘܢܩܛܠܘܢ ܡܢܟܘܢ.
17 ܘܬܗܘܘܢ ܣܢܝܐܝܢ ܡܢ ܟܠ ܐܢܫ ܡܛܠ ܫܡܝ.
19, 20 ܒܡܣܝܒܪܢܘܬܐ ܕܝܢ ܬܩܢܘܢ ܢܦܫܟܘܢ. ܡܐ ܕܚܙܝܬܘܢ
ܕܝܢ ܠܐܘܪܫܠܡ ܕܚܕܝܪ ܠܗ̇ ܚܝܠܐ. ܕܥܘ ܕܩܪܒ ܠܗ̇
21 ܚܘܪܒܗ̇. ܘܐܝܠܝܢ ܕܒܝܗܘܕ ܐܢܘܢ ܢܥܪܩܘܢ ܠܛܘܪܐ.
ܘܕܒܓܘܗ̇ ܢܦܩܘܢ ܡܢܗ̇. ܘܐܝܠܝܢ ܕܒܩ̈ܘܪܝܐ ܠܐ ܢܥܠܘܢ
22 ܠܗ̇. ܡܛܠ ܕܝܘ̈ܡܬܐ ܐܢܘܢ ܕܬܒܥܬܐ. ܕܢܫܠܡ ܟܠ
23 ܡܐ ܕܟܬܝܒ. ܘܝ ܕܝܢ ܠܐܝܠܝܢ ܕܒ̈ܛܢܢ ܘܠܐܝܠܝܢ ܕܡ̈ܝܢܩܢ
ܒܗܘܢ ܝܘ̈ܡܬܐ. ܢܗܘܐ ܓܝܪ ܐܘܠܨܢܐ ܪܒܐ
24 ܒܐܪܥܐ. ܘܪܘܓܙܐ ܣܓܝܐܐ ܥܠ ܥܡܐ ܗܢܐ. ܘܢܦܠܘܢ

46 ܐܙܕܗܪܘ ܡܢ ܣܦܪ̈ܐ ܕܨܒܝܢ ܠܡܗܠܟܘ ܒܐܣܛܠܐ.
ܘܪܚܡܝܢ ܫܠܡܐ ܒܫܘܩܐ. ܘܡܘ̈ܬܒܐ ܩܕ̈ܡܝܐ
47 ܒܟܢ̈ܘܫܬܐ. ܘܪܝܫ ܣܡܟܐ ܒܚܫ̈ܡܝܬܐ. ܘܐܟܠܝܢ
ܒ̈ܬܐ ܕܐܪ̈ܡܠܬܐ. ܒܥܠܬܐ ܕܡܘܪܟܝܢ ܨ̈ܠܘܬܗܘܢ.
ܗܢܘܢ ܢܩܒܠܘܢ ܕܝܢܐ ܝܬܝܪܐ. ○ ◎ ○
XXI. ܘܐܪܝܡ ܒܥ̈ܝܢܘܗܝ ܘܚܙܐ ܠܥܬ̈ܝܪܐ ܕܪܡܝܢ ܗܘܘ
2 ܩܘܪ̈ܒܢܝܗܘܢ ܒܝܬ ܓܙܐ. ܘܚܙܐ ܐܦ ܐܪܡܠܬܐ
3 ܡܣܟܢܬܐ ܕܐܪܡܝܬ ܫܡ̈ܘܢܐ ܬܪ̈ܝܢ. ܐܡܪ ܒܫܪܪܬܐ
ܐܡܪܢܐ ܠܟܘܢ. ܕܗܕܐ ܐܪܡܠܬܐ ܡܣܟܢܬܐ
4 ܐܪܡܝܬ. ܝܬܝܪ ܡܢ ܟܠܗܘܢ. ܗܠܝܢ ܓܝܪ ܡܢ ܡܟܐ
ܕܝܬܝܪ ܗܘܐ ܠܗܘܢ ܐܪܡܝܘ ܒܝܬ ܓܙܐ ܩܘܪ̈ܒܢܐ.
ܗܕܐ ܕܝܢ ܡܢ ܡܟܐ ܕܚܣܝܪ ܠܗ̇ ܟܠ ܕܩܢܝܐ ܗܘܬ
ܐܪܡܝܬܗ. ○ ○ ○ ○ ○
5 ܘܟܕ ܐܡܪܘ ܐ̈ܢܫܝܢ ܥܠ ܗܝܟܠܐ ܕܒܟ̈ܐܦܐ ܫܦܝܪ̈ܬܐ
6 ܘܒܩܘܪ̈ܒܢܐ ܡܨܒܬ. ܐܡܪ ܝܫܘܥ ܐܢܬܘܢ ܗܠܝܢ.
ܢܐܬܘܢ ܝܘ̈ܡܬܐ ܕܠܐ ܬܫܬܒܩ ܗܪܟܐ ܟܐܦ ܥܠ
ܟܐܦ ܕܠܐ ܬܬܣܬܪ. ○ ○ ○ ○ ○ ○
7 ܘܫܐܠܘܗܝ ܗܘܘ ܘܐܡܪܝܢ ܠܗ. ܡܠܦܢܐ ܐܡܬܝ ܗܠܝܢ
ܢܗܘܝܢ. ܘܡܢܐ ܐܬܐ ܡܟܐ ܕܡܛܝܢ ܗܠܝܢ ܕܢܗܘܝܢ.
8 ܗܘ ܕܝܢ ܐܡܪ ܠܗܘܢ. ܚܙܘ ܕܠܐ ܬܛܥܘܢ. ܣ̈ܓܝܐܐ
ܓܝܪ ܢܐܬܘܢ ܒܫܡܝ ܘܢܐܡܪܘܢ. ܕܐܢܐ ܐܢܐ. ܘܙܒܢܐ
9 ܩܪܒ. ܠܐ ܬܐܙܠܘܢ ܒܬܪܗܘܢ. ܘܡܐ ܕܫܡܥܝܢ
ܐܢܬܘܢ ܩܪ̈ܒܐ ܘܫܓܘܫܝܐ ܠܐ ܬܬܕܚܠܘܢ. ܗܠܝܢ

32 ܘܒܚܪܬܐ ܕܝܢ ܠܐ ܫܒܩܘ ܒ̈ܢܝܐ. ܘܒܚܪܬܗ ܐܦ ܗܝ
33 ܐܢܬܬܐ. ܒܩܝܡܬܐ ܕܐܝܢܐ ܡܢܗܘܢ ܬܗܘܐ ܐܢܬܬܐ. ܗܐ
34 ܓܝܪ ܠܫܒܥܬܝܗܘܢ ܗܘܬ. ܐܡܪ ܠܗܘܢ ܝܫܘܥ. ܒ̈ܢܘܗܝ
ܕܥܠܡܐ ܗܢܐ ܝܠܕܝܢ ܘܡܬܝܠܕܝܢ. ܘܢܣܒܝܢ ܢ̈ܫܐ ܘܗܘܝܢ
35 ܢ̈ܫܐ ܠܓܒܪ̈ܐ. ܐܝܠܝܢ ܕܝܢ ܕܠܗܘ ܥܠܡܐ ܫܘܘ ܠܡܩܒܠܘ.
ܘܠܗ̇ ܩܝܡܬܐ ܕܡܢ ܒܝܬ ܡ̈ܝܬܐ. ܠܐ ܓܒܪ̈ܐ ܢܣܒܝܢ
36 ܢ̈ܫܐ. ܘܐܦܠܐ ܢ̈ܫܐ ܗܘܝܢ ܠܓܒܪ̈ܐ. ܐܦܠܐ ܠܡܡܬ
ܡܫܟܚܝܢ. ܐܫܬܘܘ ܠܗܘܢ ܓܝܪ ܥܡ ܡ̈ܠܐܟܐ. ܐܝܟ
37 ܒ̈ܢܝܐ ܕܐܠܗܐ ܒ̈ܢܝܐ ܕܩܝܡܬܐ. ܥܠ ܡ̈ܝܬܐ ܕܝܢ
ܕܩܝܡܝܢ. ܘܐܦ ܡܘܫܐ ܪܡܙ. ܟܕ ܡܠܠ ܒܣܢܝܐ
38 ܐܠܗܐ ܡܢ ܣܢܝܐ ܘܐܡܪ. ܡܪܝܐ ܐܠܗܗ ܕܐܒܪܗܡ.
ܘܐܠܗܗ ܕܐܝܣܚܩ. ܘܐܠܗܗ ܕܝܥܩܘܒ. ܘܗܐ
ܐܠܗܐ ܠܐ ܗܘܐ ܕܡ̈ܝܬܐ. ܐܠܐ ܕܚ̈ܝܐ. ܟܠܗܘܢ
ܓܝܪ ܚ̈ܝܝܢ ܐܢܘܢ ܠܗ. ◦ ◦ ◦
39 ܐܡܪܝܢ ܠܗ ܐ̈ܢܫܝܢ ܡܢ ܣ̈ܦܪܐ. ܡܠܦܢܐ ܫܦܝܪ ܐܡܪ
40 ܐܢܬ. ܘܬܘܒ ܠܐ ܐܡܪܚܘ ܠܡܫܐܠܘܬܗ ܡܕܡ. ◦ ◦ ◦
41 ܘܐܡܪ ܗܘܐ ܠܗܘܢ. ܐܝܟܢܐ ܐܡܪܝܢ ܣ̈ܦܪܐ ܥܠ
42 ܡܫܝܚܐ ܕܒܪܗ ܗܘ ܕܕܘܝܕ. ܘܗܘ ܕܘܝܕ ܐܡܪ ܒܟܬܒܐ
ܕܡ̈ܙܡܘܪܐ. ܕܐܡܪ ܡܪܝܐ ܠܡܪܝ ܕܬܒ ܠܟ ܡܢ
43 ܝܡܝܢܝ. ܥܕܡܐ ܕܐܣܝܡ ܒܥܠܕܒ̈ܒܝܟ ܬܚܝܬ ܪ̈ܓܠܝܟ.
44 ܐܢ ܗܟܝܠ ܕܘܝܕ ܡܪܝ ܩܪܐ ܠܗ. ܐܝܟܢܐ ܒܪܗ
ܗܘ. ◦ ◦ ◦
45 ܘܟܕ ܫܡܥ ܗܘܐ ܟܠܗ ܥܡܐ ܐܡܪ ܠܬܠܡ̈ܝܕܘܗܝ.

ܕܠܘܩܐ

19 ܬܫܚܩܝܘܗܝ. ܘܒܥܘ ܗܘܘ ܪ̈ܒܝ ܟܗ̈ܢܐ ܘܣ̈ܦܪܐ
ܕܢܪ̈ܡܘܢ ܥܠܘܗܝ ܐܝ̈ܕܝܐ. ܒܗ ܒܫܥܬܐ. ܝܕܥܘ ܗܘܘ
20 ܓܝܪ ܕܥܠܝܗܘܢ ܐܡܪ. ܘܕܚܠܘ ܡܢ ܥܡܐ. ܘܒܬܪܟܢ
ܫܕܪܘ ܒܢ̈ܝܢܫܐ ܕܢܬܕܡܘܢ ܒܟܐ̈ܢܐ. ܕܢܐܚܕܘܢܝܗ
21 ܒܡܠܬܐ ܘܢܫܠܡܘܢܝܗ ܠܗܓܡܘܢܐ. ܘܫܐܠܘܗܝ
ܘܐܡܪܝܢ ܠܗ. ܡܠܦܢܐ. ܝܕܥܝܢ ܚܢܢ ܕܬܪܝܨܐܝܬ ܡܡܠܠ
ܐܢܬ ܘܡܠܦ ܐܢܬ. ܘܠܐ ܢܣܒ ܐܢܬ ܒܐ̈ܦܐ ܕܐܢܫ.
22 ܐܠܐ ܒܩܘܫܬܐ ܡܠܬܗ ܕܐܠܗܐ ܡܠܦ ܐܢܬ. ܫܠܝܛ
23 ܠܢ ܠܡܬܠ ܟܣܦ ܪܫܐ ܠܩܣܪ ܐܘ ܠܐ. ܘܗܘ ܐܣܬܟܠ
ܒܢܟܠܗܘܢ ܘܐܡܪ ܠܗܘܢ. ܡܢܐ ܡܢܣܝܢ ܐܢܬܘܢ
24 ܠܝ. ܚܘܐܘܢܝ ܕܝܢܪܐ. ܨܠܡܐ ܘܟܬ̈ܒܬܐ ܕܡܢ ܐܝܬ
25 ܥܠܘܗܝ. ܘܚܘܝܘܗܝ ܘܐܡܪܝܢ ܠܗ ܕܩܣܪ. ܐܡܪ
26 ܠܗܘܢ ܗܒܘ ܕܩܣܪ ܠܩܣܪ. ܘܕܐܠܗܐ ܠܐܠܗܐ. ܘܠܐ
ܐܫܟܚܘ ܠܡܐܚܕ ܡܠܬܗ ܩܕܡ ܥܡܐ. ܘܐܬܕܡܪܘ
ܥܠ ܦܬܓܡܗ ܘܫܬܩܘ ܠܗܘܢ. ∘∘ ∘∘ ∘∘
27 ܘܩܪܒܘ ܐ̈ܢܫܝܢ ܡܢ ܙܕܘ̈ܩܝܐ. ܗܢܘܢ ܕܐܡܪܝܢ ܕܠܝܬ
28 ܩܝܡܬܐ. ܘܫܐܠܘܗܝ ܘܐܡܪܝܢ ܠܗ. ܡܠܦܢܐ ܡܘܫܐ
ܟܬܒ ܠܢ. ܕܐܢ ܢܡܘܬ ܐܚܘܗܝ ܕܐܢܫ ܟܕ ܠܝܬ ܠܗ
ܒ̈ܢܝܐ. ܘܢܫܒܘܩ ܐܢܬܬܐ. ܢܣܒ ܐܢܬܬܗ ܐܚܘܗܝ.
29 ܕܢܩܝܡ ܙܪܥܐ ܠܐܚܘܗܝ. ܫܒ̈ܥܐ ܐ̈ܚܝܢ ܐܝܬ ܗܘܘ.
30 ܩܕܡܝܐ ܢܣܒ ܐܢܬܬܐ ܘܡܝܬ ܕܠܐ ܒ̈ܢܝܢ. ܘܢܣܒܗ̇
ܐܚܘܗܝ ܠܐܢܬܬܐ ܗܝ. ܐܦ ܗܘ ܡܝܬ ܕܠܐ ܒ̈ܢܝܢ.
31 ܐܦ ܗܘ ܕܬܠܬܐ ܢܣܒܗ̇. ܘܐܦ ܫܒܥܬܝܗܘܢ ܢܣܒܘܗ̇.

ܡܬܚܫܒܝܢ ܗܘܘ ܒܝܢܬܗܘܢ ܘܐܡܪܝܢ. ܐܢ ܢܐܡܪ
ܕܡܢ ܫܡܝܐ ܗܝ، ܢܐܡܪ ܠܢ. ܘܠܡܢܐ ܠܐ ܗܝܡܢܬܘܢܝܗܝ.
6 ܘܐܢ ܢܐܡܪ ܕܡܢ ܒ̈ܢܝ ܐܢܫܐ ܗܝ. ܪ̈ܓܡܝܢ ܠܢ ܟܠܗ
7 ܥܡܐ. ܡܦܣܝܣ ܓܝܪ ܥܠ ܝܘܚܢ ܕܢܒܝܐ ܗܘ. ܐܡܪܝܢ
8 ܠܗ ܠܐ ܝܕܥܝܢ ܐܢܫ ܡܢ ܐܝܟܐ ܗܝ. ܐܡܪ ܠܗܘܢ
ܝܫܘܥ. ܘܐܦܠܐ ܐܢܐ ܐܡܪ ܐܢܐ ܠܟܘܢ ܒܐܝܢܐ
ܫܘܠܛܢܐ ܥܒܕ ܐܢܐ ܗܠܝܢ. ⁘
9 ܘܫܪܝ ܕܢܐܡܪ ܠܗܘܢ ܡܬܠܐ ܗܢܐ. ܓܒܪܐ ܚܕ ܢܨܒ
ܟܪܡܐ. ܘܐܘܚܕܗ ܠܦ̈ܠܚܐ ܘܚܙܪ ܐܬܪܐ ܦܪܝܩܐ.
10 ܘܒܙܒܢ ܐܒܐ. ܫܕܪ ܥܒܕܗ ܠܘܬ ܦ̈ܠܚܐ ܕܢܬܠܘܢ ܠܗ
ܡܢ ܦ̈ܐܪܘܗܝ ܕܟܪܡܐ. ܘܡܚܘܗܝ ܘܫܕܪܘܗܝ ܟܕ
11 ܣܪܝܩ. ܘܐܘܣܦ ܘܫܕܪ ܠܥܒܕܗ ܐܚܪܢܐ. ܘܐܦ ܠܗܢܐ
13 ܓܠܦܘܗܝ ܘܐܦܩܘܗܝ. ܐܡܪ ܡܪܐ ܟܪܡܐ ܡܢܐ
ܐܥܒܕ. ܐܫܕܪ ܠܒܪܝ ܚܒܝܒܐ. ܟܒܪ ܢܬܟܚܕܘܢ ܡܢܗ.
14 ܟܕ ܚܙܘܗܝ ܕܝܢ ܦ̈ܠܚܐ. ܡܬܚܫܒܝܢ ܗܘܘ ܘܐܡܪܝܢ.
ܗܢܘ ܝܪܬܐ. ܬܘ ܢܩܛܠܝܘܗܝ ܘܬܗܘܐ ܝܪܬܘܬܐ ܕܝܠܢ.
15 ܘܐܦܩܘܗܝ ܠܒܪ ܡܢ ܟܪܡܐ ܘܩܛܠܘܗܝ. ܡܢܐ ܢܥܒܕ
16 ܠܗܘܢ ܡܪܐ ܟܪܡܐ. ܢܐܬܐ ܘܢܘܒܕ ܠܦ̈ܠܚܐ ܗܢܘܢ.
ܘܢܬܠ ܟܪܡܐ ܠܐ̈ܚܪܢܐ. ܟܕ ܫܡܥܘ ܕܝܢ ܗܠܝܢ.
17 ܐܡܪܝܢ ܚܣ ܘܠܐ ܢܗܘܐ. ܗܘ ܕܝܢ ܚܪ ܒܗܘܢ ܘܐܡܪ.
ܘܡܢܘ ܗܢܐ ܕܟܬܝܒ. ܕܟܐܦܐ ܕܐܣܠܝܘ ܒ̈ܢܝܐ.
18 ܗܝ ܗܘܬ ܠܪܫܗ ܕܙܘܝܬܐ. ܟܠ ܐܢܫ ܓܝܪ ܕܢܦܠ ܥܠ
ܗܝ ܟܐܦܐ ܢܬܪܥܥ. ܘܟܠ ܡܢ ܕܬܦܠ ܥܠܘܗܝ

40 ܒܗܘܢ. ܐܡܪ ܠܗܘܢ ܐܡܝܢ ܐܡܪ ܐܢܐ ܠܟܘܢ. ܕܐܢ
41 ܗܠܝܢ ܢܫܬܩܘܢ ܟܐ̈ܦܐ ܗܠܝܢ ܢܩܥܘܢ. ܘܟܕ ܩܪܒ
42 ܘܚܙܐ ܠܡܕܝܢܬܐ ܒܟܐ ܥܠܝܗ ܘܐܡܪ. ܕܐܦ ܒܗܢܐ
ܝܘܡܐ ܝܕܥܬܝ ܕܝܢ ܫܠܡܟܝ. ܐܠܐ ܫܠܡܐ ܠܐ ܐܬܟܣܝ
43 ܠܗ ܡܢ ܥܝܢܝܟܝ. ܢܐܬܘܢ ܕܝܢ ܝܘܡܬܐ ܕܢܚܕܪܘܢܟܝ
ܒܥܠܕ̈ܒܒܝܟܝ. ܘܢܐܠܨܘܢܟܝ ܡܢ ܟܠ ܕܘܟܐ.
44 ܘܢܣܚܦܘܢܟܝ ܥܠ ܐܪܥܐ. ܘܠܒ̈ܢܝܟܝ ܒܓܘܟܝ. ܘܠܐ
ܢܫܒܩܘܢ ܒܟܝ ܟܐܦ ܥܠ ܟܐܦ. ܚܠܦ ܕܠܐ ܝܕܥܬܝ
ܝܘܡܐ ܕܪܘܒܬܟܝ. ◦ ◦ ◦
45 ܘܟܕ ܥܠ ܠܗܝܟܠܐ. ܫܪܝ ܠܡܦܩܘ ܠܐܝܠܝܢ ܕܡܙܒܢܝܢ
46 ܒܗ ܘܙܒܢܐ. ܘܐܡܪ ܟܬܝܒ ܗܘ ܕܒܝܬܝ ܒܝܬ ܨܠܘܬܐ
ܗܘ ܠܟܠܗܘܢ ܥܡ̈ܡܐ. ܐܢܬܘܢ ܕܝܢ ܥܒܕܬܘܢܝܗܝ
47 ܡܥܪܬܐ ܕܓܝ̈ܣܐ. ܘܡܠܦ ܗܘܐ ܟܠܝܘܡ ܒܗܝܟܠܐ.
ܘܪ̈ܒܝ ܟܗ̈ܢܐ ܘܣܦܪ̈ܐ ܘܪܫܐ ܕܥܡܐ ܒܥܝܢ ܗܘܘ
48 ܠܡܘܒܕܘܬܗ. ܘܠܐ ܡܫܟܚܝܢ ܗܘܘ ܡܢܐ ܢܥܒܕܘܢ
ܠܗ. ܟܠܗ ܓܝܪ ܥܡܐ ܬܠܐ ܗܘܐ ܒܗ ܠܡܫܡܥܗ ◦:◦
XX. ܘܗܘܐ ܒܚܕ ܡܢ ܝܘܡ̈ܬܐ. ܟܕ ܡܠܦ ܗܘܐ ܒܗܝܟܠܐ
ܠܥܡܐ. ܘܡܣܒܪ ܗܘܐ. ܩܡܘ ܥܠܘܗܝ ܪ̈ܒܝ ܟܗ̈ܢܐ
2 ܘܣܦܪ̈ܐ ܕܥܡܐ ܥܡ ܩܫ̈ܝܫܐ ܘܐܡܪܝܢ ܠܗ. ܐܡܪ ܠܢ
ܒܐܝܢܐ ܫܘܠܛܢ ܗܠܝܢ ܥܒܕ ܐܢܬ. ܐܘ ܡܢܘ ܝܗܒ
3 ܠܟ ܫܘܠܛܢܐ ܗܢܐ. ܐܡܪ ܠܗܘܢ ܐܦ ܐܢܐ
4 ܐܫܐܠܟܘܢ. ܐܡܪܘ ܠܝ. ܡܥܡܘܕܝܬܗ ܕܝܘܚܢ ܡܢ
5 ܫܡܝܐ ܗܘܬ ܐܘ ܡܢ ܒ̈ܢܝ ܐܢܫܐ. ܗܢܘܢ ܕܝܢ

ܠܗ ܢܬܝܗܒ ܠܗ ܘܢܬܬܘܣܦ ܠܗ. ܘܡܢ ܕܠܝܬ ܠܗ ܐܦ
27 ܗܘ ܕܣܒܪ ܕܐܝܬ ܠܗ ܢܫܬܩܠ ܡܢܗ. ܒܪܡ ܕܝܢ ܐܝܬܘ
ܠܗܪܟܐ ܠܗܢܘܢ ܒ̈ܥܠܕܒܒܝ. ܐܝܠܝܢ ܕܠܐ ܨܒܘ ܕܐܗܘܐ
28 ܥܠܝܗܘܢ ܡܠܟܐ. ܘܩܛܠܘ ܐܢܘܢ ܩܕܡܝ. ܘܟܕ ܐܡܪ
ܗܠܝܢ ܢܦܩ ܡܢ ܬܡܢ ܀
29 ܘܟܕ ܩܪܒ ܗܘܐ ܠܐܘܪܫܠܡ. ܘܡܛܐ ܠܒܝܬ ܦ̈ܓܐ
ܘܠܒܝܬ ܥܢܝܐ. ܘܡܛܐ ܠܘܬ ܛܘܪܐ ܕܡܬܩܪܐ ܕܒܝܬ
30 ܙܝܬ̈ܐ. ܫܕܪ ܠܬܪ̈ܝܢ ܡܢ ܬܠܡ̈ܝܕܘܗܝ. ܘܐܡܪ ܠܗܘܢ
ܙܠܘ ܠܩܪܝܬܐ ܗܝ ܕܠܘܩܒܠܢ. ܘܟܕ ܥܠܝܢ ܐܢܬܘܢ. ܗܐ
ܡܫܟܚܝܢ ܐܢܬܘܢ ܥܝܠܐ ܟܕ ܐܣܝܪ. ܕܐܢܫ ܠܐ ܪܟܒ
31 ܥܠܘܗܝ. ܫܪܘ ܐܝܬܐܘܗܝ. ܘܐܢ ܐܢܫ ܡܫܐܠ ܠܟܘܢ
ܠܡܢܐ ܫܪܝܢ ܐܢܬܘܢ ܠܗ. ܐܡܪܘ ܠܗ ܠܡܪܗ
32, 33 ܡܬܒܥܐ. ܘܐܙܠܘ ܘܐܫܟܚܘ ܗܟܢܐ. ܘܟܕ ܫܐܠܘ
34 ܐܢܘܢ. ܐܬܡܪܘ ܐܢܘܢ ܦܬܓܡܐ ܕܠܡܪܗ ܡܬܒܥܐ.
35 ܘܐܝܬܝܘܗܝ ܠܥܝܠܐ ܠܘܬ ܝܫܘܥ. ܘܐܪܟܒܘ ܥܠܘܗܝ
36 ܡܪ̈ܛܘܛܝܗܘܢ. ܘܐܪܟܒܘܗܝ ܠܝܫܘܥ. ܘܟܕ ܪܕܐ ܗܘܐ.
37 ܦܪܣܝܢ ܗܘܘ ܡܪ̈ܛܘܛܝܗܘܢ ܒܐܘܪܚܐ. ܘܟܕ ܩܪܒ
ܠܡܚܬܬܐ ܕܛܘܪܐ ܕܒܝܬ ܙܝܬ̈ܐ. ܫܪܝܘ ܟܠܗ ܟܢܫܐ
ܚܕܝܢ ܗܘܘ ܘܡܫܒܚܝܢ ܠܐܠܗܐ. ܒܩܠܐ ܪܡܐ ܥܠ
38 ܟܠ ܡܕܡ ܕܚܙܘ. ܘܐܡܪܝܢ ܗܘܘ ܒܪܝܟ ܗܘ ܡܠܟܐ
ܕܐܬܐ ܒܫܡܗ ܕܡܪܝܐ. ܫܠܡܐ ܒܫܡܝܐ
39 ܘܬܫܒܘܚܬܐ ܒܡܪܘܡܐ. ܐܡܪܝܢ ܠܗ ܐܢܫܐ ܡܢ
ܦܪ̈ܝܫܐ ܡܢ ܒܝܢܝ ܗܘ ܟܢܫܐ. ܪܒܢ ܟܐܝ ܒܗܘܢ ܕܠܐ

ܕܠܘܩܐ

13 ܘܠܡܗܦܟܘ. ܘܩܪܐ ܠܥܣܪܐ ܥܒ̈ܕܘܗܝ. ܘܝܗܒ ܠܗܘܢ
ܥܣܪܐ ܡ̈ܢܝܢ. ܘܐܡܪ ܠܗܘܢ ܐܬܬܗܦܟܘ ܒܗܘܢ ܥܕ
14 ܐܬܐ ܐܢܐ. ܘܒ̈ܢܝ ܡܕܝܢܬܗ ܣܢܝܢ ܗܘܘ ܠܗ. ܘܫܕܪܘ
ܐܝܓܪ̈ܬܐ ܒܬܪܗ ܘܐܡܪܝܢ ܠܗ. ܠܐ ܨܒܝܢ ܚܢܢ ܕܢܡܠܟ
15 ܥܠܝܢ ܗܢܐ. ܘܟܕ ܢܣܒ ܡܠܟܘܬܐ ܘܗܦܟ. ܐܡܪ ܕܢܩܪܘܢ
ܠܗ ܠܗܢܘܢ ܥܒ̈ܕܘܗܝ ܕܝܗܒ ܗܘܐ ܠܗܘܢ ܟܣܦܐ.
16 ܕܢܕܥ ܡܢܐ ܐܬܬܓܪܘ. ܘܐܬܐ ܩܕܡܝܐ ܘܐܡܪ.
17 ܡܪܝ، ܡܢܝܢܟ ܥܣܪܐ ܡ̈ܢܝܢ ܐܘܬܪ. ܐܡܪ ܠܗ ܐܘܐ
ܥܒܕܐ ܛܒܐ ܕܒܩܠܝܠ ܐܫܬܟܚܬ ܡܗܝܡܢ. ܬܗܘܐ
18 ܫܠܝܛ ܥܠ ܥܣܪܐ ܟܪ̈ܟܝܢ. ܘܐܬܐ ܕܬܪ̈ܝܢ ܐܡܪ ܠܗ.
19 ܡܪܝ، ܡܢܝܢܟ ܚܡܫܐ ܡ̈ܢܝܢ ܥܒܕ. ܐܡܪ ܠܗ ܐܦ ܠܗܘ
ܘܐܦ ܐܢܬ ܬܗܘܐ ܫܠܝܛ ܥܠ ܚܡܫܐ ܟܪ̈ܟܝܢ.
20 ܘܐܬܐ ܐܚܪܢܐ ܘܐܡܪ. ܗܐ ܡܢܝܢܟ ܗܘ ܕܐܝܬ
21 ܗܘܐ ܠܘܬܝ، ܟܕ ܣܝܡ ܒܣܘܕܪܐ. ܕܚܠܬ ܓܝܪ ܡܢܟ
ܕܓܒܪܐ ܐܢܬ ܩܫܝܐ. ܕܫܩܠ ܐܢܬ ܡܕܡ ܕܠܐ ܣܡܬ.
22 ܘܚܨܕ ܐܢܬ ܡܕܡ ܕܠܐ ܙܪܥܬ. ܐܡܪ ܠܗ ܡܪܗ ܡܢ
ܦܘܡܟ ܐܕܘܢܟ ܥܒܕܐ ܒܝܫܐ ܕܠܐ ܡܗܝܡܢ. ܝܕܥ
ܗܘܝܬ ܠܝ ܕܓܒܪܐ ܐܢܐ ܩܫܝܐ. ܘܫܩܠ ܐܢܐ ܡܕܡ
23 ܕܠܐ ܣܡܬ. ܘܚܨܕ ܐܢܐ ܡܕܡ ܕܠܐ ܙܪܥܬ. ܐܝܟܢܐ
ܠܐ ܐܪܡܝܬ ܟܣܦܝ ܥܠ ܦܬܘܪܐ. ܘܐܢܐ ܕܝܢ ܐܬܝܬ
24 ܬܒܥܬܗ ܥܡ ܪ̈ܒܝܬܗ. ܘܐܡܪ ܠܗܢܘܢ ܕܩܝܡܝܢ ܠܘܬܗ.
ܣܒܘ ܡܢܗ ܡܢܝܐ. ܘܗܒܘܗܝ، ܠܗܘ ܕܐܝܬ ܠܘܬܗ
26 ܥܣܪܐ ܡ̈ܢܝܢ. ܐܡܪܢܐ ܠܟܘܢ ܓܝܪ ܕܠܟܠ ܐܢܫ ܕܐܝܬ

43 ܠܗ ܚܙܝ ܗܝܡܢܘܬܟ ܐܚܝܬܟ. ܘܒܪܫܥܬܗ ܚܙܐ.
ܘܐܬܐ ܗܘܐ ܒܬܪܗ ܘܡܫܒܚ ܗܘܐ ܠܐܠܗܐ.
ܘܟܠܗ ܥܡܐ ܕܚܙܐ ܫܒܚܘ ܠܐܠܗܐ. ∘ ⁘ ∘

XIX. ܘܟܕ ܥܠ ܘܥܒܪ ܒܐܝܪܝܚܘ. ܓܒܪܐ ܚܕ ܕܫܡܗ ܙܟܝ.
3 ܘܪܒ ܡ̈ܟܣܐ ܗܘܐ. ܘܥܬܝܪ ܗܘܐ. ܘܒܥܐ ܗܘܐ
ܠܡܚܙܝܗ ܠܝܫܘܥ. ܘܠܐ ܡܫܟܚ ܗܘܐ. ܡܛܠ
4 ܕܒܩܘܡܬܗ ܙܥܘܪ ܗܘܐ ܙܟܝ. ܘܪܗܛ ܩܕܡܘܗܝ.
ܘܣܠܩ ܠܬܬܐ ܦܟܝܗܬܐ ܕܢܚܙܝܘܗܝ. ܡܛܠ ܕܗܘܒܬ
5 ܥܒܪ ܗܘܐ ܝܫܘܥ. ܘܟܕ ܥܒܪ ܝܫܘܥ ܚܙܝܗܝ. ܐܡܪ
ܐܬܪܗܒ ܚܘܬ ܙܟܝ. ܕܝܘܡܢܐ ܓܝܪ ܒܒܝܬܟ ܘܠܐ
6 ܠܝ ܕܐܗܘܐ. ܘܐܬܪܗܒ ܢܚܬ ܘܩܒܠܗ ܚܕܝܐܝܬ.
7 ܘܟܕ ܚܙܘ ܟܠܗܘܢ ܪܛܢܝܢ ܗܘܘ. ܕܠܘܬ ܓܒܪܐ
8 ܚܛܝܐ ܥܠ ܕܢܫܪܐ. ܘܩܡ ܙܟܝ ܘܐܡܪ ܠܡܪܢ. ܗܐ
ܡܪܝ ܦܠܓܘܬ ܢܟ̈ܣܝ ܝܗܒ ܐܢܐ ܠܡܣ̈ܟܢܐ. ܘܟܠ
9 ܕܥܠܒܬ ܚܕ ܒܐܪ̈ܒܥܐ ܦܪܥ ܐܢܐ. ܐܡܪ ܠܗ ܝܫܘܥ
ܕܝܘܡܢܐ ܗܘܘ ܚ̈ܝܐ ܒܒܝܬܐ ܗܢܐ. ܘܐܦ ܗܢܐ ܒܪܗ
10 ܗܘ ܕܐܒܪܗܡ. ܘܕܐܬܐ ܒܪܗ ܕܐܢܫܐ ܕܢܒܥܐ ܘܢܚܐ
ܠܡܕܡ ܕܐܒܝܕ ܗܘܐ. ∘ ∘ ∘

11 ܘܟܕ ܫܡܥܝܢ ܗܘܘ ܗܠܝܢ. ܐܘܣܦ ܠܡܐܡܪ ܡܬܠܐ.
ܡܛܠ ܕܩܪܝܒ ܗܘܐ ܠܡܥܠ ܠܐܘܪܫܠܡ. ܘܣܒܪܝܢ
ܗܘܘ ܕܒܗ ܫܥܬܐ ܒܥܓܠ ܕܬܬܓܠܐ ܡܠܟܘܬܗ
12 ܕܐܠܗܐ. ܐܡܪ ܠܗܘܢ. ܓܒܪܐ ܚܕ ܒܪ ܛܘܗܡܐ
ܪܒܐ. ܐܙܠ ܠܐܬܪܐ ܪܚܝܩܐ ܠܡܣܒ ܡܠܟܘܬܐ

29 ܡܕܡ ܕܐܝܬ ܠܢ ܘܐܬܝܢ ܒܬܪܟ. ܐܡܪ ܠܗ ܝܫܘܥ.
ܐܡܝܢ ܐܡܪ ܐܢܐ ܠܟܘܢ. ܕܡܢ ܕܫܒܩ ܒܝܬܐ. ܐܘ
ܐܒ̈ܗܐ. ܐܘ ܐ̈ܚܐ. ܐܘ ܐܢܬܬܐ. ܐܘ ܒ̈ܢܝܐ. ܡܛܠ
30 ܡܠܟܘܬܐ ܕܐܠܗܐ. ܢܣܒ ܚܕ ܒܥܣܪܐ ܒܗܢܐ ܙܒܢܐ.
ܘܒܥܠܡܐ ܕܐܬܐ ܢܐܪܬ ܚܝ̈ܐ ܕܠܥܠܡ ◦
31 ܘܕܒܪ ܠܬܪ̈ܥܣܪܬܗ ܘܐܡܪ ܠܗܘܢ. ܗܐ ܣܠܩܝܢ ܚܢ
ܠܐܘܪܫܠܡ. ܘܡܫܬܠܡܢ ܟܠܗܝܢ ܐܝܠܝܢ ܕܟ̈ܬܝܒܢ ܒܢܒ̈ܝܐ
32 ܥܠ ܒܪܗ ܕܐܢܫܐ. ܡܫܬܠܡ ܓܝܪ ܠܥܡ̈ܡܐ ܘܒܙܚܘܢ
33 ܒܗ ܘܢܓܕܘܢܗ. ܘܢܪܩܘܢ ܒܐ̈ܦܘܗܝ. ܘܢܙܩܦܘܢܗ
34 ܘܢܩܛܠܘܢܗ. ܘܠܝܘܡܐ ܕܬܠܬܐ ܢܩܘܡ. ܘܗܢܘܢ ܚܕܐ
ܡܢ ܗܠܝܢ ܠܐ ܐܣܬܟܠܘ. ܐܠܐ ܡܟܣܝܐ ܗܘܬ
ܡܢܗܘܢ ܡܠܬܐ. ܘܠܐ ܐܫܬܘܕܥܘ ܐܝܠܝܢ ܕܐܬܡܠܠ
ܥܡܗܘܢ ◦ ◦ ◦
35 ܘܟܕ ܩܪܒ ܗܘܐ ܠܝܪܝܚܘ. ܓܒܪܐ ܚܕ
36 ܣܡܝܐ ܝܬܒ ܗܘܐ ܥܠ ܝܕ ܐܘܪܚܐ ܘܡܚܕܪ. ܘܟܕ
ܫܡܥ ܩܠ ܟܢܫܐ ܕܥܒܪ. ܡܫܐܠ ܗܘܐ ܕܡܢܘ ܗܢܐ.
37, 38 ܐܡܪܝܢ ܠܗ ܝܫܘܥ ܢܨܪܝܐ ܥܒܪ. ܘܩܥܐ ܘܐܡܪ ܝܫܘܥ
39 ܒܪܗ ܕܕܘܝܕ ܐܬܪܚܡ ܥܠܝ. ܘܐܝܠܝܢ ܕܐܙܠܝܢ ܗܘܘ
ܩܕܡܘܗܝ، ܕܝܫܘܥ ܟܐܝܢ ܗܘܘ ܒܗ ܕܢܫܬܘܩ ܠܗ. ܘܗܘ
ܝܬܝܪܐܝܬ ܩܥܐ ܗܘܐ. ܒܪܗ ܕܕܘܝܕ ܐܬܪܚܡ ܥܠܝ.
40 ܘܩܡ ܗܘ ܝܫܘܥ. ܘܦܩܕ ܗܘܐ ܕܢܝܬܘܢܝܗܝ. ܘܟܕ ܩܪܒ
41 ܠܘܬܗ. ܫܐܠܗ ܘܐܡܪ ܠܗ. ܡܢܐ ܨܒܐ ܐܢܬ ܐܥܒܕ
42 ܠܟ. ܐܡܪ ܠܗ ܡܪܝ، ܕܢܬܦܬܚܢ ܥܝ̈ܢܝ ܘܐܚܙܝܟ. ܐܡܪ

17 ܡܠܟܘܬܐ ܕܫܡܝܐ. ܐܡܝܢ ܐܡܪ ܐܢܐ ܠܟܘܢ. ܕܡܢ
ܕܠܐ ܢܩܒܠ ܡܠܟܘܬܐ ܕܐܠܗܐ ܐܝܟ ܗܢܐ ܛܠܝܐ.
ܠܐ ܢܥܘܠ ܠܗ̇ ܀
18 ܘܫܐܠܗ ܗܘܐ ܚܕ ܡܢ ܪܫܐ ܕܦܪ̈ܝܫܐ ܘܐܡܪ ܠܗ.
ܡܠܦܢܐ ܛܒܐ ܡܢܐ ܐܥܒܕ ܕܐܝܪܬ ܚ̈ܝܐ ܕܠܥܠܡ.
19 ܐܡܪ ܠܗ ܝܫܘܥ. ܡܢܐ ܩܪܐ ܐܢܬ ܠܝ ܛܒܐ. ܘܡܢܐ
ܡܫܐܠ ܐܢܬ ܠܝ ܥܠ ܛܒܐ. ܠܝܬ ܛܒܐ ܐܠܐ ܐܢ ܚܕ
20 ܐܠܗܐ. ܦܘܩ̈ܕܢܐ ܕܝܢ ܝܕܥ ܐܢܬ ܠܗܘܢ. ܐܢ. ܓܒܪܐ
ܐܢܬ ܠܢܫܐ ܠܚܒܪܟ. ܠܐ ܬܩܛܘܠ. ܘܠܐ ܬܓܘܪ. ܘܠܐ
ܬܓܢܘܒ. ܘܠܐ ܬܣܗܕ ܣܗܕܘܬܐ ܕܫܘܩܪܐ. ܝܩܪ
21 ܠܐܒܘܟ ܘܠܐܡܟ. ܐܡܪ ܠܗ ܗܠܝܢ ܟܠܗܝܢ ܢܛܪܬ ܐܢܝܢ
22 ܗܐ ܡܢ ܕܛܠܝܐ ܐܢܐ. ܟܕ ܫܡܥ ܝܫܘܥ ܐܡܪ ܠܗ ܚܕܐ
ܬܘܒ ܚܣܝܪܐ ܠܟ. ܙܠ ܟܘܠ ܡܕܡ ܕܐܝܬ ܠܟ ܘܗܒ
ܠܡ̈ܣܟܢܐ. ܘܬܗܘܐ ܠܟ ܣܝܡܬܐ ܒܫܡܝܐ. ܘܬܐ
23 ܒܬܪܝ. ܗܘ ܕܝܢ ܟܕ ܫܡܥ ܗܠܝܢ ܟܪܝܬ ܠܗ. ܛܒ ܥܬܝܪ
24 ܗܘܐ ܓܝܪ. ܟܕ ܚܙܐ ܝܫܘܥ ܕܟܪܝܬ ܠܗ. ܐܡܪ. ܐܝܟܢܐ
ܥܛܠܐ ܗܝ ܠܐܝܠܝܢ ܕܐܝܬ ܠܗܘܢ ܢܟ̈ܣܐ ܕܢܥܠܘܢ
25 ܠܡܠܟܘܬܐ ܕܐܠܗܐ. ܕܩܠܝܠܐ ܗܝ ܠܓܡܠܐ ܕܢܥܒܪ
ܒܚܪܘܪܐ ܕܡܚܛܐ. ܐܘ ܥܬܝܪܐ ܕܢܥܘܠ ܠܡܠܟܘܬܗ
26 ܕܐܠܗܐ. ܘܐܡܪܝܢ ܗܘܘ ܐܝܠܝܢ ܕܫܡܥܘ. ܡܢܘ
27 ܡܫܟܚ ܠܡܚܝܐ. ܐܡܪ ܠܗܘܢ. ܐܝܠܝܢ ܕܠܘܬ ܒ̈ܢܝ
ܐ̈ܢܫܐ ܠܐ ܡܫܟܚܢ ܠܡܗܘܐ. ܠܘܬ ܐܠܗܐ ܕܝܢ
28 ܡܫܟܚܢ. ܐܡܪ ܠܗ ܟܐܦܐ. ܗܐ ܐܚܢܢ ܫܒܩܢ ܟܠ

ܒܐܝܡܡܐ ܘܒܠܠܝܐ. ܘܡܓܪ ܪܘܚܗ ܥܡܗܘܢ.
8 ܐܡܪܢܐ ܠܟܘܢ ܕܥܒܕ ܬܒܥܬܗܘܢ ܒܥܓܠ. ܒܪܡ
ܢܐܬܐ ܗܘ ܒܪܗ ܕܐܢܫܐ ܘܢܫܟܚ ܗܝܡܢܘܬܐ ܥܠ
ܐܪܥܐ. ∘∘ ∘∘ ∘∘
9 ܘܐܡܪ ܗܘܐ ܡܬܠܐ ܗܢܐ. ܠܘܩܒܠ ܐܢܫܐ ܕܬܟܝܠܝܢ
ܥܠ ܢܦܫܗܘܢ ܕܙܕܝ̈ܩܐ ܐܢܘܢ. ܘܒܣܝܢ ܗܘܘ ܥܠ
10 ܟܠܢܫ̈ܐ. ܬܪ̈ܝܢ ܐܢ̈ܫܝܢ ܣܠܩܘ ܠܗܝܟܠܐ ܠܡܨܠܝܘ. ܚܕ
11 ܦܪܝܫܐ ܘܐܚܪܢܐ ܡܟܣܐ. ܘܗܘ ܦܪܝܫܐ ܘܩܐܡ ܗܘܐ
ܒܝܢܘܗܝ ܠܢܦܫܗ ܘܗܟܢ ܡܨܠܐ ܗܘܐ. ܡܘܕܐ ܐܢܐ
ܠܟ ܐܠܗܐ ܕܠܐ ܗܘܝܬ ܐܝܟ ܫܪܟܐ ܕܒܢܝ̈ܢܫܐ
ܚܛ̈ܘܦܐ ܘܥܘ̈ܠܐ ܘܓܝ̈ܪܐ. ܘܠܐ ܐܝܟ ܗܢܐ
12 ܡܟܣܐ. ܐܠܐ ܨܐܡ ܐܢܐ ܬܪ̈ܝܢ ܒܫܒܬܐ. ܘܡܥܣܪ
13 ܐܢܐ ܒܟܠܡܕܡ ܕܩܢܐ ܐܢܐ. ܗܘ ܕܝܢ ܡܟܣܐ ܩܐܡ
ܗܘܐ ܡܢ ܪܘܚܩܐ. ܘܠܐ ܡܬܒܝܢ ܗܘܐ ܐܦܠܐ
ܥܝ̈ܢܘܗܝ ܢܪܝܡ ܠܫܡܝܐ. ܐܠܐ ܡܚܐ ܗܘܐ ܥܠ ܚܕܝܗ
14 ܘܐܡܪ. ܐܠܗܐ ܐܬܪܚܡ ܥܠ ܚܛܝܐ. ܐܡܪ ܐܢܐ
ܠܟܘܢ ܕܢܚܬ ܠܒܝܬܗ ܗܢܐ ܡܙܕܕܩ ܝܬܝܪ ܡܢ ܗܘ. ܟܠ
ܐܢܫ ܓܝܪ ܕܢܪܝܡ ܢܦܫܗ ܢܬܡܟܟ. ܘܟܠ ܕܢܡܟ ܢܦܫܗ
ܢܬܬܪܝܡ ∘ ∘ ∘ ∘ ∘
15 ܘܡܝܬܝܢ ܗܘܘ ܠܗ ܐܦ ܛܠܝ̈ܐ ܕܢܩܪܒ ܐܢܘܢ. ܘܟܕ ܚܙܘ
16 ܬܠܡ̈ܝܕܘܗܝ ܟܐܝܢ ܗܘܘ ܒܗܘܢ. ܘܗܘ ܝܫܘܥ ܐܡܪ
ܠܗܘܢ. ܫܒܘܩܘ ܛܠܝ̈ܐ ܕܢܐܬܘܢ ܠܘܬܝ ܘܠܐ ܬܟܠܘܢ
ܐܢܘܢ. ܐܝܠܝܢ ܓܝܪ ܕܐܟܘܬ ܗܠܝܢ ܐܢܘܢ ܕܠܗܘܢ ܗܝ

31 ܒܗܿܘ ܕܝܢ ܝܘܡܐ ܡܢ ܕܥܠ ܐܓܪܐ ܗܘ ܠܐ ܢܚܘܬ
ܢܫܩܘܠ ܡܐܢܘܗܝ ܡܢ ܒܝܬܐ. ܘܡܢ ܕܒܚܩܠܐ ܗܘ
32 ܠܐ ܢܬܗܦܟ ܠܒܣܬܪܗ. ܐܬܕܟܪܘ ܠܐܢܬܬܗ
33 ܕܠܘܛ. ܡܢ ܕܨܒܐ ܕܢܚܐ ܢܦܫܗ ܢܘܒܕܝܗ. ܘܡܢ ܕܢܘܒܕ
34 ܢܦܫܗ ܢܚܝܝܗ. ܐܡܪ ܐܢܐ ܠܟܘܢ ܕܝܢ ܕܒܗܿܘ ܠܠܝܐ
ܢܗܘܘܢ ܬܪܝܢ ܒܥܪܣܐ ܚܕܐ. ܚܕ ܢܬܕܒܪ ܘܚܕ ܢܫܬܒܩ.
35 ܘܢܗܘܝܢ ܬܪܬܝܢ ܛܚܢܢ ܒܚܕܐ ܪܚܝܐ ܐܟܚܕܐ. ܚܕܐ
36 ܬܬܕܒܪ ܘܚܕܐ ܬܫܬܒܩ. ܘܢܗܘܘܢ ܬܪܝܢ ܒܚܩܠܐ.
37 ܚܕ ܢܬܕܒܪ ܘܚܕ ܢܫܬܒܩ. ܥܢܝܢ ܠܗ ܠܐܝܟܐ ܡܪܢ.
ܐܡܪ ܠܗܘܢ ܐܝܟܐ ܕܦܓܪܐ ܬܡܢ ܢܬܟܢܫܘܢ ܢܫܪܐ ◦
XVIII. ܐܡܪ ܠܗܘܢ ܬܘܒ ܐܦ ܡܬܠܐ ܗܢܐ. ܕܢܨܠܘܢ
2 ܡܛܠ ܒܟܠܥܕܢ ܘܠܐ ܗܘܬ ܡܡܐܢܐ ܠܗܘܢ. ܕܝܢܐ
ܚܕ ܐܝܬ ܗܘܐ ܒܡܕܝܢܬܐ ܚܕܐ. ܕܡܢ ܐܠܗܐ ܠܐ
ܕܚܠ ܗܘܐ. ܘܡܢ ܒܢܝܢܫܐ ܠܐ ܡܬܟܚܕ ܗܘܐ.
3 ܘܐܪܡܠܬܐ ܚܕܐ ܐܝܬ ܗܘܬ ܒܗܿ ܒܗܝ ܡܕܝܢܬܐ.
ܘܐܬܝܐ ܗܘܬ ܠܘܬܗ ܢܓܪܐ ܦܠܘܐܐ. ܘܐܡܪܐ
4 ܠܗ ܬܒܥܝܢ ܡܢ ܒܥܠܕܒܒܝ. ܘܠܐ ܨܒܐ ܗܘܐ. ܘܒܬܪܟܢ
ܐܡܪ ܒܢܦܫܗ ܗܘ ܕܝܢܐ. ܐܢ ܡܢ ܐܠܗܐ ܠܐ ܕܚܠ
5 ܐܢܐ. ܘܡܢ ܒܢܝܢܫܐ ܠܐ ܡܬܟܚܕ ܐܢܐ. ܘܗܕܐ
ܐܪܡܠܬܐ ܒܟܠܥܕܢ ܡܠܐܝܐ ܠܝ. ܐܬܒܥܝܗ ܕܠܐ
6 ܒܟܠܥܕܢ ܬܗܘܐ ܐܬܝܐ ܡܗܡܪܐ ܠܝ. ܘܐܡܪ ܡܪܢ
7 ܫܡܥܘ ܡܢܐ ܐܡܪ ܕܝܢܐ ܕܥܘܠܐ. ܐܠܗܐ ܗܟܝܠ
ܠܐ ܢܬܪܐܬ ܢܥܒܕ ܬܒܥܬܐ ܠܓܒܝܘܗܝ. ܕܩܪܝܢ ܠܗ

ܕܠܘܩܐ

ܫܘܐ ܐܢܐ ܡܟܝܠ ܕܒܪܟ ܐܬܩܪܐ. ܥܒܕܝܢܝ ܐܝܟ ܚܕ
20 ܡܢ ܐ̈ܓܝܪܝܟ. ܘܩܡ ܐܬܐ ܠܘܬ ܐܒܘܗܝ. ܘܟܕ ܗܘ
ܪܚܝܩ. ܚܙܝܗܝ ܐܒܘܗܝ ܘܐܬܪܚܡ ܥܠܘܗܝ. ܘܪܗܛ
21 ܢܦܠ ܥܠ ܨܘܪܗ ܘܢܫܩܗ. ܘܐܡܪ ܠܗ ܒܪܗ. ܐܒܝ
ܚܛܝܬ ܒܫܡܝܐ ܘܩܕܡܝܟ. ܘܡܟܝܠ ܠܐ ܫܘܐ ܐܢܐ
ܕܒܪܟ ܐܬܩܪܐ. * * * * * * * *

* * * * * * * * * * * *

* * * * * * * * * * * *

* * * * * * * * * * * *

* * * * * * * * * * * *

24 ܗܘ. ܠܐ ܬܐܙܠܘܢ ܘܠܐ ܬܬܪܗܛܘܢ. ܐܝܟܢܐ ܓܝܪ
ܕܒܪܩܐ ܒܪܩ ܡܢ ܪܘܡܐ ܕܫܡܝܐ ܘܡܢܗܪܐ ܠܬܚܬܝܗ.
25 ܗܟܢܐ ܢܗܘܐ ܒܝܘܡܗ ܕܒܪܗ ܕܐܢܫܐ. ܠܘܩܕܡ ܕܝܢ
ܥܬܝܕ ܗܘ ܕܢܚܫ ܣܓܝܐܬܐ. ܘܕܢܣܬܠܐ ܡܢ ܫܪܒܬܐ
26 ܗܕܐ. ܘܐܝܟܢܐ ܕܗܘܐ ܒܝܘܡܝ ܢܘܚ. ܗܟܢܐ ܢܗܘܐ
27 ܒܝܘܡܬܗ ܕܒܪܗ ܕܐܢܫܐ. ܕܐܟܠܝܢ ܗܘܘ ܘܫܬܝܢ.
ܘܢܣܒܝܢ ܗܘܘ ܢܫ̈ܐ ܘܝܗܒܝܢ ܗܘܘ ܠܓܒܪ̈ܐ. ܥܕܡܐ
ܠܝܘܡܐ ܕܥܠ ܢܘܚ ܠܟܘܠܐ. ܘܐܬܐ ܛܘܦܢܐ ܘܐܘܒܕ
28 ܐܢܘܢ ܠܟܠܗܘܢ. ܗܟܢܐ ܐܝܟܢܐ ܕܗܘܐ ܒܝܘܡܝ
ܠܘܛ. ܕܐܟܠܝܢ ܗܘܘ ܘܫܬܝܢ. ܘܙܒܢܝܢ ܗܘܘ ܘܡܙܒܢܝܢ.
29 ܘܢܨܒܝܢ ܗܘܘ ܘܒܢܝܢ. ܘܒܝܘܡܐ ܕܢܦܩ ܠܘܛ ܡܢ ܣܕܘܡ.
ܐܡܛܪ ܢܘܪܐ ܡܢ ܫܡܝܐ ܘܐܘܒܕ ܐܢܘܢ ܠܟܠܗܘܢ.
30 ܗܟܢܐ ܢܗܘܐ ܒܝܘܡܐ ܕܡܬܓܠܐ ܒܪܗ ܕܐܢܫܐ.

ܥܣܪܐ ܙܘ̈ܙܝܢ. ܘܬܘܒܕ ܚܕ ܡܢܗܘܢ. ܠܐ ܡܢܗܪܐ
ܫܪܓܐ ܘܡܟܢܫܐ ܒܝܬܐ. ܘܒܥܝܐ ܠܗ ܒܛܝܠܐܝܬ
9 ܥܕܡܐ ܕܬܫܟܚܝܗܝ. ܘܡܐ ܕܐܫܟܚܬܗ ܩܪܝܐ
ܠܪ̈ܚܡܬܗ ܘܠܫ̈ܒܒܬܗ. ܘܐܡܪܐ ܠܗܝܢ ܚܕܝ ܥܡܝ
10 ܕܐܫܟܚܬ ܙܘܙܝ ܕܐܒܝܕ ܗܘܐ. ܐܡܪܢܐ ܠܟܘܢ
ܕܗܟܢܐ ܬܗܘܐ ܚܕܘܬܐ ܩܕܡ ܟܠܗܘܢ ܡ̈ܠܐܟܐ
ܕܐܠܗܐ. ܥܠ ܚܕ ܚܛܝܐ ܕܬܐܒ ◦◦
11 ܐܡܪ ܗܘܐ ܠܗܘܢ ܬܘܒ. ܠܓܒܪܐ ܚܕ ܐܝܬ ܗܘܘ ܠܗ
12 ܬܪ̈ܝܢ ܒܢܝ̈ܢ. ܐܡܪ ܠܗ ܙܥܘܪܐ. ܐܒܝ ܗܒ ܠܝ ܝܪܬܘܬܐ
ܕܡܛܝܐ ܠܝ ܡܢ ܒܝܬܟ. ܘܦܠܓ ܠܗܘܢ ܟܠܗ ܩܢܝܢܗ.
13 ܘܡܢ ܒܬܪ ܝܘܡ̈ܬܐ ܩܠܝܠ. ܟܢܫ ܗܘ ܒܪܗ ܙܥܘܪܐ
ܟܠܡܕܡ ܕܡܛܝܗܝ. ܘܐܙܠ ܠܐܬܪܐ ܪܚܝܩܐ. ܘܬܡܢ
ܒܕܪ ܩܢܝܢܗ ܒܦܚܙܘܬܐ ܐܠܝܢ ܕܠܐ ܩ̈ܠܝܢ. ܡܚܠܠ
14 ܕܚܝܐ ܗܘܐ ܦܪܢܣܬܗ ܥܡ ܙܢܝ̈ܬܐ. ܘܟܕ ܓܡܪ ܟܠ
ܡܕܡ ܕܐܝܬ ܠܗ. ܘܗܘܐ ܟܦܢܐ ܥܫܝܢܐ ܒܐܬܪܐ
15 ܗܘ. ܐܙܠ ܢܩܦ ܠܗ ܠܚܕ ܡܢ ܒܢܝ ܐܬܪܐ ܗܘ. ܘܫܕܪܗ
16 ܠܩܪܝܬܐ ܠܡܪܥܐ ܚ̈ܙܝܪܐ. ܘܡܬܪܓܪܓ ܗܘܐ
ܠܡܐܟܠ ܡܢ ܚܪ̈ܘܒܐ ܗܢܘܢ ܕܐܟܠܝܢ ܗܘܘ
17 ܚ̈ܙܝܪܐ. ܘܠܐ ܐܢܫ ܝܗܒ ܗܘܐ ܠܗ. ܘܟܕ ܐܬܐ ܠܘܬ
ܢܦܫܗ ܐܡܪ. ܟܡܐ ܐܓܝ̈ܪܐ ܐܝܬ ܗܫܐ ܒܝܬ
ܐܒܝ ܕܝܬܝܪ ܠܗܘܢ ܠܚܡܐ. ܘܐܢܐ ܐܒܕ ܐܢܐ
18 ܗܪܟܐ ܡܢ ܟܦܢ. ܐܠܐ ܐܩܘܡ ܐܙܠ ܠܘܬ ܐܒܝ
19 ܘܐܡܪ ܠܗ. ܐܒܝ ܚܛܝܬ ܒܫܡܝܐ ܘܩܕܡܝܟ. ܘܠܐ

ܡܠܟܐ ܕܐܙܠ ܠܡܬܟܬܫܘ ܥܡ ܡܠܟܐ ܐܚܪܢܐ.
ܘܠܐ ܠܘܩܕܡ ܡܬܪܥܐ. ܕܐܢ ܡܫܟܚ ܒܥܣܪܐ ܐܠܦܝܢ
ܠܡܐܪܥ ܠܗܘ ܕܐܬܐ ܥܠܘܗܝ ܒܥܣܪܝܢ ܐܠܦܝܢ.
32 ܘܐܠܐ ܥܕ ܪܚܝܩ ܡܢ ܟܠܬ ܦܪܘܣܐ. ܡܫܕܪ ܐܝܙܓܕܐ
33 ܘܒܥܐ ܡܢܗ ܥܠ ܫܠܡܐ. ܗܟܢܐ ܟܠ ܐܢܫ ܡܢܟܘܢ
ܕܠܐ ܫܒܩ ܟܘܠܗ ܩܢܝܢܗ. ܬܠܡܝܕܝ ܠܐ ܡܫܟܚ
34 ܕܢܗܘܐ. ܛܒܐ ܗܝ ܡܠܚܐ. ܐܢ ܕܝܢ ܐܦ ܡܠܚܐ
35 ܬܦܟܗ ܒܡܢܐ ܬܬܡܠܚ. ܠܐ ܠܐܪܥܐ ܐܘܠܐ
ܐܦܠܐ ܠܙܒܠܐ. ܐܠܐ ܠܒܪ ܡܫܬܕܝܐ. ܡܢ ܕܐܝܬ ܠܗ
ܐܕ̈ܢܐ ܕܢܫܡܥ ܢܫܡܥ ⊙ ○ ⊙

XV. ܘܡܟ̈ܣܐ ܘܚ̈ܛܝܐ ܡܬܩܪܒܝܢ ܗܘܘ ܠܗ ܕܢܫܡܥܘܢܗ.
2 ܘܦ̈ܪܝܫܐ ܘܣ̈ܦܪܐ ܪܛܢܝܢ ܗܘܘ ܘܐܡܪܝܢ. ܗܢܐ ܓܒܪܐ
3 ܠܚ̈ܛܝܐ ܡܩܒܠ ܘܐܟܠ ܥܡܗܘܢ. ܐܡܪ ܠܗܘܢ ܗܘ
4 ܡܬܠܐ ܗܢܐ. ܡܢܘ ܡܢܟܘܢ ܕܐܝܬ ܠܗ ܐܥ̈ܢܐ
ܒ̈ܢܝܢ. ܘܐܒܕ ܚܕ ܡܢܗܘܢ. ܠܐ ܫܒܩ ܬܫܥܝܢ
ܘܬܫܥܐ ܒܛܘܪܐ. ܘܐܙܠ ܒܥܐ ܠܗܘ ܕܐܒܕ ܥܕܡܐ
5 ܕܢܫܟܚܝܘܗܝ. ܘܡܐ ܕܐܫܟܚܗ ܫܩܠ ܠܗ ܥܠ
6 ܟܬ̈ܦܬܗ. ܘܚܕܐ ܘܐܬܐ ܠܒܝܬܗ. ܘܩܪܐ ܠܪ̈ܚܡܘܗܝ
ܐܦ ܠܫܒ̈ܒܘܗܝ ܘܐܡܪ ܠܗܘܢ. ܚܕܘ ܥܡܝ ܕܐܫܟܚܬ
7 ܥܢܝ ܕܐܒܝܕ ܗܘܐ. ܐܡܪܢܐ ܠܟܘܢ ܕܗܟܢܐ
ܬܗܘܐ ܚܕܘܬܐ ܒܫܡܝܐ ܥܠ ܚܕ ܚܛܝܐ ܕܬܐܒ.
ܝܬܝܪ ܡܢ ܬ̈ܫܥܝܢ ܘܬ̈ܫܥܐ ܙ̈ܕܝܩܝܢ ܕܠܐ ܡܬܒܥܝܐ
8 ܠܗܘܢ ܬܝܒܘܬܐ. ܐܘ ܐܝܕܐ ܗܝ ܐܢܬܬܐ ܕܐܝܬ ܠܗ̇

ܐܫܬܐܠܢܝ. ܘܐܚܪܢܐ ܐܡܪ ܚܡܫܐ ܙܘܓܝܢ ܬܘܪܐ 19
ܙܒܢܬ. ܘܐܙܠ ܐܢܐ ܕܐܒܩܐ ܐܢܘܢ. ܒܥܐ ܐܢܐ ܡܢܟ
ܐܫܬܐܠܢܝ. ܘܕܬܠܬܐ ܐܡܪ ܐܢܬܬܐ ܢܣܒܬ. ܠܐ 20
ܡܫܟܚܢܐ ܕܐܬܐ. ܘܐܬܐ ܗܘ ܥܒܕܐ ܐܡܪ ܗܠܝܢ 21
ܠܡܪܗ. ܗܝܕܝܢ ܪܓܙ ܡܪܐ ܒܝܬܐ. ܘܐܡܪ ܠܥܒܕܗ.
ܦܘܩ ܒܥܓܠ ܠܫܘܩܐ ܘܠܫܒܝܠܐ ܕܡܕܝܢܬܐ. ܘܐܥܠ
ܠܟܐ ܠܡܣܟܢܐ ܘܠܡܚܝܠܐ ܘܠܚܓܝܣܐ ܘܠܣܡܝܐ.
ܘܐܡܪ ܥܒܕܐ ܡܪܝ، ܗܐ ܗܘܐ ܡܕܡ ܕܦܩܕܬ. ܘܬܘܒ 22
ܐܝܬ ܐܬܪܐ ܒܡܫܬܘܬܐ. ܐܡܪ ܡܪܐ ܠܥܒܕܗ. ܦܘܩ 23
ܠܐܘܪܚܬܐ ܘܠܒܝܬ ܣܝܓܐ. ܘܟܒܘܫ ܕܢܥܠܘܢ. ܕܢܬܡܠܐ
ܒܝܬܝ. ܐܡܪ ܐܢܐ ܠܟܘܢ ܓܝܪ ܕܐܢܫ ܡܢ ܗܠܝܢ ܐܢܫܐ 24
ܕܩܪܝܢ ܗܘܘ ܠܐ ܢܛܥܡܘܢ ܐܫܬܘܬܝ. ○ ○ ○
ܘܟܕ ܐܙܠܝܢ ܗܘܘ ܥܡܗ ܟܢܫܐ. ܐܬܗܦܟ ܐܡܪ 25
ܠܗܘܢ. ܡܢ ܕܐܬܐ ܠܘܬܝ ܘܠܐ ܣܢܐ ܠܐܒܘܗܝ 26
ܘܠܐܡܗ. ܘܠܐܚܘܗܝ ܘܠܐܚܘܬܗ. ܘܠܐܢܬܬܗ
ܘܠܒܢܘܗܝ. ܐܦ ܠܢܦܫܗ. ܬܠܡܝܕܐ ܠܐ ܡܫܟܚ
ܕܢܗܘܐ ܠܝ. ܘܡܢ ܕܠܐ ܫܩܠ ܨܠܝܒܗ ܘܐܬܐ ܒܬܪܝ، 27
ܬܠܡܝܕܐ ܠܐ ܡܫܟܚ ܕܢܗܘܐ ܠܝ. ܡܢܘ ܓܝܪ ܡܢܟܘܢ 28
ܕܨܒܐ ܕܢܒܢܐ ܡܓܕܠܐ. ܘܠܐ ܠܘܩܕܡ ܝܬܒ ܡܬܚܫܒ
ܢܦܩܬܗ. ܕܐܢܗܘ ܐܝܬ ܠܗ ܠܡܫܠܡܘܬܗ. ܕܠܐ 29
ܟܕ ܢܣܝܡ ܫܬܐܣܬܐ ܘܠܐ ܐܫܟܚ ܕܢܫܠܡ. ܟܠ
ܕܚܙܝܢ ܢܗܘܘܢ ܡܒܙܚܝܢ ܒܗ ܘܐܡܪܝܢ. ܗܢܐ ܓܒܪܐ 30
ܫܪܝ ܕܢܒܢܐ ܡܓܕܠܐ. ܘܠܐ ܐܫܟܚ ܕܢܫܠܡ. ܐܘ ܡܢܘ

ܘܢܐܡܪ ܠܟ ܕܗܒ ܕܘܟܬܐ ܠܗܢܐ. ܘܗܝܕܝܢ ܟܕ
10 ܒܗܝܬ ܐܢܬ ܬܣܬܡܟ ܒܕܘܟܬܐ ܐܚܪܝܬܐ. ܐܠܐ
ܡܐ ܕܐܙܕܡܢܬ. ܙܠ ܐܣܬܡܟ ܒܕܘܟܬܐ ܐܚܪܝܬܐ.
ܕܡܐ ܕܐܬܐ ܗܘ ܡܢ ܕܩܪܟ. ܢܐܡܪ ܠܟ ܪ̈ܚܡܝ
ܐܬܬܠܐ ܠܥܠ. ܘܬܗܘܐ ܠܟ ܬܫܒܘܚܬܐ ܒܝ̈ܢܝ
11 ܣ̈ܡܝܟܐ ܟܠܗܘܢ. ܟܠ ܓܝܪ ܕܪܝܡ ܢܦܫܗ ܢܬܡܟܟ.
12 ܘܟܠ ܕܡܟܟ ܢܦܫܗ ܢܬܪܝܡ. ܘܐܡܪ ܗܘܐ ܐܦ ܠܡܙܡܢܐ
ܐܚܫܡܝܬܐ. ܡܐ ܕܥܒܕ ܐܢܬ ܫܪܘܬܐ ܐܘ
ܐܚܫܡܝܬܐ. ܠܐ ܬܩܪܐ ܪ̈ܚܡܝܟ. ܘܐܦ ܠܐ
ܠܐܚ̈ܝܟ. ܘܠܐ ܠܐܚ̈ܝܢܝܟ. ܘܠܐ ܠܫ̈ܒܒܝܟ ܐܝܠܝܢ
ܕܥ̈ܬܝܪܐ ܐܢܘܢ. ܕܠܡܐ ܐܦ ܗܢܘܢ ܢܩܪܘܢܟ. ܘܢܗܘܐ
13 ܠܟ ܦܘܪܥܢܐ. ܐܠܐ ܡܐ ܕܥܒܕ ܐܢܬ ܚܫܡܝܬܐ.
ܩܪܝ ܠܡܣ̈ܟܢܐ ܘܠܚ̈ܓܝܪܐ ܠܣ̈ܡܝܐ ܘܠܡܟ̈ܐܒܐ.
14 ܘܛܘܒܝܟ ܕܠܝܬ ܠܗܘܢ ܕܢܦܪܥܘܢܟ. ܘܢܗܘܐ ܦܘܪܥܢܟ
15 ܒܩܝܡܬܐ ܕܙܕ̈ܝܩܐ. ܘܟܕ ܫܡܥ ܗܘܐ ܗܠܝܢ ܚܕ ܡܢ
ܗܠܝܢ ܕܣܡܝܟܝܢ ܗܘܘ. ܐܡܪ ܠܗ ܛܘܒܘܗܝ ܠܡܢ
16 ܕܢܐܟܘܠ ܫܪܘܬܐ ܒܡܠܟܘܬܗ ܕܐܠܗܐ. ܐܡܪ ܠܗ
ܡܪܢ. ܓܒܪܐ ܚܕ ܥܒܕ ܗܘܐ ܐܚܫܡܝܬܐ ܪܒܬܐ.
17 ܘܩܪܐ ܠܡܙ̈ܡܢܐ. ܘܫܕܪ ܥܒܕܗ ܒܥܕܢܐ ܕܚܫܡܝܬܐ
ܕܢܐܡܪ ܠܗܘܢ ܕܡܙܡܢܝܢ. ܕܐܬܘ. ܗܐ ܠܡ ܟܠ
18 ܟܠ ܡܕܡ ܡܛܝܒ ܗܘ. ܘܫܪܝܘ ܗܘܘ ܡܚܕܐ
ܠܡܫܬܐܠܘ. ܐܡܪ ܠܗ ܩܕܡܝܐ ܩܪܝܬܐ ܙܒܢܬ.
ܘܐܠܝܨܐ ܐܢܐ ܕܐܦܘܩ ܐܚܙܝܗ. ܒܥܐ ܐܢܐ ܡܢܟ

ܘܒܬܪ ܡܚܪ ܐܪܕܐ. ܡܛܠ ܕܠܐ ܡܫܟܚܐ ܕܢܒܝܐ
34 ܢܐܒܕ ܠܒܪ ܡܢ ܐܘܪܫܠܡ. ܐܘܪܫܠܡ ܐܘܪܫܠܡ ܕܩܛܠܬ
ܠܢ̈ܒܝܐ. ܘܪܓܡܬܝ ܠܐܝܠܝܢ ܕܐܫܬܠܚܘ ܠܘܬܟܝ. ܟܡܐ
ܙܒܢܝܢ ܨܒܝܬ ܠܡܟܢܫܘ ܠܒ̈ܢܝܟܝ. ܐܝܟ ܬܪܢܓܘܠܬܐ
35 ܕܟܢܫܐ ܦܪ̈ܘܓܝܗ ܬܚܝܬ ܓܦ̈ܝܗ ܘܠܐ ܨܒܝܬܘܢ. ܗܐ
ܫܒܝܩ ܠܟܘܢ ܒܝܬܟܘܢ ܚܪܒ. ܐܡܪܢܐ ܠܟܘܢ ܕܠܐ
ܬܚܙܘܢܢܝ ܥܕܡܐ ܕܢܐܬܐ ܝܘܡܐ ܕܬܐܡܪܘܢ. ܒܪܝܟ
XIV. ܗܘ ܕܐܬܐ ܒܫܡܗ ܕܡܪܝܐ. ܘܟܕ ܥܠ ܠܒܝܬܐ ܕܚܕ
ܡܢ ܪ̈ܫܐ ܕܦܪ̈ܝܫܐ. ܕܢܐܟܘܠ ܠܚܡܐ ܒܝܘܡܐ
2 ܕܫܒܬܐ. ܢܛܪܝܢ ܗܘܘ ܕܢܚܙܘܢ ܡܢܐ ܥܒܕ. ܘܓܒܪܐ ܚܕ
3 ܗܕܪܘܦܝܩܘܣ ܐܝܬ ܗܘܐ ܩܕܡܘܗܝ. ܥܢܐ ܝܫܘܥ
ܘܐܡܪ ܠܣܦܪ̈ܐ ܘܠܦܪ̈ܝܫܐ. ܕܐܢ ܫܠܝܛ ܠܡܐܣܝܘ
4 ܒܫܒܬܐ ܐܘ ܠܐ. ܘܗܢܘܢ ܫܬܩܝܢ ܗܘܘ. ܘܗܘ
5 ܐܚܕܗ ܘܐܣܝܗ. ܘܫܪܝܗܝ. ܘܐܡܪ ܠܗܘܢ ܡܢܘ
ܡܢܟܘܢ ܕܢܦܠ ܒܪܗ ܐܘ ܬܘܪܗ. ܐܘ ܚܡܪܗ
ܒܒܪܐ ܒܝܘܡܐ ܕܫܒܬܐ. ܘܠܐ ܡܚܕܐ ܢܓܕ ܡܣܩ
6 ܠܗ. ܘܠܐ ܐܫܟܚܘ ܠܡܬܠ ܠܗ ܦܬܓܡܐ ܥܠ
ܗܠܝܢ ◦ ◦ ◦
7 ܘܐܡܪ ܗܘܐ ܡܬܠܐ ܗܢܐ. ܠܘܬ ܗܢܘܢ ܕܡܙܡܢܝܢ
8 ܗܘܘ. ܘܓܒܝܢ ܗܘܘ ܪܝܫ ܣ̈ܡܟܐ. ܐܡܪ ܠܗܘܢ ܐܡܬܝ
ܕܡܙܕܡܢ ܐܢܬ ܠܡܫܬܘܬܐ. ܠܐ ܬܐܙܠ ܬܣܬܡܟ
ܒܕܘܟܬܐ ܡܝܩܪܬܐ. ܕܠܐ ܢܗܘܐ ܬܡܢ ܡܢܘ
9 ܕܡܝܩܪ ܡܢܟ. ܘܢܐܬܐ ܗܘ ܡܢ ܕܠܟ ܘܠܗ ܩܪܐ.

24 ܘܐܡܪ. ܡܪܝ ܙܥܘܪ̈ܝܢ ܐܢܘܢ ܕܚܝܝܢ. ܐܡܪ ܠܗ ܝܫܘܥ.
ܐܬܟܬܫܘ ܠܡܥܠ ܒܬܪܥܐ ܐܠܝܨܐ. ܐܡܪܢܐ ܠܟܘܢ
25 ܓܝܪ ܕܣܓܝ̈ܐܐ ܢܒܥܘܢ ܠܡܥܠ ܘܠܐ ܢܫܟܚܘܢ. ܡܢ
ܫܥܬܐ ܕܢܩܘܡ ܡܪܗ ܒܝܬܐ ܘܢܐܚܘܕ: ܬܪܥܐ.
ܘܬܫܪܘܢ ܩܝܡܝܢ ܠܒܪ ܘܢܩܫܝܢ ܒܬܪܥܐ. ܘܐܡܪܝܢ
ܡܪܢ ܡܪܢ ܦܬܚ ܠܢ. ܘܢܥܢܐ ܘܢܐܡܪ ܠܟܘܢ ܠܐ
26 ܝܕܥ ܐܢܐ ܠܟܘܢ ܐܝܡܟܐ ܐܢܬܘܢ. ܗܝܕܝܢ ܬܫܪܘܢ
ܠܡܐܡܪ. ܩܕܡܝܟ ܠܥܣܢ ܘܐܫܬܝܢ. ܘܒܫܘ̈ܩܝܢ
27 ܗܠܟܬ. ܗܝܕܝܢ ܢܐܡܪ ܠܟܘܢ. ܐܡܝܢ ܐܡܪܢܐ ܠܟܘܢ
ܕܠܐ ܝܕܥܢܐ ܠܟܘܢ ܐܝܡܟܐ ܐܢܬܘܢ. ܦܪܘܩܘ ܠܟܘܢ
28 ܡܢܝ. ܟܠܟܘܢ ܓܝܪ ܐܢܬܘܢ ܦܠ̈ܚܐ ܕܥܘܠܐ. ܬܡܢ
ܢܗܘܐ ܒܟܝܐ ܘܚܘܪܩ ܫ̈ܢܐ. ܟܕ ܬܚܙܘܢ ܠܐܒܪܗܡ
ܘܠܐܝܣܚܩ ܘܠܝܥܩܘܒ. ܘܠܟܠܗܘܢ ܢܒ̈ܝܐ. ܒܡܠܟܘܬܐ
29 ܕܐܠܗܐ. ܘܐܢܬܘܢ ܬܗܘܘܢ ܡܦܩܝܢ ܠܒܪ. ܘܢܐܬܘܢ
ܡܢ ܡܕܢܚܐ ܘܡܢ ܡܥܪܒܐ. ܘܡܢ ܬܝܡܢܐ ܘܡܢ
30 ܓܪܒܝܐ. ܘܢܣܬܡܟܘܢ ܒܡܠܟܘܬܗ ܕܐܠܗܐ. ܘܐܝܬ
ܐܚܪ̈ܝܐ ܕܢܗܘܘܢ ܩܕܡ̈ܝܐ. ܘܩܕܡ̈ܝܐ ܐܚܪ̈ܝܐ. ◦ ◦ ◦
31 ܘܒܗܘܢ ܒܝܘܡܬܐ ܗܢܘܢ. ܩܪܒܘ ܐܢ̈ܫܐ ܡܢ ܦܪ̈ܝܫܐ
ܘܐܡܪܝܢ ܠܗ. ܦܘܩ ܙܠ ܠܟ ܡܟܐ. ܡܛܠ ܕܗܪܘܕܣ
32 ܒܥܐ ܠܡܩܛܠܟ. ܐܡܪ ܠܗܘܢ ܙܠܘ ܐܡܪܘ ܠܗ
ܠܬܥܠܐ ܗܢܐ. ܗܐ ܡܦܩ ܐܢܐ ܫܐ̈ܕܐ. ܘܐܣܘܬܐ
ܡܫܠܡ ܐܢܐ ܝܘܡܢܐ ܘܡܚܪ. ܘܠܝܘܡܐ ܕܬܠܬܐ
33 ܡܫܬܠܡ ܐܢܐ. ܒܪܡ ܘܠܐ ܠܝ ܕܝܘܡܢܐ ܘܡܚܪ.

ܕܠܘܩܐ

ܥܠܝܗ. ܘܒܪ ܫܥܬܗ ܐܬܦܫܛܬ ܩܘܡܬܗ. ܘܡܫܒܚܐ
14 ܗܘܬ ܠܐܠܗܐ. ܘܥܢܐ ܪܒ ܟܢܘܫܬܐ ܟܕ ܡܬܚܡܬ
ܗܘܐ ܥܠ ܕܡܐܣܐ ܗܘܐ ܝܫܘܥ ܒܫܒܬܐ ܘܐܡܪ
ܠܟ̈ܢܫܐ. ܫܬܐ ܐܢܘܢ ܝܘ̈ܡܝܢ ܕܒܗܘܢ ܘܠܐ ܠܡܦܠܚ.
ܒܗܘܢ ܗܘܝܬܘܢ ܐܬܝܢ ܘܡܬܐܣܝܢ ܘܠܐ ܒܝܘܡܐ
15 ܕܫܒܬܐ. ܥܢܐ ܝܫܘܥ ܘܐܡܪ ܠܗ. ܢܣܒ ܒܐ̈ܦܐ. ܚܕ
ܚܕ ܡܢܟܘܢ ܠܐ ܫܪܐ ܬܘܪܗ ܐܘ ܚܡܪܗ ܡܢ ܐܘܪܝܐ
16 ܒܝܘܡܐ ܕܫܒܬܐ ܘܐܙܠ ܡܫܩܐ ܠܗ. ܗܕܐ ܕܝܢ
ܕܒܪܬܗ ܗܝ ܕܐܒܪܗܡ. ܕܐܣܪܗ ܐܟܠ ܩܪ̈ܨܐ ܗܐ
ܬܡܢܥܣܪܐ ܫ̈ܢܝܢ. ܠܐ ܘܠܐ ܗܘܐ ܕܬܫܬܪܐ ܡܢ
17 ܗܢܐ ܐܣܘܪܐ ܒܝܘܡܐ ܕܫܒܬܐ. ܘܟܕ ܗܠܝܢ ܐܡܪ
ܗܘܐ. ܒܗܬܝܢ ܗܘܘ ܟܠܗܘܢ ܐܝܠܝܢ ܕܩܝܡܝܢ ܗܘܘ
ܠܘܩܒܠܗ. ܘܟܠܗ ܥܡܐ ܚܕܐ ܗܘܐ ܒܟܠܗܝܢ
ܬܕ̈ܡܪܬܐ ܕܗܘܝܢ ܗܘܝ ܒܐܝܕܗ. ⁘ ⁘
18 ܘܐܡܪ ܗܘܐ ܠܡܢܐ ܕܡܝܐ ܡܠܟܘܬܐ ܕܐܠܗܐ
19 ܘܠܡܢܐ ܐܕܡܝܗ. ܕܡܝܐ ܠܦܪܕܬܐ ܕܚܪܕܠܐ ܕܢܣܒ
ܓܒܪܐ ܐܪܡܝܗ ܒܓܢܬܗ. ܘܪܒܬ ܘܗܘܬ ܐܝܠܢܐ.
ܘܐܫܟܢܬ ܦܪܚܬܐ ܕܫܡܝܐ ܒܣ̈ܘܟܝܗ ◦ ◦ ◦
20 ܬܘܒ ܐܡܪ ܠܡܢܐ ܐܕܡܝܗ ܡܠܟܘܬܐ ܕܐܠܗܐ.
21 ܕܡܝܐ ܠܚܡܝܪܐ ܕܛܫܬ ܐܢܬܬܐ ܘܛܡܪܬ ܒܬܠܬ
22 ܣܐ̈ܝܢ ܕܩܡܚܐ. ܥܕܡܐ ܕܟܠܗ ܚܡܥ. ܘܪܕܐ ܗܘܐ
ܒܩ̈ܘܪܝܐ ܘܒܡ̈ܕܝܢܬܐ. ܘܡܠܦ ܗܘܐ. ◦ ◦ ◦
23 ܘܟܕ ܐܙܠ ܠܐܘܪܫܠܡ. ܐܬܐ ܚܕ ܘܡܫܐܠ ܗܘܐ ܠܗ

ܕܠܘܩܐ

ܓ̈ܠܝܠܝܐ. ܗܢܘܢ ܕܦܝܠܛܘܣ ܚܠܛ ܕܡܗܘܢ ܥܡ
2 ܕܒ̈ܚܝܗܘܢ. ܥܢܐ ܘܐܡܪ ܠܗܘܢ ܝܫܘܥ. ܣܒܪܝܢ ܐܢܬܘܢ
ܕܗܠܝܢ ܓ̈ܠܝܠܝܐ ܚܛܝܢ ܗܘܘ ܝܬܝܪ ܡܢ ܟܠܗܘܢ
3 ܓ̈ܠܝܠܝܐ ܕܗܟܢܐ ܗܘܐ ܠܗܘܢ. ܐܡܪܢܐ ܠܟܘܢ ܕܠܐ.
ܐܠܐ ܐܦ ܐܢܬܘܢ ܐܠܐ ܬܬܘܒܘܢ ܗܟܢܐ ܬܐܒ̈ܕܘܢ
4 ܟܠܟܘܢ. ܘܗܢܘܢ ܬܡܢܬܥܣܪ ܕܢܦܠ ܥܠܝܗܘܢ ܡܓܕܠܐ
ܒܫܝܠܘܚܐ ܘܩܛܠ ܐܢܘܢ. ܣܒܪܝܢ ܐܢܬܘܢ ܕܚܛܝܢ
ܗܘܘ ܝܬܝܪ ܡܢ ܟܠܗܘܢ ܒܢ̈ܝܐܢܫܐ ܕܥܡܪܝܢ ܒܐܘܪܫܠܡ.
5 ܐܡܪܢܐ ܠܟܘܢ ܕܠܐ. ܐܠܐ ܐܦ ܐܢܬܘܢ ܐܠܐ
ܬܬܘܒܘܢ ܗܟܢܐ ܬܐܒ̈ܕܘܢ ∘ ∘ ⁘ ∘ ∘
6 ܘܐܡܪ ܗܘܐ ܡܬܠܐ ܗܢܐ. ܓܒܪܐ ܚܕ ܐܝܬ
ܗܘܬ ܠܗ ܬܬܐ ܒܟܪܡܗ. ܘܐܬܐ ܒܥܐ ܒܗ ܦܐܪ̈ܐ
7 ܘܠܐ ܐܫܟܚ. ܐܡܪ ܠܦܠܚܐ ܗܐ ܬܠܬ ܫ̈ܢܝܢ ܗܐ ܡܢ
ܕܐܬܐ ܐܢܐ ܒܥܐ ܐܢܐ ܒܗ ܦܐܪ̈ܐ ܒܬܬܐ ܗܕܐ
ܘܠܐ ܡܫܟܚ ܐܢܐ. ܦܣܘܩܝܗ ܠܡܢܐ ܡܒܛܠܐ
8 ܐܪܥܐ. ܐܡܪ ܠܗ ܗܘ ܦܠܚܐ. ܡܪܝ ܫܒܘܩܝܗ ܐܦ
9 ܗܕܐ ܫܢܬܐ. ܥܕ ܐܦܠܚܝܗ ܘܐܙܒܠܝܗ. ܘܐܢ ܥܒܕܬ
ܦܐܪ̈ܐ ܘܐܠܐ ܠܫܢܬ ܬܦܣܩܝܗ ∘∘ ∘∘ ∘∘ ∘∘
10, 11 ܘܟܕ ܡܠܦ ܗܘܐ ܒܫ̈ܒܬܐ ܒܚܕܐ ܡܢ ܒܟܢܘ̈ܫܬܐ. ܘܐܝܬ
ܗܘܬ ܬܡܢ ܐܢܬܬܐ ܚܕܐ ܕܐܝܬ ܗܘܬ ܠܗ ܪܘܚܐ
ܫ̈ܢܝܢ ܬܡܢܥܣܪܐ. ܘܟܦܝܦܐ ܗܘܬ ܘܠܐ ܡܫܟܚܐ
12 ܗܘܬ ܕܬܬܦܫܛ ܠܓܡܪ. ܘܚܙܗ ܝܫܘܥ ܘܩܪܗ ܘܐܡܪ
13 ܠܗ̇. ܐܢܬܬܐ ܫܪܝܬܝ ܡܢ ܟܘܪܗܢܟܝ. ܘܣܡ ܐܝ̈ܕܘܗܝ

49 ܝܬܝܪܐܝܬ ܢܬܒܥܘܢܗܝ. ܢܘܪܐ ܗܘ̇ ܓܝܪ ܐܬܝܬ
ܕܐܪܡܐ ܒܐܪܥܐ. ܘܗܟܐ ܨܒܐ ܐܢܐ ܐܠܘ ܡܢ ܟܕܘ
50 ܝܩܕܬ. ܘܡܥܡܘܕܝܬܐ ܐܝܬ ܠܝ ܕܐܥܡܕ. ܘܟܡܐ
51 ܐܠܝܨ ܐܢܐ ܥܕܡܐ ܕܬܫܬܠܡ. ܣܒܪܝܢ ܐܢܬܘܢ ܕܫܝܢܐ
ܐܬܝܬ ܕܐܥܒܕ ܒܐܪܥܐ. ܐܡܪ ܐܢܐ ܠܟܘܢ ܕܠܐ.
52 ܐܠܐ ܦܠܓܘ̈ܬܐ. ܡܢ ܗܫܐ ܓܝܪ ܢܗܘܘܢ ܚܡܫܐ
ܒܚܕ ܒܝܬܐ. ܡܬܦܠܓܝܢ ܬܠܬܐ ܥܠ ܬܪ̈ܝܢ. ܘܬܪ̈ܝܢ ܥܠ
53 ܬܠܬܐ. ܡܬܦܠܓ ܐܒܐ ܥܠ ܒܪܗ. ܘܒܪܐ ܥܠ ܐܒܘܗܝ.
ܐܢܬܐ ܥܠ ܒܪܬܗ̇. ܘܒܪܬܐ ܥܠ ܐܡܗ̇. ܘܚܡܬܐ
ܥܠ ܟܠܬܗ̇. ܘܟܠܬܐ ܥܠ ܚܡܬܗ̇ ◎ ○ ◎
54 ܘܐܡܪ ܗܘܐ ܠܟܢ̈ܫܐ. ܡܐ ܕܚܙܝܬܘܢ ܥܢܢܐ ܕܣܠܩܐ
ܡܢ ܡܥܪܒܐ. ܐܡܪܝܢ ܐܢܬܘܢ ܕܡܛܪܐ ܗܘܐ ܘܗܘܐ
55 ܗܘܐ. ܘܡܐ ܕܢܫܒܐ ܬܝܡܢܐ. ܐܡܪܝܢ ܐܢܬܘܢ
56 ܕܫܘܪܒܐ ܗܘܐ ܘܗܘܐ. ܢܣܒܝ ܒܐ̈ܦܐ ܦܪܨܘܦܐ
ܕܫܡܝܐ ܘܕܐܪܥܐ ܝܕܥܝܢ ܐܢܬܘܢ ܠܡܒܩܘ. ܙܒܢܐ
57 ܗܢܐ ܘܐ̈ܬܘܬܗ ܠܐ ܝܕܥܝܢ ܐܢܬܘܢ. ܘܡܢ̈ܦܫܬܟܘܢ
58 ܠܐ ܕܢܝܢ ܐܢܬܘܢ ܩܘܫܬܐ. ܡܐ ܕܐܙܠ ܐܢܬ ܥܡ
ܒܥܠ ܕܝܢܟ ܠܘܬ ܐܪܟܘܢܐ. ܥܕ ܒܡܟܗ ܐܢܬ ܒܐܘܪܚܐ
ܗܒ ܠܗ ܗܘܫܥܗ ܕܬܬܦܪܩ ܡܢܗ. ܕܠܡܐ ܢܫܚܒܟ
ܩܕܡ ܕܝܢܐ. ܘܕܝܢܐ ܢܫܠܡܟ ܠܓܒܝܐ. ܘܓܒܝܐ ܢܪܡܝܟ
59 ܒܝܬ ܐܣܝܪܐ. ܐܡܪܢܐ ܠܟ ܕܠܐ ܬܦܘܩ ܡܢ ܬܡܢ
ܥܕܡܐ ܕܬܦܪܘܥ ܫܡܘܢܐ ܐܚܪܝܐ ·⊙· ○
XIII. ܘܒܗ ܒܗ̇ܘ ܙܒܢܐ. ܐܬܘ ܐܢ̈ܫܝܢ ܘܐܡܪܘ ܠܗ ܥܠ

ܐܢܘܢ ܟܕ ܥܝܪܝܢ. ܛܘܒܝܗܘܢ ܕܢܣܡܟ ܐܢܘܢ ܘܢܫܡܫ.
ܐܘ ܐܢ ܒܡܛܪܬܐ ܕܬܪ̈ܬܝܢ ܐܘ ܕܬܠܬ ܢܐܬܐ ܘܢܫܟܚ
39 ܐܢܘܢ ܟܕ ܥܝܪܝܢ. ܛܘܒܝܗܘܢ ܠܗܘܢ. ܗܕܐ ܕܝܢ ܕܥܘ.
ܕܐܠܘ ܝܕܥ ܗܘܐ ܡܪܐ ܒܝܬܐ ܒܐܝܕܐ ܫܥܬܐ ܐܬܐ
40 ܓܢܒܐ. ܠܐ ܫܒܩ ܗܘܐ ܕܢܬܦܠܫ ܒܝܬܗ. ܐܦ ܐܢܬܘܢ
ܗܘܬܘܢ ܡܛܝܒܝܢ. ܕܒܫܥܬܐ ܕܠܐ ܣܒܪܝܢ ܐܢܬܘܢ
41 ܢܐܬܐ ܒܪܗ ܕܐܢܫܐ. ܐܡܪ ܠܗ ܟܐܦܐ. ܡܪܝ ܠܢ ܗܘ
42 ܐܡܪ ܐܢܬ ܠܗ ܡܬܠܐ ܗܢܐ. ܐܘ ܐܦ ܠܟܠܢ. ܐܡܪ
ܠܗ ܡܪܢ. ܐܝܢܐ ܗܘ ܫܠܝܛܐ ܡܗܝܡܢܐ ܘܚܟܝܡܐ
ܘܛܒܐ. ܕܢܩܝܡܝܘܗܝ ܡܪܗ ܥܠ ܥܒ̈ܕܘܗܝ. ܕܢܬܠ
43 ܠܗܘܢ ܦܪܣܐ ܒܙܒܢܗ. ܛܘܒܘܗܝ ܠܗܘ ܥܒܕܐ ܗܘ.
44 ܢܐܬܐ ܡܪܗ ܢܫܟܚܝܘܗܝ ܕܥܒܕ ܗܟܢܐ. ܫܪܝܪܐܝܬ
45 ܐܡܪ ܐܢܐ ܠܟܘܢ ܕܢܩܝܡܝܘܗܝ ܥܠ ܟܘܠܗ ܩܢܝܢܗ. ܐܢ
ܕܝܢ ܢܐܡܪ ܗܘ ܥܒܕܐ ܒܠܒܗ. ܕܡܪܝ ܡܘܚܪ ܠܡܐܬܐ.
ܘܢܫܪܐ ܠܡܡܚܐ ܠܥܒ̈ܕܐ ܗܢܘܢ ܘܠܐܡ̈ܗܬܐ.
46 ܘܠܡܐܟܠ ܘܠܡܫܬܐ ܘܠܡܪܘܐ. ܘܢܐܬܐ ܡܪܗ
ܕܥܒܕܐ ܗܘ ܒܝܘܡܐ ܕܠܐ ܣܒܪ. ܘܒܫܥܬܐ ܕܠܐ
ܝܕܥ. ܘܢܦܠܓܝܘܗܝ. ܘܢܣܝܡ ܡܢܬܗ ܥܡ ܐܝܠܝܢ ܕܠܐ
47 ܡܗܝܡܢܝܢ. ܥܒܕܐ ܕܝܕܥ ܨܒܝܢܐ ܕܡܪܗ ܘܠܐ ܛܝܒ
48 ܠܗ ܐܝܟ ܨܒܝܢܗ. ܢܠܩܐ ܡܚ̈ܘܬܐ ܣ̈ܓܝܐܬܐ. ܘܗܘ
ܕܠܐ ܝܕܥ ܘܥܒܕ ܡܕܡ ܕܫܘܐ ܠܡܚ̈ܘܬܐ ܢܠܩܐ
ܡܚ̈ܘܬܐ ܙܥܘܪ̈ܬܐ. ܟܠ ܕܝܗܝܒ ܠܗ ܣܓܝ ܣܓܝ
ܣܓܝ ܢܬܒܥ ܒܐܝܕܗ. ܘܠܡܢ ܕܐܓܥܠܘ ܠܗ ܣܓܝ

28 ܬܫܒܘܚܬܗ ܐܬܟܣܝ، ܐܟܘܬܗܝܢ. ܐܢ ܕܝܢ ܠܥܡܝܪܐ
ܕܛܘܪ̈ܐ ܕܝܘܡܢܐ ܐܝܬܘܗܝ، ܒܛܘܪ̈ܐ. ܘܡܚܪ ܝܒܫ
ܘܢܦܠ ܒܬܢܘܪܐ ܐܠܗܐ ܡܠܒܫ. ܟܡܐ ܗܟܝܠ
29 ܝܬܝܪܐܝܬ ܠܟܘܢ ܚܣܝܪ̈ܝ، ܗܝܡܢܘܬܐ. ܠܐ ܗܐ ܗܟܝܠ
ܬܒܥܘܢ ܡܢܐ ܬܐܟܠܘܢ. ܘܡܢܐ ܬܫܬܘܢ. ܘܡܢܐ
30 ܬܬܟܣܘܢ. ܘܬܬܒܥܘܢ ܒܗܠܝܢ. ܗܠܝܢ ܓܝܪ ܟܠܗܝܢ
ܒܥܡ̈ܡܐ ܗܘ ܕܐܪܥܐ ܒܥܝܢ ܠܗܝܢ. ܐܒܘܟܘܢ ܕܝܢ
31 ܝܕܥ ܕܐܦ ܠܟܘܢ ܡܬܒܥܝܢ. ܐܢܬܘܢ ܡܟܝܠ ܒܥܘ
ܡܠܟܘܬܗ ܕܐܠܗܐ. ܘܗܠܝܢ ܡܢ ܒܬܪ ܢܬܬܘܣܦ
ܠܟܘܢ ⁘
32 ܠܐ ܬܕܚܠ ܓܙܪܐ ܙܥܘܪܐ. ܕܨܒܐ ܐܒܘܟܘܢ ܕܢܬܠ
33 ܠܟܘܢ ܡܠܟܘܬܐ. ܙܒܢܘ ܟܠܡܕܡ ܕܐܝܬ ܠܟܘܢ ܘܗܒܘ
ܙܕܩܬܐ. ܘܥܒܕܘ ܠܟܘܢ ܟܝ̈ܣܐ ܕܠܐ ܒܠܝܢ. ܘܐܦ
ܣܝܡܬܐ ܕܠܐ ܚܣܪܐ ܒܫܡܝܐ. ܐܬܪ ܕܠܐ
34 ܓܢܒܐ ܡܛܐ. ܘܐܦܠܐ ܣܣܐ ܡܚܒܠ. ܘܐܬܪ
ܕܣܝܡܬܟܘܢ ܬܡܢ ܘܐܦ ܠܒܟܘܢ ܬܡܢ ܢܗܘܐ.
35 ܢܗܘܘܢ ܐܣܝܪܝܢ ܚܨ̈ܝܟܘܢ ܘܡܫܪܓܝܢ ܫܪ̈ܓܝܟܘܢ.
36 ܘܬܗܘܘܢ ܕܡܝܢ ܠܐܢܫܐ ܕܡܣܟܝܢ ܠܡܪܗܘܢ. ܐܡܬܝ
ܕܢܗܦܘܟ ܡܢ ܒܝܬ ܡܫܬܘܬܐ. ܕܡܐ ܕܐܬܐ ܘܢܩܫ
37 ܒܪܫܥܬܗ ܢܦܬܚܘܢ ܠܗ. ܛܘܒܝܗܘܢ ܠܥܒ̈ܕܐ ܗܠܝܢ
ܐܝܠܝܢ ܕܐܬܐ ܡܪܗܘܢ ܢܫܟܚ ܐܢܘܢ ܕܥܝܪܝܢ. ܐܡܝܢ
ܐܡܪܢܐ ܠܟܘܢ ܕܢܐܣܘܪ ܚܨ̈ܘܗܝ، ܘܢܣܡܟ ܐܢܘܢ
38 ܘܢܥܒܪ. ܘܐܢ ܒܡܛܪܬܐ ܕܡܨܥܬܐ ܢܐܬܐ ܘܢܫܟܚ

16 ܘܐܡܪ ܗܘܐ ܡܬܠܐ ܗܢܐ ܠܘܬܗܘܢ. ܓܒܪܐ ܚܕ
ܥܬܝܪܐ ܐܥܠܬ ܗܘܬ ܠܗ ܐܪܥܗ ܥ̈ܠܠܬܐ ܣܓܝ̈ܐܬܐ.
17 ܘܡܬܚܫܒ ܗܘܐ ܒܢܦܫܗ ܘܐܡܪ. ܡܢܐ ܐܥܒܕ. ܕܠܝܬ
18 ܠܝ ܐܝܟܐ ܕܐܟܢܘܫ ܥ̈ܠܠܬܝ. ܐܣܬܘܪ ܒܝܬ ܩ̈ܦܣܝ
ܘܐܒܢܐ ܘܐܘܪܒ ܐܢܘܢ. ܘܐܟܢܫ ܒܗܘܢ ܥ̈ܠܠܬܝ.
19 ܘܐܡܪ ܠܢܦܫܗ. ܕܗܐ ܛܒ̈ܬܐ ܣܓܝ̈ܐܬܐ ܣܝ̈ܡܢ
ܠܟܝ ܠܫ̈ܢܝܐ ܣܓܝ̈ܐܬܐ. ܐܬܢܝܚܝ ܘܐܟܘܠܝ ܘܐܫܬܝ
20 ܘܐܬܒܣܡܝ. ܐܡܪ ܠܗ ܐܠܗܐ ܚܣܝܪ ܪܥܝܢܐ. ܗܕܐ
ܒܗܢܐ ܠܠܝܐ ܢܦܫܟ ܬܒܥܝܢ ܠܗ̇ ܡܢܟ. ܗܠܝܢ ܕܛܝܒܬ
21 ܠܡܢ ܢܗܘܘܢ. ܗܟܢܐ ܗܘ ܡܢ ܕܣܐܡ ܠܗ ܣܝ̈ܡܬܐ
ܘܒܐܠܗܐ ܠܐ ܥܬܪ ܀
22 ܘܐܡܪ ܠܬܠܡܝܕܘܗܝ. ܡܛܠ ܗܢܐ ܐܡܪ ܐܢܐ ܠܟܘܢ.
ܠܐ ܬܐܨܦܘܢ ܕܢܦܫܟܘܢ ܡܢܐ ܬܐܟܠܘܢ. ܘܐܦܠܐ
23 ܕܦܓܪܐ ܡܢܐ ܬܠܒܫܘܢ. ܢܦܫܐ ܓܝܪ ܝܬܝܪܐ ܗܝ ܡܢ
24 ܣܝܒܪܬܐ ܘܦܓܪܐ ܡܢ ܠܒܘܫܐ. ܐܬܒܩܘ ܒܥ̈ܘܪܒܐ
ܕܠܐ ܙܪܥܝܢ ܘܠܐ ܚܨܕܝܢ. ܘܠܝܬ ܠܗܘܢ ܬܘ̈ܢܐ.
ܘܐܦܠܐ ܒܝܬ ܩ̈ܦܣܐ. ܘܐܠܗܐ ܡܬܪܣܐ ܠܗܘܢ.
25 ܒܟܡܐ ܗܟܝܠ ܐܢܬܘܢ ܡܝܬܪܝܢ ܡܢܗܘܢ. ܐܝܢܐ ܓܝܪ
ܡܢܟܘܢ ܟܕ ܝܨܦ. ܡܫܟܚ ܠܡܘܣܦܘ ܥܠ ܩܘܡܬܗ
26 ܐܡܬܐ ܚܕܐ. ܐܢ ܕܝܢ ܐܦ ܠܐ ܠܙܥܘܪܬܐ ܡܫܟܚܝܢ
ܐܢܬܘܢ ܠܡܥܒܕ. ܡܢܐ ܝܨܦܝܢ ܐܢܬܘܢ ܥܠ ܫܪܟܐ.
27 ܐܬܒܩܘ ܒܫܘ̈ܫܢܐ ܕܕܒܪܐ ܐܝܟܢܐ ܠܐ ܠܐܝܢ ܘܠܐ
ܥܙܠܢ. ܘܐܡܪ ܐܢܐ ܠܟܘܢ ܕܐܦܠܐ ܫܠܝܡܘܢ ܒܟܠܗ̇

5 ܠܡܥܒܕ. ܐܚܘܝܟܘܢ ܕܝܢ ܡܢ ܡܢܘ ܬܕܚܠܘܢ. ܕܚܠܘ ܡܢ
ܗܘ ܕܡܢ ܒܬܪ ܕܩܛܠ ܫܠܝܛ ܠܗ ܠܡܪܡܝܘ ܒܓܗܢܐ.
6 ܐܝܢ ܐܡܪܢܐ ܠܟܘܢ ܕܡܢ ܗܢܐ ܘܠܐ ܠܡܕܚܠ. ܚܡ̈ܫ
ܨ̈ܦܪܝܢ ܡܙܕܒܢܢ ܒܐܣܪ. ܘܚܕܐ ܡܢܗܝܢ ܠܐ ܛܥܝܐ ܩܕܡ
7 ܐܠܗܐ. ܐܦ ܡ̈ܢܝܢܐ ܓܝܪ ܕܣܥܪܐ ܕܪܫܟܘܢ ܡܢܝܢ ܐܢܝܢ
ܠܗ. ܠܐ ܗܟܝܠ ܬܕܚܠܘܢ. ܡܛܠ ܕܡܢ ܣܘܓܐܐ
8 ܕܨ̈ܦܪܐ ܣܓܝ ܡܝܬܪܝܢ ܐܢܬܘܢ. ܐܡܪܢܐ ܠܟܘܢ ܕܝܢ
ܕܟܠ ܕܢܘܕܐ ܒܝ ܩܕܡ ܒ̈ܢܝ ܐܢܫܐ. ܐܦ ܒܪܗ ܕܐܢܫܐ
9 ܢܘܕܐ ܒܗ ܩܕܡ ܡܠܐܟ̈ܘܗܝ ܩ̈ܕܝܫܐ. ܘܐܝܢܐ ܕܟܦܪ
ܒܝ ܩܕܡ ܒ̈ܢܝ ܐܢܫܐ. ܢܬܟܦܪ ܒܗ ܩܕܡ ܡܠܐܟ̈ܘܗܝ
10 ܕܐܠܗܐ. ܘܟܠ ܕܢܐܡܪ ܡܠܬܐ ܥܠ ܒܪܗ ܕܐܢܫܐ
ܢܫܬܒܩ ܠܗ. ܡܢ ܕܥܠ ܪܘܚܐ ܕܝܢ ܕܩܘܕܫܐ ܢܓܕܦ ܠܐ
11 ܢܫܬܒܩ ܠܗ. ܡܐ ܕܡܩܪܒܝܢ ܠܟܘܢ ܕܝܢ ܠܟܢ̈ܘܫܬܐ
ܩܕܡ ܐܪ̈ܟܘܣ ܘܫ̈ܠܝܛܢܐ. ܠܐ ܬܐܨܦܘܢ ܕܐܝܟܢܐ
12 ܬܦܩܘܢ ܪܘܚܐ. ܐܘ ܡܢܐ ܬܡܠܠܘܢ. ܪܘܚܐ ܓܝܪ
ܕܩܘܕܫܐ ܬܠܦܟܘܢ ܒܗ ܫܥܬܐ ܡܕܡ ܕܘܠܐ
ܕܬܐܡܪܘܢ. ○○ ○○○○ ○○
13 ܘܐܡܪ ܠܗ ܓܒܪܐ ܚܕ ܡܢ ܗܘ ܟܢܫܐ. ܡܠܦܢܐ. ܐܡܪ
14 ܠܐܚܝ ܦܠܓ ܥܡܝ ܐܪܥܐ ܘܝܪܬܘܬܐ. ܗܘ ܕܝܢ ܐܡܪ
15 ܠܗ. ܓܒܪܐ ܡܢ ܐܩܝܡܢܝ ܥܠܝܟܘܢ ܕܝܢܐ. ܘܐܡܪ
ܠܟ̈ܢܫܐ. ܐܙܕܗܪܘ ܡܢ ܟܘܠܗ̇ ܥܠܘܒܘܬܐ. ܡܛܠ ܕܠܐ
ܗܘܐ ܒܡܘ̈ܬܪܢܐ ܕܢܟ̈ܣܐ ܗܘܝܢ ܚ̈ܝܐ ܠܒ̈ܢܝ
ܐܢ̈ܫܐ. ⁘

49 ܘܐܢܬܘܢ ܒܢܝܢ ܐܢܬܘܢ ܕܗܢܘܢ ܩ̈ܒܘܪܐ. ܡܛܠ
ܗܢܐ ܚܟܡܬܗ ܕܐܠܗܐ ܐܡܪܬ. ܐܫܕܪ ܒܗܘܢ
50 ܢܒ̈ܝܐ ܘܫ̈ܠܝܚܐ. ܡܢܗܘܢ ܢܩܛܠܘܢ ܘܢܪܕܦܘܢ. ܕܢܬܬܒܥ
ܕܡܐ ܕܟܠܗܘܢ ܢܒ̈ܝܐ ܕܐܬܐܫܕ. ܗܘܐ ܡܢ ܕܐܬܒܪܝ
51 ܥܠܡܐ. ܒܕܪܐ ܠܗܕܐ ܫܪܒܬܐ. ܡܢ ܕܡܗ ܕܗܒܝܠ
ܘܥܕܡܐ ܠܕܡܗ ܕܙܟܪܝܐ ܒܪ ܒܪܟܝܐ. ܗܘ ܕܐܬܩܛܠ
ܒܝܬ ܡܕܒܚܐ ܠܗܝܟܠܐ. ܐܡܝܢ ܐܡܪܢܐ ܠܟܘܢ
ܕܢܬܬܒܥ ܡܢܗ ܡܢ ܫܪܒܬܐ ܗܕܐ. ܀ ܀
52 ܘܝ ܠܟܘܢ ܣ̈ܦܪܐ ܕܐܚܕܬܘܢ ܐܩܠܝܕܐ ܕܝܕܥܬܐ.
53 ܐܢܬܘܢ ܠܐ ܥܠܬܘܢ ܘܠܐܝܠܝܢ ܕܥܠܝܢ ܟܠܝܬܘܢ. ܘܟܕ
ܐܡܪ ܗܘܐ ܗܠܝܢ ܠܘܩܒܠܗܘܢ ܠܥܝܢ ܒܗܘܢ ܒܥܡܐ.
ܫܪܝܘ ܡܬܬܟܐܫ ܗܘܘ ܠܣ̈ܦܪܐ ܘܦ̈ܪܝܫܐ. ܘܒܥܝܢ ܗܘܘ
54 ܒܡܕܡ ܥܠ ܦܓܥ̈ܬܐ. ܘܟܡܝܢ ܗܘܘ ܠܡܐܚܕ. ܥܠܘܗܝ
XII. ܡܠܬܐ ܕܢܫܟܚܘܢ ܢܐܟܠܘܢ ܩܪ̈ܨܘܗܝ. ܘܟܕ ܟܢܫ ܥܠܘܗܝ
ܟܢܫܐ ܣܓܝܐܐ. ܐܟܚܕܐ ܕܢܕܘܫܘܢ ܚܕ ܠܚܕ. ܫܪܝ ܗܘܐ
ܠܡܐܡܪ ܠܬܠܡܝܕܘܗܝ. ܠܘܩܕܡ ܐܙܕܗܪܘ ܡܢ
2 ܚܡܝܪܐ ܕܦ̈ܪܝܫܐ ܕܐܝܬܘܗܝ ܡܣܒ ܒܐ̈ܦܐ. ܠܝܬ
ܓܝܪ ܡܕܡ ܕܟܣܐ ܕܠܐ ܢܬܓܠܐ. ܘܠܐ ܕܡܛܫܐ ܕܠܐ
3 ܢܬܝܕܥ. ܐܝܠܝܢ ܓܝܪ ܕܒܚܫܘܟܐ ܐܡܪܬܘܢ ܒܢܘܗܪܐ
ܢܬܫܡܥܘܢ. ܘܡܕܡ ܕܒܬܘܢܐ ܒܐܕ̈ܢܐ ܠܚܫܬܘܢ ܥܠ
ܐܓ̈ܪܐ ܢܬܟܪܙ ܀
4 ܐܡܪܢܐ ܠܟܘܢ ܕܝܢ ܪ̈ܚܡܝ. ܠܐ ܬܕܚܠܘܢ ܡܢ ܐܝܠܝܢ
ܕܩܛܠܝܢ ܦܓܪܐ. ܘܡܢ ܒܬܪܟܢ ܡܕܡ ܠܐ ܡܫܟܚܝܢ

37 ܘܒܥܐ ܗܘܐ ܡܢܗ ܦܪܝܫܐ ܚܕ ܕܢܫܬܪܐ ܠܘܬܗ. ܘܥܠ
38 ܐܣܬܡܟ. ܘܫܪܝ ܗܘܐ ܦܪܝܫܐ ܗܘ ܐܡܪ ܒܪܥܝܢܗ.
39 ܕܠܡܢܐ ܠܐ ܥܡܕ ܡܢ ܩܕܡ ܫܪܘܬܗ. ܐܡܪ ܠܗ
ܡܪܢ. ܐܢܬܘܢ ܦܪ̈ܝܫܐ ܒܪܗ ܗܘ ܕܟܣܐ ܘܕܦܝܢܟܐ
ܡܕܟܝܢ ܐܢܬܘܢ. ܘܓܘܟܘܢ ܡܠܐ ܚܛܘܦܝܐ ܘܒܝܫܘܬܐ.
40 ܚܣ̈ܝܪܝ ܪܥܝܢܐ ܠܐ ܗܘܐ ܡܢ ܕܥܒܕ ܕܠܒܪ ܘܐܦ ܕܠܓܘ
41 ܗܘ ܥܒܕ. ܐܠܐ ܡܕܡ ܕܐܝܬ ܠܟܘ ܡܢܟܘܢ ܗܒܘܗܝ
42 ܙܕܩܬܐ. ܘܗܐ ܟܠ ܡܕܡ ܕܟܐ ܗܘ ܠܟܘܢ. ܐܠܐ
ܘܝ ܠܟܘܢ ܣܦ̈ܪܐ ܘܦܪ̈ܝܫܐ. ܕܡܥܣܪܝܢ ܐܢܬܘܢ ܢܢܥܐ
ܘܦܓܢܐ ܘܟܠܗܘܢ ܝܪ̈ܩܘܢܐ. ܘܥܒܪܝܢ ܐܢܬܘܢ ܥܠ
ܕܝܢܐ ܘܥܠ ܚܘܒܐ ܕܐܠܗܐ. ܗܠܝܢ ܕܝܢ ܥܒܕܬܘܢ
ܘܗܠܝܢ ܕܝܢ ܠܐ ܫܒܩܬܘܢ ܀
43 ܘܝ ܠܟܘܢ ܣܦ̈ܪܐ ܘܦܪ̈ܝܫܐ. ܕܪܚܡܝܢ ܐܢܬܘܢ ܡܘܬ̈ܒܐ
44 ܩܕ̈ܡܝܐ ܒܟܢܘܫܬܐ. ܘܫܠܡܐ ܒܫܘ̈ܩܐ. ܘܝ ܠܟܘܢ
ܕܐܝܬܝܟܘܢ ܩܒ̈ܪܐ. ܘܒ̈ܢܝ ܐܢܫܐ ܡܗܠܟܝܢ ܠܥܠ
45 ܡܢܗܘܢ ܘܠܐ ܝܕܥܝܢ. ܘܥܢܐ ܚܕ ܡܢ ܣܦ̈ܪܐ ܘܐܡܪ
ܠܗ. ܡܠܦܢܐ. ܟܕ ܗܠܝܢ ܐܡܪ ܐܢܬ ܘܐܦ ܠܢ ܡܨܥܪ
46 ܐܢܬ. ܐܡܪ ܠܗ ܐܦ ܠܟܘܢ ܘܝ ܣܦ̈ܪܐ. ܕܡܥܠܝܢ ܐܢܬܘܢ
ܡܘܒ̈ܠܐ ܝܩ̈ܝܪܬܐ. ܘܣܝܡܝܢ ܐܢܬܘܢ ܥܠ ܟܬ̈ܦܬܐ
ܕܒ̈ܢܝ ܐܢܫܐ. ܘܐܢܬܘܢ ܐܦܠܐ ܒܚܕܐ ܡܢ ܨܒ̈ܥܬܟܘܢ
47 ܩܪܒܝܢ ܐܢܬܘܢ ܠܗܝܢ. ܘܝ ܠܟܘܢ ܕܒܢܝܢ ܐܢܬܘܢ ܩܒ̈ܪܐ
48 ܕܢ̈ܒܝܐ. ܕܐܒ̈ܗܝܟܘܢ ܩܛܠܘ ܐܢܘܢ. ܡܟܝܠ ܣܗܕܝܢ
ܐܢܬܘܢ ܘܡܫܬܘܕܝܢ ܐܢܬܘܢ ܒܥܒ̈ܕܐ ܕܐܒ̈ܗܝܟܘܢ.

27 ܘܟܕ ܐܡܪ ܗܠܝܢ. ܐܢܬܬܐ ܚܕܐ ܡܢ ܓܘ ܟܢܫܐ.
ܒܩܠܐ ܪܡܐ ܐܡܪܬ ܠܗ. ܛܘܒܝܗ ܠܟܪܣܐ ܕܛܥܢܬܟ.
28 ܘܬ̈ܕܝܐ ܕܐܝܢܩܘܟ. ܐܡܪ ܠܗ̇ ܝܫܘܥ. ܛܘܒܝܗܘܢ
ܠܐܝܠܝܢ ܕܫܡܥܝܢ ܡܠܬܗ ܕܐܠܗܐ ܘܢܛܪܝܢ ܠܗ̇ ◦ ◦ ◦
29 ܘܟܕ ܡܬܟܢܫܝܢ ܗܘܘ ܟܢ̈ܫܐ. ܫܪܝ ܠܡܐܡܪ. ܫܪܒܬܐ
ܗܕܐ ܫܪܒܬܐ ܗܝ ܒܝܫܬܐ. ܐܬܐ ܒܥܝܐ ܘܐܬܐ ܠܐ
30 ܬܬܝܗܒ ܠܗ̇. ܐܠܐ ܐܝܟܢܐ ܕܗܘܐ ܝܘܢܢ ܐܬܐ
ܠܢܝ̈ܢܘܝܐ. ܗܟܢܐ ܘܐܦ ܒܪܗ ܕܐܢܫܐ ܠܫܪܒܬܐ ܗܕܐ.
31 ܡܠܟܬܐ ܕܬܝܡܢܐ ܬܩܘܡ ܒܕܝܢܐ ܥܡ ܫܪܒܬܐ ܗܕܐ
ܘܬܚܝܒܝܗ̇. ܕܐܬܬ ܡܢ ܥܒ̈ܪܘܗ̇ ܕܐܪܥܐ. ܕܬܫܡܥ
ܚܟܡܬܗ ܕܫܠܝܡܘܢ. ܘܗܐ ܕܝܬܝܪ ܡܢ ܫܠܝܡܘܢ
32 ܗܪܟܐ. ܓ̈ܒܪܐ ܒ̈ܢܝ ܢܝܢܘܐ ܢܩܘܡܘܢ ܒܕܝܢܐ ܥܡ
ܫܪܒܬܐ ܗܕܐ ܘܢܚܝܒܘܢܗ̇. ܕܗܢܘܢ ܬܒܘ ܒܟܪܘܙܘܬܗ
ܕܝܘܢܢ. ܘܗܐ ܕܝܬܝܪ ܡܢ ܝܘܢܢ ܗܪܟܐ ◦ ◦
33 ܠܐ ܐܢܫ ܡܢܗܪ ܫܪܓܐ ܘܣܐܡ ܠܗ ܬܚܝܬ ܣܐܬܐ.
ܐܦ ܒܐܬܪܐ ܛܫܝܐ. ܐܠܐ ܣܐܡ ܠܗ ܠܥܠ ܡܢ
34 ܡܢܪܬܐ. ܕܐܝܠܝܢ ܕܥܐܠܝܢ ܢܚܙܘܢ ܢܘܗܪܗ. ܫܪܓܗ ܓܝܪ
ܕܦܓܪܐ ܥܝܢܐ ܗܝ. ܐܡܬܝ ܕܥܝܢܟ ܡܫܠܡ ܬܗܘܐ
ܦܫܝܛܐ ܐܦ ܦܓܪܟ ܟܠܗ ܢܗܝܪ ܗܘ. ܐܢ ܕܝܢ
ܒܝܫܐ ܬܗܘܐ ܥܝܢܐ ܐܦ ܦܓܪܟ ܟܠܗ ܚܫܘܟ
35 ܗܘ. ܬܗܘܐ ܗܟܝܠ ܙܗܝܪ ܕܠܡܐ ܢܘܗܪܐ ܕܒܟ
36 ܚܫܘܟ ܠܗ. ܘܐܢ ܢܘܗܪܐ ܕܒܟ ܚܫܘܟ ܗܘ. ܚܫܘܟܟ
ܒܟܡܐ ܢܗܘܐ. ◦ ◦ ◦

17 ܗܘ ܕܝܢ ܟܕ ܝܕܥ ܬܪܥܝܬܗܘܢ ܐܡܪ ܠܗܘܢ. ܟܠ
ܡܠܟܘ ܕܬܬܦܠܓ ܥܠ ܢܦܫܗ̇ ܬܚܪܒ. ܘܟܠ ܒܝܬܐ
18 ܕܥܠ ܒܝܬܐ ܡܬܦܠܓ ܢܦܠ ܠܗ. ܐܢ ܗܘ ܣܛܢܐ ܥܠ
ܢܦܫܗ ܐܬܦܠܓ ܐܝܟܢܐ ܬܩܘܡ ܡܠܟܘܬܗ. ܕܐܡܪܝܢ
19 ܐܢܬܘܢ ܕܒܒܥܠܙܒܘܒ ܡܦܩ ܐܢܐ ܫܐܕ̈ܐ. ܐܢ ܕܝܢ
ܐܢܐ ܒܒܥܠܙܒܘܒ ܡܦܩ ܐܢܐ ܫܐܕ̈ܐ ܡܢ ܒܢܝ̈ܟܘܢ.
ܒܢܝ̈ܟܘܢ ܒܡܢܐ ܡܦܩܝܢ ܠܗܘܢ. ܡܛܠ ܗܢܐ ܗܢܘܢ
20 ܢܗܘܘܢ ܠܟܘܢ ܕܝܢܐ. ܐܢ ܕܝܢ ܒܨܒܥܐ ܕܐܠܗܐ ܡܦܩ
ܐܢܐ ܫܐܕ̈ܐ. ܡܛܠ ܩܪܒܬ ܥܠܝܟܘܢ ܡܠܟܘܬܗ
21 ܕܐܠܗܐ. ܐܡܬܝ ܕܝܢ ܕܥܫܝܢܐ ܟܕ ܙܝܢ ܢܛܪ ܕܪܬܗ
22 ܒܫܝܢܐ ܗܘ ܩܢܝܢܗ. ܐܢ ܕܝܢ ܢܐܬܐ ܡܢ ܕܥܫܝܢ
ܡܢܗ ܘܢܙܟܝܘܗܝ. ܘܢܫܩܘܠ ܙܝܢܗ ܗܘ ܕܬܟܝܠ ܗܘܐ
23 ܥܠܘܗܝ. ܘܒܙܬܗ ܬܦܠܘܓ ܡܦܠܓ ܠܗ. ܡܢ ܕܠܐ ܗܘܐ
ܥܡܝ ܠܘܩܒܠܝ ܗܘ. ܘܡܢ ܕܠܐ ܟܢܫ ܥܡܝ ܡܒܕܪܘ
ܡܒܕܪ ○ ○ ○

24 ܪܘܚܐ ܛܢܦܬܐ ܡܐ ܕܢܦܩܬ ܡܢ ܒܪ ܐܢܫܐ. ܐܙܠܐ
ܡܬܟܪܟܐ ܒܐܬܪ̈ܘܬܐ ܕܡ̈ܝܐ ܠܝܬ ܒܗܘܢ. ܕܬܫܟܚ
ܠܗ̇ ܢܝܚܐ. ܘܟܕ ܠܐ ܐܫܟܚܬ ܐܡܪܐ. ܐܗܦܘܟ
ܐܙܠ ܠܒܝܬܝ ܡܢ ܐܝܟܐ ܕܢܦܩܬ. ܘܟܕ ܐܬܬ
25, 26 ܘܐܫܟܚܬܗ ܕܟܢܝܫ ܘܡܨܒܬ. ܐܙܠܐ ܕܒܪܐ ܫܒܥ
ܪ̈ܘܚܝܢ ܐ̈ܚܪܢܝܢ ܕܒܝܫܢ ܡܢܗ̇. ܘܥܠܢ ܘܥܡܪ̈ܢ
ܒܗ. ܘܗܘܝܐ ܐܚܪܝܬܗ ܕܗܘ ܓܒܪܐ ܒܝܫܐ ܡܢ
ܩܕܡܝܬܗ. ○ ○ ○

6 ܠܗ ܪܚܡܝ ܐܬܐ ܠܘܬܝ ܒܪܡܫܐ. ܡܛܠ ܕܪܚܡܝ
ܐܬܐ ܠܘܬܝ ܡܢ ܐܘܪܚܐ. ܘܠܝܬ ܠܝ ܡܕܡ ܕܐܣܝܡ
7 ܩܕܡܘܗܝ. ܘܗܘܝܐ ܡܢ ܠܓܘ ܘܐܡܪ ܠܗ ܠܐ ܬܗܪܢܝ.
ܡܛܠ ܕܬܪܥܐ ܐܚܝܕ ܗܘ. ܘܒܢ̈ܝܐ ܥܡܝ ܒܥܪܣܐ.
8 ܠܐ ܡܫܟܚܢܐ ܕܐܩܘܡ ܐܬܠ ܠܟ. ܐܡܪ ܐܢܐ ܠܟܘܢ
ܕܐܢ ܡܛܠ ܪܚܡܘܬܐ ܠܐ ܢܩܘܡ ܢܬܠ ܠܗ. ܡܛܠ
ܚܨܝܦܘܬܗ ܢܩܘܡ ܘܢܬܠ ܠܗ ܟܡܐ ܕܡܬܒܥܐ ܠܗ.
9 ܘܐܦ ܐܢܐ ܐܡܪ ܐܢܐ ܠܟܘܢ. ܫܐܠܘ ܘܢܬܝܗܒ ܠܟܘܢ.
10 ܒܥܘ ܘܬܫܟܚܘܢ ܠܟܘܢ. ܟܠ ܐܢܫ ܓܝܪ ܕܫܐܠ ܢܣܒ.
ܘܡܢ ܕܒܥܐ ܡܫܟܚ. ܘܡܢ ܕܢܩܫ ܡܬܦܬܚ ܠܗ.
11 ܐܝܢܐ ܕܝܢ ܡܢܟܘܢ ܕܢܫܐܠܘܗܝ ܒܪܗ ܠܚܡܐ. ܠܡܐ
ܗܘ ܟܐܦܐ ܡܘܫܛ ܠܗ. ܐܘ ܐܢ ܢܘܢܐ ܢܫܐܠܢܗܝ.
12 ܕܠܡܐ ܚܠܦ ܢܘܢܐ ܚܘܝܐ ܡܘܫܛ ܠܗ. ܐܘ ܒܝܥܬܐ
13 ܢܫܐܠܢܗܝ. ܕܠܡܐ ܥܩܪܒܐ ܡܘܫܛ ܠܗ. ܐܢ
ܐܢܬܘܢ ܕܒ̈ܝܫܐ ܐܢܬܘܢ. ܝܕܥܝܢ ܐܢܬܘܢ ܡܘܗܒܬܐ
ܛܒܬܐ ܠܡܬܠ ܠܒܢ̈ܝܟܘܢ. ܟܡܐ ܝܬܝܪܐܝܬ ܐܒܐ
ܡܢ ܫܡܝܐ. ܢܬܠ ܪܘܚܐ ܕܩܘܕܫܐ ܠܐܝܠܝܢ ܕܫܐܠܝܢ
ܠܗ. ⁘

14 ܘܗܘܐ ܟܕ ܡܦܩ ܗܘܐ ܫܐܕܐ ܡܢ ܚܪܫܐ. ܘܟܕ ܢܦܩ
ܗܘ ܫܐܕܐ ܡܠܠ ܗܘ ܚܪܫܐ. ܘܐܬܕܡܪܘ ܗܘܘ
15 ܟܢ̈ܫܐ ܗܘܝܢ. ܘܐܢܫܝܢ ܡܢ ܦܪ̈ܝܫܐ ܐܡܪܘ. ܒܒܥܠܙܒܘܒ
16 ܪܫܐ ܕܫܐ̈ܕܐ ܡܦܩ ܗܘܐ ܫܐ̈ܕܐ. ܐܚܪ̈ܢܐ ܕܝܢ ܟܕ
ܡܢܣܝܢ ܗܘܘ ܠܗ ܐܬܐ ܡܢ ܫܡܝܐ ܫܐܠܝܢ ܗܘܘ ܠܗ.

ܕܐܬܪܚܡ ܥܠܘܗܝ. ܐܡܪ ܠܗ ܝܫܘܥ. ܙܠ ܐܦ ܐܢܬ
ܗܟܢܐ ܗܘܝܬ ܥܒܕ ◦◦◦
38 ܘܟܕ ܐܙܠܝܢ ܗܘܘ ܒܐܘܪܚܐ. ܥܠ ܠܩܪܝܬܐ ܚܕܐ.
ܘܐܢܬܬܐ ܚܕܐ ܕܫܡܗ̇ ܡܪܬܐ ܩܒܠܬܗ ܒܒܝܬܗ̇.
39 ܘܐܝܬ ܗܘܬ ܠܗ̇ ܚܬܐ ܕܫܡܗ̇ ܡܪܝܡ. ܘܐܬܬ
ܝܬܒܬ ܠܘܬ ܪ̈ܓܠܘܗܝ ܕܡܪܢ. ܘܫܡܥܐ ܗܘܬ
40 ܡ̈ܠܘܗܝ. ܡܪܬܐ ܕܝܢ ܒܛܝܠܐ ܗܘܬ ܒܬܫܡܫܬܐ
ܣܓܝܐܬܐ. ܘܐܬܬ ܐܡܪܐ ܠܗ. ܡܪܝ ܠܐ ܒܛܝܠ ܠܟ
ܥܠܝ ܕܚܬܝ ܫܒܩܬܢܝ ܒܠܚܘܕܝ ܕܐܫܡܫ. ܐܡܪܝ ܠܗ̇
41 ܡܥܕܪܐ ܠܝ. ܐܡܪ ܠܗ̇ ܡܪܢ ܡܪܬܐ ܡܪܬܐ ܝܨܦܬܝ
42 ܘܛܘܪܦܐ ܕܠܝ ܐܝܬ ܠܟܝ ܠܘܬܟܝ ܥܠ ܣ̈ܓܝܐܬܐ. ܚܕܐ
ܗܘ ܕܝܢ ܡܬܒܥܝܐ. ܡܪܝܡ ܡܢܬܐ ܛܒܬܐ ܓܒܬ ܠܗ̇
ܘܠܐ ܬܫܬܩܠ ܡܢܗ̇. ◦:◦
XI. ܘܟܕ ܡܨܠܐ ܗܘܐ ܕܝܢ ܒܕܘܟܬܐ ܚܕܐ. ܒܬܪ ܕܦܪܩ
ܫܠܠ ܡܢ ܨܠܘܬܗ. ܐܡܪ ܠܗ ܚܕ ܡܢ ܬܠܡ̈ܝܕܘܗܝ.
ܡܪܢ ܐܠܦܝܢ ܠܡܨܠܝܘ ܐܝܟܢܐ ܕܝܘܚܢܢ ܐܠܦ
2 ܠܬܠܡ̈ܝܕܘܗܝ. ܐܡܪ ܠܗܘܢ ܐܡܬܝ ܕܡܨܠܝܢ ܐܢܬܘܢ
ܗܘܝܬܘܢ ܐܡܪܝܢ. ܐܒܘܢ ܕܒܫܡܝܐ ܢܬܩܕܫ ܫܡܟ.
3 ܘܬܐܬܐ ܡܠܟܘܬܟ. ܘܗܒ ܠܢ ܠܚܡܐ ܐܡܝܢܐ
4 ܕܟܠܝܘܡ. ܘܫܒܘܩ ܠܢ ܚ̈ܛܗܝܢ. ܘܐܦ ܚܢܢ ܫܒܩܝܢ ܠܟܠ
ܕܚܝܒ ܠܢ. ܘܠܐ ܬܥܠܢ ܠܢܣܝܘܢܐ. ܐܠܐ ܦܨܢ ܡܢ
5 ܒܝܫܐ. ܘܐܡܪ ܠܗܘܢ ܝܫܘܥ. ܡܢܘ ܡܢܟܘܢ ܕܢܗܘܐ
ܠܗ ܪ̈ܚܡܐ. ܘܢܐܙܠ ܠܘܬܗ ܒܦܠܓܘܬ ܠܠܝܐ. ܘܢܐܡܪ

ܚܙܘ. ܘܠܡܫܡܥ ܡܕܡ ܕܫܡܥܝܢ ܐܢܬܘܢ ܘܠܐ ܫܡܥܘ.
25 ܘܟܕ ܐܡܪ ܗܠܝܢ. ܩܪܒ ܡܠܦ ܢܡܘܣܐ ܚܕ ܕܩܐܡ ܗܘܐ
ܕܢܣܝܘܗܝ. ܐܡܪ ܠܗ ܡܠܦܢܐ ܡܢܐ ܐܥܒܕ ܕܐܝܪܬ ܚܝ̈ܐ
26 ܕܠܥܠܡ. ܐܡܪ ܠܗ ܝܫܘܥ ܒܢܡܘܣܐ ܐܝܟܢܐ ܟܬܝܒ
27 ܘܐܝܟܢܐ ܩܪܝܬ. ܐܡܪ ܠܗ ܕܬܪܚܡ ܠܡܪܝܐ ܐܠܗܟ ܡܢ
ܟܠܗ ܠܒܟ. ܘܡܢ ܟܠܗ ܚܝܠܟ. ܘܡܢ ܟܠܗ̇ ܢܦܫܟ. ܘܡܢ
28 ܟܠܗ ܪܥܝܢܟ. ܘܠܩܪܝܒܟ ܐܝܟ ܢܦܫܟ. ܐܡܪ ܠܗ
ܝܫܘܥ ܬܪܝܨܐܝܬ ܐܡܪܬ. ܗܠܝܢ ܥܒܕ ܘܚܝܐ ܐܢܬ.
29 ܗܘ ܕܝܢ ܨܒܐ ܗܘܐ ܠܡܙܕܩܘ ܢܦܫܗ. ܐܡܪ ܠܝܫܘܥ
30 ܘܡܢܘ ܩܪܝܒܝ. ܐܡܪ ܠܗ ܝܫܘܥ. ܓܒܪܐ ܚܕ ܢܚܬ
ܗܘܐ ܡܢ ܐܘܪܫܠܡ ܠܐܝܪܝܚܘ. ܘܢܦܠ ܒܐܝ̈ܕܝ ܓܝ̈ܣܐ.
ܘܐܫܠܚܘܗܝ ܘܡܚܘܗܝ. ܘܫܒܩܘܗܝ ܒܝܬ ܡܝܬ
31 ܠܚܝ. ܘܐܙܠܘ ܠܗܘܢ. ܘܓܕܫ ܟܗܢܐ ܚܕ ܢܚܬ ܗܘܐ
32 ܒܐܘܪܚܐ ܗܝ ܘܚܙܝܗܝ ܘܥܒܪܗ. ܘܐܦ ܠܘܝܐ ܟܕ
33 ܡܛܐ ܗܘ ܕܘܟܬܐ ܚܙܝܗܝ ܘܥܒܪܗ. ܫܡܪܝܐ ܕܝܢ ܚܕ
ܟܕ ܪܕܐ ܗܘܐ ܒܗ̇ ܒܐܘܪܚܐ ܘܡܛܐ ܠܘܬܗ. ܚܙܝܗܝ
34 ܘܐܬܪܚܡ ܥܠܘܗܝ. ܘܐܬܩܪܒ ܘܚܒܫ ܡܚ̈ܘܬܗ.
ܘܢܛܦ ܥܠܝܗܝܢ ܚܡܪܐ ܘܡܫܚܐ. ܘܐܪܟܒܗ ܥܠ
35 ܚܡܪܗ. ܘܐܝܬܝܗ ܠܦܘܬܩܐ ܘܬܪܣܝܗ. ܘܠܨܦܪܗ
ܕܝܘܡܐ ܐܦܩ ܬܪܝܢ ܕܝ̈ܢܪܝܢ ܝܗܒ ܠܦܘܬܩܝܐ. ܘܐܡܪ
ܬܪܣܝܘܗܝ. ܘܡܕܡ ܕܢܦܩ ܠܟ ܬܘܒ ܦܪܥ
36 ܐܢܐ ܠܟ. ܡܢܘ ܡܢ ܗܠܝܢ ܬܠܬܐ ܡܬܚܙܐ ܠܟ ܕܗܘܐ
ܩܪܝܒܐ ܕܗܘ ܕܢܦܠ ܒܐܝ̈ܕܝ ܓܝ̈ܣܐ. ܐܡܪ ܠܗ ܗܘ

15 ܕܕܝܢܐ. ܝܬܝܪ ܡܢ ܕܠܟܘܢ. ܘܐܦ ܐܢܬܝ ܟܦܪܢܚܘܡ ܠܐ
ܥܕܡܐ ܠܫܡܝܐ ܬܬܪܝܡܝܢ. ܐܠܐ ܥܕܡܐ ܠܫܝܘܠ
16 ܬܚܘܬܝܢ. ܡܢ ܕܠܟܘܢ ܫܡܥ ܠܝ ܗܘ ܫܡܥ. ܘܡܢ ܕܠܟܘܢ
ܛܠܡ ܠܝ ܗܘ ܛܠܡ. ܘܡܢ ܕܠܝ ܛܠܡ ܠܡܢ ܕܫܕܪܢܝ ܛܠܡ. ܘܡܢ
ܕܠܝ ܫܡܥ ܠܡܢ ܕܫܕܪܢܝ ܫܡܥ ◎ ○ ○
17 ܘܗܦܟܘ ܗܘܘ ܗܢܘܢ ܫܒܥܝܢ ܕܫܕܪ ܒܚܕܘܬܐ
ܘܐܡܪܝܢ. ܡܪܢ. ܘܐܦ ܫܐܕ̈ܐ ܡܫܬܥܒܕܝܢ ܠܢ ܒܫܡܟ.
18 ܐܡܪ ܠܗܘܢ ܝܫܘܥ. ܚܙܐ ܗܘܝܬ ܠܗ ܠܣܛܢܐ ܕܢܦܠ
19 ܐܝܟ ܒܪܩܐ ܕܢܦܠ ܡܢ ܫܡܝܐ. ܗܐ ܝܗܒ ܐܢܐ ܠܟܘܢ
ܫܘܠܛܢܐ. ܕܬܗܘܘܢ ܕܝܫܝܢ ܚܘ̈ܘܬܐ ܘܥܩܪ̈ܒܐ.
ܘܟܠܗ ܚܝܠܗ ܕܒܥܠܕܒܒܐ. ܘܡܕܡ ܠܐ ܢܗܪܟܘܢ.
20 ܒܪܡ ܒܗܕܐ ܠܐ ܬܚܕܘܢ ܕܫܐ̈ܕܐ ܡܫܬܥܒܕܝܢ ܠܟܘܢ.
21 ܐܠܐ ܚܕܘ ܒܫ̈ܡܗܝܟܘܢ ܕܟܬܝܒܝܢ ܒܫܡܝܐ. ܘܒܗ̇
ܒܫܥܬܐ ܐܪܘܙ ܒܪܘܚܐ ܕܩܘܕܫܐ ܘܐܡܪ. ܡܘܕܐ
ܐܢܐ ܠܟ ܐܒܐ ܡܪܗ ܕܫܡܝܐ ܘܕܐܪܥܐ. ܕܟܣܝܬ
ܗܠܝܢ ܡܢ ܚܟ̈ܝܡܐ ܘܡܢ ܣܟ̈ܘܠܬܢܐ. ܘܓܠܝܬ ܐܢܝܢ
ܠܫܒ̈ܪܐ. ܐܝܢ ܐܒܐ ܕܗܟܢܐ ܗܘܐ ܨܒܝܢܐ ܩܕܡܝܟ.
22 ܟܠ ܡܕܡ ܐܫܬܠܡ ܠܝ ܡܢ ܐܒܝ. ܘܠܐ ܐܢܫ ܝܕܥ ܡܢܘ
ܒܪܐ ܐܠܐ ܐܢ ܐܒܐ. ܘܠܐ ܡܢܘ ܐܒܐ ܐܠܐ ܐܢ
23 ܒܪܐ. ܘܠܡܢ ܕܨܒܐ ܒܪܐ ܕܢܓܠܐ ܠܗ. ܘܐܬܦܢܝ ܠܘܬ
ܬܠܡܝ̈ܕܘܗܝ ܘܐܡܪ ܠܗܘܢ. ܛܘܒܝܗܝܢ ܠܥܝ̈ܢܐ ܕܚܙܝܢ
24 ܡܕܡ ܕܚܙܝܬܘܢ. ܐܡܪܢܐ ܠܟܘܢ ܕܣܓ̈ܝܐܐ ܢܒ̈ܝܐ
ܘܡ̈ܠܟܐ ܨܒܘ ܕܢܚܙܘܢ ܡܕܡ ܕܚܙܝܬܘܢ ܐܢܬܘܢ ܘܠܐ

ܘܦ̈ܥܠܐ ܙܥܘܪܝܢ. ܒܥܘ ܗܟܝܠ ܡܢ ܡܪܗ ܕܚܨܕܐ ܐܝܟ
3 ܕܢܦܩ ܦ̈ܥܠܐ ܠܚܨܕܗ. ܙܠܘ ܗܫܐ ܗܐ ܡܫܕܪ ܐܢܐ
4 ܠܟܘܢ ܐܝܟ ܐܡܪ̈ܢܐ ܒܝܬ ܕܐ̈ܒܐ. ܠܐ ܬܫܩܠܘܢ ܠܟܘܢ
ܟܝܣܐ ܘܠܐ ܬܪ̈ܡܠܐ. ܘܠܐ ܡܣ̈ܐܢܐ. ܘܒܫܠܡܐ ܕܐܢܫ
5 ܒܐܘܪܚܐ ܠܐ ܬܫܐܠܘܢ. ܘܠܐܝܢܐ ܒܝܬܐ ܡܕܥܐ
ܕܥܠܝܢ ܐܢܬܘܢ ܠܗ. ܗܘܝܬܘܢ ܐܡܪܝܢ ܫܠܡܐ
6 ܒܒܝܬܐ ܗܢܐ. ܘܐܢ ܐܝܬ ܬܡܢ ܒܪ ܫܠܡܐ ܢܬܬܢܝܚ
ܥܠܘܗܝ ܫܠܡܟܘܢ. ܘܐܢ ܕܝܢ ܠܐ ܥܠܝܟܘܢ ܢܗܦܘܟ.
7 ܘܒܗ ܒܒܝܬܐ ܗܘܝܬܘܢ ܠܥܣܝܢ ܘܫܬܝܢ ܡܢ ܕܠܘܬܗܘܢ.
ܫܘܐ ܗܘ ܦܥܠܐ ܠܐܓܪܗ. ܘܠܐ ܬܫܢܘܢ ܡܢ ܒܝܬܐ
8 ܠܚܒܪܗ. ܘܠܐܝܕܐ ܡܕܝܢܬܐ ܕܥܠܝܢ ܐܢܬܘܢ ܠܗ̇
ܘܡܩܒܠܝܢ ܠܟܘܢ. ܠܥܣܘ ܟܘܠ ܡܕܡ ܕܡܬܬܣܝܡ
9 ܩܕܡܝܟܘܢ. ܘܐܣܘ ܡܪ̈ܥܐ ܕܐܝܬ ܒܗ. ܘܗܘܝܬܘܢ
ܐܡܪܝܢ ܕܩܪܒܬ ܠܘܬܟܘܢ ܡܠܟܘܬܗ ܕܐܠܗܐ.
10 ܠܐܝܕܐ ܡܕܝܢܬܐ ܕܝܢ ܕܥܠܝܢ ܐܢܬܘܢ ܠܗ ܘܠܐ
11 ܢܩܒܠܘܢܟܘܢ ܒܗ̇. ܦܘܩܘ ܘܐܡܪܘ ܒܫܘ̈ܩܝܗ. ܘܗܘܐ
ܐܦ ܚܠܐ ܕܕܒܩ ܒܪ̈ܓܠܝܢ ܢܦܨܝܢ ܐܢܚܢ ܠܟܘܢ. ܒܪܡ
ܕܝܢ ܗܕܐ ܕܥܘ. ܕܩܪܒܬ ܠܗ ܡܠܟܘܬܗ ܕܐܠܗܐ.
12 ܐܡܪܢܐ ܠܟܘܢ ܕܠܣܕܘܡ ܢܗܘܐ ܢܝܚ ܒܝܘܡܐ
ܕܕܝܢܐ ܛܒ ܡܢ ܕܠܗ̇ ܡܕܝܢܬܐ. ◎ ○ ◎
13 ܘܝ ܠܟܝ ܟܘܪܙܝܢ. ܘܝ ܠܟܝ ܒܝܬ ܨܝܕܐ. ܕܐܠܘ ܒܨܘܪ ܘܒܨܝܕܢ
ܗܘܘ ܚ̈ܝܠܐ ܕܗܘܘ ܒܟܝ. ܟܒܪ ܕܝܢ ܒܣܩܐ ܘܒܩܛܡܐ
14 ܬܒܘ. ܒܪܡ ܠܨܘܪ ܘܠܨܝܕܢ ܢܗܘܐ ܢܝܚ ܒܝܘܡܐ

53 ܕܫ̈ܡܪܝܐ ܕܢܛܝܒܘܢ ܠܗ. ܘܠܐ ܩܒܠܘܗܝ. ܡܛܠ
54 ܕܦܪ̈ܨܘܦܗ ܠܐܘܪܫܠܡ ܣܡ ܗܘܐ ܠܡܐܙܠ. ܘܟܕ ܕܝܢ
ܚܙܘ ܬܠܡ̈ܝܕܘܗܝ ܝܥܩܘܒ ܘܝܘܚܢܢ. ܐܡܪܘ ܠܗ ܡܪܢ
ܨܒܐ ܐܢܬ ܕܢܐܡܪ. ܕܬܚܘܬ ܢܘܪܐ ܡܢ ܫܡܝܐ
55 ܘܬܣܦܐܢܘܢ. ܘܗܘ ܐܬܦܢܝ ܘܟܐܐ ܒܗܘܢ. ܘܐܡܪ
ܠܗܘܢ. ܠܐ ܝܕܥܝܢ ܐܢܬܘܢ ܕܐܝܢܐ ܐܢܬܘܢ ܪܘܚܐ.
56 ܒܪܗ ܓܝܪ ܕܐܢܫܐ ܠܐ ܐܬܐ ܠܡܘܒܕܘ ܢܦ̈ܫܬܐ. ܐܠܐ
ܠܡܚܝܘ. ܘܐܙܠܘ ܠܗܘܢ ܠܩܪܝܬܐ ܐܚܪܬܐ. ⁘
57 ܘܟܕ ܐܙܠܝܢ ܒܐܘܪܚܐ. ܐܬܐ ܓܒܪܐ ܚܕ ܐܡܪ ܠܗ.
58 ܐܬܐ ܒܬܪܟ ܠܐܬܪ ܕܐܙܠ ܐܢܬ. ܐܡܪ ܠܗ ܝܫܘܥ
ܠܬܥ̈ܠܐ ܢܩ̈ܥܐ ܐܝܬ ܠܗܘܢ. ܘܠܦܪ̈ܚܬܐ ܕܫܡܝܐ
ܡܛܠܠܐ. ܠܒܪܗ ܕܝܢ ܕܐܢܫܐ ܠܝܬ ܠܗ ܐܬܪ ܕܢܣܡܘܟ
59 ܪܫܗ. ܘܐܡܪ ܠܐܚܪܢܐ ܬܐ ܒܬܪܝ. ܐܡܪ ܠܗ ܡܪܝ
60 ܐܦܣ ܠܝ ܠܘܩܕܡ ܐܙܠ ܐܩܒܘܪ ܠܐܒܝ ܘܐܬܐ. ܐܡܪ
ܠܗ ܝܫܘܥ ܫܒܘܩ ܡ̈ܝܬܐ ܩܒܪܝܢ ܡ̈ܝܬܝܗܘܢ. ܘܐܢܬ
61 ܙܠ ܣܒܪ ܡܠܟܘܬܗ ܕܐܠܗܐ. ܐܡܪ ܠܗ ܐܚܪܢܐ
ܐܬܐ ܒܬܪܟ ܡܪܝ. ܠܘܩܕܡ ܕܝܢ ܐܦܣ ܠܝ ܐܙܠ ܐܫܠܡ
62 ܠܒ̈ܢܝ ܒܝܬܝ ܘܐܬܐ. ܐܡܪ ܠܗ ܝܫܘܥ. ܠܐ ܐܢܫ ܪܡܐ
ܐܝܕܗ ܥܠ ܚܪܒܐ ܕܦܕܢܐ ܘܚܐܪ ܠܒܣܬܪܗ. ܘܗܘܐ
ܬܘܒ ܚܫܚ ܠܡܠܟܘܬܐ ܕܐܠܗܐ ◎ ◎
X. ܘܡܢ ܒܬܪ ܗܠܝܢ ܦܪܫ ܐܦ ܠܐܚܪ̈ܢܐ ܫܒܥܝܢ ܘܬܪ̈ܝܢ. ܘܫܕܪ
ܐܢܘܢ ܬܪ̈ܝܢ ܬܪ̈ܝܢ ܩܕܡ ܐ̈ܦܘܗܝ. ܠܟܠ ܐܬܪ ܘܡܕܝܢܐ
2 ܕܥܬܝܕ ܗܘܐ ܠܡܐܙܠ. ܐܡܪ ܠܗܘܢ ܚܨܕܐ ܗܘ ܣܓܝ

ܠܗ ܐܪܥܗ ܫܐܕܐ ܗܘ. ܘܡܫܚܩ ܗܘܐ ܠܗ. ܘܟܐܐ
ܒܗ̇ ܝܫܘܥ ܒܪܘܚܐ ܗܝ ܛܢܦܬܐ. ܘܐܣܝܗ ܠܛܠܝܐ
43 ܘܐܫܠܡܗ ܠܐܒܘܗܝ. ܘܐܬܕܡܪܘ ܟܠܗܘܢ ܥܠ
ܪܒܘܬܗ ܕܐܠܗܐ. ܘܟܕ ܟܠܢܫ ܡܬܕܡܪ ܗܘܐ ܥܠ
44 ܟܠ ܕܥܒܕ ܗܘܐ. ܐܡܪ ܠܬܠܡܝܕܘܗܝ. ܣܝܡܘ
ܐܢܬܘܢ ܡܠܐ ܗܠܝܢ ܒܐ̈ܕܢܝܟܘܢ. ܒܪܗ ܓܝܪ ܕܐܢܫܐ
45 ܥܬܝܕ ܗܘ ܕܢܫܬܠܡ ܒܐ̈ܝܕܝ ܒܢ̈ܝ ܐܢܫܐ. ܘܗܢܘܢ ܠܐ
ܡܫܬܘܕܥܝܢ ܗܘܘ ܠܗ̇ ܠܡܠܬܐ ܗܕܐ. ܡܛܠ
ܕܡܟܣܝܐ ܗܘܬ ܡܢܗܘܢ. ܕܠܐ ܢܫܬܘܕܥܘܢܗ̇. ܘܗܢܘܢ
ܕܚܠܝܢ ܗܘܘ ܕܢܫܐܠܘܢܝܗܝ ܥܠܝܗ̇ ܥܠ ܗܕܐ ܡܠܬܐ.
46 ܘܥܠܬ ܗܘܬ ܒܗܘܢ ܡܚܫܒܬܐ ܗܕܐ ܕܡܢܘ ܢܗܘܐ
47 ܪܒ ܒܗܘܢ. ܝܫܘܥ ܕܝܢ ܟܕ ܝܕܥ ܡܚܫ̈ܒܬܗܘܢ. ܐܚܕ
48 ܛܠܝܐ ܚܕ. ܘܐܩܝܡܗ ܠܘܬܗ ܘܐܡܪ. ܡܢ ܕܡܩܒܠ
ܛܠܝܐ ܗܢܐ ܒܫܡܝ ܠܝ ܗܘ ܡܩܒܠ. ܘܡܢ ܕܠܝ ܡܩܒܠ
ܠܡܢ ܕܫܕܪܢܝ ܡܩܒܠ. ܐܝܢܐ ܕܙܥܘܪ ܓܝܪ ܒܟܘܢ ܐܝܟ
49 ܗܢܐ ܛܠܝܐ ܗܢܘ ܪܒ. ܘܥܢܐ ܝܘܚܢܢ ܘܐܡܪ ܠܗ. ܚܙܝܢ
ܓܒܪܐ ܚܕ ܕܡܦܩ ܫܐ̈ܕܐ ܒܫܡܟ ܘܟܠܝܢܗܝ. ܥܠ
50 ܕܠܐ ܐܬܐ ܒܬܪܢ. ܐܡܪ ܠܗ ܝܫܘܥ ܠܐ
ܬܟܠܘܢ. ܡܢ ܕܠܐ ܗܘܐ ܓܝܪ ܠܘܩܒܠܟܘܢ ܥܡܟܘܢ
ܗܘ. ⊙ ○ ⊙

51 ܘܗܘܐ ܟܕ ܡܬܡܠܝܢ ܗܘܘ ܝܘ̈ܡܬܐ ܕܡܣܩܢܘܬܗ.
52 ܐܬܩܢ ܦܪܨܘܦܗ ܕܢܐܙܠ ܠܗ ܠܐܘܪܫܠܡ. ܘܫܕܪ ܗܘܐ
ܡܠܐ̈ܟܐ ܩܕܡ ܐ̈ܦܘܗܝ. ܘܐܙܠܘ ܥܠܘ ܠܩܪܝܬܐ ܚܕܐ

32 ܒܡܦܩܢܗ ܕܥܬܝܕ ܗܘܐ ܕܢܫܬܠܡ ܒܐܘܪܫܠܡ. ܘܫܡܥܘܢ
ܟܐܦܐ ܘܗܢܘܢ ܕܥܡܗ ܝܩܪܘ ܗܘܘ ܠܗܘܢ ܒܫܢܬܐ
ܦܨܐܬܐ. ܘܟܕ ܐܬܥܝܪܘ ܚܙܘ ܬܫܒܘܚܬܗ. ܘܠܗܘܢ
33 ܬܪ̈ܝܢ ܐܢܫܝܢ ܕܩܝܡܝܢ ܗܘܘ ܠܘܬܗ. ܘܟܕ ܫܪܝܘ ܠܡܦܪܫ
ܡܢܗ. ܐܡܪ ܟܐܦܐ ܠܝܫܘܥ. ܪܒܝ ܫܦܝܪ ܗܘ ܕܢܗܘܐ
ܗܪܟܐ. ܘܢܥܒܕ ܬܠܬ ܡ̈ܛܠܠܢ. ܠܟ ܚܕܐ. ܘܠܡܘܫܐ
ܚܕܐ. ܘܠܐܠܝܐ ܚܕܐ. ܘܠܐ ܝܕܥ ܗܘܐ ܡܢܐ ܐܡܪ
34 ܗܘܐ. ܘܟܕ ܐܡܪ ܗܠܝܢ. ܗܘܬ ܥܢܢܐ ܘܛܠܠܬ
ܥܠܝܗܘܢ. ܘܟܕ ܚܙܘ ܠܗܠܝܢ ܕܥܠܝܢ ܒܥܢܢܐ ܕܚܠܘ.
35 ܘܩܠܐ ܐܫܬܡܥ ܡܢ ܥܢܢܐ ܗܘ ܕܐܡܪ. ܗܢܘ ܒܪܝ
36 ܘܚܒܝܒܝ ܠܗ ܫܡܥܘ. ܘܟܕ ܗܘܐ ܩܠܐ ܐܫܬܟܚ
ܝܫܘܥ ܒܠܚܘܕܘܗܝ. ܘܗܢܘܢ ܫܬܩܘ ܠܗܘܢ. ܘܠܐܢܫ
ܐܦ ܠܐ ܐܡܪܘ ܡܕܡ ܕܚܙܘ ܗܘܘ ܒܗܢܘܢ ܝܘܡ̈ܬܐ.
37 ܘܒܗܘ ܝܘܡܐ ܬܘܒ ܟܕ ܢܚܬܘ ܡܢ ܛܘܪܐ. ܦܓܥ ܒܗ
38 ܟܢܫܐ ܣܓܝܐܐ. ܘܓܒܪܐ ܚܕ ܡܢ ܟܢܫܐ ܗܘ ܩܥܐ
ܘܐܡܪ. ܡܠܦܢܐ ܒܥܐ ܐܢܐ ܡܢܟ ܐܬܪܚܡ ܥܠ ܒܪܝ.
39 ܝܚܝܕܝܐ ܗܘ ܠܝ. ܘܪܘܚܐ ܗܘܐ ܠܗ. ܘܡܢ ܫܠܝܬ
ܥܠܝܐ ܪܘܚܐ ܠܗ ܘܡܪܥܬ. ܘܠܚܫܘܟ ܦܘܡܐ ܡܢܗ
40 ܡܟܐ ܕܥܫܘܬܗ. ܘܒܥܝܬ ܡܢ ܬܠܡ̈ܝܕܝܟ ܘܠܐ
41 ܐܫܟܚܘ ܠܡܐܣܝܘܬܗ ܘܠܡܦܩܘܬܗ̇. ܘܥܢܐ
ܝܫܘܥ ܘܐܡܪ. ܐܘ ܫܪܒܬܐ ܡܥܩܠܬܐ ܘܕܠܐ
ܗܝܡܢܘ. ܥܕܡܐ ܠܐܡܬܝ ܐܗܘܐ ܠܘܬܟܘܢ
42 ܘܐܣܝܒܪܟܘܢ. ܩܪܒܝܗܝ ܠܝ ܠܒܪܟ ܠܗܪܟܐ. ܘܟܕ ܡܩܪܒ

ܘܐܢܬܘܢ ܡܢܐ ܐܡܪܝܢ ܐܢܬܘܢ ܕܐܝܬܝ. ܥܢܐ
ܫܡܥܘܢ ܟܐܦܐ ܘܐܡܪ ܠܗ. ܐܢܬ ܗܘ ܡܫܝܚܐ.
21 ܘܗܘ ܟܐܐ ܒܗܘܢ ܘܦܩܕ ܐܢܘܢ ܕܗܕܐ ܠܐܢܫ ܠܐ
22 ܢܐܡܪܘܢ. ܘܐܡܪ ܕܥܬܝܕ ܗܘ ܠܒܪܗ ܕܐܢܫܐ
ܕܢܚܫ ܣܓܝ. ܘܢܣܬܠܐ ܡܢ ܩܫ̈ܝܫܐ ܘܣܦ̈ܪܐ ܘܟܗ̈ܢܐ.
ܘܢܬܩܛܠ ܘܠܝܘܡܐ ܕܬ̈ܠܬܐ ܢܩܘܡ. ○○ ○○ ○○
23 ܘܐܡܪ ܗܘܐ ܟܠ ܡܢ ܕܨܒܐ ܕܢܐܬܐ ܒܬܪܝ، ܢܟܦܘܪ
ܒܢܦܫܗ. ܘܢܫܩܘܠ ܙܩܝܦܗ ܒܟܠܝܘܡ ܘܢܐܬܐ ܒܬܪܝ.
24 ܡܢ ܕܨܒܐ ܓܝܪ ܕܢܚܐ ܢܦܫܗ ܢܘܒܕܝܗ. ܘܡܢ ܕܢܘܒܕ
25 ܢܦܫܗ ܡܛܠܬܝ، ܢܚܝܝܗ. ܡܢܐ ܓܝܪ ܢܬܝܬܪ ܒܪܐܢܫܐ ܐܢ
26 ܠܥܠܡܐ ܟܠܗ ܢܩܢܐ ܘܢܦܫܗ ܢܚܣܪ. ܡܢ ܕܢܒܗܬ ܒܝ ܓܝܪ
ܡܢܝ ܒܒܢ̈ܝܢܫܐ ܘܒܡ̈ܠܝܢ ܕܕܝܠܝ ܐܢܫ. ܢܒܗܬ ܒܗ
ܒܪܗ ܕܐܢܫܐ ܡܐ ܕܐܬܐ ܒܬܫܒܘܚܬܐ ܕܐܒܘܗܝ،
27 ܘܕܡ̈ܠܐܟܘܗܝ ܩ̈ܕܝܫܐ. ܐܡܪܢܐ ܠܟܘܢ ܕܝܢ ܫܪܝܪܐܝܬ.
ܕܐܝܬ ܐܢܫܐ ܕܩܝܡܝܢ ܗܪܟܐ. ܕܠܐ ܢܛܥܡܘܢ
ܡܘܬܐ. ܥܕܡܐ ܕܢܚܙܘܢ ܡܠܟܘܬܗ ܕܐܠܗܐ
ܕܐܬܝܐ ܒܫܘܒܚܐ ○○○
28 ܘܗܘܐ ܒܬܪ ܡ̈ܠܐ ܗܠܝܢ ܐܝܟ ܬܡ̈ܢܝܐ ܝܘܡܝܢ. ܘܕܒܪ
ܠܟܐܦܐ ܘܠܝܘܚܢܢ ܘܠܝܥܩܘܒ. ܘܣܠܩ ܠܛܘܪܐ
29 ܠܡܨܠܝܘ. ܘܟܕ ܡܨܠܐ ܐܫܬܚܠܦ ܚܙܘܐ ܕܐܦ̈ܘܗܝ.
ܘܠܒ̈ܘܫܘܗܝ ܚ̈ܘܪܝܢ ܘܡܒܪܩܝܢ ܗܘܘ ܐܝܟ ܬܠܓܐ.
30 ܘܗܐ ܬܪ̈ܝܢ ܓܒ̈ܪܝܢ ܡܡܠܠܝܢ ܥܡܗ. ܡܘܫܐ ܘܐܠܝܐ
31 ܕܐܬܚܙܝܘ ܒܬܫܒܘܚܬܐ. ܘܐܡܪܝܢ ܗܘܘ ܥܠ

ܡܠܟܘܬܐ ܕܐܠܗܐ. ܘܠܐܝܠܝܢ ܕܣܢܝܩܝܢ ܗܘܘ ܠܐ
ܐܣܝܘܬܐ ܡܐܣܐ ܗܘܐ ܠܗܘܢ. . . .
12 ܘܟܕ ܪܟܢ ܗܘܐ ܠܡܥܪܒ ܝܘܡܐ. ܩܪܒܘ ܬܠܡܝ̈ܕܘܗܝ
ܘܐܡܪܝܢ ܠܗ ܒܚܘܪܒܐ ܐܝܬܝܢ. ܫܪܝ ܠܟܢ̈ܫܐ
ܗܠܝܢ ܕܢܐܙܠܘܢ ܠܩܘܪܝܐ ܗܠܝܢ ܕܚ̈ܕܪܝܢ ܘܠܟܦܪܢܐ
13 ܕܢܫܪܘܢ ܒܗܝܢ. ܐܘ ܕܢܫܟܚܘܢ ܠܗܘܢ ܣܝܒܪܬܐ. ܐܡܪ
ܠܗܘܢ ܝܫܘܥ ܐܢܬܘܢ ܗܒܘ ܠܗܘܢ ܠܡܐܟܠ.
ܐܡܪܝܢ ܠܗ ܠܝܬ ܠܢ ܝܬܝܪ ܡܢ ܚܡܫܐ ܠܚܡ̈ܝܢ
ܘܬܪ̈ܝܢ ܢܘܢ̈ܝܢ. ܐܠܐ ܢܐܙܠ ܐܚܢܢ ܢܙܒܢ ܣܝܒܪܬܐ
14 ܠܗܢܐ ܟܠܗ ܥܡܐ. ܗܘܝܢ ܗܘܘ ܓܝܪ ܚܡܫܐ ܐ̈ܠܦܝܢ
ܓܒܪ̈ܝܢ. ܐܡܪ ܠܬܠܡܝ̈ܕܘܗܝ. ܐܣܡܟܘ ܐܢܘܢ ܣܡ̈ܟܝܢ
15 ܣܡ̈ܟܝܢ ܚܡ̈ܫܝܢ ܒܣܡܟܐ. ܘܥܒܕܘ ܗܟܢܐ. ܘܐܣܡܟܘ
16 ܐܢܘܢ ܠܟܠܗܘܢ. ܘܢܣܒ ܗܘ ܝܫܘܥ ܚܡܫܐ ܠܚܡ̈ܝܢ
ܘܬܪ̈ܝܢ ܢܘܢ̈ܝܢ. ܘܚܪ ܒܫܡܝܐ ܘܒܪܟ ܥܠܝܗܘܢ. ܘܩܨܐ
17 ܘܝܗܒ ܠܬܠܡܝ̈ܕܘܗܝ ܕܢܣܝܡܘܢ ܩܕܡ ܟܢ̈ܫܐ. ܘܐܟܠܘ
ܟܠܗܘܢ ܘܣܒܥܘ. ܘܫܩܠܘ ܩܨ̈ܝܐ ܕܡܢ ܕܐܘܬܪܘ ܡܠܐ
ܬܪ̈ܬܥܣܪ ܩܘ̈ܦܝܢ. ܘܐܬܬܢܝܚܘܢ ܗܘܘ ܐܢܫܐ ܗܠܝܢ
ܕܐܟܠܘ ܡܢ ܠܚܡܐ ܗܘ. ܐܝܟ ܚܡܫܐ ܐ̈ܠܦܝܢ. ܓܒܪ
ܡܢ ܢܫ̈ܐ ܘܛ̈ܠܝܐ. . . .
18 ܘܟܕ ܗܘܐ ܒܠܚܘܕܘܗܝ ܘܬܠܡܝ̈ܕܘܗܝ ܥܡܗ. ܫܐܠ
ܐܢܘܢ ܘܐܡܪ. ܡܢܐ ܐܡܪܝܢ ܥܠܝ ܟܢ̈ܫܐ ܕܐܝܬܝ.
19 ܐܡܪܝܢ ܠܗ. ܐܝܬ ܕܐܡܪܝܢ ܕܝܘܚܢܢ ܗܘ ܡܥܡܕܢܐ.
20 ܐ̈ܚܪܢܐ ܐܡܪܝܢ ܕܐܠܝܐ ܗܘ. ܐܡܪ ܠܗܘܢ ܗܘ

ܕܠܘܩܐ

ܚܝܠܐ ܘܫܘܠܛܢܐ ܥܠ ܟܠ ܕ̈ܝܘܐ ܘܡܟ̈ܐܒܐ. ܘܟܪ̈ܝܗܐ
2 ܠܡܐܣܝܘ. ܘܫܕܪ ܐܢܘܢ ܕܢܟܪܙܘܢ ܡܠܟܘܬܗ ܕܐܠܗܐ
3 ܘܠܡܐܣܝܘ. ܘܐܡܪ ܠܗܘܢ ܡܕܡ ܠܐ ܬܫܩܠܘܢ
ܠܟܘܢ ܠܐܘܪܚܐ. ܠܐ ܫܒܛܐ ܘܠܐ ܬܪܡܠܐ. ܘܠܐ
ܠܚܡܐ ܘܠܐ ܟܣܦܐ. ܘܠܐ ܬܪ̈ܬܝܢ ܟܘ̈ܬܝܢܝܢ ܢܗܘܝܢ
4 ܠܟܘܢ. ܘܠܒܝܬܐ ܐܝܢܐ ܕܥܠܝܢ ܐܢܬܘܢ ܬܡܢ ܗܘܘ. ܘܡܢ
5 ܬܡܢ ܦܘܩܘ. ܘܐܝܠܝܢ ܕܠܐ ܡܩܒܠܝܢ ܠܟܘܢ. ܟܕ
ܕܢܦܩܝܢ ܐܢܬܘܢ ܡܢ ܡܕܝܢܬܐ ܗܝ. ܘܐܦ ܚܠܐ
ܕܪ̈ܓܠܝܟܘܢ ܦܨܘ. ܕܬܗܘܐ ܠܗܘܢ ܠܣܗܕܘܬܐ ܀
6 ܘܟܕ ܢܦܩܘ ܫ̈ܠܝܚܘܗܝ. ܘܡܬܟܪܟܝܢ ܒܩܘ̈ܪܝܐ
ܘܡܕ̈ܝܢܬܐ. ܘܡܣܒܪܝܢ ܗܘܘ ܘܡܐܣܝܢ ܒܟܠ ܕܘܟ.
7 ܘܫܡܥ ܗܪܘܕܣ ܛܛܪܪܟܐ ܟܠܗܝܢ ܗܠܝܢ ܕܗܘܝ
ܘܡܬܕܡܪ ܗܘܐ. ܡܛܠ ܕܐܡܪܝܢ ܗܘܘ ܐ̈ܢܫܝܢ ܡܢܗܘܢ.
8 ܕܝܘܚܢܢ ܩܡ ܡܢ ܒܝܬ ܡ̈ܝܬܐ. ܘܐܚܪ̈ܢܐ ܐܡܪܝܢ ܕܐܠܝܐ
ܐܬܚܙܝ. ܐ̈ܚܪܢܐ ܐܡܪܝܢ ܕܚܕ ܡܢ ܢܒ̈ܝܐ ܩܕ̈ܡܝܐ
9 ܩܡ ܡܢ ܒܝܬ ܡ̈ܝܬܐ. ܘܐܡܪ ܗܘܐ ܗܪܘܕܣ. ܪܫܗ
ܕܝܘܚܢܢ ܐܢܐ ܦܣܩܬ. ܡܢܘ ܗܢܐ ܕܗܠܝܢ ܫܡܥ ܐܢܐ
ܥܠܘܗܝ. ܘܒܥܐ ܗܘܐ ܕܢܚܙܝܘܗܝ. ܀
10 ܘܗܦܟܘ ܗܢܘܢ ܫ̈ܠܝܚܐ. ܘܐܫܬܥܝܘ ܠܗ ܟܠ ܡܕܡ
ܕܥܒܕܘ. ܘܕܒܪ ܐܢܘܢ ܒܠܚܘܕܝܗܘܢ. ܘܐܙܠ ܠܐܬܪܐ
11 ܚܘܪܒܐ. ܘܟܕ ܝܕܥܘ ܟܢ̈ܫܐ. ܐܙܠܘ ܠܗܘܢ ܒܬܪܗ
ܒܪ̈ܓܠ. ܘܩܒܠ ܐܢܘܢ. ܘܡܡܠܠ ܗܘܐ ܥܡܗܘܢ ܥܠ

46 ܘܐܡܪ ܐܢܬ ܡܢܘ ܩܪܒ ܠܝ. ܐܡܪ ܠܗ ܝܫܘܥ. ܐܢܫ
47 ܩܪܒ ܠܝ. ܐܢܐ ܓܝܪ ܝܕܥ ܐܢܐ ܕܚܝܠܐ ܢܦܩ ܡܢܝ. ܟܕ
ܚܙܬ ܕܝܢ ܗܝ ܐܢܬܬܐ ܕܐܦܠܐ ܗܘܐ ܠܓܒܗ. ܐܬܬ
ܟܕ ܕܚܝܠܐ ܘܪܬܝܬܐ ܢܦܠܬ ܣܓܕܬ ܠܗ. ܘܐܡܪܬ
ܠܗܝܢ ܒܥܠܬܐ ܗܘ ܒܟܠܗ ܡܛܠ ܐܝܕܐ ܓܒܗ ܩܪܒܬ.
ܘܐܝܟܢܐ ܒܪ ܫܥܬܗ ܐܬܐܣܝܬ ܡܕܡ ܟܠ ܐܝܟ ܐܘܕܝܬ.
48 ܘܗܘ ܕܝܢ ܐܡܪ ܠܗ̇ ܒܪܬܝ. ܗܝܡܢܘܬܟܝ ܐܚܝܬܟܝ ܙܠܝ
49 ܒܫܠܡܐ. ܘܟܕ ܡܡܠܠ. ܐܬܘ ܡܢ ܕܒܝܬ ܪܒ ܟܢܘܫܬܐ
ܘܐܡܪܝܢ ܠܗ. ܡܝܬܬ ܠܗ̇ ܒܪܬܟ ܠܐ ܬܥܡܠ
50 ܠܡܠܦܢܐ. ܟܕ ܫܡܥ ܕܝܢ ܝܫܘܥ ܕܡܝܬܬ ܐܡܪܘ. ܐܡܪ
ܠܗ ܠܐ ܬܕܚܠ. ܒܠܚܘܕ ܡܗܝܡܢܘ ܗܝܡܢ ܘܬܚܐ
51 ܒܪܬܟ. ܘܟܕ ܐܬܐ ܠܒܝܬܗ ܕܗܘ ܓܒܪܐ. ܠܐ ܫܒܩ
ܠܐܢܫ ܕܢܥܘܠ. ܐܠܐ ܠܟܐܦܐ ܘܠܝܥܩܘܒ ܘܠܝܘܚܢܢ.
52 ܘܠܐܒܘܗ̇ ܘܠܐܡܗ̇ ܕܛܠܝܬܐ. ܘܟܠܗܘܢ ܐܢܫܐ
ܒܟܝܢ ܗܘܘ ܥܠܝܗ̇ ܘܡܪܩܕܝܢ ܗܘܘ. ܐܡܪ ܠܗܘܢ
ܝܫܘܥ ܠܐ ܬܒܟܘܢ. ܛܠܝܬܐ ܓܝܪ ܠܐ ܡܝܬܬ. ܡܕܡܟ
53 ܘܗܘ ܕܡܟܐ. ܗܢܘܢ ܕܝܢ ܓܚܟܝܢ ܗܘܘ ܥܠܘܗܝ ܕܝܕܥܝܢ
54 ܗܘܘ ܕܡܝܬܬ ܠܗ̇. ܘܗܘ ܐܚܕܗ̇ ܒܐܝܕܗ̇ ܘܩܪܗ̇
55 ܘܐܡܪ ܠܗ̇. ܛܠܝܬܐ ܩܘܡܝ. ܘܗܦܟܬ ܪܘܚܗ̇
ܘܒܪܫܥܬܗ ܩܡܬ. ܘܦܩܕ ܕܢܬܠܘܢ ܠܗ̇ ܠܡܐܟܠ.
56 ܘܬܡܗܘ ܗܘܘ ܐܒܗ̈ܝܗ̇. ܘܗܘ ܦܩܕ ܐܢܘܢ ܕܠܐܢܫ
ܠܐ ܢܐܡܪܘܢ ܡܕܡ ܕܗܘܐ ◎
IX. ܘܩܪܐ ܐܢܘܢ ܝܫܘܥ ܠܬܪ̈ܥܣܪܬܗ. ܘܝܗܒ ܠܗܘܢ

ܠܘܬܗܘܢ. ܡܛܠ ܕܕܚܠܬܐ ܪܒܬܐ ܐܚܝܕܐ ܗܘܬ
ܠܗܘܢ. ܗܘ ܕܝܢ ܣܠܩ ܠܗ ܠܣܦܝܢܬܐ ܘܗܦܟ ܡܢ
38 ܠܘܬܗܘܢ. ܗܘ ܕܝܢ ܓܒܪܐ ܕܢܦܩܘ ܗܘܘ ܡܢܗ
ܫܐ̈ܕܐ. ܒܥܐ ܗܘܐ ܡܢܗ ܕܠܘܬܗ ܢܗܘܐ. ܘܫܪܝܗܝ
39 ܝܫܘܥ ܘܐܡܪ ܠܗ. ܗܦܘܟ ܠܒܝܬܟ ܘܠܒܢܝ̈ ܐܢܫܝܟ.
ܘܐܫܬܥܐ ܠܗܘܢ ܐܝܠܝܢ ܕܥܒܕ ܠܟ ܡܪܝܐ. ܘܐܙܠ
ܗܘܐ ܘܡܟܪܙ ܗܘܐ ܒܟܠܗ̇ ܡܕܝܢܬܐ ܡܢܐ ܕܥܒܕ
40 ܠܗ ܝܫܘܥ. ܘܟܕ ܗܦܟ ܝܫܘܥ ܩܒܠܗ ܟܢܫܐ ܣܓܝܐܐ.
ܠܗ ܓܝܪ ܣܟܝܢ ܗܘܘ. ० ० ०
41 ܘܐܬܐ ܓܒܪܐ ܚܕ ܝܐܝܪܘܣ ܫܡܗ ܗܘܐ. ܘܪܫ
ܟܢܘܫܬܐ ܗܘܐ. ܘܢܦܠ ܩܕܡ ܪ̈ܓܠܘܗܝ ܕܝܫܘܥ. ܘܒܥܐ
42 ܗܘܐ ܡܢܗ ܕܢܥܘܠ ܠܒܝܬܗ. ܒܪܬܐ ܓܝܪ ܝܚܝܕܝܬܐ
ܐܝܬ ܗܘܬ ܠܗ. ܘܐܝܬܝܗ̇ ܗܘܬ ܐܝܟ ܒܪܬ ܫ̈ܢܝܢ
ܬܪܬܥܣܪܐ. ܘܡܪܥܐ ܗܘܬ ܠܡܡܬ. ܘܟܕ ܐܙܠ
43 ܝܫܘܥ ܒܐܘܪܚܐ ܚܒܨ ܗܘܐ ܠܗ. ܘܐܢܬܬܐ ܚܕܐ ܕܪܕܐ
ܗܘܐ ܕܡܗ̇ ܫ̈ܢܝܢ ܬܪܬܥܣܪܐ. ܘܟܠܗ ܢܟܣܝܗ̇
ܐܦܩܬ ܥܠ ܐܣܘ̈ܬܐ. ܘܠܐ ܐܫܟܚܬ ܕܬܬܐܣܐ
ܡܢ ܐܢܫ. ܘܐܬܩܪܒܬ ܒܣܦܗ̇ ܘܐܚܕܬܗ. ܐܦ ܠܟܢܦܘܬܗܝ
ܕܐܡܪܐ ܐܡܪܐ ܐܢܐ ܩܪܒܐ ܐܢܐ ܡܬܐܣܝܐ ܐܢܐ.
44 ܘܡܚܕܐ ܩܡ ܡܒܘܥܗ̇. ܘܐܚܣܬ ܒܦܓܪܐ ܕܚܠܝܡܬ.
45 ܘܡܚܕܐ ܡܬܪܕܝܬܐ ܕܕܡܗ̇. ܘܐܬܦܢܝ ܝܫܘܥ ܘܐܡܪ
ܡܢܘ ܩܪܒ ܠܝ.. ܘܟܕ ܟܠܗܘܢ ܟܦܪܝܢ ܗܘܘ.
ܐܡܪ ܠܗ ܟܐܦܐ. ܪܒܢ ܟܢ̈ܫܐ ܚܒܨܝܢ ܠܟ ܘܐܠܨܝܢ.

ܚܙܐ ܠܝܫܘܥ. ܩܥܐ ܘܢܦܠ ܣܓܕ ܠܗ. ܘܒܩܠܐ ܪܡܐ
ܐܡܪ. ܡܢܐ ܠܝ ܘܠܟ ܝܫܘܥ ܒܪܗ ܕܐܠܗܐ ܪܡܐ.
29 ܒܥܐ ܐܢܐ ܡܢܟ ܠܐ ܬܫܢܩܢܝ. ܦܩܕ ܗܘܐ ܠܗ ܓܝܪ
ܠܗ̇ ܪܘܚܐ ܛܢܦܬܐ ܠܡܦܩ ܡܢ ܒܪ ܐܢܫܐ. ܣܓܝ ܓܝܪ
ܙܒܢܝܢ ܢܣܒ ܗܘܐ ܠܗ. ܘܡܬܐܣܪ ܗܘܐ ܒܫ̈ܫܠܬܐ
ܘܒܟ̈ܒܠܐ ܕܢܛܪ̈ܝܢ. ܘܡܬܒܪ ܗܘܐ ܐ̈ܣܘܪܘܗܝ
ܘܡܦܩܦܩ ܗܘܐ. ܘܡܬܕܒܪ ܗܘܐ ܡܢܗ ܡܢ ܫܐ̈ܕܐ
30 ܠܚܘܪܒܐ. ܫܐܠܗ ܕܝܢ ܝܫܘܥ ܘܐܡܪ ܡܢ ܫܡܟ.
31 ܘܐܡܪ ܠܗ ܠܓܝܘܢ. ܡܛܠ ܕܫ̈ܐܕܐ ܥܐܠܝܢ ܒܗ. ܘܒܥܝܢ
ܗܘܘ ܡܢܗ ܗܢܘܢ ܫ̈ܐܕܐ ܕܠܐ ܢܦܩܕ ܐܢܘܢ ܠܬܗܘܡܐ
32 ܘܠܐ ܢܗܡܐܢܘܢ. ܐܝܬ ܗܘܬ ܕܝܢ ܬܡܢ ܒܛܘܪܐ ܥܕܪܐ
ܚܕܐ ܕܚ̈ܙܝܪܐ ܣ̈ܓܝܐܐ ܕܪܥܝܢ ܗܘܘ ܬܡܢ. ܘܒܥܝܢ ܗܘܘ
ܡܢܗ ܗܢܘܢ ܫ̈ܐܕܐ ܕܢܦܣ ܠܗܘܢ ܠܡܥܠ ܒܗܘܢ
33 ܒܥܕܪܐ ܕܚ̈ܙܝܪܐ. ܘܐܦܣ ܠܗܘܢ. ܘܢܦܩܘ ܫ̈ܐܕܐ ܡܢ
ܓܒܪܐ ܗܘ ܘܥܠܘ ܒܚ̈ܙܝܪܐ. ܘܐܬܪܡܝܬ ܗܝ ܟܠܗ̇ ܥܕܪܐ
34 ܠܝܡܬܐ. ܘܢܦܠܘ ܒܡܝܐ ܘܐܬܚܢܩܘ. ܟܕ ܚܙܘ ܕܝܢ
ܗܢܘܢ ܪ̈ܥܘܬܐ ܡܕܡ ܕܗܘܐ ܥܪܩܘ. ܘܐܫܬܥܝܘ
35 ܒܡܕ̈ܝܢܬܐ ܘܒܩܘ̈ܪܝܐ. ܘܢܦܩܘ ܐܢܫܐ ܕܢܚܙܘܢ ܡܕܡ
ܕܗܘܐ. ܘܐܬܘ ܠܘܬ ܝܫܘܥ. ܘܐܫܟܚܘ ܠܗܿܘ ܓܒܪܐ
ܕܢܦܩܘ ܡܢܗ ܗܢܘܢ ܫ̈ܐܕܐ. ܟܕ ܠܒܝܫ ܘܡܢܟܦ ܘܝܬܒ
36 ܠܘܬ ܪ̈ܓܠܘܗܝ ܕܝܫܘܥ ܘܕܚܠܘ. ܘܐܫܬܥܝܘ ܠܗܘܢ
37 ܐܝܟܢܐ ܚܝܐ ܓܒܪܐ ܗܘ. ܘܐܡܠܟܘ ܕܢܫܘ ܬܘܒ ܒܥܝܢ
ܗܘܘ ܡܢܗ ܟܠܗ ܒܢܝܐ ܗܘ ܕܓܕ̈ܪܝܐ. ܕܢܐܙܠ ܠܗ ܡܢ

19 ܘܐܬܬ ܗܘܐ ܠܘܬܗ ܕܝܫܘܥ ܐܡܗ ܘܐܚ̈ܘܗܝ.
ܘܩܝܡܝܢ ܗܘܘ ܠܒܪ. ܘܠܐ ܡܫܟܚܝܢ ܗܘܘ ܕܢܚܙܘܢܗ.
20 ܡܛܠ ܟܢܫܐ ܕܐܢܫܐ. ܘܐܡܪܘ ܠܗ ܐܡܟ ܘܐܚ̈ܝܟ
21 ܩܝܡܝܢ ܠܒܪ. ܘܒܥܝܢ ܠܡܚܙܝܟ. ܗܘ ܕܝܢ ܥܢܐ ܘܐܡܪ
ܠܗܘܢ. ܗܠܝܢ ܐܢܘܢ ܐܡܝ ܘܐܚ̈ܝ. ܐܝܠܝܢ ܕܫܡܥܝܢ
ܡܠܬܗ ܕܐܠܗܐ ܘܥܒܕܝܢ ܠܗ̇. ◦○◦
22 ܘܗܘܐ ܗܘܐ ܒܚܕ ܡܢ ܝܘܡ̈ܬܐ ܗܢܘܢ. ܣܠܩ ܝܫܘܥ
ܝܬܒ ܒܣܦܝܢܬܐ. ܗܘ ܘܬܠܡ̈ܝܕܘܗܝ ܥܡܗ. ܘܐܡܪ
23 ܠܗܘܢ. ܢܥܒܪ ܠܢ ܠܥܒܪܗ ܕܝܡܬܐ. ܘܟܕ ܪܕܝܢ ܗܘܘ
ܒܝܡܐ ܕܡܟ ܠܗ. ܘܗܘܬ ܥܠܥܠܐ ܕܪܘܚܐ ܒܝܡܬܐ.
ܘܐܬܬܡܠܝܬ ܣܦܝܢܬܗܘܢ ܡܢ ܓܠ̈ܠܐ. ܘܪܕܝܐ ܗܘܬ
24 ܠܡܛܒܥ. ܘܩܪܒܘ ܐܥܝܪܘܗܝ ܘܐܡܪܝܢ ܠܗ ܪܒܢ
ܐܒܕܝܢ ܐܢܚܢ. ܘܩܡ ܘܟܐܐ ܒܪܘܚܐ ܘܒܡܚܫܘܠܐ
25 ܕܝ̈ܡܐ. ܘܗܘܐ ܫܠܝܐ. ܘܐܡܪ ܠܗܘܢ ܐܝܟܐ ܗܝ
ܗܝܡܢܘܬܟܘܢ. ܗܢܘܢ ܕܝܢ ܟܕ ܕܚܠܝܢ. ܡܬܕܡܪܝܢ
ܗܘܘ ܘܐܡܪܝܢ ܚܕ ܠܚܕ. ܡܢܘ ܟܝ ܗܢܐ ܕܐܦ ܠܪ̈ܘܚܐ
ܘܠܝܡܐ ܦܩܕ. ܘܡܫܬܡܥܝܢ ܠܗ. ◦○◦
26 ܘܪܕܘ ܗܘܘ ܠܐܬܪܐ ܕܓܕܪ̈ܝܐ. ܗܘ ܕܐܝܬܘܗܝ ܠܘܩܒܠ
27 ܥܒܪܐ ܕܓܠܝܠܐ. ܟܕ ܢܦܩ ܕܝܢ ܠܐܪܥܐ. ܦܓܥ ܒܗ
ܓܒܪܐ ܚܕ ܕܐܝܬ ܗܘܐ ܒܠܘܗܝ ܫܐܕ̈ܐ ܡܢ ܙܒܢܐ
ܣܓܝܐܐ. ܘܢܚ̈ܬܐ ܠܐ ܠܒܫ ܗܘܐ. ܘܒܒܝܬܐ ܠܐ
ܥܡܪ ܗܘܐ. ܐܠܐ ܒܝܬ ܩܒܘܪܐ. ܘܟܠ ܥܕܢܐ
28 ܩܥܐ ܗܘܐ. ܘܡܬܟܬܫܐ ܗܘܐ ܢܦܫܗ ܒܟܐ̈ܦܐ. ܘܟܕ

11 ܢܣܬܟܠܘܢ. ܗܢܐ ܕܝܢ ܡܬܠܐ ܐܝܬܘܗܝ. ܙܪܥܐ ܡܠܬܗ
12 ܗܝ ܕܐܠܗܐ. ܘܗܢܘܢ ܕܥܠ ܝܕ ܐܘܪܚܐ. ܗܠܝܢ
ܐܢܘܢ ܕܫܡܥܝܢ ܡܠܬܐ ܕܐܠܗܐ. ܘܐܬܐ ܒܥܠܕܒܒܐ
ܫܩܠ ܠܗ̇ ܡܠܬܐ ܡܢ ܠܒܗܘܢ. ܕܠܐ ܢܗܝܡܢܘܢ
13 ܘܢܚܘܢ. ܘܗܘ ܕܥܠ ܫܘܥܐ. ܗܠܝܢ ܐܢܘܢ ܕܡܐ
ܕܫܡܥܘ ܡܠܬܐ. ܒܚܕܘܬܐ ܡܩܒܠܝܢ ܠܗ̇.
ܘܥܩܪܐ ܠܝܬ ܠܗܘܢ ܒܗ̇. ܘܒܙܒܢ ܡܗܝܡܢܝܢ. ܘܒܙܒܢ
14 ܢܣܝܘܢܐ ܡܬܥܠܝܢ. ܘܗܘ ܕܢܦܠ ܒܝܬ ܟܘ̈ܒܐ. ܗܠܝܢ
ܐܢܘܢ ܐܝܠܝܢ ܕܫܡܥܝܢ ܡܠܬܐ. ܘܒܨܦܬܐ ܐܢܘܢ.
ܘܒܥܘܬܪܐ ܕܥܠܡܐ. ܘܒܪܓܝܓܬܐ ܕܒܣܪܐ
15 ܡܬܚܢܩܝܢ. ܘܡܬܚܢܩܝܢ ܘܦܐܪܐ ܠܐ ܝܗܒܝܢ. ܘܗܘ
ܕܢܦܠ ܒܐܪܥܐ ܛܒܬܐ. ܗܠܝܢ ܐܢܘܢ ܕܒܠܒܐ ܫܦܝܐ
ܘܛܒܐ ܫܡܥܘ ܡܠܬܐ. ܘܐܚܕܘ. ܘܝܗܒܝܢ ܦܐܪܐ
ܒܡܣܝܒܪܢܘܬܐ. ·:·
16 ܡܬܠܐ ܐܚܪܢܐ ܐܡܪ ܗܘܐ. ܠܐ ܐܢܫ ܡܢܗܪ ܫܪܓܐ
ܘܡܟܣܐ ܠܗ ܒܡܐܢܐ. ܐܘ ܣܐܡ ܠܗ ܬܚܝܬ
ܥܪܣܐ. ܐܘ ܒܐܬܪܐ ܡܛܫܝܐ. ܐܠܐ ܣܐܡ ܠܗ ܠܥܠ
17 ܡܢ ܡܢܪܬܐ. ܕܟܠ ܐܢܫ ܕܥܐܠ ܢܚܙܐ ܢܘܗܪܗ. ܠܝܬ
ܓܝܪ ܡܕܡ ܕܟܣܐ. ܕܠܐ ܢܬܓܠܐ. ܘܐܦܠܐ ܕܡܛܫܝ
18 ܕܠܐ ܢܬܝܕܥ ܘܢܐܬܐ ܠܓܠܝܐ. ܚܙܘ ܡܟܝܠ ܐܝܟܢܐ ܫܡܥܝܢܬܘܢ.
ܡܢ ܕܐܝܬ ܠܗ ܓܝܪ ܢܬܝܗܒ ܠܗ ܘܢܬܬܘܣܦ ܠܗ. ܘܗܘ
ܕܠܝܬ ܠܗ. ܐܦ ܗܘ ܡܕܡ ܕܣܒܪ ܗܘܐ ܕܐܝܬ ܠܗ
ܢܬܢܣܒ ܠܗ ܡܢܗ. ·:·

VIII. ܘܗܘܐ ܒܬܪ ܗܠܝܢ܂ ܡܟܪܙ ܗܘܐ ܒܩܘܪܝܐ
ܘܒܡܕ̈ܝܢܬܐ܂ ܘܡܣܒܪ ܡܠܟܘܬܗ ܕܐܠܗܐ܂ ܐܦ
2 ܬܪ̈ܥܣܪܬܗ ܥܡܗ܂ ܘܢܫ̈ܐ ܗܠܝܢ ܕܐܬܐܣܝ̈ܘ ܗܘܝ ܡܢ
ܪ̈ܘܚܐ ܒ̈ܝܫܬܐ܂ ܘܡܢ ܟܘ̈ܪܗܢܐ܂ ܡܪܝܡ ܕܡܬܩܪܝܐ
ܡܓܕܠܝܬܐ܂ ܗܝ ܕܫܒܥܐ ܫ̈ܐܕܝܢ ܐܦܩ ܗܘܐ ܡܢܗ܂
3 ܘܝܘܚܢ ܐܢܬܬ ܟܘܙܐ ܐܦܝܛܪܘܦܗ ܕܗܪܘܕܣ܂ ܘܫܘܫܢ
ܘܐܚܪ̈ܢܝܬܐ ܣܓܝ̈ܐܬܐ ܕܡܫܡܫܢ ܗܘܝ ܠܗܘܢ ܡܢ
ܩܢܝܢ ܕܐܝܬ ܗܘܐ ܠܗܝܢ܂ ܀
4 ܘܟܕ ܐܬܟܢܫ ܟܢܫܐ ܣܓܝܐܐ܂ ܘܐܬܝܢ ܕܡܢ ܡܕ̈ܝܢܬܐ
5 ܐܬܝܢ ܗܘܘ ܠܘܬܗ܂ ܐܡܪ ܠܗܘܢ ܒܡܬ̈ܠܐ܂ ܗܐ
ܢܦܩ ܙܪܘܥܐ ܠܡܙܪܥ܂ ܘܟܕ ܙܪܥ܂ ܐܝܬ ܕܢܦܠ ܥܠ ܝܕ
6 ܐܘܪܚܐ ܘܐܬܕܝܫ܂ ܘܐܟܠܬܗ ܦܪܚܬܐ܂ ܘܐܚܪܢܐ
ܢܦܠ ܥܠ ܫܘܥܐ܂ ܘܡܛܠ ܕܠܝܬ ܗܘܬ ܠܗ ܛܠܠܐ ܡܢ
7 ܘܝܒܫ܂ ܐܚܪܢܐ ܢܦܠ ܒܝܬ ܟܘ̈ܒܐ܂ ܘܟܒܐ ܥܡܗ
8 ܘܚܢܩܘܗܝ܂ ܘܐܚܪܢܐ ܢܦܠ ܒܐܪܥܐ ܛܒܬܐ ܘܝܥܒܬ
ܦܐܪ̈ܐ܂ ܘܟܒܐ ܘܥܒܕ ܦܐܪ̈ܐ܂ ܚܕ ܒܡܐܐ܂ ܘܟܕ
ܐܡܪ ܗܠܝܢ܂ ܒܩܠܐ ܪܡܐ ܐܡܪ ܗܘܐ܂ ܕܡܢ ܕܐܝܬ
ܠܗ ܐ̈ܕܢܐ ܕܢܫܡܥ ܢܫܡܥ ◦◦◦
9 ܘܫܐܠܘܗܝ ܗܘܘ ܬܠܡܝ̈ܕܘܗܝ܂ ܡܢܘ ܡܬܠܐ ܗܢܐ܂
10 ܐܡܪ ܠܗܘܢ܂ ܠܟܘܢ ܗܘ ܝܗܝܒ ܠܡܕܥ ܐܪ̈ܙܐ
ܕܡܠܟܘܬܗ ܕܐܠܗܐ܂ ܠܗܢܘܢ ܕܝܢ ܕܒܪܐ ܠܐ ܝܗܝܒ
ܠܗܘܢ ܠܡܕܥ܂ ܡܛܠ ܗܢܐ ܒܡܬ̈ܠܐ ܡܡܠܠܐ ܐܢܐ
ܠܗܘܢ܂ ܕܟܕ ܚܙܝܢ ܠܐ ܢܚܙܘܢ܂ ܘܟܕ ܫܡܥܝܢ ܠܐ

ܚܙܐ ܕܝܢ ܦܪܝܫܐ ܗܘ ܕܩܪܝܗܝ ܐܬܚܫܒ ܒܢܦܫܗ
ܘܐܡܪ. ܗܢܐ ܐܠܘ ܢܒܝܐ ܗܘܐ ܝܕܥ ܗܘܐ ܡܢ ܗܝ.
ܐܘ ܡܢܐ ܦܠܚܢ ܕܐܢܬܬܐ ܗܝ ܚܛܝܬܐ ܕܩܪܒܬ ܠܗ.
40 ܐܡܪ ܠܗ ܝܫܘܥ. ܫܡܥܘܢ. ܐܝܬ ܠܝ ܡܕܡ ܕܐܡܪ ܠܟ.
41 ܐܡܪ ܠܗ ܐܡܪ ܪܒܝ. ܐܡܪ ܠܗ ܝܫܘܥ. ܬܪ̈ܝܢ ܚܝ̈ܒܝܢ
ܐܝܬ ܗܘܘ ܠܚܕ ܡܪܐ ܚܘܒܐ. ܚܕ ܚܝܒ ܗܘܐ ܠܗ
42 ܕܝ̈ܢܪܐ ܚܡܫܡܐܐ. ܘܚܕ ܕܝ̈ܢܪܐ ܚܡܫܝܢ. ܘܟܕ ܠܐ
ܐܝܬ ܗܘܐ ܠܗܘܢ ܠܡܦܪܥ ܠܬܪ̈ܝܗܘܢ ܫܒܩ. ܐܝܢܐ
43 ܡܢܗܘܢ ܢܚܒܝܗܝ ܝܬܝܪܐܝܬ. ܐܡܪ ܠܗ ܫܡܥܘܢ.
ܣܒܪ ܐܢܐ ܕܗܘ ܕܝܬܝܪ ܐܫܬܒܩ ܠܗ. ܐܡܪ ܠܗ
44 ܝܫܘܥ. ܬܪܝܨ ܕܢܬ. ܘܐܬܦܢܝ ܠܘܬ ܐܢܬܬܐ ܘܐܡܪ
ܠܫܡܥܘܢ. ܚܙܐ ܐܢܬ ܐܢܬܬܐ ܗܕܐ. ܠܒܝܬܟ ܥܠܬ.
ܡ̈ܝܐ ܠܪ̈ܓܠܝ ܠܐ ܝܗܒܬ ܠܝ. ܗܝ ܕܝܢ ܒܕܡ̈ܥܝܗ ܪ̈ܓܠܝ
45 ܨܒܥܬ. ܘܒܣܥܪܗ ܕܪܫܗ ܫܘܝܬ ܐܢܝܢ. ܐܢܬ ܠܐ
ܢܫܩܬܢܝ. ܗܝ ܕܝܢ ܡܢ ܕܥܠܬ ܠܐ ܫܠܝܬ ܪ̈ܓܠܝ ܠܡܢܫܩܘ.
46 ܐܢܬ ܠܐ ܡܫܚܬܢܝ. ܗܝ ܕܝܢ ܒܡܫܚܐ ܕܒܣܡܐ
47 ܡܫܚܬ ܪ̈ܓܠܝ. ܡܛܠ ܗܢܐ ܐܡܪܢܐ ܠܟ ܕܫܒܝܩܝܢ
ܠܗ̇ ܚܛܗ̈ܝܗ ܣ̈ܓܝܐܐ. ܡܛܠ ܕܣܓܝ ܐܚܒܬ. ܡܢ
48 ܕܩܠܝܠ ܓܝܪ ܐܫܬܒܩ ܠܗ. ܩܠܝܠ ܗܘ ܡܚܒ. ܐܡܪ
49 ܠܗ̇ ܠܗܝ ܐܢܬܬܐ. ܕܫܒܝܩܝܢ ܠܟܝ ܚܛܗ̈ܝܟܝ. ܘܫܪܝܘ
ܗܢܘܢ ܕܣܡܝܟܝܢ ܐܡܪܝܢ ܒܢܦܫܗܘܢ. ܡܢܘ ܗܢܐ
50 ܕܐܦ ܚ̈ܛܗܐ ܫܒܩ. ܘܐܡܪ ܠܐܢܬܬܐ ܗܝ ܗܝܡܢܘܬܟܝ
ܐܚܝܬܟܝ ܙܠܝ ܒܫܠܡܐ ܀

12 ܗܟܢܐ ܢܥܒܕ. ܘܐܬܘ ܐܦ ܡܟ̈ܣܐ ܠܡܥܡܕ. ܐܡܪܝܢ
13 ܠܗ ܡܢܐ ܢܥܒܕ. ܐܡܪ ܠܗܘܢ ܠܐ ܬܒܥܘܢ ܡܕܡ ܝܬܝܪ
14 ܥܠ ܡܕܡ ܕܦܣܝܩ ܠܟܘܢ. ܘܫܐܠܘܗܝ ܗܘܘ ܐܦ
ܐܣ̈ܛܪܛܝܘܛܐ ܘܐܡܪܝܢ ܠܗ. ܡܢܐ ܢܥܒܕ ܐܦ ܐܢܚܢ.
ܐܡܪ ܠܗܘܢ. ܠܐܢܫ ܠܐ ܬܥܫܩܘܢ. ܘܠܐܢܫ ܠܐ
15 ܬܛܠܡܘܢ. ܘܣܦܩ ܠܟܘܢ ܐܦ̈ܣܘܢܝܬܟܘܢ. ܘܐܢܫܐ
ܕܡܣܟܝܢ ܗܘܘ ܠܗ ܡܬܪܥܝܢ ܗܘܘ ܒܠܒܗܘܢ ܘܐܡܪܝܢ
16 ܠܡܐ ܕܝ ܗܘܝܘ ܡܫܝܚܐ. ܐܡܪ ܠܗܘܢ ܐܢܐ ܗܐ
ܡܥܡܕܢܐ ܠܟܘܢ ܒܡ̈ܝܐ * * * * * *

* * * * * * * * * * * *

VII. * * * * * * * * * * * *

ܐܟܠ ܘܠܐ ܫܬܐ. ܐܡܪܝܢ ܐܢܬܘܢ ܫܐܕܐ ܒܗ.
34 ܘܐܬܐ ܒܪܗ ܕܐܢܫܐ ܐܟܠ ܘܫܬܐ. ܐܡܪܝܢ ܐܢܬܘܢ
ܗܐ ܓܒܪܐ ܐܟܘܠܐ ܘܪܘܝܐ. ܘܪܚܡܐ ܕܡ̈ܟܣܐ
35 ܘܕܚ̈ܛܝܐ. ܘܐܙܕܕܩܬ ܚܟܡܬܐ ܡܢ ܒ̈ܢܝܗ ◎ ○ ◎
36 ܘܐܬܐ ܦܪܝܫܐ ܚܕ ܒܥܐ ܡܢܗ ܕܢܠܥܣ ܠܘܬܗ. ܘܥܠ
37 ܠܒܝܬܗ ܕܦܪܝܫܐ ܗܘ. ܘܟܕ ܐܣܬܡܟ. ܐܢܬܬܐ ܚܕܐ
ܚܛܝܬܐ ܐܝܬ ܗܘܬ ܒܗ̇ ܡܕܝܢܬܐ. ܟܕ ܝܕܥܬ
ܕܒܒܝܬܗ ܕܗܘ ܦܪܝܫܐ ܣܡܝܟ. ܢܣܒܬ ܫܛܝܦܬܐ
38 ܕܡܫܝܚܐ ܕܒܣܡܐ. ܘܩܡܬ ܡܢ ܒܣܬܪܗ ܠܘܬ
ܪ̈ܓܠܘܗܝ ܘܒܟܝܐ ܗܘܬ. ܘܒܕ̈ܡܥܝܗ ܪ̈ܓܠܘܗܝ ܨܒܥܬ.
ܘܒܣܥܪܐ ܕܪܫܗ̇ ܡܫܘܐ ܗܘܬ ܠܗܝܢ. ܘܡܢܫܩܐ
39 ܗܘܬ ܪ̈ܓܠܘܗܝ. ܘܡܫܚܐ ܗܘܬ ܡܢ ܗܘ ܡܫܚܐ. ܟܕ

ܕܠܘܩܐ

2 ܕܪ̈ܒܟܗܢܐ. ܒܪܒܘܬ ܟܗܢܘܬܐ ܕܚܢܢ ܘܕܩܝܦܐ. ܗܘܬ
ܡܠܬܗ ܕܐܠܗܐ ܥܠ ܝܘܚܢܢ ܒܪ ܙܟܪܝܐ. ܘܡܕܒܪ ܗܘܐ
ܒܡܕܒܪܐ ܘܒܟܠܗ ܐܬܪܐ ܕܥܒܪ ܝܘܪܕܢ. ܡܥܡܘܕܝܬܐ
4 ܕܬܝܒܘܬܐ ܠܫܘܒܩܢܐ ܕܚܛ̈ܗܐ. ܐܝܟܢܐ ܕܟܬܝܒ
ܒܢܒܘܬܗ ܕܐܫܥܝܐ ܢܒܝܐ. ܩܠܐ ܕܩܪܐ ܒܡܕܒܪܐ.
ܦܢܘ ܐܘܪܚܐ ܠܡܪܝܐ. ܘܬܪܨܘ ܒܦܫܝܛܘܬܐ ܫܒܝܠܐ
5 ܠܐܠܗܢ. ܟܠܗܘܢ ܢܚ̈ܠܐ ܢܬܡܠܘܢ ܘܟܠܗܘܢ ܛܘܪ̈ܐ
ܘܪ̈ܡܬܐ ܢܬܡܟܟܘܢ. ܘܢܗܘܐ ܥܪܩܐ ܠܦܫܝܩܐ.
6 ܘܐܬܪܐ ܥܣܩܐ ܠܦܩܥܬܐ. ܘܢܬܓܠܐ ܐܝܩܪܗ
ܕܡܪܝܐ ܘܢܚܙܘܢܗ ܐܟܚܕܐ ܟܘܠ ܒܣܪ. ܡܛܠ
ܕܦܘܡܗ ܕܡܪܝܐ ܡܠܠ ◦ ◦ ◦
7 ܘܐܡܪ ܗܘܐ ܠܟܢ̈ܫܐ ܐܝܠܝܢ ܕܐܬܝܢ ܗܘܘ ܠܘܬܗ.
ܝܠܕܐ ܕܐܟܕ̈ܢܐ ܡܢܘ ܚܘܝܟܘܢ ܠܡܥܪܩ ܡܢ ܪܘܓܙܐ
8 ܕܐܬܐ. ܥܒܕܘ ܗܟܝܠ ܦܐܪ̈ܐ ܕܫܘܝܢ ܠܬܝܒܘܬܐ.
ܘܠܐ ܬܫܪܘܢ ܠܡܐܡܪ ܕܐܒܐ ܐܝܬ ܠܢ ܐܒܪܗܡ.
ܐܡܪܢܐ ܠܟܘܢ ܓܝܪ ܕܡܫܟܚ ܐܠܗܐ ܕܡܢ ܗܠܝܢ
9 ܟܐ̈ܦܐ ܠܡܩܡܘ ܒ̈ܢܝܐ ܠܐܒܪܗܡ. ܘܗܐ ܡܛܠ
ܠܗ ܢܪܓܐ ܠܘܬ ܥܩܪ̈ܝܗܘܢ ܕܐ̈ܝܠܢܐ. ܟܘܠ ܐܝܠܢܐ
ܕܡ ܕܦܐܪ̈ܐ ܛܒ̈ܐ ܠܐ ܥܒܕ ܡܬܦܣܩ ܘܒܢܘܪܐ
ܢܦܠ ◦ ◦ ◦
10, 11 ܘܡܫܐܠܝܢ ܗܘܘ ܠܗ ܟܢ̈ܫܐ. ܡܢܐ ܢܥܒܕ ܘܢܚܐ. ܐܡܪ
ܠܗܘܢ ܡܢ ܕܐܝܬ ܠܗ ܬܪ̈ܬܝܢ ܟܘܬܝ̈ܢܝܢ ܢܬܠ ܚܕܐ
ܡܢܗܝܢ ܠܡܢ ܕܠܝܬ ܠܗ. ܘܡܢ ܕܐܝܬ ܠܗ ܣܝܒܪܬܐ

ܕܠܘܩܐ

* * * * * * * * * * * *

* * * * * * * * * * * *

* * * * * * * * * * * *

..܀.. ܐܘܢܓܠܝܘܢ. ܕܠܘܩܐ ..܀..

* * * * * * * * * * * *

* * * * * * * * * * * *

ܥܒܕܬ ܠܢ ܗܟܢܐ. ܕܗܐ ܐܒܘܟ ܒܥܩܬܐ ܘܒܨܘܪܦܐ

49 ܩܥܐܐ ܒܥܝܢ ܗܘܝܢ ܠܟ. ܐܡܪ ܠܗܘܢ ܡܢܐ ܒܥܝܢ

ܐܢܬܘܢ ܠܝ. ܠܐ ܝܕܥܝܢ ܐܢܬܘܢ ܕܒܝܬ ܐܒܐ ܘܠܐ ܠܝ

50 ܕܐܗܘܐ. ܗܢܘܢ ܕܝܢ ܠܐ ܐܣܬܟܠܘ ܒܗ̇ ܠܡܠܬܐ

51 ܕܐܡܪ ܠܗܘܢ. ܘܢܚܬ ܥܡܗܘܢ ܘܐܬܐ ܠܢܨܪܬ.

ܘܡܫܬܥܒܕ ܗܘܐ ܠܗܘܢ. ܐܡܗ ܕܝܢ ܟܠܗܝܢ ܗܠܝܢ

52 ܡ̈ܠܐ ܢܛܪܐ ܗܘܬ ܒܠܒܗ̇. ܝܫܘܥ ܕܝܢ ܪܒܐ ܗܘܐ

ܒܩܘܡܬܗ. ܘܣܓܐ ܒܚܟܡܬܗ ܘܒܛܝܒܘܬܗ. ܠܘܬ

ܐܠܗܐ ܘܠܘܬ ܒ̈ܢܝ ܐܢܫܐ ○ ○ ○

III. ܒܫܢܬ ܚܡܫܥܣܪܐ ܕܝܢ. ܒܡܕܒܪܢܘܬܐ ܕܛܝܒܪܝܘܣ

ܩܣܪ. ܘܒܗܓܡܘܢܘܬܐ ܕܦܝܠܛܘܣ ܦܢܛܝܘܣ ܒܝܗܘܕ.

ܟܕ ܪܫܐ ܐܪܒܥܝܐ ܗܪܘܕܣ ܒܓܠܝܠܐ. ܘܦܝܠܝܦܘܣ

ܐܚܘܗܝ، ܪܫܐ ܐܪܒܥܝܐ ܒܐܬܪܐ ܕܐܝܛܘܪܝܐ: ܘܒܟܘܪ

ܕܛܪܟܘܢܐ. ܘܠܘܣܢܝܐ ܪܫܐ ܐܪܒܥܝܐ ܒܐܬܪܐ

28 ܘܐܪܝܡ ܗܘܐ ܝܫܘܥ ܩܠܗ ܒܗܝܟܠܐ. ܟܕ ܡܠܦ
ܘܐܡܪ. ܠܝ ܝܕܥܝܢ ܐܢܬܘܢ. ܘܡܢ ܐܝܡܟܐ ܐܢܐ
ܝܕܥܝܢ ܐܢܬܘܢ. ܡܢ ܨܒܘܬ ܢܦܫܝ ܠܐ ܐܬܝܬ. ܐܠܐ
ܫܪܝܪ ܗܘ ܡܢ ܕܫܕܪܢܝ. ܗܘ ܐܢܐ ܕܐܢܬܘܢ ܠܐ ܝܕܥܝܢ
29 ܐܢܬܘܢ ܠܗ. ܐܢܐ ܕܝܢ ܝܕܥ ܐܢܐ ܠܗ ܕܠܘܬܗ ܐܢܐ.
30 ܘܗܘ ܫܕܪܢܝ. ܘܒܥܘ ܠܡܐܚܕܗ. ܘܠܐ ܐܢܫ ܐܪܡܝ
ܒܗ ܐܝܕܐ. ܡܛܠ ܕܠܐ ܐܬܬ ܗܘܬ ܫܥܬܗ.
31 ܘܣܓܝܐܐ ܡܢ ܟܢܫܐ ܗܝܡܢܘ ܗܘܘ ܒܗ. ܘܐܡܪܝܢ
ܗܘܘ ܡܟܐ ܕܐܬܐ ܡܫܝܚܐ ܕܠܡܐ ܕܝܬܝܪ̈ܢ ܡܢ ܗܠܝܢ
32 ܐܬܘ̈ܬܐ ܕܥܒܕ ܗܢܐ ܥܒܕ. ܘܫܡܥܘ ܦܪ̈ܝܫܐ ܕܪܛܢܝܢ
ܥܠܘܗܝ ܐܟܢܐ. ܘܫܕܪܘ ܪ̈ܒܝ ܟܗ̈ܢܐ ܘܦܪ̈ܝܫܐ
33 ܕܢܐܚܕܘܢܗ. ܘܐܡܪ ܝܫܘܥ ܩܠܝܠ ܐܚܪܢ ܙܒܢܐ
ܥܡܟܘܢ ܐܢܐ. ܘܐܙܠ ܐܢܐ ܠܝ ܠܘܬ ܡܢ ܕܫܕܪܢܝ.
34 ܘܬܒܥܘܢܢܝ ܘܠܐ ܬܫܟܚܘܢܢܝ. ܘܐܝܟܐ ܕܐܢܐ ܐܙܠܢܐ
35 ܐܢܬܘܢ ܠܐ ܡܫܟܚܝܢ ܐܢܬܘܢ ܠܡܐܬܐ. ܐܡܪܝܢ
ܝܗܘ̈ܕܝܐ ܚܕ ܠܚܕ. ܠܐܝܟܐ ܟܝ ܐܙܠ ܗܢܐ ܕܠܐ
ܡܫܟܚܝܢ ܐܢܚܢ ܠܗ. ܠܡܐ ܟܝ ܠܙܪܥܐ ܕܐܪ̈ܡܝܐ
36 ܐܙܠ ܡܠܦ. ܕܠܐ ܡܫܟܚܝܢ ܐܢܚܢ ܠܗ. ܐܘ ܡܢܐ ܗܝ
ܡܠܬܐ ܗܕܐ ܕܐܡܪ ܕܬܒܥܘܢܢܝ ܘܠܐ ܬܫܟܚܘܢܢܝ.
ܘܐܝܟܐ ܕܐܢܐ ܠܐ ܡܫܟܚܝܢ ܐܢܬܘܢ ܠܡܐܬܐ ◦ ◦ ◦
37 ܘܒܝܘܡܐ ܪܒܐ ܕܥܐܕܐ ܩܐܡ ܗܘܐ ܝܫܘܥ ܘܩܥܐ
ܘܐܡܪ. ܡܢ ܕܨܗܐ ܢܐܬܐ ܠܘܬܝ * * * * *

* * * * * * * * * * * *

17 ܕܡܢ ܕܫܕܪܢܝ. ܘܡܢ ܕܨܒܐ ܕܢܥܒܕ ܨܒܝܢܗ. ܢܕܥ ܝܘܠܦܢܐ
ܗܢܐ ܐܢ ܡܢ ܐܠܗܐ ܗܘ. ܐܘ ܐܢܐ ܡܢ ܨܒܘܬ ܢܦܫܝ
18 ܡܡܠܠ ܐܢܐ. ܡܢ ܕܡܢ ܨܒܘܬ ܪܥܝܢܗ ܚܢ ܡܡܠܠ.
ܫܘܒܚܐ ܕܢܦܫܗ ܒܥܐ. ܘܡܢ ܕܫܘܒܚܐ ܕܡܢ ܕܫܕܪܗ
19 ܒܥܐ. ܫܪܝܪ ܗܘ ܘܥܘܠܐ ܠܝܬ ܒܗ. ܠܐ ܗܘܐ
ܡܘܫܐ ܝܗܒ ܠܟܘܢ ܐܘܪܝܬܐ. ܘܠܐ ܐܢܫ ܡܢܟܘܢ
20 ܢܛܪ ܦܘܩܕܢܗ. ܠܝ ܠܡܢܐ ܒܥܝܢ ܐܢܬܘܢ ܠܡܩܛܠܢܝ.
ܐܡܪܝܢ ܠܗ ܐܢܫܐ ܕܝܘܐ ܐܝܬ ܒܟ. ܡܢܘ ܒܥܐ
21 ܠܡܩܛܠܟ. ܐܡܪ ܠܗܘܢ ܝܫܘܥ. ܚܕ ܥܒܕܐ ܥܒܕܬ
22 ܠܥܝܢܝܟܘܢ. ܘܟܠܟܘܢ ܡܬܕܡܪܝܢ ܐܢܬܘܢ. ܡܛܠ ܗܢܐ
ܡܘܫܐ ܝܗܒ ܠܟܘܢ ܓܙܘܪܬܐ. ܠܐ ܗܘܐ ܡܛܠ ܕܡܢܗ
ܗܝ ܡܢ ܡܘܫܐ. ܐܠܐ ܡܛܠ ܕܡܢ ܐܒܗ̈ܝܟܘܢ ܗܝ.
23 ܘܒܝܘܡܐ ܕܫܒܬܐ ܓܙܪܝܢ ܐܢܬܘܢ ܒܪܢܫܐ. ܘܐܢ
ܒܪܢܫܐ ܡܬܓܙܪ ܒܫܒܬܐ ܕܠܐ ܢܫܬܪܐ ܢܡܘܣܐ
ܕܡܘܫܐ. ܥܠܝ ܪܓܙܝܢ ܐܢܬܘܢ ܕܟܠܗ ܒܪܢܫܐ
24 ܐܚܠܡܬ ܒܝܘܡܐ ܕܫܒܬܐ. ܠܐ ܬܗܘܘܢ ܕܝܢܝܢ
25 ܒܐ̈ܦܐ. ܐܠܐ ܕܝܢܐ ܟܐܢܐ ܕܘܢܘ. ܘܐܡܪܝܢ ܗܘܘ
ܐܢܫܐ ܡܢ ܒ̈ܢܝ ܐܘܪܫܠܡ. ܠܐ ܗܘܐ ܗܢܐ ܗܘ ܕܒܥܝܢ
26 ܗܘܘ ܠܡܩܛܠܗ. ܘܗܐ ܚܢ ܓܠܝܐ ܩܐܡ ܘܡܡܠܠ.
ܘܐܢܫ ܡܕܡ ܠܐ ܐܡܪ ܠܗ. ܒܪ ܫܪܝܪܐܝܬ ܝܕܥܘ
27 ܩܫ̈ܝܫܐ ܕܗܢܐ ܗܘ ܡܫܝܚܐ. ܐܠܐ ܠܗܢܐ ܗܘ
ܝܕܥܝܢ ܚܢ ܠܗ ܡܢ ܐܝܟܐ ܗܘ. ܘܡܫܝܚܐ ܐܡܬܝ
ܕܐܬܐ. ܠܐ ܐܢܫ ܝܕܥ ܡܢ ܐܝܟܐ ܗܘ.

4 ܕܢܚܙܘܢ ܬܠܡܝ̈ܕܝܟ ܥܒ̈ܕܐ ܕܥܒܕ ܐܢܬ. ܠܝܬ ܓܝܪ ܐܢܫ
ܕܥܒܕ ܡܕܡ ܒܛܘܫܝܐ ܘܒܥܐ ܕܢܗܘܐ ܒܓܠܝܐ. ܐܢ
5 ܗܠܝܢ ܥܒܕ ܐܢܬ ܚܘܐ ܢܦܫܟ ܠܥܠܡܐ. ܥܕܡܐ ܓܝܪ
6 ܠܗܕܡ ܐܦܠܐ ܐ̈ܚܘܗܝ ܡܗܝܡܢܝܢ ܗܘܘ ܒܗ. ܐܡܪ
ܠܗܘܢ ܝܫܘܥ. ܙܒܢܝ ܥܕܡܐ ܠܗܫܐ ܠܐ ܡܛܐ.
7 ܕܝܠܟܘܢ ܕܝܢ ܙܒܢܟܘܢ ܒܟܠܙܒܢ ܡܛܝܒ ܗܘ. ܘܠܐ
ܡܫܟܚ ܥܠܡܐ ܠܡܣܢܝܟܘܢ. ܠܝ ܕܝܢ ܣܢܐ ܠܝ ܥܠܡܐ.
ܡܛܠ ܕܡܣܗܕ ܐܢܐ ܥܠܘܗܝ ܕܒܝܫܝܢ ܐܢܘܢ ܥܒ̈ܕܘܗܝ.
8 ܐܢܬܘܢ ܣܩܘ ܠܥܐܕܐ ܗܢܐ. ܐܢܐ ܠܐ ܣܠܩ ܐܢܐ
ܠܥܐܕܐ. ܡܛܠ ܕܠܐ ܥܕܡܐ ܠܗܫܐ ܫܠܡ ܙܒܢܐ
9, 10 ܕܝܠܝ. ܟܕ ܗܠܝܢ ܐܡܪ. ܦܫ ܠܗ ܒܓܠܝܠܐ. ܘܟܕ ܣܠܩܘ
ܐ̈ܚܘܗܝ. ܗܝܕܝܢ ܐܦ ܗܘ ܣܠܩ ܠܥܐܕܐ. ܠܐ
11 ܒܡ ܒܓܠܝܐ ܐܠܐ ܒܛܘܫܝܐ. ܝܗܘ̈ܕܝܐ ܕܝܢ ܒܥܝܢ
ܗܘܘ ܠܗ ܒܥܐܕܐ. ܘܐܡܪܝܢ ܗܘܘ ܐܝܟܘ ܗܘ.
12 ܘܪܛܢܐ ܣܓܝܐܐ ܐܝܬ ܗܘܐ ܥܠܘܗܝ ܒܟܢܫܐ. ܘܐܝܬ
ܗܘܘ ܕܐܡܪܝܢ ܕܛܒܐ ܗܘ. ܘܐܝܬ ܗܘܘ ܕܐܡܪܝܢ ܠܐ
13 ܗܘܐ ܛܒܐ. ܐܠܐ ܡܛܥܐ ܠܥܡܐ ܗܘ. ܐܢܫ ܕܝܢ
ܒܓܠܝܐ ܠܐ ܡܡܠܠ ܗܘܐ ܥܠܘܗܝ. ܡܛܠ
ܕܚܠܬܐ ܕܝܗܘ̈ܕܝܐ ◎ ◎
14 ܘܟܕ ܦܠܓܘ ܝܘ̈ܡܬܐ ܕܥܐܕܐ ܕܡ̈ܛܠܐ. ܣܠܩ ܝܫܘܥ
15 ܠܗܝܟܠܐ. ܘܡܠܦ ܗܘܐ. ܘܡܬܕܡܪܝܢ ܗܘܘ ܝܗܘ̈ܕܝܐ
ܘܐܡܪܝܢ. ܐܝܟܢܐ ܝܕܥ ܗܢܐ ܣܦܪܐ ܕܠܐ ܝܠܦ.
16 ܐܡܪ ܠܗܘܢ ܝܫܘܥ. ܝܘܠܦܢܝ ܠܐ ܗܘܐ ܕܝܠܝ. ܐܠܐ

62 ܐܡܪ ܠܗܘܢ ܗܕܐ ܡܟܫܠܐ ܠܟܘܢ. ܐܢ ܕܝܢ ܬܚܙܘܢܝܗܝ
ܠܒܪܗ ܕܐܢܫܐ ܟܕ ܣܠܩ ܠܐܬܪ ܕܐܝܬܘܗܝ ܗܘܐ ܡܢ
63 ܩܕܝܡ. ܪܘܚܐ ܗܝ ܕܡܚܝܐ ܐܘ ܦܓܪܐ ܠܐ ܡܕܡ
ܐܗܢܝ. ܡ̈ܠܐ ܕܐܢܐ ܡܠܠܬ ܥܡܟܘܢ ܪܘܚܐ ܐܢܝܢ
64 ܘܚܝܐ ܐܢܝܢ. ܐܠܐ ܐܝܬ ܡܢܟܘܢ ܐܢܫܝܢ ܕܠܐ
ܡܗܝܡܢܝܢ. ܝܕܥ ܗܘܐ ܓܝܪ ܝܫܘܥ ܡܢ ܩܕܝܡ ܡܢ
65 ܕܡܫܠܡ ܠܗ. ܐܡܪ ܠܗܘܢ ܡܛܠ ܗܢܐ ܐܡܪܬ ܠܟܘܢ.
ܕܠܐ ܐܢܫ ܡܫܟܚ ܕܢܐܬܐ ܠܘܬܝ ܐܠܐ ܐܢ ܝܗܝܒ ܠܗ
66 ܡܢ ܐܒܐ. ܡܛܠ ܗܕܐ ܣ̈ܓܝܐܐ ܡܢ ܬܠܡ̈ܝܕܘܗܝ
ܐܙܠܘ ܠܗܘܢ ܡܢ ܠܘܬܗ. ܘܠܐ ܡܗܠܟܝܢ ܗܘܘ ܥܡܗ.
67 ܐܡܪ ܝܫܘܥ ܠܬܪ̈ܥܣܪܬܗ. ܕܠܡܐ ܘܐܦ ܐܢܬܘܢ ܨܒܝܢ
68 ܐܢܬܘܢ ܠܡܐܙܠ ܠܟܘܢ. ܐܡܪ ܠܗ ܫܡܥܘܢ ܟܐܦܐ.
ܡܪܝ ܠܘܬ ܡܢ ܢܐܙܠ. ܡ̈ܠܬܐ ܕܚ̈ܝܐ ܕܠܥܠܡ ܐܝܬ ܠܟ.
69, 70 ܘܚܢܢ ܗܝܡܢܢ ܘܝܕܥܢ ܕܐܢܬ ܗܘ ܒܪܗ ܕܐܠܗܐ. ܐܡܪ
ܠܗܘܢ ܝܫܘܥ. ܠܐ ܗܘܐ ܐܢܐ ܓܒܝܬܟܘܢ ܠܟܠܟܘܢ.
71 ܘܗܘܐ ܐܦ ܡܢܟܘܢ ܚܕ ܣܛܢܐ ܗܘ. ܐܡܪ ܗܘܐ ܕܝܢ
ܥܠ ܝܗܘܕܐ ܒܪ ܫܡܥܘܢ ܐܣܟܪܝܘܛܐ. ܗܢܘ ܓܝܪ
ܥܬܝܕ ܗܘܐ ܠܡܫܠܡܘܬܗ ܚܕ ܡܢ ܬܪ̈ܥܣܪ ◦ ◦ ◦
VII. ܒܬܪ ܗܠܝܢ ܡܗܠܟ ܗܘܐ ܝܫܘܥ ܒܓܠܝܠܐ. ܠܐ ܓܝܪ
ܐܝܬ ܗܘܐ ܠܗ ܫܘܠܛܢܐ ܠܡܗܠܟܘ ܒܝܗܘܕ. ܡܛܠ
ܕܝ̈ܗܘܕܝܐ ܒܥܝܢ ܗܘܘ ܠܡܩܛܠܗ ◦ ◦ ◦
2, 3 ܘܩܪܒ ܗܘܐ ܥܐܕܐ ܕܝ̈ܗܘܕܝܐ ܕܡ̈ܛܠܠܐ. ܘܐܡܪܝܢ
ܗܘܘ ܠܗ ܐ̈ܚܘܗܝ. ܫܢܐ ܠܟ ܡܟܐ ܘܙܠ ܠܝܗܘܕ.

49 ܐܢܐ ܠܚܡܐ ܕܚܝܐ ܕܢܚܬ ܡܢ ܫܡܝܐ ܐܒܗ̈ܝܟܘܢ
50 ܐܟܠܘ ܠܚܡܐ ܒܡܕܒܪܐ ܘܡܝܬܘ ܗܢܘ ܕܝܢ ܠܚܡܐ
51 ܕܢܚܬ ܡܢ ܫܡܝܐ ܕܢܐܟܘܠ ܐܢܫ ܡܢܗ ܘܢܡܘܬ ܐܢܐ
ܐܢܐ ܠܚܡܐ ܚܝܐ ܕܢܚܬ ܡܢ ܫܡܝܐ ܕܡܢ ܕܢܐܟܘܠ
ܡܢ ܠܚܡܐ ܗܢܐ ܚܝܐ ܠܥܠܡ ܘܠܚܡܐ ܐܢܐ ܕܐܢܐ
52 ܐܬܠ ܦܓܪܝ ܗܘ ܕܥܠ ܐܦ̈ܝ ܚܝܘܗܝ ܕܥܠܡܐ. ܘܢܨܝܢ
ܗܘܘ ܝܗܘ̈ܕܝܐ ܚܕ ܥܡ ܚܕ ܘܐܡܪܝܢ ܗܘܘ ܐܝܟܢܐ
53 ܡܫܟܚ ܗܢܐ ܕܢܬܠ ܠܢ ܦܓܪܗ ܠܡܐܟܠ ܐܡܪ
ܠܗܘܢ ܝܫܘܥ ܐܡܝܢ ܐܡܝܢ ܐܡܪ ܐܢܐ ܠܟܘܢ. ܕܐܠܐ
ܬܐܟܠܘܢ ܦܓܪܗ ܕܒܪܗ ܕܐܢܫܐ ܘܬܫܬܘܢ ܕܡܗ.
54 ܠܝܬ ܠܟܘܢ ܚܝܐ ܒܟܘܢ. ܘܡܢ ܕܐܟܠ ܦܓܪܝ ܘܫܬܐ
ܕܡܝ. ܐܝܬ ܠܗ ܚܝܐ ܕܠܥܠܡ. ܘܐܢܐ ܐܩܝܡܝܘܗܝ
55 ܒܝܘܡܐ ܐܚܪܝܐ. ܦܓܪܝ ܫܪܝܪܐܝܬ ܡܐܟܘܠܬܐ ܗܘ.
56 ܘܕܡܝ ܫܪܝܪܐܝܬ ܡܫܬܝܬܐ ܗܘ. ܡܢܘ ܕܐܟܠ ܦܓܪܝ
57 ܘܫܬܐ ܕܡܝ ܒܝ ܡܩܘܐ ܘܐܢܐ ܒܗ. ܐܝܟܢܐ ܕܫܕܪܢܝ
ܐܒܐ ܚܝܐ. ܘܐܢܐ ܚܝ ܡܛܠ ܐܒܐ. ܡܢ ܕܢܐܟܠܢܝ
58 ܢܚܘܐ ܚܝ ܡܛܠܬܝ. ܗܢܐ ܗܘ ܠܚܡܐ ܕܢܚܬ ܡܢ
ܫܡܝܐ. ܠܐ ܗܘܐ ܐܝܟ ܗܘ ܕܐܟܠܘ ܐܒܗ̈ܝܟܘܢ
ܘܡܝܬܘ. ܡܢܘ ܕܝܢ ܗܢܐ ܠܚܡܐ ܢܐܟܘܠ ܚܝܐ
59 ܠܥܠܡ. ܗܠܝܢ ܐܡܪ ܒܟܢܘܫܬܐ. ܟܕ ܡܠܦ ܒܟܦܪܢܚܘܡ.
60 ܘܣ̈ܓܝܐܐ ܡܢ ܬܠܡ̈ܝܕܘܗܝ. ܟܕ ܫܡܥܘ. ܐܡܪܝܢ ܗܘܘ
ܩܫܝܐ ܗܝ ܡܠܬܐ ܗܕܐ. ܡܢܘ ܡܫܟܚ ܠܡܫܡܥܗ.
61 ܝܕܥ ܕܝܢ ܟܕ ܝܫܘܥ ܕܪܛܢܝܢ ܬܠܡ̈ܝܕܘܗܝ ܥܠ ܗܕܐ.

ܕܐܬܐ ܠܘܬܝ ܠܐ ܢܟܦܢ ܘܡܢ ܕܡܗܝܡܢ ܒܝ ܠܐ ܢܨܗܐ
36 ܡܬܘܡ ܐܠܐ ܐܡܪܬ ܠܟܘܢ ܕܚܙܝܢ ܐܢܬܘܢ ܘܠܐ
37 ܡܗܝܡܢܝܢ ܐܢܬܘܢ ܟܠ ܡܢ ܕܝܗܒ ܠܝ ܐܒܝ ܠܘܬܝ
38 ܢܐܬܐ ܘܡܢ ܕܠܘܬܝ ܢܐܬܐ ܠܐ ܐܦܩܝܘܗܝ ܕܢܚܬܬ
ܡܢ ܫܡܝܐ ܠܐ ܗܘܐ ܕܐܥܒܕ ܨܒܝܢܝ ܐܠܐ ܕܐܥܒܕ
ܨܒܝܢܗ ܕܡܢ ܕܫܕܪܢܝ ܗܘ ܕܝܢ ܨܒܝܢܗ ܕܐܒܐ ܕܫܕܪܢܝ
39 ܕܟܠ ܡܕܡ ܕܝܗܒ ܠܝ ܠܐ ܐܘܒܕ ܡܢܗ ܡܕܡ ܐܠܐ
40 ܐܩܝܡܝܘܗܝ ܒܝܘܡܐ ܐܚܪܝܐ ܗܢܘ ܓܝܪ ܨܒܝܢܗ
ܕܐܒܝ ܕܟܠ ܐܢܫ ܕܚܙܐ ܠܒܪܐ ܘܡܗܝܡܢ ܒܗ ܐܝܬ
ܠܗ ܚ̈ܝܐ ܕܠܥܠܡ ܘܐܢܐ ܐܩܝܡܝܘܗܝ ܒܝܘܡܐ
41 ܐܚܪܝܐ ܝܗܘ̈ܕܝܐ ܕܝܢ ܪܛܢܝܢ ܗܘܘ ܥܠܘܗܝ ܕܐܡܪ
42 ܕܐܢܐ ܐܢܐ ܠܚܡܐ ܕܢܚܬ ܡܢ ܫܡܝܐ ܘܐܡܪܝܢ
ܗܘܘ ܠܐ ܗܘܐ ܗܢܐ ܝܫܘܥ ܒܪܗ ܕܝܘܣܦ ܘܐܚܝܢ
ܝܕܥܝܢ ܐܚܢܢ ܠܐܒܘܗܝ ܐܝܟܢܐ ܐܡܪ ܕܐܢܐ ܡܢ
43 ܫܡܝܐ ܢܚܬܬ ܐܡܪ ܠܗܘܢ ܝܫܘܥ ܠܐ ܬܬܪܛܢܘܢ ܚܕ
44 ܥܡ ܚܕ. ܠܐ ܓܝܪ ܐܢܫ ܡܫܟܚ ܕܢܐܬܐ ܠܘܬܝ ܐܠܐ
ܐܢܐ ܕܢܓܕ ܠܗ ܐܒܐ ܕܫܕܪܢܝ ܘܐܢܐ ܐܩܝܡܝܘܗܝ
45 ܒܝܘܡܐ ܐܚܪܝܐ ܟܬܝܒ ܓܝܪ ܒܢܒܝܐ ܕܢܗܘܘܢ
ܟܠܗܘܢ ܡ̈ܠܦܐ ܕܐܠܗܐ ܟܠ ܡܢ ܕܫܡܥ ܗܟܝܠ
46 ܡܢ ܐܒܐ ܘܝܠܦ ܐܬܐ ܠܘܬܝ ܠܐ ܗܘܐ ܡܛܠ ܕܚܙܐ
ܐܢܫ ܠܐܒܐ ܐܠܐ ܡܢ ܕܠܘܬ ܐܠܗܐ ܐܝܬܘܗܝ ܗܘ
47 ܗܘ ܚܙܐ ܠܐܒܐ ܐܡܝܢ ܐܡܝܢ ܐܡܪܢܐ ܠܟܘܢ ܕܟܠ
48 ܡܢ ܕܡܗܝܡܢ ܠܐܠܗܐ ܐܝܬ ܠܗ ܚ̈ܝܐ ܕܠܥܠܡ ܐܢܐ

24 ܦܪܘܩܢ ܠܐܬܪ ܕܐܟܠܘ ܠܚܡܐ. ܘܚܙܘ ܕܠܐ ܗܘܐ
ܬܡܢ ܝܫܘܥ ܘܐܦ ܠܐ ܬܠܡܝܕܘܗܝ. ܣܠܩܘ ܠܗܘܢ
ܠܣܦܝܢܬܐ. ܘܐܬܘ ܗܘܘ ܠܟܦܪܢܚܘܡ. ܘܒܥܝܢ ܗܘܘ
25 ܠܗ ܠܝܫܘܥ. ܘܟܕ ܕܝܢ ܐܫܟܚܘܗܝ ܒܥܒܪܐ ܕܝܡܬܐ.
26 ܐܡܪܝܢ ܠܗ ܪܒܢ ܐܡܬܝ ܐܬܝܬ ܠܟܐ. ܐܡܪ ܠܗܘܢ
ܝܫܘܥ. ܐܡܝܢ ܐܡܝܢ ܐܡܪܢܐ ܠܟܘܢ. ܕܠܐ ܗܘܐ
ܡܛܠ ܕܚܙܝܬܘܢ ܐܬܘ̈ܬܐ ܒܥܝܬܘܢܢܝ. ܐܠܐ ܡܛܠ
27 ܕܐܟܠܬܘܢ ܠܚܡܐ ܘܣܒܥܬܘܢ. ܠܐ ܬܦܠܚܘܢ
ܡܐܟܘܠܬܐ ܕܐܒܕܐ. ܐܠܐ ܦܠܘܚܘ ܡܐܟܘܠܬܐ
ܕܡܩܘܝܐ ܠܚܝܐ ܕܠܥܠܡ. ܐܝܕܐ ܕܒܪܗ ܕܐܢܫܐ ܢܬܠ
28 ܠܟܘܢ. ܠܗܢܐ ܓܝܪ ܚܬܡ ܐܠܗܐ ܐܒܐ. ܐܡܪܝܢ ܠܗ
29 ܡܢܐ ܢܥܒܕ ܕܢܦܠܘܚ ܥܒ̈ܕܐ ܕܐܠܗܐ. ܐܡܪ ܠܗܘܢ
ܝܫܘܥ. ܗܢܐ ܗܘ ܥܒܕܐ ܕܐܠܗܐ. ܕܬܗܝܡܢܘܢ ܒܡܢ
30 ܕܫܕܪ ܗܘ. ܐܡܪܝܢ ܠܗ ܡܢܐ ܗܟܝܠ ܐܬܐ ܥܒܕ ܐܢܬ
31 ܕܢܚܙܐ ܘܢܗܝܡܢ ܒܟ ܡܢܐ ܦܠܚ ܐܢܬ ܐܒ̈ܗܝܢ ܡܢܢܐ
ܐܟܠܘ ܒܡܕܒܪܐ ܐܝܟ ܕܟܬܝܒ. ܕܠܚܡܐ ܡܢ ܫܡܝܐ
32 ܝܗܒ ܠܗܘܢ ܠܡܐܟܠ ܐܡܪ ܠܗܘܢ ܝܫܘܥ ܐܡܝܢ
ܐܡܝܢ ܐܡܪܢܐ ܠܟܘܢ. ܕܠܐ ܗܘܐ ܡܘܫܐ ܝܗܒ
ܠܟܘܢ ܠܚܡܐ ܡܢ ܫܡܝܐ ܐܠܐ ܐܒܝ ܝܗܒ ܠܟܘܢ
33 ܠܚܡܐ ܕܩܘܫܬܐ ܡܢ ܫܡܝܐ ܠܚܡܗ ܓܝܪ ܕܐܠܗܐ
ܢܚܬ ܡܢ ܫܡܝܐ ܘܚܝ ܗܘ ܘܡܬܝܗܒ ܠܥܠܡܐ
34 ܐܡܪܝܢ ܠܗ ܡܪܢ. ܒܟܠ ܙܒܢ ܗܒ ܠܢ ܠܚܡܐ ܗܢܐ
35 ܐܡܪ ܠܗܘܢ ܝܫܘܥ ܐܢܐ ܐܢܐ ܠܚܡܐ ܕܚ̈ܝܐ ܡܢܘ

13 ܕܠܓܡܪ ܡܕܡ ܠܐ ܢܐܒܕ. ܘܟܢܫܘ ܘܡܠܘ ܬܪܬܥܣܪ
ܩܘܦܝܢ ܕܩܨܝܐ. ܡܢ ܚܡܫܐ ܠܚܡܝܢ ܕܣܥܪܐ.
14 ܡܕܡ ܕܐܬܪܘ ܡܢ ܗܢܘܢ ܕܐܟܠܘ. ܗܢܘܢ ܕܝܢ ܐܢܫܐ ܟܕ
ܚܙܘ ܐܬܐ ܗܕܐ ܕܥܒܕ. ܐܡܪܝܢ ܗܘܘ. ܫܪܝܪܐܝܬ
15 ܗܢܐ ܗܘ ܢܒܝܐ ܕܐܬܐ ܠܥܠܡܐ. ܘܝܕܥ ܗܘܐ ܝܫܘܥ
ܕܥܬܝܕܝܢ ܗܘܘ ܕܢܚܛܦܘܢܝܗܝ ܘܢܥܒܕܘܢܝܗܝ ܡܠܟܐ. ܥܪܩ
16 ܐܢܘܢ. ܘܥܪܩ ܠܗ ܛܘܒ ܠܛܘܪܐ ܒܠܚܘܕܘܗܝ. ܟܕ
ܗܘܐ ܕܝܢ ܪܡܫܐ. ܢܚܬܘ ܗܘܘ ܬܠܡܝܕܘܗܝ ܠܝܡܐ.
17 ܘܣܠܩܘ ܒܣܦܝܢܬܐ. ܘܐܬܝܢ ܗܘܘ ܠܥܒܪܐ ܕܝܡܬܐ
ܠܟܦܪܢܚܘܡ. ܘܚܫܟܬ ܗܘܬ ܠܗ̇. ܘܠܐ ܐܬܐ ܗܘܐ ܠܘܬܗܘܢ
18 ܝܫܘܥ. ܘܪܘܚܐ ܢܫܒܬ ܗܘܬ ܠܗ̇ ܒܝܡܬܐ.
19 ܘܐܫܬܓܫܬ ܒܠܫܘܢ ܡܫܘܬܐ. ܘܕܒܪܘܗ̇ ܗܘܘ
ܠܐܣܛܕܘܬܐ ܐܣܛܕܘܬܐ ܥܣܪܝܢ ܘܚܡܫܐ ܐܘ ܬܠܬܝܢ.
ܘܚܙܘ ܠܝܫܘܥ ܟܕ ܡܗܠܟ ܥܠ ܡ̈ܝܐ. ܘܟܕ ܩܪܒ ܠܘܬ
20 ܣܦܝܢܬܐ. ܕܚܠܘ. ܗܘ ܕܝܢ ܝܫܘܥ ܐܡܪ ܠܗܘܢ ܐܢܐ
21 ܐܢܐ. ܘܨܒܝܢ ܗܘܘ ܕܢܩܒܠܘܢܝܗܝ ܒܣܦܝܢܬܐ. ܘܒܗ̇
ܒܫܥܬܐ ܗܝ ܣܦܝܢܬܐ ܡܛܬ ܗܘܬ ܠܘܬ ܐܪܥܐ. ܗܝ
ܕܐܙܠܝܢ ܗܘܘ ܠܗ̇ ◦ ◦ ◦
22 ܘܠܝܘܡܐ ܐܚܪܢܐ ܗܘ ܟܢܫܐ ܕܒܥܒܪܐ ܗܘܐ
ܕܝܡܬܐ. ܕܚܙܐ ܕܣܦܝܢܬܐ ܐܚܪܬܐ ܠܝܬ ܗܘܐ
ܬܡܢ. ܐܠܐ ܐܢ ܚܕܐ ܕܥܒܪܘ ܒܗ̇ ܬܠܡܝܕܘܗܝ
ܕܝܫܘܥ. ܘܝܫܘܥ ܠܐ ܗܘܐ ܥܡ ܬܠܡܝܕܘܗܝ ܗܘܐ
23 ܒܣܦܝܢܬܐ. ܘܟܕ ܐܬܝ̈ ܣܦܝ̈ܢܐ ܐܚܪ̈ܢܝܬܐ ܡܢ

ܕܐܢ ܒܟܬܒܘܗܝ ܕܗܘ ܠܐ ܡܗܝܡܢܝܢ ܐܢܬܘܢ. ܐܝܟܢܐ
ܠܡܠܝ ܡܗܝܡܢܝܢ ܐܢܬܘܢ ◦◦◦
VI. ܒܬܪ ܗܠܝܢ. ܐܙܠ ܝܫܘܥ ܠܥܒܪܐ ܕܝܡܬܐ ܕܓܠܝܠܐ
2 ܕܛܒܪܝܘܣ. ܘܐܙܠ ܒܬܪܗ ܟܢܫܐ ܣܓܝܐܐ. ܡܛܠ
ܕܚܙܝܢ ܗܘܘ ܐܬܘܬܐ ܕܥܒܕ ܗܘܐ ܒܟܪܝܗܐ.
3 ܘܣܠܩ ܗܘܐ ܝܫܘܥ ܠܛܘܪܐ. ܘܬܡܢ ܝܬܒ ܗܘܐ
4 ܥܡ ܬܠܡܝܕܘܗܝ. ܘܩܪܝܒܐ ܗܘܬ ܦܨܚܐ ܥܐܕܐ
5 ܕܝܗܘܕܝܐ. ܘܐܪܝܡ ܥܝܢܘܗܝ ܝܫܘܥ. ܘܚܙܐ ܟܢܫܐ
ܣܓܝܐܐ ܕܐܬܐ ܠܘܬܗ. ܘܐܡܪ ܠܦܝܠܝܦܘܣ ܐܝܟܢܐ
6 ܢܙܒܢ ܠܚܡܐ ܕܢܐܟܠܘܢ ܗܠܝܢ ܐܢܫܐ. ܗܘ ܕܝܢ ܐܡܪ
ܡܢܣܐ ܠܗ ܐܡܪܗ. ܗܘ ܓܝܪ ܝܕܥ ܗܘܐ ܡܢܐ ܥܬܝܕ
7 ܠܡܥܒܕ. ܐܡܪ ܠܗ ܦܝܠܝܦܘܣ. ܕܡܐܬܝܢ ܕܝܢܪܝܢ
ܠܚܡܐ ܠܐ ܣܦܩ ܠܗܘܢ. ܟܕ ܚܕ ܚܕ ܢܐܟܘܠ.
8 ܐܡܪ ܠܗ ܚܕ ܡܢ ܬܠܡܝܕܘܗܝ. ܐܢܕܪܐܘܣ ܫܡܗ
9 ܗܘܐ. ܐܚܘܗܝ ܕܫܡܥܘܢ ܟܐܦܐ. ܐܝܬ ܬܢܢ ܛܠܝܐ
ܘܐܝܬ ܥܠܘܗܝ ܚܡܫ ܓܪܝܨܢ ܕܣܥܪܐ. ܘܬܪܝܢ ܢܘܢܝܢ.
10 ܐܠܐ ܗܠܝܢ ܡܢܐ ܐܢܘܢ ܠܗܠܝܢ ܟܠܗܘܢ. ܐܡܪ ܗܘ
ܝܫܘܥ. ܐܠܐ ܐܣܬܡܟܘ ܐܢܘܢ ܠܐܢܫܐ ܣܬܡܟܝܢ.
ܒܕܘܟܐ ܕܝܢ ܥܣܒ ܗܘܐ ܒܗ ܒܕܘܟܬܐ ܗܝ. ܘܐܣܬܡܟܘ
11 ܐܢܫܐ ܡܢܝܢܐ ܐܝܟ ܚܡܫܐ ܐܠܦܝܢ. ܘܢܣܒ ܝܫܘܥ
ܠܚܡܐ ܗܢܘܢ ܘܒܪܟ. ܘܝܗܒ ܠܗܘܢ ܕܡܣܬܡܟܝܢ.
12 ܘܗܟܢܐ ܘܐܦ ܥܠ ܢܘܢܐ ܟܡܐ ܕܨܒܘ. ܘܟܕ ܣܒܥܘ
ܐܡܪ ܠܬܠܡܝܕܘܗܝ. ܟܢܫܘ ܩܨܝܐ ܡܕܡ ܕܝܬܪ.

35 ܗܘ ܫܪܓܐ ܗܘܐ ܕܝܩܕ ܘܡܢܗܪ. ܐܢܬܘܢ ܕܝܢ
36 ܨܒܝܬܘܢ ܕܬܫܬܒܗܪܘܢ ܕܫܥܬܐ ܒܢܘܗܪܗ. ܐܝܬ ܠܝ
ܕܝܢ ܣܗܕܘܬܐ ܕܪܒܐ ܡܢ ܕܝܘܚܢܢ. ܥܒ̈ܕܐ ܓܝܪ ܕܝܗܒ
ܠܝ ܐܒܝ ܕܐܫܠܡ ܐܢܘܢ. ܗܢܘܢ ܥܒ̈ܕܐ ܕܥܒܕ ܐܢܐ
37 ܣܗܕܝܢ ܥܠܝ ܕܐܒܐ ܫܠܚܢܝ. ܘܐܒܐ ܕܫܠܚܢܝ ܗܘ
ܣܗܕ ܥܠܝ. ܠܐ ܩܠܗ ܡܢ ܡܬܘܡ ܫܡܥܬܘܢ. ܘܠܐ
38 ܚܙܘܗ ܚܙܝܬܘܢ. ܘܠܐ ܡܠܬܗ ܡܩܘܝܐ ܒܟܘܢ.
ܡܛܠ ܕܒܐܝܢܐ ܕܗܘ ܫܕܪ ܐܢܬܘܢ ܠܐ ܡܗܝܡܢܝܢ
39 ܐܢܬܘܢ. ܒܨܘ ܠܟ̈ܬܒܐ ܕܒܗܘܢ ܣܒܪܝܢ ܐܢܬܘܢ
ܕܬܚܝܘܢ ܠܥܠܡ. ܘܗܢܘܢ ܟ̈ܬܒܐ ܥܠܝ ܗܘ ܣܗܕܝܢ.
ܗܢܘܢ ܕܣܒܪܝܢ ܐܢܬܘܢ ܕܒܗܘܢ ܐܝܬ ܠܟܘܢ ܚ̈ܝܐ.
40 ܗܢܘܢ ܣܗܕܝܢ ܥܠܝ. ܘܠܘܬܝ ܠܐ ܨܒܝܢ ܐܢܬܘܢ
41 ܕܬܐܬܘܢ. ܕܢܗܘܘܢ ܠܟܘܢ ܚ̈ܝܐ. ܫܘܒܚܐ ܡܢ
42 ܒ̈ܢܝ ܐܢܫܐ ܠܐ ܢܣܒ ܐܢܐ. ܐܠܐ ܝܕܥܬܟܘܢ ܕܚܘܒܐ
43 ܕܐܠܗܐ ܠܝܬ ܒܟܘܢ. ܐܢܐ ܐܬܝܬ ܒܫܡܗ ܕܐܒܝ
ܘܠܐ ܡܩܒܠܝܢ ܐܢܬܘܢ ܠܝ. ܘܐܢ ܐܚܪܢ ܢܐܬܐ ܒܫܡ
44 ܢܦܫܗ ܠܗܘ ܬܩܒܠܘܢ. ܐܝܟܢܐ ܡܫܟܚܝܢ ܐܢܬܘܢ
ܠܡܗܝܡܢܘ. ܕܫܘܒܚܐ ܚܕ ܡܢ ܚܕ ܡܩܒܠܝܢ ܐܢܬܘܢ.
45 ܘܫܘܒܚܐ ܕܡܢ ܚܕ ܐܠܗܐ ܠܐ ܒܥܝܢ ܐܢܬܘܢ. ܠܡܐ
ܣܒܪܝܢ ܐܢܬܘܢ ܕܐܢܐ ܗܘ ܐܟܠ ܩܪ̈ܨܝܟܘܢ. ܡܘܫܐ
ܗܘ ܐܟܠ ܩܪ̈ܨܝܟܘܢ. ܗܘ ܕܒܗ ܡܣܒܪܝܢ ܐܢܬܘܢ.
46 ܐܠܘ ܓܝܪ ܒܡܘܫܐ ܗܝܡܢܬܘܢ ܗܘܝܬܘܢ. ܘܐܦ ܒܝ
47 ܡܗܝܡܢܝܢ ܗܘܝܬܘܢ. ܗܘ ܓܝܪ ܥܠܝ ܗܘ ܟܬܒ. ܘܐܢ

ܕܡܝܩܪܝܢ ܠܐܒܐ. ܘܡܢ ܕܠܒܪܐ ܠܐ ܡܝܩܪ ܐܦܠܐ
24 ܠܐܒܐ ܕܫܕܪܗ ܡܝܩܪ. ܐܡܝܢ ܐܡܝܢ ܐܡܪܢܐ ܠܟܘܢ.
ܕܡܢ ܕܫܡܥ ܡܠܬܝ ܘܡܗܝܡܢ ܠܡܢ ܕܫܕܪܢܝ. ܐܝܬ ܠܗ
ܚ̈ܝܐ ܕܠܥܠܡ: ܘܠܕܝܢܐ ܠܐ ܐܬܐ. ܡܛܠ ܕܫܢܝ ܠܗ ܡܢ
25 ܡܘܬܐ ܠܚ̈ܝܐ. ܐܡܝܢ ܐܡܝܢ ܐܡܪܢܐ ܠܟܘܢ. ܕܐܬܝܐ
ܫܥܬܐ ܘܐܦ ܗܫܐ ܐܝܬܝܗ. ܕܐܦ ܡ̈ܝܬܐ ܢܫܡܥܘܢ
26 ܩܠܗ ܕܒܪܗ ܕܐܠܗܐ ܘܢܚܘܢ. ܐܝܟܢܐ ܓܝܪ ܕܠܐܒܐ
ܐܝܬ ܚ̈ܝܐ ܒܩܢܘܡܗ. ܗܟܢܐ ܝܗܒ ܐܦ ܠܒܪܐ
27 ܕܢܗܘܘܢ ܐܝܬ ܠܗ ܚ̈ܝܐ ܒܩܢܘܡܗ. ܘܐܫܠܛܗ ܟܠ
28 ܕܝܢܐ ܕܒܪܗ ܗܘ ܕܐܢܫܐ. ܘܠܐ ܬܬܕܡܪܘܢ ܒܗܕܐ.
ܕܗܐ ܟܠܗܘܢ ܐܝܠܝܢ ܕܒܩ̈ܒܪܐ ܐܢܘܢ. ܢܫܡܥܘܢ
29 ܩܠܗ ܕܐܠܗܐ ܘܢܚܘܢ ܘܢܦܩܘܢ. ܘܐܝܠܝܢ ܕܥ̈ܒܕܘ
ܛ̈ܒܬܐ ܐܢܘܢ ܢܦܩܘܢ ܠܩܝܡܬܐ ܕܚ̈ܝܐ. ܘܐܝܠܝܢ
30 ܕܥ̈ܒܕܘ ܒ̈ܝܫܬܐ ܐܢܘܢ ܢܦܩܘܢ ܠܩܝܡܬܐ ܕܕܝܢܐ. ܠܐ
ܡܫܟܚ ܐܢܐ ܡܕܡ ܡܢ ܨܒܘܬ ܢܦܫܝ ܠܡܥܒܕ. ܐܠܐ
ܐܝܟܢܐ ܕܫܡܥ ܐܢܐ ܕܐܢ ܐܢܐ. ܘܕܝܢܝ ܟܐܢ ܗܘ.
ܠܐ ܓܝܪ ܒܥܐ ܐܢܐ ܨܒܝܢܝ. ܐܠܐ ܒܥܐ ܐܢܐ ܨܒܝܢܗ
31 ܕܡܢ ܕܫܕܪܢܝ. ܐܢ ܐܢܐ ܡܣܗܕ ܐܢܐ ܥܠ ܢܦܫܝ.
32 ܣܗܕܘܬܝ ܠܐ ܗܘܬ ܫܪܝܪܐ. ܐܚܪܢ ܗܘ ܣܗܕ ܥܠܝ.
ܘܝܕܥܝܢ ܐܢܬܘܢ ܕܫܪܝܪܐ ܗܝ ܣܗܕܘܬܗ ܕܐܣܗܕ
33 ܥܠܝ. ܐܢܬܘܢ ܫܕܪܬܘܢ ܠܘܬ ܝܘܚܢܢ. ܘܐܣܗܕ ܒܫܪܪܐ.
34 ܐܢܐ ܕܝܢ ܠܐ ܗܘܐ ܡܢ ܒܪ ܐܢܫܐ ܢܣܒ ܐܢܐ
ܣܗܕܘܬܐ. ܐܠܐ ܗܠܝܢ ܐܡܪ ܐܢܐ ܕܐܢܬܘܢ ܬܚܘܢ.

ܗܘܐ ܠܗ ܡܢ ܕܗܒܠܬܐ ܠܚܒܪܬܗ̇. ܡܛܠ ܟܢܫܐ
14 ܕܐܢܫܐ. ܒܬܪ ܗܠܝܢ ܐܫܟܚܗ ܗܘܐ ܝܫܘܥ ܠܗ̇ܘ
ܕܐܬܐܣܝ، ܒܗܝܟܠܐ. ܘܐܡܪ ܠܗ. ܗܐ ܚܠܝܡ ܐܢܬ
ܬܘܒ ܠܐ ܬܣܟܠ. ܕܠܡܐ ܢܓܕܫ ܠܟ ܕܒܝܫ ܡܢ
15 ܩܕܡܝܐ. ܘܐܙܠ ܓܒܪܐ ܗܘ ܘܐܡܪ ܠܝܗ̈ܘܕܝܐ. ܕܝܫܘܥ
16 ܗܘ ܗܘ ܕܐܚܠܡܗ. ܘܡܛܠܬܗ ܪ̈ܕܦܝܢ ܗܘܘ ܝ̈ܗܘܕܝܐ
17 ܠܝܫܘܥ. ܥܠ ܕܠܡܥܒܕܐ ܥܒܕ ܗܠܝܢ ܒܫܒܬܐ. ܗܘ ܕܝܢ
ܝܫܘܥ ܐܡܪ ܠܗܘܢ. ܐܒܝ ܥܕܡܐ ܠܗܫܐ ܒܥ̈ܒܕܐ
18 ܥܒܕ. ܡܛܠ ܗܢܐ ܘܐܦ ܐܢܐ ܥܒܕܢܐ. ܝܗ̈ܘܕܝܐ ܕܝܢ
ܡܛܠ ܗܕܐ ܡܠܬܐ ܒܥܝܢ ܗܘܘ ܠܡܩܛܠܗ. ܠܐ
ܒܠܚܘܕ ܡܛܠ ܕܫܪܐ ܗܘܐ ܫܒܬܐ. ܐܠܐ ܡܛܠ
ܕܠܐܠܗܐ ܐܒܐ ܩܪܐ ܗܘܐ. ܘܡܫܘܐ ܗܘܐ ܢܦܫܗ
19 ܥܡ ܐܠܗܐ. ܐܡܪ ܠܗܘܢ ܝܫܘܥ. ܐܡܝܢ ܐܡܝܢ
ܐܡܪܢܐ ܠܟܘܢ. ܕܠܐ ܡܫܟܚ ܒܪܐ ܡܕܡ ܡܢ ܨܒܘܬ
ܢܦܫܗ ܠܡܥܒܕ. ܐܦܠܐ ܡܕܡ ܕܠܐ ܚܙܐ ܠܐܒܘܗܝ
ܕܥܒܕ. ܐܠܐ ܡܟܐ ܕܐܒܘܗܝ ܥܒܕ ܘܐܦ ܒܪܐ ܒܗ
20 ܡܬܕܡܐ. ܐܒܐ ܓܝܪ ܪܚܡ ܗܘ ܠܒܪܗ. ܘܟܠܡܕܡ
ܕܥܒܕ ܡܚܘܐ ܠܗ. ܕܗܘ ܢܥܒܕ. ܘܕܬܝܪܢ ܡܢ ܗܠܝܢ
ܥܒ̈ܕܐ ܡܚܘܐ ܠܗ. ܘܠܐ ܬܬܕܡܪܘܢ. ܕܐܡܪܬ ܠܟܘܢ.
21 ܐܝܟܢܐ ܓܝܪ ܕܐܒܐ ܡܚܝܐ ܡ̈ܝܬܐ ܘܡܩܝܡ ܠܗܘܢ.
ܗܟܢܐ ܐܦ ܒܪܐ ܡܚܝܐ ܠܐܝܠܝܢ ܕܗܘ ܨܒܐ ܒܗ.
22 ܐܦܠܐ ܓܝܪ ܠܐܢܫ ܠܐ ܕܐܢ. ܐܠܐ ܟܠܗ ܕܝܢܐ
23 ܠܒܪܗ ܝܗܒܗ̇. ܕܟܠ ܐܢܫ ܢܝܩܪ ܠܒܪܐ ܐܝܟܢܐ

53 ܐܫܬܐ. ܘܝܕܥ ܐܒܘܗܝ ܕܒܗ̇ ܒܫܥܬܐ ܕܐܡܪ ܠܗ
ܝܫܘܥ ܕܒܪܟ ܚܝܐ. ܘܗܝܡܢ ܗܘ ܘܟܠܗ ܒܝܬܗ.
54 ܗܕܐ ܗܝ ܐܬܐ ܕܬܪ̈ܬܝܢ ܕܥܒܕ ܝܫܘܥ. ܟܕ ܐܬܐ ܡܢ
ܝܗܘܕ ܠܓܠܝܠܐ ° °
V. ܒܬܪ ܗܠܝܢ ܗܘܐ ܗܘܐ ܥܐܕܐ ܕܝܗܘ̈ܕܝܐ. ܘܣܠܩ
2 ܗܘܐ ܝܫܘܥ ܠܐܘܪܫܠܡ. ܘܐܝܬ ܗܘܐ ܒܐܘܪܫܠܡ
ܕܘܟܬܐ ܚܕܐ ܕܡܥܡܘܕܝܬܐ ܕܡܬܩܪܝܐ ܒܥܒܪܝܬ
ܒܝܬ ܚܣܕܐ. ܘܐܝܬ ܒܗ̇ ܚܡ̈ܫܐ ܐܣ̈ܛܘܐܝܢ.
3 ܘܪܡܝܢ ܗܘܘ ܒܐܣ̈ܛܘܐ ܣܘܓܐܐ ܕܟܪ̈ܝܗܐ.
5 ܘܚܓ̈ܝܣܐ ܘܫ̈ܚܝܦܐ ܘܡܬܚܢ̈ܩܐ. ܘܐܝܬ ܗܘܐ ܬܡܢ
6 ܓܒܪܐ ܚܕ ܕܬܠܬܝܢ ܘܬܡܢܐ ܫ̈ܢܝܢ ܒܟܘܪܗ ܗܘܐ. ܘܟܕ
ܚܙܝܗܝ ܝܫܘܥ ܕܪܡܐ. ܝܕܥ ܕܙܒܢܐ ܣܓܝܐܐ ܐܝܬ ܠܗ.
7 ܐܡܪ ܠܗ ܨܒܐ ܐܢܬ ܕܬܗܘܐ ܚܠܝܡ. ܐܡܪ ܠܗ ܡܪܝ
ܠܝܬ ܠܝ ܐܢܫ ܕܡܐ ܕܡܬܬܙܝܥܝܢ ܡ̈ܝܐ ܢܚܬܢܝ
ܠܡܥܡܘܕܝܬܐ. ܘܥܕ ܐܢܐ ܐܬܐ ܐܚܪܢ ܡܢ ܩܕܡܝ
8 ܢܚܬ. ܐܡܪ ܠܗ ܝܫܘܥ. ܩܘܡ ܫܩܘܠ ܥܪܣܟ ܘܗܠܟ
9 ܘܐܠ ܠܒܝܬܟ. ܘܒܗ̇ ܒܫܥܬܐ ܐܬܚܠܡ ܓܒܪܐ ܗܘ
10 ܘܗܠܟ. ܘܗܘ ܝܘܡܐ ܫܒܬܐ ܗܘܐ. ܐܡܪܝܢ ܠܗ
ܝܗܘ̈ܕܝܐ. ܫܒܬܐ ܗܘ ܠܐ ܫܠܝܛ ܠܟ ܕܬܫܩܘܠ
11 ܥܪܣܟ. ܐܡܪ ܠܗܘܢ ܗܘ ܗܘ ܕܐܚܠܡܢܝ. ܗܘ ܐܡܪ
12 ܠܝ ܕܫܩܘܠ ܥܪܣܟ ܘܗܠܟ. ܐܡܪܝܢ ܠܗ ܡܢܘ ܗܢܐ
13 ܓܒܪܐ ܕܐܡܪ ܠܟ ܕܫܩܘܠ ܥܪܣܟ ܘܗܠܟ. ܘܗܘ
ܕܐܬܐܣܝ ܠܐ ܝܕܥ ܗܘܐ ܡܢܘ. ܗܘ ܓܝܪ ܝܫܘܥ ܫܢܝ

41 ܠܘܬܗܘܢ ܬܪ̈ܝܢ ܝܘ̈ܡܝܢ. ܘܣ̈ܓܝܐܐ ܗܝܡܢܘ ܒܗ.
42 ܡܛܠ ܡܠܬܗ. ܘܐܡܪܝܢ ܗܘܘ ܠܐܢܬܬܐ ܗܝ.
ܕܡܟܝܠ ܠܐ ܗܘܐ ܡܛܠ ܡܠܬܟܝ ܡܗܝܡܢܝܢ ܐܢܚܢ
ܒܗ. ܐܢܚܢ ܓܝܪ ܫܡܥܢ ܡܢܗ. ܘܝܕܥܝܢ ܕܫܪܪܐܝܬ
ܗܘܘ ܡܚܝܢܗ ܕܥܠܡܐ ܀ ܀
43 ܡܢ ܒܬܪ ܗܠܝܢ ܬܪ̈ܝܢ ܝܘ̈ܡܝܢ. ܢܦܩ ܡܢ ܬܡܢ ܝܫܘܥ
44 ܠܓܠܝܠܐ. ܗܘ ܓܝܪ ܝܫܘܥ ܣܗܕ ܗܘܐ ܕܢܒܝܐ
45 ܒܡܕܝܢܬܗ ܠܐ ܡܬܝܩܪ. ܘܟܕ ܐܬܐ ܩܒܠܘܗܝ ܓ̈ܠܝܠܝܐ.
ܟܕ ܚܙܘ ܡܕܡ ܕܥܒܕ ܒܐܘܪܫܠܡ ܒܥܐܕܐ. ܘܐܦ
46 ܗܢܘܢ ܓܝܪ ܐܬܘ ܗܘܘ ܠܥܐܕܐ. ܘܐܬܐ ܗܘܐ ܬܘܒ
ܠܩܛܢܐ ܕܓܠܝܠܐ. ܐܬܪ ܕܥܒܕ ܗܘܐ ܡ̈ܝܐ ܗܢܘܢ
ܚܡܪܐ ◉
ܘܐܝܬ ܗܘܐ ܒܟܦܪܢܚܘܡ ܥܒܕ ܡܠܟܐ ܚܕ ܕܒܪܗ
47 ܟܪܝܗ ܗܘܐ. ܟܕ ܫܡܥ ܕܝܫܘܥ ܐܬܐ ܡܢ ܓܠܝܠܐ
ܠܗܘܢ. ܐܬܐ ܠܘܬܗ. ܘܒܥܐ ܗܘܐ ܡܢܗ ܕܢܚܘܬ
48 ܘܢܐܣܐ ܠܒܪܗ. ܡܛܠ ܕܩܪܝܒ ܗܘܐ ܠܡܡܬ. ܐܡܪ ܠܗ
ܝܫܘܥ. ܐܢ ܢܝܫܐ ܘܬܕܡܪ̈ܬܐ ܠܐ ܚܙܝܬܘܢ ܠܐ
49 ܬܗܝܡܢܘܢ. ܐܡܪ ܠܗ ܥܒܕ ܡܠܟܐ ܡܪܝ ܚܘܬ ܥܕ ܠܐ
50 ܢܡܘܬ ܠܗ ܛܠܝܐ. ܐܡܪ ܠܗ ܝܫܘܥ. ܐܙܠ ܠܒܝܬܟ ܗܐ
ܒܪܟ ܚܝܐ. ܘܗܝܡܢ ܗܘ ܓܒܪܐ ܒܡܠܬܗ ܕܝܫܘܥ. ܘܟܕ
51 ܐܙܠ ܐܪܥܘܗܝ ܥܒ̈ܕܘܗܝ ܘܣܒܪܘܗܝ. ܘܐܡܪܘ ܠܗ
52 ܕܒܪܟ ܚܝܐ. ܘܫܐܠ ܐܢܘܢ ܕܒܐܝܕܐ ܫܥܬܐ ܗܘܐ
ܥܦܪ. ܐܡܪܝܢ ܠܗ ܐܬܡܠ ܒܫܥܬ ܫ̈ܒܥ ܫܒܩܬܗ

28 ܡܢܐ ܐܡܪ ܗܘܝܬ ܠܗ̇. ܘܗܝ ܐܢܬܬܐ ܫܒܩܬܗ̇
ܘܩܠܬܗ̇ ܘܐܙܠܬ ܗܘܬ ܠܡܕܝܢܬܐ. ܘܐܡܪܐ ܠܒܢܝܢܫܐ
29 ܬܘ ܚܙܘ ܓܒܪܐ ܕܐܡܪ ܠܝ ܟܠ ܡܕܡ ܕܥܒܕܬ. ܕܠܡܐ
30 ܗܘܐ ܡܫܝܚܐ. ܘܢܦܩܘ ܡܢ ܡܕܝܢܬܐ. ܘܐܬܝܢ ܗܘܘ
31 ܠܘܬܗ. ܘܬܠܡܝܕܘܗܝ ܕܝܢ ܒܥܝܢ ܗܘܘ ܡܢܗ ܕܢܐܟܘܠ
32 ܪܒܘܢ ܠܥܣܐ. ܐܡܪ ܠܗܘܢ. ܐܝܬ ܠܝ ܡܐܟܘܠܬܐ
33 ܕܐܟܘܠ ܐܢܐ ܕܐܢܬܘܢ ܠܐ ܝܕܥܝܢ ܠܗ̇. ܐܡܪܝܢ
ܗܘܘܢ ܚܕ ܠܚܕ. ܠܡܐ ܟܝ ܐܢܫ ܐܝܬܝ ܠܗ ܡܕܡ
34 ܠܡܐܟܠ. ܐܡܪ ܠܗܘܢ ܗܘ ܝܫܘܥ. ܡܐܟܘܠܬܝ ܕܝܠܝ
ܕܐܥܒܕ ܗܘ ܨܒܝܢܗ ܕܡܢ ܕܫܕܪܢܝ. ܘܐܫܠܡܝܘܗܝ
35 ܠܥܒܕܗ. ܠܐ ܐܢܬܘܢ ܐܡܪܝܢ ܕܐܪ̈ܒܥܐ ܐܝܠܝܢ ܝ̈ܪܚܝܢ
ܘܐܬܐ ܚܨܕܐ. ܗܐ ܐܡܪܢܐ ܠܟܘܢ ܕܐܪܝܡܘ
ܥ̈ܝܢܝܟܘܢ ܘܚܙܘ. ܕܐܪ̈ܥܬܐ ܚܘܪ ܘܡܛܝ ܠܚܨܕܐ. ܘܡܢ
36 ܟܕܘ ܚܨܘܕܐ ܐܓܪܐ ܢܣܒ. ܘܟܢܫ ܦܐܪ̈ܐ ܠܚܝܐ ܕܠܥܠܡ.
37 ܘܙܪܘܥܐ ܘܚܨܘܕܐ ܐܟܚܕܐ ܚܕܘܢ. ܒܗܕܐ ܓܝܪ
ܐܝܬܝܗ̇ ܡܠܬܐ ܕܫܪܪܐ. ܕܐܚܪܢ ܗܘ ܙܪܥ ܘܐܚܪܢ
38 ܗܘ ܚܨܕ. ܘܐܢܐ ܫܕܪܬܟܘܢ ܠܡܚܨܕ ܡܕܡ ܕܠܐ
ܗܘܐ ܐܢܬܘܢ ܠܐܝܬܘܢ ܒܗ. ܐܠܐ ܐܠܝܡ ܕܠܐܘ.
39 ܘܐܢܬܘܢ ܥܠܬܘܢ ܥܠ ܥܡܠܗܘܢ ܕܗܠܝܢ. ܘܡܢ
ܡܕܝܢܬܐ ܗܝ ܣܓܝܐܐ ܗܝܡܢܘ ܒܗ ܡܢ ܫܡܪ̈ܝܐ.
ܡܛܠ ܫܘܥܝܬܗ̇ ܕܗܝ ܐܢܬܬܐ. ܕܐܡܪܐ ܗܘܬ ܕܟܠ
40 ܡܕܡ ܕܥܒܕܬ ܐܡܪ ܠܝ. ܘܟܕ ܐܬܘ ܠܘܬܗ ܗܢܘܢ
ܫܡܪ̈ܝܐ. ܒܥܝܢ ܗܘܘ ܡܢܗ ܕܢܗܘܐ ܠܘܬܗܘܢ. ܘܗܘܐ

16 ܡܢ ܡܘܗܒܬܐ. ܐܡܪ ܠܗ̇ ܝܫܘܥ ܐܙܠܝ ܩܪܝ ܠܒܥܠܟܝ ܘܬܝ
17 ܠܗܪܟܐ. ܐܡܪܐ ܠܗ ܠܝܬ ܠܝ ܒܥܠܐ. ܐܡܪ ܠܗ̇ ܝܫܘܥ
18 ܫܦܝܪ ܐܡܪܬܝ. ܕܠܝܬ ܠܝ ܒܥܠܐ. ܚܡܫܐ ܓܝܪ ܒ̈ܥܠܝܢ
ܗܘܘ ܠܟܝ ܘܗܢܐ ܕܐܝܬ ܠܟܝ ܗܫܐ ܠܐ ܗܘܐ ܒܥܠܟܝ.
19 ܗܕܐ ܫܪܝܪܬܐ ܐܡܪܬܝ. ܐܡܪܐ ܠܗ ܗܝ ܐܢܬܬܐ.
20 ܡܪܝ ܚܙܝܐ ܐܢܐ ܕܢܒܝܐ ܐܢܬ. ܐܒ̈ܗܝܢ ܒܗܢܐ ܛܘܪܐ
ܣܓܕܘ. ܘܐܢܬܘܢ ܕܝܢ ܐܡܪܝܢ ܐܢܬܘܢ ܕܒܐܘܪܫܠܡ
21 ܗܘ ܒܝܬ ܣܓܕܬܐ. ܐܡܪ ܠܗ̇ ܝܫܘܥ. ܐܢܬܬܐ
ܗܝܡܢܝܢܝ ܕܐܬܝܐ ܫܥܬܐ. ܕܠܐ ܒܗܢܐ ܛܘܪܐ.
22 ܐܦܠܐ ܒܐܘܪܫܠܡ ܬܣܓܕܘܢ ܠܐܒܐ. ܐܢܬܘܢ ܣܓܕܝܢ
ܐܢܬܘܢ ܠܡܕܡ ܕܠܐ ܝܕܥܝܢ ܐܢܬܘܢ. ܘܐܢܚܢ ܣܓܕܝܢ
ܐܢܚܢ ܠܡܕܡ ܕܝܕܥܝܢ ܐܢܚܢ. ܕܚ̈ܝܐ ܡܢ ܝܗܘܕܝܐ
ܐܢܘܢ. ܐܠܐ ܐܬܝܐ ܫܥܬܐ ܘܗܫܐ ܐܝܬܝܗ.
ܕܣ̈ܓܘܕܐ ܫܪ̈ܝܪܐ ܢܣܓܕܘܢ ܠܐܒܐ ܒܪܘܚܐ ܘܒܫܪܪܐ.
ܘܐܦ ܐܒܐ ܓܝܪ ܐܝܟ ܗܠܝܢ ܗܘ ܣ̈ܓܘܕܐ ܒܥܐ.
24 ܐܠܗܐ ܓܝܪ ܪܘܚܐ ܗܘ. ܘܐܝܠܝܢ ܕܣܓܕܝܢ ܠܗ ܒܪܘܚܐ.
ܘܠܡܣܓܕ ܠܗܘܢ ܘܠܐ ܠܐܝܠܝܢ ܕܒܪܘܚܐ ܘܒܫܪܪܐ
25 ܣܓܕܝܢ ܠܗ. ܐܡܪܐ ܠܗ ܗܝ ܐܢܬܬܐ. ܝܕܥܐ ܐܢܐ ܐܢܐ
ܕܡܫܝܚܐ ܐܬܐ. ܘܡܐ ܕܐܬܐ ܗܘ ܡܚܘܐ ܠܢ ܟܠ
26 ܡܕܡ. ܐܡܪ ܠܗ̇ ܝܫܘܥ. ܐܢܐ ܐܢܐ ܕܡܡܠܠ ܐܢܐ
27 ܥܡܟܝ. ܘܟܕ ܗܠܝܢ ܡܡܠܠ. ܐܬܘ ܬܠܡ̈ܝܕܘܗܝ
ܘܡܬܕܡܪܝܢ ܗܘܘ ܕܥܡ ܐܢܬܬܐ ܡܡܠܠ ܗܘܐ.
ܡܟܐܡܪ ܕܝܢ ܠܐ ܐܡܪܘ ܠܗ ܕܐܘ ܡܢܐ ܒܥܬ ܐܘ

6 ܗܘܐ *********ܣܦ ܒܪܗ. ******** ܕܝܢ ܬܡܢ
**********ܐ ܕܝܥܩܘܒ. **********ܒ ܝܬܒ*******
ܕܡܥܝܢܐ. ****ܫ ܡܢ ܥܡܠܐ ܕܐܘܪܚܐ. ܘܬܠܡ̈ܝܕܘܗܝ
ܥܠܘ ܗܘܘ ܠܩܪܝܐ ܗܘ ܕܢܙܒܢܘܢ ܠܗܘܢ ܣܝܒܪܬܐ. ܘܟܕ
7 ܗܘ ܝܫܘܥ ܝܬܒ ܐܝܬ ܗܘܝ ܐܝܟ ܫ̈ܥܐ ܫܬ. ܘܐܬܬ
ܗܘܬ ܐܢܬܬܐ ܚܕܐ ܡܢ ܫܡܪܝܢ ܕܬܡܠܐ ܡ̈ܝܐ. ܐܡܪ
9 ܠܗ̇ ܝܫܘܥ ܗܒ ܠܝ ܡ̈ܝܐ ܐܢܬܬܐ. ܐܡܪܐ ܠܗ ܗܝ
ܐܢܬܬܐ ܫܡܪܝܬܐ. ܗܐ ܝܗܘܕܝܐ ܐܢܬ. ܐܝܟܢܐ
ܫܐܠܐ ܐܢܬ ܠܝ ܡ̈ܝܐ ܠܡܫܬܐ. ܕܗܘܝܐ ܐܢܐ ܫܡܪܝܬܐ
ܐܢܐ. ܝܗܘ̈ܕܝܐ ܓܝܪ ܠܐ ܡܬܚܠܛܝܢ ܥܡ ܫܡܪ̈ܝܐ.
10 ܐܡܪ ܠܗ̇ ܝܫܘܥ. ܐܠܘ ܝܕܥܐ ܗܘܝܬ ܡܘܗܒܬܗ
ܕܐܠܗܐ. ܘܡܢܘ ܗܢܐ ܕܐܡܪ ܠܟܝ ܗܒܝ ܠܝ ܐܫܬܐ.
ܐܢܬܝ ܫܐܠܐ ܗܘܝܬܝ ܠܗ. ܘܝܗܒ ܗܘܐ ܠܟܝ ܡ̈ܝܐ
11 ܚ̈ܝܐ. ܐܡܪܐ ܠܗ ܗܝ ܐܢܬܬܐ. ܡܪܝ ܐܦܠܐ ܕܘܠܐ
ܐܝܬ ܠܟ. ܘܒܪܐ ܥܡܝܩܐ ܗܝ. ܐܝܟܢܐ ܐܝܬ ܠܟ
12 ܡ̈ܝܐ ܚ̈ܝܐ. ܕܠܡܐ ܐܢܬ ܪܒ ܐܢܬ ܡܢ ܐܒܘܢ ܝܥܩܘܒ.
ܕܗܘ ܝܗܒ ܠܢ ܒܐܪܐ ܗܕܐ. ܘܐܦ ܗܘ ܡܢܗ̇ ܐܫܬܝ
13 ܘܒ̈ܢܘܗܝ ܘܒܥܝܪܗ. ܐܡܪ ܠܗ̇ ܝܫܘܥ ܟܘܠ ܕܢܫܬܐ ܡܢ
14 ܗܠܝܢ ܡ̈ܝܐ ܬܘܒ ܨܗܐ. ܘܟܠ ܕܢܫܬܐ ܡܢ ܡ̈ܝܐ
ܐܝܠܝܢ ܕܐܢܐ ܐܬܠ ܠܗ ܬܘܒ ܠܐ ܨܗܐ ܠܥܠܡ. ܐܠܐ
ܡ̈ܝܐ ܗܢܘܢ ܕܐܬܠ ܠܗ ܢܗܘܘܢ ܒܗ ܡܒܘܥܐ ܕܡ̈ܝܐ
15 ܚ̈ܝܐ ܕܠܥܠܡ. ܐܡܪܐ ܠܗ ܐܢܬܬܐ ܗܝ. ܡܪܝ ܗܒ
ܠܝ ܡܢ ܗܠܝܢ ܡ̈ܝܐ. ܕܠܐ ܗܘܝܬ ܨܗܝܐ ܘܐܬܝܐ ܕܠܐ

28 ܐܢ ܝܗܝܒ ܠܗ ܡܢ ܫܡܝܐ. ܐܢܬܘܢ ܕܝܢ ܣܗܕܝܢ ܠܝ
ܕܐܢܐ ܐܡܪܬ ܕܠܐ ܗܘܝܬ ܡܫܝܚܐ. ܐܠܐ ܫܠܝܚܐ
29 ܐܢܐ ܩܕܡܘܗܝ. ܡܢ ܕܐܝܬ ܠܗ ܓܝܪ ܟܠܬܐ ܗܘܝܘ
ܚܬܢܐ. ܘܪܚܡܗ ܕܚܬܢܐ ܗܘ ܡܢ ܕܩܐܡ ܘܨܐܬ
ܠܗ. ܘܚܕܘܬܐ ܪܒܬܐ ܚܕܐ. ܡܛܠ ܩܠܗ ܕܚܬܢܐ.
30 ܗܕܐ ܗܟܝܠ ܚܕܘܬܝ ܗܐ ܡܫܬܠܡܐ ܗܝ. ܠܗ ܗܘ ܓܝܪ
31 ܘܠܐ ܠܡܪܒܐ *** ܠܡܒܨܪ. ܗܘ ܓܝܪ *** ܠܥܠ ܐܬܐ
ܠܥܠ ܡܢ ** ܗܘ. ܘܗܘ ܕܡܢ ܐ*** ܗܘ ܡܢ ܐܪܥܐ ܗ*
*** ܐܪܥܐ ܗܘ ܡ*** ܘܗܘ ܕܡܢ ܫ*** ܐܬܐ.
32 ܡܕܡ **** ܘܫܡܥ ܡܣܗܕ. ******* ܠܐ ܟܠ
33 ܐܢܫ **** ܐܝܢܐ ܕܡ** ܣܗܕܘܬܗ *** ܕܐܠܗܐ
34 ܫ****** ܐܝܢܐ ܓܝܪ ***** ܫܕܪܗ ܡ̈ܠ****
**** ܡܡܠܠ. ܠܐ ******* ܒܟܝܠܬܐ ***
35 ******* ܐܒܐ ܠܒ**** ܪܚܡ ܗܘ ***** ܡܕܡ
36 ܗܘ ********* ܡܢ ܕܒܗ ********* ܐܝܬ ܠܗ ***
***** ܘܡܢ ܕ** ******* **ܪܐ ܠܐ ܚܙܐ ܚܝ̈ܐ.
*ܠܐ ܪܘܓܙܗ ܕܐܠܗܐ **ܘܐ ܥܠܘܗܝ ◦ ◦ ◦
IV. ** ܝܕܥ ܕܝܢ ܝܫܘܥ ***ܥܘ ܦܪ̈ܝܫܐ ***ܘ ܕܬܠܡ̈ܝܕܘܗܝ
2 ******* ܡܥܡܕ ܗܘܐ ܣܓܝ*****ܢ. ܘܠܐ ܗܘܐ ***ܒ
3 ܡܥܡܕ ܗܘܐ *** ܬܠܡ̈ܝܕܘܗܝ. ***** ܠܝܗܘܕ
4 ܘܐܙܠ*****ܒ ܠܓܠܝܠܐ. ***** ܗܘܬ ܠܗ ***
5 **** ܕܢܥܒܪ ܥܠ *** ***ܐ. ܘܐܬܐ ******ܕܐ
ܕܡ̈ܬܩܪܝܐ ******* ܗܘܬ ****ܬ ܡܪܥܝܬܐ***ܒ

17 ܕܠܥܠܡ. ܠܐ ܓܝܪ ܫܕܪ ܐܠܗܐ ܠܒܪܗ ܠܥܠܡܐ
18 ܕܢܕܘܢܝܘܗܝ ܠܥܠܡܐ. ܐܠܐ ܕܥܠܡܐ ܒܗ ܢܚܐ. ܡܢ
ܕܡܗܝܡܢ ܒܗ ܠܐ ܡܬܕܝܢ. ܘܡܢ ܕܠܐ ܕܝܢ ܡܗܝܡܢ
ܡܚܝܒ ܗܘ. ܕܠܐ ܗܝܡܢ ܒܫܡܗ ܕܒܪܗ ܕܐܠܗܐ
19 ܝܚܝܕܐ. ܗܢܐ ܗܘ ܕܝܢ ܕܝܢܐ ܕܢܘܗܪܐ ܐܬܐ ܠܥܠܡܐ.
ܘܥܠܡܐ ܝܬܝܪܐ ܪܚܡ ܠܚܫܘܟܐ. ܝܬܝܪ ܡܢ
20 ܕܠܢܘܗܪܐ. ܡܛܠ ܕܒܝܫܝܢ ܗܘܘ ܥܒ̈ܕܘܗܝ. ܡܢ ܕܒ̈ܝܫܬܐ
ܥܒܕ ܣܢܐ ܠܢܘܗܪܐ. ܘܠܐ ܐܬܐ ܠܢܘܗܪܐ. ܕܠܐ
21 ܬܗܘܐ ܡܟܣܢܘܬܐ ܠܥܒ̈ܕܘܗܝ. ܗܘ ܕܝܢ ܕܥܒܕ
ܩܘܫܬܐ. ܐܬܐ ܠܘܬ ܢܘܗܪܐ. ܕܢܬܚܙܘܢ ܥܒ̈ܕܘܗܝ
ܕܒܐܠܗܐ ܥܒܝܕܝܢ ◦ ◦ ◦
22 ܒܬܪ ܗܠܝܢ ܢܦܩ ܝܫܘܥ ܘܬܠܡܝ̈ܕܘܗܝ ܠܐܪܥܐ ܕܝܗܘܕ.
ܘܬܡܢ ܡܬܗܦܟ ܗܘܐ ܥܡܗܘܢ. ܘܡܥܡܕ ܗܘܐ.
23 ܐܦ ܝܘܚܢܢ ܡܥܡܕ ܗܘܐ ܒܥܝܢ ܢܘܢ ܕܠܓܒ ܫܠܝܡ.
ܡܛܠ ܕܡ̈ܝܐ ܣܓܝ̈ܐܐ ܐܝܬ ܗܘܘ ܬܡܢ. ܘܐܬܝܢ
24 ܗܘܘ ܐܢܫܐ ܘܥܡܕܝܢ. ܠܐ ܓܝܪ ܥܕܡܐ ܠܗܫܐ ܢܦܠ
ܗܘܐ ܝܘܚܢܢ ܒܝܬ ܐ̈ܣܝܪܐ ܀ ܀
25 ܗܘܬ ܗܘܬ ܕܝܢ ܒܥܬܐ ܒܝܢܬ ܬܠܡܝ̈ܕܘܗܝ ܕܝܘܚܢܢ.
26 ܥܡ ܝܗܘ̈ܕܝܐ ܥܠ ܬܕܟܝܬܐ. ܘܐܬܘ ܠܘܬ ܝܘܚܢܢ
ܘܐܡܪܝܢ ܠܗ. ܪܒܢ. ܗܘ ܕܥܡܟ ܗܘܐ ܒܥܒܪܐ ܕܝܘܪܕܢ.
ܘܐܢܬ ܣܗܕܬ ܥܠܘܗܝ. ܗܐ ܐܦ ܗܘ ܡܥܡܕ.
27 ܘܥܠܝܢ ܐܢܫܐ ܠܘܬܗ ܐܬܝܢ. ܐܡܪ ܠܗܘܢ ܝܘܚܢܢ.
ܠܐ ܡܫܟܚ ܒܪ ܐܢܫܐ ܠܡܣܒ ܐܦܠܐ ܡܕܡ. ܐܠܐ

6 ܠܡܠܟܘܬܐ ܕܐܠܗܐ. ܡܕܡ ܕܝܠܝܕ ܡܢ ܒܣܪܐ ܒܣܪܐ
ܗܘ. ܡܛܠ ܕܡܢ ܒܣܪ ܝܠܝܕ. ܘܡܕܡ ܕܝܠܝܕ ܡܢ ܪܘܚܐ
ܪܘܚܐ ܗܘ. ܡܛܠ ܕܐܠܗܐ ܪܘܚܐ ܗܘ. ܘܡܢ ܐܠܗܐ
7 ܐܬܝܠܕ. ܘܠܐ ܬܬܕܡܪ ܕܐܡܪܬ ܠܟ. ܕܘܠܐ ܗܘ ܠܟܘܢ
8 ܠܡܬܝܠܕܘ ܡܢ ܠܥܠ. ܪܘܚܐ ܐܬܪ ܕܨܒܝܐ ܢܫܒܐ.
ܘܩܠܗ ܗܘ ܒܠܚܘܕ ܫܡܥ ܐܢܬ. ܐܠܐ ܠܐ ܡܢ
ܐܝܟܢܐ ܐܬܬ ܝܕܥ ܐܢܬ. ܘܠܐ ܠܐܝܟܐ ܐܙܠܐ.
ܗܟܢܐ ܐܝܬܘܗܝ ܟܠ ܐܢܫ ܕܡܬܝܠܕ ܡܢ ܪ̈ܘܚܐ ܘܡܢ
9 ܪܘܚܐ. ܥܢܐ ܢܩܕܝܡܘܣ ܘܐܡܪ ܠܗ. ܐܝܟܢܐ
10 ܡܫܟܚܐ ܗܕܐ ܠܡܗܘܐ. ܥܢܐ ܝܫܘܥ ܘܐܡܪ ܠܗ.
ܐܢܬ ܗܘ ܡܠܦܢܗ ܕܐܝܣܪܝܠ ܘܗܠܝܢ ܠܐ ܝܕܥ ܐܢܬ.
11 ܐܡܝܢ ܐܡܝܢ ܐܡܪܢܐ ܠܟ. ܕܡܕܡ ܕܝܕܥܝܢ ܐܢܚܢ
ܡܡܠܠܝܢ ܐܢܚܢ. ܘܡܕܡ ܕܚܙܝܢ ܐܢܚܢ ܡܣܗܕܝܢ
12 ܐܢܚܢ. ܘܣܗܕܘܬܢ ܠܐ ܡܩܒܠܝܢ ܐܢܬܘܢ. ܐܢ ܟܠ
ܐܠܝܢ ܕܒܐܪܥܐ ܐܡܪܬ ܠܟܘܢ ܘܠܐ ܡܗܝܡܢܝܢ
ܐܢܬܘܢ. ܐܝܟܢܐ ܐܢ ܟܠ ܐܠܝܢ ܕܒܫܡܝܐ ܐܡܪ
13 ܠܟܘܢ ܬܗܝܡܢܘܢ. ܠܐ ܐܢܫ ܣܠܩ ܠܫܡܝܐ ܐܠܐ ܗܘ
ܕܢܚܬ ܡܢ ܫܡܝܐ. ܒܪܗ ܕܐܢܫܐ ܗܘ ܕܐܝܬܘܗܝ ܗܘܐ
14 ܒܫܡܝܐ. ܘܐܝܟܢܐ ܕܐܪܝܡ ܡܘܫܐ ܚܘܝܐ ܒܡܕܒܪܐ.
15 ܗܟܢܐ ܘܠܐ ܠܡܬܬܪܝܡܘ ܠܒܪܗ ܕܐܢܫܐ. ܕܟܠ ܐܢܫ
16 ܕܡܗܝܡܢ ܒܗ ܢܗܘܘܢ ܠܗ ܚ̈ܝܐ ܕܠܥܠܡ. ܗܟܢܐ
ܓܝܪ ܐܚܒ ܐܠܗܐ ܠܥܠܡܐ. ܐܝܟܢܐ ܕܠܒܪܗ ܝܚܝܕܐ
ܢܬܠ. ܕܟܠ ܐܢܫ ܕܡܗܝܡܢ ܒܗ ܢܗܘܘܢ ܠܗ ܚ̈ܝܐ

ܐܝܬ ܕܢܫܬܐ ܪܘܡܚܐ ܘܡܚܡܘܐ ܒܠܘܗܝ. ܗܘ ܗܘ
34 ܡܚܡܒܝ ܒܪܘܡܚܐ ܕܩܘܕܙܐ. ܘܐܙܠ ܢܦܩ ܘܐܬܗܦܟܬ
ܕܗܘܠ ܥܒܝܗ ܕܐܠܗܐ ◦
35 ܘܠܡܘܡܝܐ ܚܙܝܐ ܡܐܡ ܗܘܐ ܢܡܘܣ. ܘܐܘܪܝܡ ܡܢ
36 ܬܠܬܚܝܕܘܗܝ ܠܗܬܗ. ܘܚܪ ܒܢܡܘܣ ܒܢ ܡܗܠܟ. ܘܐܡܪ
37 ܗܘܐ ܡܫܝܚܐ. ܗܘ ܐܡܪܗ ܕܐܠܗܐ. ܘܒܢ ܢܡܘܣ
ܗܘܝ ܬܠܬܚܝܕܘܗܝ ܕܝܘܚܢܢ. ܐܘܠܐ ܠܗܘܢ ܒܬܪܗ
38 ܕܢܡܘܣ. ܘܐܬܦܩܝܢ ܗܘ ܢܡܘܣ ܘܚܙܐ ܐܢܘܢ ܕܐܬܘܢ
ܒܬܪܗ. ܘܐܡܪ ܠܗܘܢ ܡܢܐ ܒܥܝܢ ܐܢܬܘܢ. ܐܡܪܝܢ
39 ܠܗ ܪܒܢ ܐܝܟܐ ܗܘܐ ܐܢܬ. ܐܡܪ ܠܗܘܢ ܬܘ
ܘܬܚܙܘܢ. ܘܗܘܢ ܐܬܘ ܒܬܪܗ ܘܚܙܘ ܐܝܟܐ ܕܗܘܐ.
ܘܠܘܬܗ ܗܘܘ ܝܘܡܐ ܗܘ. ܘܐܡܪ ܗܘܘ ܐܝܟ ܫܥܐ
40 ܥܣܪ. ܘܚܕ ܡܢܗܘܢ ܡܢ ܬܠܝܢ ܬܠܬܚܝܕܘܗܝ ܕܝܘܚܢܢ.
41 ܐܢܕܪܘܣ ܫܡܗ ܗܘܐ. ܐܚܘܗܝ ܕܫܡܥܘܢ ܟܐܦܐ.
ܘܗܘ ܐܢܕܪܘܣ ܚܙܐ ܠܫܡܥܘܢ ܟܐܦܐ. ܘܐܡܪ
42 ܠܗ ܐܫܟܚܢܗܝ ܠܡܫܝܚܐ. ܘܕܒܪܗ ܘܐܬܐ ܠܘܬ
ܢܡܘܣ. ܘܚܪ ܒܗ ܢܡܘܣ ܘܐܡܪ * * * * *
* * * * * * * * * * * *
* * * * * * * * * * * *
* * * * * * * * * * * *
* * * * * * * * * * * *
* * * * * * * * * * * *
* * * * * * * * * * * *

21 ܠܐ ܗܘܝܬ ܡܫܝܚܐ. ܘܐܡܪܝܢ ܠܗ ܘܠܡܐ ܢܒܝܐ
22 ܐܢܬ. ܐܡܪ ܠܗܘܢ ܠܐ. ܐܡܪܝܢ ܠܗ ܘܡܢ ܐܢܬ. ܐܡܪ
ܠܢ ܕܢܬܠ ܦܬܓܡܐ ܠܗܢܘܢ ܕܫܕܪܘܢ. ܡܢܐ ܐܡܪ
23 ܐܢܬ ܥܠ ܢܦܫܟ. ܐܡܪ ܐܢܐ ܩܠܐ ܕܩܪܐ ܒܡܕܒܪܐ.
ܬܩܢܘ ܐܘܪܚܐ ܠܡܪܝܐ. ܐܝܟܢܐ ܕܐܡܪ ܐܫܥܝܐ
24, 25 ܢܒܝܐ. ܘܡܫܕܪܝܢ ܗܘܘ ܘܐܡܪܝܢ ܠܗ. ܡܢܐ ܗܟܝܠ
ܡܥܡܕ ܐܢܬ ܐܠܐ ܗܘܝܬ ܐܢܬ ܡܫܝܚܐ. ܐܦܠܐ
26 ܐܠܝܐ. ܐܦܠܐ ܢܒܝܐ. ܐܡܪ ܠܗܘܢ ܝܘܚܢܢ. ܐܢܐ
ܡܥܡܕ ܐܢܐ ܒ̈ܡܝܐ. ܒܝܢܬܟܘܢ ܕܝܢ ܩܐܡ ܗܘ ܐܢܐ
27 ܕܐܢܬܘܢ ܠܐ ܝܕܥܝܢ ܐܢܬܘܢ ܠܗ. ܗܘ ܕܐܬܐ ܒܬܪܝ.
ܗܘ ܕܠܐ ܫܘܐ ܐܢܐ ܕܐܫܪܐ ܥܪܩܐ ܕܡ̈ܣܐܢܘܗܝ.
28 ܗܠܝܢ ܡܠܠ ܒܝܬ ܥܢܝܐ. ܒܥܒܪܗ ܕܝܘܪܕܢܢ ܢܗܪܐ.
ܐܝܟܐ ܕܡܥܡܕ ܗܘܐ ܝܘܚܢܢ ◦
29 ܘܠܝܘܡܐ ܐܚܪܢܐ ܚܙܐ ܠܝܫܘܥ ܟܕ ܐܬܐ ܠܘܬܗ.
ܘܐܡܪ ܗܐ ܐܡܪܗ ܕܐܠܗܐ. ܗܢܘ ܡܢ ܕܫܩܠ
30 ܚܛܝܬܗ ܕܥܠܡܐ. ܗܢܘ ܕܐܡܪܬ ܥܠܘܗܝ ܕܓܒܪܐ
ܐܬܐ ܒܬܪܝ، ܘܗܘܐ ܠܗ ܩܕܡܝ. ܡܛܠ ܕܩܕܡܝ ܗܘ
31 ܗܘܐ. ܘܐܢܐ ܠܐ ܝܕܥ ܗܘܝܬ ܠܗ. ܐܠܐ ܡܛܠ
ܕܢܬܝܕܥ ܠܐܝܣܪܝܠ. ܡܛܠ ܗܢܐ ܐܬܝܬ ܐܢܐ
32 ܕܒ̈ܡܝܐ ܐܥܡܕ. ܘܣܗܕ ܝܘܚܢܢ ܘܐܡܪ. ܚܙܝܬ
ܠܪܘܚܐ ܕܐܝܟ ܝܘܢܐ ܢܚܬܬ ܡܢ ܫܡܝܐ ܘܩܘܝܬ
33 ܥܠܘܗܝ. ܘܐܢܐ ܠܐ ܝܕܥ ܗܘܝܬ ܠܗ. ܐܠܐ ܡܢ
ܕܫܕܪܢܝ ܠܡܥܡܕܘ ܒ̈ܡܝܐ. ܗܘ ܐܡܪ ܠܝ. ܕܐܝܢܐ ܕܚܙܐ

6 ܗܘܐ ܓܒܪܐ ܕܐܫܬܕܪ ܡܢ ܐܠܗܐ. ܫܡܗ ܗܘܐ
7 ܝܘܚܢܢ. ܗܢܐ ܐܬܐ ܠܣܗܕܘܬܐ ܕܢܣܗܕ ܥܠ ܢܘܗܪܐ.
8 ܘܕܟܠܐܢܫ ܢܗܝܡܢ ܒܐܝܕܗ. ܠܐ ܗܘܐ ܗܘ ܢܘܗܪܐ.
9 ܐܠܐ ܣܗܕܐ ܗܘ ܕܢܘܗܪܐ. ܐܝܬܘܗܝ ܕܝܢ ܢܘܗܪܐ
ܕܫܪܪܐ. ܕܡܢܗܪ ܠܟܠ ܒܪ ܐܢܫ ܕܐܬܐ ܠܥܠܡܐ.
10 ܒܥܠܡܐ ܗܘܐ. ܘܗܘ ܥܠܡܐ ܒܗ ܗܘܐ. ܘܥܠܡܐ
11, 12 ܠܐ ܝܕܥܗ. ܠܕܝܠܗ ܐܬܐ ܘܕܝܠܗ ܠܐ ܩܒܠܘܗܝ. ܐܝܠܝܢ
ܕܝܢ ܕܩܒܠܘܗܝ ܝܗܒ ܠܗܘܢ ܫܘܠܛܢܐ ܕܒܢܝܐ ܕܐܠܗܐ
13 ܢܗܘܘܢ. ܐܝܠܝܢ ܕܒܫܡܗ ܡܗܝܡܢܝܢ. ܐܝܠܝܢ ܕܠܐ
ܒܕܡܐ ܘܠܐ ܡܢ ܨܒܝܢܐ ܕܒܣܪܐ. ܘܠܐ ܡܢ ܨܒܝܢܐ
14 ܕܓܒܪܐ. ܐܠܐ ܡܢ ܐܠܗܐ ܐܬܝܠܕܘ. ܘܡܠܬܐ ܦܓܪܐ
ܗܘܬ ܘܐܓܢܬ ܒܢ. ܘܚܙܝܢ ܫܘܒܚܗ ܐܝܟ ܫܘܒܚܐ
ܕܝܚܝܕܝܐ ܕܡܢ ܐܒܐ. ܕܡܠܐ ܛܝܒܘܬܐ ܘܩܘܫܬܐ ܀
15 ܘܝܘܚܢܢ ܐܣܗܕ ܥܠܘܗܝ ܘܩܥܐ ܘܐܡܪ. ܗܢܐ ܗܘ
ܕܐܡܪܬ ܗܘܝܬ ܕܒܬܪܝ ܐܬܐ ܘܗܘܐ ܠܗ ܩܕܡܝ.
16 ܡܛܠ ܕܩܕܡܝ ܗܘ ܡܢܝ. ܘܡܢ ܡܠܝܘܬܗ ܐܚܢܢ ܟܠܢ
17 ܢܣܒܢ ܐܚܢܢ. ܘܛܝܒܘܬܐ ܚܠܦ ܛܝܒܘܬܐ. ܕܢܡܘܣܐ
ܒܝܕ ܡܘܫܐ ܐܬܝܗܒ. ܘܛܝܒܘܬܐ ܘܩܘܫܬܐ ܒܝܕ
18 ܝܫܘܥ ܡܫܝܚܐ ܗܘܬ. ܠܐܠܗܐ ܡܢ ܡܬܘܡ ܐܢܫ
ܠܐ ܚܙܝܗܝ. ܝܚܝܕܝܐ ܒܪܐ ܕܡܢ ܒܥܘܒܗ ܕܐܒܘܗܝ. ܗܘ
19 ܐܫܬܥܝ ܠܢ. ܘܗܕܐ ܗܝ ܣܗܕܘܬܗ ܕܝܘܚܢܢ. ܟܕ ܫܕܪܘ
ܠܘܬܗ ܡܢ ܐܘܪܫܠܡ. ܝܗܘܕܝܐ ܟܗܢ̈ܐ ܘܠܘܝܐ.
20 ܘܫܐܠܘܗܝ ܠܗ ܐܢܬ ܡܢ ܐܢܬ. ܘܐܘܕܝ ܘܐܡܪ ܕܐܢܐ

ܕܡܗܝܡܢܝܢ ܒܝ. ܗܠܝܢ ܒܫܡܝ ܫ̈ܐܕܐ ܢܦܩܘܢ. ܒܠܫܢܐ
18 ܚܕܬܐ ܢܡܠܠܘܢ. ܚܘ̈ܘܬܐ ܢܫܩܠܘܢ ܒܐܝ̈ܕܝܗܘܢ. ܘܐܢ
ܡܕܡ ܣܡܐ ܕܡܡܝܬܐ ܢܫܬܘܢ ܠܐ ܢܗܪܐ ܐܢܘܢ. ܥܠ
ܟܪ̈ܝܗܐ ܢܣܝܡܘܢ ܐܝ̈ܕܝܗܘܢ ܘܢܬܚܠܡܘܢ ◦
19 ܡܪܢ ܕܝܢ ܝܫܘܥ ܡܢ ܒܬܪ ܕܦܩܕ ܠܬܠܡܝ̈ܕܘܗܝ ܐܣܬܠܩ
20 ܠܫܡܝܐ. ܘܝܬܒ ܡܢ ܝܡܝܢܐ ܕܐܠܗܐ. ܗܢܘܢ ܕܝܢ
ܢܦܩܘ ܘܐܟܪܙܘ ܒܟܠ ܕܘܟܐ. ܟܕ ܡܪܢܐ ܒܥܕܪܗܘܢ
ܒܟܠ. ܘܡܫܠܡܗܘܢ ܡܒܪ ܗܘܐ ܒܐ̈ܬܘܬܐ ܕܥܒܕܝܢ
ܗܘܘ ◦ ⁘ ◦

ܫܠܡ. ܐܘܢܓܠܝܘܢ.

ܕܡܪܩܘܣ.

ܐܘܢܓܠܝܘܢ. ܕܝܘܚܢܢ.

1. ܒܪܫܝܬ ܐܝܬܘܗܝ ܗܘܐ ܡܠܬܐ. ܘܗܘ ܡܠܬܐ
ܐܝܬܘܗܝ ܗܘܐ ܠܘܬ ܐܠܗܐ. ܘܐܠܗܐ ܐܝܬܘܗܝ
2 ܗܘܐ ܗܘ ܡܠܬܐ. ܗܢܐ ܐܝܬܘܗܝ ܗܘܐ ܒܪܫܝܬ
3 ܠܘܬ ܐܠܗܐ. ܟܠܡܕܡ ܒܗ ܗܘܐ. ܘܒܠܥܕܘܗܝ ܐܦ
4 ܠܐ ܚܕܐ ܗܘܬ. ܗܘ ܕܝܢ ܡܕܡ ܕܗܘܐ ܒܗ ܚ̈ܝܐ
ܐܝܬܝ. ܘܚ̈ܝܐ ܐܝܬܝܗܘܢ ܢܘܗܪܐ ܕܒ̈ܢܝ ܐܢܫܐ.
5 ܘܗܘ ܢܘܗܪܐ ܒܚܫܘܟܐ ܡܢܗܪ ܗܘܐ. ܘܚܫܘܟܐ
ܠܐ ܐܕܪܟܗ. ◦ ◦ ◦

ܕܡܬܝ

ܘܝ ܠܟܘܢ ܣܦܪ̈ܐ ܘܦܪ̈ܝܫܐ ܢܣܒܝ ܒܐ̈ܦܐ. ܕܡܕܟܝܢ 25
ܐܢܬܘܢ ܒܪܗ ܕܟܣܐ ܘܕܦܝܠܣܐ. ܘܡܢ ܠܓܘ * *

* * * * * * * * * * * *
* * * * * * * * * * * *
* * * * * * * * * * * *
* * * * * * * * * * * *
* * * * * * * * * * * *
* * * * * * * * * * * *
* * * * * * * * * * * *

* * * * * * * * * * * *
* * * * * * * * * * * *
* * * * * * * * * * * *
* * * * * * * * * * * *
* * * * * * * * * * * *
* * * * * * * * * * * *
* * * * * * * * * * * *
* * * * * * * * * * * *

ܐܢܬܘܢ ܒ̈ܬܐ ܕܐܪܡܠܬܐ. ܒܥܠܬܐ ܕܡܘܪܟܝܢ
ܐܢܬܘܢ ܨܠܘܬܟܘܢ. ܡܛܠ ܗܢܐ ܬܩܒܠܘܢ ܕܝܢܐ
ܝܬܝܪܐ ◦◦ ◦◦ ◦◦

15 ܘܝ ܠܟܘܢ ܣܦܪ̈ܐ ܘܦܪ̈ܝܫܐ ܢܣܒܝ ܒܐܦܐ. ܕܡܬܟܪܟܝܢ
ܐܢܬܘܢ ܝܡܐ ܘܝܒܫܐ ܠܡܥܒܕܘ ܚܕ ܓܝܘܪܐ. ܘܡܐ
ܕܗܘܐ ܥܒܕܝܢ ܐܢܬܘܢ ܠܗ ܒܪܗ ܕܓܗܢܐ ܐܥܦܐ
ܥܠܝܟܘܢ ◦◦◦◦

16 ܘܝ ܠܟܘܢ ܡܕܒܪ̈ܢܐ ܥܘܝܪ̈ܐ. ܕܐܡܪܝܢ ܐܢܬܘܢ ܡܢ
ܕܝܡܐ ܒܗܝܟܠܐ ܠܐ ܡܕܡ. ܘܡܢ ܕܝܡܐ ܒܕܗܒܐ
17 ܕܒܗܝܟܠܐ ܚܝܒ. ܘܣܟ̈ܠܐ ܥܘܝܪ̈ܐ ܡܢܘ ܓܝܪ ܪܒ ܕܗܒܐ
18 ܐܘ ܗܝܟܠܐ ܕܗܘ ܡܩܕܫ ܠܗ ܠܕܗܒܐ. ܘܡܢ ܕܝܡܐ
19 ܒܩܘܪܒܢܐ ܕܥܠ ܡܕܒܚܐ ܚܝܒ. ܥܘܝܪ̈ܐ ܡܢܘ ܓܝܪ ܪܒ
ܩܘܪܒܢܐ ܐܘ ܡܕܒܚܐ ܕܗܘ ܡܩܕܫ ܠܗ ܠܩܘܪܒܢܐ.
20 ܡܢ ܕܝܡܐ ܗܟܝܠ ܒܡܕܒܚܐ ܝܡܐ ܒܗ ܘܒܟܠ ܡܐ
21 ܕܐܝܬ ܥܠܘܗܝ. ܘܡܢ ܕܝܡܐ ܒܗܝܟܠܐ ܝܡܐ ܒܗ
22 ܘܒܡܢ ܕܥܡܪ ܒܗ. ܘܡܢ ܕܝܡܐ ܒܫܡܝܐ ܝܡܐ
ܒܟܘܪܣܝܗ ܕܐܠܗܐ ܘܒܡܢ ܕܝܬܒ ܥܠܘܗܝ ܀

23 ܘܝ ܠܟܘܢ ܣܦܪ̈ܐ ܘܦܪ̈ܝܫܐ ܢܣܒܝ ܒܐܦܐ. ܕܡܥܣܪܝܢ
ܐܢܬܘܢ ܢܢܥܐ ܘܫܒܬܐ ܘܟܡܘܢܐ. ܘܫܒܩܬܘܢ
ܝܩܝܪ̈ܬܗ ܕܐܘܪܝܬܐ. ܕܝܢܐ ܘܚܢܢܐ ܘܗܝܡܢܘܬܐ.
ܗܠܝܢ ܕܝܢ ܥܒܕܬܘܢ ܘܗܠܝܢ ܕܝܢ ܠܐ ܫܒܩܬܘܢ.
24 ܡܕܒܪ̈ܢܐ ܥܘܝܪ̈ܐ ܕܡܨܠܠܝܢ ܐܢܬܘܢ ܡܢ ܒܩܐ. ܘܓܡܠܐ
ܐܢܬܘܢ ܒܠܥܝܢ܀

XXIII. ܗܝܕܝܢ ܐܡܪ ܝܫܘܥ ܠܟܢܫܐ ܘܠܬܠܡܝܕܘܗܝ. ܥܠ
2, 3 ܟܘܪܣܝܐ ܕܡܘܫܐ ܝܬܒܘ ܣܦܪܐ ܘܦܪܝܫܐ. ܟܠܡܕܡ
ܕܐܡܪܝܢ ܠܟܘܢ ܗܘܝܬܘܢ ܢܛܪܝܢ ܘܥܒܕܝܢ. ܐܝܟ
ܥܒܕܝܗܘܢ ܕܝܢ ܠܐ ܬܥܒܕܘܢ. ܐܡܪܝܢ ܓܝܪ ܘܠܐ
4 ܥܒܕܝܢ. ܘܐܣܪܝܢ ܡܘܒܠܐ ܝܩܝܪܬܐ ܘܣܝܡܝܢ ܥܠ
ܟܬܦܬܐ ܕܒܢܝܢܫܐ. ܘܗܢܘܢ ܒܚܕܐ ܡܢ ܨܒܥܬܗܘܢ
5 ܠܐ ܩܪܒܝܢ ܠܗܝܢ. ܟܠ ܡܕܡ ܓܝܪ ܕܥܒܕܝܢ ܕܢܬܚܙܘܢ
ܠܒܢܝܢܫܐ. ܘܡܦܬܝܢ ܒܪܡܐ ܕܬܦܠܝܢܝܗܘܢ. ܘܡܘܪܟܝܢ
6 ܬܟܠܬܐ ܕܡܪܛܘܛܝܗܘܢ. ܘܪܚܡܝܢ ܪܝܫ ܣܡܟܐ
ܒܚܫܡܝܬܐ. ܘܡܘܬܒܐ ܩܕܡܝܐ ܒܟܢܘܫܬܐ
7 ܘܫܠܡܐ ܒܫܘܩܐ. ܘܨܒܝܢ ܕܢܗܘܘܢ ܩܪܝܢ ܠܗܘܢ ܪܒܝ
8 ܐܢܫܐ ܪܒܝ ܪܒܝ. ܐܢܬܘܢ ܕܝܢ ܠܐ ܬܬܩܪܘܢ ܪܒܝ. ܚܕ ܗܘ
ܓܝܪ ܪܒܟܘܢ ܡܫܝܚܐ. ܘܐܢܬܘܢ ܐܚܐ ܐܢܬܘܢ.
9 ܘܐܒܐ ܠܐ ܬܩܪܘܢ ܠܟܘܢ ܒܐܪܥܐ. ܚܕ ܗܘ ܓܝܪ
10 ܐܒܘܟܘܢ ܕܒܫܡܝܐ. ܘܠܐ ܬܬܩܪܘܢ ܡܕܒܪܢܐ. ܡܛܠ
11 ܕܡܕܒܪܢܟܘܢ ܡܫܝܚܐ ܗܘ. ܘܡܢ ܕܪܒ ܒܟܘܢ ܢܗܘܐ
12 ܪܒ. ܢܗܘܐ ܠܟܘܢ ܡܫܡܫܢܐ. ܟܠ ܐܢܫ ܓܝܪ ܕܢܪܝܡ
ܢܦܫܗ ܢܬܡܟܟ. ܘܡܢ ܕܢܡܟ ܢܦܫܗ ܢܬܬܪܝܡ ◎ ○ ◎
14 ܘܝ ܠܟܘܢ ܣܦܪܐ ܘܦܪܝܫܐ ܢܣܒܝ ܒܐܦܐ. ܕܐܚܕܝܢ
ܐܢܬܘܢ ܡܠܟܘܬܐ ܕܫܡܝܐ ܩܕܡ ܒܢܝ ܐܢܫܐ. ܠܐ
ܓܝܪ ܐܢܬܘܢ ܥܠܝܢ. ܘܠܐ ܠܐܝܠܝܢ ܕܐܬܝܢ ܠܡܥܠ
ܫܒܩܝܢ ܐܢܬܘܢ ◎ ○ ◎
13 ܘܝ ܠܟܘܢ ܣܦܪܐ ܘܦܪܝܫܐ ܢܣܒܝ ܒܐܦܐ. ܕܐܟܠܝܢ

31 ܐܠܐ ܐܝܟ ܡ̈ܠܐܟܐ ܐܢܘܢ ܕܒܫܡܝܐ. ܘܥܠ
ܩܝܡܬܐ ܕܝܢ ܕܡ̈ܝܬܐ ܠܐ ܩܪܝܬܘܢ. ܕܐܡܪ ܐܠܗܐ
32 ܕܐܢܐ ܐܢܐ ܐܠܗܗ ܕܐܒܪܗܡ. ܘܐܠܗܗ ܕܐܝܣܚܩ.
ܘܐܠܗܗ ܕܝܥܩܘܒ. ܘܗܘܐ ܐܠܗܐ ܠܐ ܗܘܐ ܕܡ̈ܝܬܐ
ܐܠܐ ܕܚ̈ܝܐ ⊙ ○ ⊙
33 ܘܟܕ ܫܡܥܘ ܟܢ̈ܫܐ ܗܢܘܢ. ܡܬܕܡܪܝܢ ܗܘܘ ܒܝܘܠܦܢܗ.
34 ܦܪ̈ܝܫܐ ܕܝܢ ܟܕ ܫܡܥܘ ܕܫܬܩ ܐܢܘܢ ܠܙܕ̈ܘܩܝܐ. ܐܬܟܢܫܘ
35 ܠܘܬܗ. ܘܫܐܠܗ ܗܘܐ ܚܕ ܡܢܗܘܢ ܣܦܪܐ ܟܕ
36 ܡܢܣܐ ܠܗ ܘܐܡܪ ܠܗ. ܡܠܦܢܐ ܐܝܢܐ ܦܘܩܕܢܐ
37 ܪܒ ܘܡܩܕܡ ܒܐܘܪܝܬܐ. ܐܡܪ ܠܗ ܝܫܘܥ. ܕܬܪܚܡ
ܠܡܪܝܐ ܐܠܗܟ ܡܢ ܟܠܗ ܠܒܟ. ܘܡܢ ܟܠܗ̇ ܢܦܫܟ.
38 ܘܡܢ ܟܠܗ ܚܝܠܟ. ܗܢܐ ܗܘ ܦܘܩܕܢܐ ܪܒܐ ܘܩܕܡܝܐ.
39 ܘܕܬܪܬܗ ܕܕܡܐ ܠܗ. ܕܬܪܚܡ ܠܩܪܝܒܟ ܐܝܟ ܢܦܫܟ.
40, 41 ܒܗܠܝܢ ܬܪ̈ܬܝܢ ܦܘ̈ܩܕܢܝܢ ܬܠܝܐ ܐܘܪܝܬܐ ܘܢܒ̈ܝܐ. ܘܟܕ
42 ܟܢ̈ܝܫܝܢ ܦܪ̈ܝܫܐ. ܡܫܐܠ ܗܘܐ ܠܗܘܢ ܘܐܡܪ. ܡܢܐ
ܐܡܪܝܢ ܐܢܬܘܢ ܥܠ ܡܫܝܚܐ ܒܪ ܡܢܘ. ܐܡܪܝܢ
43 ܠܗ ܒܪ ܕܘܝܕ. ܐܡܪ ܠܗܘܢ ܐܝܟܢܐ ܗܟܝܠ ܕܘܝܕ
44 ܒܪܘܚܐ ܕܩܘܕܫܐ ܩܪܐ ܠܗ ܡܪܝ. ܐܡܪ ܓܝܪ ܕܐܡܪ
ܡܪܝܐ ܠܡܪܝ. ܬܒ ܠܟ ܡܢ ܝܡܝܢܝ. ܥܕܡܐ ܕܐܣܝܡ
45 ܒܥܠܕܒ̈ܒܝܟ ܬܚܝܬ ܪ̈ܓܠܝܟ. ܐܢ ܗܟܝܠ ܕܘܝܕ ܡܪܝ
46 ܩܪܐ ܠܗ ܐܝܟܢܐ ܒܪܗ ܗܘ. ܘܠܐ ܐܢܫ ܐܫܟܚ ܕܢܬܠ
ܠܗ ܦܬܓܡܐ. ܘܐܦܠܐ ܐܢܫ ܐܡܪܚ ܡܢ ܗܘ ܝܘܡܐ
ܠܡܫܐܠܘܬܗ ܬܘܒ ⊙

17 ܒܐ̈ܦܐ ܕܐܢܫ. ܐܡܪ ܠܢ ܡܢܐ ܡܬܚܙܐ ܠܟ. ܫܠܝܛ
18 ܠܡܬܠ ܟܣܦ ܪܫܐ ܠܩܣܪ ܐܘ ܠܐ. ܝܕܥ ܕܝܢ ܝܫܘܥ
ܒܒܝܫܘܬܗܘܢ ܘܐܡܪ ܠܗܘܢ. ܢܣ̈ܒܝ ܒܐ̈ܦܐ ܡܢܐ
19 ܡܢܣܝܢ ܐܢܬܘܢ ܠܝ. ܚܘܐܘܢܝ ܕܝܢܪܐ ܕܟܣܦ ܪܫܐ.
20 ܘܗܢܘܢ ܩܪܒܘ ܠܗ ܕܝܢܪܐ. ܘܐܡܪ ܠܗܘܢ ܝܫܘܥ.
ܨܠܡܐ ܗܢܐ ܘܟ̈ܬܒܬܐ ܕܡܢ. ܐܡܪܝܢ ܠܗ ܕܩܣܪ.
21 ܗܝܕܝܢ ܐܡܪ ܠܗܘܢ. ܗܒܘ ܕܩܣܪ ܠܩܣܪ ܘܕܐܠܗܐ
22 ܠܐܠܗܐ. ܘܟܕ ܫܡܥܘ ܐܬܕܡܪܘ ܘܫܒܩܘܗܝ
ܘܐܙܠܘ ○○○

23 ܒܗܘ ܝܘܡܐ ܩܪܒܘ ܩܕܡܘܗܝ ܙܕܘܩܝ̈ܐ ܘܐܡܪܝܢ ܠܗ.
24 ܕܠܝܬ ܩܝܡܬܐ. ܘܫܐܠܘܗܝ ܘܐܡܪܝܢ ܠܗ. ܡܠܦܢܐ.
ܡܘܫܐ ܐܡܪ ܠܢ. ܕܐܢ ܗܘ ܕܢܡܘܬ ܐܢܫ ܟܕ ܠܝܬ ܠܗ
ܒܢ̈ܝܐ. ܬܗܘܐ ܐܢܬܬܗ ܠܐܚܘܗܝ. ܘܢܩܝܡ ܙܪܥܐ
25 ܠܐܚܘܗܝ. ܐܝܬ ܗܘܘ ܕܝܢ ܠܘܬܢ ܫܒܥܐ ܐܚ̈ܝܢ.
ܩܕܡܝܗܘܢ ܢܣܒ ܐܢܬܬܐ ܘܡܝܬ. ܘܠܐ ܥܒܕ ܒܢ̈ܝܐ.
26 ܘܗܘܬ ܐܢܬܬܗ ܠܐܚܘܗܝ. ܐܦ ܐܚܪܢܐ ܗܟܘܬ.
27 ܘܐܦ ܕܬܠܬܐ. ܥܕܡܐ ܠܫܒܥܬܝܗܘܢ. ܘܐܚܪܝܬ
28 ܒܬܪ ܟܠܗܘܢ ܡܝܬܬ ܠܗ̇ ܗ̇ܝ ܐܢܬܬܐ. ܒܩܝܡܬܐ
ܗܟܝܠ ܠܐܝܢܐ ܡܢܗܘܢ ܬܗܘܐ ܐܢܬܬܐ. ܗܐ ܓܝܪ
29 ܠܫܒܥܬܝܗܘܢ ܗܘܬ ܗܘܬ. ܥܢܐ ܝܫܘܥ ܘܐܡܪ ܠܗܘܢ.
ܛܥܝܢ ܐܢܬܘܢ. ܘܠܐ ܝܕܥܝܢ ܐܢܬܘܢ ܟܬ̈ܒܐ.
30 ܐܦܠܐ ܚܝܠܗ ܕܐܠܗܐ. ܒܩܝܡܬ ܡ̈ܝܬܐ ܓܝܪ ܠܐ
ܓܒܪ̈ܐ ܢܣܒܝܢ ܢܫ̈ܐ. ܐܦ ܠܐ ܢܫ̈ܐ ܗܘ̈ܝܢ ܠܓܒܪ̈ܐ.

5 ܠܡܫܬܘܬܐ. ܗܢܘܢ ܕܝܢ ܒܣܘ. ܘܐܝܬ ܕܐܙܠ ܠܩܪܝܬܐ.
6 ܘܐܝܬ ܕܐܙܠ ܠܬܓܘܪܬܐ. ܫܪܟܐ ܕܝܢ ܕܐܫܬܚܪܘ.
7 ܐܚܕܘ ܠܥܒ̈ܕܘܗܝ ܘܨܥܪܘ ܐܢܘܢ ܘܩܛܠܘ. ܘܪܓܙ ܡܠܟܐ
ܗܘ ܘܫܕܪ ܠܚܝܠܘܬܗ. ܘܐܘܒܕ ܐܢܘܢ ܠܩܛܘ̈ܠܐ ܗܠܝܢ.
ܘܠܡܕܝܢܬܗܘܢ ܐܘܩܕ ܒܢܘܪܐ ◦◦◦
8 ܗܝܕܝܢ ܐܡܪ ܠܥܒ̈ܕܘܗܝ. ܡܫܬܘܬܐ ܡܛܝܒܐ ܗܝ.
ܘܗܢܘܢ ܕܡܙܡܢܝܢ ܗܘܘ ܠܐ ܫܘܝܢ ܗܘܘ ܠܗ̇. ܡܛܠ
9 ܦܘܩܘ ܠܘܬ ܐܦ̈ܪܫܘܬܐ. ܘܟܠ ܡܢ ܕܡܫܟܚܝܢ ܐܢܬܘܢ
10 ܩܪܘ ܠܘܬ ܡܫܬܘܬܐ. ܘܢܦܩܘ ܥܒ̈ܕܐ ܗܢܘܢ ܠܘܬ
ܐܘܪ̈ܚܬܐ. ܘܟܢܫܘ ܟܠ ܕܐܫܟܚܘ ܒ̈ܝܫܐ ܘܛ̈ܒܐ.
11 ܘܐܬܡܠܝ ܒܝܬ ܡܫܬܘܬܐ ܣ̈ܡܘܟܐ. ܘܥܠ ܡܠܟܐ
ܕܢܚܙܐ ܣ̈ܡܘܟܐ. ܘܚܙܐ ܬܡܢ ܓܒܪܐ ܕܠܐ ܠܒܝܫ
12 ܠܒ̈ܘܫܐ ܕܡܫܬܘܬܐ. ܐܡܪ ܠܗ ܚܒܪܝ ܐܝܟܢܐ ܐܬܝܬ
ܠܗܪܟܐ. ܕܠܒ̈ܘܫܐ ܕܡܫܬܘܬܐ ܠܝܬ ܠܟ. ܘܗܘ ܫܬܩ
13 ܠܗ. ܗܝܕܝܢ ܐܡܪ ܡܠܟܐ ܠܡܫ̈ܡܫܢܐ. ܐܣܘܪܘܗܝ
ܒܐܝ̈ܕܘܗܝ ܘܒܪ̈ܓܠܘܗܝ. ܘܐܦܩܘܗܝ ܠܚܫܘܟܐ ܒܪܝܐ.
14 ܬܡܢ ܢܗܘܐ ܒܟܝܐ ܘܚܘܪܩ ܫ̈ܢܐ. ܣܓܝܐܝܢ ܐܢܘܢ ܓܝܪ
ܩܪ̈ܝܐ ܘܒܚܝ̈ܪܝܢ ܙ̈ܥܘܪܐ ◦◦◦
15 ܗܝܕܝܢ ܐܙܠܘ ܦܪ̈ܝܫܐ. ܘܢܣܒܘ ܡܠܟܐ ܕܐܝܟܢܐ
16 ܢܨܘܕܘܢܗ ܒܡܠܬܐ. ܘܫܕܪܘ ܠܘܬܗ ܬܠܡ̈ܝܕܝܗܘܢ ܥܡ
ܒܢ̈ܝܐ ܕܗܪܘܕܣ ܘܐܡܪܝܢ ܠܗ. ܡܠܦܢܐ ܝܕܥܝܢ ܚܢܢ
ܕܫܪܝܪ ܐܢܬ. ܘܐܘܪܚܐ ܕܐܠܗܐ ܒܩܘܫܬܐ ܡܠܦ
ܐܢܬ. ܘܠܐ ܒܛܝܠ ܠܟ ܒܐܢܫ. ܠܐ ܓܝܪ ܢܣܒ ܐܢܬ

39 ܢܩܛܠܝܘܗܝ. ܘܢܗܘܐ ܠܢ ܝܪܬܘܬܐ ܕܝܠܗ. ܘܐܚܕܘܗܝ
40 ܘܐܦܩܘܗܝ ܠܒܪ ܡܢ ܟܪܡܐ ܘܩܛܠܘܗܝ. ܐܡܬܝ ܗܟܝܠ
ܕܢܐܬܐ ܡܪܗ ܕܟܪܡܐ ܡܢܐ ܢܥܒܕ ܠܗܘܢ ܠܦܠܚܐ
41 ܗܠܝܢ. ܐܡܪܝܢ ܠܗ ܕܒܝܫ ܒܝܫ ܢܘܒܕ ܐܢܘܢ. ܘܟܪܡܐ
ܢܫܠܡ ܠܦܠܚܐ ܐ̈ܚܪܢܐ. ܐܝܠܝܢ ܕܢܗܒܘܢ ܦܐܪ̈ܐ
42 ܒܙܒܢܗܘܢ. ܐܡܪ ܠܗܘܢ ܝܫܘܥ. ܠܐ ܡܡܬܘܡ ܩܪܝܬܘܢ
ܒܟܬܒܐ. ܕܟܐܦܐ ܗܝ ܕܐܣܠܝܘ ܒ̈ܢܝܐ. ܗܝ ܗܘܬ
ܠܪܫ ܙܘܝܬܐ. ܡܢ ܠܘܬ ܡܪܝܐ ܗܘܬ ܗܕܐ. ܘܐܝܬܝܗ
43 ܬܕܡܘܪܬܐ ܒܥ̈ܝܢܝܢ. ܡܛܠ ܗܢܐ ܐܡܪ ܐܢܐ ܠܟܘܢ.
ܕܬܫܬܩܠ ܡܢܟܘܢ ܡܠܟܘܬܐ ܕܐܠܗܐ. ܘܬܬܝܗܒ
44 ܠܥܡܐ ܕܥܒܕ ܦܐܪ̈ܐ. ܟܠ ܡܢ ܕܢܦܠ ܥܠ ܗܝ ܟܐܦܐ
ܢܬܬܒܪ. ܘܟܠ ܕܬܦܠ ܥܠܘܗܝ ܬܫܚܩܝܘܗܝ. ܪ̈ܒܝ ܟܗ̈ܢܐ
45 ܕܝܢ ܘܦܪ̈ܝܫܐ ܟܕ ܫܡܥܘ ܦܠܐܬܐ. ܝܕܥܘ ܕܥܠܝܗܘܢ
46 ܗܘ ܐܡܪ. ܘܒܥܘ ܗܘܘ ܕܢܐܚܕܘܢܗ ܘܕܚܠܘ ܡܢ
ܥܡܐ. ܡܛܠ ܕܐܝܟ ܕܠܢܒܝܐ ܐܚܝܕܝܢ ܗܘܘ
ܠܗ. ◦◦◦

XXII. ܬܘܒ ܥܢܐ ܝܫܘܥ ܘܐܡܪ ܠܗܘܢ ܦ̈ܠܐܬܐ.
2 ܐܬܕܡܝܬ ܡܠܟܘܬܐ ܕܫܡܝܐ ܠܓܒܪܐ ܡܠܟܐ. ܕܥܒܕ
3 ܡܫܬܘܬܐ ܠܒܪܗ. ܘܫܕܪ ܠܥܒ̈ܕܘܗܝ ܕܢܩܪܘܢ ܠܗܢܘܢ
ܕܡܙܡܢܝܢ ܠܡܫܬܘܬܐ. ܘܠܐ ܨܒܘ ܠܡܐܬܐ ◦◦◦
4 ܬܘܒ ܫܕܪ ܥܒ̈ܕܐ ܐ̈ܚܪܢܐ ܘܐܡܪ. ܐܡܪܘ ܠܗܢܘܢ
ܕܡܙܡܢܝܢ ܗܘܘ. ܗܐ ܐܛܝܒܬ ܡܫܬܘܬܝ. ܬ̈ܘܪܝ
ܘܦܛ̈ܡܝ ܢܟܝܣܝܢ ܐܢܘܢ. ܘܟܠܡܕܡ ܡܛܝܒ ܗܘ ܬܘ

ܠܗ ܬܪ̈ܝܢ ܒ̈ܢܝܢ. ܐܡܪ ܠܩܕܡܝܐ ܙܠ ܒܪܝ ܝܘܡܢܐ ܥܒܕ
29 ܥܒܕܐ ܒܟܪܡܐ. ܐܡܪ ܠܗ ܠܐ ܨܒܐ ܐܢܐ. ܐܚܪܝܬ
30 ܕܝܢ ܬܘܬܗ ܢܦܫܗ ܘܐܙܠ ܠܟܪܡܐ. ܘܐܡܪ ܠܐܚܪܢܐ
31 ܗܟܘܬ. ܘܗܢܐ ܘܐܡܪ ܐܢܐ ܡܪܝ. ܘܠܐ ܐܙܠ. ܡܢ ܡܢ
ܗܠܝܢ ܬܪ̈ܝܢ ܡܬܚܙܐ ܠܟܘܢ ܕܥܒܕ ܨܒܝܢܐ ܕܐܒܘܗܝ.
ܐܡܪܝܢ ܠܗ ܗܘ ܩܕܡܝܐ. ܐܡܪ ܠܗܘܢ ܝܫܘܥ. ܐܡܝܢ
ܐܡܪܢܐ ܠܟܘܢ. ܕܡ̈ܟܣܐ ܘܙܢ̈ܝܬܐ ܡܩܕܡܝܢ ܠܟܘܢ
32 ܠܡܠܟܘܬܐ ܕܐܠܗܐ. ܐܬܐ ܓܝܪ ܠܘܬܟܘܢ ܝܘܚܢܢ
ܒܐܘܪܚܐ ܕܟܐܢܘܬܐ ܘܠܐ ܗܝܡܢܬܘܢܝܗܝ.
ܡ̈ܟܣܐ ܕܝܢ ܘܙܢ̈ܝܬܐ ܗܝܡܢܘ ܒܗ. ܐܢܬܘܢ ܕܝܢ
ܐܦ ܠܐ ܟܕ ܚܙܝܬܘܢ ܬܘܬܒܘܢ ܢܦܫܟܘܢ ܐܚܪܝܬ
ܕܬܗܝܡܢܘܢܝܗܝ. ◦ ◦ ◦
33 ܫܡܥܘ ܡܬܠܐ ܐܚܪܢܐ. ܓܒܪܐ ܚܕ ܡܪܐ ܒܝܬܐ
ܐܝܬ ܗܘܐ. ܢܨܒ ܟܪܡܐ ܘܐܚܕܪܗ ܣܝܓܐ. ܘܚܦܪ
ܒܗ ܡܥܨܪܬܐ. ܘܒܢܐ ܒܗ ܡܓܕܠܐ. ܘܐܫܠܡܗ
34 ܠܦ̈ܠܚܐ ܘܐܙܠ. ܘܟܕ ܩܪܒ ܙܒܢܐ ܕܦܐܪ̈ܐ. ܫܕܪ
35 ܥܒ̈ܕܘܗܝ ܠܘܬ ܦ̈ܠܚܐ. ܕܢܣܒܘܢ ܠܗ ܦܐܪ̈ܐ. ܘܐܚܕܘ
ܐܢܘܢ ܦ̈ܠܚܐ ܗܢܘܢ ܠܥܒ̈ܕܘܗܝ. ܐܝܬ ܕܡܚܘܗܝ.
36 ܘܐܝܬ ܕܪ̈ܓܡܘܗܝ. ܘܐܝܬ ܕܩܛܠܘܗܝ. ܬܘܒ ܫܕܪ
ܥܒ̈ܕܘܗܝ ܣܓܝ̈ܐܐ ܕܡܝܬܪܝܢ ܡܢ ܩܕܡܝܐ. ܘܥܒܕܘ
37 ܠܗܘܢ ܗܟܘܬ. ܒܚܪܬܐ ܕܝܢ ܫܕܪ ܠܘܬܗܘܢ ܠܒܪܗ
38 ܘܐܡܪ. ܒܪܡ ܢܒܗܬܘܢ ܡܢ ܒܪܝ. ܗܢܘܢ ܕܝܢ ܦ̈ܠܚܐ ܟܕ
ܚܙܘܗܝ ܠܒܪܗ. ܐܡܪܘ ܒܝܢܬܗܘܢ. ܗܢܘ ܝܪܬܐ ܬܘ

21 ܐܝܟܢܐ ܒܪܫܥܬܗ ܝܒܫܬ ܬܬܐ ܗܕܐ. ܥܢܐ ܝܫܘܥ
ܘܐܡܪ ܠܗܘܢ. ܐܡܝܢ ܐܡܪ ܐܢܐ ܠܟܘܢ. ܕܐܢ ܬܗܘܐ
ܒܟܘܢ ܗܝܡܢܘܬܐ ܘܠܐ ܬܬܦܠܓܘܢ. ܠܐ ܒܠܚܘܕ
ܐܝܟ ܗܕܐ ܕܬܬܐ ܬܥܒܕܘܢ. ܐܠܐ ܐܢ ܬܐܡܪܘܢ
ܠܛܘܪܐ ܗܢܐ ܕܐܫܬܩܠ ܘܦܠ ܒܝܡܐ. ܢܗܘܐ
22 ܠܟܘܢ ܗܟܢܐ. ܘܟܘܠ ܡܕܡ ܕܬܫܐܠܘܢ ܒܨܠܘܬܐ
ܘܬܗܝܡܢܘܢ ܬܣܒܘܢ ܀
23 ܘܟܕ ܐܬܐ ܠܗܝܟܠܐ. ܩܪܒܘ ܠܗ ܪ̈ܒܝ ܟܗܢܐ ܘܩܫ̈ܝܫܐ
ܕܥܡܐ ܘܐܡܪܝܢ ܠܗ. ܒܐܝܢܐ ܫܘܠܛܢܐ ܗܠܝܢ ܥܒܕ
24 ܐܢܬ. ܘܡܢ ܝܗܒ ܠܟ ܫܘܠܛܢܐ ܗܢܐ. ܥܢܐ ܝܫܘܥ
ܘܐܡܪ ܠܗܘܢ. ܐܦ ܐܢܐ ܐܫܐܠܟܘܢ ܡܠܬܐ ܚܕܐ
ܕܬܐܡܪܘܢ ܠܝ. ܘܐܡܪ ܠܟܘܢ ܒܐܝܢܐ ܫܘܠܛܢܐ
25 ܥܒܕܐ ܗܠܝܢ. ܡܥܡܘܕܝܬܗ ܕܝܘܚܢܢ ܡܢ ܐܝܟܐ
ܗܘܬ. ܡܢ ܫܡܝܐ ܐܘ ܡܢ ܒ̈ܢܝ ܐܢܫܐ. ܗܢܘܢ ܕܝܢ
ܡܬܚܫܒܝܢ ܗܘܘ ܒܢܦܫܗܘܢ ܘܐܡܪܝܢ ܗܘܘ. ܕܐܢ
ܢܐܡܪ ܠܗ ܕܡܢ ܫܡܝܐ ܗܝ. ܢܐܡܪ ܠܢ ܘܠܡܢܐ ܠܐ
26 ܗܝܡܢܬܘܢ ܒܗ. ܘܐܢ ܢܐܡܪ ܕܡܢ ܒ̈ܢܝ ܐܢܫܐ ܗܝ
ܕܚܠܝܢ ܐܢܚܢ ܡܢ ܟܢܫܐ. ܟܠܗܘܢ ܓܝܪ ܐܢܫܐ ܐܝܟ
27 ܕܠܢܒܝܐ ܐܚܝܕܝܢ ܗܘܘ ܠܗ ܠܝܘܚܢܢ. ܘܐܡܪܝܢ ܠܗ ܠܐ
ܝܕܥܝܢ ܐܢܚܢ. ܐܡܪ ܠܗܘܢ ܝܫܘܥ. ܘܐܦ ܠܐ ܐܢܐ
ܐܡܪ ܐܢܐ ܠܟܘܢ. ܒܐܝܢܐ ܫܘܠܛܢܐ ܥܒܕ ܐܢܐ
ܗܠܝܢ ܀
28 ܐܝܟܢܐ ܕܝܢ ܡܬܚܙܝܐ ܠܟܘܢ. ܓܒܪܐ ܚܕ ܐܝܬ ܗܘܐ

ܠܐܠܗܐ. ܥܠ ܟܠ ܡܐ ܕܚܙܘ ◦ ◦ ◦
10 ܘܟܕ ܥܠ ܠܐܘܪܫܠܡ. ܐܬܪܥܫܬ ܟܠܗ ܡܕܝܢܬܐ.
11 ܘܐܡܪܝܢ ܡܢܘ ܗܢܐ. ܐܡܪܝܢ ܠܗܘܢ ܟܢ̈ܫܐ ܗܠܝܢ.
12 ܗܢܘ ܝܫܘܥ ܢܒܝܐ ܕܡܢ ܢܨܪܬ ܕܓܠܝܠܐ. ܘܥܠ
ܝܫܘܥ ܠܗܝܟܠܐ ܕܐܠܗܐ. ܘܐܦܩ ܡܢ ܗܝܟܠܐ
ܕܐܠܗܐ ܠܟܠܗܘܢ ܙܒ̈ܢܐ ܘܙܒ̈ܢܝܢܐ. ܘܗܦܟ ܝܫܘܥ
ܦܬܘܪ̈ܐ ܕܡ̈ܥܪܦܢܐ. ܘܟܘܪ̈ܣܘܬܗܘܢ ܕܗܢܘܢ ܕܡܙܒܢܝܢ
13 ܝܘ̈ܢܐ. ܘܐܡܪ ܠܗܘܢ ܟܬܝܒ ܗܘ ܕܒܝܬܝ ܒܝܬ ܨܠܘܬܐ
ܢܬܩܪܐ ܠܟܠܗܘܢ ܥܡ̈ܡܐ. ܐܢܬܘܢ ܕܝܢ ܥܒܕܬܘܢܝܗܝ
14 ܡܥܪܬܐ ܕܠܣ̈ܛܝܐ. ܘܩܪܒܘ ܠܗ ܒܗܝܟܠܐ ܥܘܝܪ̈ܐ
15 ܘܚܓܝܪ̈ܐ ܘܐܣܝ ܐܢܘܢ. ܘܟܕ ܚܙܘ ܟܘܡܪ̈ܐ ܘܣܦܪ̈ܝ ܥܡܐ
ܬܕܡܪ̈ܬܐ ܕܥܒܕ. ܘܛܠܝ̈ܐ ܕܩܥܝܢ ܗܘܘ ܒܗ ܒܗܝܟܠܐ.
ܘܐܡܪܝܢ ܗܘܘ ܐܘܫܥܢܐ ܠܒܪܗ ܕܕܘܝܕ. ܐܬܟܐܒ
16 ܠܗܘܢ ܘܐܡܪܝܢ. ܠܐ ܫܡܥ ܐܢܬ ܡܢܐ ܐܡܪܝܢ
ܗܠܝܢ. ܐܡܪ ܠܗܘܢ ܝܫܘܥ. ܐܝܢ. ܠܐ ܡܩܪܝܬܘܢ
ܩܪܝܬܘܢ ܕܡܢ ܦܘܡܐ ܕܛ̈ܠܝܐ ܘܕܝ̈ܢܩܐ ܐܬܩܢܬ
17 ܬܫܒܘܚܬܐ. ܘܫܒܩ ܐܢܘܢ ܘܢܦܩ ܠܗ ܠܒܪ ܡܢ
18 ܡܕܝܢܬܐ. ܠܒܝܬ ܥܢܝܐ ܕܢܒܘܬ ܬܡܢ. ܒܨܦܪܐ ܕܝܢ ܟܕ
19 ܗܦܟ ܗܘܐ ܠܡܕܝܢܬܐ. ܟܦܢ. ܘܚܙܐ ܬܬܐ ܚܕܐ
ܒܐܘܪܚܐ. ܘܐܬܐ ܠܘܬܗ ܘܠܐ ܐܫܟܚ ܒܗ ܡܕܡ.
ܐܠܐ ܐܢ ܛܪ̈ܦܐ ܒܠܚܘܕ. ܘܐܡܪ ܠܗ ܬܘܒ ܦܐܪ̈ܐ
ܠܐ ܢܗܘܘܢ ܒܟ ܠܥܠܡ. ܘܒܗ ܒܫܥܬܐ ܝܒܫܬ ܬܬܐ
20 ܗܝ. ܘܟܕ ܚܙܘ ܬܠܡܝ̈ܕܘܗܝ ܐܬܕܡܪܘ. ܘܐܡܪܝܢ ܗܘܘ

ܐܢܬܘܢ ܕܐܥܒܕ ܠܟܘܢ. ܐܡܪܝܢ ܠܗ ܡܪܢ. ܕܢܬܦܬܚ 33
ܥܝ̈ܢܝܢ ܘܢܚܙܝܢ. ܘܐܬܪܚܡ ܥܠܝܗܘܢ. ܘܩܪܒ 34
ܠܥܝ̈ܢܝܗܘܢ. ܘܒܗ ܒܫܥܬܐ ܚܙܘ ܘܐܙܠܘ ܒܬܪܗ ◎○◎
ܘܟܕ ܩܪܒ ܠܐܘܪܫܠܡ. ܘܐܬܐ ܠܒܝܬ ܦܓܐ. ܥܠ ܓܢܒ XXI.
ܛܘܪܐ ܕܒܝܬ ܙܝܬܐ. ܗܝܕܝܢ ܫܕܪ ܝܫܘܥ ܬܪ̈ܝܢ ܡܢ
ܬܠܡ̈ܝܕܘܗܝ ܘܐܡܪ ܠܗܘܢ. ܙܠܘ ܠܩܪܝܬܐ ܗܕܐ 2
ܕܠܩܘܒܠܟܘܢ. ܘܗܐ ܡܫܟܚܝܢ ܐܢܬܘܢ ܚܡܪܐ ܚܕܐ
ܟܕ ܐܣܝܪܐ. ܘܥܝܠܗ ܥܠ ܓܒܗ. ܫܪܘ ܐܝܬܘ ܐܢܘܢ
ܠܝ. ܘܐܢ ܐܢܫ ܢܐܡܪ ܠܟܘܢ ܡܕܡ. ܐܡܪܘ ܠܗ 3
ܠܡܪܢ ܡܬܒܥܝܢ. ܘܡܚܕܐ ܡܫܕܪ ܠܗܘܢ. ܗܕܐ 4
ܕܝܢ ܕܗܘܬ. ܕܢܬܡܠܐ ܡܕܡ ܕܐܬܐܡܪ ܡܢ ܢܒܝܐ
ܕܐܡܪ ܗܘܐ. ܐܡܪܘ ܠܒܪܬ ܨܗܝܘܢ. ܗܐ ܡܠܟܟܝ 5
ܐܬܐ ܠܟܝ. ܙܕܝܩ ܘܡܟܝܟ. ܘܪܟܝܒ ܥܠ ܚܡܪܐ ܘܥܠ
ܥܝܠܐ ܒܪ ܐܬܢܐ. ܘܐܙܠܘ ܗܟܢ ܬܠܡ̈ܝܕܘܗܝ. 6
ܘܥܒܕܘ ܐܝܟ ܕܦܩܕ ܐܢܘܢ ܝܫܘܥ. ܘܐܝܬܝܘ ܠܚܡܪܐ 7
ܘܠܥܝܠܐ. ܘܣܡܘ ܗܘܘ ܡܪ̈ܛܘܛܝܗܘܢ. ܘܪܟܒ ܝܫܘܥ
ܥܠ ܡܢܗܘܢ. ܘܣܓܝܐܐ ܕܟܢܫܐ ܗܘ ܦܪܣܘ ܗܘܘ 8
ܡܪ̈ܛܘܛܝܗܘܢ ܒܐܘܪܚܐ. ܐ̈ܚܪܢܐ ܕܝܢ ܦܣܩܝܢ ܗܘܘ
ܣܘ̈ܟܐ ܡܢ ܐ̈ܝܠܢܐ ܘܪܡܝܢ ܗܘܘ ܒܐܘܪܚܐ. ܘܟ̈ܢܫܐ 9
ܗܢܘܢ ܕܐܙܠܝܢ ܗܘܘ ܩܕܡܘܗܝ ܘܒܬܪܗ. ܩܥܝܢ ܗܘܘ
ܘܐܡܪܝܢ. ܐܘܫܥܢܐ ܠܒܪܗ ܕܕܘܝܕ. ܒܪܝܟ ܗܘ ܕܐܬܐ
ܒܫܡܗ ܕܡܪܝܐ. ܐܘܫܥܢܐ ܒܡܪ̈ܘܡܐ. ܘܟܕ ܥܠ
ܠܐܘܪܫܠܡ ܩ̈ܠܝܠܐ. ܘܚܕܝܢ ܗܘܘ ܡܫܒܚܝܢ

ܡܪ̈ܝܗܘܢ ܐܢܘܢ. ܘܪ̈ܘܪܒܢܝܗܘܢ ܫܠܝܛܝܢ ܐܢܘܢ
26 ܥܠܝܗܘܢ. ܒܝܢܬܟܘܢ ܕܝܢ ܠܐ ܢܗܘܐ ܗܟܢܐ.
ܐܠܐ ܡܢ ܕܨܒܐ ܒܟܘܢ ܕܢܗܘܐ ܪܒܐ. ܢܗܘܐ ܠܟܘܢ
27 ܡܫܡܫܢܐ. ܘܡܢ ܕܨܒܐ ܒܟܘܢ ܕܢܗܘܐ ܩܕܡܝܐ.
28 ܢܗܘܐ ܠܟܘܢ ܥܒܕܐ. ܐܝܟܢܐ ܕܒܪܗ ܕܐܢܫܐ ܠܐ
ܐܬܐ ܕܢܬܫܡܫ. ܐܠܐ ܕܢܫܡܫ. ܘܕܢܬܠ ܢܦܫܗ ܦܘܪܩܢܐ
ܚܠܦ ܣܓ̈ܝܐܐ. ܐܢܬܘܢ ܕܝܢ ܒܥܘ ܕܡܢ ܙܥܘܪܘܬܐ
ܬܪܒܘܢ. ܘܠܐ ܡܢ ܪܒܘܬܐ ܬܒܨܪܘܢ. ◦ ◦ ◦
ܡܟܐ ܕܡܬܩܪܝܢ ܐܢܬܘܢ ܠܒܝܬ ܐܫܬܘܬܐ. ܠܐ
ܬܗܘܘܢ ܡܣܬܡܟܝܢ ܒܕܘܟܬܐ ܡܝܬܪܬܐ. ܕܠܐ
ܢܐܬܐ ܡܢ ܕܡܝܬܪ ܡܢܟ. ܘܢܐܡܪ ܠܟ ܡܙܡܢܐ
ܐܫܬܘܬܐ ܐܬܩܪܒ ܠܬܚܬ. ܘܬܒܗܬ ܩܕܡ
ܣ̈ܡܝܟܐ. ܐܢ ܕܝܢ ܬܬܡܟܟ ܒܕܘܟܬܐ ܒܨܝܪܬܐ. ܘܢܐܬܐ
ܡܢ ܕܒܨܝܪ ܡܢܟ. ܘܢܐܡܪ ܠܟ ܡܙܡܢܐ ܐܫܬܘܬܐ
ܐܬܩܪܒ ܘܐܬܥܠܐ. ܘܬܗܘܐ ܠܟ
ܬܫܒܘܚܬܐ ܡܝܬܪܬܐ ܩܕܡ ܣ̈ܡܝܟܐ. ◦ ◦ ◦ ◦
29 ܘܟܕ ܢܦܩܝܢ ܗܘܘ ܡܢ ܐܝܪܝܚܘ. ܐܬܐ ܗܘܐ ܒܬܪܗ
30 ܟܢܫܐ ܣܓܝܐܐ. ܘܬܪ̈ܝܢ ܣ̈ܡܝܐ ܝܬܒܝܢ ܗܘܘ ܥܠ
ܝܕ ܐܘܪܚܐ. ܘܟܕ ܫܡܥܘ ܕܝܫܘܥ ܥܒܪ. ܩܥܝܢ ܗܘܘ
31 ܘܐܡܪܝܢ. ܐܬܪܚܡ ܥܠܝܢ ܒܪܗ ܕܕܘܝܕ. ܘܟܢ̈ܫܐ ܗܢܘܢ
ܟܐܝܢ ܗܘܘ ܒܗܘܢ ܕܢܫܬܩܘܢ. ܗܢܘܢ ܕܝܢ ܐܪܝܡܘ
ܩܠܗܘܢ ܘܐܡܪܝܢ. ܐܬܪܚܡ ܥܠܝܢ ܡܪܢ ܒܪܗ ܕܕܘܝܕ.
32 ܘܩܡ ܝܫܘܥ ܘܩܪܐ ܐܢܘܢ. ܘܐܡܪ ܡܢܐ ܨܒܝܢ

ܩܕ̈ܡܝܐ. ܘܩ̈ܕܡܝܐ ܢܗܘܘܢ ܐ̈ܚܪܝܐ. ܣܓܝ̈ܐܐ ܐܢܘܢ
ܓܝܪ ܩ̈ܪܝܐ ܘܒܨܝܪܝܢ ܓ̈ܒܝܐ
17 ܘܟܕ ܣܠܩ ܗܘܐ ܝܫܘܥ ܠܐܘܪܫܠܡ. ܕܒܪ ܗܘܐ
ܒܚܒܗ ܠܬ̈ܠܡܝܕܘܗܝ ܒܐܘܪܚܐ. ܘܐܡܪ ܠܗܘܢ
18 ܒܝܢܘܗܝ ܘܠܗܘܢ. ܗܐ ܣܠܩܝܢ ܚܢܢ ܠܐܘܪܫܠܡ. ܘܒܪܗ
ܕܐܢܫܐ ܡܫܬܠܡ ܠܪ̈ܒܝ ܟܗ̈ܢܐ ܘܠܣ̈ܦܪܐ. ܘܢܚܝܒܘܢܗ
19 ܠܡܘܬܐ. ܘܢܫܠܡܘܢܗ ܠܥ̈ܡܡܐ. ܘܢܒܙܚܘܢ ܒܗ
ܘܢܢܓܕܘܢܗ. ܘܢܙܩܦܘܢܗ. ܘܠܝܘܡܐ ܕܬܠܬܐ ܢܩܘܡ
20 ܗܝܕܝܢ ܩܪܒܬ ܠܘܬܗ ܐܡܗܘܢ ܕܒ̈ܢܝ ܙܒܕܝ ܗܝ ܘܒ̈ܢܝܗ.
21 ܘܣܓܕܬ ܠܗ. ܘܫܐܠܐ ܗܘܬ ܡܢܗ ܡܕܡ. ܗܘ
ܕܝܢ ܐܡܪ ܠܗ̇ ܡܢܐ ܨܒܝܐ ܐܢܬܝ. ܐܡܪܐ ܠܗ ܐܡܪ
ܕܢܬܒܘܢ ܗܠܝܢ ܬܪ̈ܝܗܘܢ ܒ̈ܢܝ ܚܕ ܡܢ ܝܡܝܢܟ ܘܚܕ ܡܢ
22 ܣܡܠܟ ܒܡܠܟܘܬܟ ܘܒܫܘܒܚܟ. ܥܢܐ ܝܫܘܥ ܘܐܡܪ
ܠܗ̇. ܠܐ ܝܕܥܝܢ ܐܢܬܘܢ ܡܢܐ ܫܐܠܝܢ ܐܢܬܘܢ.
ܡܫܟܚܝܢ ܐܢܬܘܢ ܠܡܫܬܝܐ ܟܣܐ ܗܢܐ ܕܐܢܐ ܥܬܝܕ
23 ܠܡܫܬܝܗ. ܐܡܪܝܢ ܡܫܟܚܝܢ ܐܢܚܢ. ܐܡܪ ܠܗܘܢ
ܝܫܘܥ. ܕܬܫܬܘܢ ܟܣܐ ܗܢܐ ܡܫܟܚܝܢ ܐܢܬܘܢ.
ܕܬܬܒܘܢ ܕܝܢ ܚܕ ܡܢ ܝܡܝܢܝ ܘܚܕ ܡܢ ܣܡܠܝ. ܗܕܐ
ܠܐ ܗܘܬ ܕܝܠܝ ܕܐܬܠ ܠܟܘܢ. ܐܠܐ ܠܐܝܠܝܢ ܕܐܬܛܝܒ
24 ܠܗܘܢ ܡܢ ܠܘܬ ܐܒܝ. ܘܟܕ ܫܡܥܘ ܥܣ̈ܪܐ ܪܓܙܘ ܥܠ
25 ܗܠܝܢ ܬܪ̈ܝܢ ܐ̈ܚܝܢ. ܘܩܪܐ ܐܢܘܢ ܝܫܘܥ ܘܐܡܪ
ܠܗܘܢ. ܝܕܥܝܢ ܐܢܬܘܢ ܕܪ̈ܫܢܝܗܘܢ ܕܥ̈ܡܡܐ

3 ܒܝܘܡܐ ܚܕ. ܘܫܕܪ ܐܢܘܢ ܠܟܪܡܗ. ܘܢܦܩ ܒܬܠܬ
ܫ̈ܥܝܢ. ܘܚܙܐ ܐ̈ܚܪܢܐ ܕܩܝܡܝܢ ܒܫܘܩܐ ܘܒܛܝܠܝܢ.
4 ܘܐܡܪ ܠܗܘܢ ܙܠܘ ܐܦ ܐܢܬܘܢ ܠܟܪܡܐ. ܘܡܕܡ
5 ܕܘܠܐ ܐܬܠ ܠܟܘܢ. ܘܐܙܠܘ. ܘܢܦܩ ܬܘܒ ܒܫܬ ܫ̈ܥܝܢ.
6 ܘܒܬܫܥ ܫ̈ܥܝܢ. ܘܥܒܕ ܗܟܘܬ ܒܒܪ. ܘܢܦܩ ܒܚܕܥܣܪܐ
ܫ̈ܥܝܢ. ܘܐܫܟܚ ܐ̈ܚܪܢܐ ܕܩܝܡܝܢ. ܘܐܡܪ ܠܗܘܢ
7 ܡܢܐ ܩܝܡܝܢ ܐܢܬܘܢ ܘܒܛܝܠܝܢ ܝܘܡܐ ܟܠܗ. ܐܡܪܝܢ
ܠܗ ܐܢܫ ܠܐ ܐܓܪܢ. ܐܡܪ ܠܗܘܢ ܙܠܘ ܐܦ ܐܢܬܘܢ
8 ܠܟܪܡܐ. ܘܡܐ ܕܘܠܐ ܐܬܠ ܠܟܘܢ. ܘܟܕ ܗܘܐ ܪܡܫܐ
ܐܡܪ ܡܪܐ ܟܪܡܐ ܠܪܒ ܒܝܬܗ. ܩܪܝ ܠܦܥ̈ܠܐ
ܘܗܒ ܠܗܘܢ ܐܓܪܗܘܢ. ܘܫܪܐ ܡܢ ܐ̈ܚܪܝܐ ܥܕܡܐ
9 ܠܩ̈ܕܡܝܐ. ܟܕ ܐܬܘ ܕܝܢ ܗܠܝܢ ܕܒܚܕܥܣܪܐ ܫ̈ܥܝܢ
10 ܫܩܠܘ ܕܝܢܪܐ ܕܝܢܪܐ. ܘܟܕ ܐܬܘ ܩ̈ܕܡܝܐ ܣܒܪܝܢ ܗܘܘ
ܕܠܗܘܢ ܝܬܝܪ ܝܬܠ. ܘܢܣܒܘ ܐܦ ܗܢܘܢ ܕܝܢܪܐ ܕܝܢܪܐ.
11, 12 ܘܟܕ ܢܣܒܘ ܪܛܢܘ ܥܠ ܡܪܐ ܒܝܬܐ ܘܐܡܪܝܢ ܠܗ. ܗܠܝܢ
ܐ̈ܚܪܝܐ ܚܕܐ ܫܥܐ ܦܠܚܘ. ܘܐܫܘܝܬ ܐܢܘܢ ܥܡܢ
13 ܕܣܒܠܢ ܝܘܩܪܗ ܕܝܘܡܐ ܟܠܗ ܘܚܘܡܐ. ܗܘ ܕܝܢ ܥܢܐ
ܘܐܡܪ ܠܚܕ ܡܢܗܘܢ. ܚܒܪܝ ܠܐ ܛܠܡܬܟ. ܠܐ ܗܘܐ
14 ܒܕܝܢܪܐ ܩܨܬ ܥܡܝ. ܣܒ ܕܝܠܟ ܘܙܠ. ܘܐܢܐ ܨܒܐ ܐܢܐ
15 ܕܐܬܠ ܠܗܢܐ ܐ̈ܚܪܝܐ ܐܝܟ ܕܠܟ. ܠܐ ܫܠܝܛ ܐܢܐ
ܕܐܥܒܕ ܒܕܝܠܝ ܡܕܡ ܕܨܒܐ ܐܢܐ. ܐܘ ܕܠܡܐ ܥܝܢܟ
16 ܒܝܫܐ ܕܐܢܐ ܛܒ ܐܢܐ. ܗܟܢܐ ܢܗܘܘܢ ܐ̈ܚܪܝܐ

ܕܝܢ ܐܡܪ ܠܬܠܡܝܕܘܗܝ. ܐܡܝܢ ܐܡܪ ܐܢܐ ܠܟܘܢ.
24 ܕܥܛܠܐ ܗܝ ܠܥܬܝܪܐ ܕܢܥܘܠ ܠܡܠܟܘܬ ܫܡܝܐ. ܬܘܒ
ܕܝܢ ܐܡܪ ܐܢܐ ܠܟܘܢ. ܕܦܫܝܩ ܗܘ ܠܓܡܠܐ ܕܢܥܒܪ
ܒܚܪܘܪܐ ܕܡܚܛܐ. ܐܘ ܠܥܬܝܪܐ ܠܡܠܟܘܬܐ
25 ܕܫܡܝܐ. ܬܘܒ ܕܝܢ ܟܕ ܫܡܥܘ ܬܠܡܝܕܘܗܝ ܬܡܝܗܝܢ
ܗܘܘ ܘܕܚܝܠܝܢ ܛܒ. ܘܐܡܪܝܢ ܗܘܘ ܡܢܘ ܟܝ ܡܫܟܚ
26 ܠܡܚܐ. ܚܪ ܒܗܘܢ ܝܫܘܥ ܘܐܡܪ ܠܗܘܢ. ܗܕܐ
ܠܘܬ ܒܢ̈ܝ ܐܢܫܐ ܠܐ ܡܫܟܚܐ ܕܬܗܘܐ. ܐܠܗܐ ܕܝܢ
27 ܟܠ ܡܕܡ ܡܫܟܚ ܠܡܥܒܕ. ܗܝܕܝܢ ܥܢܐ ܫܡܥܘܢ ܟܐܦܐ
ܘܐܡܪ ܠܗ. ܗܐ ܚܢܢ ܫܒܩܢ ܟܠ ܡܕܡ ܘܐܬܝܢ ܒܬܪܟ.
28 ܡܢܐ ܟܝ ܢܗܘܐ ܠܢ. ܐܡܪ ܠܗܘܢ ܝܫܘܥ. ܐܡܝܢ
ܐܡܪ ܐܢܐ ܠܟܘܢ. ܕܐܢܬܘܢ ܕܐܬܝܬܘܢ ܒܬܪܝ. ܒܥܠܡܐ
ܚܕܬܐ. ܡܐ ܕܝܬܒ ܒܪܗ ܕܐܢܫܐ ܥܠ ܬܪܘܢܘܣ
ܕܫܘܒܚܗ. ܬܬܒܘܢ ܐܦ ܐܢܬܘܢ ܥܠ ܬܪ̈ܥܣܪ
ܟܘܪ̈ܣܘܢ. ܘܬܕܘܢܘܢ ܬܪ̈ܬܥܣܪܐ ܫܒ̈ܛܝܢ ܕܒܝܬ ܐܝܣܪܝܠ.
29 ܘܟܠ ܐܢܫ ܕܫܒܩ ܒ̈ܬܐ ܘܐܚ̈ܐ. ܐܘ ܐܚ̈ܘܬܐ.
ܐܘ ܐܡܐ. ܐܘ ܐܢܬܬܐ. ܐܘ ܒܢ̈ܝܐ. ܐܘ ܩܘܪ̈ܝܐ.
ܡܛܠ ܫܡܝ ܕܝܠܝ. ܢܣܒ ܚܕ ܒܡܐܐ. ܘܒܥܠܡܐ
30 ܕܐܬܐ ܢܐܪܬ ܚܝ̈ܐ ܕܠܥܠܡ. ܣܓܝ̈ܐܐ ܕܝܢ ܩܕ̈ܡܝܐ
ܕܢܗܘܘܢ ܐܚܪ̈ܝܐ. ܘܐܚܪ̈ܝܐ ܕܢܗܘܘܢ ܩܕ̈ܡܝܐ ◌ ◌ ◌
XX. ܕܡܝܐ ܕܝܢ ܡܠܟܘܬܐ ܕܫܡܝܐ. ܠܓܒܪܐ ܡܪܐ ܒܝܬܐ.
2 ܕܢܦܩ ܒܨܦܪܐ ܠܡܐܓܪ ܦܥ̈ܠܐ ܠܟܪܡܗ. ܘܦܣܩ
ܥܡܗܘܢ ܥܡ ܦܥ̈ܠܐ. ܡܢ ܕܝܢܪܐ ܚܕ ܠܦܥܠܐ ܚܕ.

ܥܒܕܘ ܐܢܘܢ. ܘܐܝܬ ܕܗܢܘܢ ܥܒܕܘ ܢܦܫܗܘܢ
ܡܗ̈ܝܡܢܐ ܡܛܠ ܡܠܟܘܬܐ ܕܫܡܝܐ. ܡܢ ܕܡܨܐ
ܕܢ ܒܫܠܡܐ ܕܢܫܡܥ ܢܫܡܥ ◦◦◦
13 ܗܝܕܝܢ ܩܪܒܘ ܠܗ ܛ̈ܠܝܐ ܕܢܣܝܡ ܐܝܕܗ ܥܠܝܗܘܢ
14 ܘܢܨܠܐ. ܘܟܐܐܘ ܒܗܘܢ ܬܠܡ̈ܝܕܘܗܝ. ܐܡܪ ܠܗܘܢ
ܝܫܘܥ. ܫܒܘܩܘ ܛ̈ܠܝܐ ܐܬܝܢ ܠܘܬܝ ܘܠܐ ܬܟܠܘܢ
ܐܢܘܢ ܕܢܐܬܘܢ ܠܘܬܝ. ܐܝܠܝܢ ܓܝܪ ܕܐܟܘܬܗܘܢ ܗܠܝܢ ܐܢܘܢ
15 ܕܝܠܗܘܢ ܗܝ ܡܠܟܘܬܐ ܕܫܡܝܐ. ܘܣܡ ܐܝܕܗ
ܥܠܝܗܘܢ ܘܐܙܠ ܡܢ ܬܡܢ. ◦◦◦
16 ܘܩܪܒ ܓܒܪܐ ܚܕ ܘܐܡܪ ܠܗ. ܡܠܦܢܐ ܛܒܐ ܡܢܐ
17 ܐܥܒܕ ܕܐܝܪܬ ܚ̈ܝܐ ܕܠܥܠܡ. ܐܡܪ ܠܗ ܝܫܘܥ ܡܢܐ
ܡܫܐܠ ܐܢܬ ܠܝ ܥܠ ܛܒܐ. ܚܕ ܗܘ ܓܝܪ ܛܒܐ
ܐܠܗܐ. ܐܢ ܨܒܐ ܐܢܬ ܕܝܢ ܕܬܥܘܠ ܠܚ̈ܝܐ ܛܪ
18 ܦܘܩ̈ܕܢܐ. ܐܡܪ ܠܗ ܐܝܠܝܢ. ܐܡܪ ܠܗ ܝܫܘܥ. ܠܐ
ܬܩܛܘܠ. ܘܠܐ ܬܓܘܪ. ܘܠܐ ܬܓܢܘܒ. ܘܠܐ ܬܣܗܕ
19 ܣܗܕܘܬܐ ܕܫܘܩܪܐ. ܝܩܪ ܠܐܒܘܟ ܘܠܐܡܟ. ܘܐܚܒ
20 ܠܩܪܝܒܟ ܐܝܟ ܢܦܫܟ. ܐܡܪ ܠܗ ܗܘ ܥܠܝܡܐ ܗܠܝܢ
ܟܠܗܝܢ ܢܛܪܬ ܐܢܝܢ ܗܐ ܡܢ ܕܛܠܝܐ ܐܢܐ. ܡܢܐ ܬܘܒ
21 ܚܣܝܪܐ. ܐܡܪ ܠܗ ܝܫܘܥ. ܐܢ ܨܒܐ ܐܢܬ ܕܬܗܘܐ
ܓܡܝܪ. ܙܠ ܙܒܢ ܩܢܝܢܟ ܘܗܒ ܠܡܣ̈ܟܢܐ. ܘܬܗܘܐ
ܠܟ ܣܝܡܬܐ ܒܫܡܝܐ. ܘܣܒ ܨܠܝܒܟ ܘܬܐ ܒܬܪܝ.
22 ܘܟܕ ܫܡܥ ܥܠܝܡܐ ܗܘ ܡܠܬܐ ܗܕܐ. ܐܙܠ ܟܕ ܟܪܝܐ
23 ܠܗ. ܡܛܠ ܕܐܝܬ ܗܘܐ ܠܗ ܩܢܝܢܐ ܣܓܝܐܐ. ܝܫܘܥ

ܓܠܝܠܐ. ܘܐܬܐ ܠܗ ܠܬܚܘܡܐ ܕܝܗܘܕ. ܠܥܒܪܐ
2 ܕܝܘܪܕܢ. ܘܐܬܐ ܒܬܪܗ ܟܢܫܐ ܣܓܝܐܐ. ܘܐܣܝ
ܐܢܘܢ ܬܡܢ ° ° °
3 ܘܩܪܒܘ ܠܘܬܗ ܦܪ̈ܝܫܐ. ܘܡܢܣܝܢ ܗܘܘ ܠܗ ܘܐܡܪܝܢ
ܗܘܘ. ܕܐܢ ܗܘ ܕܫܠܝܛ ܠܓܒܪܐ ܕܢܫܪܐ ܐܢܬܬܗ ܥܠ
4 ܟܠ ܥܠܐ. ܗܘ ܕܝܢ ܥܢܐ ܘܐܡܪ ܠܗܘܢ. ܠܐ ܩܪܝܬܘܢ
ܕܡܢ ܕܒܪܐ ܠܒܪܢܫܐ ܡܢ ܒܪܫܝܬ ܐܦ ܠܢܩܒܬܐ ܗܘ ܒܪܐ.
5 ܘܐܡܪ ܕܡܛܠ ܗܕܐ ܢܫܒܘܩ ܓܒܪܐ ܠܐܒܘܗܝ
ܘܠܐܡܗ ܘܢܩܦ ܠܐܢܬܬܗ. ܘܢܗܘܘܢ ܬܪ̈ܝܗܘܢ ܚܕ
6 ܦܓܪ. ܡܟܝܠ ܠܐ ܗܘܘ ܬܪ̈ܝܢ. ܐܠܐ ܚܕ ܐܢܘܢ ܦܓܪ.
ܡܕܡ ܕܐܠܗܐ ܗܘ ܙܘܓ ܒܪܢܫܐ ܠܐ ܢܦܪܫ.
7 ܐܡܪܝܢ ܠܗ ܠܡܢܐ ܗܟܝܠ ܦܩܕ ܡܘܫܐ. ܕܡܢ ܕܨܒܐ
ܕܢܫܪܐ ܐܢܬܬܗ ܢܬܠ ܠܗ ܐܓܪܬܐ ܕܫܘܒܩܐ. ܐܡܪ
8 ܠܗܘܢ. ܡܘܫܐ ܡܛܠ ܩܫܝܘܬ ܠܒܟܘܢ ܗܘ ܐܦܣ ܠܟܘܢ
ܕܬܫܪܘܢ ܢܫ̈ܝܟܘܢ. ܡܢ ܒܪܫܝܬ ܕܝܢ ܠܐ ܗܘܐ ܗܟܢܐ
9 ܗܘܐ. ܐܡܪܢܐ ܠܟܘܢ ܕܝܢ ܕܡܢ ܕܫܒܩ ܐܢܬܬܗ ܕܠܐ
ܡܠܬܐ ܕܙܢܘܬܐ ܘܢܣܒ ܐܚܪܬܐ ܓܡܪ ܓܐܪ ܠܗ.
10 ܐܡܪܝܢ ܠܗ ܬܠܡ̈ܝܕܘܗܝ. ܐܢ ܗܟܢܐ ܐܝܬ ܥܠܬܐ
ܒܝܢ ܓܒܪܐ ܠܐܢܬܬܐ. ܠܐ ܦܩܚ ܠܡܣܒ ܐܢܬܬܐ.
11 ܐܡܪ ܠܗܘܢ ܝܫܘܥ. ܠܐ ܗܘܐ ܟܠ ܐܢܫ ܣܦܩ ܠܗ
ܠܡܠܬܐ ܗܕܐ. ܐܠܐ ܐܝܠܝܢ ܕܝܗܝܒ ܠܗܘܢ ܡܢ ܠܥܠ
12 ܐܠܗܐ. ܐܝܬ ܓܝܪ ܡܗ̈ܝܡܢܐ ܕܡܢ ܟܪܣܐ ܕܐܡܗܘܢ
ܗܘܘ ܡܗ̈ܝܡܢܐ. ܘܐܝܬ ܡܗ̈ܝܡܢܐ ܕܒ̈ܢܝ ܐܢܫܐ

ܫܪܝ ܠܡܚܫܒ ܚܘܫܒܢܐ. ܩܪܒ ܩܕܡܘܗܝ ܚܕ ܡܚܝܒܘܗܝ
25 ܕܚܝܒ ܗܘܐ ܠܗ ܪ̈ܒܘ ܟܟ̈ܪܝܢ. ܘܟܕ ܠܝܬ ܗܘܐ ܠܗ
ܠܡܦܪܥ. ܦܩܕ ܕܢܙܕܒܢ ܗܘ ܘܐܢܬܬܗ ܘܒ̈ܢܘܗܝ.
26 ܘܢܬܦܪܥ ܟܠ ܕܐܝܬ ܠܗ. ܘܢܦܠ ܥܒܕܐ ܗܘ ܘܣܓܕ
ܠܡܪܗ. ܘܐܡܪ ܐܓܪ ܥܠܝ ܪܘܚܐ ܘܟܠ ܡܕܡ ܦܪܥ
27 ܐܢܐ ܠܟ. ܘܐܬܪܚܡ ܥܠܘܗܝ ܡܪܗ ܘܫܪܝܗܝ. ܐܦ
28 ܚܘܒܬܐ ܫܒܩ ܠܗ. ܘܢܦܩ ܥܒܕܐ ܗܘ ܘܐܫܟܚ ܠܚܕ
ܡܢ ܟܢ̈ܘܬܗ. ܕܚܝܒ ܗܘܐ ܠܗ ܕ̈ܢܪܐ ܡܐܐ.
ܘܐܚܕܗ ܘܚܢܩ ܗܘܐ ܠܗ. ܘܐܡܪ ܗܘܐ ܠܗ
29 ܦܪܘܥܢܝ ܡܕܡ ܕܚܝܒ ܐܢܬ ܠܝ. ܘܢܦܠ ܗܘ ܟܢܬܗ
ܘܒܥܐ ܗܘܐ ܡܢܗ ܘܐܡܪ ܗܘܐ ܠܗ. ܐܓܪ ܥܠܝ
30 ܪܘܚܐ ܘܐܦ ܐܢܐ ܦܪܥ ܐܢܐ. ܗܘ ܕܝܢ ܠܐ ܩܒܠ
ܒܥܘܬܗ. ܐܠܐ ܐܙܠ ܐܪܡܝܗ ܒܝܬ ܐܣܘ̈ܪܐ. ܥܕܡܐ
31 ܕܢܦܪܥܝܘܗܝ ܡܕܡ ܕܚܝܒ. ܟܕ ܚܙܘ ܕܝܢ ܟܢ̈ܘܬܗ
ܐܠܝܢ ܕܗܘܝ. ܟܪܝܬ ܠܗܘܢ ܛܒ. ܘܐܬܘ ܘܚܘܘ
32 ܠܡܪܗܘܢ ܟܠ ܡܕܡ ܕܗܘܐ. ܗܝܕܝܢ ܩܪܝܗܝ ܡܪܗ
ܘܐܡܪ ܠܗ. ܥܒܕܐ ܒܝܫܐ. ܗܝ ܟܠܗ ܚܘܒܬܐ ܫܒܩܬ
33 ܠܟ ܡܛܠ ܕܒܥܝܬ ܡܢܝ. ܠܐ ܙܕܩ ܗܘܬ ܐܦ ܐܢܬ
34 ܕܬܚܘܢ ܠܟܢܬܟ ܐܝܟܢܐ ܕܐܢܐ ܚܢܬܟ. ܘܪܓܙ ܥܠܘܗܝ
ܡܪܗ. ܘܐܫܠܡܗ ܕܢܗܘܐ ܡܬܢܓܕ. ܥܕܡܐ ܕܢܦܪܘܥ
35 ܟܠܗ ܚܘܒܬܐ. ܗܟܢܐ ܢܥܒܕ ܠܟܘܢ ܐܒܝ ܕܒܫܡܝܐ.
ܐܠܐ ܬܫܒܩܘܢ ܐܢܫ ܠܐܚܘܗܝ ܡܢ ܠܒ̈ܘܬܟܘܢ ◦◦◦
XIX. ܘܗܘܐ ܟܕ ܫܠܡ ܝܫܘܥ ܡ̈ܠܐ ܗܠܝܢ. ܫܢܐ ܠܗ ܡܢ

ܕܐܫܟܚܝܗ. ܐܡܝܢ ܐܡܪ ܐܢܐ ܠܟܘܢ ܕܚܕܐ ܒܗ ܝܬܝܪ
14 ܡܢ ܗܢܘܢ ܬܫܥܝܢ ܘܬܫܥܐ ܐܝܠܝܢ ܕܠܐ ܛܥܘ. ܗܟܢܐ
ܠܐ ܨܒܐ ܐܒܘܟܘܢ ܕܒܫܡܝܐ ܕܢܐܒܕ ܚܕ ܡܢ ܗܠܝܢ
ܙܥܘܪ̈ܐ ◦ • ◦

15 ܐܢ ܕܝܢ ܐܣܟܠ ܒܟ ܐܚܘܟ ܐܟܣܝܗܝ ܒܝܢܝܟ ܘܠܗ
16 ܒܠܚܘܕ. ܐܢ ܫܡܥܟ ܝܬܪܬ ܐܚܘܟ. ܘܐܢ ܠܐ
ܢܫܡܥܟ ܕܒܪ ܥܡܟ ܬܘܒ ܚܕ ܐܘ ܬܪ̈ܝܢ. ܕܥܠ ܦܘܡ
17 ܬܪ̈ܝܢ ܬ̈ܠܬܐ ܣܗ̈ܕܝܢ ܬܩܘܡ ܟܠ ܡܠܐ. ܐܢ ܕܝܢ
ܠܐ ܢܫܡܥ ܐܢܘܢ ܐܡܪ ܠܥܕܬܐ. ܘܐܢ ܠܥܕܬܐ ܠܐ
ܢܫܡܥ. ܢܗܘܐ ܚܫܝܒ ܠܟ ܐܝܟ ܚܢܦܐ ܘܐܝܟ
18 ܡܟܣܐ. ܘܐܡܝܢ ܐܡܪ ܐܢܐ ܠܟܘܢ ܕܟܠ ܡܐ
ܕܬܐܣܪܘܢ ܒܐܪܥܐ ܢܗܘܐ ܐܣܝܪ ܒܫܡܝܐ. ܘܡܕܡ
19 ܕܬܫܪܘܢ ܒܐܪܥܐ ܢܗܘܐ ܫܪܐ ܒܫܡܝܐ ◦ ܬܘܒ
ܐܡܝܢ ܐܡܪ ܐܢܐ ܠܟܘܢ. ܕܐܢ ܬܪ̈ܝܢ ܡܢܟܘܢ ܢܫܬܘܘܢ
ܒܐܪܥܐ ܥܠ ܟܠ ܨܒܘ ܕܢܫܐܠܘܢ. ܢܗܘܐ ܠܗܘܢ ܡܢ ܠܘܬ
20 ܐܒܝ ܕܒܫܡܝܐ. ܐܝܟܐ ܓܝܪ ܕܟܢܝܫܝܢ ܬܪ̈ܝܢ ܐܘ ܬܠܬܐ
ܒܫܡܝ. ܬܡܢ ܐܢܐ ܒܡܨܥܬܗܘܢ ◦ ◦ ◦

21 ܗܝܕܝܢ ܩܪܒ ܠܘܬܗ ܫܡܥܘܢ ܟܐܦܐ ܘܐܡܪ ܠܗ.
ܡܪܝ، ܟܡܐ ܙܒ̈ܢܝܢ ܐܢ ܗܘ ܕܢܣܟܠ ܒܝ ܐܚܝ ܐܫܒܘܩ
22 ܠܗ. ܥܕܡܐ ܠܫܒܥ ܙܒ̈ܢܝܢ. ܐܡܪ ܠܗ ܠܐ ܫܒܥ. ܐܠܐ
ܥܠ ܫܒܥܝܢ ܫ̈ܒܥ ܫ̈ܒܥ ◦ ◦

23 ܡܛܠ ܗܢܐ ܕܡܝܐ ܡܠܟܘܬܐ ܕܫܡܝܐ ܠܓܒܪܐ
24 ܡܠܟܐ. ܕܨܒܐ ܠܡܣܒ ܚܘܫܒܢܐ ܡܢ ܥܒ̈ܕܘܗܝ. ܘܟܕ

4 ܬܥܠܘܢ ܠܡܠܟܘܬܐ ܕܫܡܝܐ. ܡܢ ܕܡܟܟ ܓܝܪ ܢܦܫܗ
ܐܝܟ ܗܢܐ ܛܠܝܐ ܗܘ ܪܒ ܒܡܠܟܘܬܐ ܕܫܡܝܐ.
5 ܘܡܢ ܕܢܩܒܠ ܐܝܟ ܚܕ ܡܢ ܗܠܝܢ ܛ̈ܠܝܐ ܒܫܡܝ ܠܝ ܗܘ
6 ܡܩܒܠ. ܘܟܠ ܕܢܟܫܠ ܠܚܕ ܡܢ ܗܠܝܢ ܙ̈ܥܘܪܐ ܐܝܠܝܢ
ܕܡܗܝܡܢܝܢ ܒܝ. ܦܩܚ ܗܘܐ ܠܗ ܕܬܗܘܐ ܬܠܝܐ
ܪܚܝܐ ܕܚܡܪܐ ܒܨܘܪܗ. ܘܢܬܛܒܥ ܒܥܘ̈ܡܩܘܗܝ
7 ܕܝܡܐ. ܘܝ ܠܥܠܡܐ ܡܢ ܡܟ̈ܫܘܠܐ ܕܐܬܝܢ. ܐܢܢܩܐ ܗܝ
ܓܝܪ ܕܢܐܬܘܢ ܡܟ̈ܫܘܠܐ. ܐܠܐ ܘܝ ܠܓܒܪܐ ܕܒܐܝܕܗ
8 ܢܐܬܘܢ ܡܟ̈ܫܘܠܐ. ܐܢ ܕܝܢ ܐܝܕܟ ܐܘ ܪܓܠܟ ܡܟܫܠܐ
ܠܟ ܦܣܘܩ ܫܕܝܗ ܡܢܟ. ܦܩܚ ܠܟ ܓܝܪ ܕܬܐܬܐ
ܠܚܝܐ ܟܕ ܚܓܝܪ ܐܢܬ ܐܘ ܟܕ ܦܣܝܩ ܐܢܬ. ܘܠܐ ܟܕ
ܐܝܬ ܠܟ ܬܪ̈ܬܝܢ ܐܝ̈ܕܝܢ ܘܬܪ̈ܬܝܢ ܪ̈ܓܠܝܢ ܬܦܠ ܒܓܗܢܐ
9 ܕܢܘܪܐ. ܘܐܢ ܗܘ ܕܥܝܢܟ ܡܟܫܠܐ ܠܟ ܚܨܝ ܫܕܝܗ
ܡܢܟ. ܦܩܚ ܠܟ ܕܬܥܘܠ ܠܚܝܐ ܟܕ ܐܝܬ ܠܟ
ܚܕܐ ܥܝܢܐ. ܘܠܐ ܟܕ ܐܝܬ ܠܟ ܬܪ̈ܬܝܢ ܥܝ̈ܢܝܢ ܬܦܘܠ
10 ܒܓܗܢܐ ܕܢܘܪܐ. ܚܙܘ ܕܠܡܐ ܬܒܣܘܢ ܒܚܕ ܡܢ ܗܠܝܢ
ܙ̈ܥܘܪܐ ܐܝܠܝܢ ܕܡܗܝܡܢܝܢ ܒܝ. ܐܡܪܢܐ ܠܟܘܢ ܓܝܪ
ܕܡ̈ܠܐܟܝܗܘܢ ܒܫܡܝܐ ܒܟܠܙܒܢ ܚܙܝܢ ܦܪ̈ܨܘܦܗ ܕܐܒܝ
11 ܕܒܫܡܝܐ. ܘܐܬܐ ܒܪܗ ܕܐܢܫܐ ܕܢܚܐ ܗܘ ܡܕܡ
ܕܐܒܝܕ ܗܘܐ ◦ ◦ ◦
12 ܡܢܐ ܕܝܢ ܡܬܚܙܐ ܠܟܘܢ. ܐܢ ܢܗܘܘܢ ܠܓܒܪ
ܡܐܐ ܥ̈ܪܒܝܢ ܘܛܥܐ ܚܕ ܡܢܗܘܢ. ܠܐ ܫܒܩ ܬܫܥܝܢ
13 ܘܬܫܥܐ ܒܛܘܪܐ. ܘܐܙܠ ܒܥܐ ܠܗܘ ܕܛܥܐ. ܘܐܢ

ܠܟܘܢ. ܕܐܢ ܗܘ ܕܬܗܘܐ ܒܟܘܢ ܗܝܡܢܘܬܐ ܐܝܟ
ܦܪܕܬܐ ܕܚܪܕܠܐ. ܬܐܡܪܘܢ ܠܛܘܪܐ ܗܢܐ ܕܫܢܐ
ܡܢ ܗܪܟܐ ܘܢܫܢܐ. ܘܡܕܡ ܠܐ ܢܚܣܘܟܘܢ ...
22 ܘܟܕ ܗܢܘܢ ܡܬܗܦܟܝܢ ܒܓܠܝܠܐ. ܐܡܪ ܠܗܘܢ ܝܫܘܥ.
ܥܬܝܕ ܗܘ ܕܝܢ ܒܪܗ ܕܐܢܫܐ ܕܢܫܬܠܡ ܒܐܝ̈ܕܝ ܒ̈ܢܝ
23 ܐܢܫܐ ܘܢܩܛܠܘܢܗ. ܘܠܝܘܡܐ ܕܬܠܬܐ ܢܩܘܡ. ܘܟܪܝܬ
ܠܗܘܢ ܛܒ ...
24 ܘܟܕ ܐܬܘ ܠܟܦܪܢܚܘܡ. ܐܬܘ ܗܢܘܢ ܕܓܒܝܢ ܬܪ̈ܝܢ
ܙܘ̈ܙܝܢ ܠܘܬ ܫܡܥܘܢ. ܘܐܡܪܝܢ ܠܗ ܪܒܟܘܢ ܠܐ ܝܗܒ
25 ܬܪ̈ܝܢ ܙܘ̈ܙܘܗܝ. ܘܐܡܪ ܫܡܥܘܢ ܐܝܢ. ܘܟܕ ܥܠ ܠܒܝܬܐ
ܩܕܡܗ ܝܫܘܥ. ܘܐܡܪ ܠܗ ܡܢܐ ܡܬܚܙܝܐ ܠܟ
ܫܡܥܘܢ. ܡ̈ܠܟܝܗ ܕܐܪܥܐ ܡܢ ܡܢ ܫܩܠܝܢ ܡܟܣܐ
26 ܘܟܣܦ ܪܝܫܐ. ܡܢ ܒܢܝ̈ܗܘܢ ܐܘ ܡܢ ܢܘܟ̈ܪܝܐ. ܐܡܪ ܠܗ
ܫܡܥܘܢ ܡܢ ܢܘܟ̈ܪܝܐ. ܐܡܪ ܠܗ ܝܫܘܥ ܡܕܝܢ ܒ̈ܢܝ
27 ܚܐܪ̈ܐ ܐܢܘܢ ܒܢܝ̈ܐ. ܕܠܐ ܕܝܢ ܢܟܫܠ ܐܢܘܢ. ܙܠ ܠܝܡܐ
ܘܐܪܡܐ ܓܪܓܬܐ. ܘܢܘܢܐ ܩܕܡܝܐ ܕܣܠܩ. ܗܘ ܘܦܬܚ
ܦܘܡܗ. ܘܬܫܟܚ ܬܡܢ ܐܣܬܪܐ. ܗܒܝܗ ܘܗܒܝܗ
ܚܠܦܝ ܘܚܠܦܝܟ ...
XVIII. ܘܒܗܘ ܫܥܬܐ ܩܪܒܘ ܗܢܘܢ ܬܠܡ̈ܝܕܘܗܝ ܕܝܫܘܥ
ܘܐܡܪܝܢ ܠܗ. ܡܢܘ ܟܝ ܪܒ ܒܡܠܟܘܬܐ
2 ܕܫܡܝܐ. ܘܩܪܐ ܝܫܘܥ ܠܛܠܝܐ ܚܕ. ܘܐܩܝܡܗ
3 ܒܡܨܥܬܗܘܢ. ܘܐܡܪ. ܐܡܝܢ ܐܡܪ ܐܢܐ ܠܟܘܢ. ܕܐܢ ܠܐ
ܬܬܗܦܟܘܢ ܘܬܗܘܘܢ ܐܝܟ ܚܕ ܡܢ ܗܠܝܢ ܛ̈ܠܝܐ. ܠܐ

ܠܗܘܢ ܝܫܘܥ ܘܐܡܪ ܠܗܘܢ. ܕܠܡܐ ܠܐܢܫ ܐܡܪܝܢ
ܐܢܬܘܢ ܚܙܘܐ. ܥܕܡܐ ܕܢܩܘܡ ܒܪܗ ܕܐܢܫܐ ܡܢ
ܒܝܬ ܡ̈ܝܬܐ ◎ ○ ◎
10 ܘܡܫܐܠܝܢ ܗܘܘ ܠܗ ܬܠܡ̈ܝܕܘܗܝ ܘܐܡܪܝܢ. ܠܡܢܐ
11 ܐܡܪܝܢ ܣ̈ܦܪܐ ܕܐܠܝܐ ܐܬܐ ܠܘܩܕܡ. ܐܡܪ ܠܗܘܢ
12 ܐܠܝܐ ܐܬܐ ܕܢܬܩܢ ܟܠܡܕܡ. ܐܡܪܢܐ ܠܟܘܢ ܕܗܐ
ܐܠܝܐ ܐܬܐ ܘܠܐ ܝܕܥܘܗܝ. ܐܠܐ ܥܒܕܘ ܒܗ ܟܠ
ܡܐ ܕܨܒܘ. ܗܟܢܐ ܐܦ ܒܪܗ ܕܐܢܫܐ ܥܬܝܕ ܗܘ
13 ܕܢܚܫ ܡܢܗܘܢ. ܗܝܕܝܢ ܐܣܬܟܠܘ ܬܠܡ̈ܝܕܘܗܝ ܕܥܠ
14 ܝܘܚܢܢ ܗܘ ܡܥܡܕܢܐ ܐܡܪ ܠܗܘܢ ܗܟܢܐ. ܘܟܕ
ܐܬܐ ܝܫܘܥ ܠܘܬ ܟܢܫܐ. ܐܬܐ ܓܒܪܐ ܚܕ ܘܢܦܠ
15 ܥܠ ܒܘܪ̈ܟܘܗܝ. ܘܒܥܐ ܗܘܐ ܡܢܗ ܘܐܡܪ ܠܗ. ܡܪܝ
ܐܬܪܚܡ ܥܠܝ. ܒܪܝ ܒܪ ܐܓܪܐ ܐܝܬ ܠܗ. ܘܒܝܫܐܝܬ
ܡܫܬܢܩ. ܙܒܢܐ ܓܝܪ ܣ̈ܓܝܐܢ ܒܢܘܪܐ ܢܦܠ. ܘܙܒܢܐ
16 ܣ̈ܓܝܐܢ ܒܡ̈ܝܐ. ܘܩܪܒܬܗ ܠܬܠܡ̈ܝܕܝܟ ܘܠܐ ܐܫܟܚܘ
17 ܠܡܐܣܝܘܬܗ. ܥܢܐ ܝܫܘܥ ܘܐܡܪ ܠܗܘܢ. ܐܘ
ܫܪܒܬܐ ܡܥܩܠܬܐ ܘܕܠܐ ܗܝܡܢܘ. ܥܕܡܐ ܠܐܡܬܝ
ܐܗܘܐ ܠܘܬܟܘܢ ܘܐܣܝܒܪܟܘܢ. ܐܝܬܝܘܗܝ ܠܝ ܠܗܪܟ
18 ܠܟܐ. ܘܟܐܐ ܒܗ ܝܫܘܥ. ܘܢܦܩ ܡܢܗ ܫܐܕܐ. ܘܡܢ
19 ܗܝ ܫܥܬܐ ܐܬܐܣܝ ܛܠܝܐ ܗܘ. ܗܝܕܝܢ ܩܪܒܘ ܠܘܬ
ܝܫܘܥ ܬܠܡ̈ܝܕܘܗܝ ܘܐܡܪܝܢ ܠܗ ܒܝܢܝܗܘܢ ܘܠܗ.
20 ܠܡܢܐ ܚܢܢ ܠܐ ܐܫܟܚܢ ܠܡܐܣܝܘܬܗ. ܐܡܪ ܠܗܘܢ
ܡܛܠ ܙܥܘܪܘܬ ܗܝܡܢܘܬܟܘܢ. ܐܡܝܢ ܓܝܪ ܐܡܪܢܐ

27 ܡܢܐ ܢܬܠ ܒܪܢܫܐ ܬܘܠܦܐ ܕܢܦܫܗ. ܥܬܝܕ ܗܘ ܓܝܪ
ܒܪܗ ܕܐܢܫܐ ܕܐܬܐ ܒܬܫܒܘܚܬܐ ܕܐܒܘܗܝ ܥܡ
ܡܠܐ̈ܟܘܗܝ. ܘܗܝܕܝܢ ܢܦܪܘܥ ܠܐܢܫ ܐܢܫ ܐܝܟ
28 ܥܒ̈ܕܘܗܝ. ܐܡܝܢ ܐܡܪܢܐ ܠܟܘܢ ܕܐܝܬ ܐܢܫܐ ܡܢ
ܗܠܝܢ ܕܩܝܡܝܢ ܗܪܟܐ. ܕܠܐ ܢܛܥܡܘܢ ܡܘܬܐ.
ܥܕܡܐ ܕܢܚܙܘܢ ܠܒܪܗ ܕܐܢܫܐ. ܟܕ ܐܬܐ ܒܡܠܟܘܬܗ
ܘܒܫܘܒܚܗ. ∘∘ ∘∘ ∘∘
XVII. ܒܬܪ ܫܬܐ ܝܘ̈ܡܝܢ. ܕܒܪ ܝܫܘܥ ܠܫܡܥܘܢ ܟܐܦܐ.
ܘܠܝܥܩܘܒ ܘܠܝܘܚܢܢ ܐܚܘܗܝ. ܘܐܣܩ ܐܢܘܢ ܠܛܘܪܐ
2 ܪܡܐ ܒܠܚܘܕܝܗܘܢ. ܘܐܫܬܚܠܦ ܚܙܘܐ ܕܐܦ̈ܘܗܝ
ܠܥܝ̈ܢܝܗܘܢ. ܘܐܢܗܪ ܦܪܨܘܦܗ ܐܝܟ ܫܡܫܐ.
3 ܘܢ̈ܚܬܘܗܝ ܚܘܪܘ ܐܝܟ ܬܠܓܐ. ܘܐܬܚܙܝ ܠܗܘܢ
4 ܡܘܫܐ ܘܐܠܝܐ ܟܕ ܡܡܠܠܝܢ ܥܡܗ. ܐܡܪ ܫܡܥܘܢ
ܟܐܦܐ ܠܝܫܘܥ. ܫܦܝܪ ܗܘ ܠܢ ܕܗܪܟܐ ܢܗܘܐ. ܐܢ
ܨܒܐ ܐܢܬ ܢܥܒܕ ܗܪܟܐ ܬܠܬ ܡܛ̈ܠܠܝܢ. ܠܟ ܚܕܐ.
5 ܘܠܡܘܫܐ ܚܕܐ. ܘܠܐܠܝܐ ܚܕܐ. ܘܟܕ ܗܘ ܡܡܠܠ.
ܗܐ ܥܢܢܐ ܕܢܘܗܪܐ ܐܛܠܠܬ ܥܠܝܗܘܢ. ܘܩܠܐ
ܐܫܬܡܥ ܡܢ ܥܢܢܐ ܗܝ ܕܐܡܪ. ܗܢܐ ܗܘ ܒܪܝ
6 ܘܚܒܝܒܝ ܕܒܗ ܨܒܝܬ. ܠܗ ܫܡܥܘ. ܘܟܕ ܫܡܥܘ
7 ܬܠܡ̈ܝܕܘܗܝ ܕܚܠܘ ܛܒ. ܘܢܦܠܘ ܥܠ ܐ̈ܦܝܗܘܢ. ܘܩܪܒ
ܝܫܘܥ ܘܐܩܝܡ ܐܢܘܢ ܘܐܡܪ ܠܗܘܢ. ܠܐ ܬܕܚܠܘܢ.
8 ܘܐܪܝܡܘ ܥܝ̈ܢܝܗܘܢ ܘܠܐ ܚܙܘ ܐܠܐ ܠܝܫܘܥ
9 ܒܠܚܘܕܘܗܝ. ܘܟܕ ܢܚܬܝܢ ܡܢ ܛܘܪܐ. ܦܩܕ ܗܘܐ

17 ܡܫܝܚܐ ܒܪܗ ܕܐܠܗܐ ܚܝܐ. ܐܡܪ ܠܗ ܝܫܘܥ
ܛܘܒܝܟ ܫܡܥܘܢ ܒܪܗ ܕܝܘܢܐ. ܕܒܣܪܐ ܘܕܡܐ ܠܐ
18 ܓܠܐ ܠܟ. ܐܠܐ ܐܒܝ ܕܒܫܡܝܐ. ܐܦ ܐܢܐ ܐܡܪ
ܐܢܐ ܠܟ ܕܐܢܬ ܗܘ ܟܐܦܐ. ܘܥܠ ܗܕܐ ܟܐܦܐ
19 ܐܒܢܝܗ ܠܥܕܬܝ. ܘܬܪ̈ܥܐ ܕܫܝܘܠ ܠܐ ܢܚܣܢܘܢܗ̇. ܠܟ
ܐܬܠ ܐܩܠܝ̈ܕܐ ܕܬܪ̈ܥܐ ܕܡܠܟܘܬܐ ܕܫܡܝܐ. ܘܟܠ
ܡܕܡ ܕܬܐܣܘܪ ܒܐܪܥܐ ܢܗܘܐ ܐܣܝܪ ܒܫܡܝܐ.
ܘܡܕܡ ܕܬܫܪܐ ܒܐܪܥܐ ܢܗܘܐ ܫܪܐ ܒܫܡܝܐ.
20 ܗܝܕܝܢ ܟܐܐ ܒܗܘܢ ܒܬܠܡܝ̈ܕܘܗܝ ܕܠܐܢܫ ܠܐ
ܢܐܡܪܘܢ ܥܠܘܗܝ ܕܗܘܝܘ ܡܫܝܚܐ ◎ ◦ ◎
21 ܡܢ ܗܝܕܝܢ ܫܪܝ ܗܘܐ ܝܫܘܥ ܠܡܚܘܝܘ ܐܢܘܢ
ܠܬܠܡܝ̈ܕܘܗܝ. ܕܥܬܝܕ ܗܘ ܕܢܐܙܠ ܠܐܘܪܫܠܡ. ܘܢܣܒܪ
ܣܓܝ. ܘܢܚܫ ܡܢ ܩܫܝ̈ܫܐ ܘܪ̈ܒܝ ܟܗ̈ܢܐ ܘܣܦ̈ܪܐ.
22 ܘܢܩܛܠܘܢܗ. ܘܠܝܘܡܐ ܕܬܠܬܐ ܢܩܘܡ. ܘܢܣܒ
ܫܡܥܘܢ ܟܐܦܐ ܘܐܡܪ ܚܣ ܠܟ ܡܪܝ. ܠܐ ܬܗܘܐ
23 ܗܕܐ. ܗܘ ܕܝܢ ܝܫܘܥ ܐܬܦܢܝ ܘܚܙܐ ܒܗ ܒܫܡܥܘܢ
ܘܐܡܪ ܠܗ. ܙܠ ܠܟ ܠܒܣܬܪܝ ܣܛܢܐ ܬܘܩܠܬܐ ܐܢܬ
ܠܝ. ܕܠܐ ܡܬܪܥܐ ܐܢܬ ܕܐܠܗܐ ܐܠܐ ܕܒ̈ܢܝ ܐܢܫܐ.
24 ܗܝܕܝܢ ܐܡܪ ܝܫܘܥ ܠܬܠܡܝ̈ܕܘܗܝ. ܡܢ ܕܨܒܐ ܕܢܐܬܐ
ܒܬܪܝ ܢܟܦܘܪ ܒܢܦܫܗ. ܘܢܫܩܘܠ ܙܩܝܦܗ ܘܢܐܬܐ
25 ܒܬܪܝ. ܡܢ ܕܨܒܐ ܓܝܪ ܕܢܚܐ ܢܦܫܗ ܢܘܒܕܝܗ. ܘܡܢ
26 ܕܢܘܒܕ ܢܦܫܗ ܡܛܠܬܝ ܢܫܟܚܝܗ. ܡܢܐ ܓܝܪ ܡܬܗܢܐ
ܒܪ̈ܢܫܐ ܐܢ ܠܥܠܡܐ ܟܠܗ ܢܩܢܐ ܘܢܦܫܗ ܢܚܣܪ. ܐܘ

7 ܚܡܝܪܐ ܕܦܪ̈ܝܫܐ ܘܕܙܕܘ̈ܩܝܐ. ܘܗܢܘܢ ܡܬܚܫܒܝܢ
8 ܗܘܘ ܒܢܦܫܗܘܢ. ܕܠܐ ܢܣܒܘ ܠܗܘܢ ܠܚܡܐ. ܝܕܥ
ܕܝܢ ܝܫܘܥ ܘܐܡܪ ܠܗܘܢ. ܡܢܐ ܡܬܚܫܒܝܢ ܐܢܬܘܢ
ܒܢܦܫܟܘܢ ܚܣܝܪܝ ܗܝܡܢܘܬܐ. ܕܠܐ ܢܣܒܬܘܢ ܠܟܘܢ
9 ܠܚܡܐ. ܥܕܡܐ ܠܗܫܐ ܠܐ ܡܣܬܟܠܝܢ ܐܢܬܘܢ.
ܘܠܐ ܥܗܕܝܢ ܐܢܬܘܢ ܠܚܡܫܐ ܠܚ̈ܡܝܢ. ܐܦ
ܠܚܡܫܐ ܐܠܦܝܢ ܕܐܟܠܘ ܡܢܗܘܢ. ܘܟܡܐ ܩܘ̈ܦܝܢ
10 ܫܩܠܬܘܢ ܡܢ ܩܨ̈ܝܗܘܢ. ܘܐܦ ܠܐ ܠܗܠܝܢ ܫܒܥܐ
ܠܚ̈ܡܝܢ ܕܐܪ̈ܒܥܐ ܐ̈ܠܦܝܢ ܐܟܠܘ ܡܢܗܘܢ. ܘܟܡܐ
11 ܕܝܢ ܐ̈ܣܦܝܪܝܢ ܫܩܠܬܘܢ. ܐܝܟܢ ܠܐ ܡܣܬܟܠܝܢ
ܐܢܬܘܢ ܕܠܐ ܗܘܐ ܥܠ ܠܚܡܐ ܐܡܪܬ ܠܟܘܢ.
12 ܕܐܙܕܗܪܘ ܡܢ ܚܡܝܪܐ ܕܦܪ̈ܝܫܐ ܘܕܙܕܘ̈ܩܝܐ. ܗܝܕܝܢ
ܐܣܬܟܠܘ ܕܠܐ ܗܘܐ ܥܠ ܚܡܝܪܐ ܕܦܪ̈ܝܫܐ
ܘܕܙܕܘ̈ܩܝܐ ܐܡܪ ܠܗܘܢ ܕܐܙܕܗܪܘ. ܐܠܐ ܡܢ
ܝܘܠܦܢܗܘܢ ܕܦܪ̈ܝܫܐ ܘܕܙܕܘ̈ܩܝܐ ◎ ○ ◎
13 ܘܟܕ ܐܬܐ ܕܝܢ ܝܫܘܥ ܠܐܬܪܐ ܕܩܣܪܝܐ ܕܦܝܠܝܦܘܣ.
ܡܫܐܠ ܗܘܐ ܠܬܠܡܝܕܘܗܝ ܘܐܡܪ. ܡܢܐ ܐܡܪܝܢ
ܐܢܫܐ ܥܠܝ ܕܐܝܬܝ. ܡܢܘ ܠܡ ܗܢܐ ܒܪܗ ܕܐܢܫܐ.
14 ܐܡܪܝܢ ܠܗ ܬܠܡܝܕܘܗܝ. ܐܝܬ ܕܐܡܪܝܢ ܕܝܘܚܢܢ ܗܘ
ܡܥܡܕܢܐ. ܐܚܪ̈ܢܐ ܐܡܪܝܢ ܕܐܠܝܐ ܗܘ. ܐܚܪ̈ܢܐ
ܐܡܪܝܢ ܐܪܡܝܐ ܗܘ. ܐܚܪ̈ܢܐ ܐܡܪܝܢ ܚܕ ܡܢ ܢܒ̈ܝܐ
15 ܗܘ. ܐܡܪ ܠܗܘܢ ܘܐܢܬܘܢ ܡܢܐ ܐܡܪܝܢ ܐܢܬܘܢ
16 ܕܐܝܬܝ. ܥܢܐ ܫܡܥܘܢ ܟܐܦܐ ܘܐܡܪ. ܐܢܬ ܗܘ

ܩܪܐ ܠܬܠܡܝܕܘܗܝ ܘܐܡܪ ܠܗܘܢ. ܡܬܪܚܡ ܐܢܐ
ܥܠ ܟܢܫܐ ܗܢܐ. ܕܗܐ ܬܠܬܐ ܝܘ̈ܡܝܢ ܩܘܘ ܠܘܬܝ.
ܘܠܝܬ ܠܗܘܢ ܡܕܡ ܕܢܐܟܠܘܢ. ܘܕܐܫܪܐ ܐܢܘܢ ܟܕ
ܨܝܡܝܢ ܐܢܘܢ ܠܐ ܨܒܐ ܐܢܐ. ܕܠܐ ܢܫܬܪܘܢ ܠܗܘܢ
33 ܒܐܘܪܚܐ. ܐܡܪܝܢ ܠܗ ܬܠܡܝ̈ܕܘܗܝ. ܡܢ ܐܝܟܐ
ܠܢ ܒܡܕܒܪܐ ܚܘܪܒܐ ܠܚܡܐ ܠܡܣܒܥܘ ܠܟܠܗ ܟܢܫܐ
34 ܗܢܐ. ܐܡܪ ܠܗܘܢ ܝܫܘܥ ܟܡܐ ܠܚܡ̈ܝܢ ܐܝܬ
ܠܟܘܢ. ܐܡܪܝܢ ܠܗ ܫܒܥܐ ܠܚܡ̈ܝܢ. ܘܩܠܝܠ ܢܘ̈ܢܐ.
35, 36 ܘܦܩܕ ܠܟܢܫܐ ܕܢܣܬܡܟܘܢ ܥܠ ܐܪܥܐ. ܘܢܣܒ
ܠܫܒܥܐ ܠܚܡ̈ܝܢ ܘܠܢܘ̈ܢܐ. ܘܒܪܟ ܘܩܨܐ ܘܝܗܒ
37 ܠܬܠܡܝ̈ܕܘܗܝ ܘܬܠܡܝ̈ܕܘܗܝ ܝܗܒܘ ܠܟܢܫܐ. ܘܐܟܠܘ
ܟܠܗܘܢ ܘܣܒܥܘ. ܘܫܩܠܘ ܡܢ ܩܨ̈ܝܗܘܢ ܘܝܬܪܐ
38 ܕܩ̈ܨܐ ܡܠܝܐ ܫܒܥܐ ܐ̈ܣܦܪܝܕܝܢ ܟܕ ܡܠܝܢ. ܘܗܢܘܢ
ܗܘܘ ܐܢܫܐ ܐܝܠܝܢ ܕܐܟܠܘ ܐܪ̈ܒܥܐ ܐ̈ܠܦܝܢ ܓܒ̈ܪܝܢ.
ܣܛܪ ܡܢ ܛ̈ܠܝܐ ܘܢ̈ܫܐ. ◦ ◦ ◦
39 ܘܟܕ ܫܪܐ ܠܟܢܫܐ. ܣܠܩ ܝܬܒ ܠܗ ܒܣܦܝܢܬܐ. ܘܐܬܐ
XVI. ܠܗ ܠܬܚܘܡܐ ܕܡܓܕܘ. ܘܩܪܒܘ ܦܪ̈ܝܫܐ ܘܙ̈ܕܘܩܝܐ
ܘܡܢܣܝܢ ܗܘܘ ܠܗ. ܘܫܐܠܝܢ ܠܗ ܐܬܐ ܡܢ ܫܡܝܐ
2, 4 ܕܢܚܘܐ ܐܢܘܢ. ܗܘ ܕܝܢ ܐܡܪ ܠܗܘܢ. ܫܪܒܬܐ ܒܝܫܬܐ
ܘܓܝܪܬܐ. ܐܬܐ ܒܥܝܐ ܘܐܬܐ ܠܐ ܬܬܝܗܒ ܠܗ.
ܐܠܐ ܐܢ ܐܬܐ ܕܝܘܢܢ ܢܒܝܐ. ܘܫܒܩ ܐܢܘܢ ܘܐܙܠ
5 ܠܗ. ܘܟܕ ܐܬܘ ܠܥܒܪܐ. ܛܥܘ ܬܠܡܝ̈ܕܘܗܝ ܕܢܣܒܘܢ
6 ܠܗܘܢ ܠܚܡܐ. ܐܡܪ ܠܗܘܢ ܝܫܘܥ. ܐܙܕܗܪܘ ܡܢ

22 ܘܕܨܝܕܢ. ܘܗܐ ܐܢܬܬܐ ܚܕܐ ܟܢܥܢܝܬܐ ܢܦܩܬ
ܡܢܗܘܢ ܡܢ ܬܚܘ̈ܡܐ ܗܠܝܢ. ܘܩܥܝܐ ܗܘܬ
ܘܐܡܪܐ. ܐܬܪܚܡ ܥܠܝ ܡܪܝ ܒܪܗ ܕܕܘܝܕ. ܒܪܬܝ
23 ܒܝܫܐܝܬ ܡܬܕܒܪܐ ܡܢ ܫܐ̈ܕܝ ܥܐܕܐ. ܘܗܘ ܠܐ ܝܗܒ
ܠܗ ܦܬܓܡܐ. ܘܩܪܒܘ ܬܠܡܝ̈ܕܘܗܝ ܘܒܥܝܢ ܗܘܘ ܡܢܗ
ܘܐܡܪܝܢ ܗܘܘ ܠܗ. ܫܪܝܗ ܕܗܐ ܡܩܥܝܐ ܘܐܬܝܐ
24 ܒܬܪܢ. ܗܘ ܕܝܢ ܥܢܐ ܘܐܡܪ ܠܗܘܢ. ܠܐ ܐܫܬܕܪܬ
ܐܠܐ ܒܬܪ ܥܢܐ ܗܠܝܢ ܕܐܒܕ. ܡܢ ܒܝܬ ܐܝܣܪܝܠ
25 ܗܝܕܝܢ ܗܝ ܩܪܒܬ ܣܓܕܬ ܠܗ ܘܐܡܪܐ ܠܗ ܡܪܝ ܥܕܪܝܢܝ.
26 ܗܘ ܕܝܢ ܥܢܐ ܘܐܡܪ ܠܗ̇. ܠܐ ܘܠܐ ܠܡܣܒ ܠܚܡܐ
27 ܕܒܢ̈ܝܐ ܘܠܡܪܡܝܘ ܠܟܠ̈ܒܐ. ܐܡܪܐ ܠܗ ܐܝܢ ܡܪܝ. ܐܦ
ܟܠ̈ܒܐ ܒܪܢ ܐܟܠܝܢ ܡܢ ܦܪ̈ܬܘܬܐ ܕܢܦܠܝܢ ܡܢ ܦܬܘܪ̈ܐ
28 ܕܡܪ̈ܝܗܘܢ ܘܚܝܝܢ. ܘܥܢܐ ܘܐܡܪ ܠܗ̇. ܐܘ ܐܢܬܬܐ
ܪܒܐ ܗܝ ܗܝܡܢܘܬܟܝ. ܢܗܘܐ ܠܟܝ ܐܝܟ ܕܨܒܝܐ ܐܢܬܝ.
ܘܐܬܐܣܝܬ ܒܪܬܗ̇ ܡܢ ܗܝ ܫܥܬܐ ◦
29 ܘܫܢܝ ܝܫܘܥ ܡܢ ܬܡܢ. ܘܐܬܐ ܠܗ ܥܠ ܓܢܒ ܝܡܬܐ
30 ܕܓܠܝܠܐ. ܘܣܠܩ ܝܬܒ ܠܗ ܒܛܘܪܐ. ܘܩܪܒܘ ܠܗ ܟܢ̈ܫܐ
ܣܓ̈ܝܐܐ. ܟܕ ܐܝܬ ܗܘܘ ܥܡܗܘܢ ܚܓ̈ܝܪܐ ܘܣܡ̈ܝܐ
ܘܚܪ̈ܫܐ ܘܦܟ̈ܝܚܐ. ܘܣܓ̈ܝܐܐ ܕܟܐ̈ܒܐ ܐܚܪ̈ܢܐ.
ܘܐܪܡܝܘ ܐܢܘܢ ܠܘܬ ܪ̈ܓܠܘܗܝ. ܘܐܣܝ ܐܢܘܢ.
31 ܘܡܬܕܡܪܝܢ ܗܘܘ ܟܢ̈ܫܐ ܗܢܘܢ. ܟܕ ܚܙܝܢ ܗܘܘ ܚܪ̈ܫܐ
ܕܡܡܠܠܝܢ. ܘܚܓ̈ܝܪܐ ܕܡܗܠܟܝܢ. ܘܣܡ̈ܝܐ ܕܚܙܝܢ.
32 ܘܡܫܒܚܝܢ ܗܘܘ ܠܐܠܗܐ ܕܐܝܣܪܝܠ. ܗܘ ܕܝܢ ܝܫܘܥ

ܗܢܐ ܒܣܦ̈ܘܬܗ ܗܘ ܡܝܩܪ ܠܝ. ܘܠܒܗ ܪܚܝܩ ܡܢܝ.
9 ܣܪܝܩܐܝܬ ܕܝܢ ܕܚܠܝܢ ܠܝ. ܘܡܠܦܝܢ ܝ̈ܘܠܦܢܐ ܕܦ̈ܘܩܕܢܐ
ܕܒܢ̈ܝܢܫܐ ܀
10 ܘܩܪܐ ܠܟܢܫܐ ܘܐܡܪ ܠܗܘܢ. ܫܡܥܘ ܘܐܣܬܟܠܘ
11 ܕܠܐ ܗܘܐ ܡܕܡ ܕܥܐܠ ܠܦܘܡܐ ܡܣܝܒ ܠܗ ܠܒܪ
ܐܢܫܐ. ܐܠܐ ܡܕܡ ܕܢܦܩ ܡܢ ܦܘܡܐ ܗܘ ܗܘ
12 ܡܣܝܒ ܠܗ ܠܒܪܢܫܐ. ܗܝܕܝܢ ܩܪܒܘ ܬܠܡܝ̈ܕܘܗܝ
ܘܐܡܪܝܢ ܠܗ. ܝܕܥ ܐܢܬ ܕܦܪ̈ܝܫܐ ܟܕ ܫܡܥܘ ܡܠܬܐ
13 ܗܕܐ ܐܬܟܫܠܘ. ܗܘ ܕܝܢ ܥܢܐ ܘܐܡܪ ܠܗܘܢ. ܟܠ
14 ܢܨܒܬܐ ܕܐܒܝ ܕܒܫܡܝܐ ܠܐ ܢܨܒܗ̇ ܬܬܥܩܪ. ܫܒܘܩܘ
ܠܗܘܢ. ܣܡ̈ܝܐ ܐܢܘܢ ܗ̈ܕܝܐ. ܣܡܝܐ ܕܝܢ ܕܠܣܡܝܐ
15 ܡܕܒܪ ܬܪܝܗܘܢ ܒܓܘܡܨܐ ܢܦܠ. ܥܢܐ ܫܡܥܘܢ ܟܐܦܐ
16 ܘܐܡܪ ܠܗ. ܦܫܩ ܠܢ ܡܬܠܐ ܗܢܐ. ܐܡܪ ܠܗ ܐܦ
ܠܐ ܐܢܬܘܢ ܥܕܟܐ ܠܗܢܐ ܡܣܬܟܠܝܢ ܐܢܬܘܢ.
17 ܠܐ ܝܕܥܝܢ ܐܢܬܘܢ ܕܟܠ ܡܕܡ ܕܥܐܠ ܠܦܘܡܐ
ܠܟܪܣܐ ܗܘ ܐܙܠ. ܘܡܢ ܬܡܢ ܡܫܬܕܐ ܒܬܕܟܝܬܐ.
18 ܡܕܡ ܕܝܢ ܕܢܦܩ ܡܢ ܦܘܡܐ ܡܢ ܠܒܐ ܗܘ ܢܦܩ. ܘܗܘ
19 ܗܘ ܡܣܝܒ ܠܗ ܠܒܪܢܫܐ. ܡܢ ܠܒܐ ܗܘ ܓܝܪ ܢܦܩ
ܡܚܫܒ̈ܬܐ ܒܝ̈ܫܬܐ. ܕܩܛܠܐ ܘܓܘܪܐ. ܘܙܢܝܘܬܐ.
20 ܘܓܢܒܘܬܐ. ܘܣܗܕܘܬܐ ܕܫܘܩܪܐ ܘܓܘܕܦܐ. ܗܠܝܢ
ܐܢܝܢ ܕܡܣܝܒܢ ܠܒܪܢܫܐ. ܟܕ ܐܢܫ ܓܝܪ ܢܐܟܘܠ ܠܚܡܐ
ܟܕ ܠܐ ܡܫܝܓ ܐܝ̈ܕܘܗܝ ܠܐ ܡܣܬܝܒ ◌
21 ܘܢܦܩ ܝܫܘܥ ܡܢ ܬܡܢ. ܘܐܙܠ ܠܗ ܠܬܚܘܡܐ ܕܨܘܪ

31 ܡܪܝ ܐܚܝܢ. ܘܒܗ̇ ܒܫܥܬܐ ܐܘܫܛ ܝܫܘܥ ܐܝܕܗ
ܘܐܚܕܗ. ܘܐܡܪ ܠܗ ܚܣܝܪ ܗܝܡܢܘܬܐ ܠܡܢܐ
32 ܐܬܦܠܓܬ. ܘܟܕ ܣܠܩ ܠܣܦܝܢܬܐ ܫܠܝܬ ܪܘܚܐ.
33 ܘܩܪܒܘ ܗܢܘܢ ܕܒܣܦܝܢܬܐ ܣܓܕܘ ܠܗ. ܘܐܡܪܝܢ
34 ܫܪܝܪܐܝܬ ܒܪܗ ܐܢܬ ܕܐܠܗܐ. ܘܟܕ ܣܠܩ ܠܝܒܫܐ.
35 ܐܬܘ ܠܗܘܢ ܠܓܢܣܪ. ܘܐܫܬܘܕܥܘܗܝ ܒ̈ܢܝ ܐܬܪܐ ܗܘ.
ܘܫܕܪܘ ܠܟܠܗ̇ ܒܘܪ ܕܠܗܘܢ. ܘܩܪܒܘ ܩܕܡܘܗܝ
36 ܟܠܗܘܢ ܐܝܠܝܢ ܕܒܝܫ ܒܝܫ ܒܟܘܪܗܢ. ܘܒܥܝܢ ܗܘܘ ܡܢܗ
ܕܢܩܪܒܘܢ ܒܠܒܘܫܗ ܠܬܟܠܬܐ ܕܐܣܛܠܗ. ܘܐܝܠܝܢ ܕܩܪܒܘ
ܗܘܘ ܐܬܐܣܝܘ ܗܘܘ ◎ ◦ ◎

XV. ܗܝܕܝܢ ܩܪܒܘ ܠܘܬܗ ܕܝܫܘܥ ܣܦ̈ܪܐ ܘܦܪ̈ܝܫܐ ܕܡܢ
2 ܐܘܪܫܠܡ ܘܐܡܪܝܢ ܠܗ. ܠܡܢܐ ܥܒܪܝܢ ܬܠܡܝ̈ܕܝܟ ܥܠ
ܦܘܩܕܢܐ ܕܩܕ̈ܡܝܢ. ܠܐ ܓܝܪ ܡܫܝܓܝܢ ܐܝ̈ܕܝܗܘܢ ܡܐ
3 ܕܐܟܠܝܢ ܠܚܡܐ. ܗܘ ܕܝܢ ܥܢܐ ܘܐܡܪ ܠܗܘܢ. ܠܡܢܐ
ܘܐܦ ܐܢܬܘܢ ܥܒܪܝܢ ܐܢܬܘܢ ܥܠ ܦܘܩܕܢܐ ܕܐܠܗܐ
4 ܡܛܠ ܕܬܩܝܡܘܢ ܦܘܩ̈ܕܢܝܟܘܢ. ܐܠܗܐ ܓܝܪ ܐܡܪ
ܝܩܪ ܠܐܒܘܟ ܘܠܐܡܟ. ܘܡܢ ܕܡܨܚܐ ܠܐܒܘܗܝ
5 ܐܘ ܠܐܡܗ ܢܬܩܛܠ. ܐܢܬܘܢ ܕܝܢ ܐܡܪܝܢ ܐܢܬܘܢ
ܐܢܫ ܠܐܒܘܗܝ ܘܠܐܡܗ. ܩܘܪܒܢ ܬܬܗܢܐ ܡܢܝ.
6 ܗܢܐ ܠܐ ܝܩܪ ܠܐܒܘܗܝ. ܘܒܛܠܬܘܢ ܡܠܬܐ ܕܐܠܗܐ
7 ܡܛܠ ܕܬܩܝܡܘܢ ܦܘܩ̈ܕܢܝܟܘܢ. ܢܣܒܝ ܒܐܦ̈ܐ. ܫܦܝܪ
8 ܐܬܢܒܝ ܥܠܝܟܘܢ ܐܫܥܝܐ ܢܒܝܐ ܕܐܡܪ ܗܘܐ. ܥܡܐ

ܒܫܡܝܐ ܘܒܪܟ. ܘܩܨܐ ܠܚܡܐ ܘܝܗܒ ܠܬܠܡܝܕܘܗܝ.
20 ܘܗܢܘܢ ܬܠܡܝܕܘܗܝ ܣܡܘ ܠܟܢܫܐ. ܘܐܟܠܘ ܟܠܗܘܢ
ܘܣܒܥܘ. ܘܫܩܠܘ ܬܘܬܪܐ ܕܩܨܝܐ ܡܢ ܦܬܘܪܝܗܘܢ
21 ܬܪܬܥܣܪ ܩܘ̈ܦܝܢ ܟܕ ܡܠܝܢ. ܘܗܢܘܢ ܐܢܫܐ ܕܐܟܠܘ
ܗܘܘܢ ܗܘܘ ܚܡܫܐ ܐ̈ܠܦܝܢ ܓܒ̈ܪܝܢ. ܣܛܪ ܡܢ ܢ̈ܫܐ
22 ܘܛ̈ܠܝܐ. ܘܦܩܕ ܠܬܠܡܝܕܘܗܝ ܕܢܣܩܘܢ ܒܐܠܦܐ.
ܘܢܐܙܠܘܢ ܩܕܡܘܗܝ ܠܥܒܪܐ. ܥܕ ܫܪܐ ܠܟ̈ܢܫܐ ܗܠܝܢ.
23 ܘܟܕ ܫܪܐ ܐܢܘܢ. ܣܠܩ ܠܗ ܠܛܘܪܐ ܒܠܚܘܕܘܗܝ
ܠܡܨܠܝܘ. ܘܟܕ ܗܘܐ ܪܡܫܐ ܒܠܚܘܕܘܗܝ ܗܘܐ ܬܡܢ.
24 ܘܐܠܦܐ ܪܚܝܩܐ ܗܘܬ ܡܢ ܐܪܥܐ ܐܣܛܕ̈ܘܬܐ
ܣܓܝܐܬܐ. ܘܡܫܬܢܕܐ ܗܘܬ ܡܢ ܓ̈ܠܠܐ. ܡܛܠ ܕܪܘܚܐ
25 ܠܩܘܒܠܗܘܢ ܗܘܬ. ܒܡܛܪܬܐ ܕܝܢ ܪܒܝܥܝܬܐ ܕܠܠܝܐ.
ܐܬܐ ܠܘܬܗܘܢ ܝܫܘܥ ܟܕ ܡܗܠܟ ܥܠ ܡ̈ܝܐ.
26 ܘܟܕ ܚܙܐܘܗܝ ܬܠܡܝܕܘܗܝ ܕܡܗܠܟ ܥܠ ܓ̈ܠܠܐ
ܫܓܫܘ ܐܬܕܠܚܘ. ܘܐܡܪܝܢ ܗܘܘ ܕܓܠܝܐ ܗܘ. ܘܡܢ
27 ܕܚܠܬܗܘܢ ܩܥܘ ܗܘܘ. ܘܡܚܕܐ ܒܝܕܥܬܐ ܡܠܠ
28 ܥܡܗܘܢ. ܐܬܚܝܠܘ ܐܢܐ ܐܢܐ ܠܐ ܬܕܚܠܘܢ. ܐܡܪ
ܠܗ ܫܡܥܘܢ ܟܐܦܐ. ܡܪܝ ܐܢ ܐܢܬ ܗܘ ܦܩܘܕ ܠܝ
29 ܐܬܐ ܠܘܬܟ ܥܠ ܡ̈ܝܐ. ܐܡܪ ܠܗ ܬܐ. ܘܢܚܬ
ܫܡܥܘܢ ܟܐܦܐ ܡܢ ܐܠܦܐ. ܘܡܗܠܟ ܗܘܐ ܥܠ
30 ܡ̈ܝܐ. ܘܐܬܐ ܠܘܬ ܝܫܘܥ. ܘܟܕ ܚܙܐ ܪܘܚܐ ܕܥܫܝܢܐ
ܗܝ. ܕܚܠ ܘܫܪܝ ܠܡܛܒܥ. ܘܩܥܐ ܒܩܠܐ ܪܒܐ ܘܐܡܪ.

ܕܗܪܘܕܝܐ ܒܡܨܥܬ ܣܡܟܐ. ܘܫܦܪܬ ܠܗ ܠܗܪܘܕܣ.
7 ܡܛܠ ܗܢܐ ܐܫܬܘܝ ܠܗ ܒܡܘܡܬܐ ܕܟܠ ܡܐ
8 ܕܬܫܐܠܝܘܗܝ ܢܬܠ ܠܗ. ܗܝ ܕܝܢ ܡܛܠ ܕܡܠܦܐ ܗܘܬ
ܡܢ ܐܡܗ. ܐܡܪܬ. ܗܒ ܠܝ ܗܪܟܐ ܒܦܝܢܟܐ ܪܫܗ
9 ܕܝܘܚܢܢ ܡܥܡܕܢܐ. ܘܟܪܝܬ ܠܗ ܠܡܠܟܐ. ܘܡܛܠ
10 ܡܘܡܬܐ ܘܡܛܠ ܣܡܝܟܐ. ܦܩܕ ܕܢܬܝܗܒ ܠܗ. ܘܫܕܪ
11 ܦܣܩ ܪܫܗ ܕܝܘܚܢܢ ܒܒܝܬ ܐܣܝܪܐ. ܘܐܝܬܝܘ ܪܫܗ
ܕܝܘܚܢܢ ܒܦܝܢܟܐ. ܘܐܬܝܗܒ ܠܛܠܝܬܐ. ܘܗܝ ܛܠܝܬܐ
12 ܐܘܒܠܬܗ ܠܐܡܗ. ܘܩܪܒܘ ܬܠܡ̈ܝܕܘܗܝ ܕܝܘܚܢܢ
ܘܫܩܠܘ ܫܠܕܗ ܘܩܒܪܘܗܝ. ܘܐܬܘ ܘܚܘܘ ܠܝܫܘܥ.
13 ܫܡܥ ܕܝܢ ܟܕ ܝܫܘܥ ܫܢܝ ܠܗ ܡܢ ܬܡܢ ܠܐܬܪܐ
ܚܘܪܒܐ ܒܠܚܘܕܘܗܝ. ܘܟܕ ܫܡܥܘ ܟܢ̈ܫܐ ܕܡܢ
ܡܕ̈ܝܢܬܐ ܘܡܢ ܩܘܪ̈ܝܐ. ܐܙܠܘ ܠܗܘܢ ܒܬܪܗ ܒܪܓܠ.
14 ܘܟܕ ܢܦܩ ܚܙܐ ܟܢ̈ܫܐ ܣܓܝ̈ܐܐ. ܐܬܪܚܡ ܥܠܝܗܘܢ.
ܘܠܟܪ̈ܝܗܘܢ ܐܣܝ ◎○◎
15 ܘܟܕ ܗܘܐ ܪܡܫܐ. ܩܪܒܘ ܬܠܡ̈ܝܕܘܗܝ ܘܐܡܪܝܢ ܠܗ.
ܐܬܪܐ ܚܪܒܐ ܗܘ. ܘܥܕܢܐ ܥܒܪ. ܫܪܝ ܟܢ̈ܫܐ ܗܢܘܢ
16 ܢܐܙܠܘܢ ܠܩܘܪ̈ܝܐ ܘܢܙܒܢܘܢ ܠܗܘܢ ܣܒܪܬܐ. ܘܐܡܪ
ܠܗܘܢ ܠܐ ܡܬܒܥܐ ܠܗܘܢ ܠܡܐܙܠ. ܗܒܘ ܠܗܘܢ
17 ܐܢܬܘܢ ܠܡܐܟܠ. ܐܡܪܝܢ ܠܗ ܠܝܬ ܠܢ ܬܢܢ. ܐܠܐ
18 ܚܡܫ ܓܪ̈ܝܨܢ ܘܬܪ̈ܝܢ ܢܘ̈ܢܝܢ. ܐܡܪ ܠܗܘܢ ܐܝܬܘ
19 ܐܢܘܢ ܠܝ. ܘܦܩܕ ܠܟܢ̈ܫܐ ܠܡܣܬܡܟܘ ܥܠ ܥܣܒܐ.
ܘܢܣܒ ܗܠܝܢ ܚܡܫܐ ܓܪ̈ܝܨܢ ܘܬܪ̈ܝܢ ܢܘ̈ܢܝܢ. ܘܚܪ

ܠܓܒܪܐ ܡܪܐ ܒܝܬܐ. ܕܡܦܩ ܡܢ ܣܝܡܬܗ ܚܕܬܬܐ
ܘܥܬܝܩܬܐ. ◦◦◦
53 ܘܟܕ ܫܠܡ ܝܫܘܥ ܡ̈ܬܠܐ ܗܠܝܢ. ܫܢܝ ܠܗ ܡܢ ܬܡܢ.
54 ܘܐܬܐ ܠܗ ܠܡܕܝܢܬܗ. ܘܡܠܦ ܗܘܐ ܠܗܘܢ ܝܫܘܥ
ܒܟ̈ܢܘܫܬܗܘܢ. ܐܝܟܢܐ ܕܢܬܕܡܪܘܢ. ܘܗܘܢ ܐܡܪܝܢ
ܐܝܡܟܐ ܠܗ ܠܗܢܐ ܚܟܡܬܐ ܗܕܐ ܘܚܝܠܐ ܗܢܐ.
55 ܠܐ ܗܘܐ ܗܢܐ ܒܪ ܝܘܣܦ ܢܓܪܐ. ܘܫܡܗ̇ ܠܐܡܗ̇
ܡܪܝܡ. ܘܐܚ̈ܘܗܝ ܝܥܩܘܒ ܘܝܘܣܦ ܘܫܡܥܘܢ
56 ܘܝܗܘܕܐ. ܘܐܚ̈ܘܬܗ ܟܠܗܝܢ ܠܘܬܢ ܐܝܢ. ܐܝܡܟܐ
57 ܠܗ ܗܠܝܢ ܟܠܗܝܢ ܠܗܢܐ. ܘܡܬܟܫܠܝܢ ܗܘܘ ܒܗ. ܗܘ
ܕܝܢ ܝܫܘܥ ܐܡܪ ܠܗܘܢ. ܠܝܬ ܢܒܝܐ ܕܡܨܛܥܪ ܐܠܐ
58 ܐܢ ܒܡܕܝܢܬܗ. ܘܒܒܝܬܗ. ܘܠܐ ܥܒܕ ܬܡܢ ܚ̈ܝܠܐ
ܣ̈ܓܝܐܐ. ܡܛܠ ܚܣܝܪܘܬ ܗܝܡܢܘܬܗܘܢ ◦◦ ◦◦ ◦◦
XIV. ܒܗܘ ܕܝܢ ܙܒܢܐ ܫܡܥ ܗܪܘܕܣ ܛܛܪܪܟܐ ܫܡܥܗ
2 ܕܝܫܘܥ. ܘܐܡܪ ܠܥܒ̈ܕܘܗܝ. ܗܢܐ ܝܘܚܢܢ ܗܘ ܡܥܡܕܢܐ
3 ܩܡ ܡܢ ܒܝܬ ܡ̈ܝܬܐ. ܡܛܠ ܗܢܐ ܚ̈ܝܠܐ ܣܥܪܝܢ ܒܗ. ܗܘ
ܓܝܪ ܗܪܘܕܣ ܐܚܕܗ ܗܘܐ ܠܝܘܚܢܢ ܘܐܣܪܗ.
ܘܐܪܡܝܗ ܒܒܝܬ ܐ̈ܣܝܪܐ. ܡܛܠ ܗܪܘܕܝܐ ܐܢܬܬ
4 ܦܝܠܝܦܘܣ ܐܚܘܗܝ. ܐܡܪ ܗܘܐ ܠܗ ܓܝܪ ܝܘܚܢܢ.
5 ܕܠܐ ܫܠܝܛ ܠܟ ܕܬܗܘܐ ܠܟ ܐܢܬܬܐ. ܘܨܒܐ ܗܘܐ
ܠܡܩܛܠܗ ܘܕܚܠ ܗܘܐ ܡܢ ܥܡܐ. ܡܛܠ ܕܐܝܟ
ܕܠܢܒܝܐ ܐܚܝܕܝܢ ܗܘܘ ܠܗ ܠܝܘܚܢܢ. ◦◦◦
6 ܘܟܕ ܗܘܐ ܒܝܬ ܡܘܠܕܗ ܕܗܪܘܕܣ ܥܠܬ ܪܩܕܬ ܒܪܬܗ̇

42 ܘܟܠܗܘܢ ܐܝܠܝܢ ܕܥܒܕܝܢ ܥܘܠܐ. ܘܢܪܡܘܢ ܐܢܘܢ
ܒܐܬܘܢܐ ܕܢܘܪܐ. ܬܡܢ ܢܗܘܐ ܒܟܝܐ ܘܚܘܪܩ ܫܢ̈ܐ.
ܗܝܕܝܢ ܙܕܝ̈ܩܐ ܢܢܗܪܘܢ ܐܝܟ ܫܡܫܐ ܒܡܠܟܘܬܗ
43 ܕܐܒܘܗܘܢ. ܡܢ ܕܐܝܬ ܠܗ ܐܕܢ̈ܐ ܠܡܫܡܥ
ܢܫܡܥ ◦◦◦
44 ܕܡܝܐ ܡܠܟܘܬܐ ܕܫܡܝܐ ܠܣܝܡܬܐ ܕܛܡܝܪܐ
ܒܩܪܝܬܐ. ܘܟܕ ܐܫܟܚܗ̇ ܓܒܪܐ ܛܫܝܗ̇. ܘܡܢ ܚܕܘܬܗ
ܐܙܠ ܙܒܢ ܟܠ ܡܕܡ ܕܐܝܬ ܠܗ. ܘܙܒܢܗ̇ ܠܗ ܩܪܝܬܐ
ܗܝ. ◦◦◦
45 ܬܘܒ ܕܡܝܐ ܡܠܟܘܬܐ ܕܫܡܝܐ. ܠܓܒܪܐ ܬܓܪܐ
46 ܕܒܥܐ ܗܘܐ ܡܪ̈ܓܢܝܬܐ ܛܒ̈ܬܐ. ܘܟܕ ܐܫܟܚ
ܡܪܓܢܝܬܐ ܛܒܬܐ ܘܝܩܝܪܬ ܕܡܝ̈ܐ. ܐܙܠ ܘܙܒܢ ܟܠ
ܡܕܡ ܕܐܝܬ ܠܗ. ܘܐܬܐ ܘܙܒܢܗ̇ ܠܗ. ◦◦◦
47 ܬܘܒ ܕܡܝܐ ܡܠܟܘܬܐ ܕܫܡܝܐ ܠܡܨܝܕܬܐ ܪܒܬܐ
48 ܕܢܦܠܬ ܒܝܡܐ. ܘܡܢ ܟܠ ܓܢܣ ܟܢܫܬ. ܘܟܕ ܕܝܢ ܡܠܬ
ܐܣܩܘܗ̇ ܥܠ ܣܦܪ ܝܡܐ. ܘܝܬܒܘ ܓܒܘ ܛܒ̈ܐ
49 ܒܡ̈ܐܢܐ. ܘܐܝܠܝܢ ܕܒܝܫܝܢ ܫܕܘ ܐܢܘܢ ܠܒܪ. ܗܟܢܐ
ܢܗܘܐ ܒܫܘܠܡܗ ܕܥܠܡܐ. ܢܦܩܘܢ ܡ̈ܠܐܟܐ ܘܢܦܪܫܘܢ
50 ܠܒ̈ܝܫܐ ܡܢ ܒܝܬ ܙܕܝ̈ܩܐ. ܘܢܪܡܘܢ ܐܢܘܢ ܒܐܬܘܢܐ
ܕܢܘܪܐ. ܬܡܢ ܢܗܘܐ ܒܟܝܐ ܘܚܘܪܩ ܫܢ̈ܐ. ◦◦◦
51 ܐܡܪ ܠܗܘܢ ܝܫܘܥ ܠܬܠܡܝ̈ܕܘܗܝ، ܐܣܬܟܠܬܘܢ ܗܠܝܢ
52 ܟܠܗܝܢ. ܐܡܪܝܢ ܠܗ ܐܝܢ. ܐܡܪ ܠܗܘܢ ܡܛܠ ܗܢܐ
ܟܠ ܣܦܪܐ ܕܡܬܬܠܡܕ ܠܡܠܟܘܬܐ ܕܫܡܝܐ. ܕܡܐ

ܡܠܟܘܬܐ ܕܫܡܝܐ ܠܦܪܕܬܐ ܕܚܪܕܠܐ. ܕܢܣܒ ܓܒܪܐ
32 ܘܙܪܥܗ ܒܩܪܝܬܗ. ܘܗܝ ܙܥܘܪܐ ܗܝ ܡܢ ܟܠܗܘܢ
ܙܪ̈ܥܘܢܐ. ܘܡܐ ܕܪܒܬ ܪܒܐ ܗܝ ܡܢ ܟܠܗܘܢ ܝܪ̈ܘܩܐ.
ܘܗܘܝܐ ܐܝܠܢܐ. ܘܐܬܝܐ ܣܘܦܬ ܒܥܘܦܐ ܕܫܡܝܐ
ܘܥܫܢܐ ܒܣܘ̈ܟܘܗܝ ܀
33 ܡܬܠܐ ܐܚܪܢܐ. ܕܡܝܐ ܡܠܟܘܬܐ ܕܫܡܝܐ ܠܚܡܝܪܐ
ܕܢܣܒܬ ܐܢܬܬܐ ܛܫܝܬܗ. ܘܦܪܣܬ ܒܩܡܚܐ
ܥܕܡܐ ܕܗܘܐ ܟܠܗ ܚܡܝܪ ܀
34 ܗܠܝܢ ܟܠܗܝܢ ܡܠܠ ܝܫܘܥ ܒܡ̈ܬܠܐ ܠܟ̈ܢܫܐ. ܘܕܠܐ
35 ܡܬ̈ܠܐ ܠܐ ܡܡܠܠ ܗܘܐ ܥܡܗܘܢ. ܘܢܫܬܠܡ
ܡܠܬܐ ܕܐܬܐܡܪܬ ܒܢܒܝܐ ܕܐܡܪ ܗܘܐ. ܐܦܬܚ
ܦܘܡܝ ܒܡ̈ܬܠܐ. ܘܐܡܠܠ ܟܣܝ̈ܬܐ ܕܡܢ ܩܕܝܡ ܀
36 ܗܝܕܝܢ ܫܒܩ ܠܟ̈ܢܫܐ ܘܐܬܐ ܠܒܝܬܐ. ܘܩܪܒܘ ܠܘܬܗ
ܬܠܡܝ̈ܕܘܗܝ ܘܐܡܪܝܢ ܠܗ. ܦܫܘܩ ܠܢ ܡܬܠܐ ܗܘ
37 ܕܙܝ̈ܙܢܐ ܕܩܪܝܬܐ. ܗܘ ܕܝܢ ܥܢܐ ܘܐܡܪ ܠܗܘܢ. ܙܪܘܥܗ
38 ܕܙܪܥܐ ܛܒܐ ܒܪܗ ܗܘ ܕܐܢܫܐ. ܘܩܪܝܬܐ ܥܠܡܐ
ܗܘ. ܗܘ ܕܝܢ ܙܪܥܐ ܛܒܐ ܗܠܝܢ ܐܢܘܢ ܒ̈ܢܝܗ
39 ܕܡܠܟܘܬܐ. ܘܙ̈ܝܙܢܐ ܒ̈ܢܘܗܝ ܐܢܘܢ ܕܒܝܫܐ. ܘܙܪܘܥܐ
ܗܘܘ ܣܛܢܐ. ܘܚܨܕܐ ܫܘܠܡܗ ܗܘ ܕܥܠܡܐ.
40 ܘܚ̈ܨܘܕܐ ܡ̈ܠܐܟܐ ܐܢܘܢ. ܐܝܟܢܐ ܗܟܝܠ
ܕܡܬܠܩܛܝܢ ܙܝ̈ܙܢܐ ܘܝܩܕܝܢ ܒܢܘܪܐ. ܗܟܢܐ ܢܗܘܐ
41 ܒܫܘܠܡܗ ܕܥܠܡܐ. ܢܫܕܪ ܒܪܗ ܕܐܢܫܐ ܠܡ̈ܠܐܟܘܗܝ
ܘܢܠܩܛܘܢ ܡܢ ܒܝܬ ܡܠܟܘܬܗ ܟܠܗܘܢ ܡ̈ܟܫܘܠܐ.

22 ܐܪܕܘܦܝܐ ܡܛܠ ܡܠܬܐ ܥܓܠ ܡܬܟܫܠ. ܘܗܘ ܕܢܦܠ
ܒܝܬ ܟܘ̈ܒܐ. ܗܢܐ ܗܘ ܕܫܡܥ ܡܠܬܐ. ܘܪܢܝܐ ܗܘ
ܕܥܠܡܐ ܗܢܐ. ܘܛܘܥܝܝ ܕܥܘܬܪܐ. ܘܗܢܝܢ ܚܢܩܝܢ
23 ܠܗ. ܘܕܠܐ ܦܐܪ̈ܐ ܗܘܐ. ܘܗܘ ܕܢܦܠ ܒܐܪܥܐ
ܛܒܬܐ. ܗܘ ܗܘ ܕܫܡܥ ܡܠܬܐ ܘܡܣܬܟܠ ܒܗ̇.
ܘܝܗܒ ܦܐܪ̈ܐ. ܐܝܬ ܕܡܐܐ. ܘܐܝܬ ܕܫܬܝܢ. ܘܐܝܬ
ܕܬܠܬܝܢ ◦ ◦ ◦
24 ܐܚܪܢܐ ܕܝܢ ܡܬܠܐ ܐܘܣܦ ܘܐܡܪ ܠܗܘܢ. ܕܡܝܐ
ܡܠܟܘܬܐ ܕܫܡܝܐ. ܠܓܒܪܐ ܕܙܪܥ ܙܪܥܐ ܛܒܐ
25 ܒܩܪܝܬܗ. ܘܟܕ ܕܡܟܘ ܐܢܫܐ. ܐܬܐ ܒܥܠܕܒܒܐ ܘܙܪܥ
26 ܙܝܙܢܐ ܒܝܬ ܚܛܐ ܘܐܙܠ. ܘܟܕ ܝܥܐ ܥܣܒܐ ܘܥܒܕ
27 ܦܐܪ̈ܐ. ܗܝܕܝܢ ܐܬܚܙܝܘ ܙܝܙܢܐ. ܘܩܪܒܘ ܥܒ̈ܕܘܗܝ
ܕܡܪܐ ܒܝܬܐ ܘܐܡܪܝܢ ܠܗ. ܡܪܢ ܠܐ ܗܘܐ ܙܪܥܐ
28 ܛܒܐ ܙܪܥܬ ܒܩܪܝܬܟ. ܐܝܡܟܢܐ ܐܝܬ ܒܗ ܙܝܙܢܐ. ܗܘ
ܕܝܢ ܐܡܪ ܠܗܘܢ. ܓܒܪܐ ܒܥܠܕܒܒܐ ܥܒܕ ܗܕܐ.
ܐܡܪܝܢ ܠܗ ܥܒ̈ܕܘܗܝ. ܨܒܐ ܐܢܬ ܢܐܙܠ ܢܠܩܛ
29 ܐܢܘܢ. ܐܡܪ ܠܗܘܢ ܠܐ. ܕܠܡܐ ܟܕ ܠܩܛܝܢ ܐܢܬܘܢ
30 ܙܝܙܢܐ ܬܥܩܪܘܢ ܐܦ ܚܛܐ ܥܡܗܘܢ. ܐܠܐ ܫܒܘܩܘ
ܢܪܒܘܢ ܐܟܚܕܐ ܥܕܡܐ ܠܚܨ̈ܕܐ. ܘܒܗܘ ܙܒܢܐ ܕܚܨ̈ܕܐ
ܐܡܪ ܐܢܐ ܠܚ̈ܨܘܕܐ. ܠܩܘܛܘ ܠܘܩܕܡ ܙܝܙܢܐ. ܘܐܣܘܪܘ
ܐܢܘܢ ܡܩ̈ܛܪܢܬܐ ܐܝܟ ܕܠܝܩܕܐ. ܘܚܛܐ ܟܢܫܘ ܐܢܘܢ
ܠܐܘܨܪܐ ܕܝܠܝ ◦ ◦ ◦
31 ܘܐܚܪܢ ܗܘܐ ܠܗܘܢ ܡܬܠܐ ܐܚܪܢܐ. ܕܡܝܐ

12 ܕܫܡܝܐ. ܠܗܢܘܢ ܕܝܢ ܠܐ ܝܗܝܒ ܠܗܘܢ ܠܡܕܥ. ܡܢ
13 ܕܐܝܬ ܠܗ ܓܝܪ ܢܬܝܗܒ ܠܗ ܘܢܬܬܘܣܦ ܠܗ. ܘܡܢ
ܕܠܝܬ ܠܗ ܐܦ ܗܘ ܡܕܡ ܕܐܝܬ ܠܗ ܢܫܬܩܠ ܡܢܗ.
ܡܛܠ ܗܢܐ ܒܡ̈ܬܠܐ ܡܡܠܠ ܐܢܐ ܥܡܗܘܢ.
ܕܚܙܝܢ ܕܚܙܝܢ ܠܐ ܚܙܝܢ. ܘܫܡܥܝܢ ܕܫܡܥܝܢ ܠܐ ܫܡܥܝܢ
14 ܘܠܐ ܡܣܬܟܠܝܢ. ܕܠܐ ܢܬܦܢܘܢ ܢܬܐܣܘܢ. ܘܬܫܠܡ
ܢܒܘܬܗ ܕܐܫܥܝܐ ܢܒܝܐ ܕܐܡܪ ܗܘܐ. ܕܡܫܡܥ
ܬܫܡܥܘܢ ܘܠܐ ܬܣܬܟܠܘܢ. ܘܚܙܘܐ ܬܚܙܘܢ ܘܠܐ
15 ܬܚܙܘܢ. ܐܬܥܒܝ ܠܗ ܓܝܪ ܠܒܗ ܕܥܡܐ ܗܢܐ.
ܘܐܕ̈ܢܝܗܘܢ ܐܘܩܪܘ ܕܠܐ ܢܫܡܥܘܢ. ܘܥ̈ܝܢܝܗܘܢ
ܥܡܨܘ. ܕܠܐ ܢܚܙܘܢ ܒܥ̈ܝܢܝܗܘܢ ܘܢܫܡܥܘܢ
ܒܐܕ̈ܢܝܗܘܢ. ܘܢܣܬܟܠܘܢ ܒܠܒܗܘܢ. ܘܢܬܦܢܘܢ ܘܐܐܣܐ
16 ܐܢܘܢ. ܕܝܠܟܘܢ ܕܝܢ ܛܘܒܝܗܝܢ ܠܥ̈ܝܢܝܟܘܢ ܕܚܙܝܢ. ܘܛܘܒ
17 ܠܐܕ̈ܢܝܟܘܢ ܕܫܡܥܢ. ܐܡܝܢ ܓܝܪ ܐܡܪ ܐܢܐ ܠܟܘܢ
ܕܣ̈ܓܝܐܐ ܢܒܝ̈ܐ ܘܙܕ̈ܝܩܐ ܐܬܪܓܪܓܘ ܕܢܚܙܘܢ ܡܕܡ
ܕܚܙܝܢ ܐܢܬܘܢ ܘܠܐ ܚܙܘ. ܘܠܡܫܡܥ ܡܕܡ ܕܫܡܥܝܢ
18 ܐܢܬܘܢ ܘܠܐ ܫܡܥܘ. ܐܢܬܘܢ ܕܝܢ ܫܡܥܘ ܡܬܠܐ
19 ܕܙܪܘܥܐ. ܟܘܠ ܐܢܫ ܕܫܡܥ ܡܠܬܐ ܕܡܠܟܘܬܐ ܘܠܐ
ܡܣܬܟܠ. ܐܬܐ ܒܝܫܐ ܘܚܛܦ ܠܗ ܠܙܪܥܐ ܡܢ ܠܒܗ.
20 ܗܢܐ ܗܘ ܕܐܙܕܪܥ ܥܠ ܝܕ ܐܘܪܚܐ. ܘܗܘ ܕܐܙܕܪܥ
ܥܠ ܫܘܥܐ. ܗܢܐ ܗܘ ܕܫܡܥ ܡܠܬܐ. ܘܒܚܕܘܬܐ
21 ܡܣܒܪܐܝܬ ܡܩܒܠ ܠܗ. ܘܡܛܠ ܕܠܝܬ ܠܗ ܥܩܪܐ.
ܐܠܐ ܠܙܒܢ ܡܩܘܝܐ ܗܘ. ܡܐ ܕܗܘܐ ܕܝܢ ܐܘܠܨܢܐ ܐܘ

47, 48 ܒܥܘܗ. ܗܘ ܕܝܢ ܥܢܐ ܘܐܡܪ ܠܗܘ ܡܢ ܕܐܡܪ ܠܗ.
49 ܡܢ ܗܝ ܐܡܝ ܘܡܢ ܐܢܘܢ ܐܚ̈ܝ. ܘܦܫܛ ܐܝܕܗ ܠܘܬ
50 ܬܠܡ̈ܝܕܘܗܝ ܘܐܡܪ. ܗܐ ܐܡܝ ܘܗܐ ܐܚ̈ܝ. ܟܠ ܡܢ
ܕܥܒܕ ܨܒܝܢܗ ܕܐܒܝ ܕܒܫܡܝܐ. ܗܢܐ ܗܘ ܐܚ̈ܝ
ܘܐܚ̈ܘܬܝ ܘܐܡܝ ◎ ○ ◎

XIII. ܘܒܗܘ ܝܘܡܐ ܢܦܩ ܝܫܘܥ ܡܢ ܒܝܬܐ. ܘܝܬܒ ܠܗ
2 ܥܠ ܝܕ ܝܡܐ. ܘܐܬܟܢܫܘ ܠܘܬܗ ܟܢܫܐ ܣܓܝܐܐ.
ܘܣܠܩ ܘܝܬܒ ܠܗ ܒܣܦܝܢܬܐ. ܘܟܠܗ ܟܢܫܐ ܩܐܡ
3 ܗܘܐ ܥܠ ܣܦܪ ܝܡܐ. ܘܡܠܠ ܥܡܗܘܢ ܣܓܝ
4 ܒܦܠܐ̈ܬܐ ܘܐܡܪ. ܗܐ ܢܦܩ ܙܪܘܥܐ ܠܡܙܪܥ. ܘܟܕ
ܙܪܥ. ܐܝܬ ܕܢܦܠ ܥܠ ܝܕ ܐܘܪܚܐ ܘܐܬܬ ܦܪܚܬܐ
5 ܕܫܡܝܐ ܘܐܟܠܬܗ. ܐܚܪܢܐ ܕܝܢ ܢܦܠ ܥܠ ܫܘܥܐ.
ܘܠܝܬ ܗܘܐ ܐܪܥܐ ܣܓܝܐܐ. ܘܒܗ̇ ܒܫܥܬܐ ܫܘܚܬ.
6 ܡܛܠ ܕܠܝܬ ܒܥܘܡܩܐ ܕܐܪܥܐ ܣܓܝܐܐ. ܘܒܡܚܡܫܐ
ܕܫܡܫܐ ܕܗܘܐ ܒܠܗ ܫܚܬ. ܘܡܛܠ ܕܠܐ ܐܪܡܝܬ
7 ܥܩܪܐ ܒܐܪܥܐ ܝܒܫܬ. ܐܚܪܢܝܬܐ ܢܦܠܬ ܒܝܬ ܟܘ̈ܒܐ.
8 ܘܣܠܩܘ ܟܘ̈ܒܐ ܥܡܗ̇ ܘܚܢܩܘܗ̇. ܘܐܚܪܢܝܬܐ ܕܝܢ ܢܦܠܬ
ܒܐܪܥܐ ܛܒܬܐ ܘܝܗܒܬ ܦܐܪ̈ܐ. ܘܪܒܬ ܘܝܗܒܬ.
9 ܐܝܬ ܕܡܐܐ ܘܐܝܬ ܕܫܬܝܢ ܘܐܝܬ ܕܬܠܬܝܢ. ܡܢ
10 ܕܐܝܬ ܠܗ ܐܕ̈ܢܐ ܠܡܫܡܥ ܢܫܡܥ ◎ ◎
ܘܩܪܒܘ ܬܠܡ̈ܝܕܘܗܝ ܘܐܡܪܝܢ ܠܗ. ܠܡܢܐ ܒܦ̈ܠܐܬܐ
11 ܡܡܠܠ ܐܢܬ ܥܡܗܘܢ. ܗܘ ܕܝܢ ܥܢܐ ܘܐܡܪ ܠܗܘܢ.
ܡܛܠ ܕܠܟܘܢ ܗܘ ܝܗܝܒ ܠܡܕܥ ܐܪ̈ܙܐ ܕܡܠܟܘܬܐ

39 ܗܘ ܕܝܢ ܥܢܐ ܘܐܡܪ ܠܗܘܢ. ܫܪܒܬܐ ܗܕܐ ܒܝܫܬܐ
ܘܓܝܪܬܐ. ܐܬܐ ܒܥܝܐ ܘܐܬܐ ܠܐ ܬܬܝܗܒ ܠܗ.
40 ܐܠܐ ܐܢ ܐܬܗ ܕܝܘܢܢ ܢܒܝܐ. ܐܝܟܢܐ ܓܝܪ ܕܗܘܐ
ܝܘܢܢ ܒܟܪܣܗ ܕܢܘܢܐ ܬܠܬܐ ܝܘ̈ܡܝܢ ܘܬܠ̈ܬܐ ܠܠ̈ܝܐ.
ܗܟܢܐ ܐܦ ܒܪܗ ܕܐܢܫܐ ܢܗܘܐ ܒܠܒܗ̇ ܕܐܪܥܐ
41 ܬ̈ܠܬܐ ܝܘ̈ܡܝܢ ܘܬܠܬܐ ܠܠ̈ܝܐ. ܓܒܪ̈ܐ ܒܢ̈ܝ ܢܝܢܘܐ
ܢܩܘܡܘܢ ܒܕܝܢܐ ܥܡ ܫܪܒܬܐ ܗܕܐ ܘܢܚܝܒܘܢܗ̇.
ܕܗܢܘܢ ܬܒܘ ܒܟܪܘܙܘܬܗ ܕܝܘܢܢ. ܘܗܐ ܕܪܒ ܡܢ ܝܘܢܢ
42 ܗܪܟܐ. ܡܠܟܬܐ ܕܬܝܡܢܐ ܬܩܘܡ ܒܕܝܢܐ ܥܡ
ܫܪܒܬܐ ܗܕܐ ܘܬܚܝܒܝܗ̇. ܕܐܬܬ ܡܢ ܥܒܪ̈ܝܗ̇
ܕܐܪܥܐ ܕܬܫܡܥ ܚܟܡܬܗ ܕܫܠܝܡܘܢ. ܘܗܐ ܕܪܒ
ܡܢ ܫܠܝܡܘܢ ܗܪܟܐ ܀
43 ܪܘܚܐ ܕܝܢ ܛܢܦܬܐ ܡܐ ܕܢܦܩܬ ܡܢ ܒܪܢܫܐ. ܐܙܠܐ
ܡܬܟܪܟܐ ܒܐܬܪ̈ܘܬܐ ܕܡ̈ܝܐ ܠܝܬ ܒܗܘܢ. ܕܬܫܟܚ
44 ܠܗ̇ ܢܝܚܐ. ܘܡܐ ܕܠܐ ܐܫܟܚܬ ܠܗ̇. ܗܝܕܝܢ ܐܡܪܐ.
ܐܗܦܘܟ ܐܙܠ ܠܒܝܬܝ ܡܢ ܐܬܪ ܕܢܦܩܬ. ܘܐܢ ܐܬܬ
45 ܐܫܟܚܬܗ ܕܪܝܩ ܘܡܟܢܫ ܘܡܨܒܬ. ܗܝܕܝܢ ܐܙܠܐ
ܕܒܪܐ ܥܡܗ̇ ܫܒܥ ܪ̈ܘܚܝܢ ܐ̈ܚܪܢܝܢ ܕܒܝܫܢ ܡܢܗ̇. ܘܥܠܝܢ
ܘܥܡܪܢ ܒܗ. ܘܗܘܝܐ ܐܚܪܝܬܗ ܕܓܒܪܐ ܗܘ ܒܝܫܐ
ܡܢ ܩܕܡܝܬܗ. ܗܟܢܐ ܢܗܘܐ ܠܗ̇ ܠܫܪܒܬܐ ܗܕܐ
ܒܝܫܬܐ. ܀
46 ܘܥܕ ܗܘ ܡܡܠܠ ܗܘܐ ܠܟܢܫܐ. ܘܐܬܘ ܐܡܗ
ܘܐܚ̈ܘܗܝ ܩܝܡܝܢ ܗܘܘ ܠܒܪ. ܘܒܥܝܢ ܗܘܘ ܠܡܡܠܠܘ

ܡܦܩ ܐܢܐ ܫܐܕ̈ܐ. ܡܟܝܠ ܡܛܬ ܥܠܝܟܘܢ
29 ܡܠܟܘܬܗ ܕܐܠܗܐ. ܐܝܟܢܐ ܓܝܪ ܡܫܟܚ ܐܢܫ ܕܢܥܘܠ
ܠܒܝܬܗ ܕܚܣܝܢܐ ܘܢܒܘܙ ܡ̈ܐܢܘܗܝ. ܐܠܐ ܐܢ ܠܘܩܕܡ
30 ܠܗ ܠܚܣܝܢܐ ܢܐܣܘܪ. ܘܗܝܕܝܢ ܢܒܘܙ ܒܝܬܗ. ܡܢ ܕܠܐ
ܗܘܐ ܥܡܝ ܠܘܩܒܠܝ ܗܘ. ܘܡܢ ܕܠܐ ܟܢܫ ܥܡܝ ܡܒܕܪܘ
31 ܡܒܕܪ. ܡܛܠܗܢܐ ܐܡܪ ܐܢܐ ܠܟܘܢ. ܕܟܠ ܚ̈ܛܗܝܢ
ܘܓܘ̈ܕܦܝܢ ܢܫܬܒܩܘܢ ܠܒ̈ܢܝ ܐܢܫܐ. ܟܠ ܕܥܠ ܪܘܚܐ ܕܝܢ
32 ܕܩܘܕܫܐ ܢܓܕܦ ܠܐ ܢܫܬܒܩ ܠܗ. ܘܟܠ ܕܢܐܡܪ ܡܠܬܐ
ܥܠ ܒܪܗ ܕܐܢܫܐ ܢܫܬܒܩ ܠܗ. ܟܠ ܕܥܠ ܪܘܚܐ ܕܝܢ
ܕܩܘܕܫܐ ܢܓܕܦ ܠܐ ܢܫܬܒܩ ܠܗ. ܠܐ ܒܗܢܐ ܥܠܡܐ
33 ܘܠܐ ܒܥܠܡܐ ܕܥܬܝܕ. ܐܘ ܥܒܕܘ ܐܝܠܢܐ ܛܒܐ
ܘܦܐܖ̈ܘܗܝ ܛܒ̈ܝܢ. ܐܘ ܥܒܕܘ ܐܝܠܢܐ ܒܝܫܐ ܘܦܐܖ̈ܘܗܝ
34 ܒܝܫܝܢ. ܡܢ ܦܐܖ̈ܘܗܝ ܕܝܢ ܡܬܝܕܥ ܐܝܠܢܐ. ܝܠܕ̈ܐ
ܕܐܟ̈ܕܢܐ. ܐܝܟܢܐ ܡܫܟܚܝܢ ܐܢܬܘܢ ܛܒ̈ܬܐ ܠܡܡܠܠܘ
ܕܒ̈ܝܫܐ ܐܢܬܘܢ. ܡܢ ܬܘܬܪ̈ܘܗܝ ܓܝܪ ܕܠܒܐ ܡܡܠܠ
35 ܦܘܡܐ. ܓܒܪܐ ܛܒܐ ܡܢ ܣܝܡ̈ܬܐ ܛܒ̈ܬܐ ܕܠܒܗ
ܡܦܩ ܛܒ̈ܬܐ. ܘܓܒܪܐ ܒܝܫܐ ܡܢ ܣܝܡ̈ܬܐ ܒܝ̈ܫܬܐ
36 ܕܠܒܗ ܒܝ̈ܫܬܐ ܡܡܠܠ. ܐܡܪܢܐ ܠܟܘܢ ܕܝܢ. ܕܟܠ ܡܠܐ
ܒܛܠܐ ܕܢܐܡܪܘܢ ܒ̈ܢܝ ܐܢܫܐ. ܢܬܠܘܢ ܒܠܝܗ ܦܬܓܡܐ
37 ܒܝܘܡܐ ܕܕܝܢܐ. ܡܢ ܡ̈ܠܝܟ ܓܝܪ ܬܙܕܕܩ. ܘܡܢ ܡ̈ܠܝܟ
ܬܬܚܝܒ ܀

38 ܗܝܕܝܢ ܥܢܘ ܠܗ ܐܢܫܐ ܡܢ ܣ̈ܦܪܐ ܘܦܪ̈ܝܫܐ ܘܐܡܪܝܢ
ܠܗ. ܡܠܦܢܐ. ܨܒܝܢ ܐܢܚܢ ܕܢܚܙܐ ܡܢܟ ܡܕܡ ܐܬܐ.

15 ܕܢܘܒܕܘܢܝܗܝ. ܝܫܘܥ ܕܝܢ ܝܕܥ ܘܫܢܝ ܠܗ ܡܢ ܬܡܢ.
ܘܐܙܠܘ ܒܬܪܗ ܐܢܫܐ ܣܓܝ̈ܐܐ. ܘܐܣܝ ܠܟܠܗܘܢ.
16 ܘܟܐܐ ܒܗܘܢ ܕܗܘܢ ܠܐܢܫ ܠܐ ܢܓܠܘܢܝܗܝ.
17 ܕܢܬܡܠܐ ܡܕܡ ܕܐܬܐܡܪ ܒܦܘܡ ܐܫܥܝܐ ܢܒܝܐ
18 ܕܐܡܪ ܗܘܐ. ܕܗܐ ܥܒܕܝ ܕܐܨܛܒܝܬ ܒܗ. ܘܚܒܝܒܝ
ܕܨܒܝܬ ܒܗ ܢܦܫܝ. ܪܘܚܝ ܐܣܝܡ ܥܠܘܗܝ. ܘܢܣܒܪ ܕܝܢܐ
19 ܠܥܡ̈ܡܐ. ܠܐ ܢܬܚܪܐ ܘܠܐ ܢܩܥܐ. ܘܠܐ ܐܢܫ ܢܫܡܥ
20 ܩܠܗ ܒܫܘܩܐ. ܩܢܝܐ ܪܥܝܥܐ ܠܐ ܢܬܒܪ. ܘܫܪܓܐ
ܕܡܛܦܛܦ ܠܐ ܢܕܥܟ. ܥܕܡܐ ܕܢܦܩ ܕܝܢܐ ܠܙܟܘܬܐ.
21 ܘܠܫܡܗ ܥܡ̈ܡܐ ܢܣܒܪܘܢ ◦◦◦
22 ܗܝܕܝܢ ܩܪܒܘ ܩܕܡܘܗܝ ܓܒܪܐ ܚܕ ܕܐܝܬ ܗܘܐ
ܥܠܘܗܝ ܫܐܕܐ. ܘܣܡܐ ܘܚܪܫ. ܘܐܣܝܗ ܘܡܠܠ
23 ܚܪܫܐ ܗܘ ܘܚܙܐ ܘܫܡܥ. ܘܡܬܕܡܪܝܢ ܗܘܘ
ܟܠܗܘܢ ܟܢ̈ܫܐ. ܘܐܡܪܝܢ ܗܘܘ ܕܕܠܡܐ ܗܢ ܗܘܝܘ ܒܪܗ
24 ܕܕܘܝܕ. ܦܪ̈ܝܫܐ ܕܝܢ ܟܕ ܫܡܥܘ ܐܡܪܘ. ܗܢܐ ܠܐ ܡܦܩ
25 ܫܐ̈ܕܐ ܐܠܐ ܒܒܥܠܙܒܘܒ ܪܫܗܘܢ ܕܕܝ̈ܘܐ. ܟܕ ܚܙܐ
ܕܝܢ ܪܥܝܢܝܗܘܢ ܐܡܪ ܠܗܘܢ. ܟܠ ܡܠܟܘ ܕܬܬܦܠܓ ܥܠ
ܢܦܫܗ ܬܬܚܪܒ. ܘܟܠ ܒܝܬ ܘܡܕܝܢܐ ܕܬܬܦܠܓ ܥܠ ܢܦܫܗ
26 ܠܐ ܢܩܘܡ. ܘܐܢ ܣܛܢܐ ܠܣܛܢܐ ܡܦܩ ܥܠ ܢܦܫܗ
27 ܡܬܦܠܓ. ܐܝܟܢܐ ܗܟܝܠ ܬܩܘܡ ܡܠܟܘܬܗ. ܘܐܢ
ܐܢܐ ܒܒܥܠܙܒܘܒ ܡܦܩ ܐܢܐ ܫܐ̈ܕܐ ܡܢ ܒܢ̈ܝܟܘܢ.
ܒܢ̈ܝܟܘܢ ܒܡܢܐ ܡܦܩܝܢ ܠܗܘܢ. ܡܛܠ ܗܢܐ ܗܢܘܢ
28 ܢܗܘܘܢ ܠܟܘܢ ܕܝ̈ܢܐ. ܐܢ ܕܝܢ ܐܢܐ ܒܪܘܚܐ ܕܐܠܗܐ

ܕܡܬܝ

ܘܦܪܟܝܢ ܒܐܝ̈ܕܝܗܘܢ ܘܐܟܠܝܢ. ܟܕ ܚܙܘ ܐܢܘܢ ܦܪ̈ܝܫܐ 2
ܐܡܪܝܢ ܠܗ. ܡܛܠܐ ܥܒܕܝܢ ܬܠܡ̈ܝܕܝܟ ܡܕܡ ܕܠܐ
ܫܠܝܛ ܠܡܥܒܕ. ܐܡܪ ܠܗܘܢ ܠܐ ܩܪܝܬܘܢ ܡܢܐ ܥܒܕ 3
ܕܘܝܕ ܟܕ ܟܦܢ ܘܐܝܠܝܢ ܕܥܡܗ. ܐܝܟܢܐ ܥܠ ܠܒܝܬܗ 4
ܕܐܠܗܐ. ܘܐܟܠ ܠܚܡ ܐ̈ܦܝܐ. ܕܠܐ ܠܗ ܫܠܝܛ
ܗܘܐ ܠܡܐܟܠ ܐܦܠܐ ܠܐܝܠܝܢ ܕܥܡܗ. ܐܠܐ ܐܢ
ܠܟܗ̈ܢܐ ܒܠܚܘܕ. ܐܘ ܠܐ ܩܪܝܬܘܢ ܒܐܘܪܝܬܐ. 5
ܕܟ̈ܗܢܐ ܒܗܝܟܠܐ ܗܘܘ ܡܚܠܝܢ ܠܗ̇ ܠܫܒܬܐ. ܘܕܠܐ
ܚܛܗܝܢ ܐܢܘܢ. ܐܡܪܢܐ ܠܟܘܢ ܕܝܢ ܕܗܪܐ ܪܒ ܡܢ 6
ܗܝܟܠܐ ܗܪܟܐ. ܘܐܠܘ ܝܕܥܝܢ ܗܘܝܬܘܢ ܡܢܘ ܚܢܢܐ 7
ܒܥܐ ܐܢܐ ܘܠܐ ܕܒܚܬܐ. ܠܐ ܡܚܝܒܝܢ ܗܘܝܬܘܢ
ܠܙܟܝܐ. ܡܪܗ̇ ܓܝܪ ܕܫܒܬܐ ܒܪܗ ܗܘ ܕܐܢܫܐ ◌ ◌ ◌ 8
ܘܟܕ ܥܒܪ ܡܢ ܬܡܢ ܘܐܬܐ ܠܟܢܘܫܬܗܘܢ. ܘܗܘܐ ܓܒܪܐ 9, 10
ܚܕ ܕܐܝܕܗ ܕܝܒܝܫܐ ܡܝܒܫܐ ܗܘܬ. ܘܡܫܐܠܝܢ ܗܘܘ
ܠܗ ܘܐܡܪܝܢ. ܕܐܢ ܗܘ ܕܫܠܝܛ ܒܫܒܬܐ ܕܢܐܣܐ
ܠܡܐܣܝܘ. ܕܢܫܟܚܘܢ ܢܐܟܠܘܢ ܩ̈ܪܨܘܗܝ. ܐܡܪ 11
ܠܗܘܢ. ܡܢܘ ܓܒܪܐ ܡܢܟܘܢ ܕܐܝܬ ܠܗ ܥܪܒܐ. ܘܢܦܠ
ܒܚܒܪܐ ܒܝܘܡܐ ܕܫܒܬܐ. ܘܠܐ ܐܚܕ ܡܩܝܡ ܠܗ.
ܟܡܐ ܗܟܝܠ ܝܬܝܪ ܒܪ ܐܢܫܐ ܡܢ ܥܪܒܐ. ܡܛܠ 12
ܫܠܝܛ ܗܘ ܒܫܒܬܐ ܠܡܥܒܕ ܕܫܦܝܪ. ܗܝܕܝܢ ܐܡܪ 13
ܠܓܒܪܐ ܗܘ ܦܫܘܛ ܐܝܕܟ. ܘܦܫܛ ܐܝܕܗ ܘܬܩܢܬ
ܐܝܟ ܚܒܪܬܗ̇. ◌ ◌ ◌ ◌ ◌ ◌
ܘܟܕ ܢܦܩܘ ܦܪ̈ܝܫܐ. ܢܣܒܘ ܡܠܟܐ ܥܠܘܗܝ ܐܝܟܢܐ 14

ܠܟܝ ܟܘܪܙܝܢ ܘܝ ܠܟܝ ܒܝܬ ܨܝܕܐ. ܕܐܠܘ ܒܨܘܪ ܘܒܨܝܕܢ
ܗܘܘ ܚܝܠܐ ܕܗܘܘ ܒܟܝܢ. ܟܒܪ ܕܝܢ ܒܣ̈ܩܐ ܘܒܩܛܡܐ
22 ܬܒܘ. ܒܪܡ ܗܢܐ ܐܡܪܢܐ ܠܟܘܢ. ܕܠܨܘܪ ܘܠܨܝܕܢ
23 ܢܗܘܐ ܢܝܚ ܒܝܘܡܐ ܕܕܝܢܐ ܝܬܝܪ ܡܢ ܕܠܟܝܢ. ܘܐܢܬܝ
ܟܦܪܢܚܘܡ ܠܐ ܥܕܡܐ ܠܫܡܝܐ ܐܬܬܪܝܡܬܝ. ܐܠܐ
ܥܕܡܐ ܠܫܝܘܠ ܬܬܚܬܝܢ. ܕܐܠܘ ܒܣܕܘܡ ܗܘܘ ܚܝܠܐ
24 ܐܝܠܝܢ ܕܗܘܘ ܒܟܝ. ܩܝܡܐ ܗܘܬ ܥܕܡܐ ܠܝܘܡܢܐ.
ܒܪܡ ܗܢܐ ܐܡܪܢܐ. ܕܠܐܪܥܐ ܕܣܕܘܡ ܢܗܘܐ ܢܝܚ
ܒܝܘܡܐ ܕܕܝܢܐ ܝܬܝܪ ܡܢ ܕܠܟܝ ◦ ◦ ◦
25 ܒܗܘ ܕܝܢ ܙܒܢܐ ܥܢܐ ܝܫܘܥ ܘܐܡܪ. ܡܘܕܐ ܐܢܐ
ܠܟ ܐܒܐ ܡܪܐ ܕܫܡܝܐ ܘܕܐܪܥܐ. ܕܟܣܝܬ ܗܠܝܢ
26 ܡܢ ܚܟܝ̈ܡܐ ܘܓܠܝܬ ܐܢܝܢ ܠܛܠܝ̈ܐ. ܐܝܢ ܐܒܝ ܕܗܟܢܐ
27 ܗܘܐ ܨܒܝܢܐ ܩܕܡܝܟ. ܟܠ ܡܕܡ ܐܫܬܠܡ ܠܝ ܡܢ
ܐܒܝ. ܘܠܐ ܐܢܫ ܝܕܥ ܠܒܪܐ ܐܠܐ ܐܢ ܐܒܐ. ܘܐܦ
ܠܐ ܠܐܒܐ ܐܠܐ ܐܢ ܒܪܐ. ܘܡܢ ܕܨܒܐ ܒܪܐ
ܕܢܓܠܐ ܠܗ. ◦ ◦ ◦
28 ܬܘ ܠܘܬܝ ܟܠܟܘܢ ܠܐܝ̈ܢܐ ܘܫܩܝܠܝ ܡܘܒ̈ܠܐ ܝܩܝܪ̈ܬܐ
29 ܘܐܢܐ ܐܢܝܚܟܘܢ. ܘܫܩܘܠܘ ܢܝܪܝ ܥܠܝܟܘܢ. ܘܝܠܦܘ
ܡܢܝ ܕܢܝܚ ܐܢܐ ܘܡܟܝܟ ܐܢܐ ܒܠܒܝ. ܘܬܫܟܚܘܢ
30 ܢܝܚܐ ܠܢܦ̈ܫܬܟܘܢ. ܢܝܪܝ ܓܝܪ ܒܣܝܡ ܗܘ. ܘܡܘܒܠܝ
ܩܠܝܠܐ. ◦ ◦ ◦
XII. ܒܗܘ ܙܒܢܐ ܡܗܠܟ ܗܘܐ ܝܫܘܥ ܒܫܒܬܐ ܒܝܬ
ܙܪ̈ܥܐ. ܘܬܠܡܝܕܘܗܝ ܟܦܢܘ. ܘܫܪܝܘ ܡܠܩܛܝܢ ܫܒ̈ܠܐ

ܗܐ ܐܝܠܝܢ ܕܪ̈ܟܝܟܐ ܠܒܫܝܢ ܒܝܬ ܡ̈ܠܟܐ ܐܢܘܢ.
9 ܘܐܠܐ ܡܢܐ ܢܦܩܬܘܢ ܠܡܚܙܐ ܢܒܝܐ. ܐܝܢ ܐܡܪܢܐ
10 ܠܟܘܢ ܕܝܬܝܪ ܗܘ ܡܢ ܢܒܝܐ. ܗܢܘ ܕܟܬܝܒ ܥܠܘܗܝ.
ܕܗܐ ܡܫܕܪ ܐܢܐ ܡܠܐܟܝ ܩܕܡ ܦܪ̈ܨܘܦܟ. ܕܢܬܩܢ
11 ܐܘܪܚܐ ܩܕܡܝܟ. ܐܡܝܢ ܐܡܪܢܐ ܠܟܘܢ ܕܠܐ ܩܡ
ܒܝ̈ܠܕܝ ܢܫ̈ܐ ܕܪܒ ܡܢ ܝܘܚܢܢ ܡܥܡܕܢܐ. ܙܥܘܪܐ ܕܝܢ
12 ܒܡܠܟܘܬܐ ܕܫܡܝܐ ܪܒ ܗܘ ܡܢܗ. ܡܢ ܝܘ̈ܡܝ ܝܘܚܢܢ
ܕܝܢ ܡܥܡܕܢܐ ܘܥܕܡܐ ܠܗܫܐ. ܐܠܝܨܐ ܗܝ
ܡܠܟܘܬܐ ܕܫܡܝܐ. ܘܐ̈ܠܝܨܐ ܡܚܛܦܝܢ ܠܗ.
13 ܟܠܗܘܢ ܓܝܪ ܢܒ̈ܝܐ ܘܐܘܪܝܬܐ ܥܕܡܐ ܠܝܘܚܢܢ
14 ܐܬܢܒܝܘ. ܘܐܢ ܨܒܝܢ ܐܢܬܘܢ ܠܡܩܒܠܘ ܗܘܝܘ ܐܠܝܐ
15 ܕܥܬܝܕ ܠܡܐܬܐ. ܡܢ ܕܐܝܬ ܠܗ ܐܕ̈ܢܐ ܠܡܫܡܥ
ܢܫܡܥ ◦◦◦
16 ܠܡܢ ܕܝܢ ܐܕܡܝܗ ܠܫܪܒܬܐ ܗܕܐ. ܕܡܝܐ ܠܛ̈ܠܝܐ
17 ܕܝܬܒܝܢ ܒܫܘܩܐ ܘܩܥܝܢ ܠܚܒܪ̈ܝܗܘܢ. ܘܐܡܪܝܢ.
ܙܡܪܢ ܠܟܘܢ ܘܠܐ ܪܩܕܬܘܢ. ܘܐܠܝܢ ܠܟܘܢ ܘܠܐ
18 ܐܪܩܕܬܘܢ. ܐܬܐ ܓܝܪ ܠܘܬܟܘܢ ܝܘܚܢܢ ܟܕ ܠܐ ܐܟܠ
19 ܘܐܦܠܐ ܫܬܐ. ܘܐܡܪܝܢ ܐܢܬܘܢ ܫܐܕܐ ܒܗ. ܘܐܬܐ
ܒܪܗ ܕܐܢܫܐ ܐܟܠ ܘܫܬܐ. ܘܐܡܪܝܢ ܐܢܬܘܢ ܗܐ
ܓܒܪܐ ܐܟܘܠܐ ܫܬܝܐ. ܘܪܚܡܐ ܕܡ̈ܟܣܐ
ܘܕܚ̈ܛܝܐ. ܘܐܙܕܕܩܬ ܚܟܡܬܐ ܡܢ ܥ̈ܒܕܝܗ. ◦◦◦
20 ܗܝܕܝܢ ܫܪܝ ܗܘܐ ܝܫܘܥ ܠܡܚܣܕܘ ܡ̈ܕܝܢܬܐ. ܐܝܠܝܢ
21 ܕܗܘܝ ܒܗܝܢ ܚܝܠܐ ܣ̈ܓܝܐܐ ܘܠܐ ܬܒ. ܘܐܡܪ ܘܝ

38 ܡܢ ܕܠܝ ܗܘ ܠܐ ܫܘܐ ܠܝ. ܘܟܠ ܕܠܐ ܫܩܠ ܙܩܝܦܗ
39 ܘܐܬܐ ܒܬܪܝ ܠܐ ܫܘܐ ܠܝ. ܡܢ ܕܡܫܟܚ ܓܝܪ ܢܦܫܗ
40 ܢܘܒܕܝܗ. ܘܡܢ ܕܢܘܒܕ ܢܦܫܗ ܡܛܠܬܝ ܢܫܟܚܝܗ. ܡܢ
ܕܡܩܒܠ ܠܟܘܢ ܠܝ ܗܘ ܡܩܒܠ. ܘܡܢ ܕܠܝ ܡܩܒܠ ܠܡܢ
41 ܕܫܕܪܢܝ ܡܩܒܠ. ܡܢ ܕܡܩܒܠ ܢܒܝܐ ܒܫܡ ܢܒܝܐ ܐܓܪܐ
ܕܢܒܝܐ ܢܣܒ. ܘܡܢ ܕܡܩܒܠ ܙܕܝܩܐ ܒܫܡ ܙܕܝܩܐ
42 ܐܓܪܐ ܕܙܕܝܩܐ ܢܣܒ. ܘܟܠ ܡܢ ܕܢܫܩܐ ܠܚܕ ܡܢ ܗܠܝܢ
ܙܥܘܪܐ ܟܣܐ ܕܡܝܐ ܩܪ̈ܝܪܐ ܒܫܡܐ ܕܬܠܡܝܕܘܬܐ.
ܐܡܝܢ ܐܡܪ ܐܢܐ ܠܟܘܢ ܕܠܐ ܢܐܒܕ ܐܓܪܗ ⊙ ○ ⊙

XI. ܘܗܘܐ ܟܕ ܫܠܡ ܝܫܘܥ ܠܡܦܩܕܘ ܠܬܪ̈ܥܣܪ ܬܠܡܝܕܘܗܝ
ܫܢܝ ܠܗ ܡܢ ܬܡܢ. ܠܡܠܦܘ ܘܠܡܟܪܙܘ ܒܡܕ̈ܝܢܬܗܘܢ ⊙
2 ܝܘܚܢܢ ܕܝܢ ܟܕ ܫܡܥ ܒܒܝܬ ܐܣ̈ܝܪܐ ܒܥܒ̈ܕܘܗܝ
3 ܕܝܫܘܥ. ܫܕܪ ܠܬܠܡܝܕܘܗܝ ܘܫܐܠ ܠܗ. ܐܢܬ
ܗܘ ܗܘ ܕܐܬܐ ܐܘ ܠܐܚܪܝܢ ܗܘ ܡܣܟܝܢ ܐܢܚܢ.
4 ܘܥܢܐ ܝܫܘܥ ܘܐܡܪ ܠܗܘܢ. ܐܙܠܘ ܚܘܘ ܠܝܘܚܢܢ ܡܕܡ
5 ܕܚܙܝܢ ܐܢܬܘܢ ܘܡܕܡ ܕܫܡܥܝܢ ܐܢܬܘܢ. ܗܐ ܓܝܪ
ܣܡ̈ܝܐ ܚܙܝܢ. ܘܚܓܝ̈ܪܐ ܡܗܠܟܝܢ. ܘܓܪ̈ܒܐ ܡܬܕܟܝܢ.
ܘܚܪ̈ܫܐ ܫܡܥܝܢ. ܘܡܝ̈ܬܐ ܡܬܬܥܝܪܝܢ. ܘܡܣ̈ܟܢܐ
6 ܡܣܒܪܝܢ. ܘܛܘܒܘܗܝ ܐܠܐ ܢܬܟܫܠ ܒܝ ⊙ ○ ⊙
7 ܡܢ ܒܬܪ ܕܐܙܠܘ ܕܝܢ ܗܠܝܢ. ܫܪܝ ܗܘܐ ܝܫܘܥ ܠܡܐܡܪ
ܠܟ̈ܢܫܐ ܥܠ ܝܘܚܢܢ. ܡܢܐ ܢܦܩܬܘܢ ܠܡܕܒܪܐ
8 ܠܡܚܙܐ. ܩܢܝܐ ܕܡܢ ܪܘܚܐ ܡܬܬܙܝܥ. ܘܐܠܐ ܡܢܐ
ܢܦܩܬܘܢ ܠܡܚܙܐ. ܓܒܪܐ ܕܢܚ̈ܬܐ ܪ̈ܟܝܟܐ ܠܒܝܫ.

ܬܠܡܝܕܘܗܝ ܐܡܪ ܠܗ. ܡܪܝ ܐܦܣ ܠܝ ܠܘܩܕܡ ܐܙܠ
22 ܐܩܒܘܪ ܠܐܒܝ ܘܐܬܐ. ܐܡܪ ܠܗ ܝܫܘܥ ܫܒܘܩ
ܡ̈ܝܬܐ ܢܩܒܪܘܢ ܡ̈ܝܬܝܗܘܢ. ܘܐܢܬ ܬܐ ܒܬܪܝ ○ ○ ○

* * * * * * * * * * * *

* * * * * * * * * * * *

IX. * * * * * * * * * * * *

* * * * * * * * * * * *

* * * * * * * * * * * *

* * * * * * * * * * * *

* * * * * * * * * * * *

X. * * * * * * * * * * * *

* * * * * * * * * * * *

* * * * * * * * * * * *

32 ܟܠ ܐܢܫ ܗܟܝܠ ܕܢܘܕܐ ܒܝ ܩܕܡ ܒ̈ܢܝ ܐܢܫܐ. ܐܘܦ
33 ܐܢܐ ܐܘܕܐ ܒܗ ܩܕܡ ܐܒܐ ܕܒܫܡܝܐ. ܘܡܢ ܕܢܟܦܘܪ
ܒܝ ܩܕܡ ܒ̈ܢܝ ܐܢܫܐ. ܐܦ ܐܢܐ ܐܟܦܘܪ ܒܗ ܩܕܡ ܐܒܝ
34 ܕܒܫܡܝܐ. ܘܩܕܡ ܡ̈ܠܐܟܘܗܝ. ܠܐ ܐܬܝܬ ܕܐܪܡܐ
ܫܝܢܐ ܒܐܪܥܐ. ܐܠܐ ܦܠܓܘܬܐ ܕܪ̈ܥܝܢܐ ܘܣܝܦܐ.
35 ܐܬܝܬ ܓܝܪ ܕܐܦܠܓ ܒܪܐ ܥܠ ܐܒܘܗܝ. ܘܒܪܬܐ ܥܠ
36 ܐܡܗ̇. ܘܟܠܬܐ ܥܠ ܚܡܬܗ̇. ܘܒ̈ܥܠܕܒܒܘܗܝ ܕܓܒܪܐ
ܒ̈ܢܝ ܒܝܬܗ ○ ○ ○
37 ܡܢ ܕܪܚܡ ܕܝܢ ܠܐܒܘܗܝ ܐܘ ܠܐܡܗ ܝܬܝܪ ܡܢ ܕܠܝ
ܗܘ ܠܐ ܫܘܐ ܠܝ. ܘܡܢ ܕܪܚܡ ܒܪܗ ܐܘ ܒܪܬܗ ܝܬܝܪ

ܕܐܦܠܐ ܒܐܢܫ ܒܟܠܗ ܐܝܣܪܝܠ ܐܫܟܚܬ ܐܝܟ ܗܕܐ
11 ܗܝܡܢܘܬܐ. ܐܡܪ ܐܢܐ ܠܟܘܢ ܕܝܢ. ܕܣܓܝ̈ܐܐ
ܢܐܬܘܢ ܡܢ ܡܕܢܚܐ ܘܡܢ ܡܥܪܒܐ. ܘܢܣܬܡܟܘܢ ܥܡ
ܐܒܪܗܡ ܘܐܝܣܚܩ ܘܝܥܩܘܒ ܒܡܠܟܘܬܐ ܕܫܡܝܐ
12 ܘܒܢܘܗܝ ܕܡܠܟܘܬܐ ܢܦܩܘܢ ܠܚܫܘܟܐ ܒܪܝܐ. ܬܡܢ
13 ܢܗܘܐ ܒܟܝܐ ܘܚܘܪܩ ܫ̈ܢܐ. ܗܝܕܝܢ ܐܡܪ ܝܫܘܥ
ܠܩܢܛܪܘܢܐ ܗܘ. ܙܠ ܐܝܟܢܐ ܕܗܝܡܢܬ ܢܗܘܐ ܠܟ.
ܘܒܗ ܒܫܥܬܐ ܐܬܐܣܝ ܛܠܝܗ ○○○
14 ܘܐܬܐ ܝܫܘܥ ܠܒܝܬܗ ܕܫܡܥܘܢ ܟܐܦܐ. ܘܚܙܐ
15 ܠܚܡܬܗ ܕܪܡܝܐ ܘܐܚܝܕܐ ܠܗ ܐܫܬܐ. ܘܩܪܒ
ܠܐܝܕܗ. ܘܒܗ ܒܫܥܬܐ ܫܒܩܬܗ ܐܫܬܐ. ܘܩܡܬ
ܘܡܫܡܫܐ ܗܘܬ ܠܗܘܢ ○○ ○○ ○○
16 ܡܕܒܪ ܪܡܫܐ ܕܝܢ. ܩܪܒܘ ܩܕܡܘܗܝ ܟܠܗܘܢ ܐܝܠܝܢ
ܕܐܝܬ ܗܘܐ ܠܗܘܢ ܫܐܕ̈ܐ. ܘܐܣܝ ܐܢܘܢ ܒܡܠܬܗ.
17 ܘܐܝܠܝܢ ܕܒܝܫ ܒܝܫ ܒܟܘܪܗܢܝܢ ܗܘܘ ܐܣܝ ܐܢܘܢ. ܕܢܬܡܠܐ
ܡܕܡ ܕܐܬܐܡܪ ܒܝܕ ܐܫܥܝܐ ܢܒܝܐ ܕܐܡܪ ܗܘܐ.
ܕܗܘ ܢܣܒ ܟܐ̈ܒܝܢ. ܘܫܩܠ ܟܘܪܗ̈ܢܝܢ ○○○
18 ܟܕ ܚܙܐ ܕܝܢ ܝܫܘܥ ܟܢܫܐ ܣܓܝܐܐ ܕܚܕܪܝܢ ܠܗ. ܦܩܕ
19 ܠܬܠܡܝܕܘܗܝ ܕܢܐܙܠܘܢ ܠܥܒܪܐ ܕܝܡܐ. ܘܩܪܒ ܣܦܪܐ
ܚܕ ܘܐܡܪ ܠܗ. ܡܠܦܢܐ ܐܬܐ ܒܬܪܟ ܠܐܬܪ ܕܐܙܠ
20 ܐܢܬ. ܐܡܪ ܠܗ ܝܫܘܥ. ܠܬܥܠܐ ܢܩܥܐ ܐܝܬ ܠܗܘܢ.
ܘܠܦܪܚܬܐ ܕܫܡܝܐ ܡܛܠܠܐ. ܠܒܪܗ ܕܝܢ ܕܐܢܫܐ ܠܝܬ
21 ܠܗ ܐܬܪ ܕܢܣܡܘܟ ܪܫܗ. ܐܚܪܢܐ ܕܝܢ ܡܢ

28 ܘܟܕ ܫܠܡ ܝܫܘܥ ܡ̈ܠܘܗܝ ܗܠܝܢ. ܬܡܗܝܢ ܗܘܘ ܟܢ̈ܫܐ
29 ܥܠ ܝܘܠܦܢܗ. ܕܐܝܟ ܡܫܠܛܐ ܡܠܦ ܗܘܐ ܠܗܘܢ.
VIII. ܘܠܐ ܐܝܟ ܣܦܪ̈ܝܗܘܢ ܘܦܪ̈ܝܫܐ. ܘܟܕ ܢܚܬ ܡܢ ܛܘܪܐ.
2 ܐܬܝܢ ܗܘܘ ܒܬܪܗ ܟܢ̈ܫܐ ܣ̈ܓܝܐܐ ܘܗܐ ܓܪܒܐ ܚܕ.
+ܩܪܒ ܐܬܐ ܢܦܠ ܣܓܕ ܠܗ. ܘܐܡܪ ܠܗ ܡܪܝ. ܐܢ ܨܒܐ
3 ܐܢܬ ܡܫܟܚ ܐܢܬ ܠܡܕܟܝܘܬܢܝ. ܘܦܫܛ ܐܝܕܗ ܝܫܘܥ
ܘܩܪܒ ܠܗ. ܘܐܡܪ ܠܗ ܨܒܐ ܐܢܐ ܐܬܕܟܐ. ܘܒܗ̇
4 ܒܫܥܬܐ ܐܬܕܟܝ ܡܢܗ ܓܪܒܐ. ܘܐܡܪ ܠܗ ܝܫܘܥ.
ܕܠܡܐ ܠܐܢܫ ܐܡܪ ܐܢܬ. ܐܠܐ ܙܠ ܚܘܐ ܢܦܫܟ
ܠܟ̈ܗܢܐ. ܘܩܪܒ ܩܘܪܒܢܐ ܐܝܟ ܕܦܩܕ ܡܘܫܐ.
ܕܢܗܘܐ ܠܗܘܢ ܠܣܗܕܘܬܐ ◦◦◦
5 ܒܬܪ ܗܠܝܢ ܕܝܢ ܥܠ ܠܟܦܪܢܚܘܡ. ܩܪܒ ܠܗ ܩܢܛܪܘܢܐ
6 ܚܕ. ܘܒܥܐ ܗܘܐ ܡܢܗ ܘܡܬܟܫܦ ܠܗ ܘܐܡܪ.
ܒܒܝ ܡܪܝ. ܘܐܪܒܐ ܒܒܝܬܐ ܒܬܫܪܝܐ ܪܡܐ.
7, 8 ܐܡܪ ܠܗ ܝܫܘܥ ܐܢܐ ܐܬܐ ܘܐܣܝܘܗܝ. ܥܢܐ ܗܘ
ܩܢܛܪܘܢܐ ܘܐܡܪ ܠܗ. ܡܪܝ. ܠܐ ܫܘܐ ܐܢܐ ܕܬܥܘܠ
ܬܚܝܬ ܡܛܠܠܝ. ܐܠܐ ܒܠܚܘܕ ܐܡܪ ܒܡܠܬܐ
9 ܘܢܬܐܣܐ ܛܠܝܝ. ܐܦ ܐܢܐ ܓܝܪ ܓܒܪܐ ܐܢܐ ܕܬܚܝܬ
ܫܘܠܛܢܐ. ܘܐܝܬ ܠܝ ܫܘܠܛܢܐ ܐܦ ܠܝ. ܘܐܣܛܪ̈ܛܝܘܛܐ
ܐܝܬ ܬܚܝܬ ܐܝܕܝ. ܘܐܡܪ ܐܢܐ ܠܗܢܐ ܕܙܠ ܘܐܙܠ.
ܘܠܐܚܪܢܐ ܕܬܐ ܘܐܬܐ. ܘܠܥܒܕܝ ܐܡܪ ܐܢܐ ܕܥܒܕ
10 ܕܦܠܚ ܘܥܒܕ. ܟܕ ܫܡܥ ܕܝܢ ܝܫܘܥ ܐܬܕܡܪ. ܘܐܡܪ
ܠܐܝܠܝܢ ܕܐܬܝܢ ܒܬܪܗ. ܐܡܝܢ ܐܡܪܢܐ ܠܟܘܢ.

ܠܩܛܝܢ ܡܢ ܟܘܒܐ ܥܢܒ̈ܐ. ܐܘ ܬܐ̈ܢܐ ܡܢ ܕܖ̈ܕܖܐ.
17 ܟܠ ܐܝܠܢܐ ܛܒܐ ܦܐܖ̈ܐ ܛܒ̈ܐ ܥܒܕ. ܘܐܝܠܢܐ ܒܝܫܐ
18 ܦܐܖ̈ܐ ܒܝ̈ܫܐ ܥܒܕ. ܠܐ ܡܫܟܚ ܐܝܠܢܐ ܛܒܐ
ܕܢܥܒܕ ܦܐܖ̈ܐ ܒܝ̈ܫܐ. ܘܐܦܠܐ ܐܝܠܢܐ ܒܝܫܐ ܕܢܥܒܕ
19 ܦܐܖ̈ܐ ܛܒ̈ܐ. ܟܠ ܐܝܠܢܐ ܗܟܝܠ ܕܦܐܖ̈ܐ ܛܒ̈ܐ ܠܐ
20 ܥܒܕ. ܡܬܦܣܩ ܘܒܢܘܪܐ ܢܦܠ. ܡܢ ܦܐܖ̈ܝܗܘܢ ܗܟܝܠ
ܬܫܬܘܕܥܘܢ ܐܢܘܢ ⁘
21 ܠܐ ܗܘܐ ܗܟܝܠ ܟܠ ܕܐܡܪ ܠܝ ܡܪܝ ܡܪܝ ܥܐܠ
ܠܡܠܟܘܬܐ ܕܫܡܝܐ. ܐܠܐ ܗܘ ܕܥܒܕ ܨܒܝܢܗ ܕܐܒܝ
22 ܕܒܫܡܝܐ. ܗܘ ܢܥܘܠ ܠܡܠܟܘܬ ܫܡܝܐ. ܣܓܝܐ̈ܐ ܓܝܪ
ܢܐܡܪܘܢ ܠܝ ܒܗܘ ܝܘܡܐ. ܡܪܢ ܡܪܢ. ܠܐ ܒܫܡܟ
ܐܟܠܢ ܘܐܫܬܝܢ. ܘܒܫܡܟ ܐܬܢܒܝܢ. ܘܒܫܡܟ ܫܐ̈ܕܐ
23 ܐܦܩܢ. ܘܒܫܡܟ ܚܝ̈ܠܐ ܣܓܝܐ̈ܐ ܥܒܕܢ. ܗܝܕܝܢ ܐܡܪ
ܠܗܘܢ. ܕܠܐ ܡܢ ܡܬܘܡ ܝܕܥܬܟܘܢ. ܙܠܘ ܠܟܘܢ ܡܢܝ
ܦ̈ܠܚܝ ܥܘܠܐ ⁘
24 ܟܠ ܐܢܫ ܕܫܡܥ ܡ̈ܠܝ ܗܠܝܢ ܘܥܒܕ ܠܗܝܢ. ܐܕܡܝܘܗܝ
25 ܠܓܒܪܐ ܚܟܝܡܐ. ܕܒܢܐ ܒܝܬܗ ܥܠ ܫܘܥܐ. ܘܢܚܬ
ܡܛܪܐ. ܘܐܬܘ ܢܗܖ̈ܘܬܐ. ܘܢܫܒ ܖ̈ܘܚܐ ܘܐܬܛܪܦܘ ܒܗ
ܒܒܝܬܐ ܘܠܐ ܢܦܠ. ܡܛܠ ܕܫ̈ܬܐܣܘܗܝ ܥܠ ܫܘܥܐ
26 ܣܝܡܢ ܗܘܝ. ܘܟܠ ܐܢܫ ܕܫܡܥ ܡ̈ܠܝ ܗܠܝܢ ܘܠܐ ܥܒܕ
ܠܗܝܢ. ܕܡܐ ܠܓܒܪܐ ܣܟܠܐ. ܕܒܢܐ ܒܝܬܗ ܥܠ ܚܠܐ.
27 ܘܢܚܬ ܡܛܪܐ. ܘܐܬܘ ܢܗܖ̈ܘܬܐ. ܘܢܫܒ ܖ̈ܘܚܐ ܘܐܬܛܪܦܝ
ܒܗ ܒܒܝܬܐ ܗܘ ܘܢܦܠ. ܘܗܘܬ ܡܦܘܠܬܗ ܪܒܐ ⁘

ܩܪܝܬܐ ܡܢ ܥܝܢܟ. ܘܗܝܕܝܢ ܬܬܚܙܐ ܠܟ ܠܡܦܩܘ ܓܠܐ
ܡܢ ܥܝܢܗ ܕܐܚܘܟ ◌ ◌ ◌
ܠܐ ܬܬܠܘܢ ܩܘܕܫܐ ܠܟܠ̈ܒܐ. ܘܠܐ ܬܪܡܘܢ 6
ܡܪ̈ܓܢܝܬܟܘܢ ܩܕܡ ܚܙܝܪ̈ܐ. ܕܠܐ ܢܕܘܫܘܢ ܐܢܝܢ
ܒܪ̈ܓܠܝܗܘܢ. ܘܢܬܗܦܟܘܢ ܢܚܒܠܘܢܟܘܢ. ܫܐܠܘ ܘܢܬܝܗܒ ܠܟܘܢ. 7
ܒܥܘ ܘܬܫܟܚܘܢ. ܢܩܘܫܘ ܘܢܬܦܬܚ ܠܟܘܢ. ܟܠ ܡܢ ܓܝܪ 8
ܕܫܐܠ ܢܣܒ. ܘܡܢ ܕܒܥܐ ܡܫܟܚ. ܘܡܢ ܕܢܩܫ ܡܬܬܦܬܚ
ܠܗ. ܡܢܘ ܓܝܪ ܡܢܟܘܢ ܕܢܫܐܠܝܘܗܝ ܒܪܗ ܠܚܡܐ. 9
ܠܡܐ ܟܐܦܐ ܡܘܫܛ ܠܗ. ܐܘ ܐܢ ܢܘܢܐ ܢܫܐܠܝܘܗܝ 10
ܠܡܐ ܚܘܝܐ ܡܘܫܛ ܠܗ. ܐܢ ܗܟܝܠ ܐܢܬܘܢ ܕܒ̈ܝܫܐ 11
ܐܢܬܘܢ. ܝܕܥܝܢ ܐܢܬܘܢ ܡܘܗ̈ܒܬܐ ܛܒ̈ܬܐ ܠܡܬܠ
ܠܒ̈ܢܝܟܘܢ. ܟܡܐ ܝܬܝܪܐܝܬ ܐܒܘܟܘܢ ܕܒܫܡܝܐ.
ܢܬܠ ܛܒ̈ܬܐ ܠܐܝܠܝܢ ܕܫܐܠܝܢ ܠܗ. ܟܠܡܕܡ ܗܟܝܠ 12
ܕܨܒܝܢ ܐܢܬܘܢ ܕܢܥܒܕܘܢ ܠܟܘܢ ܒܢ̈ܝܢܫܐ. ܗܟܘܬܗܘܢ
ܥܒܕܘ ܠܗܘܢ. ܗܢܘ ܓܝܪ ܢܡܘܣܐ ܘܢܒ̈ܝܐ. ܥܘܠܘ 13
ܒܬܪܥܐ ܥܠܝܩܐ. ܡܛܠ ܕܦܬܝܐ ܬܪܥܐ ܘܪܘܝܚܐ
ܐܘܪܚܐ ܕܡܘܒܠܐ ܠܐܒܕܢܐ. ܘܣܓܝܐܐ ܐܢܘܢ ܕܐܙܠܝܢ
ܒܗ̇. ܡܐ ܐܠܝܨ ܬܪܥܐ ܘܐܠܝܨܐ ܐܘܪܚܐ ܕܡܘܒܠܐ 14
ܠܚܝ̈ܐ. ܘܙܥܘܪܝܢ ܐܢܘܢ ܐܝܠܝܢ ܕܡܫܟܚܝܢ ܠܗ̇ ◌ ◌
ܛܪܘ ܢܦܫܟܘܢ ܡܢ ܢܒ̈ܝܐ ܕܟܕܒܘܬܐ. ܕܐܬܝܢ ܠܘܬܟܘܢ 15
ܒܠܒܘܫܐ ܕܐܡܪ̈ܐ. ܘܡܢ ܠܓܘ ܕܐܒ̈ܐ ܐܢܘܢ ܚܛܘ̈ܦܐ.
ܡܢ ܦܐܪ̈ܝܗܘܢ ܗܟܝܠ ܬܫܬܘܕܥܘܢ ܐܢܘܢ. ܠܐ ܓܝܪ 16

27 ܐܢܬܘܢ ܝܬܝܪܝܢ ܡܢܗܘܢ. ܡܢܘ ܕܝܢ ܡܢܟܘܢ ܡܫܟܚ
28 ܠܡܘܣܦܘ ܥܠ ܩܘܡܬܗ ܐܡܬܐ ܚܕܐ. ܕܥܠ ܠܒܘܫܐ
ܝܨܦܝܢ ܐܢܬܘܢ. ܚܙܘ ܠܫܘܫܢܐ ܕܕܒܪܐ ܐܝܟܢܐ ܡܬܪܒܝܢ.
29 ܕܠܐ ܥܡܠܝܢ ܘܠܐ ܠܐܝܢ. ܘܐܡܪ ܐܢܐ ܠܟܘܢ
ܕܐܦܠܐ ܫܠܝܡܘܢ ܒܟܠܗ ܬܫܒܘܚܬܗ ܐܬܟܣܝ
30 ܐܝܟ ܚܕ ܡܢܗܘܢ. ܘܐܢ ܕܝܢ ܠܥܡܝܪܐ ܕܕܒܪܐ ܕܝܘܡܢܐ ܐܝܬܘܗܝ.
ܘܡܚܪ ܡܬܬܠܩ ܘܢܦܠ ܒܬܢܘܪܐ ܐܠܗܐ ܡܠܒܫ.
ܟܡܐ ܗܟܝܠ ܠܟܘܢ ܢܬܟܠܠ ܠܗ ܚܣܝܪܝ
31 ܗܝܡܢܘܬܐ. ܠܐ ܗܟܝܠ ܬܐܨܦܘܢ ܘܬܐܡܪܘܢ. ܡܢܐ
32 ܢܐܟܘܠ ܘܡܢܐ ܢܫܬܐ. ܘܡܢܐ ܢܬܟܣܐ. ܗܠܝܢ ܓܝܪ
ܟܠܗܝܢ ܒܥ̈ܡܡܐ ܗܘ ܕܐܪܥܐ ܒܥܝܢ ܠܗܝܢ. ܝܕܥ ܗܘ
33 ܓܝܪ ܐܒܘܟܘܢ ܕܐܦ ܠܟܘܢ ܡܬܒܥܝܢ ܗܠܝܢ. ܐܢܬܘܢ
ܕܝܢ ܒܥܘ ܠܘܩܕܡ ܡܠܟܘܬܗ ܕܐܠܗܐ ܘܙܕܝܩܘܬܗ.
34 ܘܗܠܝܢ ܟܠܗܝܢ ܢܬܬܘܣܦܢ ܠܟܘܢ. ܠܐ ܗܟܝܠ ܬܐܨܦܘܢ
ܕܡܚܪ. ܡܛܠ ܕܡܚܪ ܓܝܪ ܕܝܠܗ ܝܨܦ. ܣܦܩ ܠܗ
VII. ܠܝܘܡܐ ܒܝܫܬܗ. ܠܐ ܬܕܘܢܘܢ. ܕܠܐ ܬܬܕܝܢܘܢ. ܒܗܘ
ܓܝܪ ܕܝܢܐ ܕܕܝܢܝܢ ܐܢܬܘܢ ܡܬܕܝܢܝܢ ܐܢܬܘܢ. ܘܒܟܝܠܬܐ
3 ܕܟܝܠܝܢ ܐܢܬܘܢ ܡܬܟܝܠ ܠܟܘܢ. ܡܢܐ ܕܝܢ ܚܙܐ
ܕܟܝܠܗ ܕܐܚܘܟ ܚܙܐ ܐܢܬ. ܘܩܪܝܬܐ ܕܐܝܬ ܒܥܝܢܟ
4 ܠܐ ܒܚܪ ܐܢܬ. ܐܘ ܐܝܟܢܐ ܡܫܟܚ ܐܢܬ ܠܡܐܡܪ
ܠܐܚܘܟ. ܫܒܘܩ ܐܦܩ ܟܝܠܐ ܡܢ ܥܝܢܟ. ܕܗܐ ܩܪܝܬܐ ܒܥܝܢܟ
5 ܕܠܟ ܩܪܝܬܐ ܗܘܝܐ. ܢܣܒ ܒܐ̈ܦܐ ܐܦܩ ܠܘܩܕܡ

ܐܝܟܢܐ ܕܨܐܡ ܨܝܡܝܢ. ܘܐܡܝܢ ܐܡܪܢܐ ܠܟܘܢ ܕܩܒܠܘ
17 ܐܓܪܗܘܢ. ܐܢܬ ܕܝܢ ܐܡܬܝ ܕܨܐܡ ܐܢܬ. ܐܫܝܓ
18 ܐܦ̈ܝܟ ܘܡܫܘܚ ܪܫܟ. ܕܠܐ ܬܬܚܙܐ ܠܒܢ̈ܝ ܐܢܫܐ
ܕܨܐܡ ܐܢܬ. ܐܠܐ ܠܐܒܘܟ ܕܝܕܥ ܒܟܣܝܐ.
19 ܘܐܒܘܟ ܕܚܙܐ ܒܟܣܝܐ ܢܦܪܥܟ. ܠܐ ܬܣܝܡܘܢ ܠܟܘܢ
ܣܝܡܬܐ ܒܐܪܥܐ. ܐܬܪ ܕܢܦܠ ܣܣܐ ܘܡܚܒܠ. ܘܐܬܪ
20 ܕܦܠܫܝܢ ܓܢ̈ܒܐ ܘܓܢܒܝܢ. ܐܠܐ ܣܝܡܘ ܠܟܘܢ ܣܝܡܬܐ
ܒܫܡܝܐ. ܐܬܪ ܕܠܐ ܣܣܐ ܡܚܒܠ. ܘܐܦܠܐ ܓܢ̈ܒܐ
21 ܦܠܫܝܢ ܘܓܢܒܝܢ. ܐܬܪ ܓܝܪ ܕܣܝܡܬܟܘܢ ܬܗܘܐ ܐܦ
22 ܠܒܟܘܢ ܬܡܢ ܢܗܘܐ. ܫܪܓܗ ܓܝܪ ܕܦܓܪܐ ܥܝܢܐ ܗܝ.
ܐܢ ܥܝܢܟ ܬܗܘܐ ܦܫܝܛܐ. ܐܦ ܦܓܪܟ ܟܠܗ ܢܗܝܪܐ
23 ܢܗܝܪ. ܐܢ ܕܝܢ ܥܝܢܟ ܬܗܘܐ ܒܝܫܐ. ܐܦ ܦܓܪܟ ܟܠܗ
ܚܫܘܟ ܗܘ. ܐܢ ܗܟܝܠ ܢܘܗܪܐ ܕܒܟ ܚܫܘܟ ܗܘ.
ܚܫܘܟܟ ܟܡܐ ܢܗܘܐ ◦ ◦ ◦
24 ܠܐ ܐܢܫ ܡܫܟܚ ܦܠܚ ܬܪ̈ܝܢ ܡܪ̈ܘܢ. ܕܠܐ ܠܚܕ
ܢܣܢܐ ܘܠܐܚܪܢܐ ܢܪܚܡ. ܐܘ ܠܚܕ ܢܣܒܪ ܘܠܐܚܪܢܐ
ܢܒܣܐ. ܠܐ ܡܫܟܚܝܢ ܐܢܬܘܢ ܠܐܠܗܐ ܠܡܦܠܚ
25 ܘܠܡܡܘܢܐ. ܡܛܠ ܗܢܐ ܐܡܪ ܐܢܐ ܠܟܘܢ. ܕܠܐ
ܬܐܨܦܘܢ ܠܢܦܫܟܘܢ ܡܢܐ ܬܐܟܠܘܢ. ܘܐܦܠܐ
ܠܦܓܪ̈ܟܘܢ ܡܢܐ ܬܠܒܫܘܢ. ܢܦܫܐ ܓܝܪ ܝܬܝܪܐ ܗܝ ܡܢ
26 ܣܝܒܪܬܐ. ܘܦܓܪܐ ܡܢ ܠܒܘܫܐ. ܚܙܘ ܒܦܪ̈ܚܬܐ
ܕܫܡܝܐ. ܕܠܐ ܙܪܥܝܢ ܘܠܐ ܚܨܕܝܢ ܘܠܐ ܟܢܫܝܢ.
ܘܐܒܘܟܘܢ ܕܒܫܡܝܐ ܡܬܪܣܐ ܠܗܘܢ. ܠܐ ܗܟܝܠ

ܘܒܙ̈ܘܝܬܐ ܕܫ̈ܘܩܐ ܠܡܨܠܝܘ. ܕܢܬܚܙܘܢ ܠܒܢ̈ܝ ܐܢܫܐ.
6 ܐܡܪ ܐܢܐ ܠܟܘܢ ܕܩܒܠܘ ܐܓܪܗܘܢ. ܐܢܬ ܕܝܢ
ܐܡܬܝ ܕܡܨܠܐ ܐܢܬ. ܥܘܠ ܠܟ ܠܬܘܢܐ. ܘܐܚܘܕ
ܬܪܥܐ ܒܐܦ̈ܝܟ. ܘܨܠܝ ܠܐܒܘܟ ܕܒܟܣܝܐ. ܘܐܒܘܟ
ܕܚܙܐ ܒܟܣܝܐ ܢܦܪܥܟ ◦◦◦
7 ܘܐܡܬܝ ܕܡܨܠܝܢ ܐܢܬܘܢ. ܠܐ ܗܘܝܬܘܢ ܡܦܩܩܝܢ
ܐܝܟ ܢܣܒ̈ܝ ܒܐ̈ܦܐ. ܕܣܒܪܝܢ ܓܝܪ ܕܒܡܡܠܠܐ
8 ܣܓܝܐܐ ܡܫܬܡܥܝܢ. ܠܐ ܗܟܝܠ ܬܬܕܡܘܢ ܠܗܘܢ.
ܝܕܥ ܗܘ ܓܝܪ ܐܒܘܟܘܢ ܡܢܐ ܡܬܒܥܐ ܠܟܘܢ
9 ܥܕܠܐ ܬܫܐܠܘܢܝܗܝ. ܗܟܢܐ ܕܝܢ ܗܘܝܬܘܢ
10 ܡܨܠܝܢ. ܐܒܘܢ ܕܒܫܡܝܐ ܢܬܩܕܫ ܫܡܟ. ܬܐܬܐ
11 ܡܠܟܘܬܟ. ܘܢܗܘܐ ܨܒܝܢܟ ܒܐܪܥܐ ܐܝܟ
12 ܕܒܫܡܝܐ. ܠܚܡܐ ܕܣܘܢܩܢܢ ܝܘܡܢܐ ܗܒ ܠܢ. ܘܫܒܘܩ
ܠܢ ܚܘ̈ܒܝܢ. ܐܝܟܢܐ ܕܐܦ ܚܢܢ ܫܒܩܢ ܠܚܝ̈ܒܝܢ.
13 ܘܠܐ ܬܥܠܢ ܠܢܣܝܘܢܐ. ܐܠܐ ܦܨܢ ܡܢ ܒܝܫܐ.
ܡܛܠ ܕܕܝܠܟ ܗܝ ܡܠܟܘܬܐ ܘܬܫܒܘܚܬܐ. ܠܥܠܡ
ܥܠܡܝܢ ܐܡܝܢ ◦◦◦
14 ܐܢ ܓܝܪ ܬܫܒܩܘܢ ܠܒܢ̈ܝ ܐܢܫܐ ܣܟ̈ܠܘܬܗܘܢ. ܐܦ
15 ܐܒܘܟܘܢ ܕܒܫܡܝܐ ܢܫܒܘܩ ܠܟܘܢ. ܐܢ ܕܝܢ ܐܢܬܘܢ
ܠܐ ܬܫܒܩܘܢ ܠܒܢܝ ܐܢܫܐ ܣܟ̈ܠܘܬܗܘܢ. ܘܐܦܠܐ
ܐܒܘܟܘܢ ܢܫܒܘܩ ܠܟܘܢ ܣܟ̈ܠܘܬܟܘܢ ◦◦◦
16 ܘܐܡܬܝ ܕܨܝܡܝܢ ܐܢܬܘܢ. ܠܐ ܬܗܘܘܢ ܐܝܟ ܢܣܒ̈ܝ
ܒܐ̈ܦܐ. ܕܡܚܒܠܝܢ ܐܦ̈ܝܗܘܢ. ܕܢܬܚܙܘܢ ܠܒܢ̈ܝ

ܐܚܪܢܝܢ. ܘܡܢ ܕܫܐܠ ܠܟ ܗܒ ܠܗ. ܘܡܢ ܕܨܒܐ ܕܢܙܦ 42
ܡܢܟ ܠܐ ܬܟܠܝܘܗܝ. ܫܡܥܬܘܢ ܕܐܬܐܡܪ ܠܩ̈ܕܡܝܐ. 43
ܕܬܪܚܡ ܠܩܪܝܒܟ ܘܬܣܢ ܠܒܥܠܕܒܒܟ. ܐܢܐ ܕܝܢ ܐܡܪ 44
ܐܢܐ ܠܟܘܢ ܕܐܚܒܘ ܠܒܥܠܕܒ̈ܒܝܟܘܢ. ܘܨܠܘ ܥܠ ܐܝܠܝܢ
ܕܪ̈ܕܦܝܢ ܠܟܘܢ. ܐܝܟܢܐ ܕܬܗܘܘܢ ܒ̈ܢܘܗܝ ܕܐܒܘܟܘܢ 45
ܕܒܫܡܝܐ. ܗܘ ܕܡܕܢܚ ܫܡܫܗ ܥܠ ܛ̈ܒܐ ܘܥܠ
ܒ̈ܝܫܐ. ܘܡܚܬ ܡܛܪܗ ܥܠ ܟܐ̈ܢܐ ܘܥܠ ܥ̈ܘܠܐ. ܐܢ 46
ܓܝܪ ܡܚܒܝܢ ܐܢܬܘܢ ܠܐܝܠܝܢ ܕܡܚܒܝܢ ܠܟܘܢ ܡܢܘ
ܐܓܪܟܘܢ. ܗܕܐ ܓܝܪ ܐܦ ܡ̈ܟܣܐ ܥܒܕܝܢ. ܘܐܢ 47
ܫܐܠܝܢ ܐܢܬܘܢ ܒܫܠܡܐ ܕܐܚ̈ܝܟܘܢ ܒܠܚܘܕ. ܡܢܐ ܗܝ
ܝܬܝܪܘܬܟܘܢ. ܠܐ ܗܐ ܐܦ ܡ̈ܟܣܐ ܗܕܐ ܥܒܕܝܢ
ܗܘܘ ܗܟܝܠ ܓܡܝܪ̈ܐ. ܐܝܟܢܐ ܕܐܒܘܟܘܢ ܕܒܫܡܝܐ 48
ܓܡܝܪ ܗܘ. ܐܙܕܗܪܘ ܕܠܐ ܬܥܒܕܘܢ ܙܕܩܬܟܘܢ VI.
ܩܕܡ ܒ̈ܢܝܢܫܐ. ܐܝܟܢܐ ܕܬܬܚܙܘܢ ܠܗܘܢ. ܘܐܠܐ
ܐܓܪܐ ܠܝܬ ܠܟܘܢ ܠܘܬ ܐܒܘܟܘܢ ܕܒܫܡܝܐ. ܐܡܬܝ 2
ܗܟܝܠ ܕܥܒܕ ܐܢܬ ܙܕܩܬܐ. ܠܐ ܬܩܪܐ ܩܪܢܐ
ܩܕܡܝܟ. ܐܝܟܢܐ ܕܥܒܕܝܢ ܢܣ̈ܒܝ ܒܐܦܐ ܒܟܢ̈ܘܫܬܐ
ܘܒܫ̈ܘܩܐ. ܐܝܟܢܐ ܕܢܫܬܒܚܘܢ ܡܢ ܒ̈ܢܝܢܫܐ. ܐܡܝܢ
ܐܡܪ ܐܢܐ ܠܟܘܢ ܕܩܒܠܘ ܐܓܪܗܘܢ. ܐܢܬ ܕܝܢ ܡܐ ܕܥܒܕ 3
ܐܢܬ ܙܕܩܬܐ. ܠܐ ܬܕܥ ܣܡܠܟ ܡܢܐ ܥܒܕܐ ܝܡܝܢܟ.
ܕܬܗܘܐ ܙܕܩܬܟ ܒܟܣܝܐ. ܘܐܒܘܟ ܕܚܙܐ ܒܟܣܝܐ 4
ܢܦܪܥܟ ܒܓܠܝܐ. ܘܡܐ ܕܡܨܠܐ ܐܢܬ. ܠܐ ܬܗܘܐ ܐܝܟ 5
ܗܢܘܢ ܢܣ̈ܒܝ ܒܐܦܐ. ܕܪܚܡܝܢ ܕܢܩܘܡܘܢ ܒܟܢ̈ܘܫܬܐ

ܐܝܕܟ ܕܝܡܝܢܐ ܡܟܫܠܐ ܠܟ ܦܣܘܩ ܫܕܝܗ ܡܢܟ.
ܦܩܚ ܠܟ ܓܝܪ ܕܢܐܒܕ ܚܕ ܡܢ ܗܕܡܝܟ. ܘܠܐ ܟܠܗ
31 ܦܓܪܟ ܢܐܙܠ ܠܓܗܢܐ. ܐܬܐܡܪ ܕܡܢ ܕܫܪܐ ܐܢܬܬܗ
32 ܢܬܠ ܠܗ̇ ܐܓܪܬܐ ܕܫܘܒܩܐ. ܐܢܐ ܕܝܢ ܐܡܪ ܐܢܐ
ܠܟܘܢ ܕܡܢ ܕܫܪܐ ܐܢܬܬܗ ܕܠܐ ܐܬܐܡܪ ܥܠܝܗ̇
ܙܢܝܐ. ܗܘܝܘ ܡܓܪ ܠܗ̇. ܘܡܢ ܕܫܩܠ ܫܒܝܩܬܐ ܡܓܪ
33 ܓܒܪ܀ ܬܘܒ ܫܡܥܬܘܢ ܕܐܬܐܡܪ ܠܩ̈ܕܡܝܐ. ܠܐ
ܬܐܡܐ ܡܘܡܬܐ ܕܫܘܩܪܐ. ܐܠܐ ܬܬܠ ܠܡܪܝܐ
34 ܡܘܡܬܟ. ܐܢܐ ܕܝܢ ܐܡܪܢܐ ܠܟܘܢ ܕܠܡܘܡܘ ܠܐ
ܬܐܡܘܢ. ܠܐ ܒܫܡܝܐ ܕܟܘܪܣܝܗ ܐܝܬܘ ܕܐܠܗܐ.
35 ܘܐܦ ܠܐ ܒܐܪܥܐ ܡܛܠ ܕܟܘܒܫܐ ܗܝ ܕܬܚܝܬ
ܪ̈ܓܠܘܗܝ. ܘܐܦ ܠܐ ܒܐܘܪܫܠܡ ܡܛܠ ܕܡܕܝܢܬܗ ܗܝ
36 ܕܡܠܟܐ ܪܒܐ. ܘܐܦܠܐ ܒܪܫܟ ܬܐܡܐ. ܡܛܠ ܕܠܐ
ܡܫܟܚ ܐܢܬ ܠܡܥܒܕ ܒܗ ܡܢܬܐ ܚܕܐ ܕܣܥܪܐ
37 ܐܘܟܡܬܐ ܐܘ ܚܘܪܬܐ. ܐܠܐ ܬܗܘܐ ܡܠܬܟܘܢ
ܐܝܢ ܐܝܢ ܘܠܐ ܠܐ. ܡܝܬܪ ܕܝܢ ܕܡܢ ܗܠܝܢ ܣܛܪ ܡܢ
ܒܝܫܐ ܗܘ ܀܀܀
38 ܫܡܥܬܘܢ ܕܐܬܐܡܪ ܕܥܝܢܐ ܚܠܦ ܥܝܢܐ. ܘܫܢܐ
39 ܚܠܦ ܫܢܐ. ܐܢܐ ܕܝܢ ܐܡܪ ܐܢܐ ܠܟܘܢ ܕܠܐ
ܬܩܘܡܘܢ ܠܘܩܒܠ ܒܝܫܐ. ܐܠܐ ܡܢ ܕܡܚܐ ܠܟ ܥܠ
40 ܦܟܟ [ܐܦܝܐ] ܠܗ ܐܚܪܢܐ. ܘܡܢ ܕܒܥܐ ܕܢܕܘܢ ܥܡܟ
ܘܢܣܒ ܟܘܬܝܢܟ. ܫܒܘܩ ܠܗ ܫܩܠ ܐܦ ܡܪܛܘܛܟ.
41 ܡܢ ܕܐܡܪ ܠܟ ܕܬܐܙܠ ܥܡܗ ܡܝܠ. ܙܠ [ܥܡܗ] ܬܪܝܢ

20 ܕܫܡܝܐ. ܐܡܪܢܐ ܠܟܘܢ ܓܝܪ. ܕܐܠܐ ܬܝܬܪ
ܙܕܝܩܘܬܟܘܢ ܝܬܝܪ ܡܢ ܣܦܪ̈ܐ ܘܦܪ̈ܝܫܐ. ܠܐ ܬܥܠܘܢ
21 ܠܡܠܟܘܬܐ ܕܫܡܝܐ. ܫܡܥܬܘܢ ܕܐܬܐܡܪ ܠܩܕܡ̈ܝܐ
ܕܠܐ ܬܩܛܘܠ. ܘܟܠ ܡܢ ܕܢܩܛܘܠ ܢܬܚܝܒ ܒܕܝܢܐ.
22 ܐܢܐ ܕܝܢ ܐܡܪ ܐܢܐ ܠܟܘܢ. ܕܟܠ ܡܢ ܕܢܪܓܙ ܥܠ
ܐܚܘܗܝ ܐܝܩܐ ܢܗܘܐ ܡܚܝܒ ܠܕܝܢܐ. ܘܡܢ ܕܢܐܡܪ
ܠܐܚܘܗܝ ܪܩܐ ܢܗܘܐ ܡܚܝܒ ܠܟܢܘܫܬܐ. ܘܟܠ ܡܢ
ܕܢܐܡܪ ܠܐܚܘܗܝ ܫܛܝܐ ܢܗܘܐ ܡܚܝܒ ܠܓܗܢܐ
23 ܕܢܘܪܐ ◦ ܐܢܗܘ ܗܟܝܠ ܕܡܩܪܒ ܐܢܬ ܩܘܪܒܢܟ ܩܕܡ
ܡܕܒܚܐ. ܘܬܡܢ ܬܬܕܟܪ ܕܡܕܡ ܐܚܝܕ ܐܚܘܟ ܥܠܝܟ
24 ܐܬܡܢ. ܫܒܘܩ ܩܘܪܒܢܟ ܬܡܢ ܩܕܡܘܗܝ ܕܡܕܒܚܐ.
ܘܙܠ ܠܘܩܕܡ ܐܬܪܥܐ ܥܡ ܐܚܘܟ. ܘܗܝܕܝܢ ܬܐ
ܘܩܪܒ ܩܘܪܒܢܟ ◦ ◦ ◦
25 ܗܘܝܬ ܡܫܬܘܐ ܥܡ ܒܥܠܕܝܢܟ. ܥܕܟܠ ܟܕ ܒܥܡܗ
ܐܢܬ ܒܐܘܪܚܐ. ܕܠܡܐ ܒܥܠܕܝܢܟ ܢܫܠܡܟ ܠܕܝܢܐ.
26 ܘܕܝܢܐ ܢܫܠܡܟ ܠܓܒܝܐ. ܘܬܦܠ ܒܒܝܬ ܐܣܝܪ̈ܐ. ܘܐܡܝܢ
ܐܡܪ ܐܢܐ ܠܟ. ܕܠܐ ܬܦܘܩ ܡܢ ܬܡܢ. ܥܕܡܐ
ܕܬܬܠ ܫܡܘܢܐ ܐܚܪܝܐ ◦ ◦ ◦
27, 28 ܫܡܥܬܘܢ ܕܐܬܐܡܪ ܠܩܕܡ̈ܝܐ ܕܠܐ ܬܓܘܪ. ܐܢܐ ܕܝܢ
ܐܡܪ ܐܢܐ ܠܟܘܢ. ܕܟܠ ܡܢ ܕܚܙܐ ܐܢܬܬܐ ܘܪܓ
29 ܠܗ̇ ܓܪܗ̇ ܒܠܒܗ. ܐܢ ܕܝܢ ܥܝܢܟ ܕܝܡܝܢܐ ܡܟܫܠܐ
ܠܟ ܚܨܝܗ̇ ܘܫܕܝܗ̇ ܡܢܟ. ܦܩܚ ܠܟ ܓܝܪ ܕܐܒܕ ܚܕ ܗܕܡܝܟ
30 ܢܐܒܕ. ܘܠܐ ܟܠܗ ܦܓܪܟ ܢܐܙܠ ܠܓܗܢܐ. ܘܐܢ

ܕܕܝܠܗܘܢ ܗܝ ܡܠܟܘܬܐ ܕܫܡܝܐ ܀
11 ܛܘܒܝܟܘܢ ܡܐ ܕܪܕܦܝܢ ܠܟܘܢ ܒ̈ܢܝ ܐܢܫܐ ܘܡܚܣܕܝܢ
ܠܟܘܢ. ܘܐܡܪܝܢ ܥܠܝܟܘܢ ܟܠ ܡܕܡ ܕܒܝܫ ܒܕܓܠܘܬܐ
12 ܡܛܠ ܫܡܝ. ܐܢܬܘܢ ܕܝܢ ܚܕܘ ܘܪܘܙܘ ܒܗܿܘ ܝܘܡܐ.
ܕܐܓܪܟܘܢ ܣܓܝ ܒܫܡܝܐ. ܗܟܢܐ ܓܝܪ ܪ̈ܕܦܘ ܗܘܘ
13 ܐܒܗ̈ܬܗܘܢ ܠܢܒ̈ܝܐ. ܐܝܠܝܢ ܕܩܕܡܝܟܘܢ ܗܘܘ. ܐܢܬܘܢ
ܐܢܘܢ ܡܠܚܗ ܕܐܪܥܐ. ܐܢ ܕܝܢ ܡܠܚܐ ܬܦܟܗ ܘܬܬܛܦܠ
ܒܡܢܐ ܬܬܡܠܚ. ܠܡܕܡ ܠܐ ܐܘܠܐ. ܐܠܐ ܕܢܫܬܕܐ ܠܒܪ.
14 ܘܢܕܘܫܘܢ ܕܢܫܠܗ ܒ̈ܢܝ ܐܢܫܐ. ܐܢܬܘܢ ܐܢܘܢ ܢܘܗܪܗ
ܕܥܠܡܐ. ܘܠܐ ܡܫܟܚܐ ܡܕܝܢܬܐ ܕܥܠ ܛܘܪܐ ܒܢܝܐ
15 ܕܬܛܫܐ. ܘܠܐ ܐܢܫ ܡܢܗܪ ܫܪܓܐ ܘܣܐܡ ܠܗ ܬܚܝܬ
ܡܘܕܝܐ. ܐܠܐ ܣܐܡ ܠܗ ܥܠ ܡܢܪܬܐ. ܘܡܢܗܪ
16 ܠܟܠܗܘܢ ܐܝܠܝܢ ܕܒܒܝܬܐ ܐܢܘܢ. ܗܟܢܐ ܢܢܗܪ
ܢܘܗܪܟܘܢ ܩܕܡ ܒ̈ܢܝ ܐ̈ܢܫܐ ܕܢܚܙܘܢ ܥ̈ܒܕܝܟܘܢ ܛ̈ܒܐ.
17 ܘܢܫܒܚܘܢ ܠܐܒܘܟܘܢ ܕܒܫܡܝܐ ◦ ܠܐ ܬܣܒܪܘܢ
ܕܐܬܝܬ ܕܐܫܪܐ ܢܡܘܣܐ ܘܢܒ̈ܝܐ. ܠܐ ܐܬܝܬ
18 ܕܐܫܪܐ ܐܢܘܢ. ܐܠܐ ܠܡܫܠܡܘ ܐܢܘܢ. ܐܡܝܢ ܓܝܪ
ܐܡܪܢܐ ܠܟܘܢ. ܕܥܕܡܐ ܕܢܥܒܪܘܢ ܫܡܝܐ ܘܐܪܥܐ.
ܝܘܕ ܐܬܘܬܐ ܚܕܐ ܐܘ ܣܪܛܐ ܚܕܐ ܠܐ ܬܥܒܪ ܡܢ
19 ܢܡܘܣܐ. ܥܕܡܐ ܕܟܠ ܡܕܡ ܢܗܘܐ. ܟܠ ܕܢܫܪܐ
ܗܟܝܠ ܚܕ ܡܢ ܦܘ̈ܩܕܢܐ ܗܠܝܢ ܙܥܘܪܐ. ܘܢܠܦ ܗܟܢܐ
ܠܒ̈ܢܝ ܐܢܫܐ. ܒܨܝܪܐ ܢܬܩܪܐ ܒܡܠܟܘܬܐ ܕܫܡܝܐ.
ܟܠ ܕܢܥܒܕ ܕܝܢ ܘܢܠܦ. ܗܢܐ ܪܒܐ ܢܬܩܪܐ ܒܡܠܟܘܬܐ

24 ܒܥܡܐ. ܘܐܫܬܡܥ ܛܒܗ ܒܟܠܗ ܣܘܪܝܐ. ܘܩܪܒܘ
ܠܗ ܟܠܗܘܢ ܐܝܠܝܢ ܕܒܝܫ ܒܝܫ ܥܒܝܕܝܢ. ܘܐܝܠܝܢ
ܕܐܚܝܕܝܢ ܒܟܘܪ̈ܗܢܐ ܡܫܚ̈ܠܦܐ. ܘܒܬܫܢܝ̈ܩܐ ܩܫ̈ܝܐ.
ܘܦܓܝ̈ܥܐ ܕܩ̈ܠܝܚܐ ܙܢܚ ܗܘܘ ܒܟܠܗܘܢ. ܘܐܣܝ
ܟܐ̈ܒܐ. ܘܗܘܐ ܟܠ ܚܕ ܚܕ ܡܢܗܘܢ ܐܝܕܗ ܣܐܡ
25 ܗܘܐ. ܘܠܟܠܗܘܢ ܡܟܐܣܐ ܗܘܐ. ܘܐܙܠܘ ܒܬܪܗ
ܟܢ̈ܫܐ ܣܓ̈ܝܐܐ. ܡܢ ܓܠܝܠܐ ܘܡܢ ܥܣܪ̈ܬ ܡܕ̈ܝܢܬܐ.
ܘܡܢ ܐܘܪܫܠܡ. ܘܡܢ ܝܗܘܕ. ܘܡܢ ܥܒܪܐ ܕܝܘܪܕܢ.
V. ܟܕ ܚܙܐ ܕܝܢ ܠܟܢ̈ܫܐ. ܣܠܩ ܝܬܒ ܠܗ ܒܛܘܪܐ. ܘܩܪܒܘ
2 ܠܘܬܗ ܬܠܡ̈ܝܕܘܗܝ. ܘܦܬܚ ܦܘܡܗ ܘܡܠܦ ܗܘܐ
ܠܗܘܢ ܘܐܡܪ ܀

3 ܛܘܒܝܗܘܢ ܠܡ̈ܣܟܢܐ ܒܪܘܚܗܘܢ ܕܕܝܠܗܘܢ ܗܝ
ܡܠܟܘܬܐ ܕܫܡܝܐ ܀

4 ܛܘܒܝܗܘܢ ܠܡܟ̈ܝܟܐ ܕܗܢܘܢ ܢܐܪܬܘܢ ܠܐܪܥܐ ܀

5 ܛܘܒܝܗܘܢ ܠܐܒ̈ܝܠܐ ܕܗܢܘܢ ܢܬܒܝܐܘܢ ܀

6 ܛܘܒܝܗܘܢ ܠܐܝܠܝܢ ܕܟܦܢܝܢ ܘܨܗܝܢ ܠܟܐܢܘܬܐ
ܕܗܢܘܢ ܢܣܒܥܘܢ ܀

7 ܛܘܒܝܗܘܢ ܠܡܪ̈ܚܡܢܐ ܕܥܠܝܗܘܢ ܢܗܘܘܢ ܪ̈ܚܡܐ.

8 ܛܘܒܝܗܘܢ ܠܐܝܠܝܢ ܕܕܟܝܢ ܒܠܒܗܘܢ ܕܗܢܘܢ
ܢܚܙܘܢܝܗܝ ܠܐܠܗܐ ܀

9 ܛܘܒܝܗܘܢ ܠܥܒ̈ܕܝ ܫܠܡܐ ܕܗܢܘܢ ܒ̈ܢܘܗܝ ܕܐܠܗܐ
ܢܬܩܪܘܢ ܀

10 ܛܘܒܝܗܘܢ ܠܐܝܠܝܢ ܕܪܕܝܦܝܢ ܡܛܠ ܙܕܝܩܘܬܐ

ܕܡܬܝ

13 ܘܫܒܩܗ ܠܢܨܪܬ. ܘܐܬܐ ܥܡܪ ܒܟܦܪܢܚܘܡ. ܕܥܠ ܝܕ
14 ܝܡܐ. ܒܬܚܘܡܐ ܕܙܒܘܠܘܢ ܘܕܢܦܬܠܝ. ܕܢܬܡܠܐ ܡܕܡ
15 ܕܐܬܐܡܪ ܒܝܕ ܐܫܥܝܐ ܢܒܝܐ ܕܐܡܪ ܗܘܐ. ܐܪܥܐ
ܕܙܒܘܠܘܢ ܘܐܪܥܐ ܕܢܦܬܠܝ. ܐܘܪܚܐ ܕܝܡܐ. ܥܒܪ̈ܘܗܝ
16 ܕܝܘܪܕܢ ܢܗܪܐ. ܓܠܝܠܐ ܕܥ̈ܡܡܐ. ܥܡܐ ܕܝܬܒ ܗܘܐ
ܒܚܫܘܟܐ ܚܙܘ ܢܘܗܪܐ ܪܒܐ. ܘܐܝܠܝܢ ܕܝܬܒܝܢ ܗܘܘ
ܒܛܠܠܐ ܕܡܘܬܐ. ܢܘܗܪܐ ܪܒܐ ܕܢܚ ܥܠܝܗܘܢ ◦◦◦
17 ܡܢ ܗܝܕܝܢ ܫܪܝ ܝܫܘܥ ܠܡܟܪܙܘ ܘܠܡܐܡܪ. ܩܪܒܬ ܠܗ
18 ܡܠܟܘܬܐ ܕܫܡܝܐ. ܘܟܕ ܡܗܠܟ ܗܘܐ ܡܪܢ ܥܠ ܝܕ
ܝܡܐ ܕܓܠܝܠܐ. ܚܙܐ ܬܪ̈ܝܢ ܐܚ̈ܝܢ. ܠܫܡܥܘܢ ܕܡܬܩܪܐ
ܟܐܦܐ. ܘܠܐܢܕܪܐܘܣ ܐܚܘܗܝ. ܟܕ ܪܡܝܢ ܗܘܘ
19 ܡܨܝ̈ܕܬܗܘܢ ܒܝܡܐ ܡܛܠ ܕܨܝ̈ܕܐ ܗܘܘ. ܐܡܪ ܠܗܘܢ
ܫܡܥܘܢ. ܬܘ ܒܬܪܝ ܘܐܥܒܕܟܘܢ ܨܝ̈ܕܐ ܕܒ̈ܢܝ ܐܢܫܐ.
20 ܘܗܢܘܢ ܒܗ ܒܫܥܬܐ. ܫܒܩܘ ܡܨܝ̈ܕܬܗܘܢ ܘܐܙܠܘ
ܒܬܪܗ ◦◦◦
21 ܘܟܕ ܥܒܪ ܡܢ ܬܡܢ. ܚܙܐ ܠܬܪ̈ܝܢ ܐܚ̈ܝܢ ܐܚܪ̈ܢܝܢ.
ܠܝܥܩܘܒ ܘܠܝܘܚܢܢ ܐܚܘܗܝ ܒ̈ܢܝ ܙܒܕܝ. ܟܕ ܝܬܒܝܢ
ܗܘܘ ܒܣܦܝܢܬܐ ܥܡ ܙܒܕܝ ܐܒܘܗܘܢ. ܘܡܬܩܢܝܢ
22 ܡܨܝ̈ܕܬܗܘܢ. ܘܩܪܐ ܐܢܘܢ ܝܫܘܥ. ܘܗܢܘܢ ܒܗ
23 ܒܫܥܬܐ ܫܒܩܘ ܡܨܝ̈ܕܬܗܘܢ ܘܐܙܠܘ ܒܬܪܗ. ܘܗܘ
ܡܬܟܪܟ ܗܘܐ ܒܟܠܗ ܓܠܝܠܐ. ܘܡܠܦ ܗܘܐ
ܒܟܢ̈ܘܫܬܐ. ܘܡܟܪܙ ܗܘܐ ܣܒܪܬܐ ܕܡܠܟܘܬܐ.
ܘܡܐܣܐ ܗܘܐ ܟܠ ܬܫ̈ܢܝܩܝܢ ܘܟܠ ܟܘܪ̈ܗܢܝܢ

ܐܫܬܡܥ ܡܢ ܫܡܝܐ ܕܐܡܪ ܠܗ. ܐܢܬ ܗܘ ܒܪܝ
IV. ܘܚܒܝܒܝ ܕܒܟ ܐܨܛܒܝܬ. ܗܝܕܝܢ ܝܫܘܥ ܐܬܕܒܪ ܡܢ
2 ܪܘܚܐ ܕܩܘܕܫܐ ܠܡܕܒܪܐ. ܕܢܬܢܣܐ ܡܢ ܣܛܢܐ. ܘܨܡ
3 ܒܬܪ ܐܪ̈ܒܥܝܢ ܝܘ̈ܡܝܢ ܕܐܟܦܢ ܗܘܐ ܒܗܢ. ܘܩܪܒ ܠܘܬܗ
ܗܘ ܕܡܢܣܐ ܘܐܡܪ ܠܗ. ܐܢ ܒܪܗ ܐܢܬ ܕܐܠܗܐ
4 ܐܡܪ ܕܗܠܝܢ ܟܐ̈ܦܐ ܢܗܘܝܢ ܠܚܡܐ. ܗܢܐ ܝܫܘܥ
ܘܐܡܪ ܠܗ. ܟܬܝܒ ܗܘ ܕܠܐ ܗܘܐ ܒܠܚܡܐ ܒܠܚܘܕ
ܚܝܐ ܒܪܢܫܐ. ܐܠܐ ܒܟܠ ܦܬܓܡ ܕܢܦܩ ܡܢ ܦܘܡܗ
5 ܕܡܪܝܐ. ܗܝܕܝܢ ܕܒܪܗ ܐܟܠ ܩܪܨܐ ܘܐܝܬܝܗ ܠܡܕܝܢܬ
6 ܩܘܕܫܐ. ܘܐܩܝܡܗ ܥܠ ܩܪܢܐ ܕܗܝܟܠܐ. ܘܐܡܪ
ܠܗ ܐܢ ܒܪܗ ܐܢܬ ܕܐܠܗܐ ܐܪܡܐ ܢܦܫܟ ܠܬܚܬ.
ܟܬܝܒ ܓܝܪ ܕܠܡܠܐ̈ܟܘܗܝ ܢܦܩܕ ܥܠܝܟ. ܕܥܠ
ܐ̈ܝܕܝܗܘܢ ܢܛܠܘܢܟ. ܕܠܐ ܡܬܬܩܘܡ ܬܬܩܠ ܪܓܠܟ
7 ܒܟܐܦܐ. ܬܘܒ ܐܡܪ ܠܗ ܝܫܘܥ. ܟܬܝܒ ܗܘ ܕܠܐ
8 ܬܢܣܐ ܠܡܪܝܐ ܐܠܗܟ. ܬܘܒ ܕܒܪܗ ܐܟܠ ܩܪܨܐ
ܠܛܘܪܐ ܐܝܢܐ ܕܪܡ ܛܒ. ܘܚܘܝܗ ܟܠܗܝܢ ܡ̈ܠܟܘܬܐ
9 ܕܥܠܡܐ ܘܫܘܒܚܗܝܢ. ܘܐܡܪ ܠܗ ܗܠܝܢ ܟܠܗܝܢ
10 ܐܬܠ ܠܟ ܐܢ ܗܘ ܕܬܦܠ ܘܬܣܓܘܕ ܩܕܡܝ. ܗܝܕܝܢ
ܐܡܪ ܠܗ ܝܫܘܥ. ܙܠ ܠܟ ܒܣܬܪܝ ܣܛܢܐ. ܟܬܝܒ ܗܘ
ܓܝܪ ܕܠܡܪܝܐ ܐܠܗܟ ܬܣܓܘܕ. ܘܠܗ ܒܠܚܘܕܘܗܝ
11 ܬܦܠܘܚ. ܗܝܕܝܢ ܫܒܩܗ ܐܟܠ ܩܪܨܐ ܥܕ ܙܒܢܐ. ܘܗܐ
ܡ̈ܠܐܟܐ ܩܪܒܘ ܘܡܫܡܫܝܢ ܗܘܘ ܠܗ ܠܝܫܘܥ. ◦◦◦◦◦
12 ܟܕ ܫܡܥ ܕܝܢ ܝܫܘܥ ܕܝܘܚܢܢ ܐܫܬܠܡ. ܐܙܠ ܠܗ ܠܓܠܝܠܐ.

ܡܥܡܕܐ ܗܘܐ ܐܢܫ ܐܢܫ ܒܫ̈ܘܠܦܗܘܗܝ. ܟܕ ܚܙܐ ܕܝܢ 7
ܟܢ̈ܫܐ ܘܦܪ̈ܝܫܐ ܘܙܕ̈ܘܩܝܐ ܕܐܬܝܢ ܠܡܥܡܘܕܝܬܗ.
ܐܡܪ ܠܗܘܢ: ܝܠܕܐ ܕܐܟܕ̈ܢܐ ܡܢܘ ܚܘܝܟܘܢ ܠܡܥܪܩ
ܡܢ ܪܘܓܙܐ ܕܐܬܐ. ܥܒܕܘ ܗܟܝܠ ܦܐܪ̈ܐ ܕܫܘܝܢ 8
ܠܬܝܒܘܬܐ. ܘܠܐ ܬܐܡܪܘܢ ܒܢܦܫܟܘܢ ܕܐܒܐ ܐܝܬ 9
ܠܢ ܐܒܪܗܡ. ܐܡܪ ܐܢܐ ܠܟܘܢ ܓܝܪ ܕܡܫܟܚ ܐܠܗܐ ܡܢ
ܗܠܝܢ ܟܐܦ̈ܐ ܠܡܩܡܘ ܒܢ̈ܝܐ ܠܐܒܪܗܡ. ܘܗܐ ܡܛܠ 10
ܠܗ ܢܪܓܐ ܥܠ ܥܩܪ̈ܝܗܘܢ ܕܐܝ̈ܠܢܐ. ܟܠ ܐܝܠܢܐ ܗܟܝܠ
ܕܦܐܪ̈ܐ ܛܒ̈ܐ ܠܐ ܥܒܕ. ܡܬܦܣܩ ܘܠܢܘܪܐ ܐܙܠ.
ܐܢܐ ܕܝܢ ܗܐ ܡܥܡܕ ܐܢܐ ܠܟܘܢ ܒܡ̈ܝܐ ܠܬܝܒܘܬܐ. 11
ܗܘ ܕܝܢ ܐܢܐ ܕܐܬܐ ܒܬܪܝ ܚܝܠܬܢ ܗܘ ܡܢܝ. ܘܠܐ
ܫܘܐ ܐܢܐ ܐܢܐ ܡܣ̈ܐܢܘܗܝ ܠܡܫܩܠ. ܗܘ ܢܥܡܕܟܘܢ
ܒܪܘܚܐ ܕܩܘܕܫܐ ܘܒܢܘܪܐ. ܗܘ ܕܐܚܝܕ ܪܦܫܐ 12
ܒܐܝܕܗ ܘܡܕܟܐ ܐܕܪܗ. ܘܚ̈ܛܐ ܢܚܠ ܒܐܘ̈ܨܪܘܗܝ.
ܘܬܒܢܐ ܡܘܩܕ ܒܢܘܪܐ ܕܠܐ ܕܥܟܐ ○ ○ ○
ܗܝܕܝܢ ܐܬܐ ܝܫܘܥ ܡܢ ܓܠܝܠܐ ܠܝܘܪܕܢܢ. ܠܘܬ ܝܘܚܢܢ 13
ܕܢܥܡܕܝܘܗܝ. ܘܟܠܝܗܝ ܝܘܚܢܢ ܘܐܡܪ ܠܗ. ܐܢܐ ܣܢܝܩ 14
ܐܢܐ ܕܐܢܬ ܬܥܡܕܝܢܝ. ܘܐܢܬ ܠܘܬܝ ܐܬܝܬ. ܐܡܪ ܠܗ 15
ܝܫܘܥ ܫܒܘܩ ܗܫܐ. ܡܛܠ ܕܗܟܢܐ ܘܠܐ ܠܢ ܕܢܡܠܐ
ܟܠܗ ܟܐܢܘܬܐ. ܗܝܕܝܢ ܫܒܩܗ ܠܡܥܡܕ. ܘܥܡܕ
ܗܘܐ ܝܫܘܥ. ܘܟܕ ܥܡܕ. ܒܗ̇ ܒܫܥܬܐ ܕܣܠܩ ܝܫܘܥ 16
ܡܢ ܡ̈ܝܐ. ܘܗܐ ܐܬܦܬܚܘ ܫܡܝܐ. ܘܚܙܐ ܪܘܚܐ
ܕܐܠܗܐ ܕܢܚܬܐ ܐܝܟ ܝܘܢܐ ܘܩܘܝܬ ܥܠܘܗܝ. ܘܩܠܐ 17

ܡܝܬ ܕܝܢ ܗܪܘܕܣ ܡܠܟܐ. ܐܬܚܙܝ ܠܝܘܣܦ ܒܡܨܪܝܢ
20 ܡܠܐܟܐ ܕܡܪܝܐ ܒܚܠܡܐ ܘܐܡܪ ܠܗ. ܩܘܡ ܕܒܪ
ܠܛܠܝܐ ܘܠܐܡܗ ܘܙܠ ܠܐܪܥܐ ܕܐܝܣܪܝܠ. ܡܛܠ
ܕܡܝܬܘ ܠܗܘܢ ܗܢܘܢ ܕܒܥܝܢ ܗܘܘ ܢܦܫܗ ܕܛܠܝܐ
21 ܠܡܘܒܕܘ. ܗܘ ܕܝܢ ܩܡ ܫܩܠܗ ܠܛܠܝܐ ܘܠܐܡܗ.
ܘܐܬܐ ܠܗ ܠܐܪܥܐ ܕܐܝܣܪܝܠ ◦

22 ܟܕ ܫܡܥ ܕܝܢ ܝܘܣܦ ܕܐܪܟܠܐܘܣ ܗܘܐ ܡܠܟܐ
ܒܝܗܘܕ. ܒܕܘܟܬ ܗܪܘܕܣ ܐܒܘܗܝ. ܕܚܠ ܕܢܐܙܠ
ܠܬܡܢ. ܘܐܬܚܙܝ ܠܗ ܒܚܠܡܐ ܕܢܐܙܠ ܠܗ ܠܐܬܪܐ
23 ܕܓܠܝܠܐ. ܘܐܬܐ ܠܬܡܢ. ܘܥܡܪ ܗܘܐ ܒܡܕܝܢܬܐ
ܚܕܐ ܕܡܬܩܪܝܐ ܢܨܪܬ. ܘܐܬܡܠܝܬ ܡܠܬܐ ܕܐܡܝܪܐ
ܒܢܒܝܐ. ܕܢܨܪܝܐ ܢܬܩܪܐ ◦◦◦

III. ܘܒܗܘܢ ܝܘ̈ܡܬܐ. ܐܬܐ ܝܘܚܢ ܡܥܡܕܢܐ. ܘܡܟܪܙ
2 ܗܘܐ ܒܡܕܒܪܐ ܕܝܗܘܕ ܘܐܡܪ ܗܘܐ. ܕܬܘܒܘ. ܡܛܠ
3 ܕܩܪܒܬ ܠܗ̇ ܡܠܟܘܬܐ ܕܫܡܝܐ. ܗܢܘ ܓܝܪ ܕܟܬܝܒ
ܥܠܘܗܝ ܒܐܫܥܝܐ ܢܒܝܐ ܕܐܡܪ ܗܘܐ. ܩܠܐ ܕܩܪܐ
ܒܡܕܒܪܐ. ܛܝܒܘ ܐܘܪܚܐ ܠܡܪܝܐ. ܘܬܪܘܨܘ
4 ܫܒܝ̈ܠܘܗܝ ܕܐܠܗܢ. ܗܘ ܕܝܢ ܝܘܚܢ ܠܒܝܫ ܗܘܐ
ܠܒܘܫܐ ܕܣܥܪܐ ܕܓܡ̈ܠܐ. ܘܐܣܝܪ ܗܘܐ ܒܪܘܨܬܐ
ܒܚܨ̈ܘܗܝ. ܘܡܐܟܘܠܬܗ ܐܝܬܝܗ̇ ܗܘܬ ܩܡ̈ܨܐ
5 ܘܕܒܫܐ ܕܒܪܐ. ܗܝܕܝܢ ܐܬܝܢ ܗܘܘ ܠܘܬܗ ܟ̈ܠ
ܐܘܪܫܠܡ ܘܟܠܗ̇ ܝܗܘܕ. ܘܟܠܗ̇ ܒܪܐ ܕܝܘܪ̈ܕܢ ܘܥܡܕܝܢ
6 ܢܗܪܐ. ܘܡܥܡܕ ܗܘܐ ܠܗܘܢ ܒܝܘܪܕܢ ܢܗܪܐ. ܟܕ

11 ܚܕܘܬܐ ܪܒܬܐ ܚܕܝܘ. ܘܥܠܘ ܠܒܝܬܐ ܘܚܙܘܗܝ
ܠܛܠܝܐ ܥܡ ܡܪܝܡ ܐܡܗ. ܘܢܦܠܘ ܣܓܕܘ ܠܗ. ܘܦܬܚܘ
ܣ̈ܝܡܬܗܘܢ ܘܩܪܒܘ ܠܗ ܩܘܪܒܢܐ. ܕܗܒܐ ܘܡܘܪܐ
12 ܘܠܒܘܢܬܐ. ܘܐܬܚܙܝ ܠܗܘܢ ܒܚܠܡܐ ܕܠܐ ܢܗܦܟܘܢ
ܠܘܬ ܗܪܘܕܣ. ܘܗܢܘܢ ܒܐܘܪܚܐ ܐܚܪܬܐ ܐܙܠܘ
13 ܗܘܘ ܠܐܬܪܗܘܢ. ܘܡܢ ܒܬܪܗܘܢ ܐܬܚܙܝ ܠܝܘܣܦ
ܡܠܐܟܐ ܕܡܪܝܐ ܒܚܠܡܐ ܘܐܡܪ ܠܗ. ܩܘܡ ܫܩܘܠ
ܠܛܠܝܐ ܘܠܐܡܗ ܘܥܪܘܩ ܠܡܨܪܝܢ. ܘܬܡܢ ܗܘܝ ܥܕܡܐ
ܕܐܡܪܢܐ ܠܟ. ܡܛܠ ܕܥܬܝܕ ܗܘ ܗܪܘܕܣ ܠܡܒܥܝܗ
ܠܛܠܝܐ ܐܝܟܢܐ ܕܢܘܒܕܝܘܗܝ ∘∘∘
14 ܝܘܣܦ ܕܝܢ ܩܡ ܘܫܩܠܗ ܠܛܠܝܐ ܘܠܐܡܗ ܒܠܠܝܐ
15 ܘܐܙܠ ܠܗ ܠܡܨܪܝܢ. ܘܗܘܐ ܬܡܢ ܥܕܡܐ ܕܡܝܬ
ܗܪܘܕܣ ܡܠܟܐ. ܕܢܬܡܠܐ ܡܕܡ ܕܐܬܐܡܪ ܡܢ
ܡܪܝܐ ܒܝܕ ܢܒܝܐ ܕܐܡܪ ܗܘܐ. ܕܡܢ ܡܨܪܝܢ ܩܪܝܬ
ܠܒܪܝ ∘∘∘
16 ܗܝܕܝܢ ܗܪܘܕܣ ܟܕ ܚܙܐ ܕܒܙܚܘ ܒܗ ܡ̈ܓܘܫܐ.
ܐܬܚܡܬ ܛܒ. ܘܫܕܪ ܩܛܠ ܠܟܠܗܘܢ ܛ̈ܠܝܐ ܕܒܝܬ
ܠܚܡ ܘܒܟܠܗܘܢ ܬܚܘܡܝܗ. ܡܢ ܒܪ ܬܪ̈ܬܝܢ
ܫ̈ܢܝܢ ܘܠܬܚܬ. ܠܙܒܢܐ ܕܐܬܚܦܛ ܠܗ ܡܢ
17 ܡ̈ܓܘܫܐ. ܗܝܕܝܢ ܐܫܬܠܡܬ ܡܠܬܐ ܗܝ ܕܐܡܪ ܐܪܡܝܐ
18 ܢܒܝܐ. ܩܠܐ ܐܫܬܡܥ ܒܪܡܬܐ. ܐܒܠܐ ܘܒܟܝܐ
ܘܐܠܝܬܐ ܣܓܝ̈ܐܬܐ. ܩܠܐ ܕܪܚܝܠ ܕܒܟܝܐ ܥܠ ܒ̈ܢܝܗ.
19 ܘܠܐ ܨܒܝܐ ܠܡܬܒܝܐܘ. ܡܛܠ ܕܠܐ ܐܝܬܝܗܘܢ. ܟܕ

ܘܗܘܐ ܥܡܗ ܒܕܟܝܘ ܥܕܡܐ ܕܝܠܕܬܗ ܠܒܪܐ ܘܩܪܬ ܫܡܗ
ܝܫܘܥ ܀

II. ܘܟܕ ܐܬܝܠܕ ܝܫܘܥ ܒܒܝܬ ܠܚܡ ܕܝܗܘܕܐ ܒܝܘܡܝ
ܗܪܘܕܣ ܡܠܟܐ. ܘܗܐ ܡܓܘܫܐ ܐܬܘ ܡܢ ܡܕܢܚܐ
2 ܠܐܘܪܫܠܡ. ܘܐܡܪܝܢ ܐܝܟܐ ܗܘ ܡܠܟܐ ܕܝܗܘܕܝܐ
ܕܐܬܝܠܕ. ܐܚܙܝܢ ܓܝܪ ܚܙܝܢ ܟܘܟܒܗ ܒܡܕܢܚܐ. ܘܐܬܝܢ
ܠܡܣܓܕ ܠܗ ܀

3 ܟܕ ܫܡܥ ܕܝܢ ܗܪܘܕܣ ܡܠܟܐ ܐܬܬܙܝܥ. ܘܟܠܗ
4 ܐܘܪܫܠܡ ܥܡܗ. ܘܟܢܫ ܠܟܠܗܘܢ ܪ̈ܒܝ ܟܗ̈ܢܐ ܘܣ̈ܦܪܐ
ܕܥܡܐ ܘܫܐܠ ܠܗܘܢ ܐܝܟܐ ܡܬܝܠܕ ܡܫܝܚܐ
5 ܐܡܪܝܢ ܠܗ ܒܒܝܬ ܠܚܡ ܕܝܗܘܕܐ ܗܟܢܐ ܓܝܪ ܟܬܝܒ
6 ܒܢܒܝܐ. ܐܦ ܐܢܬܝ ܒܝܬ ܠܚܡ ܕܝܗܘܕܐ ܠܐ ܗܘܝܬܝ
ܙܥܘܪܐ ܡܢ ܡܠܟܘܬܐ ܕܝܗܘܕܐ. ܡܢܟܝ ܓܝܪ ܢܦܘܩ
7 ܡܠܟܐ ܕܗܘ ܢܪܥܝܘܗܝ ܠܥܡܝ ܐܝܣܪܐܝܠ. ܗܝܕܝܢ ܗܪܘܕܣ
ܡܛܫܝܐܝܬ ܩܪܐ ܠܗܘܢ ܠܡܓܘܫܐ. ܘܡܚܡܛ ܗܘܐ
ܠܗܘܢ. ܙܒܢ ܒܐܝܢܐ ܥܕܢܐ ܐܬܚܙܝ ܠܗܘܢ ܟܘܟܒܐ.
8 ܘܫܕܪ ܐܢܘܢ ܠܒܝܬ ܠܚܡ. ܘܐܡܪ ܠܗܘܢ ܙܠܘ ܒܥܘ
ܥܠܘܗܝ ܥܠ ܛܠܝܐ ܚܦܝܛܐܝܬ. ܘܡܐ ܕܐܫܟܚܬܘܢܝܗܝ
9 ܬܘ ܚܘܐܘܢܝ. ܕܐܙܠ ܐܦ ܐܢܐ ܐܣܓܘܕ ܠܗ. ܗܢܘܢ ܕܝܢ
ܟܕ ܫܡܥܘ ܦܘܩܕܢܐ ܡܢ ܡܠܟܐ ܐܙܠܘ. ܘܐܬܚܙܝ ܠܗܘܢ
ܟܘܟܒܐ ܗܘ ܕܚܙܘ ܗܘܘ ܒܡܕܢܚܐ ܐܙܠ ܗܘܐ
ܡܕܒܪ ܠܗܘܢ: ܥܕܡܐ ܕܐܬܐ ܘܩܡ ܠܥܠ ܡܢ ܒܪ ܕܐܝܬܘܗܝ
10 ܗܘܐ ܛܠܝܐ. ܗܢܘܢ ܕܝܢ ܟܕ ܚܙܘܗܝ ܠܟܘܟܒܐ

16 ܠܡܬܢ ܡܬܢ ܐܘܠܕ ܠܝܥܩܘܒ ܝܥܩܘܒ ܐܘܠܕ ܠܝܘܣܦ
ܗܘ ܕܡܟܝܪܐ ܗܘܬ ܠܗ ܡܪܝܡ ܒܬܘܠܬܐ ܗܝ ܕܝܠܕܬ
ܠܝܫܘܥ ܡܫܝܚܐ ◎
17 ܟܠܗܝܢ ܗܟܝܠ ܫܪܒܬܐ ܡܢ ܐܒܪܗܡ ܘܥܕܡܐ ܠܕܘܝܕ
ܗܘܝ ܫܪܒܬܐ ܐܪܒܥܣܪܐ ܘܡܢ ܕܘܝܕ ܘܥܕܡܐ
ܠܓܠܘܬܐ ܕܒܒܠ ܫܪܒܬܐ ܐܪܒܥܣܪܐ ܘܡܢ ܓܠܘܬܐ
ܕܒܒܠ ܥܕܡܐ ܠܡܫܝܚܐ ܫܪܒܬܐ ܐܪܒܥܣܪܐ ◎○◎
18 ܡܘܠܕܗ ܕܝܢ ܕܡܫܝܚܐ ܗܟܢܐ ܗܘܐ ܟܕ ܡܟܝܪܐ ܗܘܬ
ܡܪܝܡ ܐܡܗ ܠܝܘܣܦ ܟܕ ܠܐ ܢܬܩܪܒܘܢ ܚܕ ܠܘܬ ܚܕ
19 ܐܫܬܟܚܬ ܒܒܛܢܐ ܡܢ ܪܘܚܐ ܕܩܘܕܫܐ ܝܘܣܦ ܕܝܢ
ܡܛܠ ܕܓܒܪܐ ܗܘܐ ܟܐܢܐ ܠܐ ܨܒܐ ܗܘܐ ܕܢܦܪܣܝܗ
20 ܠܡܪܝܡ ܘܐܬܪܥܝ ܗܘܐ ܕܒܫܠܐܝܬ ܢܫܠܝܗ ܟܕ ܗܠܝܢ
ܕܝܢ ܐܬܪܥܝ ܐܬܚܙܝ ܠܗ ܠܝܘܣܦ ܡܠܐܟܐ ܕܡܪܝܐ
ܒܚܙܘܐ ܕܠܠܝܐ ܘܐܡܪ ܠܗ ܝܘܣܦ ܒܪܗ ܕܕܘܝܕ ܠܐ
ܬܕܚܠ ܠܡܕܒܪ ܠܡܪܝܡ ܡܟܝܪܬܟ ܗܘ ܓܝܪ ܕܡܬܝܠܕ
21 ܡܢܗ ܡܢ ܪܘܚܐ ܗܘ ܕܩܘܕܫܐ ܟܠܗ ܬܐܠܕ ܠܟ ܕܝܢ
ܒܪܐ ܘܬܩܪܐ ܫܡܗ ܝܫܘܥ ܗܘ ܓܝܪ ܢܚܝܘܗܝ ܠܥܠܡܐ
22 ܡܢ ܚܛܗܝܗܘܢ ܗܕܐ ܕܝܢ ܕܗܘܬ ܕܢܬܡܠܐ ܡܕܡ
ܕܐܬܐܡܪ ܡܢ ܡܪܝܐ ܒܦܘܡ ܐܫܥܝܐ ܢܒܝܐ ܕܐܡܪ
23 ܗܘܐ ܗܐ ܒܬܘܠܬܐ ܬܒܛܢ ܘܬܐܠܕ ܒܪܐ ܘܬܩܪܐ
ܫܡܗ ܥܡܢܘܐܝܠ ܕܡܬܬܪܓܡ ܐܠܗܢ ܥܡܢ ◎○◎
24 ܟܕ ܩܡ ܕܝܢ ܝܘܣܦ ܡܢ ܫܢܬܗ ܥܒܕ ܐܝܟܢܐ ܕܦܩܕ ܠܗ
25 ܡܠܐܟܐ ܕܡܪܝܐ ܘܕܒܪܗ ܠܡܪܝܡ ܘܕܟܝܐܝܬ ܥܡܪ

ܐܘܢܓܠܝܘܢ ܕܡܦܪܫܐ ܡܬܝ

ܟܬܒܐ ܕܬܘܠܕܬܗ ܕܝܫܘܥ ܡܫܝܚܐ ܒܪܗ ܕܕܘܝܕ ܒܪܗ I.
ܕܐܒܪܗܡ ܐܒܪܗܡ ܐܘܠܕ ܠܐܝܣܚܩ ܐܝܣܚܩ ܐܘܠܕ 2
ܠܝܥܩܘܒ ܝܥܩܘܒ ܐܘܠܕ ܠܝܗܘܕܐ ܘܠܐܚܘܗܝ
ܝܗܘܕܐ ܐܘܠܕ ܠܦܪܨ ܘܠܙܪܚ ܡܢ ܬܡܪ ܦܪܨ ܐܘܠܕ 3
ܠܚܨܪܘܢ ܚܨܪܘܢ ܐܘܠܕ ܠܐܪܡ ܐܪܡ ܐܘܠܕ ܠܥܡܝܢܕܒ 4
ܥܡܝܢܕܒ ܐܘܠܕ ܠܢܚܫܘܢ ܢܚܫܘܢ ܐܘܠܕ ܠܫܠܐ ܫܠܐ 5
ܐܘܠܕ ܠܒܥܙ ܡܢ ܪܚܒ ܒܥܙ ܐܘܠܕ ܠܥܘܒܕ ܡܢ ܪܥܘܬ
ܥܘܒܕ ܐܘܠܕ ܠܐܝܫܝ ܐܝܫܝ ܐܘܠܕ ܠܕܘܝܕ ܡܠܟܐ ܕܘܝܕ 6
ܐܘܠܕ ܠܫܠܝܡܘܢ ܡܢ ܐܢܬܬܗ ܕܐܘܪܝܐ ܫܠܝܡܘܢ 7
ܐܘܠܕ ܠܪܚܒܥܡ ܪܚܒܥܡ ܐܘܠܕ ܠܐܒܝܐ ܐܒܝܐ ܐܘܠܕ
ܠܐܣܐ ܐܣܐ ܐܘܠܕ ܠܝܗܘܫܦܛ ܝܗܘܫܦܛ ܐܘܠܕ 8
ܠܝܗܘܪܡ ܝܗܘܪܡ ܐܘܠܕ ܠܐܚܙܝܐ ܐܚܙܝܐ ܐܘܠܕ
ܠܝܘܐܫ ܝܘܐܫ ܐܘܠܕ ܠܐܡܘܨܝܐ ܐܡܘܨܝܐ ܐܘܠܕ
ܠܥܘܙܝܐ ܥܘܙܝܐ ܐܘܠܕ ܠܝܘܬܡ ܝܘܬܡ ܐܘܠܕ ܠܐܚܙ 9
ܐܚܙ ܐܘܠܕ ܠܚܙܩܝܐ ܚܙܩܝܐ ܐܘܠܕ ܠܡܢܫܐ ܡܢܫܐ 10
ܐܘܠܕ ܠܐܡܘܢ ܐܡܘܢ ܐܘܠܕ ܠܝܘܫܝܐ ܝܘܫܝܐ 11
ܐܘܠܕ ܠܝܘܟܢܝܐ ܘܠܐܚܘܗܝ ܒܓܠܘܬܐ ܕܒܒܠ ܡܢ 12
ܒܬܪ ܓܠܘܬܐ ܕܝܢ ܕܒܒܠ ܝܘܟܢܝܐ ܐܘܠܕ ܠܫܠܬܐܝܠ
ܫܠܬܐܝܠ ܐܘܠܕ ܠܙܘܪܒܒܠ ܙܘܪܒܒܠ ܐܘܠܕ ܠܐܒܝܘܪ 13
ܐܒܝܘܪ ܐܘܠܕ ܠܐܠܝܩܝܡ ܐܠܝܩܝܡ ܐܘܠܕ ܠܥܙܘܪ ܥܙܘܪ 14
ܐܘܠܕ ܠܨܕܘܩ ܨܕܘܩ ܐܘܠܕ ܠܐܟܝܢ ܐܟܝܢ ܐܘܠܕ
ܠܐܠܝܘܕ ܐܠܝܘܕ ܐܘܠܕ ܠܐܠܝܥܙܪ ܐܠܝܥܙܪ ܐܘܠܕ 15